# HITLER'S ARMY

DAVID STONE
THE MEN, MACHINES AND ORGANIZATION

# HITLER'S ARMY

## 1939–1945

ZENITH PRESS

## Acknowledgments

My thanks are due to all those who so willingly and generously provided or permitted the use of quotations or illustrations from their own works or organizations. Amongst these, I should mention especially George Forty, who permitted me to use several quotations from his excellent study of the German infantryman 1939–45; Brian Davis for enabling the use of many photographs – a number of them previously unpublished – drawn from his private archive; and Major Rodney Goodinson, who very kindly provided photographs of several German army documents. In some cases a source could not be contacted, notwithstanding every reasonable effort to do so; all such material is of course fully credited where used, and in the bibliography where appropriate. Much of the research for this book was necessarily carried out in Germany, and particular mention should be made of the outstanding assistance provided by the military and civilian staff of the Bundeswehr Militärhistorisches Museum at Dresden, especially the access to the museum archives and artifacts so willingly provided, together with the generous provision of original images of uniform insignia, equipment and other items. Also in Germany, I am most grateful to Anne Dorte-Krause and other staff of the Deutsches Historisches Museum in Berlin for their assistance, particularly with identifying and sourcing illustrations to support specific parts of the text. Other museums and organizations in Germany and elsewhere that contributed directly or indirectly to the development of this work are shown at the end of the bibliography. However, the significant assistance provided to me in Germany by my friend and former professional colleague Oberstleutnant Peter Hellerling, a serving officer in the German Bundeswehr, deserves particular mention, and his invaluable contribution is indicated more fully in the Author's Note. Next, special thanks are due to Terry Hughes and David Green for battling their way through the several early drafts of this work; the final manuscript has benefited enormously from their ever-constructive criticism, advice and corrections. Any errors, misinterpretations, or misplaced assertions that might still remain in the work are therefore mine alone. My wife Prue also proofread the early drafts, while as an artist in her own right she also provided the original artwork for some of the insignia illustrations. Once again, Jeremy Whitehorn at Heartland Old Books in Tiverton, Devon, provided access to various pre-war publications dealing with the German rearmament process from 1933, as well as to some more recent but none the less rare reference material. Also in Tiverton, the support provided once again by Twyford Photographic and Print, but by Keith Luxton especially, to print, reproduce, scan and modify text and illustrations alike was as usual first-rate. I was also delighted that this project enabled me to renew and continue my seven-year association with David Gibbons and Tony Evans at DAG Publications in London. In addition to processing the book on behalf of Anova Books, David Gibbons also edited the final manuscript, and the resulting book has benefited enormously from his always constructive suggestions, ideas and proposed amendments. Finally, my thanks go as always to my ever-supportive, infinitely patient and unfailingly enthusiastic publisher John Lee, as well as to Komal Patel and the other members of the staff at Anova Books.

David Stone

---

# Contents

# Author's Note

This book is about one of the best-known, consistently professional, frequently controversial, and – initially – most successful armies ever to take to the battlefield, the German army that went to war in 1939. Much has been written about this remarkable fighting force ever since 1945, but this work seeks to contribute significantly to these publications and analyzes by providing the reader with a clear (and in some cases quite detailed) account and visual picture of the development, organization, operational procedures, training, equipment and officers and soldiers of what might justifiably be called 'Hitler's Army' from 1933 to 1945. It also addresses some of the less tangible issues affecting this army, such as morale, motivation, honor and discipline, as well as the army's sometimes difficult relationship with the Nazi-led state that it served, and with Hitler as its supreme commander. However, it does not seek to explore the philosophy of Nazism or the history of what has often been termed the 'SS State'. It focuses absolutely upon the army, with coverage of the Allgemeine SS and Waffen-SS – never a part of the army or indeed of the Wehrmacht – included only where this is essential to the story of the development of the army. As well as providing a comprehensive overview of the development of Hitler's army, this work has been structured to serve as an authoritative companion to many of the existing historical works, personal memoirs and more specifically focused battlefield accounts of Germany and its armed forces during the Third Reich era.

The Führer and his soldiers – Hitler visiting army and air force troops at Jaroslaw, south-east Poland on 22 September, 1939.

An overview of the German army at war is necessarily included in order to set the main part of this work in context, although a detailed account of each campaign and battle in which the army was engaged between 1939 and 1945 is beyond the intended scope of this work. None the less, the influence of wider international and domestic events upon the development of the army, not only during the war but also since 1918, was highly significant. The impact of such influences – political, economic and military – is very evident throughout the historical overview, dealing as it does with the two decades that followed World War I and then with the almost six years of warfare that began in September 1939.

Not surprisingly, the army's organization changed extensively between 1933, when the Nazis came to power in Germany, and 1945; but to document each and every such change in this work would be both impracticable and, arguably, positively confusing. Accordingly, most organizations have been considered at divisional level, with particular examples focused first upon the period soon after the Nazis came to power, then upon the immediate pre-war years, and finally upon the last two years of the war; with the organization of the high command of the army during the final few years of the conflict described in some detail. Generally, contemporary German publications and documents and Allied intelligence reports and assessments provided much of the organizational detail as at 1944–5, and where appropriate these have been utilized to show the army as it was, or as it was perceived to be, instead of merely reflecting the often over-optimistic planning and organizational aspirations of the German high command at the time.

Athough written primarily for the English-language reader, the inclusion within the text of a large number of German words was inevitable. Usually, the meaning of these words has been indicated on first use, with this explanation being repeated later only where essential, and a comprehensive German–English glossary is provided, in which virtually every German word used in the main text is also explained. In order to maintain clarity, however, the necessary expedient of 'anglicizing' most of the unit designations and titles has been adopted. The German–English glossary provides absolute accuracy, and I am especially indebted to Oberstleutnant Peter Hellerling for meticulously checking, correcting, and advising me on all aspects of the glossary throughout its development, as well as assisting me with many other aspects of my research for this work within Germany. He was also largely responsible for the accuracy of the appendix that describes the OKH organization in 1944–5. Meanwhile, my discussions with him in recent times and my frequent contact with other officers and soldiers of the Bundeswehr over many years have provided me with an invaluable German perspective on the former fighting force that was, arguably, an historical forerunner of the army upon which the defense of Germany depends today.

David Stone

# PART I
# The German Army in Peacetime, 1918–1939

## 1. Setting the Stage

In 1939 the German army was quite simply the best war-fighting force in Europe – or so it was regarded by most contemporary military analysts. Certainly it was not the largest European army; neither did it necessarily possess the technologically best or most extensive equipment. The French army, for example, was larger overall and had significantly more tanks and artillery than its German neighbor. And some would undoubtedly argue that Britain's small professional army was better than that which could be fielded by Germany. However, while the British army enjoyed a formidable reputation for its discipline, its traditions and regimental system, and its success in preserving the security of one of the greatest empires in world history, it had rested upon its laurels after 1918. Consequently, as the dark clouds of conflict massed over Europe in the autumn of 1939, Britain was generally ill-prepared to fight a modern industrialized war of maneuver and all-arms and inter-service cooperation.

Similarly, France had been traumatized by its army's crippling losses in the Great War. One result of this was that in 1939 many of its senior commanders were still mesmerized by the primacy of the defense over the offense – a concept and principle exemplified by the construction of the Maginot Line from 1928, designed to strengthen the existing static defenses on France's eastern border, parts of which had originally been built more than fifty years earlier. Paris was also just as preoccupied with the preservation of the French colonial empire (especially in North Africa and the Far East) as London was with policing the vast array of Britain's overseas territories. Inevitably, British and French government priorities and policies were reflected in their respective military deployments and activities. In consequence of this, as Germany mobilized for war, only a few British and French commanders, tacticians and strategists really understood the changed nature of the coming conflict – amongst them officers such as Basil Liddell-Hart in England and Charles de Gaulle in France.

While the two principal imperial European powers were ill-prepared for war in 1939, on the other side of the Atlantic the United States resembled a sleeping giant. Late to arrive on the battlefields of the Great War in 1917 and then one of the victors in 1918, Washington adopted isolationist foreign policies to ensure that never again would Americans have to fight and die to resolve another of Europe's interminable nationalistic squabbles. Consequently, the US Army of 1939 was proportionally too small even to defend the nation it served, let alone to conduct significant expeditionary operations, being for many years largely disregarded by the US population and ignored by the US government. The general perception was that the continental US borders were secure, and there were few votes to be gained promoting defense issues. As a result, in 1939 the US Army was undermanned, poorly

equipped, inadequately trained, and suffering the low self-esteem that years of neglect had engendered. However, America's financial strength, manpower reserves, natural resources and industrial capacity were enormous – as time would eventually show when world events finally forced the United States to apply all this potential to create a war machine of unprecedented military-industrial capability.

Elsewhere, the Soviet Union also had considerable war-fighting potential in 1939. But despite its considerable resources, a well-developed industrial base that included a thriving tank production and armaments industry, and large amounts of manpower, much of the Red Army was still reeling from the practical consequences of the communist system that had spawned both it and its then head of state, Joseph Stalin. The Soviet leader's purges during 1937 and 1938 had torn the heart out of the officer corps with the loss of much of its military talent (almost 37,000 officers of all ranks were shot or imprisoned, including three marshals, all but two army commanders, and two-thirds of the divisional commanders), so that in 1939 the Soviet Union was militarily unbalanced and over-politicized – although its longer-term strategic potential remained very evident.

While in 1939 the United States and many of the great European powers were in various states of military stagnation, denial or distraction, in the Far East and Southeast Asia the imperial Japanese army had been creating mayhem with its ruthless campaigns on the Korean peninsula, in Manchuria and in China from 1931. However, while the Japanese successes were undoubtedly striking, their opponents were generally unprepared, uncoordinated and of a lesser military quality in terms of their equipment, motivation and training. Also, the sort of war that the Japanese were already fighting in China was very different from the high-tempo form of modern warfare that would shortly break out in Europe.

Meanwhile, in just six years the German army of what had by 1939 been characterized as the "Third Reich" had overcome, or judiciously disregarded, a succession of internal obstacles and international constraints to become the most powerful and tactically innovative war machine of the day. The army that Hitler committed to war in 1939 was well-motivated and generally convinced of the rightness both of the National Socialist cause and of Hitler's foreign policies. At the forefront of these were the need to right the perceived wrongs done to Germany and its army by the Western Allies through the Versailles peace treaty in 1919 and to gain the "lebensraum" ("living space") necessary for a much expanded "Greater German Reich". By 1939 this resurrected, rearmed and reinvigorated army was once again well-trained, well-equipped and extremely well-led. Its operational doctrine was generally sound – much of it having been exercised at secret training grounds in Russia from 1925 and during the early 1930s

Adolf Hitler is shown here on the popular and well-produced cigarette card collections and albums produced by Haus Neuerburg of Köln am Rhein and others. The main heading is "Leadership – Flags [or Standards] – Tradition", the pictures being intended to portray the close connections between the "old army" and the post-1933 Nazi regime. The pictures show (top to bottom and left to right): the Führer, Adolf Hitler, and minister of war, Generalfeldmarschall von Blomberg; Generaloberst von Fritsch, commander-in-chief of the army until 1938; General-oberst von Seeckt, commander-in-chief of the Reichswehr and the army until 1926; troops honoring the standards of the old army; a company of standard bearers carrying the flags or standards of the old army alongside those of the new Wehrmacht; and finally a kettle-drummer leading a cavalry unit's mounted band on parade. Various other examples of these mid-1930s-era cards also appear elsewhere in this work.

# Führung · Fahnen · Tradition

**1** Führer und Reichskriegsminifter. Oberfter Befehls-haber der Wehrmacht ift der Führer. Unter ihm befiehlt über Heer, Kriegsmarine und Luftwaffe der Reichs-kriegsminifter und Oberbefehlshaber Generalfeldmarfchall v. Blomberg.

**2** Generaloberft Frhr. v. Fritfch. Dem Oberbefehlshaber des Heeres, Generaloberft Frhr. v. Fritfch, unterfteht das in 3 Gruppen, 12 Korps und 36 Divifionen gegliederte Heer. Territorial ift diefes auf Wehrkreife verteilt.

**3** Generaloberft v. Seeckt. Der Schöpfer der in der Nach-kriegszeit gebildeten Reichswehr wurde in Anerkennung feiner hervorragenden Verdienfte als Chef des Infanterie-regiments 67 mit der heutigen Wehrmacht aufs ehrenvollfte verbunden.

**4** Ehrung der Fahnen der alten Armee. Am 17. März 1935, dem Tag der Verkündung deutfcher Wehrhoheit, ließ der Führer die Feldzeichen der alten Armee mit dem Kriegskreuz fchmücken. Im Herbft 1936 bekam das Heer die erften der am 5. Oktober 1935 verliehenen eigenen Fahnen.

**5** Fahnenkompanie. Zu nationalen Gedenktagen werden die an hiftorifchen Stätten ruhenden Fahnen der alten Armee durch Fahnenkomponien abgeholt. Unfer Bild zeigt eine folche vor der Potsdamer Garnifonkirche.

**6** Keffelpauker. Die Kavallerieregimenter der alten Armee hatten z. T. Keffelpauken. Sie werden im heutigen Heere, meift von Reiter- und Artillerieregimentern, weiter-geführt.

and then battle-tested during the Spanish Civil War from 1936. The operational concepts of all-arms and inter-service cooperation were well understood and accepted, and the meshing of the army's infantry, artillery and armour with the air power of the Luftwaffe had been well practiced. So it was that in very many ways the German army of 1939 represented the zenith of German military achievement and the culmination of a process that had begun with the heyday of Prussia in the mid-seventeenth century and continued during the time of Frederick the Great. It had eventually progressed to the "golden age" of German militarism of the nineteenth century with Kaiser Wilhelm I, Bismarck and von Moltke, before suffering the inevitable consequences of imperial and militaristic hubris under Kaiser Wilhelm II, culminating in the catastrophe of World War I.

Military defeat always provides hard lessons for the vanquished, and Germany learnt very well the lessons of 1918 – at the same time Hitler and the Nazis also learned all too well the political and propaganda lessons that flowed quite predictably from the punishing terms that the Allies imposed upon the defeated Germany at Versailles. If 1939 was the zenith of the German army's capability, the total defeat of the Wehrmacht in 1945 was unquestionably its nadir. The "Götterdämmerung" ("Twilight of the Gods") of 1945 was a most remarkable and almost bizarre change of Germany's military fortunes, which can only be understood by appreciating the real nature of the army that Hitler created from 1933 and directed in war from 1939 to 1945. But perhaps the extremes of victory and defeat experienced by those who fought for the Fatherland between 1939 and 1945 were always unavoidable, as – notwithstanding its consummate military professionalism and virtually unrivalled war-fighting capability during the early years of the war – the Third Reich's army was based from its inception upon the fatally flawed and perverse foundations of National Socialist political ideology. Throughout, its fortunes and its ultimate destiny were bound inextricably to those of its creator and commander-in-chief, so that from 1933 to 1945 the German army of the Third Reich became and could quite properly be described as "Hitler's army."

## 2. German Militarism

The imprint of the German jackboot upon the path of history was deep and lasted for almost a century, from the mid-nineteenth century to 1945. Indeed, the jackboot, together with the spiked Pickelhaube and later the "coalscuttle"-shaped Stahlhelm helmet, were regularly used by cartoonists and propagandists alike to symbolize German military aggression and imperialism. Such symbolism was not inappropriate. The historical impact of the German armed forces – notably the army – was probably greater than that of any other European military force and this was certainly so in continental Europe. Without a doubt, German militarism has been a dominating force in European political and

Frederick II, "The Great", of Prussia (1712–1786).

military thinking and events for the last two centuries, especially so after the Prussian-led triumphs of 1866 and 1871.

But whether admired or hated, envied or emulated, lauded or reviled, over time the German army's effect on world events was frequently out of all proportion both to the size of the German armed forces and to that of the nation from which it was drawn, and this has undoubtedly contributed to the legend of German militarism. Indeed, it could be argued that the accelerating pace of German militarism was historically unavoidable, as successive invasions and conflicts turned the country into an almost constant battleground, a situation that could only be resolved through the unification of the Germanic states and their achievement of a viable military capability. This process began in 1640 and culminated in 1871, by which time militarism had – of necessity and to varying degrees – already permeated virtually every part of German society: a society that accepted unquestioningly the primacy of the military establishment within the state and the fundamental role of the German army in ensuring the future successes and evolution of that state both nationally and globally.

The origins of what eventually came to be characterized as "German militarism" were firmly rooted in a particularly violent and turbulent period of history that occurred during the early part of the seventeenth century, specifically the cataclysmic and often horrific events which afflicted central Europe and its population during the Thirty Years War between 1618 and 1648. However, while these events stood out as the catalyst which began and then

Carl Philip Gottlieb
von Clausewitz
(1780–1831).

Gerhardt Johann
David, Graf von
Scharnhorst
(1755–1813).

enabled an almost unbroken process of development that eventually culminated in the creation of the German army that went to war in 1939, other influences also directly affected the ethos of tradition and culture which contributed to the evolving nature of German militarism. Several of these well pre-dated the seventeenth century and prominent amongst them was the burgeoning number of historical facts, myths and legends that have underwritten the development of a truly German identity and awareness ever since AD 9, the year in which the Germanic tribes led by Arminius, the son of the chief of the Cherusci tribe, defeated three Roman legions at Kalkriese near Wiehengebirge in the densely forested Teutoburger Wald of northern Germany. To achieve this remarkable victory – one of the key formative battles of European history, for it subsequently led directly to Augustus Caesar abandoning Roman control of all the territory between the Rhine and the Elbe – Arminius had united many of the disparate tribes in the areas which today comprise Westphalia and Hessen. Consequently, while possibly an over-simplification of the disparate nature of the tribal structure of the time, Kalkriese was one of the first occasions on which a cohesive "German" or "Germanic" fighting force might be said to have appeared on the field of battle. The significance of Arminius as a symbol of German nationalism was in later times exploited by the imperial and the Nazi regimes alike.

Then, in later times, Germanic history became intertwined with legends – particularly those of the mighty River Rhine. Notable amongst these legends were the plentiful tales of bravery and chivalry – many with an underlying moral or religious aspect – and especially the stories of Beowulf, of Dietrich, of Lohengrin the Swan Knight of Kleve, of the Loreley, of the Lay of Hildebrand, and the poem *Parsifal*. But undoubtedly the most famous legend was the world renowned "Song of the Nibelungen" – the *Nibelunglied* – composed late in the twelfth century, which was possibly based upon a poem of Austrian or Tyrolese origin.[1]

This saga (as many others) was inspired by the Scandinavian and Germanic myths of ancient times and by their deeds, their obsession with honor, fidelity, loyalty, retribution and revenge, together with their almost superhuman skills as warriors. The Nibelungen – the heroes of the tale – provided a rich if somewhat violent cultural heritage and foundation of folklore for the people of Germany, with these warriors and demi-gods embodying the very essence of all that was judged to be truly "Germanic". The impact of the Rhine legends upon German culture is significant and the evocative deeds and images of Siegfried, Brunhilde, Kriemhilde, Gunther, Hagen, Attila and a score of other heroes and villains – male and female alike – show that they were warriors first and foremost. Amid the wholesale slaughter, the un-questioning love, the glorious triumphs and heartrending tragedies of the Rhine legends lies something of the warrior culture, the fatalism, the romanticism and the intangible sense of destiny that influenced aspects of the development of the martial nature of Germany well into the twentieth century. And it was emotive

images such as these that were from time to time exploited by the nation's military and political leaders alike, in order to promote and reinforce the German's love of his country – his "Heimat" – and his sacred role as its defender.

An organization closely linked with the perception of German militarism was the Teutonic Order of military and religious knights, originally established at Acre in 1190, during the Third Crusade. Indeed, the term "teutonic" was sometimes used by non-Germans as a somewhat derogatory term for German militarism into the mid-twentieth century, although the military capability of the Teutonic Order had in fact been abandoned at the end of the Napoleonic Wars. However, the members of this overtly military, religious and chivalrous order, who were originally known as the Hospitallers of Saint Mary of the German House in Jerusalem, provided another strand of the warrior heritage that underscored and contributed to the evolving martial nature and national character of what would one day become Germany. Indeed, the badge of the Teutonic Order was a black cross on a white background, an identifying symbol that was much later adopted by Germany's armed forces in two world wars and which continues to be used by Germany's armed forces today. Noteworthy also was the fact that the power base of the Teutonic Order in Germany was originally established at Marienburg in Prussia (whose national colors adopted in later times were also black and white). It remained there until the religious element moved to Mergentheim in the sixteenth century, while the more secular part of the community remained in Prussia, which was transformed into a principality by the Hohenzollern Grand Master of the Order. Later, Prussia played a key role in the development of Germany's military capability, while the Hohenzollerns were destined to rule first Brandenburg and Brandenburg-Prussia, then Prussia, and finally Germany itself until the demise of the German empire in 1918.

Throughout much of the Middle Ages the Germanic way of warfare was governed by a feudal system in which the emperor or king reigned supreme and exerted his authority and military power through the knights and nobles who owed their allegiance to him. These lords in turn commanded the mass of men-at-arms, serfs and vassals who lived on their land, for whom an absolute obligation of service and obedience to their lord and master existed. During this period the disparate forces of the many German states generally followed the standard of the one-headed black eagle emblazoned upon the yellow flag of the empire. But in due course, during the late twelfth century, the relative dis-organization and fragmented nature of the feudal system gave way to the development of permanently established armed forces and to a formalized concept of mercenary soldiering in Germany, from which process emerged the Landsknechts, who dominated the business of warfare in Europe for many years, right up to the Thirty Years' War.

From the wholesale devastation and slaughter that was visited upon the first German empire – the Holy Roman Empire that had

existed intermittently since the time of Charlemagne in AD 800 – during the Thirty Years' War from 1618 to 1648, there emerged the seeds of what later germinated and blossomed into German nationalism – a movement indisputably inspired and led by the state of Prussia. However, nationalistic objectives demanded both unity and a viable military capability and the development of neither of these was straightforward. Consequently, the often turbulent political evolution of Germany – headed by Prussia – was mirrored by that of its army, indicating the convergence of army and state, with their respective impacts upon each other and upon the population.

The organizational and battlefield successes achieved by Frederick William of Brandenburg, "The Great Elector", then Frederick III (later Frederick I of Prussia), Frederick William I (the "Soldier King") and finally Frederick II ("the Great") between 1640 and 1786 were often spectacular and invariably far-reaching. However, after the death of Frederick the Great the Prussian army was allowed to stagnate. As a result, over the next two decades under the rule of Frederick William III, much of the military advantage it had gained under his three predecessors was lost. However, this period of temporary decline also saw the emergence of such great military thinkers, trainers and organizers as Clausewitz, Gneisenau and Scharnhorst. External influences also

played their part: notably the rise and expansionist policies of Napoleonic France, which eventually led to the Prussian army's devastating defeat at Jena in 1806.

These three men in particular shaped not only Germany's military future but also that of the wider international profession of arms for generations to come, and thereby they gave birth to new global perceptions of German militarism and consummate military professionalism. Then, in the mid-nineteenth century, began a new "golden age" (although for some other nations it would prove to be a dark age!) of Prussian and German militarism, guided by the able hands of von Moltke, von Roon, von Bismarck, and the future King William (Wilhelm) I of Prussia. In order to support their plans for German unification it was necessary to industrialize the business of war, which resulted in the subordination of many aspects of everyday civilian life – such as the railways, certain factories, medical facilities, telegraph and postal communications, security matters and so on – to military control or supervision by the German general staff: an organization that was itself a byword for military professionalism, intellect and excellence.

The militarization of Germany paid handsome dividends as success followed success – first against Denmark over Schleswig-Holstein in 1864, then against Austria in 1866 and finally against

Full of confidence about the coming war against France, Prussian officers symbolically sharpen their swords on the steps of the French embassy in Berlin following Prussia's declaration of war in August 1806. However, just three months later on 14 October the army suffered a devastating defeat at Jena – although this catastrophe subsequently prompted a return to the Prussian military professionalism of former times.

August Wilhelm
Neithardt, Graf von
Gneisenau
(1760–1831).

Helmuth Karl
Bernhard, Graf von
Moltke (1800–1891).

Prince Otto von
Bismarck, Duke of
Lauenburg
(1815–1898).

Kaiser Wilhelm II
(1859-1941).

France in 1870–1. Indeed, by early 1871 the victorious German armies had enabled the creation of the first truly German empire (the Second Reich) on 18 January that year, an event and achievement that marked the total success of the policies and aspirations of Bismarck and Wilhelm I. However, after Wilhelm II became Kaiser (German Emperor) in 1888, it became increasingly clear that the army's remarkable achievements had also enabled Germany to embark upon an ever more ambitious imperialistic road that eventually led to 1914. This culminated in the catastrophe of World War I and Germany's defeat in 1918, which then consigned the nation and its armed forces to an uncertain future. The political maelstrom of the Weimar Republic was a period of uncertainty in which extreme political organizations prospered and the population increasingly looked to the army as the nation's savior. Implicit in this was the national perception of the army's traditional role as the restorer of order and stability and as the exemplar of the discipline, patriotism, duty and honor that had characterized German society during much of the previous century.

By that stage, of course, the process of militarization had become institutionalized and largely self-perpetuating through the ever-increasing involvement of the nation in various forms of obligatory universal military service or support for the army's activities. Also, the evidence of history was compelling, for it had been the army that – with very few exceptions – had produced or enabled many of Germany's greatest achievements ever since the late seventeenth century. For three hundred years the concept of the "Soldier's Coat" introduced during the reign of Frederick the Great meant that any Prussian, and later German, who rejected or was denied the privilege of serving in the army was indeed a lesser person, one that had failed in his duty and obligation of service to his country. Over time, but especially from Germany's military "golden age" of the mid-nineteenth century and the creation of the Second Reich, virtually every German official was uniformed, and was usually entitled to wear a ceremonial sword, dagger or other symbolic weapon indicating his rank and status. The uniform had become the norm and symbolized the virtues of order and discipline that were regarded as being the very essence of the German state and empire, with those who were not entitled to wear a uniform often regarded with disdain or suspicion.

Indeed, the "stab in the back" propaganda so actively promoted by Generalfeldmarschall von Hindenburg and most of the military leadership to preserve the post-war honor and viability of the army when the armistice was declared in 1918 was readily accepted by a defeated nation for which defeat had always been unthinkable. The "stab in the back" blamed mainly the politicians and all those civilians who had remained safely on the "home front", the people who had supposedly become ever more disaffected with the war and failed in their patriotic duty to support the fighting forces as austerity increased at home and their standard of living declined with more and more resources being diverted to support the war effort. The "stab in the back" propaganda line also blamed Germany's defeat on the war profiteers who had benefited

considerably from the conflict, as well as on a diverse range of groups and organizations, including the Bolsheviks, the Jews and even the navy. According to those who promoted the "stab in the back" concept, the army had in contrast stood firm and resolute throughout; it had done its duty, maintained its honor, and had remained undefeated in 1918. Consequently, it was represented to a traumatized German populace that the victory its army so justly deserved had been snatched from its grasp at the last minute by the self-interest and weakness of the civilian government sitting safely in Berlin. Understandably, in a country that was already so "institutionally militarized" in the widest sense, the "stab in the back" propaganda achieved widespread credibility, as the military and the post-imperial political leaders struggled to maintain a viable army as the only organization that could both save and restore Germany in the post-war world. But, as ever, wider and often unforeseen events and influences subsequently determined the direction in which Germany and its army would move after the disaster of 1914–18, while simultaneously fuelling and shaping the changing nature of German militarism during the two decades that followed World War I.

# 3. 1918 and the Legacy of Versailles

Germany's defeat in 1918 precipitated almost three decades of civil unrest and military change, much of this a direct consequence of the terms of the post-war peace treaty announced to the German delegation at Versailles the following year. The punitive, and in many ways humiliating, requirements exacted by the Allied powers in 1919 became known just as the already shaky government of the post-war Weimar Republic was managing to attain a measure of control over the country. This it achieved through its ruthless suppression of the various revolutionary movements (primarily the communists) by the use of semi-mercenary units of the blatantly right-wing but generally effective Freikorps. Very many Freikorps members were disillusioned and angry. Officers and soldiers who had marched home in November 1918 had found the Fatherland, for which they had battled during four long years, torn by revolution and political turmoil, with rampant inflation, unemployment and economic decay contrasting starkly with the fortunes that had been amassed by the war profiteers. Meanwhile the fighting force in which they had so recently found comradeship, patriotism and military success had been discarded, its cohesion dissipating with every day that passed. As a result, despite the orderly return of the army in November 1918, its subsequent disintegration meant that this force was unable to carry out the internal security role originally envisaged for it by the embryo government.

Clearly a new force was urgently required to act either in place of or alongside the army if the republic was to be saved and

**Left:** Far from guaranteeing the future peace of Europe, the punitive terms imposed upon Germany by the Allied Powers at the conference at Versailles in May 1919 later provided a significant propaganda tool to Hitler and the Nazi Party.

**Below:** A disabled World War I veteran and holder of the Iron Cross First Class is forced to beg for charity on a Berlin street, post-1918. Such scenes reinforced the "stab in the back" concept within the army, inflaming the existing feelings of injustice and political betrayal.

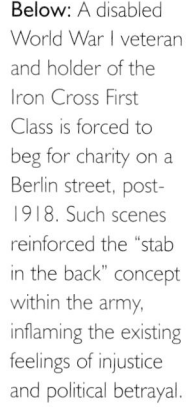

government authority restored. The government therefore authorized the general staff to raise new units (Freikorps) specifically for the purpose of suppressing revolution and disorder at home, and to defend the frontiers in the east in Silesia and along the Baltic littoral against increasingly active Polish and communist forces. These Freikorps were funded by the War Ministry, and many were based upon the now fragmented former regiments of the old army, often comprising all-arms groups of infantry, cavalry, artillery and mine-thrower (heavy mortar) troops. However, despite their nominal employment by the government and the operational direction of such units by the army high command, virtually every member of the Freikorps harbored a deep distrust of senior military officers and a "fanatical hatred of the provisional government."[2] Thus the legacy of the "betrayal" of 1918 and the army's "stab in the back" ran deep, while its active promotion would ensure that it continued to do so during the turbulent 1920s and early 1930s. Nevertheless, while their motives and occasional excesses often did not bear close scrutiny, it was undeniable that the Freikorps restored a considerable degree of order out of the chaos that ensued in the wake of Germany's defeat in 1918.

But then, with Germany just beginning to emerge from the post-war nightmare of socialist revolution and even the possibility of its becoming a communist state, the Allied powers at Versailles had promulgated the draft conditions to be imposed upon Germany by the impending peace treaty. The terms were announced to the German delegation at Versailles on 7 May 1919, and (notwithstanding the wholesale death and destruction that had taken place between 1914 and 1918, but particularly so in France and Belgium) a number of these edicts were undoubtedly excessive and ill-advised. It was hardly surprising, therefore, that

Germany was
reduced in size by
about 13 percent by
the Treaty of
Versailles. The new
borders are shown,
together with
overflow shading to
indicate Germany's
pre-1919 territorial
boundaries.

the Versailles treaty was a body-blow to the new republic and a severe shock to the German people. In Germany, its terms were seen as being unacceptably punitive, unreasonable, humiliating, intolerable and dishonorable – the treaty even required Germany to admit its "war guilt" and to submit its military leaders to trials for war crimes. For the officers and soldiers of the Freikorps and the regular army especially, the perceived political betrayals of 1918 were compounded by this treaty.

At Versailles the Allies sought to emasculate the German army (as well as disbanding the air force and neutralizing the navy) – if fully implemented the treaty would have effectively left Germany defenseless. Specifically, the army was to be manned by no more than 100,000 long-term volunteers, including a maximum of 4,000 officers. This army would be organized into two army groups with a total of seven infantry divisions and three cavalry divisions. Its operational role was to be limited to home defense and border security. Meanwhile, the legendary German general staff was to be abolished, with a "military office" (or Truppenamt) established to oversee day-to-day administrative matters, while all forms of planning and preparation for mobilization were forbidden. Furthermore, all military schools (apart from one arms school maintained for each arm), the Kriegsakademie (the higher-level staff training academy) and all the officer training academies were to be abolished.

Having effectively neutralized the army's planning, officer training and command structure, its operational capability was then negated by denying it any heavy weapons (including tanks), heavy artillery of all calibers and combat aircraft. In parallel, the German navy was reduced to little more than a coastal defense force. It was no accident that the victorious Allied powers decreed that the principal arm of Germany's post-war army was to be the cavalry, as after 1914 this was the arm that had been shown to be the least relevant or effective in a modern war. The authorized scales of all small-arms (such as rifles, pistols and light machine guns) were set at the absolute minimum essential to provide a basic military self-defense or policing capability.

The wider provisions of Versailles were no less draconian, feeding the national sense of anger and betrayal that swept through Germany in 1919, for at a stroke the treaty denied Germany secure borders, removed its colonial possessions and permitted the Poles – a nation long regarded with contempt by most Germans – to acquire large areas of territory at Germany's expense. Germany was to lose all of its overseas colonies, together with Alsace-Lorraine (which had been annexed from France in 1871) and certain other frontier territory to Belgium and France. Poland was to gain large tracts of German territory in the east, including Danzig, which was now categorized as a "Free City" under the protection of the League of Nations. A plebiscite was to take place to determine whether Silesia should in the future be under German or Polish sovereignty. France was to assume responsibility for the "protection" of the Saar coal-mining region for at least fifteen years, in compensation for the destruction of the French coal-mining industry during the war, and the Allied powers would occupy parts of the Rhineland for the same period as a guarantee of German compliance with the treaty. To the east of the occupied area a demilitarized zone some thirty miles wide was also to be established along its entire length. Finally, an Allied Control Commission would be established to oversee German compliance with all the provisions of the Treaty of Versailles.

Faced with no practicable alternatives, the government accepted the treaty and duly signed it on 28 June. By so doing it further weakened both its ability to govern and its ability to maintain the already tenuous control it exerted over the military forces of what had by then become the "Weimar Republic" – so named following the government's relocation from Berlin to the small Thuringian town of Weimar from 6 February 1919 when the deteriorating security situation in Berlin had made its continued presence there untenable. At a stroke, in their understandable but ill-judged post-war desire to exact such telling retribution upon Germany, the Allied powers had created throughout Germany a unifying sense of outrage in all sections of the population – military and non-military alike – that would in due course be successfully exploited by Adolf Hitler and the National Socialist party's propagandists.

# 4. The Weimar Republic and the Reichswehr

For the army the next two decades were dominated by three inter-related activities or events. First came the so-called "Kapp-Lüttwitz putsch" (which was led by the prominent right-wing extremist Wolfgang Kapp and by General von Lüttwitz, military commander of all troops east of the Elbe and in Saxony, Thuringia and Hanover). Next, there was General von Seeckt's largely successful reorganization and development of the new republic's standing army – the Reichswehr – notwithstanding the severe external constraints that had been placed upon it at Versailles. Finally, there was the rise to political power of the "Nationalsozialistische Deutsche Arbeiterpartei" (NSDAP) – the Nazis – and the way in which they finally gained total control of the Reichswehr. Together, these matters contributed directly to the creation and nature of the German army that eventually went to war in 1939.

The "Kapp-Lüttwitz putsch" that took place in Berlin during March 1920 in the aftermath of the furor over the Versailles treaty was an attempted military and right-wing coup born directly out

A Freikorps unit pictured on 22 May 1919 prior to a successful operation against Soviet Russian forces at Riga on the Baltic coast. The 24-year old commander at the center is Freiherr Hasso von Manteuffel, who would later distinguish himself as a Panzer commander during World War II.

of the "stab in the back" concept, together with the wider national dissent over the terms of the treaty. Although it enjoyed considerable support in some quarters and had initially seemed set for success, the "Kapp-Lüttwitz putsch" actually collapsed within just three days. But despite its final failure it had significant implications for the longer-term future of the army and the nation, as no punitive action was taken against those who had supported or taken part in the putsch. This inaction by the authorities excited the considerable anger of the trades unions, the workers and many members of the middle class alike, which triggered outbreaks of violence in Saxony, Thuringia and the Ruhr, where workers' self-defense units and the communist members of a "Red Army" battled ferociously with regular troops and the Freikorps for several weeks. This new upsurge of revolutionary violence was ruthlessly suppressed, but it was noteworthy that, whereas the army had declined to deal with the right-wing putsch, it subsequently set about the suppression of the left-wing movements with considerable enthusiasm and efficiency.

In practice, the army's position had been greatly clarified by the outcome of the putsch, as it had proved its ability both to support the government and to restore order within the state, while also demonstrating that it would not tolerate political direction that did

not match its traditional perceptions of duty, honor and the army's core role. In other words, it would not entertain any orders or instructions that were predominantly democratic or socialist in nature. Although the highly competent chief of staff and head of the army (Chef der Heeresleitung) General von Seeckt, who had been appointed in the aftermath of the putsch, later insisted that by his handling of the army's involvement in the affair he had ensured the apolitical nature of the new Reichswehr, its nature was nevertheless at best traditional and at worst blatantly right-wing – a situation that presaged the relative ease with which it would eventually achieve an accommodation with the NSDAP. In the meantime, the officer corps once again began to regard themselves and the army they led as an élite, pivotal and (in their view) independent power whose destiny was to influence the direction and conduct of Germany's domestic affairs whenever necessary. On the other hand, after the putsch the democratic and political left viewed the burgeoning capability of the Reichswehr with great misgiving and profound distrust. While the putsch failed in Berlin, its effects were much greater in Bavaria, where the move to the political right had been even more noticeable. There, local Reichswehr commanders had forced the resignation of the social democrat state government and its replacement with a hard-line

In March 1920, the right-wing Kapp-Lüttwitz putsch was launched. Here troops supporting the coup and the "Kapp government" await further orders early on the morning of 13 March, close to the Brandenburg Gate, Berlin.

right-wing government with the declared aim of making Bavaria a "focus of order" for the whole of Germany. Already the great cities of Munich and Nürnberg were well on the way to becoming veritable Meccas for German right-wing extremism, and Bavaria's future status as the ideological home of the NSDAP was already predictable.

Among the famous names of German military leaders and commanders of the twentieth century – von Hindenburg, von Ludendorff, and later Guderian, Rommel, von Manstein, Model, von Manteuffel and many more – the name of General Hans von Seeckt is perhaps less well-known. There are two reasons for this. First, his particular contribution to the development of the German army was organizational rather than on the battlefield. Second, von Seeckt died in 1936 and so was uninvolved in the events from 1939 that once again impelled Germany to prominence on the international stage. Nevertheless, by his actions during the early years of the Weimar administration up to 1926, von Seeckt created the Reichswehr as an effective fighting force and (by artfully circumventing many of the constraints imposed by Versailles) established a viable offensive capability that became the strategic and organizational cornerstone of the much-expanded Wehrmacht with which Germany went to war in 1939. Von Seeckt's contribution to the story of the German army was most significant, for ultimately his work provided Adolf Hitler with the military wherewithal for his attempt to realize his political ambitions by force of arms.

General von Seeckt came from a traditional Prussian military family and had enjoyed a distinguished military career at regimental duty and as a member of the Prussian general staff. His war record during World War I had been exemplary, and included planning the successful German breakthrough at Soissons in January 1915. In the immediate post-war period he served as military expert to the peace delegation, acting chief of the general staff, and then as head of the "Preparatory Commission for the Peace Army". He was a traditionalist and held many reactionary views, foremost amongst which was the role of the German army as a non-political but nation-shaping force and an institution vital to the future existence and nature of the German state. In broad terms, his vision was for the republic to have a modern version of the imperial army that had, in his view and that of the majority of the officer corps, served Germany so well from 1870 to 1918. However, unlike many of his more closely focused professional contemporaries, he also appreciated art, humanity and many of the intangibles of life and was described by one commentator as "a man of the world in the best sense of the term, adroit, self-possessed, skilful in the handling of men and affairs, with a great appreciation of the beautiful in every form, music, art, women, nature – he himself in later years said that vanity, sense of beauty, and the cavalier's instinct were the three outstanding traits in his character."[3]

A man of few words, his inscrutability earned him the nickname of the "sphinx", while his reputation as an organizer,

General Hans von Seeckt (1866–1936) was the principal architect of the modernized and reinvigorated Reichswehr. He is shown here with the Reichswehr minister, Dr. Gessler, during army maneuvers in January 1931.

innovator and diplomat allowed him to exert great influence upon the politicians and ministers with whom he worked and whose environment he understood all too well. This was despite his personal dislike of politicians and of a republican political system that forever threatened the stability and good order of the state during the Weimar era. His views and beliefs led him to direct that "political activity of every kind will be energetically kept out of the army. Political strife within the Reichswehr is incompatible with the spirit of comradeship and discipline and can only harm military training."[4]

The active de-politicizing of the army in the years following the Kapp-Lüttwitz putsch and the traumas inflicted upon Germany by the left-right influences that had blossomed immediately after the war (and which continued to do so to varying degrees throughout the Weimar years) was a major objective of von Seeckt's reforms. Participation in political meetings and organizations was forbidden and even the constitutional right of the soldiers to vote was suspended. However, this deliberate de-coupling of the army from the political process and awareness meant that it was also distanced from any real comprehension of the malign political influences that would emerge within Germany a few years later. This was arguably one of the factors that facilitated the relative ease with which the Reichswehr became the forerunner of "Hitler's army." The daunting task that faced von Seeckt was, therefore, to create an effective post-1920 German army against a continuing background of political unrest, while at the same time not contravening (or at least not being seen to contravene) the potentially crippling terms of the Treaty of Versailles. The military reforms he introduced can conveniently be categorized as conceptual, organizational and educational – the last of which included training in all its many forms. Predictably, all of these overlapped, were interdependent, and were implemented progressively over a number of years.

Von Seeckt's over-riding aim was to move the army into a state of political neutrality and away from the peccadilloes that had flowed from the Freikorps units, frequently at the instigation of their often charismatic and colorful but politically dangerous commanders. However, the army was to remain firmly connected to the "old army" and its traditions, so that a clear thread of historical continuity and heritage could be readily identified within the Reichswehr. To that end, companies, batteries and squadrons of the Reichswehr adopted the names and heritage of the former regiments of the Kaiser's army and were known as "tradition carriers" or Traditionsträger. For the wider German public, these links were publicized and emphasized through a wide range of commercial publications, such as the popular and well-produced cigarette card collections and albums produced by Haus Neuerburg of Köln am Rhein and others. Similarly, and not-withstanding the protests of many liberals, von Seeckt maintained the Feldgrau uniform and Stahlhelm of the war period, which had become synonymous with the image of German militarism both at home and abroad. Following its introduction on the Verdun battlefield in February 1916, the German "coalscuttle" steel helmet had supplanted the Pickelhaube as the single uniform item that most typified the German soldier, and as such its retention was a matter of considerable importance to many former soldiers. This was demonstrated by the post-war creation of the Stahlhelm organization for army veterans, which then flourished during the 1920s and early 1930s before its absorption into the NSDAP's paramilitary SA and SS organizations during 1933 and 1934.

General von Seeckt's reforms also sought to strengthen the ties between the nation and the army by reviving the system of geographical linking and the Landsmannschaften concept. Necessarily, this linking was now based upon the territory and populated areas of the Weimar Republic rather than that of the greater Germany of the pre-1914 period. From this process the separate identities of the Bavarian, Prussian, Saxon and Württemberg units that had been maintained since 1871 largely disappeared, so that the Reichswehr was at last presented as the first truly national German army. With the transfer of executive

power to the minister of war in 1923 military and civilian administrative functions blurred still further when the seven district commanders (all of whom were general officers) were given control of economic and day-to-day affairs in their areas. These included matters such as the provision of foodstuffs, labor conditions, prices, currency regulations, relief for the unemployed and (as clear evidence of the continuing Prussian influence) the "limitation of luxury." From 1923, the human face of the Reichswehr was actively promoted and widely publicized through military band concerts staged in aid of charities, and by its provision of gifts for the poor of the various military districts. In these ways the army exhibited many of the traits seen in the former Prussian army prior to the mid-nineteenth century, and von Seeckt's hand in this was very evident.

Organizationally, von Seeckt had two matters to consider. First, he was bound to create an army within the terms of the Versailles treaty – or to circumvent those terms by various means. Second, given that the constrained army organization would inevitably be much smaller than that which Germany actually needed to defend the country effectively, the Reichswehr had to be developed as the professional cadre of a considerably greater national force in embryo, rather than as a complete army. His principal objective was therefore to provide for Germany a small, well-trained professional army capable of conducting high-tempo offensive operations and achieving decisive results in short order. But behind and in support of this army there would be a large militia force capable of conducting defensive and security operations. In order to create a viable offensive capability it was necessary to create an appropriate mobile capability, but with Versailles having prohibited Germany having offensive weaponry, including tanks, combat aircraft and heavy artillery, this presented von Seeckt and his colleagues with a considerable challenge.

As ever, at the heart of the process of developing the new army was the officer corps. Of the 16,000 officers serving in the provisional Reichswehr when the Versailles terms were announced, only 4,000 were permitted to serve in the new Reichswehr. Consequently only the best and most experienced officers were retained, very many having already demonstrated their abilities on the staff and (in the case of numbers of the more junior and middle-grade officers) in combat during the war. Intakes of no more than 200 new ensigns were required annually to maintain the strength of the officer corps: so neither the numbers nor the quality of those available for officer selection gave cause for concern. Meanwhile, the Reichswehr's soldiers were now twelve-year volunteers rather than the three-year conscripts of former times. But these ordinary non-commissioned officers (NCOs) and soldiers were very different from their predecessors: of 96,000 men serving in the Reichswehr in 1930, nine percent had completed secondary education, one percent had matriculated successfully, and three percent were Einjährigen (one-year full-time service volunteers aspiring to a reserve officer commission). Their overall educational, intellectual and practical abilities reflected the fact that

The peacetime organization of the Reichswehr was based upon seven military districts or "Wehrkreise". In addition to the principal headquarters and divisions, this contemporary 1933 map also shows the German territory lost ("verlorene") at Versailles in 1919, as well as the demilitarized ("militärfreie") zone imposed on Germany's western border by the Allied Powers.

the Reichswehr now required no more than 8,000 volunteers each year and that these men could be selected from a population of sixty million.

These men of the new Reichswehr enjoyed a much better lifestyle than had their predecessors. Von Seeckt's reforms resulted in an updated and improved pay structure that included the banding of the private soldier's pay in three separate grades based on his experience and qualifications. In parallel with this came new or extensively refurbished barracks, which provided more space for the individual soldier, better recreational facilities and a much better living environment overall. A review and relaxation of army regulations also ended the long-standing late-night curfew rules for senior soldiers. Meanwhile, significant changes were made to the military code of discipline. Henceforth, the onus not to offend was placed upon the individual soldier's sense of duty and honor and the threat of dismissal from the army, rather than the fear of any traditional punishment. Lastly, in contrast to the importance of religion in day-to-day military life in the old imperial army and its Prussian predecessors, church parades were finally abolished in the Reichswehr, although somewhat anachronistically the old *"GOTT MIT UNS"* embossed on the soldier's belt plate remained until 1945. Arguably, this gradually diminishing emphasis upon the spiritual perspective (and by implication upon the moral perspective as well) contributed to the gradual desensitizing of the professional officers and soldiers of the new Reichswehr in their future approach to the business of war-fighting.

However, the army was still viewed as a somewhat less than prestigious career by much of post-1918 German society, and those men who did seek a commission were therefore particularly well motivated, following a vocation of service and duty to the Fatherland rather than hoping to gain any of the social advantages and kudos that had characterized the extravagant and often profligate lifestyle of many officers in the old imperial army. Indeed, the Reichswehr officer was now expected to live on his army pay, which was increased appropriately in the course of von Seeckt's reforms. Such attitudes entirely reflected the ethos of the new Reichswehr, in which the deliberate interpersonal barriers that had been so assiduously maintained between officers and soldiers in the imperial army were now modified, with an officer's duty of care now cited as being just as important as his ability as a tactical leader. Memories of the unprecedented breakdowns in discipline witnessed during the latter days of the final great German offensive of 1918 – the Kaiserschlacht – still haunted the German high command, and this had lent urgency to bringing the officer-soldier relationship fully into the modern military age. Implicit in this was the need to recruit a quite different sort of officer into the new Reichswehr.

The intellectual and educational standards of the officer corps were reinforced by the mandatory pre-selection requirement for an applicant to have matriculated successfully. This initial hurdle was then followed by a further four years of training before the young ensign's commission could be confirmed. Failure at any stage could result in his subsequent rejection. More advanced military training courses followed, with regular rigorous testing and assessment at all stages. Even though the officer had by then been commissioned, any subsequent decline in his performance, or a judgment that he lacked the ability to progress further, could still result in the termination of his commissioned service. Such was the nature of a highly selective meritocracy in which every officer was required and trained to command or to operate at least one level above his actual rank and appointment, and frequently at two or even three levels above. This concept was characterized as the "leadership-based army" or Führerheer concept.

A natural consequence of this might well have been a dramatic increase in the number of officers commissioned from the ranks, so many ordinary soldiers having demonstrated their ability and courage during the war. However, while the way to a commission was regularized and eased for the well-educated soldier – with success in three examinations providing access to the officer selection system – the officer corps of the late 1920s still came overwhelmingly from the traditional military families and officer class. Indeed, the terms imposed at Versailles actually provided what was still a very traditional and Prussian-influenced high command with the opportunity to discharge large numbers of officers who had been promoted from the ranks during the war, notwithstanding that many of these men had served competently and even with distinction. Consequently, whereas in 1913 only 25 percent of regular officers came from military families and from the well-established Offizierskaste, in 1929 no less than 67 percent did so. Also, an analysis of the social status of the fathers of the Reichswehr officers serving in 1930 showed that no less than 95 percent were or had been of sufficient social standing for their sons to have been eligible candidates for a commission based upon the pre-1914 criteria, while the social status of the remaining five percent (small farmers, artisans, minor officials and other workers) would have debarred their sons from gaining a commission prior to 1914. Similarly, of 195 ensigns commissioned in 1929, 164 had entered through the normal officer selection system, while only 31 had been commissioned from the ranks.[5] Thus, although change was undoubtedly the order of the day in theory, in practice certain long-established traditions still influenced a great deal of army policy. This was especially so where the officer corps and the selection of its officer candidates were concerned and would continue to be so until the Nazis gained overall power in 1933.

Thus the principles affecting the manning of the new Reichswehr were determined and developed, including the new arrangements for terms of service and selection that would enable the army to generate forces up to the levels permitted by Versailles. However, in order to carry out its role the Reichswehr also had to be properly equipped and trained. Accordingly, and in spite of the considerable obstacles imposed at Versailles, both its equipment and its training aspirations reflected the need to achieve an effective mobile offensive capability.

The volunteer soldiers now available to the army were of a high intellectual and educational quality, which (together with the ordinary soldier's twelve-year engagement) permitted a speedy progression from basic to more advanced training. The individual training system at unit level evolved progressively until in 1926 it was divided into six categories. These were based upon ability and experience, with separate training programs for recruits, for older soldiers of limited ability, for non-commissioned officer candidates, for leaders at squad and platoon level, and for leaders at company level. In 1930 this system was formally adopted throughout the Reichswehr. Meanwhile in 1927 a three-year army training cycle was introduced. This required non-specialist combat units to concentrate in succession upon the rifle, the machine gun, and other technologies (such as gas warfare, support weapons, communications and so on) in successive years, while at the same time also carrying out their normal core training activities. Although drill remained an important element of recruit training, it was drastically reduced for trained soldiers, as was gymnastics; sport and extended periods of practical field training now filled the time instead.[6]

Since Versailles had forbidden Germany to carry out any mobilization planning, von Seeckt gradually transformed the Prussian and German high command's long-standing pre-occupation with immediate readiness into a new emphasis upon raising the professional standards of the individual officer and soldier to unprecedented levels. To that end, the use of individual initiative was increasingly promoted through applying the German command concept of Auftragstaktik – mission-led operational direction, focusing upon the wider aims and objectives rather than upon the detail of how they should be achieved – but at much lower levels of command than had been the case in former times. Von Seeckt himself summarized the concept of Auftragstaktik and the responsibility it placed upon commanders and their subordinates when he stated: "Mission-type orders means assigning the objective to be reached, providing [the subordinate commander with the] the necessary means to do so, but allowing [him] complete freedom of action for the execution of the mission."[7]

Training for small-unit offensive operations was conducted extensively, building unashamedly upon the success of the former Stoßtruppen,* the highly effective German assault detachments, or shock troops, that had evolved during the combat on the Western Front during World War I. Meanwhile, at the higher levels of command it was recognized that Germany would almost certainly be confronted by superior enemy numbers in a future war, and so subjects such as mobile defense, fighting withdrawal, concentration of forces and delivery of a decisive counter-stroke were all studied and regularly exercised. All of this accorded precisely with the resolve of von Seeckt and his colleagues that never again would the army become embroiled in the strategically stultifying kind of warfare it had experienced on the Western Front from 1914 to 1918.

The demise of the military academies required by Versailles was largely circumvented by the theoretical and more intellectual training formerly carried out by those institutions now being conducted within the separate divisions of the Reichswehr. This included staff training, written exercises, command and control exercises, and exercises carried out by all levels of headquarters both with and without troops, together with all manner of war games. At the same time, the Truppenamt continued to act as a general staff in all but name, under the direction of Major General Otto Hasse. Within it was a small air planning staff for what was (in theory) Germany's non-existent combat air force. All field exercises were made as realistic as possible, with live-firing a

common feature of these, including the frequent use of overhead fire support from machine guns and from other light support weapons where these were available. In 1921 von Seeckt published a much-revised and updated edition of army field service regulations. This publication, *Command of Combined Arms Combat*, encapsulated his vision for the Reichswehr's offensive capability in the future.

Although quality was a major consideration, the development of viable military mass (the combination of manpower, weaponry, firepower and the resources to sustain them) also occupied the attention of von Seeckt and the Reichswehr's high command extensively. The army managed in various ways to exceed the manpower ceiling that had been imposed by the Allies by such practices as placing significant numbers of officers and soldiers, who would in other circumstances have served in the Reichswehr, into the paramilitary Landespolizei. Other would-be Reichswehr soldiers, among them many members of the Stahlhelm organization, also served with the Grenzschutz-Ost (border troops on Germany's eastern border) in Silesia, where continued friction with the Poles frequently resulted in violent clashes. The creation of several other paramilitary bodies enabled military skills to be acquired and trained reserves to be developed covertly outside the much more visible and closely monitored Reichswehr organization. Similarly, ordinary motor vehicles were used on exercises to represent tanks, and a number of cavalry units were allocated technical, specialist and support roles that in fact bore little resemblance to the traditional role of that arm. However, without the chance both to develop and exercise the tanks, aircraft and other heavy weapons that had been banned by Versailles, and to practice the troops who would use them, the aspirations set out in *Command of Combined Arms Combat* could never realistically be realized. But then, in 1922, the solution to this seemingly insurmountable problem emerged from a most unlikely source.

By that time, Germany had already found friends overseas who saw military, political or economic advantages for their own countries in being prepared to ignore the Versailles treaty and assist Germany to regain its military capability. In Santander, the Spanish shipyards built new submarines for the German navy and provided suitable training facilities. In Sweden, the great armaments firm of Bofors collaborated with Krupp of Essen to develop and test new artillery weapons for the German army. However, in a move that would have considerable historical irony some nineteen years later, the country that was most directly responsible for enabling the army to achieve a viable offensive capability was actually its former enemy Russia, which was now the communist-controlled Soviet Union. By a secret military agreement signed in 1922 in parallel with the Rapallo Agreement[8] concluded between Moscow and Berlin, Germany agreed to train the Red Army and to pay an annual amount to the Soviets, in return for which the Soviet Union put facilities at the disposal of the Reichswehr for it to develop and train with those weapons prohibited by Versailles. Soon Krupp and Junkers were working

---

* The German character 'ß' has been used for those words in which it usually appeared during the 1933–45 period and substitutes for 'ss'.

secretly in special Soviet factories to develop their artillery and aircraft to support the Reichswehr, while complete units of artillery and armored troops and groups of combat pilots were effectively concealed in Russia, living and training within various Red Army establishments, training areas and flying schools. Between 1925

The Versailles treaty had forbidden the Reichswehr to have any tanks. Accordingly, in order to enable it to study, develop and practice armored warfare tactics, it adopted and trained with a range of simulated tanks made of cardboard, as well as various types of tractor.

and 1933 some 130 army pilots and 80 observers were trained at Lipetsk, while in 1925 a school of armored warfare was established at Kazan, where the first German-manufactured tanks were deployed in 1928. The tactics of what eventually became the Panzer arm of Hitler's army were initially trialled by re-roling the seven innocently-named transport battalions (Kraftfahrabteilungen) of the Reichswehr. Within Germany itself during the 1920s and early 1930s the army regularly exercised with agricultural tractors and ordinary motor cars mocked-up to simulate tanks, in order to practice the tactical handling of mechanized units. At higher levels of command, senior German officers often travelled secretly to Russia in order to view the various projects then in progress as well as to observe Red Army maneuvers. Given the fundamental divergence of ideology between communist Russia and republican Germany, the Rapallo Agreement was in many ways an unlikely and unholy alliance, but von Seeckt's determination to secure this arrangement was entirely pragmatic – both countries needed military support and training facilities that only the other could provide. At the same time, both Soviet Russia and Germany still regarded the main western Allies of 1914–18, France, Britain and the United States, as unfriendly and potentially hostile powers. These perceptions were based upon Versailles in Germany's case, while Soviet antipathy toward the former Western powers stemmed from the counter-revolutionary interventionist expeditions they had launched into Russia from 1917.

So it was that between 1920 and 1926 General Hans von Seeckt was instrumental in reviving, developing and maintaining a German military capability which the Versailles treaty had specifically sought to prevent. He achieved this against a background of continuing internal political unrest that often gave way to violence and despite the army's hostility to the Weimar Republic and its political leadership. Von Seeckt generally held very similar opinions, despite his own position within the republic's governing body as military chief of staff, but he successfully sublimated his personal views on the matter for what he perceived as the greater good of the army and the country he served. At the time of his resignation from active duty in 1926 – the activities of the Freikorps and the first stirrings of the NSDAP (notably Hitler's abortive "Beer Hall putsch" of 1923) notwithstanding – he could not reasonably have foreseen the sea-change in Germany's political fortunes in the 1930s or the purpose to which the army would eventually be put by Hitler. Nevertheless, he unknowingly enabled all that would follow from 1939. Without his transformation and expansion of the Reichswehr during the 1920s, the subsequent creation of "Hitler's army" would not have been possible.

## 5. The Nazis in Power

From 1925 much political manoeuvring took place as von Hindenburg dominated the army and the government alike (and was viewed by many almost as a new Kaiser). The minister of war from 1928 was Wilhelm Groener, and the Reichswehr was headed by General Wilhelm Heye, following von Seeckt's resignation in 1926.[9]

From 1932, General Kurt von Schleicher, a man close to both von Hindenburg and Groener, exerted great influence upon a succession of chancellors, achieving that position himself in December 1932 but then being forced to resign on 28 January the following year. Professionally competent, he was a manipulative, politically ambitious and self-serving reactionary. He actively courted Hitler and the Nazis from 1930, less from any belief in the merits of the Nazi cause than as a means of achieving his goals for Germany and the army – indeed, he later tried unsuccessfully to use the Reichswehr and the trades unions together to contain the rapidly growing popularity and power of Adolf Hitler and the NSDAP. His always dangerous involvement with National Socialism placed him at the very center of much of the political chaos and civil unrest that was evident in much of Germany by the early 1930s, and this eventually provoked his own death at the hands of the Nazis. The political chaos included the demise of the minister of war, General Groener, following his unsuccessful attempt to ban the NSDAP Sturmabteilung (the Nazi SA "storm detachments", the "Brownshirts"), and the fall of Chancellor Brüning with the appointment of Franz von Papen in his place, at which time von Schleicher became minister for the Reichswehr. Then, in July 1932, von Papen was forced to call an election. As a result the Nazis became the largest single party represented in the Reichstag. Hitler refused to accept a coalition government, and von Hindenburg refused to appoint him chancellor. A further election in November 1932 did not alter the situation significantly, and this led von Hindenburg to appoint von Schleicher as

chancellor. However, his time in office lasted little more than a month, and a coalition government was finally formed early in 1933, with Hitler as chancellor and von Papen as his deputy.

This was a defining moment for Germany and its army. General Werner von Blomberg had earlier replaced von Schliecher as minister for the Reichswehr. In October 1933, General Ludwig Beck was appointed head of the Truppenamt, and in February 1934 Lieutenant General Werner von Fritsch became Chef der Heeresitleung (Chief of the Army High Command). All these generals now occupying key posts were Nazi sympathizers. Meanwhile, Hitler and the NSDAP moved to consolidate their political position and power within and over all of the principal civilian institutions of Germany. These included the police, the judiciary, the state civil services and the local administrative bodies. Neither did the army escape the attention of the Nazi political message. There, Hitler's nationalistic speeches and declared policies of rearming Germany, reintroducing military conscription, dispensing with the constraints imposed by Versailles, saving the state from the "evils of communism",[10] and restoring Germany to its former greatness found favour throughout much of the Reichswehr. Many members of the officer corps viewed his statement that the new German state – a "Third Reich", no less – would be founded jointly upon the Nazi Party and the Reichswehr as reassuring, positively stimulating and thoroughly motivating after the uncertain and turbulent years of Weimar. Surely, many of them thought, a few constraints on civil liberties and the new anti-Semitic measures now being introduced and imposed so speedily throughout the country were of little consequence if the army was once again destined to become a real power both within Germany and in the wider world?

On 15 March 1933 instructions were issued to introduce the new Reichskokarde insignia and for the adoption of the eagle and swastika (Hakenkreuz) helmet decal, which combined the traditional German eagle with the NSDAP symbol. From 17 February 1934 the black-white-red shield helmet decal was also taken into use. Finally, instructions for the wearing of the spread-eagle and swastika national emblem on the uniform jacket were issued on 30 October 1935, the national insignia having already been widely taken into use from early 1934.[11] So it was that by the end of 1935 the Nazi emblem was everywhere accepted and seen to be in everyday use as an integral part of the badge of the Reichswehr and of the German nation. It was a masterpiece of political presentation by the Nazis, one that visually reinforced the inseparable nature of the NSDAP from the nation in which it now held power.

Unquestionably, the Nazis' swift progress to power was remarkable. However, when considered within the totality of 1914–18, the shame of Versailles, the unpopularity of Weimar, the growing fear of communism, a perceived Polish threat and the (ostensibly) apolitical development of the Reichswehr by von Seeckt, the rise of the NSDAP was perhaps less of an aberration than it might at first seem to be. The political process had been

In early 1933 von Hindenburg finally agreed to the formation of a coalition government, with Hitler as chancellor and von Papen as his deputy. Here, a propaganda poster in Berlin in November 1933 seeks to portray the unity of purpose of von Hindenburg (the "Marschall") and Hitler (the "Gefreite", or lance-corporal).

"Wall Street Crash" was severe throughout Europe, but in Germany it proved to be absolutely catastrophic, and by the summer of 1931 the awful extent of this economic disaster was evident throughout Germany as business confidence collapsed and foreign investment fell away. The country's once-booming manufacturing industry swiftly disintegrated as German trade and overseas markets stagnated and then crumbled, which in turn produced mass unemployment. Banks foreclosed, there was rampant inflation, and the nation's financial system was in turmoil. Inevitably, the blend of financial chaos, unemployment, dashed hopes, lost savings, ruined lives, anger and frustration boiled over – there were regular outbreaks of violent street-fighting between political extremist groups, and by now the only groups of any consequence were the communists and the Nazis. Such was the volatile, violent, polarized political environment in which Nazism thrived. Of the two diametrically opposed political groups, the Nazis and their brown-shirted paramilitary troopers of the SA finally emerged triumphant in 1933. They did so with the tacit approval and passive support of very many members of the Reichswehr.

This support was reinforced by Hitler's rejection of a proposal made by Ernst Röhm (the commander of the Sturmabteilung) in February 1934 that the SA should provide the foundation for the creation of a new German army, a proposal that was under-standably anathema for the army. Röhm also advocated the continuance of the National Socialist revolution, something that now ran contrary to Hitler's own agenda. Indeed, Röhm's timing was particularly ill-judged, as it coincided with a power-play by two members of Hitler's inner circle, Himmler and Göring, to supplant the SA with the Schutzstaffel (or SS), the Nazi Party's own élite paramilitary self-protection and security force. On 30 June 1934, the Nazi "blood purge" – Die Nacht der langen Messer (or "Night of the Long Knives") – was launched by scores of SS murder squads. During the next few days some 77 leading Nazis were arrested and summarily executed, together with at least another 100 lesser Nazis and non-Nazi opponents of the party. However, the overall figure for those killed, including SA men, political figures, civil servants and military officers, was almost certainly much higher. Despite his well-known contempt for the SA, the recently retired General von Schleicher and his wife were among those murdered, shot down by six SS gunmen at their home in Neubabelsberg, Berlin, in front of their fourteen-year old stepdaughter. Bizarrely, Hitler and his closest associates were personally involved in the bloodbath despite the fact that numbers of those killed had variously been their friends, colleagues and comrades-in-arms in the old army, the Freikorps and the NSDAP for many years. Significantly, the Reichswehr provided some of the weapons and other facilities to the SS for these murderous operations, justifying this support with the argument that the SA's military aspirations had directly threatened the army, while at the same time Röhm's revolutionary political aspirations had also threatened the stability of the state.

so weakened in the post-1918 years that, while the German people yearned for stability and a strong, capable, democratic and (within reason) liberal government, the Reichswehr was probably the only institution of the time that could have delivered this through wholehearted support for the government and direct involvement in the political process. However, the army's often half-hearted support for Weimar and the active opposition of many officers to the republican government created a political vacuum while opening the way for the NSDAP to fill that vacuum with alacrity.

Nevertheless, the Nazis might still have failed to achieve political power and the Weimar Republic might yet have survived if other equally important factors had not militated against this. In practice the political events, turmoil, violence, and uncertainty of 1930–4 had also been conducted against the wider background of escalating economic turbulence triggered by the collapse of the Wall Street Stock Exchange in October 1929. The impact of the

The events of 30 June 1934 and the few days that followed were a defining moment both for Germany and for the army. As well as consolidating Hitler's power and establishing the Nazis' political course for the next decade, the "blood purge" also eliminated the SA and replaced it with the much more effective and ideologically focused SS, the organization that later spawned the Waffen-SS (the "armed SS"), many of whose troops would in due course fight alongside those of the army on many of Germany's World War II battlefields. Thus, 1934 marked the point from which the fortunes and fate of the German army began to converge with those of the Waffen-SS (as opposed to the Allgemeine SS, the "general SS").

Following the death of von Hindenburg on 2 August 1934, Hitler assumed the title of Führer instead of president and so took to himself absolute power throughout Germany. The Reichswehr, which had for so long abrogated its political responsibilities and denied its involvement in German politics during the formative years of the republic, now came fully within the Nazi purview. No longer were the soldiers required to swear allegiance to the state, to its constitution and lawful institutions, and obedience to the president of the republic and their superior officers, as they had under the Weimar regime. Neither were they any longer to swear allegiance to "the people of Germany and the Fatherland" when

swearing the modified and simplified oath introduced by Hitler in December 1933 soon after he gained power. Then on 2 August 1934 another version of the soldier's oath was promulgated. In this latest version every officer and soldier was required to "swear by God this sacred oath that I shall render unconditional obedience to Adolf Hitler, the Führer of the German Reich and its people, supreme commander of the armed forces, and that I shall at all times be prepared, as a brave soldier, to give my life for this oath."

On 21 May 1935 the Reichswehr was renamed "Die Wehrmacht" – the national armed forces, comprising "Die Kriegs-marine" (the navy), "Die Luftwaffe" (the air force) and "Das Heer" (the army) – within which every officer, soldier, sailor and airman now owed his duty, honor and loyalty not merely to the German state but to the man who had successfully contrived to present the very essence of the German state embodied in his own person as "Der Führer", Adolf Hitler. Thus "Hitler's army" rose at last like a phoenix from the ashes and despair of Versailles, firmly founded upon the war machine so assiduously developed by von Seeckt during the all-too-often dark days of Weimar. For the army and for Germany alike, those dark days would eventually prove to be as nothing compared with the even darker but unforeseen days that lay ahead.

Here the principal members of the 1933 coalition government attend a performance at the Berlin State Opera, in August 1933. They include (front row, left to right) Göring (minister of the interior for Prussia), von Blomberg (defense minister), Hitler (chancellor), von Hindenburg (president), von Papen (vice-chancellor), and (seated far right) Raeder (head of the navy).

"The new Europe is invincible" – a propaganda map published in *Signal* magazine encapsulated Hitler's strategic intentions and (inset) highlighted the "hostile war plans" of the nations surrounding Germany and Italy in 1939.

# PART II
# The German Army at War, 1939–1945

## 1. Opening Moves

Although the German army launched its first real offensive of the war on 1 September 1939 with its invasion of Poland, it had actually embarked upon the first of its steps along the road to war as early as 1935. In January that year a plebiscite by the population of the Saar voted overwhelmingly for the region's return to German rule. This border region and industrial mining area had been under the "protection" of France since 1919 in accordance with the arrangements directed at Versailles, but in March 1935 Germany resumed control of the Saarland; that same month Hitler introduced conscription and created a peacetime army 550,000 strong and comprising 36 divisions, a move in direct defiance of Versailles. This was the first really clear indication to the wider world that Germany, led by the Nazis, was actively moving to redress the situation that had been imposed by the Allied powers at Versailles. The lack of any effective opposition by those powers either to German repossession of the Saarland or to Hitler's announcement of a dramatic increase in Germany's military capability was certainly not lost on the Führer. A year later, in March 1936, German troops marched into the Rhineland in strength, a region that had been demilitarized by the Versailles treaty with the intention of the Allies that it should be an effective buffer zone between Germany and France. These troops were rapturously received by the German Rhinelanders, while the Allied powers again did nothing to counter this flagrant breach of the requirements mandated by Versailles. Also in 1936, the Rome–Berlin Axis treaty was signed between Italy and Germany, later being reinforced by the so-called "Pact of Steel" in May 1939, although Japan's disinclination to sign that pact weakened its wider international impact. Much later, the Tripartite Pact of 27 September 1940 would fully establish the Rome–Berlin–Tokyo Axis, with Hungary, Romania and Slovakia joining it from November 1940, Bulgaria from March 1941 and Croatia from 15 June 1941. In due course, many soldiers of Hitler's European allies served alongside those of the German army and in many cases under its direct operational command.[1]

In March 1938, Germany annexed Austria and made it part of a "Greater Germany" by the Anschluß (or "union"). Although many Austrians had long supported union with Germany, this was expressly forbidden by the Versailles treaty. Despite this, on 12 March the German army was ordered to execute *Fall Otto* ("Case" – or "Operation" – "Otto") and subsequently entered Austria to "quell disorder and re-establish the rule of law" in response to a request contrived by Hitler and initiated by Seyss-Inquart, the prominent Austrian Nazi. Within days Austria had been absorbed into Germany, and on 10 April the Austrian population sanctioned the country's new status with a plebiscite. Yet again Hitler had achieved his expansionist objectives without counter-action by France or Britain, and once more the army had been the tool by which these had been achieved. Next, in September 1938, another provision of the Versailles treaty was overturned when the Munich Agreement between Germany, Italy, Britain and France forced Czechoslovakia to cede the predominantly German-speaking Sudetenland (part of Bohemia and Moravia) to Germany. German troops began their occupation of the Sudetenland on 1 October. Then, following further political machinations by Hitler in early 1939, Czechoslovakian President Emil Hácha was coerced into inviting the Wehrmacht to occupy the rest of the country, and on 15 March the German army occupied the remainder of Czechoslovakia. German expansionism, the rejection of Versailles, a disregard for the norms and niceties of international diplomacy, and the successive appeasement of Hitler by Britain and France characterized all of these increasingly daring but astutely-judged moves by the German leader; and in every case it was ultimately the German army that carried them through, while simultaneously providing a suitably threatening backdrop to Hitler's dealings with the representatives of France and Britain and those of the territories on which he had preyed so successfully. Then, in the late summer of 1939, the army's posture changed from threatening to war-fighting when Hitler – secure in the knowledge of Soviet acquiescence due to the German-Soviet non-aggression pact signed on 23 August that year – finally demonstrated the extent of his disdain for France, Britain and the international community, as he set out to resolve Germany's long-standing territorial and post-Versailles disputes on the country's eastern borders. A new military catch-word was soon to enter the military vocabulary to describe a whole new concept of warfare – Blitzkrieg ("lightning war"). Between September 1939 and June 1940 the devastating impact of the Blitzkrieg fell upon Europe, first in the east, then in the north, and finally in the west.

Generalfeldmarschall Walther von Brauchitsch was commander-in-chief of the army from 1938 until Hitler became supreme commander of the armed forces in 1941.

## 2. The Defeat of Poland, September 1939

On the night of 31 August 1939, in the OKH (Oberkommando des Heeres, the army high command) rear headquarters at Zossen, at the OKH forward headquarters, and in the many army command posts and command vehicles concealed in the villages and woods of East Prussia and along Germany's eastern border, the officers' maps all bore the title "Polen" (Poland). At dawn next day, two German army groups crossed the border with a total of more than 2,500 tanks and one and a half million soldiers, supported by almost 10,000 artillery guns and an overwhelming amount of close air support provided by the Luftwaffe. The armored units quickly lanced through the Polish border defenses and roared on into Poland and toward its capital, Warsaw. Behind the Panzer and motorized units came the infantry divisions. Just two decades after the end of the Kaiser's war in 1918 – the "Great War" or "the war to end all wars" – German soldiers were again on the march. Once more Europe was the focus of armed conflict on a grand scale, and World War II had begun.

The spearhead of seven Panzer divisions, four motorized divisions and four light divisions cut speedily through the thinly-spread Polish defense forces, despite the fact that these same forces comprised

Despite some spirited resistance to the German invasion, the Polish army was outclassed and speedily overwhelmed by the Wehrmacht onslaught. Here justifiably self-confident German infantrymen advance into the southern Warsaw suburbs in September 1939.

Generaloberst Heinz Guderian was a master of the Blitzkrieg, a consummate professional soldier and an outstanding Panzer leader and tactician.

some 30 infantry divisions and eleven cavalry brigades. Indeed, in 1939 Poland's armed forces were the fifth largest in the world and included an army with one million men, 475 tanks and 2,800 artillery pieces, now deployed in well-established fixed fortifications and sheltered by several major river obstacles. Nevertheless, the German Panzers quickly broke through the Polish defense lines, and behind them came 40 infantry divisions and one cavalry brigade to consolidate the initial successes. The 4th and 3rd Armies of Army Group North struck from Pomerania and East Prussia, while the 8th, 10th and 14th Armies of Army Group South surged north-east from Slovakia and Silesia toward Warsaw and eastwards toward Lvov.

The 19th Army Corps, commanded by General Heinz Guderian, was in the van of the 4th Army's assault against the heavily fortified zone to the south of the Free City of Danzig. The tanks were echeloned in waves, attacking on a frontage no greater than 5,000 meters, while Stuka dive-bombers and artillery bombarded the Polish positions ahead of the Panzer units and to their flanks. In many places the Panzers rolled along routes and through close terrain that the Polish high command had believed were impassable to armored forces. Motorized infantry moved behind the tanks, ready to deal with any well-defended anti-tank positions or with strongpoints that blocked the way ahead and could not be bypassed. During these early engagements Guderian directed the corps from his own command tank at the forefront of the action, frequently coming under direct Polish fire, and on at least one occasion fire from his own artillery as well. Initially, the Panzer units suffered significant losses at the hands of the Polish anti-tank gunners, due to the relative inexperience of the German commanders dealing with the sheer speed, scale and all-arms nature (including close air support) of this new sort of combat. However, the attacking troops learned fast, and by 5 September the Danzig Corridor was in German hands. Polish resistance was crumbling everywhere, and 4th and 3rd Armies had linked up in East Prussia. Elsewhere, the armored divisions of the three armies of Army Group South, commanded by General Gerd von Rundstedt, with his chief of staff General Erich von Manstein, thrust rapidly past Lodz and toward Warsaw, past Krakow and onwards to the River Vistula, Lvov and the River Bug. In every area the Polish defenses crumbled under the onslaught, and huge

numbers of shocked Polish troops surrendered as their defenses collapsed in the face of the sheer speed, concentrated force and overwhelming firepower of the invaders.

The qualitative chasm between the German and Polish armies was exemplified by an account later related to an interviewer by a Panzer soldier. He told of Polish cavalry counterattacks early in the campaign, when his unit was attacked by enemy cavalry – "Imagine it, sabres against steel plate. A prisoner taken after one such charge is said to have told the interrogating officer that his regiment had been assured that German tanks were made either of cardboard or of wood and sacking. My Panzer informant recalled seeing one officer charge up to one of the vehicles in his squadron, rise up in his stirrups and give a vicious downward stroke with his sabre. This shattered in his hand and the Pole looked dumbfounded. Immediately he pulled out his pistol and fired several rounds at the Panzer, finally shooting himself, determined to die rather than surrender."[2] Apparently the Poles might have thought that the Germans were still using the old "paper panzer" wooden training tanks of the Reichswehr era. General Guderian recalled: "The Polish Pomorska Cavalry Brigade, in ignorance of the nature of our tanks, had charged them with swords and lances and had suffered tremendous losses."[3] In any event, the Polish defense was shattered, and with its initial objectives achieved the 3rd Army advanced on Warsaw while Guderian's 19th Corps of 4th Army now struck south toward Brest-Litovsk to the east of the River Bug, deep into Polish territory.

Only to the west of Warsaw were the Poles able to launch a counter-stroke. There, on 9 September, the Poznan Army, supported by the residue of the Pomorz Army to its north, struck the 8th Army's flank guard. This attack came just as the Germans were primarily focused upon capturing Warsaw, where the 4th Panzer Division had that same day already experienced the limitations of using armor in built-up areas, losing 57 of 120 tanks engaged during three hours of fighting. At the same time, the 10th Army had outrun its supply lines and was short of fuel. At first the Polish counter-stroke achieved some success against the German infantry divisions. However, the speedy redeployment of 1st and 4th Panzer Divisions from the Vistula and Warsaw, together with German forces from the northwest, soon enveloped and routed the Poznan Army, and by the evening of 15 September the Polish offensive had been effectively neutralized. In the meantime, Guderian's two Panzer divisions and one motorized infantry division had completed the encirclement of the strategically important communications hub of Brest-Litovsk the previous day. The city capitulated on 17 September; Warsaw fell on 27 September; and the last Polish resistance ended at Kock on 6 October. By then both France and Great Britain had declared war on Germany (on 3 September), but France had failed to make good a promise to support Poland with an attack into western Germany on 17 September. Moscow further compounded the deepening international crisis when Soviet troops unexpectedly occupied much of eastern Poland.

Generally, the Polish campaign validated the Blitzkrieg concept, although some important lessons had been learnt by the army, and it was therefore time to take stock of the four-week campaign before Hitler launched the Wehrmacht against the Third Reich's former and newly declared enemies beyond Germany's western and northern borders. In the meantime, the Wehrmacht's victory served to reinforce a growing international perception of Germany's new-found military might, together with the view within Germany that Hitler's judgment and strategic ability were indeed infallible. However, within the army it was acknowledged that the new form of war-fighting that it had brought to the battlefield carried with it its own difficulties. These were certainly not insurmountable but needed to be addressed urgently.

Despite the German army's victory – the once-proud Polish army had been virtually annihilated during just four weeks of fighting – the list of lessons learned was extensive. Many officers of the high command, geographically displaced from the fighting army groups, had neither appreciated the speed with which the armored formations moved nor the amounts of technical support and resources needed to maintain their momentum. The capability mismatch between the well-armored tanks and their supporting, but largely unprotected, motorized infantry had been very evident, as was that between the speed of the fast-moving Panzers and that of the non-motorized infantry divisions. Predictably, these infantry divisions – moving on foot and with horse-drawn artillery and other transport – were unable to move or work at the tempo of the Panzer divisions, and this was often compounded by the pedestrian and unimaginative leadership style displayed by some of their commanders. The rapid destruction of the Polish cavalry at the hands of the German armored units demonstrated clearly that the use of mounted cavalry for offensive action in war was no longer a viable option; but, of necessity, horses would continue to be widely used by the army for support and transportation tasks throughout the war.

Within the all-arms armored combat groups and divisions, the already high standards of training and battlefield cooperation still required further honing. Air-to-ground cooperation and support had worked well during the campaign, especially the close support of engaged ground formations. But many aspects of logistics support – above all else the provision of fuel – had to be improved significantly if the army's armored units were to achieve all that Hitler would demand of them in the future. In the event, despite the lessons of Poland in 1939 and the subsequent improvements that were introduced, logistics issues would continue to bedevil the Panzer forces in many of the coming campaigns as they outran their resupply arrangements time and again. The tanks themselves had generally performed well, with no more than 25 percent of these vehicles out of action due to mechanical problems at any one time. Few significant tank-versus-tank actions had taken place, but most of the 217 tanks destroyed by enemy action were the lighter tanks that had been successfully engaged by Polish anti-tank guns. Indeed, the light armored divisions had suffered heavily in action

German and Russian troops manning the Russo-German demarcation line in Poland, 1939. Comrades-in-arms in 1939, these soldiers would be bitter enemies just two years later.

and had not realized their full potential. This was due primarily to the lightness of their vehicles' armor and an insufficiency of supporting tanks and motorized infantry.

The Polish campaign confirmed the best mix of divisions in a Panzer corps to be two Panzer divisions and one motorized infantry division, all with integral supporting arms and Panzer and infantry sub-groupings. Possibly the greatest lesson of the Polish campaign was that the German army would need considerably more armored divisions than it then had if it was to achieve all that Hitler demanded of it in the future. However, in September 1939 the die had already been cast, the escalating conflict was already in progress, and it was far too late to generate such additional forces with the required numbers and level of capability. Consequently, despite the significant increases that were later implemented (including the transformation of the original four light armored divisions into the 6th, 7th, 8th and 9th Panzer Divisions) and the concentration of armored forces for specific campaigns and operations to produce local armored superiority, the continued lack of these divisions in large numbers during the next few years always constrained the army's strategic and tactical aspirations. Indeed, even where more Panzer divisions were able to be created, the balance between the pressing need for quantity and the parallel need to maintain quality would be a continuing issue within the army high command as well as a frequent source of friction between the Third Reich's political leadership and its military chiefs.

# 3. Denmark and Norway, April–May 1940

With his immediate strategic objectives in the east accomplished, Hitler directed the Wehrmacht's energies toward northern Europe: specifically, Denmark and Norway. These operations were planned and ordered by OKW (Oberkommando der Wehrmacht, the armed forces high command) in response to Hitler's concerns that Anglo-French support for the Finns (who were by then under Soviet attack) would prejudice Germany's supplies of Swedish iron ore. Accordingly, on 9 April 1940, with tank units (but not Panzer divisions) spearheading the ground assaults, the Germans launched their newly-formed airborne (or air-landed) infantry and parachute battalions against Denmark and Norway, and both countries were quickly overwhelmed. Within four weeks the fighting had ceased, despite the deployment of British and French forces to support the Norwegians. The viability of airborne forces was proved in Norway, and these troops were destined to have a key role in the initial phase of the army's forthcoming campaign in the west. But while the role of the airborne troops was clearly that of soldiers, they were by then officially Luftwaffe personnel – in a perverse and largely politically-motivated decision taken at Göring's instigation, the army parachute units that had existed since 1936 had been subsumed into the Luftwaffe in January 1938 (and in similar circumstances the army's air defense artillery had come under Luftwaffe command in 1935).

At the conclusion of the campaigns in Denmark and Norway the army consisted of 153 divisions (including ten Panzer and six motorized infantry), of which no less than 136 were available for subsequent operations in the west. Of the remainder, eight divisions were in Norway and Denmark, three in Germany and nine in eastern Germany, Poland and Czechoslovakia. In addition, three Waffen-SS divisions were available for operations alongside those of the army.

## 4. The Defeat of France, May 1940

For almost 200 years France had been first Prussia's and then Germany's main continental rival, and in more recent times – in the aftermath of the devastation of eastern France during 1914–18 – it had been one of the most intransigent and unforgiving signatories

German troops disembark from troop-carrying merchant vessels in Norway on 9 April 1940, the first day of an invasion launched under the pretense of providing German "protection" to that country.

of the Versailles treaty.[4] In fact, Hitler had originally intended to attack westwards via Belgium as soon as the Polish campaign was concluded, with a view to subduing France as soon as practicable, safeguarding the future security of the Ruhr, seizing control of the English Channel coast and then establishing the forward air bases necessary to commence a bombing campaign against Britain. The planned offensive was codenamed *Fall Gelb* ("Case Yellow"). However, particularly bad weather through the winter of 1939/40 forced a delay until the spring, by which time German operations to secure the "northern flank" in Scandinavia had been completed successfully. Hitler used the intervening months to increase his personal control of the army through the progressive marginalization of the chief of the general staff, General Franz Halder, and the army's commander-in-chief, General Walther von Brauchitsch, both of whom had expressed their reservations about an attack upon France. The growing command and control vacuum at OKH was offset at OKW by the additional power gained by Generals Keitel and Jodl, both of whom were staunch supporters of Hitler. Consequently, by early 1940 the direction of German strategic operations was firmly in the hands of Hitler and his favored generals at OKW. In just a few years the system of army command and control that had existed in the German army since the mid-nineteenth century and until 1918, with its operational direction firmly in the hands of the general staff, had changed irrevocably as operational authority over the army became increasingly centralized and focused upon the Führer himself.

Originally OKH had planned for three army groups – the predominantly armored Army Group B in the north (with four armies, including nine Panzer and four motorized divisions) and Army Group A (two armies) in the center – to strike into France through Belgium and the Ardennes respectively, while Army Group C secured the southern border area and flank and then remained in reserve. However, by May 1940 the whole emphasis had changed from the fairly conservative OKH plan to one that envisaged the main thrust, not in the north, but in the centerthrough the densely-forested Ardennes and toward Sedan. In addition to being attracted by its daring nature, Hitler was very aware that Sedan had particular historical significance for Germany and France alike – this was the fortress town at which Wilhelm I, Bismarck and von Moltke had completed the comprehensive and humiliating defeat of Napoleon III and the Second French Empire in September 1870. But certain military considerations also favored this plan, among these the proven success of the Panzers that had traversed parts of Poland originally judged unsuitable for tanks. There was much resistance from within the high command to changing the original plan, but it was no coincidence that a number of officers who had fought in Poland supported the new approach enthusiastically. Foremost amongst these were von Manstein and Guderian. However, fate finally determined the outcome of the debate when a copy of the original OKH plan was unfortunately lost to the Belgians (and was therefore revealed to France and Britain) in an air crash. This significantly undermined

continued OKH support for what was in many respects no more than a modified version of the old Schlieffen Plan.[5] This was, of course, the plan the French and British had always expected the Germans to adopt, based upon their own analysis of the ground, the perceived defensive strength of the French Maginot Line, and their own misperceptions concerning the correct use of armor on a modern battlefield and the type of war that the German army was about to unleash against them.

The much-modified *Fall Gelb* plan still called for a diversionary attack against the Netherlands, Belgium and Luxembourg in line with the original concept, and this part of the offensive would initially be spearheaded by two Panzer corps, supported by airborne and infantry units. It was designed to convince the Anglo-French forces that the long-anticipated "hook" through Belgium and then southwest to seize Paris was indeed still the German intention, and it was expected to provoke an Anglo-French counter-move into Belgium, thus extending their lines of communication and support. But in reality the main attack would now emanate from the depths of the heavily forested (and theoretically impassable for tanks) Ardennes, with some 45 divisions assigned, of which ten were Panzer divisions. The principal blow would fall upon Sedan, where the break-through and consequent dislocation of the Anglo-French forces would be achieved. Thereafter the Panzer divisions would not race for Paris. They would instead seize crossings over the River Meuse, outflank the Maginot Line, cut through the Anglo-French armies and separate them. They would then strike west and northwest to trap the British and the residue of their Belgian and French allies against the Channel coast in order to complete their destruction. The ground attacks were to be preceded by a number of daring *coup de main* operations carried out by parachute troops.

At the outset of the offensive the opposing forces were fairly evenly matched in quantitative terms, but qualitatively the Germans possessed a significant edge. The Dutch and Belgian armies comprised no more than eight and eighteen divisions respectively, in addition to which they had their various reserve forces. The British Expeditionary Force (BEF) had nine divisions under its command in northern France, with a further division grouped with the French 2nd Army Group in the south. The main strength of the Allies lay in the three French army groups. These were the 1st Army Group, with 22 divisions, including two light armored and three motorized; the 2nd Army Group with 36 divisions (including its one British division); and the 3rd Army Group, with fourteen divisions. There was also the 7th Army, with seven divisions, including one light armored and two motorized. French reserves comprised 22 divisions, three of which were armored. Within these army groups the French fielded about 3,000 modern, well-armed and well-armored tanks, with 1,292 of these grouped separately into light and heavy tank divisions. The British had 210 light and 100 heavy tanks, but all of these were allocated to support the infantry. Significantly, the relative paucity of French anti-tank guns – no more than some 8,000 in May 1940 – fell well short of the numbers needed to counter the armored threat that was even then massing just across the frontier.

On the German side, Army Group B in the north had 28 divisions (including three Panzer and two motorized) to carry out its deception mission. The southern Army Group C had nineteen divisions for its security tasks in the south opposite the Maginot Line defenses, while in the center General von Rundstedt's Army Group A deployed no less than 45 divisions (including seven Panzer and three motorized). The divisions of Army Group A were further sub-allocated within the 4th, 12th and 16th Armies. But of particular significance was the armored spearhead, grouped into

Infantrymen of the 6th and 7th Rifle Regiments, together with troops of the 7th Motorcycle Battalion, of Rommel's 7th Panzer Division advance in the area of the Somme river crossings, France, summer 1940. Once unleashed, the German Panzer units generally proved unstoppable, although the preponderance of the army's non-mechanized units frequently limited its overall rate of advance and strategic achievements.

Successful Panzer leaders such as Generalfeldmarschall Erich von Manstein (top), General Hermann Hoth (center) and Generalfeldmarschall Ewald von Kleist dominated the army's armored offensives during the campaigns in France and Russia.

Panzer Group Hoth (two Panzer divisions, one of which was commanded by Erwin Rommel, later to become one of the best-known German commanders of the war) and Panzer Group Kleist (five Panzer divisions). These were the formations that would bring about the defeat of France, and the forthcoming offensive was therefore very much centered upon their actions. Within Panzer Group Kleist were the 41st and 19th Panzer Corps, commanded by Generals Reinhardt and Guderian respectively. The German armored forces deployed with no more than 627 Pz.Kpfw.III and Pz.Kpfw.IV tanks, 1,679 Pz.Kpfw.I and Pz.Kpfw.II tanks, and 381 Czech 38(t) tanks seized in 1939 – a grand total of just 2,687 tanks. But by May 1940 Germany also possessed more than 3,000 combat aircraft, including 400 of the Ju 87 Stuka dive-bombers so vital for the support of the Panzer formations, while the French could deploy a total of about 1,200 aircraft and no dive-bombers. The relative strengths of other aircraft categories indicated that the French and British had about 800 fighters, compared with 1,000 German aircraft of this type (virtually all of which enjoyed a technological superiority), while France had just 150 medium and heavy bombers compared with Germany's 1,470. In artillery, France had less than 3,000 anti-aircraft guns while the Germans had 9,300, and although the German field artillery with some 7,700 guns possessed many fewer than the 11,000 of the French, the latter's almost total reliance on horse-drawn guns meant that France was ill-prepared to conduct or to counter motorized and mobile operations by armored forces.[6]

The ground attack against the Low Countries began on the night of 10 May, a glider-borne operation by specially trained airborne troops of Sturmabteilung Koch having already been launched. This was a daring and most successful assault directly on to the massive complex of Belgian fortifications at Eben Emael – the key to the defense of the Meuse bridges – that morning, achieving complete surprise and linking up with the advancing ground forces during the night of 10/11 May. Within four days the Netherlands had collapsed and, as anticipated, the Allies moved troops into Belgium, engaging Army Group B along the River Dyle. Then, on the morning of 13 May, the first real tank battles took place between Huy and Tirlemont, where the German 16th Panzer Corps supported by the ever-present Stukas infiltrated through the French armored screen. By 5.45 that afternoon the Germans had forced a general withdrawal, which continued during the following two days. However, this action was still no more than a continuation of the wider deception, and, in the face of more resolute opposition from the 1st French Army, the 16th Panzer Corps soon extricated itself from this battle prior to joining that which was by then developing farther to the south. In the meantime, the main blow had already smashed into France from the woods and defiles of the Ardennes as the 15th Panzer Corps struck at Dinant, the 41st at Monthermé, and the 19th at Sedan. On a frontage of no more than eighty kilometers, the three Panzer corps raced to secure the crossings over the River Meuse, and by the night of 12 May they were on the east bank of the river, preparing to

cross the next morning. Despite heavy resistance, by mid-afternoon on 13 May all three corps had secured infantry bridgeheads on the far bank, and the engineers had begun to construct the ferries and bridges necessary for the tanks to cross. By midnight the 15th and 19th Corps had these in place, using them to reinforce their bridgeheads with armor as quickly as possible. The French failed to exploit the temporary vulnerability of the German bridgeheads (especially that of the 41st Corps) and as the Panzers prepared to break out to the west and north, General Corap, commanding the French 9th Army, ordered a general withdrawal on the night of 14 May. By the following evening, elements of the 1st and 7th Panzer Divisions – the former from Guderian's 19th Panzer Corps and the latter from Hoth's 15th Panzer Corps – were respectively 24 and 42 kilometers west of the Meuse. In scenes reminiscent of the Polish campaign, the opposition collapsed wherever the German tanks appeared – prisoners surrendered in huge numbers, and French morale was shattered as the Blitzkrieg struck fear into the consciousness of the French commanders and their soldiers.

The tanks rolled on, protected and supported by the virtually unchallenged air power of the Luftwaffe. But then, with total victory well within the grasp of their enthusiastic commanders, the Panzer units became victims of their own success. The high command – specifically Hitler and von Rundstedt – began to fear for the vulnerability of the Panzer divisions that had advanced so far ahead of the rest of the invading ground forces. Certainly these divisions were indispensable and irreplaceable, but with the French and British defense crumbling it would have been worthwhile allowing the advance to continue, and the only proper decision for the high command now should have been whether to strike at Paris or for the Channel. However, caution prevailed and a halt was ordered to enable the non-Panzer formations to catch up. Despite this, Guderian did persuade his Panzer group commander, Kleist, to allow him a further 24 hours of activity, during which he advanced more than 60 kilometers farther to the River Oise. Rommel also pushed his 7th Panzer Division on another 80 kilometers, reaching Le Cateau by the morning of 17 May. At that point a complete halt was finally ordered. However, growing evidence of the rapidly escalating French collapse (notwith-standing a few local counterattacks, which were soon dealt with), and of the westwards retreat of the BEF with the residue of Belgian and French forces in northern France, later prompted the high command to order a resumption of the advance.

By mid-morning on 20 May the three leading Panzer corps occupied a line from Arleux, close to the River Scarpe, running generally south to Péronne on the River Somme. During that evening the tank crewmen of the 2nd Panzer Division had their first view of the English Channel from their positions in Abbeville; the 1st Panzer Division was well established in Amiens; and the two Panzer divisions of the 41st Corps (6th and 8th) were in positions centered upon Le Boisle and Hesdin respectively. Meanwhile, in the 15th Panzer Corps, the 7th Panzer Division had reached Arras, with the 5th Panzer Division in the Cambrai area.

Apparently, the way now lay wide open for the Panzer corps to seize the Channel ports from Dunkirk to Boulogne and so envelop the remaining undefeated Allied troops in northern France. But then the Germans suffered their first significant reverse, when the motorized infantry of Rommel's 25th Panzer Regiment – the 7th Division's spearhead – was surprised by a group of 70 British heavy tanks near Arras, just when the German tanks were moving well ahead of, and separated from, their supporting infantry. The British tanks wrought havoc among the unprotected infantry, and only when they were engaged by the German divisional artillery and by a number of 88mm anti-aircraft guns (used most effectively in the anti-tank role) did the slaughter of the Panzergrenadiers abate. Some 36 Matilda Mark I and II tanks were destroyed by the devastating fire of these 88mm guns, their barrels depressed as far as they would go. But even the speedy return of the Panzer regiment's tanks made little difference to the outcome of the engagement: they were met in their turn by a storm of fire from a number of well-concealed British anti-tank guns, which quickly reduced twenty German tanks to burning hulks. Eventually the 5th Panzer Division, urgently summoned from Cambrai, arrived on the scene, but by then the battle was more or less over.

This short, sharp and tactically insignificant engagement had much wider implications at the operational and strategic level of command. The German losses served to confirm the high command's fears about over-extending the lines of advance of the Panzer divisions, while also underlining the vulnerabilities inherent in these particular divisions as then structured and equipped. However, as well as confirming the ineffectiveness of the German 37mm PAK anti-tank gun against the armor of the latest Allied tanks, it had also shown those who witnessed this battle the enormous potential of the 88mm anti-aircraft gun utilized as an anti-armor weapon – a potential that Rommel would later employ very effectively during his campaign in North Africa.

In any event, fearful of losing its most important war-winning fighting formations, the high command now ordered a halt to the spectacular if somewhat helter-skelter advance that had taken place during the first three weeks of May 1940. A general consolidation was to take place, with flanks and lines of communication properly secured, while the remaining ground forces caught up. In the meantime, the Panzer corps prepared deliberate attacks to take Boulogne and Calais, rather than making any attempt to engage the rapidly filling Allied salient about Dunkirk – Göring had confidently asserted that the Luftwaffe would deal with this residual rump of the Allied armies in northern France. In the event, air power alone proved unable to defeat the Dunkirk salient, and, although Calais fell on 26 May, thus releasing the 19th Panzer Corps for operations against the salient, it was by then defended strongly and in depth, and it would require a major operation to overcome it. Before this attack could be mounted, however, between 26 May and 4 June a mixed fleet of British, French and Belgian naval vessels, together with a disparate armada of privately owned craft of every type, had embarked a total of 338,226

soldiers (of which 198,315 were British and 139,911 were Allied but predominantly French) and conveyed them to safety in England, while on 28 May the Panzer divisions had been withdrawn from their positions close to the Channel coast to prepare for the task of defeating the remaining French forces to the south. So it was that the opportunity for the German armored units to annihilate the Anglo-French forces at Dunkirk had been denied them by their own high command, a decision that underlined, and had been in large part precipitated by, the overall paucity of Panzer forces then available to the army.

During June the Panzers struck south and west, supported by the bulk of the *Fall Gelb* non-motorized follow-on forces, all of which were by then well-established on French territory. Although some stiff French resistance was encountered, with often spirited attacks being carried out by a number of French armored units, such action was generally isolated and unsustainable. Certainly the heart had gone from the French army, and both its high command and its government lacked the resolve to fight on. From 10 June the government was actively seeking ways in which to end the conflict, and on 13 June Paris became an open city, being entered by the Germans the next day. Elsewhere, Guderian's Panzers reached the Swiss frontier on 16 June, enveloping a huge number of French units between his corps and the French border. Cherbourg fell to Rommel's division on 19 June, where the 1st British Armoured Division belatedly and ill-advisedly had been sent from England to fight alongside the French defenders – 174 light tanks and 156 medium tanks were lost by the British at Cherbourg. Lyons fell on 20 June, and by 25 June the German line ran across southern France from Angoulême in the west, north of Limoges, through Clermont-Ferrand and St-Etienne, and then along the south side of the River Rhône to the Swiss border close to Geneva. The newly installed French president, Marshal Pétain, had already ordered an end to further resistance on 17 June, and by 25 June the battle for France was over. The Germans controlled the Low Countries and all of northern France, and a compliant French government had assumed power in the as yet unoccupied south of the country. The army's victory was complete. The Blitzkrieg concept had been well and truly validated, and what was universally seen as Hitler's strategic brilliance was acclaimed throughout Germany.

Exemplifying the success of German arms in 1940, troops parade along the Boulevard Haussmann in Paris on 14 June 1940, during the Wehrmacht's celebration of its victory over France.

With considerable strategic ability and experience of army and army group command in Poland, France and Russia, Generalfeldmarschall Gerd von Runstedt was given overall command in the West in 1944 and later masterminded the Ardennes offensive.

## 5. The Balkan Campaign, March–June 1941

The fall of France and the evacuation of the BEF to England removed the immediate threat of ground warfare on Germany's western flank, although Great Britain continued to pose a threat at sea and in the air, as well as farther overseas. The Luftwaffe was confident both of its ability to bomb Britain into submission and to achieve the level of air superiority in the Channel area that was a prerequisite for the invasion of southern England – Operation *Seelöwe* ("Sealion"); but its failure to defeat the Royal Air Force (RAF) during the Battle of Britain between July and October 1940 led to the indefinite postponement of *Seelöwe* on 17 September. Indeed, it is arguable whether the planned cross-Channel invasion was ever really viable in 1940, and Hitler frequently appeared to lack real enthusiasm for this operation. Meanwhile, the bombing of British cities and strategic targets during August 1940 to May 1941 also failed to force a British capitulation. In any event, Hitler's assessment as at June 1940 was that for all practical purposes Great Britain (whose empire the Führer much admired) had already been defeated militarily and was therefore neutralized strategically. He firmly believed that it was only a matter of time before London accepted the inevitable and sued for peace, when he anticipated that its armed forces would join Nazi Germany's great crusade against the menace of communism.

In truth, by August 1940, Hitler's attention – and that of the OKW and OKH – was becoming increasingly focused on the army's next great enterprise in the east, the defeat of the Soviet Union. Numbers of troops had already been redeployed from France in preparation for this, while that same month Hitler ordered that the army should increase its strength to 180 active divisions. However, although the number of Panzer divisions was doubled (to twenty) and no less than 205 divisions had been created by June 1941, the requirement set out for the army in Directive No. 17 of 1 August 1940 was generally achieved only by splitting up and weakening its existing formations. Consequently, the actual increase in capability was negligible and its strategic impact illusory. In the meantime, on what would soon become the southern flank of Germany's thrust eastwards, the Italian forces of Hitler's Axis ally Mussolini were proving woefully incapable of making any progress against the Greek and British forces in Greece, North Africa and the Mediterranean. This, together with the need to safeguard Romanian oil supplies for German use, led to the army's Balkan and Aegean area campaign from April 1941, the planning for which had begun on 18 November the previous year following the successful counterattack carried out by the Greek forces against the Italians.

On 6 April 1941 German forces, primarily the 12th Army (but also involved were the 2nd Army and an additional corps) struck into Yugoslavia simultaneously from Bulgaria, Austria, Romania and Hungary. Encountering weak Yugoslav resistance, the failure of the Anglo-Greek force to exploit the defensive potential of Yugoslavia's

rugged terrain, and aided by Greek animosity toward the British within the Anglo-Greek command structure, the Blitzkrieg moved swiftly to outflank the Anglo-Greek forces and cut off the Greek army in Albania. Everywhere the Allies were forced to withdraw, and on 20 April the British bowed to the inevitable and ordered the evacuation of its expeditionary force, thus consigning Greece to German occupation. Some 27,000 of the troops evacuated were transported to the island of Crete, where they joined an Anglo-Greek garrison of about 3,000 British and Commonwealth soldiers (predominantly the 6th Australian and 2nd New Zealand Divisions) and several thousand Greek troops. However, most of the Allies' heavy weapons, support equipment and artillery used in Greece were not available for the defense of Crete, having been abandoned during the evacuation of the mainland.

## 6. The Battle for Crete, May 1941

The Allies already knew from "Ultra" intelligence derived from their intercepts of German "Enigma" code messages that the Germans intended to seize Crete, in order both to prevent the bombing of the Romanian oilfields and to forestall a British offensive being launched into the region from North Africa. Accordingly, the decision had been taken to defend the island. But in order to protect the secret of "Ultra", General Freyberg, the British commander, was not permitted to enhance the airfield defenses to the extent he deemed necessary, and, deprived of the full intelligence picture, the British commanders anticipated that the main invasion would be amphibious. What followed was the first – and last – great German airborne assault of the war.

In fact, the Fallschirmjäger (paratroops) had officially been under Luftwaffe control since 1935, so it might be argued that their activities fall outside a study dealing with the development of the German army. None the less, in many of the coming campaigns these paratroopers served as élite infantrymen, "army" soldiers in all but name, alongside army units and under army command, where they demonstrated time and again their fighting spirit, determination and professionalism. Similarly, their airborne (parachute- and glider-delivered) assault operations were patently military rather than air force activities, and so it would be an omission not to take account of the rise and relatively short-lived existence of the airborne capability within the Wehrmacht, and particularly of the decisive role of these troops in the capture of Crete.

Operation *Merkur* called for the airfields at Maleme (close to the town of Canea), Heraklion and Retimo to be seized in a parachute assault by Major General Kurt Student's Fliegerkorps 11, supported by Fliegerkorps 8 (the air strike component); these two formations made up Generaloberst Alexander Löhr's Luftflotte 4. The capture of the airfields would enable the airlanding of the 5th Mountain Division shortly thereafter. The German airborne and air-landed forces together numbered 15,750 men, with a follow-on force of up to 7,000 transported by sea. The assault force was supported by 500 transports (mainly Ju 52s), about 80 gliders, 280 bombers, 180 fighters, and 40 reconnaissance aircraft.

Soon after dawn on 20 May the airborne assault against Crete began, and it initially sustained very heavy casualties at the hands of the lightly-armed and thinly-spread, but determined and well-trained British Commonwealth troops. Meanwhile, at sea the Royal Navy destroyed the 5th Mountain Division's component in their transports en route to their intended landing beaches on the island. On 21 May, however, the precipitate abandonment by its New Zealander defenders of Hill 107, which overlooked Maleme airfield, allowed Student to call in the Ju 52 transports, despite the Allied artillery fire still falling on the runway. The tide turned, and the German main effort switched from Heraklion to Maleme, where the build-up of the 5th Mountain Division continued apace, as the defense of Crete swiftly crumbled from the west. With the battle lost, the Royal Navy managed to evacuate some 7,000 British Commonwealth troops from Heraklion and Sphakia harbors to Egypt between 27 and 30 May, nine warships being sunk and a further seventeen badly damaged at the hands of the fighters and bombers of Fliegerkorps 8 during the battle. By 1 June the fighting for Crete had ended. The garrison's British and Commonwealth casualties amounted to 1,742 killed and missing, 2,225 wounded and 11,370 captured. Of the 17,530 German troops who landed on Crete between 20 and 23 May, no fewer than 8,000 had been killed, including about 6,500 of the élite Fallschirmjäger, and although the strategic mission had been accomplished, with the Balkan and Aegean flank and Romania secured against any possible British interference in the army's impending attack on Russia, such losses to the German airborne forces were unsustainable – some 56 percent overall. As a result, Hitler never again sanctioned the large-scale use of airborne units, and thereafter the Fallschirmjäger were used only for conventional ground combat and certain small-scale commando operations.

By June 1941 the main focus of the high command was already firmly fixed elsewhere, as the OKW now assumed responsibility for all operational theaters except one. The single operational theater that remained under OKH control was what would shortly become known as the Eastern Front, as the final preparations for Hitler's impending invasion of the Soviet Union were completed in Germany and in the occupied territories to the east.

# 7. The Invasion of the Soviet Union, June–December 1941

Hitler's obsession with the evils of communism, its supposed links to a wider Jewish conspiracy against Germany, and his perception of the Russians as an inferior race together shaped his foreign policy and strategic objectives, and precipitated his decision to attack his erstwhile Soviet ally in 1941. Viewed in hindsight, this was a classic example both of underestimating and of misunderstanding one's enemy, and the monumental errors of judgment, national policies, political and ideological dogma, and strategic solutions that resulted were thoroughly perverse. But, by early 1941, the perverted political ideology of the time had well and truly subsumed the legacy of common sense and pragmatism that had generally served Germany's army so well in the past. It had transformed the impending attack on the Soviet Union (Operation *Barbarossa*) into a crusade in which it was anticipated that the forces of National Socialism would finally and inevitably annihilate the evils of its ideological arch-enemy, communism, thus enabling Germany to assume at last its rightful place at the head of the civilized nations of the world. At the same time, despite the strategic inevitability of the German attack against the Soviet Union, Hitler also feared that Stalin was on the verge of supporting Great Britain against Germany and used this mistaken belief to justify his eventual decision to attack in mid-1941. In fact, Churchill had indeed already secretly proposed this course of action to Stalin, but the Soviet ruler had ignored the British overtures (believing them to be a trap) and had then dutifully informed his ally Hitler about them – which merely fuelled Hitler's existing suspicions. However, these suspicions had also been reinforced by Stalin's reluctance to join Germany in the war against Britain when Hitler had proposed this in November 1940, despite the Führer's offer to Stalin of a significant part of the British Empire's overseas territories once Britain had been defeated.

While the ever-pragmatic Soviet leader had no thoughts of embarking upon a war against Germany at that stage, he had already anticipated that such a conflict would probably take place not less than two years hence, and he suspected that Hitler's failure to launch the invasion of England in 1940 was indicative of a secret Anglo-German accommodation against the Soviet Union, with any acceptance of Hitler's invitation to declare war against Britain

The morale and propaganda value of Hitler's visits to his troops in the field was always significant, and such events were always well photographed and widely reported within Germany. Here, the Führer visits army units on the Eastern Front, probably shortly before the start of Operation Barbarossa in mid-1941.

Generalfeldmarschall Fedor von Bock performed well in Poland, France and Russia but was one of a succession of senior officers later dismissed by Hitler for expressing strategic views that differed from those of the Führer.

providing an excuse for that to happen. This view was given added validity by the bizarre, unauthorized and ill-fated flight to Scotland by Hitler's deputy, Rudolf Hess, in May 1941. In any event, Stalin remained absolutely convinced that Germany could not attack Russia in the short-term and certainly not while Britain remained undefeated. He reasoned that a German attack on Russia would involve Germany in a war on two fronts, which ran directly contrary to all military logic in light of Germany's limited resources and ability to fight a widespread and potentially lengthy war of attrition.

Hitler believed that the Soviet state was fundamentally so flawed and its armed forces so weakened (36,671 of its best military personnel having been executed, exiled or dismissed during Stalin's widespread purges of the officer corps since 1937) that the mere fact of the German offensive would precipitate its rapid demise. In addition, Stalin's repressive totalitarian regime had provoked considerable disquiet among significant sections of the population in western and southern Russia. But Hitler's assessment was soon shown to be far from accurate. Indeed, he had failed to understand that the Russian soldier's love of his motherland and readiness to obey his leaders without question (perhaps more from fear and a sense of duty to his country than as a consequence of communist ideology or respect for the leadership) were akin to the German soldier's love of his Heimat and to his obligations of duty and obedience (embodied in the soldier's oath introduced in May 1935). Had Hitler properly comprehended the true nature of the Russian soldier and his homeland, Operation *Barbarossa* might well have taken a very different form, with the German invasion almost certainly not being launched as early as mid-1941.

Given the extent of pre-war German-Soviet military cooperation, especially during the early stages of Germany's rearmament during the 1930s, it was quite incredible that German military intelligence had also misunderstood or misrepresented the military capability and true nature of its erstwhile ally. Clearly, the widely held, but misplaced, view both in the high command and throughout much of the army that the great new offensive would be another Blitzkrieg, similar to those of 1939 and 1940 and ultimately just as successful, was hopelessly optimistic. The army was destined to pay a catastrophic price for this historic miscalculation by Hitler and the increasingly politicized high command at OKW. While the early stages of the offensive would indeed mirror the Blitzkrieg successes of 1940, the sheer scale and tempo of the invasion of the Soviet Union would eventually prove unsustainable. By the end of the war in May 1945, no fewer than 80 percent of the army's total casualties from 1939 to 1945 would have been sustained during its four years' campaign against the Red Army on the Eastern Front, while the Wehrmacht as a whole would have incurred a staggering 1,015,000 fatal casualties on that front alone between June 1941 and May 1945.

As dawn broke on 22 June 1941, following a short hot and sultry night, thousands of guns were unmasked and began their bombardment of the Soviet border defenses, while overhead waves of the Luftwaffe's ground attack aircraft screamed eastwards to strike positions and headquarters in depth, and to destroy the Soviet air force on the ground. Meanwhile, thousands more tank, armored infantry carrier, truck and motorcycle engines started up, radio silence was broken, and the huge troop concentrations at last moved from their concealed hiding areas eastwards to the border and on into Russia. Despite its devastating scale, for some time after the start of the German onslaught and in the face of all the evidence to the contrary, Stalin remained in a state of denial that Hitler had reneged on the German-Soviet non-aggression pact. Nor could he be swayed from his belief that Hitler's action confounded all military common sense and strategic logic.

Initially, the impressive progress made during the first three or four months of Operation *Barbarossa* allayed any residual reservations about its advisability. At the outset, the army – four million men, 3,648 tanks (of the army's total fleet of 5,694 tanks), 600,000 other vehicles, 7,184 artillery guns, most of the Wehrmacht's 600,000 horses, and supported by some 2,000 aircraft – advanced on a front that was almost 1,600 kilometers long and ran from the Baltic in the north to the Black Sea in the south.[7]

Twenty-year-old infantryman Harald Henry, advancing with the second echelon, recorded that "we've been marching for 25 kilometers past images of terrible destruction. About 200 smashed-up, burnt-out [Russian] tanks turned upside down, guns, lorries, field kitchens, motor-cycles, anti-tank guns, a sea of weapons, helmets, items of equipment of all kinds, pianos and radios, filming vehicles, medical equipment, boxes of munitions and books, grenades, blankets, coats, knapsacks. In among them, [there are] corpses already turning black … A stench of putrefaction [from dead horses] hangs numbingly over our columns." Some six weeks later, he wrote of "endless hours of marching ahead … The strange smell everywhere, a mixture of fire, sweat and horse corpses that will probably remain with me forever as part of this campaign. [And meanwhile] the dust shrouds us all. This unending eastern land is so vast, it's quite impossible to try to gauge its extent … the featureless spaces flow endlessly as far as the horizon."[8]

Despite the significant progress made by the army against the Russians during the first days and weeks of the invasion, it is noteworthy that this was due primarily to concentration of force, surprise, and superior tactics, rather than to the application of overwhelming strength on a strategic scale. At the outset of Operation *Barbarossa* the Red Army forces defending Western Russia fielded almost three million men, supported by no fewer than 15,000 of the army's 24,000 tanks and 9,000 aircraft. Also, other than in aircraft, the qualitative imbalance was not nearly as great as has sometimes been suggested. Of the 3,648 German tanks deployed on 22 June, only 444 were the latest Pz.Kpfw.IV model, while almost 2,000 of the Russian tanks that opposed them were T-34 and KV heavy tanks, both of which types were superior to any tank then in German army service.

In the north, Army Group North (commanded by General-feldmarschall Ritter von Leeb), with three Panzer divisions, two motorized divisions and 24 infantry divisions, attacked from East Prussia, through Latvia, Lithuania and Estonia, capturing Riga on 1 July before joining with Finnish forces about Leningrad and besieging the city from 19 August. Meanwhile, Generalfeldmarschall Fedor von Bock's Army Group Center, with nine Panzer divisions, six motorized divisions, 33 infantry divisions and one cavalry division, struck eastwards from occupied Poland to capture Smolensk on 15 July. By 29 June two Panzer groups had also cut off some 300,000 soldiers at Minsk. Finally, Army Group South, under the command of Generalfeldmarschall Gerd von Rundstedt, with five Panzer divisions, three motorized divisions and 34 infantry divisions, as well as a number of units from Germany's Romanian ally, advanced into the southwest of the Soviet Union, into Bessarabia and toward Odessa and Kharkov, which fell on 24 October. By 25 November the Panzers were less than twenty miles from Moscow – they could have been there very much earlier had they not been diverted by Hitler to carry out other tasks between mid-July and early October. Indeed, as early as mid-July, evidence of the increasing discord between Hitler, OKW, OKH and some of the formation commanders in the field was emerging, as the campaign threatened to run on longer than had been envisaged but with no longer-term strategic objectives yet set for it. Then in mid-September the first snows of the winter fell in the north; in mid-October heavy rain and sleet made vehicle movement virtually impossible. The plummeting temperatures in mid-November at last froze the ground and enabled the advance

to continue, but the bitter cold brought with it many other problems.

As the months passed, the hundreds of thousands of soldiers who had originally driven, ridden and marched deep into the Soviet Union from East Prussia, occupied Poland and from start points in Hungary and Romania in June 1941 had clearly embarked upon a campaign very different from anything that they had previously experienced. Although the army at first achieved a succession of victories, the annihilation of much of the Red Army in western Russia, and thousands of prisoners taken, by the end of the summer of 1941 its lines of communication and resupply were unprecedented in length. Russian resistance was stiffening, and the army was also facing the imminent onset of the Russian winter, for which the Wehrmacht was ill-prepared – the high command had never expected the army to have to endure such a winter in the field. At the same time, with German industrial mobilization never having achieved the scale necessary to sustain a war of attrition, the army was beginning to suffer critical shortages of the spares, fuel and other resources so essential to its offensive capability, a capability exemplified by the Panzer and motorized divisions, of which there were, in any case, still too few.

In addition to the everyday military practicalities and exigencies of war-fighting, the moral nature of the army's campaign also changed in Russia as it became implicated in certain of the operations carried out by the Einsatzgruppen (task forces) and Einsatzkommandos ("killer units"). These SS units and special

All too soon the autumn of 1941 turned to winter in Russia, the first snowfalls frustrating the high command's intention to seize Moscow and conclude *Barbarossa* that year. Here infantrymen advance cautiously into a village, making the most of the armored protection and potential firepower of an accompanying Pz.Kpfw.IV tank. Despite the wintry conditions, the lack of winter clothing is very evident.

Although Generalfeldmarschall Erwin Rommel (top) was undoubtedly the best known Afrikakorps commander, some other generals who also contributed to the army's achievements in North Africa included General Walther Nehring, Generalleutnant Ludwig Crüwell and Generaloberst Jürgen von Arnim.

police units followed up the army's main advance and secured the rear areas, a task that routinely included the extermination of any partisans, saboteurs, political commissars and others designated "enemies of the Third Reich"; in addition to those categorized as Untermenschen ("subhumans"), which included Jews and gypsies. Any pretense that the army had been able to distance itself from the political dogma of the time had become illusory by mid-1941, when orders issued by senior army commanders included such statements as, "The annihilation of those same Jews who support Bolshevism and its organization for murder, the partisans, is a measure of self-preservation" (General Hermann Hoth, 4th Panzer Army), and "the Jewish-Bolshevik system must be rooted out once and for all" (General Erich von Manstein). The chief of the army's general staff, General Franz Halder, had already acknowledged the inevitability of the army having to carry out collective reprisals against Russian civilians, and that the coming campaign would be a "war of extermination." Such statements, together with numerous policy documents and directives, indicated that the campaign would routinely disregard the needs and any rights of the Russian civilian or soldier, being generally conducted as a punitive operation to eliminate a dangerous political ideology and against a lesser race that deserved nothing less than annihilation. As the campaign proceeded, such attitudes within the army became increasingly more difficult to distinguish from the quite separate Nazi ideological policies developed to resolve what was termed "the Jewish question", which eventually resulted in the Holocaust. An opponent of the Hitler regime, former ambassador Ulrich von Hassell, highlighted the consequences of these orders and policy directives when he noted that "the army must [now] assume the onus of the murders and burnings which up to now have been confined to the SS."[9]

From October the weather deteriorated rapidly, and artillery officer Siegfried Knappe noted that "by late October, the mud was so bad that nothing could move in it. All movement stopped except on railroads and paved roads ... even infantry on foot could move only with the greatest difficulty. Nothing on wheels or tracks could move at all except on the [main] post road or railroads. The only way we could move vehicles was to corduroy the roads with small tree trunks laid side-by-side to provide a solid surface. We established corduroy roads between our gun positions and our source of ammunition and supplies at division headquarters. Such roads were difficult footing for the horses, and the vehicles jolted over them, but at least we could transport supplies and ammunition. A hard freeze came on November 7, which proved both an advantage and a disadvantage. We could move again, but now we were freezing because we still did not have winter clothing. We had the same field uniforms we had worn through the summer, plus a light overcoat ... We tried to spend the nights in villages so we could get out of the weather ... The fahrers [horse handlers] would keep the horses behind houses at night, and strap blankets on them as well, to try to shelter them from the wind. The horses had [their] winter coats of fur, which helped them, although a few

of them died at night from the cold. On November 12, the temperature dropped to twelve degrees below zero Fahrenheit." As the division at last approached the outer suburbs of Moscow at the end of November, "a paralyzing blast of cold hit us, and the temperature dropped far below zero and stayed there. Our trucks and vehicles would not start, and our horses started to die from the cold in large numbers for the first time; they would just die in the bitter cold darkness of the night, and we would find them dead the next morning. The Russians knew how to cope with this weather, but we did not; their vehicles were built and conditioned for this kind of weather, but ours were not ... On December 5, the temperature plummeted to thirty degrees below zero."[10]

By late November the German offensive had ground to a halt along a generally north-south line that ran so close to one of its major objectives, the Soviet capital, that the German soldiers could see the onion-dome towers of the Kremlin from their forward positions. The campaign had reached its high-water mark. In early December the Red Army, which had by then been reinforced by the arrival of more than 30 divisions of Mongolian troops from Siberia, launched its first major counter-offensive to save Moscow with a series of concerted attacks by some 500,000 troops on a frontage of almost a thousand kilometers from Leningrad to Kursk. This forced parts of Army Group Center to withdraw into defensive positions as far westwards as 320 kilometers from their front line of a few days before.

Meanwhile, far off in the Pacific, the Japanese attack on Pearl Harbor, Hawaii, on 7 December at last brought the United States fully into the war alongside Great Britain and the Soviet Union. Germany immediately declared war against the United States, and thereby made inevitable the prospect of the two-front war its strategists had always counselled was militarily unsustainable.

# 8. The North African Campaign, February 1941 to May 1943

While the preparations for the invasion of Russia had been moving forward and the Balkan and Aegean campaigns launched to alleviate the deteriorating situation of Italy's forces in that region, another campaign was already ongoing against the British and Commonwealth forces in North Africa. As early as July 1940, General von Brauchitsch had proposed an expansion of operations in the Mediterranean theater as a means of breaking the strategic stalemate that had developed once Operation *Seelöwe* became unachievable. The new campaign would build on the Italian operations then in progress (which had enjoyed some early successes) and strike at Britain's presence in the area – including the North African littoral, Egypt and the Suez Canal – thereby displacing British control of the Mediterranean and persuading additional non-aligned states to join the Axis. Although the plan was accepted in principle, it was much debated and subsequently scaled-down by Hitler, who was concerned that it would detract from his plans for the invasion of Russia. However, by early 1941 the series of significant defeats suffered by the well-manned but inadequately equipped and poorly-led Italian forces at the hands of the British Western Desert Force prompted the urgent deployment of German military units to redress a rapidly deteriorating Axis situation in North Africa. On 14 February the first German combat troops of the newly formed Deutsches Afrikakorps (DAK) arrived at Tripoli, where they were reviewed by their commander, General Erwin Rommel. In due course the DAK comprised the 15th and 21st Panzer Divisions, 90th Light Division, 164th Infantry Division, and an airborne brigade (Fallschirmjäger-Brigade Ramke). Later, as "Panzerarmee Afrika", it operated with the 10th, 20th and 21st Corps of the Italian 1st Army. Although the build-up of the DAK to its full strength was not achieved for a number of months, Rommel launched a limited offensive with one armored division on 3 April, which first captured Bardia, then effectively neutralized the Australian garrison at Tobruk by laying siege to the port. It finally forced a British withdrawal to its bases in Egypt, and in just two weeks the army had regained Libya for the Axis and changed the course of the North African campaign. Indeed, if Hitler had not continually denied the DAK the combat strength that it needed – some four or five Panzer divisions instead of just two – Rommel would undoubtedly have been able to complete the defeat of the British and Commonwealth forces in North Africa and Egypt during 1941.

Despite an ongoing lack of resources and being permanently outnumbered in men and tanks, the DAK consistently out-thought and outfought the British from March 1941 to the late summer of 1942. This was testimony to Rommel's personal ability as a military commander, a man described by Churchill as "a very daring and skilful opponent … a great general". However, none of these German victories were strategically decisive, as Rommel lacked the necessary combat power to reinforce and exploit his successes, whereas whenever the British suffered a reverse they withdrew, built up their strength, and then launched a new offensive. Rommel was always unable to retrench or reinforce in this fashion, and so the DAK had to conduct most of the campaign with those units that were already in its order of battle by about mid-1941, although the DAK's experienced and battle-hardened 15th and 21st Panzer Divisions were undoubtedly élite units in all but name.

In December 1941 a well-planned British offensive forced the DAK back to El Agheila and enabled the relief of Tobruk, while the DAK withdrew from Cyrenaica in good order to the border of Tripolitania. Early in 1942 the arrival of some 50 new tanks by sea allowed Rommel to resume the offensive in February, and by the end of May he had reached Gazala. There, despite finding himself in a potentially perilous situation with his forces placed between a complex of strongly-held British and Free French positions and his own minefields, he regrouped and extricated the DAK successfully, forcing a British withdrawal back to Egypt and El Alamein. Meanwhile, Tobruk fell to the Germans, where about 2,000 much-needed vehicles fell into the hands of the DAK. Rommel had well and truly lived up to his nickname of the "Desert Fox", and Hitler promoted him Generalfeldmarschall.

However, success in war is as much about having adequate resources as it is about superior generalship, and although the DAK had advanced to within 100 kilometers of Alexandria by July 1942, there Rommel was confronted by the British 8th Army, now commanded by General Montgomery. By forcing the DAK to engage in a battle of attrition and denying it the sort of free-flowing mobile battle that had enabled its earlier successes, Montgomery inflicted a major defeat on the DAK at El Alamein on 23 October to 4 November. Thereafter, despite the belated arrival of reinforcements, the German retreat westwards continued during the next six months, at every stage the DAK eluding Allied attempts to outflank it. Meanwhile, Anglo-US forces landed in strength at Casablanca, Algiers and Oran on 8 November 1942, and with the 8th Army pressing hard from the east the eventual outcome was inevitable. The remaining German and Italian forces in North Africa finally surrendered in Tunisia on 12–13 May 1943 at the end of a campaign characterized by a resolute fighting withdrawal conducted over a period of several months. The defeat of the US Army 2nd Corps at Kasserine Pass in February was the only significant victory during the more than 3,000 kilometers withdrawal, and shortly after that battle Rommel had been invalided back to Germany, thus avoiding the final surrender of the DAK.

A DAK Kübelwagen pictured in Tunisia during 1943. Note the prominently displayed flag, used to avoid attack by Luftwaffe aircraft; also the pennant, indicating that this vehicle apparently belongs to a division HQ.

Nevertheless, the troops had fought on to the end in the best traditions of the German army, without attracting the accusations of excesses and atrocities that marred the army's record in some other theaters. Significantly perhaps, neither the DAK nor the other German forces in North Africa included any SS units apart from a small detachment of Sicherheitsdienst (security police), SD Einsatz-Kommando Tunis, which had been established to direct the French police operations in Tunisia, and so the Nazi ideological policies applied rigorously in Europe were hardly in evidence in North Africa.

## 9. The Eastern Front, December 1941 to September 1942

While the soldiers of the Afrikakorps had been enjoying their victories in North Africa during 1941 and early 1942, their comrades-in-arms on the Eastern Front had been suffering the severe effects of a Russian winter for which they were ill-prepared, together with the consequences of the Red Army's counter-offensive launched in December 1941. The reverses sustained that December also exacerbated the ill-feeling and distrust that existed between the OKW and the OKH and the various commanders in the field, which allowed Hitler to seize the opportunity to dismiss many of the OKH senior staff officers, together with a number of commanders in Russia, including such well-known and competent officers as von Rundstedt, von Leeb and Guderian. At the same time Hitler removed General von Brauchitsch as commander-in-chief of the army and assumed the role himself, a move that effectively gave Hitler direct operational control of the army's campaign in Russia. This was followed by a further centralization at OKW rather than OKH of several of the army's other powers and responsibilities, including its right to select and promote its own officers, so that by 1942 the army had finally lost the authority to control its own destiny, both administratively and operationally. Meanwhile, the army's toll of casualties and equipment losses on the Eastern Front mounted steadily as the harsh Russian winter gradually gave way to spring.

By the spring of 1942 the army in Russia had sustained about 900,000 casualties and lost more than 2,300 armored vehicles, as well as fifty percent of its original complement of horses. Although no fewer than 29 new divisions had been created and dispatched to the Soviet Union since June 1941, this had generally been at the expense of not replacing the casualties sustained by the original divisions, so that the impressive number of divisions now shown on the army's order of battle was mitigated by the fact that most of them were seriously below their established strength. Nevertheless, despite the often critical shortages and the hardships suffered during that first winter, the soldiers' morale generally remained high as they prepared to carry out Hitler's orders for a new summer offensive. Instead of resuming the assault to capture Moscow, this new attack – *Fall Blau* (Case Blue) – was to be

carried out by Army Group South in the Ukraine and then taken on into the Caucasus to seize its strategically vital oilfields.

On 28 June 1942, while Army Group North and Army Group Center maintained a defensive posture, 68 German divisions supported by a further 50 Italian, Romanian and Hungarian formations struck toward Voronezh on the River Don. After a week of heavy fighting Voronezh fell on 5 July, while concurrent attacks cleared the Crimea and the Kerch Peninsula and captured Sevastopol. At that stage, on 9 July, Army Group South was split into Army Groups A and B. The former had the mission of securing the Donets Basin north of Rostov before moving south into the Caucasus and advancing to a line from Baku to Batumi, thereby gaining control of the oilfields; while Army Group B advanced to capture the city and military-industrial complex on the River Volga at Stalingrad. The offensive progressed well at first, with Army Group B making rapid progress. But then, on 16 July, Hitler ordered the 4th Panzer Army to re-deploy to assist Army Group A, just as Army Group B was approaching Stalingrad. Then, realizing that this city might provide a base from which Army Group A could be threatened, Hitler countermanded his earlier order and returned the 4th Panzer Army to Army Group B. This succession of "order, counter-order and disorder" meant that neither the Caucasus oilfields nor Stalingrad had been accorded the higher priority. Consequently, neither army group had sufficient combat power to achieve its objectives, so that the offensive gradually lost its momentum. The stage was set for what would prove to be the historic battle of Stalingrad.

## 10. The Battle of Stalingrad, September 1942 to February 1943

The capture of Stavropol on 5 August and Krasnodar on 9 August marked the limit of Army Group A's progress. Meanwhile, well to the north-east in the western suburbs of the great city of Stalingrad, the infantrymen of the 6th Army, commanded by General Friedrich Paulus, who had been fighting on the city outskirts since 7 August, began to encounter growing resistance as they fought their way into the city on 23rd and 24th. This assault would subsequently prove to be the precursor to one of the defining battles of the whole war, as the five-month-long battle of Stalingrad began. On the same day, 24 August, Hitler replaced the increasingly pessimistic General Halder as chief of the army's general staff by General Kurt Zeitzler, a man acquiescent to Hitler's wishes and who has been described by one historian as "an obedient optimist."[11] By late 1942 Hitler had surrounded himself with many such officers, and this was already having fatal consequences for the many thousands of German soldiers fighting on the Eastern Front.

Within Army Group B, with Paulus' army already enmeshed in the urban fighting for Stalingrad itself, the security of the 6th Army's flanks was the responsibility of the disparate Italian,

Generalfeldmarschall Friedrich Paulus commanded the ill-fated German 6th Army at Stalingrad.

Hungarian and Romanian units. On 19 November a major counter-stroke by the Red Army cut through the Romanians, isolating 250,000 men of the 6th Army, two Romanian divisions and part of the 4th Panzer Army within the city. By 22 November these forces were effectively cut off from the rest of the German forces and became dependent upon air re-supply, something that the Luftwaffe patently lacked the capability to achieve despite Göring's assurances to the contrary. Nevertheless, Hitler ordered the 6th Army to stand and fight on until relieved. Elsewhere, Army Group A now became vulnerable, and in late December the more than a quarter of a million German troops then in the Caucasus began to withdraw northwards into the Taman Peninsula, linking up with the forces in the Crimea and removing themselves from the most immediate threat that then faced them. Not until January did Hitler formally approve a general withdrawal from the Caucasus.

In the meantime, a few divisions with about 230 tanks and commanded by General Erich von Manstein were grouped together as "Army Group Don" to relieve Stalingrad. Despite their unavoidably slow advance against the combined rigours of a second Russian winter and in the face of growing Soviet resistance, this force did manage to come within fifty kilometers of the 6th Army's defensive perimeter by mid-December. But a deteriorating situation on Army Group Don's flanks due to the collapse of the Italian 8th Army, together with Paulus' refusal to attempt a breakout to link up with the relieving force, compelled von Manstein to withdraw his army group, and by the end of December the distance between the beleaguered 6th Army and the nearest units of the main German force exceeded 160 kilometers. In practice both von Manstein and Paulus knew that, by mid-December, the 6th Army lacked the resources, stamina and determination to stage a successful breakout.

The conditions endured by the soldiers fighting within the embattled city were appalling, and even the smallest successes were viewed as victories. Following one such minor territorial gain in late autumn 1942, an infantryman wrote that "The Reich [battle] flag has been flying over the center since yesterday. The center and area around the railway station [at the city center, west of the Volga] are in German hands." This was indeed a welcome morale-booster for the soldiers as they "lay in the earth holes wrapped in our blankets. The cold north-east wind came whistling through the canvas strips of our tent. It was pouring with rain. By way of celebration we cobbled together a mixture of flour, water and some grease (intended for lubricating guns) and fried up some pancakes. We rounded off this delicious meal with tea and the last cigarettes."[12] But a few weeks later, with the city by then firmly in the grip of the Russian winter, another infantryman recorded that, "From a quarter to six until two in the morning, with only a short pause, we were out in a blizzard. It penetrated our coats, our clothing gradually got soaked through, freezing stiff against our bodies. We were feeling unbelievably ill in the stomach and bowel. The cold soon exceeded all bounds. Lice! Frost gripped my pus-

infected fingers … My gloves were so wet that I couldn't bear them any longer [and] I wrapped a towel round my ravaged hands … [When we] stood, wet and frozen … [our] boots froze solidly to the ground."[13]

Christmas in Stalingrad brought no respite, although some of the staff officers apparently fared somewhat better than the ordinary soldiers manning the forward positions. Soldier Wilhelm Raimund Beyer wrote that, "by Christmas Day there was almost no food left. What was being distributed can hardly be described as rations: tiny amounts of tinned bread, tinned sausage, occasionally meat from a horse that had met its end somehow or other … Everyone had long since furtively eaten up his 'iron ration' [officially issued and kept for emergency use only]. When just before Christmas the order reached us that iron rations could now be broken into, everyone laughed."[14] Another soldier, an infantryman, observed that "our rations are very poor at the moment. In the morning we get 200 grams of bread, five grams of butter, twenty grams of sausage and a bowl of soup, that's all … Half of us are even too weak to get up in the morning, let alone do any work."[15] Such accounts contrasted with the somewhat better conditions enjoyed by at least one group of headquarters officers in their command bunker on Christmas Eve 1942: "We sang Christmas carols and presents were distributed. Each man [all of whom were presumably officers] received three bars of chocolate, three tubes of sweets, fifty cigarettes, half a loaf of bread, 130 grams of meat and some sandwich spread … We had conjured up a Christmas tree from a few pine branches, decorated it with silver paper from cigarette boxes, cut one of the last candles into pieces,

Panzergrenadiers supported by a Pz.Kpfw.IV await the order to attack a Russian bunker during the bitterly contested battle of Stalingrad.

and used the lids from empty food tins and a nail to make holders … Thirteen of us gentlemen were there when the general arrived with a gift for everyone: a bottle of alcohol for the senior officers, and something to smoke for the others."[16] The apparent contrast in living conditions is striking, although in practice it simply reflected the different nature of the duties and the place of work of the headquarters staff officers and soldiers, compared with those of the front-line infantrymen. However, for very many officers, just a few weeks later it would prove to be a considerable disadvantage to have held such rank at Stalingrad. In any event, senior officers at OKH in Germany were by no means unaware of the dire situation affecting the beleaguered 6th Army, and in late December 1942 General Zeitzler, the army chief of staff, voluntarily adopted a "Stalingrad diet", stating that he would not eat more than that which was issued to the troops within Stalingrad. Consequently, for many days he was to be seen in the general staff officers' mess refusing to eat the normal food that was served, thereby highlighting day-by-day the failure of the Luftwaffe to supply Stalingrad as Göring had promised. The general visibly lost weight, and on 5 January Hitler ordered him to eat properly again forthwith and not "to use up his strength on such gestures."[17]

By January 1943 the 6th Army was facing annihilation as the Soviet attackers – constantly reinforced by the arrival of fresh troops ferried across the River Volga – began to consolidate their positions within the city, gaining ever more ground day by day.

The Soviet capture of the airfield removed the army's last link with the outside world, and increasing numbers of individual German troops began to surrender, despite the summary fate that befell these prisoners-of-war in very many cases. On 26 January, the two main parts of the attacking Soviet forces came together at the center of Stalingrad, thereby shattering the cohesion of what was left of the German defense. The final act in the drama came on 31 January, when Hitler announced that General Paulus had been promoted Generalfeldmarschall, mindful of the fact that no German field marshal had ever been taken alive in battle. But Paulus and his army had already endured enough. On the same day he attempted to negotiate suitable terms of surrender, and on 2 February the last of the 91,000 German and other Axis soldiers in Stalingrad still more or less alive were taken into Soviet captivity. The prisoners included one field marshal and 22 generals. Of these prisoners-of-war, almost 50 percent would be dead by the spring of 1943, many summarily shot by their captors while even more succumbed to disease, starvation and the bitter cold. In all, more than 200,000 German soldiers were killed or captured during the battles for Stalingrad, and of those captured less than 5,000 eventually returned to Germany following their release from Soviet prison camps some ten years later.

Despite some isolated instances of Russian compassion, both for the German soldiers captured at Stalingrad and those taken prisoner earlier in the campaign, conditions in the Soviet prisoner-

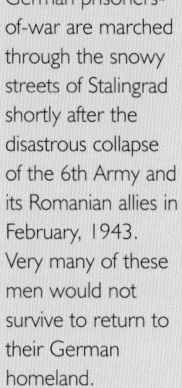

German prisoners-of-war are marched through the snowy streets of Stalingrad shortly after the disastrous collapse of the 6th Army and its Romanian allies in February, 1943. Very many of these men would not survive to return to their German homeland.

of-war camps were generally appalling, with a daily death rate of one percent in the camp hospitals. The prisoners were usually forced to build their own camps, but with underground earth bunkers rather than huts for accommodation. These regularly flooded in the spring and autumn. Suicide, disease, dysentery, summary execution and literally freezing to death were all common-place. Even those men fit when captured often succumbed later to a below-starvation diet of unground millet and a punishing program of hard labor, which included work on major construction projects such as the reconstruction of Stalingrad, hydro-electric schemes, and excavating the Don–Volga canal. In Soviet philosophy, "man was just another material" to be used to maximum effect and then discarded. Quite apart from the fact that the Germans were clearly the aggressors, Russian attitudes to their German captives were also shaped by the litany of atrocities committed by the SS and the Wehrmacht on the Eastern Front against a population the Nazi leadership had actively portrayed as Untermenschen. Remarkably, perhaps, the 6th Army's capitulation at Stalingrad destroyed neither the German army's offensive capability nor its will to fight, but it was nevertheless a major catastrophe, both psychologically and in terms of resources, with so many men and so much equipment lost in vain. Certainly it was the defining moment of the war on the Eastern Front and provided an indication of the likely outcome of the wider war for Germany – although such indications continued to go largely unheeded by Hitler and the senior officers of his generally acquiescent high command.

The comments of General Hans Doerr in late 1942 related specifically to the situation at Stalingrad, but they would soon prove prophetic in terms of the army's wider campaign on the Eastern Front. He observed that, "the time for conducting large-scale operations was gone forever. From the wide expanses of steppe-land the war moved to the jagged gullies of the Volga hills with their copses and ravines, into the factory area of Stalingrad, spread out over uneven, pitted, rugged country, covered with iron, concrete and stone buildings. The mile as a measure of distance was replaced by the yard. Headquarters' map was the map of the city."[18] Stalingrad on the river Volga was truly a watershed – the Blitzkrieg era had finally run its course.

## 11. The Battle of Kursk, July 1943

The battle of Kursk (Operation *Zitadelle*, or "Citadel") had its roots in the wider fallout from the demise of the 6th Army at Stalingrad and the earlier withdrawal of Army Group A in late December and into January 1943, together with the mounting scale and daring of the Soviet attacks. On 8 February 1943 one of these attacks recaptured Kursk and struck on west toward Kharkov. This created a salient that extended well into German-held territory and offered the army an opportunity to cut off and destroy much of the Soviet force. To that end, the 2nd SS-Panzer

Corps was ordered by Hitler to hold Kharkov, prior to a German counterattack. But, after a week of bitter fighting within the largely ruined city, the Waffen-SS troopers were finally forced to abandon Kharkov to the Red Army on 15 February. This withdrawal further extended the Soviet line and on 19 February, at Krasnograd, the 2nd SS-Panzer Corps and part of 4th Panzer Army launched a surprise armored attack which resulted in more than 23,000 Soviet casualties and about 9,000 prisoners captured. This forced the Russians to withdraw in some disarray. As a result, by late March, as winter turned to spring and iron-hard ground gradually turned to mud, Kharkov was again in German hands, together with Orel to the north, while well over a million Soviet troops were now deployed within what had become the 250-kilometer-wide Kursk salient. Once again Hitler judged that an opportunity existed to strike into the salient, isolating and then destroying the mass of units therein. What eventually followed (though not until July) culminated in the largest tank battle in the history of warfare to that date. It also signalled that the ability of the army's Panzer units to conduct their Blitzkrieg-style operations with impunity had finally ended.

The delay in launching Operation *Zitadelle* reflected the need to complete other operations in the Kharkov area beforehand. It was also occasioned by the movement constraints imposed by the spring thaw and by the need to muster sufficient quantities of the armor – principally tanks and assault guns – to carry out the operation. Although the three months delay to July was probably unavoidable, it is arguable that it fatally prejudiced the operation from the outset. This was not least because the Soviets were forewarned of the German plan – probably by the Western Allies utilizing the "take" of intelligence from their "Enigma" code intercepts (but with the source having been represented to Moscow as a highly-placed spy in the OKH, as the Russians were still officially unaware that the Anglo-US high command possessed a captured "Enigma" machine and had broken its code system). Early indications of German intentions were later followed up with the precise date that the operation was scheduled to begin, 5 July 1943. In any event, the 1,300,000 Red Army soldiers within the salient used these three months to turn the salient into a veritable fortress of anti-tank obstacles, ditches and gun emplacements, minefields and well-prepared infantry strongpoints. The whole network of defensive positions was up to 200 kilometers deep and supported by no fewer than 20,220 guns, 3,600 tanks and 2,400 aircraft, with a sizeable armored counter-stroke force held in reserve to the east of the salient. Surprisingly, quite apart from continuing to believe that the security of the forthcoming operation had not been compromised, the Germans were also largely unaware of the true extent of the Soviet defensive preparations within the Kursk salient. Certainly some German senior commanders suspected a Soviet trap, but at the same time were confident that the first-rate units earmarked for the operation were more than able to overcome the Soviet forces in the salient. The Soviet defensive battle plan at Kursk was masterminded by

General Kurt Zeitzler was chief of the general staff 1942–5; although experienced and competent, he failed to persuade Hitler of the need for tactical compromises and to adopt a more pragmatic approach to the campaign on the Eastern Front.

Generalfeldmarschall Wilhelm Keitel (top) and Generaloberst Alfred Jodl were Hitler's principal military advisers at OKW throughout the war, their unequivocal compliance with the Führer's wishes often having an adverse effect upon army operations.

Marshal Georgi K. Zhukov and was carried out by his subordinate commanders Rokossovsky, Vatutin and Konev, all of whom would later inflict a terrible retribution upon Germany and its army during the final eighteen months of the war.

In the south, the German formation deployed for the *Zitadelle* offensive was the 4th Panzer Army, reinforced following the loss of a large part of the former 4th Army during the fighting at Stalingrad in January. In July 1943 this extensively reconstituted army had six Panzer divisions, five Panzergrenadier divisions and eleven non-armored divisions, with a total of about 1,300 tanks, plus many self-propelled assault guns and other armored vehicles. The northern German force was the 9th Army, with six Panzer divisions, one Panzergrenadier division, about 800 tanks and other armored vehicles, and fourteen non-armored divisions. By 1943, in addition to the earlier Pz.Kpfw.IVs, the German tank fleet included numbers of the new Pz.Kpfw.V Panther tank with its well-sloped armor and 75mm main armament, and the formidable Pz.Kpfw.VI Tiger tank, which mounted a powerful 88mm gun. The 88mm weapon was also mounted on the heavily armored Elefant (originally titled "Ferdinand") self-propelled assault guns, which by 1943 were included in the Panzer and Panzergrenadier division's armored vehicle inventory. Ninety of these guns were committed to *Zitadelle*. With no fewer than 2,200 tanks and about 1,000 assault guns in these two armies, this meant that about 70 percent of the German armored capability on the Eastern Front had been committed to *Zitadelle*. About 1,800 combat aircraft supported the two armies, which was some 65 percent of the German air capability on the Eastern Front. In all, the two armies totalled some 900,000 men.[19]

At about 0200 hours on 5 July, with the offensive due to commence at 0500, the Soviet artillery fired a massive bombardment against the German armor and troop concentrations, indicating all too clearly that this would be no surprise attack, while many of the German units had already been subjected to frequent harassing attacks by partisans as they moved into their positions for the operation. Despite such disconcerting occurrences, the spearheads of the 9th Army and the 4th Panzer Army surged across their start lines to the north and the south at 0500 hours in accordance with the plan to reach Kursk and so cut off the Russian troops within the salient. However, both forces quickly found themselves embroiled in a morass of anti-armor defenses supported by the huge weight of fire from hundreds of tanks, anti-tank guns and other artillery. By the close of 5 July, the lead elements of the 4th Panzer Army had advanced no more than thirteen kilometers, the rest of that army having achieved even less. In the north, the 9th Army achieved little more than six kilometers of penetration. Everywhere the offensive stalled, with rapidly mounting casualties to men and armored vehicles. Although the Luftwaffe's Stukas provided close air support at the outset, this was insufficient to unlock the planned Blitzkrieg by the Panzers, while in any case the Russian Ilyushin Il-2 Sturmovik ground-attack aircraft were all the time inflicting their own punishment upon the exposed German armor. The assault quickly degenerated into a battle of attrition, with separate deliberate attacks being required to overcome each and every strongpoint, line of defense and fortified village; but many of these were so strongly held that they delayed and diverted the attacking Germans into yet other killing areas. As the battle developed, the Pz.Kpfw.V Panthers so recently introduced into service began to suffer various mechanical breakdowns, while the lumbering Elefants – armed with the powerful 88mm gun, but with only one machine gun for close protection – initially smashed through the Russian positions with relative ease, only to find themselves isolated, so that they were then destroyed piecemeal by teams of Soviet infantrymen with a variety of anti-armor weapons and explosive charges. After almost a week of bitter fighting within the salient, the forward units of the two assaulting armies were still 225 kilometers apart.

On 11 July the attacking 1st, 2nd and 3rd SS-Panzer Divisions of the Waffen-SS did at last appear to be making some progress in the area of Prokhorovka, while advancing astride the north–south rail link between Kursk and Belgorod in the vanguard of the 4th Panzer Army's attack. However, as more than 600 Pz.Kpfw.IV, Pz.Kpfw.V Panther and Pz.Kpfw.VI Tiger tanks, together with numbers of assault guns, closed up and surged forward to press their advantage on the following day, the Waffen-SS Panzer divisions suddenly found themselves facing most of the T-34/76 tanks of the 5th Guards Tank Army, held in reserve until now and with the T-34s in considerably greater numbers than the German tanks. On that day, 12 July, more than 1,500 armored vehicles maneuvered within the southern part of the salient,[20] while at its core some 250 German tanks and 600 Soviet tanks became locked within a cauldron of battle that fast assumed the appearance of "a confused, dust-shrouded mass, thickened by the billowing black, oily smoke from stricken tanks and guns".[21] Incredibly, this great armored mêlée, later acknowledged to have been the greatest tank battle of the war, took place in an area of no more than three square miles. Indeed, the first Soviet tank attack involved the T-34s literally driving straight into and diagonally through the flank of the German advance in a manner more reminiscent of a nineteenth-century cavalry charge than of twentieth-century warfare. All the time they engaged the Panzers to deadly effect, often at less than a hundred meters range – "The sound of armor on armor could be heard for miles around, punctuated by the bark of 76mm or 88mm guns and the explosions that followed."[22] The slaughter continued all day, and when night fell the scene was still illuminated by "the sparks and swirling flame from hundred upon hundred of blazing tanks and self-propelled guns, or from the wreckage of scores of the German Stuka dive-bombers or Russian Shturmovik *(sic)* tank-busting aircraft which had ranged over the battlefield, adding their own tallies of death and destruction to the holocaust below."[23] By nightfall, the 4th Panzer Army had lost 400 tanks and 10,000 men since the start of the Kursk offensive, and it could advance no farther. To the north, by 12 July the 9th Army had lost about 200 tanks and as many as 25,000 men.

Undoubtedly the Russians had lost much more – possibly as many as 1,800 tanks and 40,000 men in the southern part of the salient alone – but they still had sufficient reserves to be able to absorb such losses and to launch further attacks at the north of the salient, while the Germans had entirely exhausted their ability to advance farther. Indeed, the Soviets claimed to have killed or captured as many as half a million German soldiers and to have destroyed 1,500 tanks since 5 July. Whatever the true figures, the losses to both sides and the sheer scale of the destruction that had resulted from the week-long battle were without doubt truly appalling. Even Hitler understood that *Zitadelle* was no longer achievable, and he ordered that the operation be terminated (a decision also influenced by the fact that Anglo-US forces had landed in Sicily on 10 July). Despite the destruction inflicted upon the opposing sides – especially that sustained by the Russian forces – neither side could claim Kursk as a tactical victory. At the operational level it had signalled the end of *Zitadelle* and the German failure to envelop the salient; far more significantly for the army, Kursk marked the point at which the offensive and strategic initiative on the Eastern Front passed to the Russians. By early August, Army Group Center and Army Group South had withdrawn from the Kursk area, abandoning Orel, Kharkov and Belgorod on 5 August. Then, on 7 September, the Germans began their evacuation of the Ukraine, while far to the north the Red Army recaptured Smolensk on 25 September. Everywhere the Russian ground forces (by now organized into ten army "fronts" stretching from the Baltic to the Caucasus) were mounting coordinated offensives and advancing westwards against the much-weakened Wehrmacht.

## 12. The Italian Campaign, July 1943 to May 1945

On 10 July 1943, just five days after the start of Operation *Zitadelle* in Russia, the Western Allies followed the defeat of the Axis forces in North Africa the previous year with Operation *Husky*, the landing in Sicily of the 15th Army Group, comprising General Montgomery's British 8th Army and General Patton's US 7th Army. This opened a new front for the Axis on the southern flank of mainland Europe just as the war on the Eastern Front was turning against it. At the same time in Italy, Mussolini's position was becoming ever more tenuous (he was subsequently ousted from power on 25 July), and there were indications that the country was on the verge of signing an armistice with the Allies. Sicily was defended by an Axis garrison of 50,000 German troops in the 14th Panzer Corps, commanded by General Hube, and 315,000 troops of the Italian 6th Army. Italian General Guzzoni was nominally in overall command of the defense of Sicily, although he soon relinquished operational control to Hube. Despite some spirited resistance initially, numbers of the Italian troops fled as soon as the invaders landed, and so most of the short

but hard-fought defensive campaign was conducted by the German troops, primarily by the 15th Panzergrenadier Division and by a Luftwaffe armored formation, the Panzer Division "Hermann Göring" or "Panzerdivision HG". Gradually the Germans were forced north toward Messina, and on 10 August General Hube ordered an evacuation to mainland Italy. It was a measure of the skill with which the army conducted its withdrawal that between 11 and 17 August no less than 39,569 German troops, 9,605 vehicles, 47 tanks, 94 guns and 17,000 tons of ammunition were successfully transported across the Strait of Messina to the mainland. On 17 August the Allies entered Messina, and on 3 September the Italian government signed a secret armistice with the Allies. Italy-s unconditional surrender was announced publicly on 8 September.

The Germans had for some time anticipated Italy's collapse and quickly disarmed the Italian forces, taking over their defenses as well as increasing the number of German divisions in Italy from six in July to eighteen in September, with four more en route. This was timely, as the Italians had been responsible for the defense of the port of Salerno, and it was here that the Allies landed (Operation *Avalanche*) their main invasion force – General Mark Clark's US 5th Army (US 6th Corps and British 10th Corps) – on the morning of 9 September, with other smaller landings at Taranto, Reggio and Brindisi. The unexpected presence at Salerno of the newly-arrived German troops of General von Vietinghoff's 10th Army resulted in a hard, week-long battle for the port, and only the arrival of significant numbers of Allied reinforcements and the fire support of two additional Royal Navy battleships prevented the Germans forcing an Allied evacuation of the beachhead. However, the sheer weight of Allied numbers and resources eventually forced a well-ordered German withdrawal, and Naples finally fell on 5 October.

In Italy, as elsewhere, Allied air superiority necessitated the army investing heavily in anti-aircraft guns to protect its formations from air attack. Here a 20mm multi-barrel Flakvierling 38 anti-aircraft gun is positioned in snow-covered hills near Monte Cassino in the Gustav Line, November 1943.

So began the Italian campaign, where Generalfeldmarschall Kesselring compensated for the German army's lack of men and resources by imposing a grinding war of attrition upon the Allies, using to best advantage Italy's rugged terrain, which generally favored the defense. Between September 1943 and May 1945 the Allies were forced to retain in Italy much of the manpower and *matériel* that might otherwise have been used for the impending invasion of France, while all the time suffering often heavy casualties in a succession of battles to overcome a series of well-sited German lines of defense. Notable actions included Cassino (17 January to 11 February 1944), where General von Senger und Etterlin's troops of the 14th Panzer Corps (comprised mainly of infantry and paratroopers, with only a few tanks) halted the Allied advance in order to enable the Germans to reinforce and replace their significant losses. Meanwhile, an Allied landing (Operation *Shingle*) by the US 6th Corps at Anzio was designed to outflank the German defenses of the Gustav Line (which incorporated the hilltop monastery of Monte Cassino) and open the way to Rome. Although the strategic concept had been inspired and the landing itself was completely successful, finding the area between Anzio and Rome largely free of German combat forces, the Allies then failed to exploit that success by immediately advancing on Rome. Anzio vividly demonstrated the contrast between the tight command and control doctrine of the Allies and the flexible, or intuitive mission-orientated, doctrine of Auftragstaktik applied in the German army. While the US commander consolidated the beachhead and prepared to deal with what he anticipated would be an early German counterattack, he entirely missed the opportunity to outflank and disrupt the German defenses and lines of

communication and to capture Rome virtually unopposed, which together had been the principal objectives of Operation *Shingle*. On the other hand, although the Germans were certainly surprised by the landing at Anzio, General von Mackensen reacted speedily, moving units of his 14th Army to contain the bridgehead. A stalemate ensued, and on 30 January a Panzer-led counterattack split the Anglo-US beachheads and almost reached the sea before Allied air and naval fire forced a withdrawal. In the meantime, while 14th Army continued to hold the Allies at Anzio, farther east General von Senger und Etterlin's 14th Panzer Corps, reinforced by additional Fallschirmjäger and army units, frustrated two more Allied attempts to break through the Gustav Line at Cassino. During the first of these, from 15 to 20 February, the Monte Cassino monastery (which the Allies believed, incorrectly, was occupied by German troops) was destroyed by bombing. The second battle began on 15 March with the Allied bombing of Cassino town, and ended on the 25th. The German defenders were eventually forced to concede a few positions, although throughout the battle the fighting was exceptionally hard and frequently hand-to-hand, with very high Allied casualties. Only the committal by General Clarke of the full weight of Allied air and ground firepower on 11 May, together with every ground force unit available, finally produced a German withdrawal. On 18 May, Monte Cassino fell, and the integrity of the Gustav Line was broken. This at last enabled the Allies at Anzio to break out and link up with the advancing US 5th Army on 26 May, with Rome finally captured on 4 June.

Just two days later the Allies landed in strength in Normandy. The Allied invasion of occupied France created yet another active

During the Allied invasion of mainland Europe, German artillerymen rush to man their gun on the French coast, June 1944.

front for Germany and its already hard-pressed army, while in Italy the German 10th Army (von Vietinghoff) and 14th Army (von Mackensen) withdrew steadily northwards, all the time imposing further delays and casualties on the advancing Allies in a succession of well-prepared positions and defense lines: the Viterbo Line, the Trasimene Line, the Gothic Line, the Genghis Khan Line, the Adige or Venetian Line, and the Alpine Line. However, it was on the Gothic Line, to the north of Pisa and Florence, that Kesselring effectively halted the advance of the US 5th Army and British 8th Army in the late summer of 1944, although sporadic fighting continued and the 8th Army did manage to take Ravenna in December.

The occupation of the Gothic Line signalled the end of the army's year-long campaign of defense and withdrawal along the length of Italy as the Italian campaign became stalemated through the months of rain, flooded rivers, occasional snow and ubiquitous mud that characterized the north Italian winter. Eventually the Allies mounted an offensive into the Po Valley on 14 April 1945, subsequently striking north into the Alps toward the Brenner Pass and northwest toward Turin and Milan. But by then the war had already been lost, and the remaining German forces in Italy, still composed mainly of the 10th and 14th Armies and the paratroopers of two airborne corps, surrendered on 2 May.

# 13. The Allied Invasion of Mainland Europe, June–October 1944

In early spring of 1944 the German army in France comprised some 61 divisions including eleven armored divisions, and from these were drawn many of the units to defend Hitler's "Atlantic Wall", the massive and elaborate conglomeration of obstacles, mines, concrete bunkers, underground tunnels, artillery emplacements and defensive positions that lined the coast of the European mainland from Scandinavia and along the north coast of the occupied Netherlands, Belgium and France.

In overall command of the army in France, Holland and Belgium was Generalfeldmarschall von Rundstedt, designated Oberbefehlshaber West (OB West). His forces included Army Group G (1st Army and 19th Army) and Army Group B (7th Army and 15th Army). OB West also controlled a powerful armored reserve, Panzer Group West. Army Group B was commanded by Generalfeldmarschall Rommel, in post since November 1943, with responsibility for the coastline from Brittany, through Normandy, and to Antwerp. Panzer Group West was commanded by General von Schweppenburg and was designated as the OKW reserve, which could only be deployed on Hitler's personal authority. The quality of the forces defending the coastline varied widely, ranging from battle-seasoned armored and infantry units to "static divisions" composed of "stomach battalions" (medically downgraded troops) and even units of Russian "volunteers" formed from prisoners-of-war taken on the

Eastern Front. In planning their response to an Allied invasion, von Rundstedt and von Schweppenburg favored holding the Panzer divisions back, ready to strike the Allies as they moved inland from the beaches. But Rommel, mindful of his time as commander of the DAK and of the threat posed by the Allied air forces, believed that the sort of mobile operations enjoyed by the army earlier in the war were no longer feasible. He argued that any Allied landing would need to be defeated within 24 hours if the Allies were to be denied a lodgement, and he therefore urged strongly that the reserve Panzer units should be positioned close to the beaches and placed under his direct command.

Operation *Neptune*, the seaborne part of the Allied invasion on the morning of 6 June, was preceded during the previous night by a large-scale airborne assault into the inland areas beyond, and on the flanks of, the intended landing beaches. This attack from the air was carried out by the Allied paratroops and glider-borne infantry of the US 82nd and 101st Airborne Divisions and the British 6th Airborne Division. At 0016 hours the glider-borne British troops of D Company, Oxfordshire and Buckinghamshire Light Infantry, landed precisely on their objective, the bridge over the Caen Canal near the village of Ranville. D Company was the first Allied unit to engage the German defenders on D-Day. Their *coup de main* operation was in some ways reminiscent of that carried out by the Fallschirmjäger glider-borne assault against the Belgian fortress of Eben Emael just over four years earlier, at the beginning of the German army's Blitzkrieg against France and the Low Countries.

In the meantime, the seaborne invasion had begun when, shortly before dawn that day, the greatest invasion fleet in the history of modern warfare arrived off the coast of Normandy. By last light on D-Day, from Varreville in the west to Ouistreham in the east, the US 1st Army and British 2nd Army, which together comprised General Montgomery's 21st Army Group, had gained a foothold at the five landing beaches codenamed "Utah", "Omaha", "Gold", "Juno" and "Sword". However, for the first 24 hours this foothold was somewhat tenuous on the US beach at "Omaha". There, German artillery and the enfilade fire from numerous machine gun emplacements and soldiers of two regiments of the veteran 352nd Infantry Division created havoc

An infantry patrol moves through Caen, summer 1944. For almost a month the German defenders successfully resisted every attempt by the Anglo-Canadian forces to capture the strategically important French town.

Generalfeldmarschall Günter Hans von Kluge held a succession of important appointments in the west and on the Eastern Front, finally commanding the forces that were encircled and defeated at the Falaise gap in 1944.

amongst the US infantrymen, inflicting severe casualties upon them as they tried desperately to find cover among the obstacles and sand dunes on the fire-swept beach. Despite the initial setback at "Omaha", successive waves of Allied troops were fed into the beachheads during the day. Eventually five US, British and Canadian divisions, together with various independent brigades, Free French and other Allied and specialist units, were all safely ashore and setting about consolidating and exploiting their beachheads.

Despite increasing numbers of reports of the worsening military situation in Normandy and ever more urgent requests for reinforcements that were now reaching OKW from the German army headquarters in France – the most important of which sought permission to deploy the reserve Panzer divisions to counter the Allied landings – Hitler and the senior staff at OKW remained convinced well into 6 June that the attack in Normandy was merely a diversion to cover the yet-to-come main Allied assault across the Pas de Calais. This illustrated the particular success of the strategic deception operation (Operation *Fortitude*) that had supported the Allied invasion plan. The reserve Panzer units were finally ordered to deploy that afternoon, but the delay by OKW meant that the time at which their impact upon the invasion might have been greatest had already passed. By that stage also their distance from the coast (140 to 160 kilometers in some cases) proved to be even more telling for, just as Rommel had feared, Allied air power inflicted significant casualties upon the Panzer divisions as they moved out of their concentration areas and drove

to join the battle. As a result, they were not fully effective until 8 or 9 June, by which time their strength had already been significantly depleted.

By 7 June the British and Canadian divisions had effectively secured the Allied left (east) flank against a counter-attack by the German armored reserves, while on the right flank the US troops on "Utah" beach had started moving out to exploit and expand their bridgehead. By 12 June all five of the original landing beaches had linked up and formed a single cohesive bridgehead, while at sea a huge fleet of cargo and troop-carrying vessels constantly plied back and forth across the Channel between England and the Normandy beachheads and "Mulberry" artificial harbors. From 19 to 22 June a severe storm in the Channel temporarily disrupted the logistic flow, grounded the Allied aircraft and provided a possible opportunity for a German counterattack. But all the German forces designated for such action were either already fully committed or were still en route to the battle area. Hitler's "Atlantic Wall" had been breached irrevocably. Thereafter the Allied strength in northwest Europe increased with each week and month that passed.

Nevertheless, the army managed by and large to contain the Allied invasion through most of June and much of July, despite two major operations launched by the Anglo-Canadian forces to capture the city of Caen (originally designated as a British objective for "day one"). During these localized battles of attrition the Germans inflicted greater casualties on the Allies than they themselves suffered, but the Germans could ill afford their own losses of men and equipment. Most of this fighting took place amidst the *bocage* countryside of Normandy, with its small stone-built villages, thickly-wooded copses, and a myriad patchwork of small fields and sunken lanes, each flanked by high earth banks topped with dense hedgerows. The area's few metalled roads were typically set in deep gullies between the fields. Such terrain favored the German defenders, their infantry in particular, and was not conducive to armored movement by either side. During the final week of June, an early attempt (Operation *Epsom*) by the Allies to capture Caen stalled in the face of fierce resistance and was followed by a determined German counterattack that lasted from 29 June to 1 July. The Americans on the west flank of the beachheads experienced less resistance, and by 27 June they had captured Cherbourg and cleared the Cotentin Peninsula. Then, between 17 and 21 July, Operation *Goodwood* at last resulted in the capture of Caen by British and Canadian troops, which in turn enabled the breakout from the eastern bridgeheads and prepared the way for the Anglo-Canadian advance toward the Netherlands. Between 25 and 30 July the Americans struck out from the St-Lô area in Operation *Cobra*, and following the success of this operation there was a general re-orientation of the US divisions toward the east and southeast in preparation for their rapid advance into central France. During August, General Patton's US 3rd Army encircled most of the German 7th Army and 5th Panzer Army, already embattled with Anglo-Canadian formations about Caen and Falaise in the "Falaise

Panzergrenadiers take cover in the broken and heavily wooded *bocage* countryside of Normandy during the summer of 1944. Meanwhile, a vehicle-mounted 20mm anti-aircraft gun is being used in the ground support role to provide covering fire for the infantrymen.

Pocket", where 60,000 troops, 500 armored vehicles and thousands of other vehicles and quantities of equipment were trapped. On 20 August the pocket was sealed, and as many as 10,000 German soldiers were killed in the battle that ensued before these encircled forces were finally forced to surrender.

Although there were almost ten million men fighting with the Wehrmacht by the beginning of August 1944, they were now spread between three fronts – Eastern, Western and Italian – while with most of these troops already actively engaged there were few reserves available. On 15 August the German army's predicament was further compounded when part of the US 5th Army sent from Italy landed (Operation *Dragoon*) on the French Riviera and pushed on into southern France. Paris was liberated by the Allies on 25 August, Marseilles and Toulon fell on the 28th, and Amiens on the 31st. Dieppe and Rouen were lost on 1 September; Antwerp, Brussels and Lyons on 3–4 September; and just over a week later the US troops who had landed during Operation *Dragoon* linked up with those who had landed in Normandy. On 12 September elements of the US 1st Army at last entered Germany to the south of Aachen, although the "West Wall" was not effectively breached until 2 October, with the city of Aachen only falling to the Allies in late October after a period of bitter street fighting.

Despite its overall success, the Allied advance gradually slowed, its lines of communication and supply growing ever longer as it approached the potentially formidable natural obstacle of the River Rhine. In a matter of weeks the winter would also begin to impinge upon the vehicle movement on which the Allies depended. Accordingly, in a bid to "bounce" the Rhine and maintain the momentum of the advance, a daring but abortive airborne operation (Operation *Market Garden*) was launched to seize a crossing over the river at Arnhem in the Netherlands. However, this operation by the 1st Allied Airborne Army from 16 to 26 September resulted in the virtual destruction of the British 1st Airborne Division at Arnhem, as the advancing Allied ground forces were unable to break through the German defense lines in time to link up with the isolated airborne forces before the Germans overwhelmed the lightly-equipped paratroopers with armored, infantry and Waffen-SS units. Operation *Market Garden* illustrated very vividly that although the Allies were approaching the very core of the Third Reich, and despite the fact that everywhere the Wehrmacht was withdrawing, the German army was by no means ready to accept defeat. For German civilians and soldiers alike, this stalwart attitude had undoubtedly been reinforced by the politically necessary but pragmatically ill-advised statement by US President Roosevelt at Casablanca in January 1943 that nothing less than "the unconditional surrender of Germany, Italy and Japan" would be acceptable to the Allies, which had provided a significant motivational tool to Hitler's propaganda chief, Joseph Goebbels.

On 28 September Calais was taken by the Allies. The German forces defending Aachen surrendered on 21 October, and on 9 November US forces crossed the River Moselle, Free French units

capturing Strasbourg on 24 November. Everywhere the Germans appeared to be falling back, and as harsh winter weather swept across northern Europe the Allies discounted the possibility of any new counter-offensive by the Germans before 1945.

Clearly 1944 had not been a good year for the German forces, but this was especially so in the case of the army. In July an abortive bomb attack on Hitler at his headquarters in East Prussia had involved (with others) a number of senior and junior army officers. Hitler's rage was terrible indeed, as was the retribution inflicted by the Gestapo upon the conspirators, their associates and their families. The key conspirators, including many senior army officers, were arraigned at the "People's Court" (Volksgericht) in Berlin, summarily convicted, tortured and later savagely executed at Plötzensee Prison, while many others were consigned to concentration camps. Although Rommel had not been directly involved in the plot, he too became a victim of the Nazi purge, and on Hitler's direction was forced to commit suicide in order to avoid the humiliation of a show trial and retribution being taken against his family. As well as ending any residual resistance to Hitler, the failure of the July Plot substantially reduced any remaining influence that the army had enjoyed with Hitler and the OKW while significantly strengthening the authority of the SS within Germany. At the same time it dramatically accelerated the climate of fear that now pervaded every part of the Third Reich and its non-SS armed forces during the final nine months of the war in Europe.

Among a number of speedily-implemented measures that directly affected the army, Himmler was appointed commander-in-chief of the Replacement Army, an appointment which had the effect of making the SS responsible for the administration, training and discipline of all newly formed army units and formations. Even the army's traditional salute was replaced by the Nazi salute in accordance with an order issued on 23 July, while the political influence of the National Socialists' existing political organization within the army (the Nationalsozialistische Führungsoffiziere, or "National Socialist leadership officers", the NSFO, which had been established in 1943) was formally strengthened. Finally, on 1 August, a new law made the relatives of soldiers responsible (and therefore punishable) for the actions and any perceived wrongdoings of their serving soldier relatives. In spite of all this, the army by and large still obeyed its oath of loyalty to the letter and maintained its unquestioning faith in Hitler's ability to achieve the final victory for Germany, while many soldiers condemned the July Plot conspirators unreservedly, viewing them as traitors to Germany who had also dishonored the army.

# 14. The Ardennes Offensive, December 1944 to January 1945

By December 1944 the Allies in the west had settled into a line of defensive positions at the German border, there to plan and prepare for the crossing of the Rhine and the campaign to

General Friedrich Fromm commanded the Ersatzheer 1939–44 but was relieved as its commander by Himmler in 1944 in the aftermath of the 20 July plot, eventually being executed in 1945 for complicity in that conspiracy.

General Ludwig Beck was chief of the general staff 1935–8, a highly accomplished and morally driven officer who later headed the resistance move-ment against Hitler, being arrested and killed shortly after the failure of the 20 July plot in 1944.

complete the German defeat as soon as practicable in 1945. Christmas had almost arrived, snow and freezing temperatures had halted virtually all movement, and a general air of complacency settled over many Allied units, nowhere more so than among the American troops stationed in the "quiet sector" of the Ardennes and Eifel at the junction of the borders of Belgium, Germany and Luxembourg. This was the same area from which the Panzers had struck against France in May 1940, and, contrary to virtually every Allied intelligence assessment, German armor and infantry were once again massing in the dark forests of the Ardennes.

At dawn on 16 December the troops of US 1st Army were awakened by a tremendous artillery bombardment, followed soon after by the sound of advancing tanks, assault guns and troop carriers. Masses of German armor and infantry burst out of the misty, snow-laden woods and valleys as the Wehrmacht's last major offensive, Operation *Wacht am Rhein* (literally, "Watch [or 'Guard'] on the Rhine") gathered momentum, the name of the operation deliberately chosen to belie its offensive nature. *Wacht am Rhein* had been devised by Hitler and planned by von Rundstedt as a daring but always risky bid to split the Anglo-US armies, secure the line of the Meuse and seize Antwerp, thereby gaining time for the development, mass production and deployment of Germany's potentially devastating new V-weapons. The attack was conducted by three armies: the 5th Panzer Army, commanded by General von Manteuffel, the 7th Army, commanded by General Branden-berger, and the 6th Panzer Army, commanded by Waffen-SS Oberstgruppenführer "Sepp" Dietrich.

During its early days, the battle later dubbed the "Battle of the Bulge" by the Allies caused widespread panic among the surprised American units that bore the brunt of the initial assault, notably those of the 8th Corps. Their consequent disarray and a series of precipitate withdrawals at first threatened the whole Allied situation in the west. On 20 December no fewer than 9,000 US soldiers, mainly of the 422nd and 423rd Regiments of the 106th Infantry Division on the Schnee Eifel, surrendered to the grenadiers of the 18th Volksgrenadier Division in the worst American reverse sustained during the US Army's campaign in northwest Europe. However, while the attackers achieved a

number of tactical successes, the continuing lack of resources (especially fuel) and reserves to sustain and exploit these early victories meant that the German offensive eventually lost momentum and ground to a halt. In the meantime, while the winter weather had covered the early deployment of the ground forces very effectively, these conditions had also meant that *Wacht am Rhein* (unlike the Blitzkriegs of 1939 and 1940) initially lacked the air power needed to support such an offensive. Then, when the mist and cloud finally lifted, neither the already depleted Luftwaffe nor the German ground forces were able to counter the overwhelming weight of Allied air power that was rapidly launched against them. Eventually several factors and events combined to halt the onslaught and seal the fate of *Wacht am Rhein*. Among these were the German failure to capture the vital road junction at St. Vith until 21 December, the resolute defense of Bastogne by the US 101st Airborne Division, the eventual stabilization of the US 1st Army, which bore the brunt of the initial assault, the sheer weight of Allied air power and finally the strong counterattacks launched by Field Marshal Montgomery from the north and General Patton from the south, which enabled the Allies to restore the situation in "the Bulge". Operation *Wacht am Rhein* ended on 16 January, with those German units that had managed to escape the Allied counter-offensive and fighter-bombers having already withdrawn back into Germany. Certainly the army had inflicted enormous casualties upon the US forces, at least 10,276 dead, 47,493 wounded, and 23,218 missing. However, while the Americans were well able to replace these losses, the German army's casualties during the offensive were at least as great as those of the Americans and may have numbered as many as 120,000 dead, wounded and missing. These men were simply irreplaceable, as were the hundreds of Panzers destroyed during the army's last great offensive in the west.

## 15. The Defense of Northwest Europe, February–May 1945

Following the failure of the Ardennes offensive, the army concentrated its defenses along the Rhine, while the Allies resumed their broad-front advance in February 1945. To the north, an Anglo-Canadian attack (Operation *Veritable*) into the Reichswald forest area commenced on 8 February, where the German 1st Parachute Army, commanded by General Schlemm, inflicted heavy casualties upon the British 2nd Army and Canadian 1st Army of 21st Army Group. Using a maze of well-prepared positions, bunkers and obstacles in the darkness of the water-logged forest, and in the streets and buildings of the nearby towns of Goch and Cleve, the paratroopers first staged a determined defense and then conducted a successful fighting withdrawal to safety across the Rhine, albeit losing as many as 90,000 men killed, wounded or missing. A concurrent operation (Operation *Grenade*) by the US 9th Army farther to the south was delayed by bad weather until 23 February. It made slow progress, delayed by flooded roads and waterlogged countryside, but on 1 March these forces at last reached Düsseldorf.

Even farther south the US 12th Army Group advanced (Operation *Lumberjack*) to reach the Rhine between Köln (Cologne) and Koblenz, and on 7 March troops of the US 9th Armored Division had the good fortune to seize more or less intact the weakly defended railway bridge over the Rhine at Remagen – the German army officer responsible for the security and demolition of the bridge was summarily court-martialled and executed on Hitler's orders. By March the Allied armies, British, American, Canadian and Free French, had all closed up to the Rhine, and on 23 March advance elements of Montgomery's 21st Army Group crossed the river (Operation *Plunder*) at ten places between Rheinberg and Rees. This combined ground and airborne assault by some 80,000 men supported by more than 2,000 guns and aerial bombardment quickly overwhelmed the thinly-spread German defenders, now without significant reserves available to them. By the end of the month Montgomery had some twenty divisions and more than 1,000 tanks east of the Rhine, poised to strike for Berlin if so ordered. However, it had already been decided by the "Big Three" Allied war leaders – Roosevelt, Stalin and Churchill – that Hitler's capital would be left for the Russians to capture, while the Anglo-US armies would not move east of the Elbe River.

Consequently, the Western Allies advanced steadily onwards into the Netherlands, southern Germany and toward the industrial Ruhr. There, between 25 March and 18 April, they gradually enveloped and then forced the collapse of Army Group B within the "Ruhr Pocket". Germany's industrial heartland was devastated and more than 320,000 soldiers were captured. After four days evading Allied patrols, the erstwhile commander of Army Group B, Generalfeldmarschall Model, (who had earlier stated that "a [German] field marshal does not become a prisoner. Such a thing is just not possible"[24]) committed suicide in the forest near Duisburg. By the end of April, despite some spirited counterattacks and determined last-ditch defensive actions, the army had lost the war in the west, very many German soldiers meeting their final fate as casualties or prisoners-of-war while fighting in the devastated villages, towns, cities, fields and forests of Germany itself. Despite the clearly deteriorating situation, as late as January 1945 a British intelligence report derived from interviews with a number of recently captured German prisoners-of-war in the west had assessed that, "Few thought that Germany had any hope of final victory; most had had their fill of fighting and recognized the futility of continuing the struggle. Nevertheless, they all fought hard. The deduction would seem to be that no matter how poor the morale of the German soldier may be, he will fight hard as long as he has leaders to give him orders and see that they are obeyed."[25] In the meantime, by the early spring of 1945 the inexorable westward advance by the Russians begun soon after the great tank battle at Kursk in late 1943 had at last brought the Red Army to the very gates of Berlin.

## 16. The Eastern Front and Berlin, August 1943 to May 1945

Generalfeldmarschall Walther Model was a loyal supporter of Hitler and a highly competent army and army group commander, who chose suicide rather than capture after his command was defeated in the "Ruhr Pocket" in 1945.

Despite countless brave and often suicidal battles fought, stands made and counterattacks launched, the army's litany of reverses on the Eastern Front continued. As Germany's reserves of men and resources diminished, those of the Soviet Union (and its Western Allies) increased, so such actions did little more than delay the inevitable. Consequently, for very many of its soldiers the army's withdrawal westwards only ended once its shattered divisions eventually reached a final defensive position, or were outflanked, enveloped, overwhelmed or captured by the advancing Red Army. By the end of 1943, Orel, Kharkov, Smolensk and Kiev had all fallen and the evacuation of the Ukraine was all but complete. In early 1944 a new series of major Soviet offensives began, maximizing their tempo between June and August when Army Group Center was destroyed. The 900-day siege of Leningrad was raised in January; Sevastopol fell in May; and Soviet control of the Ukraine was restored by the late summer. In the north, part of the German army became increasingly isolated as it was forced to withdraw toward the Courland Peninsula and

In spring 1945, many areas of Berlin were necessarily defended by Volkssturm troops during the final battle for the German capital, although such units were patently ill-prepared to combat the Red Army onslaught.

East Prussia. In August, Romania changed sides, and in September Bulgaria was occupied by the Soviets. In November, Soviet troops in Hungary began a siege of Budapest. A major Soviet offensive was launched on 12 January 1945, striking toward Warsaw, the River Oder and Berlin. Budapest fell in mid-February, while in the area of Lake Balaton in southwest Hungary the Germans launched their last significant offensive of the war, and most of the remaining Waffen-SS Panzer divisions were annihilated in the heavy fighting that ensued. Subsequently, Hitler ordered that the Waffen-SS officers who had fought at Lake Balaton should be stripped of their decorations, an order greatly resented by the Waffen-SS and which indicated that by that stage of the war Hitler had lost faith not only in the army but also in even his most loyal fighting units. This particular defeat enabled the Red Army to advance into Austria – Vienna fell on 6 April – and on to Prague. Meanwhile, behind the lines the SS, the military police and "flying courts-martial" teams ranged far and wide, sweeping up and summarily executing large numbers of deserters, "defeatists", and officers who had ordered withdrawals against orders or who were perceived to have failed the Third Reich in some other way, together with anyone suspected of "undermining fighting morale". During the war no fewer than 11,700 men were executed in this way, with possibly an even greater number of unrecorded executions having taken place. During World War I just 48 German soldiers had been executed for military offenses.

Berlin was always where it would all end. The Russian offensive to reach the city began on 16 April, when almost 200 Red Army divisions were unleashed against about 50 much-weakened German divisions. Then, on 23 April, the battle for Berlin began in earnest, as the Red Army's 5th Shock Army, 8th Guards Army and 1st Guards Tank Army struck from the east and southeast in an attack that would eventually draw one and a half million Soviet troops into the onslaught against the German capital. The city was defended by just 45,000 army, other Wehrmacht and Waffen-SS troops with 60 tanks, plus about 40,000 young, old, disabled and infirm Volkssturm soldiers. A further 2,000 Waffen-SS troops of the "Leibstandarte SS Adolf Hitler" were also deployed specifically to defend the Reich Chancellery and the central government area.

From the north, the Red Army's 47th Army, 3rd Shock Army and 2nd Guards Tank Army attacked into the suburbs, while from the southwest the 3rd Guards Tank Army and 28th Army worked their way into the city. Farther to the southwest, the 4th Guards Tank Army struck northwards toward the important town of Potsdam. By then Hitler and many of his immediate entourage were closeted deep in the Führerbunker adjacent to the Reich Chancellery and the Brandenburg Gate at the very heart of Berlin. On 29 April, with the Russian assault troops in the devastated city above almost at the gates of the Reichstag, Hitler married his mistress Eva Braun and later dictated his last will and political testament. During the afternoon of 30 April 1945 the man most responsible for World War II put a pistol to his head and committed suicide. Eva Braun, Frau Hitler, lay dead beside the body of her new husband, having taken poison. Afterwards, both bodies were doused with gasoline and burned by members of the Führerbunker staff in a shallow ditch close to the main entrance to the bunker. Some of the Nazis who had been with Hitler in the bunker to the end subsequently managed to escape, while several others chose to commit suicide. The Reichstag finally fell at 1300 on 2 May. Meanwhile at 2250 hours on 30 April a group of three Red Army sergeants had made their way to a balcony at the front of the building and there unfurled the blood-red flag that signalled the Soviet Union's final victory over the forces of the Third Reich. The remaining German troops in Berlin capitulated on 2 May, having inflicted about 100,000 casualties on the attacking Soviet forces since 16 April. Many of the German prisoners of war in the long columns that marched eastwards out of the ruined city into captivity in the Soviet camps would never see Germany again. In early May 1945 the Soviets held 1,464,803 prisoners-of-war in Germany alone, while more than a million more had already been transported to the Soviet Union to join the several hundred thousand German soldiers captured since 1941. Large numbers of these men remained in Soviet captivity for many years, the last 9,626 survivors being released from the Soviet Union in 1955.

On 7 May, General Alfred Jodl signed Germany's unconditional surrender at Reims, and on 9 May Generalfeldmarschall Wilhelm Keitel formally signed the unconditional surrender documents in Berlin with Soviet Marshal Zhukov. The war that Hitler's army had fought from September 1939 to May 1945 was finally over. The process that began when Hitler and the Nazis achieved power some twelve years earlier had also run its course, having inflicted untold misery upon the world, and ended with failure, destruction and death on an almost unimaginable scale.

Exemplifying the human consequences of Hitler's ambitions for the German army, a soldier mourns the death of two of his comrades of an infantry replacement battalion during the final months of the war.

# PART III
# The Creation of Hitler's Army: Rearmament, 1933–1939

The two-and-a-half years that preceded the formal creation of the Wehrmacht on 21 May 1935 witnessed an unprecedented period of preparatory activity, in order that Germany's reinvigorated and regenerated armed forces might in due course achieve the overall military capability to support the grand designs and expansionist policies expounded by their new head of state and commander-in-chief. Fundamental to this was the urgent need to develop a modern German army that could dissuade, and if necessary counter, any moves by the Allied powers to prevent German rearmament and its inevitable contravention of the provisions of the Treaty of Versailles. The process began as soon as the Nazis came to power in January 1933 and continued apace until it was more or less complete at the end of 1938. By then the German army numbered no fewer than two million men, with intakes of 500,000 newly conscripted recruits joining for training each year. However, these impressive manpower numbers masked capability shortfalls in several important areas, notably the development of an effective armored force large enough to ensure the success of the Nazis' strategic aims. Furthermore, throughout the army's expansion from 1933 to 1939, it experienced considerable difficulties with officer and non-commissioned officer (NCO) recruitment and training, as the burgeoning numbers of battalions, regiments, divisions and corps outstripped the availability of men qualified to train and command them. The numerous expediencies to which the army resorted while resolving its manning difficulties eventually produced a German army whose nature was very different from that of its Weimar and Reichswehr predecessor, and once this process was complete, the new army – Hitler's army – was virtually unrecognizable from the army of the imperial era prior to 1918.

The army was always able to obtain the necessary numbers of soldiers to fill its lowest ranks both through conscription (from 1935) and from the numbers of young men seeking a career, and a generally better and more exciting lifestyle than many of them could have aspired to in civilian life as laborers or unskilled workers. Certainly the in-barracks living conditions of the army of the mid-1930s were much better than those in many other European armies, as was noted by the German historian Dr. Herbert Rosinski writing in 1939: "The great care devoted to the improvement of the relationship between the officer and his men in the Reichswehr has been taken over into the new army, and the material welfare of the men greatly improved in every respect. Gone are the old cheerless barracks with their dreary red brick walls. The new quarters, which have risen during the last years [i.e. since 1933], are cheery, pleasant buildings, whitewashed and gaily painted with military scenes and the portraits of famous soldiers. Reading-rooms, furnished in the style of a wood-panelled country inn, are established and the light and airy living quarters, with their running hot and cold water, are far beyond what most of the soldiers are accustomed to at home, particularly in the case of special arms, such as the air force or the tank units. The food is excellent and much superior, both in quality and quantity, even to that of highly paid workers in the heavy industries. Great care is taken to see that the food is properly cooked and as much variety introduced into the menu as possible."[1] Officers received the same quality and quantity of food as those they commanded, and when on leave the food allowance paid was the same for officers and soldiers.

After 1933 the Hitler Youth (Hitler Jugend) organization and the state labor service (Reichsarbeitsdienst or RAD) very effectively conditioned most German boys and young men for a future life of service to the Nazi state through military or other similarly institutionalized service. A contemporary commentator noted that the army "appears more like an exciting adventure" when contrasted with "the harsh treatment of youngsters in the labor camps."[2] The RAD service obligation was promulgated on 26 June 1935 and required all citizens aged between eighteen and 25 to complete six months living and working in the state labor camps. In practice, some boys began their period of RAD service as young as seventeen, although eighteen or nineteen were generally the norm, with some joining much later in order to complete higher-level education or professional training. The RAD labor camps were mainly based in rural areas, so the young men completing their RAD service were generally involved with farm work, open-cast coal mining, road construction, ditching and suchlike. The RAD was a particularly important part of the

Membership of the Hitler Jugend was invaluable preparation for military service. Youngsters such as these photographed at Witzleben railway station in Charlottenburg, Berlin, in 1939, are probably en route to a training day, possibly in the nearby Grunewald forest.

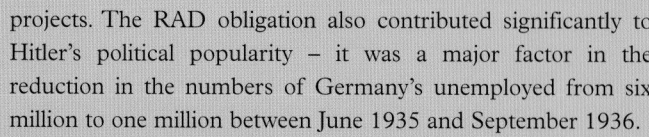

rearmament process, as the young men who shouldered their brilliantly-polished "parade spades" (ordinary spades were issued for work purposes) for six months of involuntary labor service were in all but name completing six months of military pre-conditioning and physical training immediately before they began their military service. At the same time Germany gained a huge supply of cheap manual labor for a host of essential tasks and new

projects. The RAD obligation also contributed significantly to Hitler's political popularity – it was a major factor in the reduction in the numbers of Germany's unemployed from six million to one million between June 1935 and September 1936.

The process of German rearmament between 1933 and 1939 was at the same time ambitious, innovative, speedy, pervasive and (despite some setbacks and shortfalls) generally successful. While it clearly supported the wider policies and foreign policy aspirations of Hitler and the NSDAP, it also exemplified the ability of the German military to develop and implement, during a relatively short period of time, a rearmament plan that impacted upon virtually every part of the German nation, the theoretical constraints imposed by Versailles notwithstanding. The rate of the army's expansion was quite remarkable, and the key milestones and achievements in this complex process illustrated the organizational expertise of the military staffs, together with the unwavering focus and sense of purpose with which Germany was imbued during the early years of the Nazi regime.

From the moment the Nazi Party achieved power on 30 January 1933, it was widely understood throughout Germany (but probably nowhere more so than in the army) that one of the Nazis' primary goals was to overcome or "revise" the Versailles treaty. The army also knew very well that the introduction of conscription was both a Nazi intention and all but inevitable if Germany was to fulfil its newly-declared destiny. But before conscription could begin, a suitable framework had to be put in place ready to administer, train and command these large influxes of manpower, and accordingly the numbers of administrative, support and logistic staff and instructors accelerated rapidly. At the same time, on 1 April 1933 specialist combat support sub-units were formed to complement the Reichswehr's existing organization and provide additional firepower for the newly created infantry units. Because of the constraints imposed by Versailles, these support weapons companies and communications and other specialist units had previously been found only at the expense of re-allocating much-needed combat troops from within battalions and regiments. Now however, for the first time since 1920, the German government-authorized creation of these new units moved the Reichswehr's manpower level beyond the 100,000 mandated by the Allied powers at Versailles.

The problem of increasing the size of the officer corps posed a particular challenge. At the time that its expansion was ordered, there were only 4,000 serving army officers, of whom about 450 were in the medical and veterinary branches. The army's difficulties were exacerbated by the re-assignment of some 500 officers and a number of NCOs to the newly formed Luftwaffe. Meanwhile, only one war college existed, its training intake limited to 180 officers each year. As a result of all this there was an overall shortfall of no fewer than 30,000 officers in 1933. In the short term this deficiency was addressed by recalling recently retired Reichswehr officers, by transferring paramilitary police officers into the army and by commissioning several hundred NCOs.

However, a consequence of the last of these measures was the unavoidable depletion of numbers of NCOs, whose experience was also of critical importance to the successful development of the army in the future. In October 1934 those officers who had been forced to retire in 1919 (when the full impact of Versailles had struck the post-1918 army) were recalled to duty. Where appropriate they were reinstated to their former ranks; those assessed no longer fit for active service were assigned to administrative posts, thereby releasing other officers for active duty. In the meantime, on 1 April 1934 the first large-scale enlistment of volunteers for one year of military service had already been announced. In parallel with all these activities, various subterfuges were employed both to mask the burgeoning size of the army and also to enable it to train for its future role. On 1 October 1934, as an act of deliberate policy, the true strength of the Reichswehr was concealed by allocating garrison names rather than regimental numbers to existing and projected units alike. Similarly, from 1933 the army's innocuously-titled "transport battalions" (Kraftfahrtabteilungen) that had already concealed and facilitated the covert development of the new armored forces became the nucleus of the embryo Panzer divisions.

During the Reichswehr summer maneuvers of 1932, the last such maneuvers that von Hindenburg attended, the training included both reinforced infantry regiments and tank battalions. The latter were necessarily still represented by dummy vehicles mocked-up to look like tanks, but properly armored reconnaissance cars also joined these maneuvers for the first time. These were six-wheeled truck chassis fitted with steel armored plate. Guderian, who was by then chief of staff to the inspector of motorized troops, General Lutz, recalled that, "School children, accustomed to stick their pencils through the canvas walls of our dummies in order to have a look at the inside were disappointed this time; so, too, were the infantrymen who usually defended themselves against our 'tanks' with sticks and stones and who now found themselves ruled out of action by the despised Panzers."[3] Continued criticism by numbers of officers, especially cavalry officers, was confounded by the 1932 maneuvers, which demonstrated the potential of armored and motorized forces, and Guderian was able to capitalize further on this a year later when he was allocated a 30-minute time-slot to demonstrate motorized tactical concepts and equipment to Hitler when the newly appointed chancellor visited Kummersdorf.

**Below:** At the 1935 Nazi Party rally in Nürnberg much of the army's powerful new equipment – such as the half-track carriers towing artillery shown here – was displayed and paraded on "Wehrmacht Day".

The army's reoccupation of the de-militarized Rhineland on 7 March 1936 was greeted enthusiastically by the region's German population, while Hitler's standing and reputation as a statesman were further enhanced within Germany.

Guderian showed and demonstrated a motorcycle platoon, an anti-tank platoon, a platoon of experimental Pz.Kpfw.I tanks, and one platoon each of light and heavy armored reconnaissance cars. This event would prove to be a defining moment for the future Panzer arm in light of future events – Guderian recalled that Hitler was "much impressed by the speed and precision of movement of our units, and said repeatedly: 'That's what I need! That's what I want to have!'"[4]

The introduction of universal conscription was proclaimed on 16 March 1935, together with a declared target size for the army of 550,000 men in twelve corps (or 36 divisions), and the formation of the Luftwaffe was announced at the same time. Remarkably, international disquiet at this clear evidence of Germany's rejection of the Versailles treaty was muted, while the lack of any substantive action by the Allied powers beyond a few mildly expressed protests meant that German rearmament could continue without let or hindrance. This significant achievement was soon followed by the incorporation of all of Germany's paramilitary police units into the army from 1 October, which in practice produced an army of about 480,000 men in ten corps, comprising 24 divisions and three Panzer divisions. Following the German reoccupation of the Rhineland in 1936, this measure also allowed the Landespolizei battalions from that area to be incorporated into the army without delay. As the size and capability of Germany's reinvigorated army increased apace throughout 1935, a new Kriegsheer or "war army" organizational concept was developed. This involved a professional standing or peacetime Feldheer (field army) designed to meet Germany's immediate strategic and security needs on a day-to-day basis and (ideally) to fight a short war without recourse to further military manpower. To back up the Feldheer there would be an Ersatzheer (replacement army) to provide reinforcements and a sustained depth of military capability in the post-mobilization period and

during a protracted conflict. The viability of the Kriegsheer concept was considerably strengthened by the period of obligatory military service being increased from one to two years from 24 August 1936, for this measure effectively doubled the overall size of the Feldheer within a few months of its implementation.

In parallel with the development of its structure and operational concepts, considerable attention was also paid to more aesthetic matters designed to foster military tradition and restore the army's former pride and status. The introduction of new uniforms, merit awards and insignia in 1935 had in many cases recognized particular political events and individual achievements directly or indirectly related to the rise of National Socialism. Indeed, the whole business of military tradition and perceptions of German history were central to the cultural development of the Wehrmacht, but nowhere more so than in the army. However, as with the physical manifestations of the army's renaissance as Hitler's army (such as its swastika-adorned insignia), much of the army's revived heritage from the mid-1930s was also dominated by the Nazis' often perverse interpretations of the military and social history of the German people in former times. In the same way that such symbolism was a core feature of the development and rise to power of the Nazi party, it also played a key part in the reawakening of military pride both within the army and across the nation. After more than two decades of the Weimar Republic, during which many of the old imperial army's regimental colors had remained laid up in churches, museums or government buildings, with no new colors presented, on 14 September 1936 the first sixteen new colors of Hitler's army were presented to a number of units and formations at the Nazi party's Nürnberg rally. These presentations included infantry, armored, cavalry, reconnaissance, artillery and signals units and were but the first of many such presentations, new standards or colors being issued to many other Wehrmacht units during the last months of 1936, and the final such event taking place in Danzig in 1940, when units of the Ersatzheer received their new colors.

The colors, guidons, standards and flags proudly borne by the army color bearers were based on the principal arm of service color (Waffenfarbe) – for example, white for the infantry, red for the artillery, black for engineers, green for Jäger units, pink for Panzer units, golden-yellow for the cavalry – and featured a field of the appropriate color upon which was set a large Iron Cross. The black Wehrmacht eagle and swastika emblem appeared at its center on a white background surrounded by a wreath of silver oak leaves. Swastikas were also at each corner of the color or guidon, which was usually edged with a double fringe of silver aluminium threads. The flags that flew above army barracks and government buildings from 1933 included the old red, white and black tricolor of the imperial era, the red flag of the Nazi party, with the black swastika on white circle at its center, and the national war flag or banner, the Reichskriegsflagge. This was red, with a black and white cross, a black on white swastika at the center, and a traditional Iron Cross emblem in the top left corner. Throughout Germany the traditional red, white and black colors of the imperial era appeared alongside the red, white and black swastika flags and banners of the Nazis, implying a direct connection between Germany's imperial past and an impending return under Hitler's leadership to its former military glory.

Another important milestone was passed on 1 October 1936 when the last two of the twelve army corps Hitler had declared as the new army's target size on 16 March 1935 were formed, some fifteen months earlier than had originally been anticipated. When fully mobilized, the army now fielded 36 divisions, including three armored (or Panzer) divisions (each comprising one armored brigade of two regiments, plus one motorized infantry brigade), as well as one mountain brigade and one cavalry brigade. There were also four reserve divisions and 21 Landwehr divisions. An army parachute infantry company was formed during 1936 but was transferred to the Luftwaffe in January 1938.[5] Just a year later, on 19 October 1937, 13th and 14th Corps were formed, both of which were in addition to the twelve original corps declared in 1935. These considerable achievements had been at the expense of using numerous shortcuts and expediencies, however, and various deficiencies persisted. During the army's major maneuvers carried out in 1936 most battalions still had no more than two officers per company, most platoons being led by NCOs. About 18,000 officers were in post by March 1937, but this still represented a significant shortfall against the 30,000 required, in particular the need to fill staff officer posts in the headquarters of the new corps and divisions. Inevitably, this led to much cross-posting and short-touring, which was disruptive and affected unit cohesion and team building. During the following year, the continuing lack of officers was alleviated to some extent by the government's pragmatic but far-reaching declaration that all officers (including retired officers) would henceforth be liable for indefinite military service. This edict encompassed former officers living outside Germany and over-age former officers, although where appropriate the latter would be required to serve as instructors if they were assessed as not still being fit for active service. Together, these measures increased the number of army officers to about 25,000 by the end of 1938. Meanwhile, the momentum of change and expansion had continued largely unchecked and had even accelerated with the 15th, 16th, 17th and 18th Corps formed during 1938, these particular increases being made possible by the Austrian Anschluß of March 1938 and the Munich settlement signed that September (which ceded control of the Sudetenland in Czechoslovakia to Germany). These two events enabled the immediate incorporation into the German army of five existing divisions from the former Austrian army, together with the conscription of numbers of individual Austrians and Sudeten Germans for military service in the Wehrmacht.

Left: On 12 March 1938, the Anschluß produced the annexation of Austria and brought it fully into the ambit of Hitler's "Greater Germany", enabling the immediate incorporation of Austria's five army divisions into the Wehrmacht.

In late 1938, with the military storm clouds gathering over Europe, much had been achieved during the five years since the Nazis achieved power. Not least of this was the attainment of the two-million-man army, with its continued annual intakes of no fewer than 500,000 conscripts at the start of their two years of military training. This produced an army that included five Panzer divisions, two independent Panzer brigades, four light armored (cavalry) divisions and three mountain divisions. By mid-1939, with war against Poland imminent, the fully mobilized strength of the army had in theory further increased to 103 divisions, although in practice the strength of the Feldheer remained at about 51, as the 103 divisions included many framework formations and units for which the necessary

Below: Then, on 1 October the same year, German troops occupied the Sudetenland, with Hitler's planned occupation of the rest of Czecho-slovakia (including Bohemia and Moravia) subsequently being completed during March 1939. Here, motorcycle units move into Prague on a wet and wintry Wednesday 15 March.

As the need to step up the Third Reich's armaments production became increasingly important, propaganda posters emphasized the interdependence of German military and industrial capabilities, while constantly exhorting the factory workers to ever greater efforts. Here a factory worker symbolically passes hand grenades to a front-line soldier.

manpower was still largely untrained or part-trained. There were still only seven Panzer divisions and four fully motorized infantry divisions in the army, while the larger part of the army (some 86 divisions) still relied upon horses to tow its artillery and supply wagons, and upon requisitioned civilian motor vehicles to carry out a wide range of transport tasks. As most infantry units had no integral transport, they were generally constrained to move on foot, using requisitioned and captured vehicles wherever these were available and moving by rail whenever possible. Although observers of the major maneuvers of 1936 and 1937 noted that "large units were able to accomplish marches up to forty-five miles [seventy kilometers] in twenty-four hours" such achievements hardly matched the levels of motorized mobility necessary to conduct the sort of large-scale, wide-ranging armored offensives that would be a vital part of the coming conflict.

Despite continuing difficulties in a few areas, the officer deficiency of the mid-1930s had been more or less resolved by early 1939, with five military academies by then in place and an output of 3,000 officers per year based upon a training course that had pragmatically been reduced from two years to between eleven and fourteen months. Officer recruitment was buoyant, with about 60 percent of all German boys leaving high school in 1938 declaring their wish to become army officers. However, at the same time, some of the more traditional aspects of the country's education system had stagnated because of the need to accommodate National Socialist ideology and its constraining mores in the standard curriculum, and, with so many boys lacking the necessary academic skills or intellectual aptitude traditionally required to qualify for entry to the military academies, all formal educational qualification requirements for officer candidates were increasingly disregarded (and were finally abandoned altogether in November 1942). Meanwhile, the influence of the Hitler Jugend movement and the national emphasis upon sport and other physical activities – including a whole range of military-related activities such as gymnastics, route marching, throwing dummy hand grenades, glider piloting and shooting – all contributed positively to the physical conditioning and mental hardening of German youth in advance of the coming conflict. The 1936 Berlin Olympiad also contributed indirectly to the national enthusiasm for physical perfection and the admiration of athletic excellence while simultaneously affording Hitler an unrivalled propaganda opportunity to blend sporting excellence and the promotion of an Aryan ideal with semi-military pageantry on a grand scale.

The urgent need to produce sufficient suitably qualified NCOs was also addressed, and several existing flaws in the prevailing system of NCO training and careers were dealt with at the same time. Among these was the fact that the rapidly expanding army had suffered considerably from the departure of many thoroughly competent NCOs after just two years of military service. The weakness of the two-year engagement as an NCO was that the first year of active duty was usually spent as an

assistant instructor and the second year attending specialist courses, so that the army's regiments and divisions often gained little or no direct value from an NCO's acquired expertise. And with much more emphasis on technology, two years was simply too short for an NCO to acquire the necessary skills and then apply them effectively within the Feldheer. The situation was further worsened by the fact that large numbers of poorer quality NCOs routinely stayed on for the ten years plus two years re-training to which they were entitled, while on the other hand the standard career path did not offer a satisfactory career for those men who were more capable or ambitious and who might therefore have been officer candidates in due course. Accordingly, three new NCO training schools were established to train these men on courses lasting two years. Linked to this, a mandatory four-and-a-half-year enlistment for NCOs was introduced, together with increased opportunities for these men to be considered for a commission in due course. As a result of these changes the army benefited appropriately from its fully-trained NCOs thereafter, as well as encouraging suitable NCOs to apply for a commission. Overall, the changes occasioned by German rearmament from 1933 to 1939 were seismic in their scope and affected the whole of the army, at every level of its structure, from the high command right down to the individual officer and soldier.

While these changes had been taking place in the army, the Nazi Party's own paramilitary security force, the Schutzstaffel (or

The February 1943 edition of *Signal* included pictures of self-propelled guns, tanks and artillery ammunition being produced at various industrial plants. As the war progressed, the Wehrmacht's in-house magazine *Signal* regularly featured articles on the German factories that manufactured weapons, vehicles and equipment for the army.

An Auto-Union advertisement published in *Signal* in October 1942 illustrated the close relationship between the civilian motor industry and military vehicle production. The soldier's Auto-Union motorcycle carries a Wehrmacht "WH" (army) registration plate, while the staff car has a Luftwaffe "WL" registration.

SS), had also grown significantly since its original formation in 1923 as the SS-Stabswache in Berlin. By 1936 an SS-VT (SS-Verfügungstruppe) Inspectorate had been established to oversee the administration and development of what by late 1939 had become the "armed" or Waffen-SS,* headed by Reichsführer-SS (RF-SS) Heinrich Himmler. Although by definition the Waffen-SS was neither part of the army nor of the Wehrmacht, the story of this force increasingly overlapped that of the army from 1939, with Waffen-SS units frequently fighting alongside and under the command of army formations throughout the war in every theater except North Africa, while at various stages of the war some army units also found themselves commanded by Waffen-SS headquarters. Although the Waffen-SS was understandably much more politicized than the army, its military organizations and general regulations were largely based upon those of the

* The story of the Waffen-SS falls outside the story of Hitler's army, but in recognition of the parallel nature of its history with that of the army from 1933 to 1945 a short account of the development, organization and divisions of the Waffen-SS can be found in Appendix 1.

army, modified where necessary to take account of its SS and Nazi heritage.

Organizational changes, personnel increases and the acquisition of new equipment represented only part of the story, for such a sweeping program also needed the operational concepts it supported and the equipment that it introduced to be tried, tested and (where necessary) amended and proved again during its course, with only so much of value able to be distilled out of Germany-based training activities. Certainly these had been innovative, and included the training carried out by units such as the seven so-called "transport battalions" (Kraftfahrabteilungen), which would in due course be revealed as the army's armored spearhead of the Panzer forces. Similarly, although ingenious, the widespread use of agricultural tractors and ordinary motor cars mocked-up to simulate tanks in order to practice the tactical handling of mechanized units during the army's maneuvers of the 1920s and early 1930s fell well short of the sort of training required to ready the army for war. Consequently, for Germany to recover its former military might it needed discrete weapons manufacturing and testing facilities, together with training areas and proving grounds far from the prying eyes of the Allied observers who sought to monitor and enforce the Versailles treaty. Ideally, the army also needed to exercise its new tactical theories and equipment under battlefield conditions. Fortuitously for the Nazis, in 1922 Germany had already found friends overseas in Spain, Sweden and the Soviet Union prepared to ignore the Versailles treaty and to assist the Reichswehr to regain an effective military capability, and it is arguable that if these arrangements had not been in place a full decade before Hitler achieved power the very ambitious rearmament program implemented between 1933 and 1939 might not have been viable.

In addition to the testing and production of submarines by the Spanish shipyards at Santander, and of artillery guns by the Swedish armaments firm of Bofors, the secret military agreement between Moscow and Berlin signed in 1922 in parallel with the Rapallo agreement had placed huge areas within Soviet Russia at the disposal of the German army. There, German army units could develop their operational techniques and tactics, as well as training with the full range of offensive warfare weapons prohibited by the Versailles treaty, while senior army officers frequently travelled to Russia secretly in order to view the various projects and training then in progress, as well as to observe Red Army maneuvers.

However, such activities were not limited to training exercises alone, for in 1936 the Spanish Civil War began, and this afforded the army and the newly created Luftwaffe a timely and unrivalled opportunity to take part in the conflict as units of "volunteers" fighting in support of General Franco's forces. As a result, from 1936 to 1939 the army's embryo Panzer forces and some other units were able to try, test and develop in Spain much of their new equipment, air–ground support procedures and mobile tactics under actual war conditions. The experience gained using tanks, other motor vehicles, motorcycles, aircraft, machine guns and other small-arms in combat was of incalculable benefit to the development of Hitler's army, and particularly so for the officers destined to command the armored forces during the fast-moving mobile operations that would be carried out just a few years later. A US government intelligence assessment of the state of the German army at the time of the outbreak of the war noted that the German army of 1939 was "a model of efficiency, the best product of the concentrated military genius of the most scientifically military of nations."[6] However, while the whole process of rearmament and restructuring during the 1930s finally produced the men and equipment with which the army went to war in 1939, this achievement and subsequent sustainability of that capability against all the odds also depended upon other less tangible forces that had long existed in the national consciousness. In the early spring of 1945, with Hitler's army pressed hard on all fronts and Germany's impending defeat by then inevitable, a contemporary Allied military intelligence assessment stated: "Despite [as at March 1945] the acute lack of weapons, ammunition, fuel, transport, and human reserves, the German army seems to function with its old [1939] precision and to overcome what appear to be insuperable difficulties with remarkable speed ... The cause of this toughness, even in defeat is not generally appreciated. It goes much deeper than the quality of weapons, the excellence of training and leadership, the soundness of tactical and strategic doctrine, or the efficiency of control at all echelons. It is to be found in the military tradition which is so deeply ingrained in the whole character of the German nation and

which alone makes possible the interplay of these various factors of strength to their full effectiveness."[7]

The often spectacular progress made by the armed forces during the 1930s was not replicated throughout German industry, which meant that the Wehrmacht always lacked the supporting depth of German industrial production essential for it to fight a war of attrition – which, of course, Hitler did not envisage in 1939. Indeed, the Blitzkrieg successes of 1939 and 1940 later tended to reinforce the validity of the Führer's assessment, as well as prompting his order to disband some seventeen divisions following the army's successful campaign against France in June 1940, despite his future intention to invade Russia just twelve months later. Consequently, and notwithstanding the significant output of war material from the factories of Krupp, Rheinmetall, Mauser-Werke, Polte-Werke, Daimler-Benz A.G., Hanomag, Linke-Hoffmann, Telefunken, Carl Zeiss, Dortmunder-Union and a host of other firms throughout Germany, mass production had not begun by 1939, while the total mobilization of German industry would not take place until Albert Speer gained overall control of armaments and war production in 1942. Similarly, no national-level plans existed for a "total war economy", and measures such as using female labor in the armaments factories to release men for other tasks were simply not considered. As a result the vital dovetailing of the state's industrial capacity into the needs of the national armed forces and the pre-war rearmament program never really took place, which in turn meant that effective strategic planning and industrial-military prioritization was haphazard or non-existent.

This resulted in the wastage of Germany's ever-diminishing resources as the war drew on, with Hitler's later strategic planning so often fuelled by memories of the campaigns of 1939 and 1940, which had been characterized by short, mobile campaigns with quick victories, and the ability to raid and replenish sufficient military stocks, industrial capacity and raw materials from newly-conquered territories. Such optimistic assumptions were shown to be disastrously flawed once Germany invaded the Soviet Union in June 1941, when – against all Hitler's expectations – the army found itself committed to a grinding war of attrition on the Eastern Front. Thereafter, the needs of the Wehrmacht frequently outstripped the ability of the Third Reich to produce or provide them, despite the success of the rearmament program in the pre-war years and the prodigious (but by then much too late) achievements of Albert Speer from 1942. Indeed, one of the great ironies of the war was that while the economy and industrial capacity of the Third Reich was eventually mobilized in 1942 to meet the challenges of a "total" industrial war, by that stage the army on the Eastern Front had in many ways been "de-modernized", having adapted itself to a form of warfare that was frequently little short of primitive in nature.[8]

Germany's ability to prosecute the war beyond 1942 depended in large part upon the work of Albert Speer, who successfully moved German industry on to a total war footing after his appointment as the Third Reich's armaments minister that year. Speer is seen here on Hitler's left during a visit by the Führer to a weapons demonstration in 1943.

Vehicle pennants were used to indicate the rank of a senior officer or that a vehicle was carrying an officer on official duty. These pennants were usually painted on to a metal base, or directly on to the mudguard (fender) of an armored vehicle.

**Left:** Field Marshal's pennant (Generalfeldmarschall) (actual size 30cms x 30cms)

**Center:** General's pennant (actual size 35cms x 23cms)

**Right:** Other Officer's pennant (actual size 30cms x 20cms)

# PART IV
# The Structure of Military Power

## 1. Shaping the Structure

In order to bring the armed forces entirely under Hitler's authority, and thus make them a compliant tool for implementing his foreign policies, it was first necessary to break the traditional and long-standing system of command and control at the highest levels of government and military authority. These would be removed or re-shaped so that the Third Reich could develop in accordance with National Socialist policies and ideology unconstrained by traditional German values, loyalties and traditions. Accordingly, in parallel with the expansion and rearmament of the armed forces from 1933, many other changes also took place as the army's long-standing command arrangements were progressively restructured. In the politically charged emerging Third Reich, Hitler's National Socialist agenda impacted directly upon the interface between the government and the high command as the Führer tightened his direct control over the government and its ability to direct the armed forces. This escalating process provided an increasingly uncomfortable dilemma for many officers, especially those in the army. By the middle of the decade, numbers of officers who had originally regarded the Nazis as a useful (but merely temporary) expedient, by which the prestige, power and influence enjoyed by the old imperial German army in former times might be restored, finally realized that they had lost control of the process they had supported either actively or (more usually) by their passivity and acquiescence during the late 1920s and early 1930s. Few of them, however, could deny either the remarkable extent of the military renaissance already achieved by the Nazi government or the potential future opportunities this opened up for the armed forces in the future.

In late 1937 several senior army officers spoke openly against Hitler's expansionist intentions, fearful in particular of a new war against France and Great Britain. By doing so they played directly into Hitler's hands and enabled him to achieve total control of the armed forces. Dissent within parts of the officer corps had been growing for a few years, and ever since 1935 various officers had criticized the speed of the rearmament process, correctly identifying that in many cases quantity was being achieved at the expense of quality. Foremost amongst these officers were Generaloberst Ludwig Beck, chief of the general staff, Generaloberst Werner von Fritsch, commander-in-chief of the army, and Generalfeldmarschall Werner von Blomberg, the war minister. Together, these officers wielded considerable power – control of the armed forces and matters of national defense were still the direct responsibility of the Ministry of War at that stage. In January 1938, accusations of immorality were made against von Blomberg's new wife, while separate allegations of homosexuality (then still a criminal offense) were made simultaneously against von Fritsch. As a widower, government minister and field marshal, von Blomberg's marriage to his secretary Eva Gruhn on 12 January 1938 was certainly ill-advised, as it was well known that Gruhn had enjoyed a somewhat colorful and risqué social life, a fact that was quickly brought to Hitler's attention via the Berlin chief of police, enthusiastically prompted by Göring. Von Blomberg was accused of bringing the officer corps into disrepute, and his position became untenable. In the case of von Fritsch, a confirmed bachelor, the Gestapo (Geheime Staatspolizei, the state secret police) alleged that he had committed a homosexual offense with one "Bavarian Joe", a "rent boy", near Potsdam railway station in November 1934. The allegation was made by Himmler and was entirely false, and an officers' court of honor subsequently exonerated von Fritsch absolutely. But the damage had been done. Both von Blomberg and von Fritsch were forced to resign, their retirements being announced officially on 4 February 1938.[1]

The removal of von Blomberg and von Fritsch enabled Hitler to create an armed forces high command at Zossen-Wünsdorf, located to the south of Berlin. Meanwhile, General (later Generalfeldmarschall) Walther von Brauchitsch succeeded von Fritsch as commander-in-chief of the army, while General Friedrich Fromm assumed command of the Ersatzheer. In the wake of these changes, a purge of other officers thought to be less than supportive of Hitler's plans was carried out during 1938, some sixteen generals being relieved of their commands and a further 44 senior commanders transferred to other duties.[2] Everywhere, officers known to be loyal to Hitler were immediately appointed to replace these men, and, although many of the new appointees were undoubtedly competent, their political reliability generally took precedence over their military capability. Despite remaining in post, Beck became increasingly isolated, especially after the creation of the new armed forces high command significantly reduced the power of the general staff, and he eventually resigned on 18 August 1938. He was replaced as chief of the army general staff by General Franz Halder.[3] Although he was another opponent of Hitler's policies, Halder (as did many other army officers) set his personal misgivings aside in order to carry out what was widely regarded as a German officer's immutable duty to the nation and to the Führer to whom he had sworn absolute loyalty.

## 2. Command and Control of the Armed Forces: The OKW

The principle of unity of command was central to the German military system, and this fundamental principle was applied at all levels of command. At the highest level it was intended to enable the efficient management of all aspects of the national military capability, although in due course a succession of diverging and competing political and military imperatives would affect and detract from this, particularly so from 1942. This concept meant that the army (Heer), air force (Luftwaffe) and navy (Kriegsmarine) were not separate services but existed as the three separate branches of a single service, the Wehrmacht (the national armed forces), which was commanded by the armed forces high command (Oberkommando der Wehrmacht, or OKW). The OKW was responsible for all aspects of the nation's ground, air and maritime warfare policies in peace and war, directing and coordinating the activities of the army high command (Oberkommando des Heeres, or OKH), the air force high

command (Oberkommando der Luftwaffe, or OKL) and the navy high command (Oberkommando der Kriegsmarine, or OKM) as necessary. Prior to hostilities the OKW was responsible for the national defense plans, and once war began it controlled the armed forces' operations on land, sea and in the air. In order to separate routine administrative actions from the business of war-fighting, once hostilities commenced the OKW and the various subordinate high commands divided into forward and

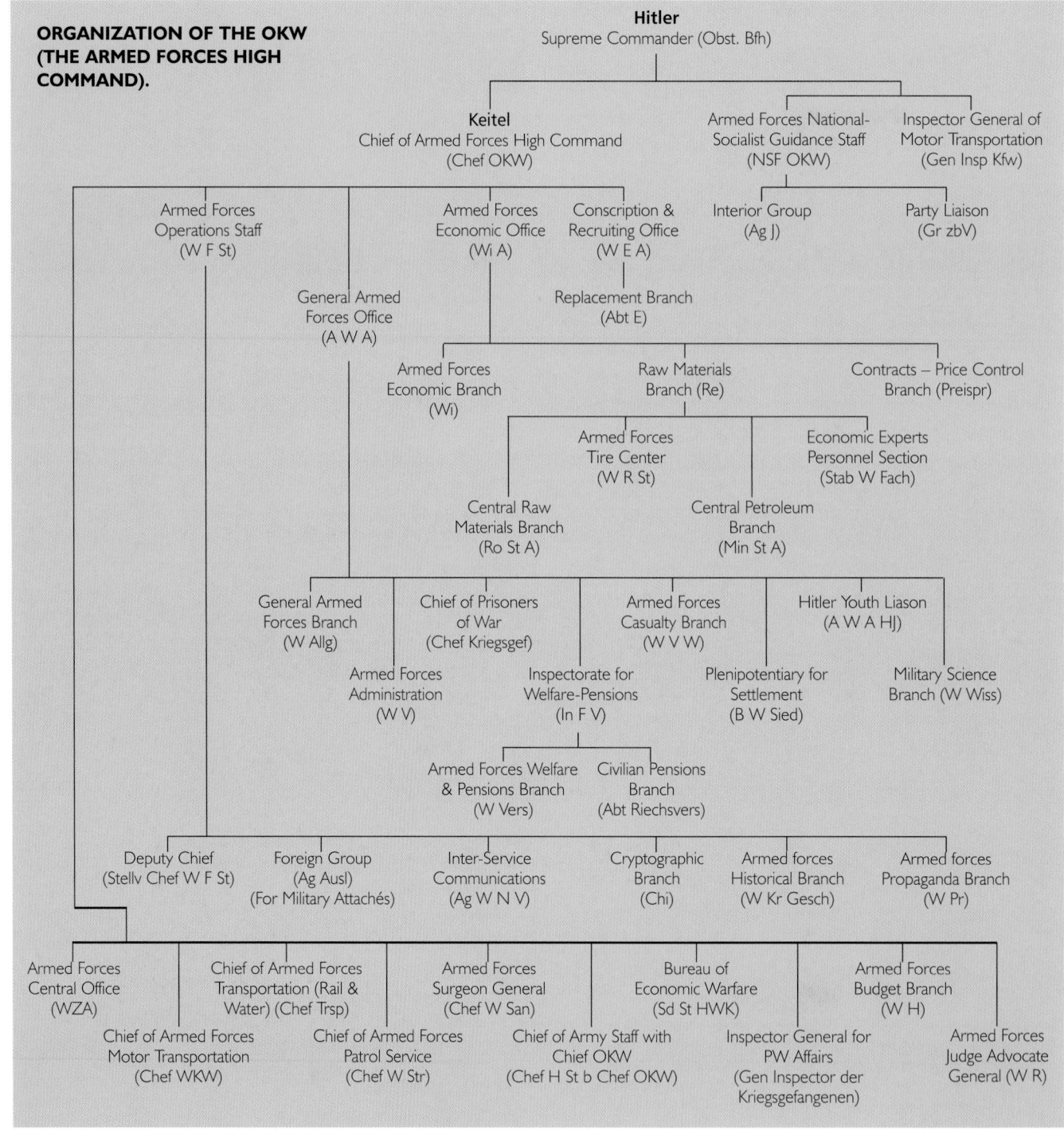

**ORGANIZATION OF THE OKW (THE ARMED FORCES HIGH COMMAND).**

rear headquarters, the latter remaining mainly in the Berlin area dealing with all non-operational and non-urgent matters while the forward headquarters staff controlled the operations in progress. Although Waffen-SS units and formations also came under operational control of the OKW or the OKH once deployed in the field, the Waffen-SS was not officially part of the Wehrmacht, and so for all non-operational purposes it remained firmly under SS control. The discrete command status of the Waffen-SS was indicated very clearly by the absence of any formalized SS representation within the otherwise comprehensive military, paramilitary, civil service, economic and political organization of the OKW.

From 4 February 1938, with the demise of the traditional war ministry in the wake of the departure of von Blomberg and von Fritsch, and the subsequent removal of many other senior officers, Hitler assumed supreme command of the German armed forces as "Führer und Oberster Befehlshaber" (leader and supreme commander). However, it was not until 19 December 1941 (following the German failure to capture Moscow) that he eventually dismissed the newly appointed commander-in-chief of the army, Generalfeldmarschall von Brauchitsch. Thereafter, Hitler personally assumed direct control of military operations, setting OKW and the armed forces on an increasingly disastrous course which began during the Russian winter of 1941 and ended in Berlin in May 1945. From 1934 to 1938, Hitler was Führer, chancellor and supreme commander (but with supreme command exerted through the commander-in-chief, who was also the minister of war); from 1938 to 1941 he was Führer, chancellor, supreme commander and minister of war; finally, from 1941 to 1945, he was Führer, chancellor, supreme commander, minister of war, and commander-in-chief of the army. Although Generalfeldmarschall Wilhelm Keitel was the principal OKW officer (Chef des OKW) from 1938, his function was always that of a chief of staff, or executive officer, rather than a commander. The other key officer at OKW was Generaloberst Alfred Jodl, who headed the operations staff branch (Wehrmachtführungsstab) throughout the war. Both Keitel and Jodl were fiercely pro-Hitler, always putting their personal loyalty to the Führer and their unquestioning obedience to his policies and demands ahead of the needs of the armed forces as a whole.

Superficially, the evidence of Hitler's apparent abilities as a strategist, diplomat and leader were clear to see. In 1936 the Rhineland had been returned to German control amid scenes of much national rejoicing; then, on a continuing tide of national euphoria, Austria had been brought into the Greater German Reich in 1938; while the Sudetenland had been returned to Germany the same year, with Germany completing the occupation of the remainder of Czechoslovakia by the spring of 1939. Hitler's diplomatic successes included the Munich Agreement of 29 September 1938 and the non-aggression pact with the Soviet Union signed by von Ribbentrop and Molotov on 23 August 1939.[4] Undoubtedly some Nazi policies and the politically-motivated actions of the SS against resistance groups, saboteurs, political activists, gypsies, Jews and others deemed to be enemies of the Third Reich in the newly-occupied territories were distasteful to some army officers. However, these matters were generally considered to be none of the army's business and inconsequential when set against the much wider future of the newly-declared Third Reich and the crucial role of the army in that future. So it was, with the potential to place four and a half million men under arms, with the Soviet Union effectively neutralized, with internal security matters in the hands of the SS, with much of German industry and the economy at last moving (albeit still too slowly) on to a war footing, and with a compliant high command in place, the stage was set for Hitler's army to go to war in Europe. With such considerations in mind, the observations of Dr. Herbert Rosinski, made in late 1938, were particularly noteworthy. He wrote: "[General] Ludendorff in his vision of the 'totally mobilized' nation [had] still thought its leader would be the 'Super General' conducting it upon sober military considerations. [However] under the new form of 'extended strategy' it is obvious that the direction of the whole must lie in the hands of the political leader [i.e., Adolf Hitler], and it is very doubtful whether considerations of a purely military character will be allowed to play in his counsels a role corresponding to their real importance. In the 'Leader-General' of the Third Reich the German army may well find the prophet who sends it to Armageddon."[5]

Until 1941, Hitler as head of state had quite correctly concerned himself primarily with strategic and diplomatic issues. During the early war years he had been open to suggestions and amenable to alternative ideas. However, as his apparent infallibility as a statesman and military leader continued prior to 1941, he became ever more intolerant of criticism and ever more certain of his own judgment. Consequently, once Hitler became directly involved in the day-to-day operational planning and decisions of the OKW, the concept of unified command became virtually unachievable. Inevitably, deep-seated inter-service rivalries already existed between the army, navy and air force, and Hitler's policy of fostering "divide and rule" in order to forestall internal opposition meant that these rivalries hardened, so that the OKW could never fulfil its potential. Similarly, the personal and political ambitions of various senior members of the OKW staff, together with those of the heads of the army, navy and air force, further weakened the effectiveness of the OKW and diluted the strength of its relationship with the OKH, OKL and OKM. With the constant replacement of competent but independently-minded staff officers and military advisers by pro-Hitler personnel, the ability of the OKW to fulfil its intended purpose to conduct strategic planning and to produce, implement and coordinate innovative operational direction was gradually transformed. As the war progressed, the OKW became little more than a conduit for endorsing and promulgating Hitler's orders and policies while simultaneously concerning itself with a multiplicity of administrative and minor or primarily presentational matters at an inappropriately high level of command.

# 3. Command and Control of the Army: The OKH

Since the second half of the nineteenth century the officers of the German general staff corps had provided the army with a foundation of outstanding professional competence that included the highest standards of military intellect, conceptual analysis and philosophy. It had also provided a relatively small pool of exceptionally talented army officers from which the army's most senior commanders were selected, trained, and eventually appointed. The general staff was the remarkable command and control machine that lay at the heart of the army and organized, supervised and directed all that it undertook. In 1939 the principal army headquarters by and through which the general staff carried this out was the OKH (the Oberkommando des Heeres). When full mobilization was ordered, the OKH divided into two parts. The main headquarters deployed to the

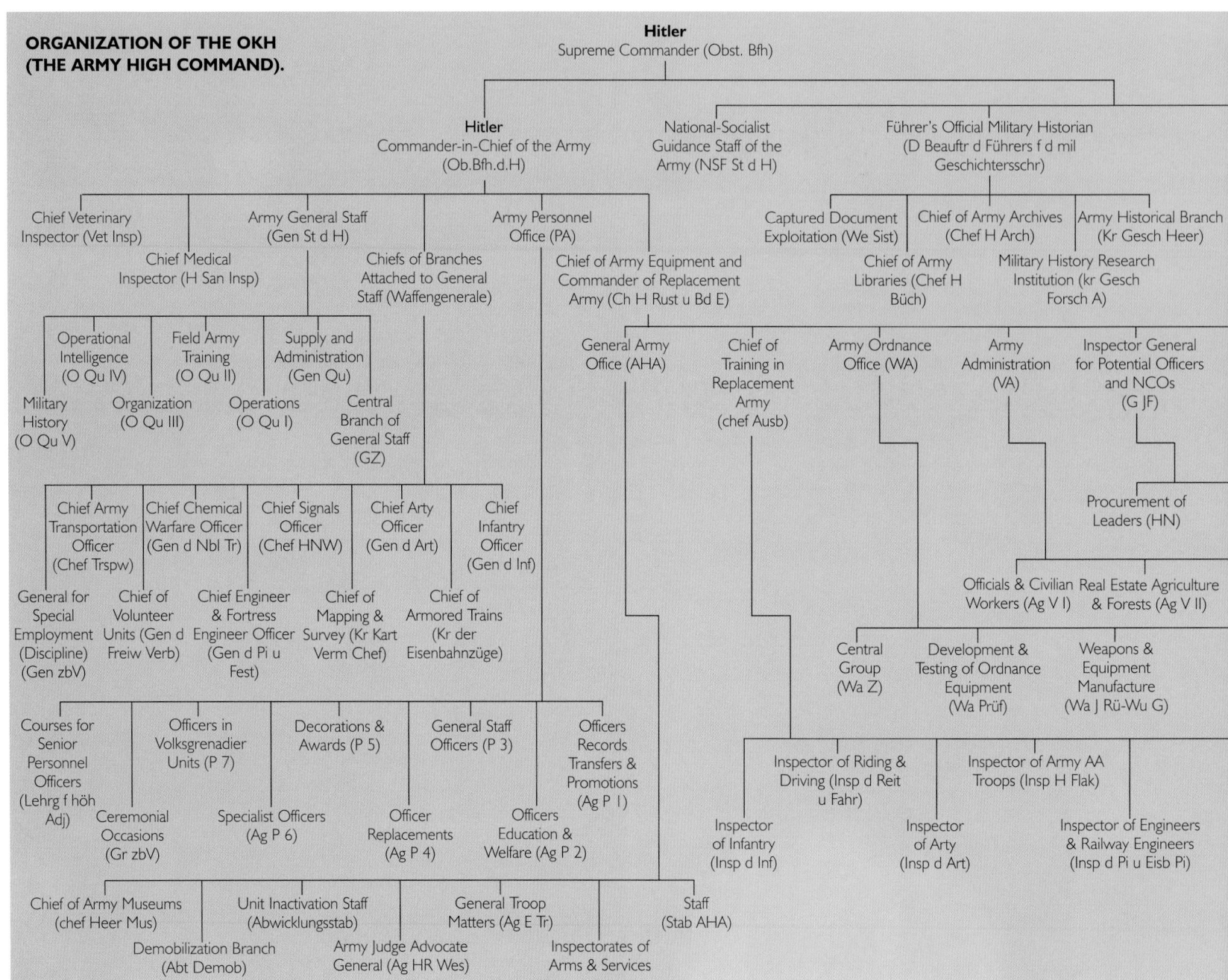

**ORGANIZATION OF THE OKH (THE ARMY HIGH COMMAND).**

field and was headed by the then commander-in-chief, von Brauchitsch. It included staff branches dealing with operations, training, organization and intelligence. Supply matters at the main headquarters were overseen by a quartermaster general who also advised the commander-in-chief. There were also OKW officers present at the main headquarters to provide advice and to coordinate transport, communications and air support. Meanwhile an OKH rear headquarters remained based in Berlin, with responsibility for the secondary and routine day-to-day staff functions usually carried out by the main headquarters, as well as for any not represented at the forward

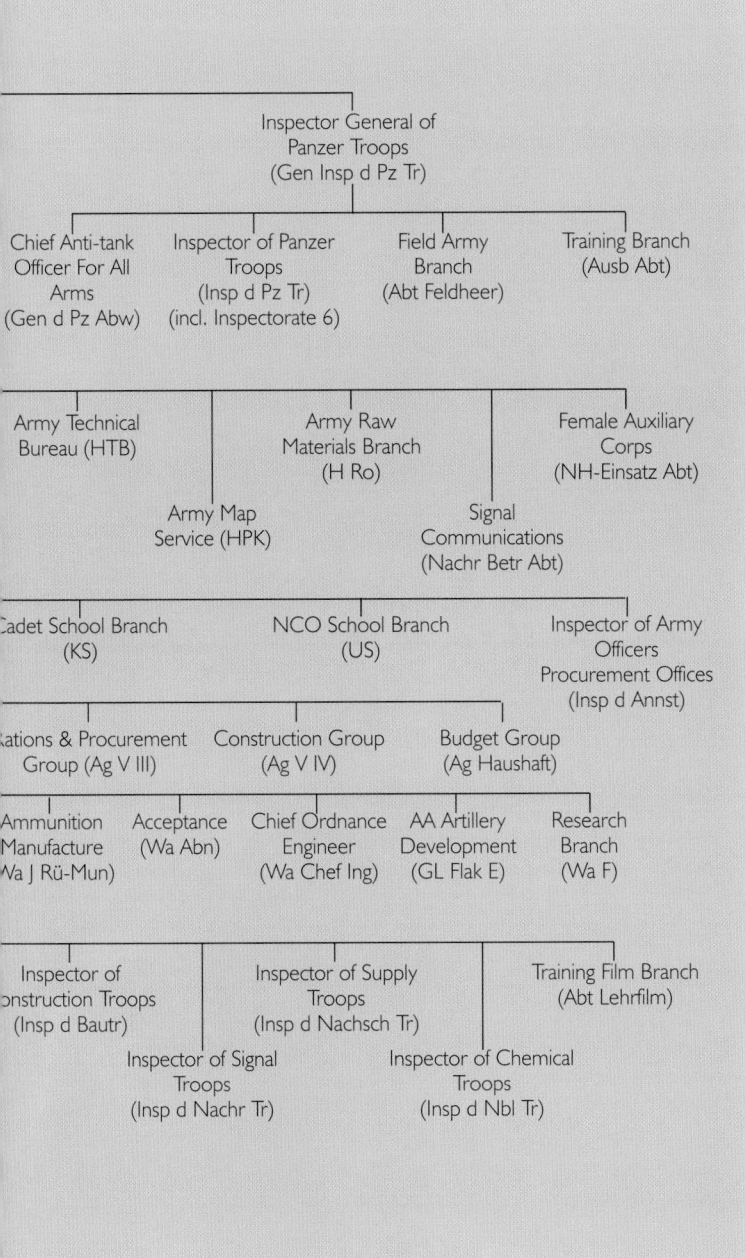

main headquarters. This was the OKH operating concept implemented at the start of the war.

When Hitler created the OKW and took to himself supreme authority over all the armed forces, the power enjoyed by the three principal subordinate headquarters diminished. Nowhere was this more so than in the army high command, where the Führer's obsessive suspicion of the army (by far the largest of the fighting services), its officer corps as a whole and the officers of the general staff in particular, meant that the traditional pre-eminence of the latter declined throughout the war. The fortunes of the general staff finally reached their nadir following the abortive attempt on Hitler's life in July 1944, when Himmler was appointed commander of the Ersatzheer and local Nazi officials (Gauleiter) were authorized to overrule the decisions and policies of local army

Hitler is greeted by Generalfeldmarschalls von Runstedt and von Brauchitsch as he arrives at a railway station (possibly Groß Börnecke) on 20 August 1938 before visiting army maneuvers on a nearby training area.

Himmler with Hitler. Himmler replaced General Fromm as head of the Ersatzheer, which in effect displaced OKH control of the Ersatzheer, giving control to the SS.

reservations about the army's traditional conservatism and reliability vis-à-vis that of the politically more reliable Luftwaffe and Kriegsmarine. Despite this, the OKH was still the headquarters to which the army groups, corps and other major formations looked for operational direction and support, with many talented officers being employed on the OKH staff, although their professional abilities were often the result of experience gained during the pre-1938 era, especially during the military revival of the Reichswehr by Generaloberst Hans von Seeckt during the 1920s. Accordingly, although it eventually became little more than a means through which Hitler imposed his will upon the army, the OKH was still able to perform its routine command functions effectively but without much of the innovative thinking and freedom of action that had characterized the German army's high command in the past. The very fact that the OKH was generally able to carry out its operational task throughout the war was evidence of the quality of many of the OKH staff officers, and their ability to operate effectively despite the often intolerable working constraints and political influences that increasingly impacted upon their daily work. Indeed, it is noteworthy that from December 1941, when the responsibility for all theaters other than the Eastern Front passed to the OKW and the OKH was left with responsibility only for the day-to-day conduct of the war on the Eastern Front, never less than 60 percent of the entire army was deployed against the Russians until the end of the war.

By late 1944 the OKH comprised three main branches – the general staff, the heads of arms and the army personnel office, plus the extensive command structure of the Ersatzheer. There was also a discrete element commanded and controlled directly by Hitler as supreme commander, rather than via the OKH general staff. Significantly, from 1943 this last element included the inspectorate of Panzer troops, which was arguably the army's most potent fighting force, certainly where offensive operations were contemplated.

An amplification of the main functions and responsibilities of each of the very many elements and staff branches that comprised the OKH during the final years of the war is to be found in Appendix 2. In the army chain of command below the OKH were the various army groups (Heeresgruppen), six in peacetime. Prior to mobilization each of the Heeresgruppen served as the superior headquarters of varying numbers of the nation's fifteen pre-war military districts, the Wehrkreise or Wehrbezirke (which were usually designated by Roman numerals, as were the army corps, although this was not mandatory). On general mobilization in 1939 the Heeresgruppen moved from their normal peacetime training role to form two operational army group commands and a number of army headquarters, while an additional army group command headquarters, Army Group South, was created from von Rundstedt's Polish campaign planning staff specifically for the invasion of Poland. Additional army-level headquarters for the Feldheer were drawn from the military districts, each of which

commanders, no matter how senior. The executive power of the general staff and the OKH suffered during the post-1938 years (especially from 1942), but the OKH still directed military ground operations at the highest level, although the work of the OKW operations staff increasingly overlapped that of the OKH general staff branch as the war progressed, and even more so after Hitler took personal control of the army from December 1941. Indeed, from the start of the war, the OKH forward headquarters in the field was always sited close to Hitler's own field headquarters (Führerhauptquartier), an arrangement that enabled Hitler's close control of army operations and emphasized his well-known

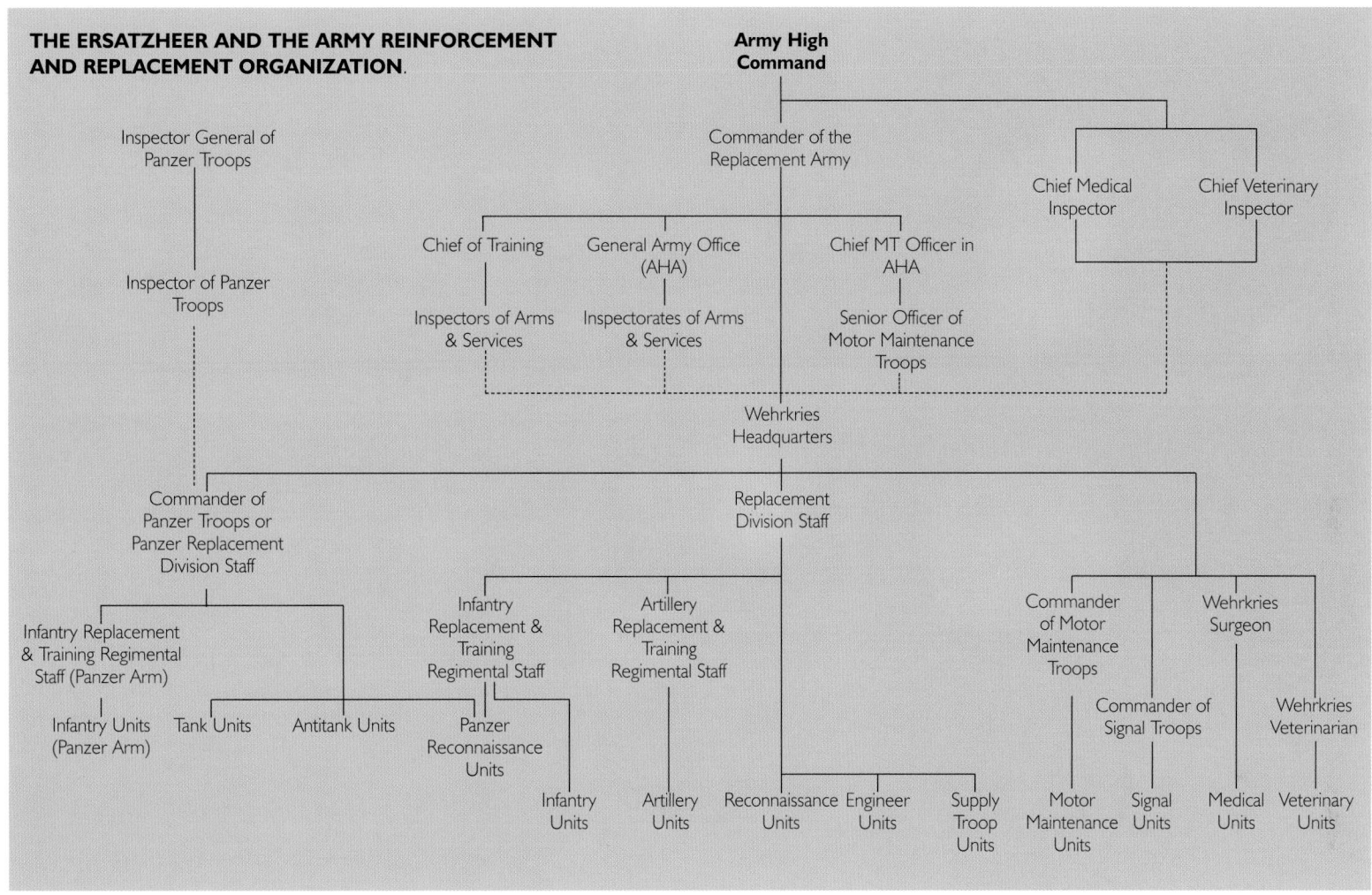

**THE ERSATZHEER AND THE ARMY REINFORCEMENT AND REPLACEMENT ORGANIZATION.**

typically administered two corps in peacetime. After the Polish campaign two more Wehrkreise were added, with others formed later, and by late 1944 eleven operational army group commands existed, controlling no fewer than 26 armies. Once hostilities had commenced, the residual Wehrkreise structure in Germany came under the control of the army's second echelon force, the Ersatzheer, which fulfilled a range of functions that were separate from, but supported those of, the Feldheer.

# 4. The Replacement Army: The Ersatzheer

The Ersatzheer was a powerful Germany-based framework organization that came fully into existence on general mobilization. Its principal task was to train and provide replacements for the Feldheer, although it also carried out many other related administrative activities.* Although many Ersatz-

heer units were eventually involved in operational tasks to varying extents, the Ersatzheer title did not indicate an intention to use it as a properly constituted reserve army that could, or would, replace the Feldheer if required. "Replacement" here referred to the fully trained individuals, groups of individuals and some formed units that the Ersatzheer was required to provide to the Feldheer as and whenever required. To achieve this, there were direct links between the specific units and formations in the Ersatzheer and the Feldheer, from regiment to corps. Thus, a division-size Feldheer formation usually had a regiment-size replacement unit (Ersatzeinheit) in the Ersatzheer, while a Feldheer regiment had an Ersatzeinheit battalion in the Ersatzheer, and so on. These formations and units were linked by common numerical designations, and in addition to being a training and replacement unit an Ersatzeinheit also had an administrative duty of care for wounded and convalescent soldiers from its affiliated Feldheer unit.

The Ersatzheer remained under OKH command until the abortive 20 July 1944 bomb plot against Hitler precipitated the removal and later execution of General Friedrich Fromm, who had been commander of the Ersatzheer and chief of army

---

* These tasks, responsibilities and activities are shown in more detail at Appendix 2.

equipment (Chef der Heeresrüstung und Befehlshaber des Ersatzheeres) from 1 September 1939 until 20 July 1944. Himmler then replaced Fromm, at which stage the SS in effect displaced OKH control of the Ersatzheer, together with its many training, administrative, manpower replacement and other support responsibilities within Germany. But by that stage the Ersatzheer concept was in any case experiencing a gradual breakdown, diminishing manpower resources in Germany meaning that the training cycle for replacements was curtailed. At the same time, numbers of Ersatzheer troops were also being committed directly to combat missions, including counter-partisan operations, rather than being assigned to the Feldheer as fully trained soldiers.

# 5. Mobilization for War

Despite some significant shortfalls in the preparation of the German population and industry for a war that eventually proved to be much longer and more demanding of resources than Hitler had originally envisaged, the armed forces made the transition speedily and efficiently from their peacetime configuration to a war footing in 1939. At the heart of this process was the army's mobilization plan. The efficiency of the German army's mobilization for the Franco-Prussian War in 1870 had proved decisive, and, although the surge of numbers reporting for duty initially overwhelmed the induction system in 1914, it was also a significant contributor to Germany's early successes in World War I. Accordingly, the mobilization plan in 1939 was well-founded, took account of the problems encountered in 1914, and was in many respects an extension of the army's peacetime deployment and command and control organization. This organization was territorially-based and founded upon the division of Germany into corps areas or Wehrkreise, each of which contained the headquarters and framework components of at least one corps and its subordinate divisions. The Wehrkreise were also largely self-contained and self-administered military districts, within which conscription, the defense of those territorial areas, civil order and security, and a host of other military and civil matters devolved on to the senior military commander of the Wehrkreise, who was also the corps commander in war. In August 1939, with Austria and the Sudetenland already firmly within the German military ambit, the peacetime Wehrkreise headquarters locations and the army divisions they administered, controlled or sponsored were as shown in the table opposite.

Army corps areas of responsibility and Wehrkreise in 1945, from a contemporary map.

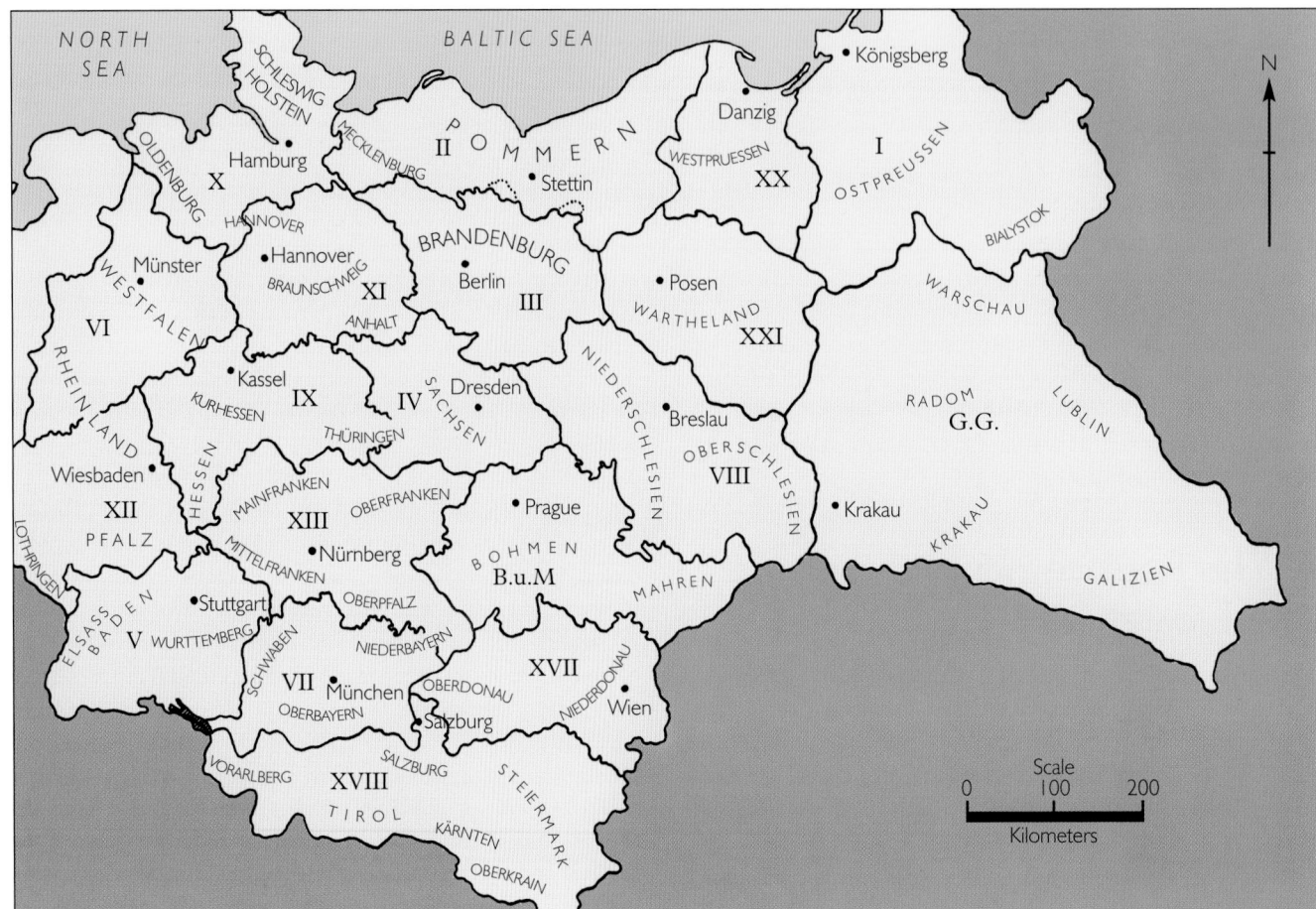

| Wehrkreis Number | Headquarters Location | Subordinate Divisions |
|---|---|---|
| 1st (I) | Königsberg | 1st, 11th, 21st Infantry Divisions |
| 2nd (II) | Stettin | 12th, 32nd Infantry Divisions |
| 3rd (III) | Berlin | 3rd, 23rd Infantry Divisions |
| 4th (IV) | Dresden | 4th, 14th, 24th Infantry Divisions |
| 5th (V) | Stuttgart | 5th, 25th, 35th Infantry Divisions |
| 6th (VI) | Münster | 6th, 16th, 26th Infantry Divisions |
| 7th (VII) | München | 7th, 27th Infantry Divisions |
| | | 1st Mountain Division |
| 8th (VIII) | Breslau | 8th, 18th, 28th Infantry Divisions |
| 9th (IX) | Kassel | 9th, 15th Infantry Divisions |
| 10th (X) | Hamburg | 22nd, 30th Infantry Divisions |
| 11th (XI) | Hanover | 19th, 31st Infantry Divisions |
| 12th (XII) | Wiesbaden | 33rd, 34th, 36th Infantry Divisions |
| 13th (XIII) | Nürnberg | 10th, 17th, 46th Infantry Divisions |
| 14th (XIV) | Magdeburg | 2nd, 13th, 20th, 29th Motorized Divisions |
| 15th (XV) | Jena | 1st, 2nd, 3rd Light Divisions |
| 16th (XVI) | Berlin | 1st, 3rd, 4th, 5th Panzer Divisions |
| 17th (XVII) | Vienna | 44th, 45th Infantry Divisions |
| 18th (XVIII) | Salzburg | 2nd, 3rd Mountain Divisions |
| 19th (XIX) | Vienna | 2nd Panzer Division |
| | | 4th Light Division |

Following the fall of Poland, a 20th (XX) Corps area was created with its headquarters at Danzig, a 21st (XXI) with its headquarters at Posen, followed by the creation of the corps-status Wehrkreise General Government (Generalgouvernement) with its headquarters at Cracow, and Bohemia (Böhmen und Mähren) with its headquarters at Prague.

By mid-1939 most of the combat divisions of the Feldheer were already more or less ready for war, capable of completing their full mobilization within twelve hours of being ordered to do so. Much of the army was mobilized progressively over a period of many months, with reservists called-up individually and taken into existing regular units to serve alongside the experienced soldiers of those units, rather than in newly-created units manned largely by inexperienced troops. During the final twelve months prior to August 1939 the older men were called up first, those who already had some military training, so that they could be returned speedily to full effectiveness by refresher training in their units during the remaining months of peace. This graduated and measured approach benefited the armed forces and the nation alike, as the disruption to national and personal life was minimized, while the army as a whole steadily achieved its war strength. During the early war years, the efficiency of the conscription system actually enabled some men to be released from their military service for medical reasons or to fulfil other high-priority war jobs as civilians, while others were able to defer or altogether avoid conscription into the armed forces. This approach continued until the later years of the war, when the deteriorating strategic situation, increasing casualties and new manpower requirements meant that virtually no forms of non-military employment remained sacrosanct. At that stage many former soldiers were recalled to active duty, while the upper and lower age limits for military service were also extended.

Once mobilized, the Feldheer structure was based upon a number of army groups, each of which nominally controlled at least two armies, each usually composed of two corps; an army corps controlled at least two divisions, but often more. This was the basic hierarchical structure for planning purposes, although at various times army groups controlled more than two armies for limited periods or for specific operations – such as the invasion of Poland in 1939 (when von Rundstedt's Army Group South comprised three armies). Other similar instances included the campaign against France in 1940 (when von Rundstedt's Army Group A again controlled three armies), the follow-on operations in Russia in 1941 following *Barbarossa* (when Army Groups Center and South controlled six and four armies respectively), and the Ardennes offensive in December 1944 (where Model's Army Group B controlled four armies). On mobilization in 1939 it had been planned to establish just ten army-level commands. However, this was increased soon afterwards when the existing 1st, 2nd, 3rd, 4th, 5th, 7th, 8th, 10th, 12th and 14th Armies were joined by the 9th, 6th, 16th and 18th Armies. New 2nd, 4th, 7th and 12th Armies were also formed.[6] To complement these major formations there was a whole range of supporting framework units, usually maintained at cadre strength in peacetime, and army and army group troops that were not permanently assigned in peacetime but which could be activated, mobilized and allocated to support Feldheer army groups and armies as necessary, depending upon the strategic or operational situation. They included a wide range of special purpose and reserve units. The assignment and employment of forces from this pool was generally determined by the OKW and subsequently controlled by the OKH in consultation with the OKW, as their allocation almost invariably reflected the needs of the strategic plan. These units typically included those with particular engineer, technical, construction or bridging and obstacle-crossing capabilities; heavy and anti-aircraft artillery; some field artillery, and railway artillery troops; some independent heavy tank units; armored trains; motorized anti-tank gun and flame-thrower units; and specialist logistics or transport units.

The mobilization plan for the infantry divisions involved a modified but standardized call-up and force-development system. These divisions were mobilized in "waves" (Wellen) which categorized each division and took account of its required speed of mobilization, fighting status and actual organization, as well as grouping together men who were of similar ages and who had completed the same amount of pre-army training in organizations such as the Hitler Jugend and the Reichsarbeits-dienst (RAD). As at 1 September 1939, four mobilization waves were already nearing completion or had been completed. Wave 1 included the 35 infantry divisions of the peacetime, pre-war, full-time, regular army, each of which numbered up to 17,734 all ranks. Wave 2 comprised a further sixteen divisions, manned primarily by reservists, while Wave 3 comprised 21 divisions of part-trained men, reservists and older soldiers of the Landwehr.

Finally, Wave 4 represented fourteen divisions based upon the reinforcement battalions of the regular army. During the war a further 31 Wellen were subsequently mobilized or projected: three in 1939, six in 1940, three in 1941, one in 1941–2, one in 1942, four in 1943, and no less than nine in 1944, with a further four (primarily Volksgrenadier units) in 1944–5. Some post-1939 mobilization waves produced as many as ten divisions, but none generated forces at the levels achieved during August–September 1939, while some (Wave 16 in July 1941, Wave 23 in January 1944, and Wave 30 in July 1944) produced no complete divisions at all, providing only a number of separate regiments or brigades, or groups of individual personnel who were subsequently incorporated piecemeal into a later wave.

# 6. Armies and Army Groups

Once the war began, the Feldheer order of battle changed frequently and extensively as the strategic and operational situation developed, necessitating the reassignment of armies, corps and divisions, including their redeployment between the eastern, western, Scandinavian, African, Balkan and Italian operational areas. At the same time, the mobilization waves produced a steady flow of reinforcing and replacement infantry divisions year-on-year, while simultaneously all sorts of new formations were being created as others were disbanded or destroyed in combat. Organizational change was constant, and there was also a continuing program of change as new equipment and weapons technology – especially the heavy tanks, artillery and V-weapons produced later in the war – spawned a plethora of experimental and special-purpose units to test and operate these potential war-winners. Meanwhile, as the war expanded, German armies frequently served alongside those of their Hungarian, Italian or Romanian allies within mixed army groups. Over the course of the war the sheer scale, flexibility and

**Army Deployments 1939–1944 (Selected Examples)**

| Date | Theater of Operations | Deployed Armies |
|---|---|---|
| Pre-war, in 1939 | Greater Germany | 1st, 2nd, 3rd, 4th, 5th, 7th, 8th, 10th, 12th, 14th (as included in the OKW/OKH mobilization plan) |
| June 1941 | Eastern Front | 2nd, 4th, 6th, 9th, 11th, 16th, 17th, 18th |
| | Western Front | 1st, 7th, 15th |
| | Balkans | 12th |
| | Norway | Army "Norway" |
| January 1944 | Eastern Front | 2nd, 4th, 6th, 8th, 9th, 16th, 17th, 18th, 20th, 1st Panzer, 2nd Panzer, 3rd Panzer, 4th Panzer |
| | Western Front | 1st, 7th, 15th, 19th |
| | Balkans | Panzer Army No. 2 |
| | Norway | Army "Norway" (later the 20th Mountain Army) |
| | Italy | 10th, 14th |

complexity of these changes produced significant control and management challenges, and this may be illustrated by the examples of Feldheer army-level structures and deployments between 1939 and 1944, together with the composition of some army groups between 1942 and 1945,[7] shown in the tables.

In January 1940 there were 27 corps-level commands, but eighteen months later this had increased to 31 infantry corps, three mountain warfare corps, twelve motorized corps, and the Deutsches Afrikakorps. As with the army groups and armies, various new corps were created as the war progressed, while others were restructured, re-titled, given a new role or deactivated. By the end of 1944, there were eleven army groups, which commanded collectively no fewer than 26 separate armies, including six Panzer armies, one mountain army, and one Luftwaffe parachute or airborne army.

# 7. The Theater of War

Once deployed, the Feldheer subdivided its operational and administrative functions into distinct areas in order to separate the business of fighting the battle from the more routine matters that supported the fighting. The theater of operations (Operationsgebiet) split into a forward combat zone (Gefechtsgebiet) and a communications zone or rear area (Rückwärtiges Gebiet). To its rear was an area known as the Gebiet der Kriegsverwaltung – a military-administered security zone of virtually any size that lay between the theater of operations and the Greater German homeland – the Gebiet der Kriegsverwaltung could encompass the whole of an occupied country or territory. Lastly, the Greater German homeland was known as the Heimatsgebiet, also termed the "zone of the interior", which was divided into military districts (Wehrkreise) in peacetime and then in time of war maintained active links with the Feldheer as

**Composition of Army Groups 1942–1945 (Selected Examples)**

| Date | Army Group (AG) | Composition |
|---|---|---|
| September 1942 | AG Fretter-Pico | 6th Army, 2nd Hungarian Army; then 5th Army, 3rd Hungarian Army |
| | AG Ruoff | 17th Army, 3rd Romanian Army |
| | AG Liguria | 14th Army, Ligurian Army (Italian) |
| December 1942 | AG Hoth | 4th Panzer Army, 4th Romanian Army |
| April 1944 | AG Woehler | 8th Army, 4th Romanian Army |
| July 1944 | AG Raus (later AG Heinrici) | 1st Panzer Army, 1st Hungarian Army |
| | AG von Weichs | 2nd Army, 2nd Panzer Army, 2nd Hungarian Army |
| | AG Balck | 5th Army, 3rd Hungarian Army |
| October 1944 | AG Woehler | 8th Army, 2nd Hungarian Army |
| November 1944 | AG Woehler | 8th Army, 1st Hungarian Army |
| | AG Student | 1st Parachute Army, 15th Army |
| March 1945 | AG Balck | 6th Army, 3rd Hungarian Army |

well as a very direct involvement with the Ersatzheer on matters of conscription, training and replacements. For planning purposes, each army group and its subordinate armies, corps and divisions occupied a specific place within a robust and infinitely flexible organizational framework that could be modified to take account of the specific area upon which it was superimposed, the operational situation and the actual numbers and types of formations and units involved.

Irrespective of the high-level arrangements for the organization and command and control of the army in wartime, success or failure always depended ultimately upon the hundreds of thousands of ordinary officers and men, the "Landser", who served in the divisions, regiments and battalions of "Das Heer". It follows that the army's operational successes after 1940 generally reflected the innate professionalism and determination of its officers and soldiers, and their loyalty to Germany, their units and the army. For almost four more years these traditional martial qualities and the resilience of many ordinary officers and soldiers offset both the strategic mismanagement and ineptitude displayed by Hitler after 1940 and the ever-increasing interference of the Nazi party and the SS in the army's business.

Therein lay much of the uniqueness and inherent strength that characterized the German army of the 1930s and 1940s, just as it had in earlier times.

# 8. Replacements and Reinforcements

Mobilization and deployment were only the first stages of going to war, for in anything other than a very short conflict there was an almost immediate requirement to start processing and training the manpower to replace those who became casualties or who would be needed as reinforcements for the Feldheer in an expanding war. This task fell to the Ersatzheer, where the twin issues of training and replacements were constantly driven by the ebb and flow of the Feldheer's battlefield successes and failures. The sheer scale of the replacements required by the Feldheer, especially once Operation *Barbarossa* was under way, and the size of the task facing the Ersatzheer, was illustrated by the casualty figures for some of the many formations fighting with the Feldheer on the Eastern Front between June 1941 and April 1942, where no fewer

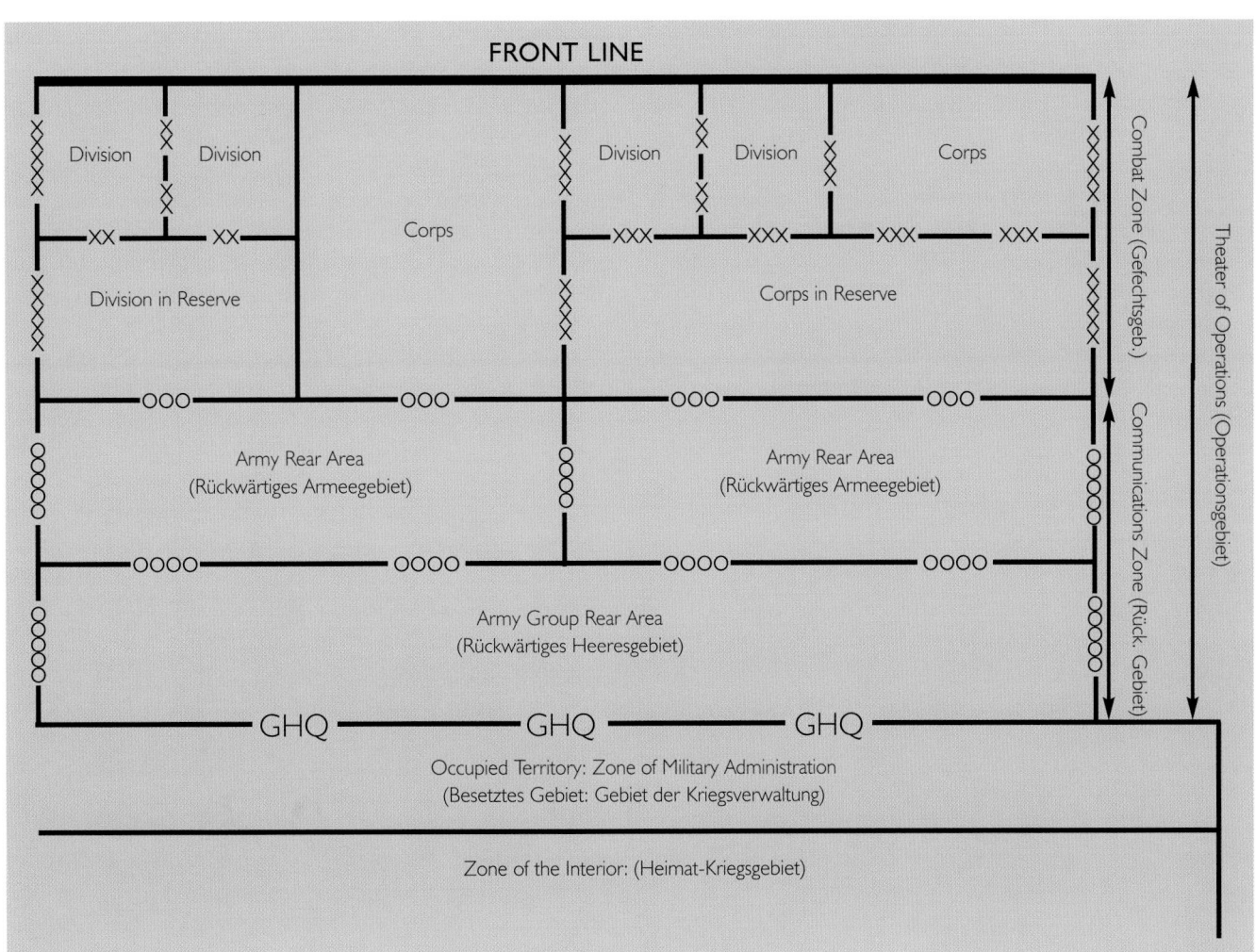

Schematic organization of a theater of war. (US Official, 1945)

than 90,000 replacements had already been committed by August 1941, with a further 132,000 urgently required.

In the first example, the "Großdeutschland" motorized infantry regiment crossed into Russia on 27 and 28 June and was almost immediately engaged in heavy fighting. During July an entire company was ambushed and annihilated. In November one battalion was reduced to just eight officers and 359 soldiers and was subsequently destroyed during further fighting in December. That month, all of the companies were reduced to ten or fifteen men during the Red Army's December counter-offensive, and by the end of the year the regiment had lost some 4,070 men, including 125 officers. This was almost three-quarters of the 6,000 men with which it had entered Russia. By mid-February just two battalions remained, their companies all commanded by NCOs, and shortly thereafter these were combined into a single battalion. By 20 February, when it was finally withdrawn from that winter's fighting, the "Großdeutschland" Regiment numbered no more than three officers and thirty NCOs and soldiers.[8]

The story of the 18th Panzer Division was similar, and within just three weeks of the start of *Barbarossa* the division had lost about 2,300 soldiers and 123 officers (including six battalion commanders), having started the campaign with 17,174 soldiers and 401 officers – a casualty rate of about fifteen percent. By the end of July the division's casualties totalled some 3,200 soldiers and 153 officers. Despite receiving some replacements, the division suffered further losses of 6,667 soldiers and 120 officers by late March 1942, and its total battle casualties from 22 June 1941 up to the end of March 1942 were 9,148 soldiers and 323 officers.[9] Finally, the 12th Infantry Division fielded 14,073 soldiers and 336 officers at the start of *Barbarossa*, but by mid-December it had lost about a third of that strength, having sustained 4,200 casualties and with a residual strength of 11,351 soldiers and 287 officers. The division was also engaged in the defensive fighting at Demjansk from February to May 1942, when the encircled German forces lost 41,212 men of an original 96,000, while the forces that relieved them also incurred a further 12,373 casualties.[10] From mid-1941, the task facing the Ersatzheer of replacing such huge losses was daunting indeed.

The system by which the Ersatzheer provided replacements to the Feldheer was complex and changed substantially during the course of the war. Time, the strategic situation, revised priorities and a dwindling pool of manpower all impacted upon it, but in essence, the system relied upon a vast framework of replacement units distributed throughout the Wehrkreise. Every replacement (Ersatz) unit (usually organized as a battalion) was affiliated to a Feldheer unit, both units having the same identification number, with the Germany-based replacement unit inducting recruits, training them and finally dispatching them to the affiliated Feldheer unit or formation as required. More than 50 different types of regular replacement unit existed, variously dealing with every aspect of processing and training the manpower for all arms of the Feldheer. Necessarily, the replacement unit liaised closely

with the Feldheer unit it supported, and the home base of the Feldheer unit was usually that of the replacement unit as well. Such territorial connections were an important aid to morale, and as a matter of policy soldiers served alongside those who came from the same Wehrkreis wherever possible (unless they had some special skill that could only be exploited in another Wehrkreis – mountaineering for example). However, during the final two or three years of the war soldiers were increasingly sent wherever they were most needed, irrespective of geographical links or (in the case of re-trained soldiers and those returning from convalescence) the unit to which they originally belonged. The Deutsches Afrikakorps was always a special case, however, and irrespective of an individual's territorial or Wehrkreis affiliation, replacements for North Africa were processed and trained within Wehrkreis II and Wehrkreis XI exclusively, so that the Ersatzheer could concentrate all the specialist desert warfare training within those replacement units. Such pragmatism became ever more necessary as the war progressed and, while the first four waves of divisional manpower produced by the Wehrkreise in the summer and autumn of 1939 by and large conformed to the established pre-war affiliations, from 1940 some infantry replacement units were also required to provide soldiers for Feldheer regiments other than their affiliated regiments. Meanwhile, as the Feldheer expanded, several replacement units were redesignated as field units, being incorporated straight away into the Feldheer order of battle.

Over time, unit affiliations changed and the original dual numbering system was much modified, but every Feldheer unit remained affiliated to a Germany-based replacement unit at all times, and it was to that Ersatzheer unit that a soldier leaving the Feldheer or reporting back for duty after convalescence was required to report in the first instance.

Another matter affecting the Ersatzheer and its replacement units was a requirement for units based in the border areas to move out of their barracks prior to the invasions of Poland, the Low Countries, France and Russia. This allowed Feldheer units to occupy these barracks and training grounds while preparing for the offensives. Later, the Ersatzheer units could return, when they often acted as garrison troops in these border regions. Other Ersatzheer units moved into the newly occupied territories, thus vacating their bases in Germany for temporary use by new units of the rapidly expanding Feldheer. Change was incessant, and in September 1942 the traditional responsibilities of the replacement units were split so that they henceforth only had responsibility for the induction and administrative processing of their soldiers before quickly passing them on to a closely-linked training unit (Ausbildungseinheit), where they were trained and then dispatched to an affiliated Feldheer unit. This generally enabled the replacement units (now with a primarily administrative function) to occupy their home stations as in the past, while the new training units could be located anywhere, including France, Denmark, Poland, the Low Countries, Lithuania, the Soviet

Union and northern Italy. These training units were organized as divisions, and as such they also provided occupation forces that released many Feldheer combat divisions from being tied down on mundane security duties. Such "training divisions" in the occupied territories were titled Reservedivisionen (reserve divisions), and in due course Reservekorps (reserve corps) were also formed from these part-trained or less experienced units and formations. During 1942 and 1943 twenty-six Reservedivisionen were formed, with thirteen in the west, seven in the east, three in Denmark, two in Croatia and one in Italy; four of these were armored divisions. Meanwhile, in line with the army's general policy of conducting training well beyond Germany whenever possible, and of holding bodies of replacements well forward in the theaters of operations wherever it was practicable to do so, supplementary training was also conducted by replacement units (principally for the infantry) and field replacement pools located in the rear areas of some Feldheer army groups and armies. These units might temporarily hold any number of troops (who would usually arrive in a group known as a Marschbataillone – or "march battalion") and provided a general training facility as well as acting as a feeder unit for a specific formation. One such training unit was operated by the Panzergrenadierdivision "Großdeutschland" near Romny in the summer of 1943, dispatching troops forward at short notice as and when required.

Inevitably perhaps, the dual role (training and operations) of the Reservedivision eventually proved unsustainable in the face of constant pressure from the high command to bring new divisions fully into operational service, while at the same time their always tenuous non-operational connection with the Wehrkreise slipped away. In the west these divisions became ever more committed to the defense of the Atlantic Wall from 1943, while in the east they became embroiled in the hard-fought counter-partisan campaigns. With more and more operational tasks imposed upon them, the Reservedivisionen soon found that, far from being able to send replacements to Feldheer divisions, they needed to retain soldiers for their own use. As a result, some Reservedivisionen were redesignated as field divisions during 1943 and 1944, while others were disbanded and their manpower redistributed; yet others suffered heavy losses and were rendered ineffective during the fighting on the Eastern Front, as well as in northern France while countering the Allied invasion in June and July 1944. By the end of 1944 only about seven Reservedivisionen still existed, of which only two were still carrying out the training role. The Reservedivision undoubtedly provided a useful operational stop-gap just when the army's fortunes on the battlefield were beginning to decline, but their general committal to operational tasks seriously disrupted the army training process, as did the fact that by late 1944 no less than two-thirds of the army's training was taking place in areas well beyond Germany, where they were increasingly threatened by direct attack. Not surprisingly, perhaps, this much-changed situation had already prompted a gradual return to a Germany-based replacement and training system

during 1944. Despite the fact that by the end of 1944 the Wehrmacht was heavily engaged in major fighting on the Eastern Front, in northwest Europe and in Italy, the army – and the OKH general staff especially so – once again demonstrated its resourcefulness by entirely reorganizing the training system yet again. It did so primarily by building upon those training units already established in Germany and by reverting to a controlling organization based upon the tried and tested Wehrkreise system.

For the Ersatzheer and OKH alike, further significant changes were occasioned by the appointment of Reichsführer-SS Heinrich Himmler as commander of the Ersatzheer in mid-1944, in the aftermath of the failed assassination attempt against Hitler on 20 July. The SS introduced a number of measures at that time; others would probably have been adopted in any case. The basic training period was universally reduced to six weeks but with longer hours worked; Luftwaffe and Kriegsmarine personnel were re-directed into the army; the Volkssturm was formed for home defense and swept virtually all remaining manpower not already in the Wehrmacht into military employment; and the Wehrkreise boundaries were adjusted. In parallel, arrangements designed to simplify and speed up the training and replacement system were also introduced. One measure that preceded the July 1944 command change was the creation of Kampfmarschbataillone (literally, "battle transfer battalions") of about 900 men, which moved from the Ersatzheer to the Feldheer as structured replacement units already armed, equipped and trained for combat. Smaller battalion- and company-size groups of replacements also moved straight to Feldheer units, although they were not categorized as ready for immediate combat. These examples illustrate the flexibility and pragmatism that the OKH and Ersatzheer necessarily adopted to ensure that the flow of replacements to the Feldheer continued largely uninterrupted during the closing years of the war. As a result, a viable training and replacement system continued to operate throughout 1944 and into 1945, with the Wehrkreise also resuming their traditional training and replacement role, albeit with some modifications.

This was a fairly remarkable achievement, for by late 1944 the army was being pressed hard in the west, on the Eastern Front and in Italy. The towns, cities, communications and industrial infrastructure of Germany were being bombed by the US Army Air Force (USAAF) by day and the Royal Air Force (RAF) by night. All the while, Germany's access to strategic raw materials and natural resources was constantly reducing, as were its remaining reserves of manpower. It follows that the strategic successes achieved between 1939 and 1943, and even those at the operational and tactical level in 1944 and 1945, in large part reflected primarily the standard of training of the troops as well as the army's ability to move its trained replacements to the right place in a timely manner. From this it is evident that the story of the Ersatzheer and its key role in supporting the Feldheer and Germany's wider war effort is perhaps one of the less well-known and understated stories of the German army during World War II.

"Victory at Any Price" – This propaganda poster, depicting a soldier bearing the Reichskriegsflagge with the Nazi swastika device shown prominently, sought to promote and reinforce the nation's absolute commitment to the army during the later years of the war.

SIEG
UM JEDEN PREIS

# PART V
# Officers and Soldiers

## 1. The Changing Army, 1935–1945

Between the introduction of conscription in March 1935 and the final months of the Third Reich in 1945 the nature and composition of the army's manpower changed considerably, such developments being virtually inevitable. The army continued to fight on until the end, often achieving quite disproportionate results against the Allied forces thrusting into Germany on all fronts by March 1945. But the steadily diminishing availability of fresh recruits from within Germany, the rising numbers of battle casualties and the ever-reducing amount of time available to train new soldiers before they were consigned to the front – all affected the physical preparedness and professional competence of the individual soldier as the war progressed.

The lack of manpower from within Germany also resulted in a dilution of what had formerly been the exclusively "German" composition of the army, and eventually significant numbers of "foreigners" were recruited from annexed and occupied territories wherever a parental or other genealogical or alternative acceptable link with Germany existed, although such links were often quite tenuous. Volunteers from the Nordic countries of Norway, Sweden and Denmark were accepted into the army without possessing or needing to acquire German citizenship, as were those from Belgium and the Netherlands, all of which countries were viewed as racially acceptable and within the Germanic ambit. Ultimately, these intakes also included numbers of Frenchmen, Czechs, Poles and others from eastern European countries that had previously been considered ethnically or racially unacceptable recruitment areas; latterly they even included "volunteers" from among the Third Reich's many Russian prisoners-of-war. However, the German citizenship rules that were applied to most of the army's Polish and eastern European volunteers imposed a ten-year probationary period and also debarred these men from promotion beyond senior private during their military service. In extremis, these individuals could then be officially categorized as ethnically Germanic peoples (Volksdeutsche), which made them racially acceptable for military service in the Wehrmacht. Indeed, among some of the first soldiers encountered by the Allies on the Normandy beaches on D-Day, 6 June 1944, were Russians who had been taken into German military service.

These individual non-Germans who served with the army should not be confused with the various national "foreign legions" deliberately recruited by Heinrich Himmler's SS as a matter of deliberate policy, and which subsequently served as formed units and formations with the Waffen-SS mainly on the Eastern Front and during the final campaigns within Germany. And, in accordance with the overarching Nazi ideology on matters of race and the concept of the "Untermenschen", Jews and gypsies continued to be rigorously excluded from German military service – even those who were only half Jewish by birth – no matter how critical the manning situation became.

The parlous manpower situation that obtained during much of the last eighteen months of the war was far removed from that which had existed in the late 1930s, or indeed during the first three years of the conflict. Initially the Nazi-led government took considerable trouble not to jeopardize the still-fragile German economy or the social life of the country by the mass or indiscriminate induction of men for military service. The creation and maintenance of a strong economy following the economic disasters of the post-1918 Weimar years had been a crucial pillar in the Nazi manifesto, and Hitler's domestic popularity was due in large part to his government's successes in this area, particularly the virtual elimination of unemployment. At the same time, promoting the essential nature of the family and its traditional place in the German Heimat lay at the very core of National Socialist culture. Although the army needed to be strong enough to support his foreign policy objectives, Hitler knew that this had to be achieved without destabilizing the economic or social order, or sowing seeds of discontent among those who were called up for military service. Accordingly, the German soldier both prior to, and at the beginning, of the war generally benefited from a system that managed the duration and timing of his obligatory military service very carefully. While the requirement to serve in some military capacity could rarely be avoided altogether, this well-regulated system also took full account of deferments for students, certain personal and wider business circumstances and those whose civilian occupation was in some other way vital to the state. In line with Hitler's belief that the war would be of short duration, this general approach lasted well into the early war years, with discharges of soldiers on medical grounds, or in order to return to their suitably essential civilian occupation, being relatively routine occurrences. As a consequence of this, the German army that went to war in 1939 was indeed "an army such as the world has never seen" (to quote Hitler), with soldiers who were thoroughly trained, well motivated, physically robust, well managed, and justifiably confident both in themselves and in their national leaders.

Once the army was fully committed in Russia this somewhat idyllic situation soon began to change. Many men who had previously been released from active service were recalled to duty, together with those deferred earlier. As a result, the composition and nature of many units gradually changed, and from 1943 – with the war of attrition on the Eastern Front consuming ever more troops – the numbers of Luftwaffe and Kriegsmarine personnel drafted into the army diluted the "army" composition of many of its units. At the same time much-cherished (by the Nazis and the civilian population alike) and legally-protected family-orientated concessions – such as exemption from military service for the only surviving son of a family, and for a father with a large dependent family – were necessarily rescinded as the toll of casualties mounted. Some convicted prisoners were even afforded the opportunity to redeem themselves through combat service in army penal units, although the advantages of this were always questionable, such units frequently being regarded as expendable. From 1943 involvement in direct combat was no longer the sole preserve of the combat arms, as service support units frequently found themselves fighting pitched battles against partisans, while other such units were often required to stem a breakthrough or defend a vital position in extremis. All the while, the numbers of men authorized for these service units were reviewed time and again, with any identified manpower surpluses speedily consigned to combat units. Simultaneously, the authorized size of divisions was reduced, these manpower reductions being offset by enhancing the division's firepower through increased allocations of automatic and anti-tank weapons. Together, the changed nature of the army's operations and its diminishing sources of manpower combined to affect the overall nature or character of the army, especially so once the tide turned on the Eastern Front following the failure of Operation *Zitadelle* in July 1943.

During 1943 individual physical fitness standards were lowered significantly, with men up to age 60 required to register for military service and others who were medically unfit drafted into so-called "stomach battalions", so named because (as far as practicable) a special diet was provided for the hundreds of soldiers in such units who had been diagnosed with severe stomach ailments! One such unit that acquitted itself particularly well despite this apparent handicap was the 70th Infantry Division (nicknamed the "White Bread Division") formed in 1944, which played a leading role in the defense of Walcheren Island. In 1944, the number of civilian occupations that exempted the worker from military service was drastically reduced, and all men aged sixteen to 60 who were not already in some form of military service became liable for home defense duties with the Volkssturm. Following the abortive assassination attempt against Hitler on 20 July, the already pervasive influence of the SS over army matters such as discipline, political reliability, loyalty and efficiency increased significantly. As a result, desertion, alleged cowardice, dereliction of duty (including withdrawals contrary to orders) almost invariably resulted in summary execution by early 1945, while flying court-martial teams of SS personnel, Feldjäger and military police roamed the rear areas dispensing summary justice – especially in cases involving any sort of failure of duty on the part of an army officer. In the face of such far-reaching changes and influences, the composition, nature and military ethos of Hitler's army changed significantly during five years of war, so that the army which went to war in 1939 was in many ways a very different army from that which surrendered to the Allies in May 1945. None the less, its individual officers and soldiers, old and young, veterans and raw recruits alike, were still essentially the same sort of German men who had fought "Mit Gott für König und Vaterland" ("with God for King and Fatherland") in times past and now fought just as determinedly for their Führer. Indeed,

Hitler had presented himself to the German people as representing the actual embodiment of Germany, and it was therefore unthinkable for the vast majority of army officers and soldiers to do otherwise than fight on to the best of their ability. Irrespective of any misgivings some might have had about the political direction in which the Nazi state was moving, to do otherwise would not only have contravened their soldier's oath but would also have meant abandoning their sacred obligation to Germany. For the men of a nation whose military culture and ethos stemmed not from the relatively short time during which the Hitler and the Nazis had been in power, but which had in practice developed over almost three centuries of Prussian and German militarism and national development, such actions would have been unpatriotic and dishonorable, and therefore thoroughly un-German. The worth and effectiveness of any army always depends upon the quality of its officers and soldiers, and duty, honor, loyalty, patriotism and a culture of obedience (but certainly not blind obedience) had long been the traditional hallmarks of the German officer and soldier. These were among the key motivating factors that hardened and unified the army, and gave it the determination and confidence which enabled it to achieve the spectacular successes of 1939–41, then to continue to fight against the odds during the increasingly dark days of late 1943 and the final desperate battles for Germany's very survival in late 1944 and early 1945.

## 2. Officers

Contrary to the popular, if frequently exaggerated, stereotype of the pre-war Prussian or German army officer (one much-exploited for propaganda purposes by the Allies in both world wars), very many of the officers who served in Hitler's army represented a break with the social traditions of the imperial army of the Second German Empire from 1871 to 1918. By enabling any man suitably qualified to gain a commission, the almost tangible social barrier that had long existed between an officer and the soldiers he commanded was all but eliminated. At the same time, this enabled many ordinary German men and serving soldiers to achieve on merit the traditional standing in the community that an officer's commission had long attracted in Germany (apart from during the immediate post-1918 period). However, a new prerequisite for would-be officers was now their perceived or proven political reliability and enthusiasm for National Socialism, although formal membership of the Nazi party (while usually a career advantage) was not considered essential. Meanwhile, the officer's duty of care and personal involvement in the welfare of his soldiers introduced into the army from the mid-1930s was also an important contribution to the process of team building and unit cohesion. Such fundamental changes were carried through and maintained despite the background disruption caused by the army's rapid expansion during the 1930s, and again

RITTERKREUZTRÄGER
*sprechen zur* HITLER-JUGEND

Eichenlaubträger **Major von Hirschfeld**
spricht am **Sonnabend, dem 13. Februar 1943,** um **18**³⁰ Uhr
im Nibelungensaal (Rosengarten) zur Jugend

This poster advertises a talk by Knight's Cross winner Major von Hirschfeld on 13 February 1943. As part of the army's recruiting program, carefully selected officers and soldiers who had distinguished themselves on the battlefield spoke about their experiences to audiences of Hitler Jugend and young men eligible for military service.

later during the war when units were virtually annihilated, disbanded and reformed in short order due to the vagaries of combat.

While reforms were carried out and positive measures were introduced, an increasingly harsh regime of military discipline was gradually imposed, largely as a consequence of the nature of the fighting in Soviet Russia and the reverses suffered there by the Wehrmacht from 1943. This reflected the high command's obsessive concern (reinforced by the first-hand memories of many senior and middle-grade officers) that widespread indiscipline and mutinies such as those experienced on the Western Front in 1918 might be repeated in the army on the Eastern Front. It also recognized that the traditional officer-soldier relationship of the old imperial German army was gone forever, and that the once unassailable authority enjoyed by the German officer, with the unquestioning obedience of those he commanded, could no longer be assumed in conditions of extreme adversity and despair. Accordingly, during the latter part of the war and especially on the Eastern Front, much evidence emerged to indicate that the fear of severe punishment for any indiscipline was only exceeded by the terror of falling into the hands of the enemy. Both of these emotions or fears were actively promoted by the high command, the former to maintain order among the troops and total obedience to their officers, the latter to ensure that the troops would fight to the end and never contemplate surrender. As a result, although Hitler's army ostensibly adopted a much more egalitarian, considered and leadership-based approach to the business of command and to the relationship between officers and soldiers than had the Kaiser's army, in practice it actually demanded a greater level of unquestioning obedience from officers and soldiers alike. This situation stemmed from the soldier's oath and his absolute allegiance to Hitler in the first instance, and from the contrived convergence of National Socialist ideology and traditional military values and norms thereafter. Eventually the high command, frequently prompted by Hitler himself, was obliged to impose a disciplinary code that brutalized the army and was largely based upon the fear of retribution. This turn of events detracted significantly from the often laudable military leadership concepts and ideals the army had expounded and adopted during the latter days of the Reichswehr, and which had continued during the rise of National Socialism in the 1930s, underscoring the development of Hitler's army and its battlefield successes during the campaigns of 1939, 1940 and 1941.

Overall, army officers were divided administratively into four groups by rank. The first included the general officers (Generale); in the second group were the field officers (Stabsoffiziere), the colonels, lieutenant colonels and majors; while the third group contained all the captains, and the fourth group the lieutenants.* In terms of employment, professional status and conditions of service, army officers broadly fell into one of three employment groups, or into a further fourth group whose members were not originally officers but who did later achieve officer status. First, there were the regular officers, who from 1942 also included the many NCOs who had received wartime temporary commissions (Kriegsoffiziere) that were then made permanent. On their retirement in wartime most regular officers were subject to recall, and in practice most regular officers discharged after 1939 were retained on active duty and employed appropriately from the time of their discharge – possibly in the training organization, in the Ersatzheer or within a headquarters. Next, there were the general staff corps officers (Generalstabsoffiziere) who were those officers selected, trained and qualified to fill staff and command appoint-

**Offiziere von morgen**

* The full range of German army officer ranks is shown in Appendix 4, together with their British and US Army equivalents.

ments, and from whom those officers destined for high command would ultimately be found.

The third group were the reserve officers (Reserveoffiziere). Before the war, most reserve officers were conscripted men who had demonstrated leadership and professional abilities during the first year of their obligatory military service, and who had the necessary academic qualifications. During their second year they were designated as Reserve-Offizier-Anwärter (officer candidates or aspirants) and were formally trained as infantry platoon commanders, being commissioned (although the German army used the word "promoted" [befördern] rather than "commissioned" for the transition to officer status) as reserve officers on discharge, and subject to attending annual periods of continuation training with their unit. Similarly, some suitably qualified regular NCOs were commissioned as reserve officers on discharge. Dependent upon age, the pre-war Reserveoffiziere were categorized either as Offiziere der Reserve (aged under 35) or as Offiziere der Landwehr (those aged above 35). However, as the men called up for military service during the war were generally not discharged at the end of the former two-year period, suitably qualified volunteers and selected conscripts were termed Reserve-Offizier-Bewerber (reserve officer applicants) and were commissioned as reserve officers once formally trained as such, subsequently serving on for the duration of the war, but not as regular career army officers. Based upon the length of their service, regular officers on discharge received a pension, lump sum payment and assistance to gain civilian employment. Rations and accommodation were provided free of charge, together with most equipment and some work or field uniform clothing, but in principle officers were expected to purchase their own uniforms, for which they received a one-time allowance of about RM 450.00 (in late 1944) and a monthly uniform upkeep allowance of about RM 30.00.* In September 1938, newly-promoted artillery Leutnant Siegfried Knappe expressed the opinion that, "my army pay was enough to maintain a fairly good standard of living … Our room and board were also provided. On our pay, we could afford to have an inexpensive car and a horse … being an officer in the peacetime German army was a very nice life."[1]

Once the war began, the training of potential officers and officer candidates was adjusted to take account of the time many had already spent on active service, as well as the pressing need to produce additional leaders as quickly as practicable, for army officers always suffered a disproportionately high rate of battle casualties. Although the standard officer training course was still planned to take place over a period of between sixteen and twenty months, provision also existed for soldiers with extensive combat experience, proven leadership qualities, and who were aged thirty and above, to be commissioned after just a few months spent as an officer candidate with a field unit. Officer candidates for regular

* Further details and examples of German army officer pay rates and allowances as at 9 November 1944 are in Appendix 5, together with those for some NCO ranks and soldiers.

Oberleutnant Hendrick Sieger, a distinguished German army pentathlon champion pictured at Nürnberg in 1934. He is wearing the pre-1936 Reichswehr-pattern officer's service dress uniform of the time, complete with the officer's sabre that was in general use until the introduction of the officer's dagger as a side-arm from 1935.

commissions were required to sign up for unlimited service, while the length of service liability of those aspiring to reserve officer commissions was for a fixed period. Slightly higher physical standards were required of candidates wishing a regular commission and a full army career.

The high rate of army officer casualties throughout the war reflected the leadership concept that underwrote every aspect of the army's activities – as a matter of principle, officers of all ranks led from the front in an army that always favored offensive action over defensive options. Consequently, senior officers were regularly in the forward battle areas, and between 1939 and 1942 more than 25 German army generals died in action, while as many as 80 had

A class of ensigns (Fähnriche) or officer cadets studying a tactical problem on a relief map model at the Kriegsschule ("war school") at Bornstedt, Potsdam, southwest of Berlin. The other three Kriegsschulen were at Dresden, München and Hannover.

died in action by May 1945. The campaign in Russia increased the toll of officer casualties dramatically: 1,253 officers died in action between September 1939 and May 1941, but from June 1941 to March 1942 at least 15,000 officers were killed in action, and although there were 12,055 Leutnante (lieutenants) in the army in July 1941, by March 1942 the records showed only 7,276.[2]

Despite such casualty figures, the determination and practical performance of the officers in all arms and branches of Hitler's army continued to demonstrate the efficacy of the selection and training system that had produced them, as well as the deeper legacy of the German military ideal and culture that had developed and shaped the officer corps during more than two centuries.

The selection and formal training cycle for most officers followed a standard pattern, and this was modified slightly to take account of whether the officer was a candidate for a regular commission or for a reserve officer commission. Regular officer candidates were selected as untrained volunteers at age sixteen or seventeen, or from serving conscripts aged less than 28 years, or by application from regular NCOs with at least two months' field service. Reserve officer candidates were selected as untrained

volunteers, or during the initial conscription process or during their basic training, or after achieving NCO rank and having already proved their leadership abilities to the satisfaction of the unit commander in a field unit. Once selected, officer candidates were generally first trained as NCOs, then as junior officers, and finally as officers for their own branch or service. The whole process was conducted within a multi-faceted but always closely coordinated officer training regime, with the potential officers or officer candidates classified and grouped as such throughout the three phases of their training. This principle was maintained despite the involvement of the Ersatzheer and the Feldheer, together with a host of training units, field units, military schools, and other agencies.

In addition to the regular and reserve officers, there were also numbers of specialist officers who completed specially modified combined training packages. These officers included medical, veterinary, ordnance and motor maintenance officers. Administrative officers and judge advocates also underwent this training once the special troop service (Truppensonderdienst) branch was created in 1944. All these officers had to meet the basic officer candidate criteria

Young officers receive instruction on reconnaissance tactics, 8 February 1943, while attending a course at the army Kriegsschule for infantry officers.

## The Regular Officer Standard Training Course

| Phase I | Phase II | Phase III |
|---|---|---|
| **Basic and NCO Training** | **Field Training and Officer Candidate Training** | **Advanced or Specialist Training** |
| (10 months) | (up to 7 months) | (3 months) |
| PART ONE (4 months): | PART ONE (up to 3 months): | Advanced or special-to-arm training at an |
| Basic infantry training. | Attachment to a field unit (culminating in | appropriate officer training special service school, |
| PART TWO (6 months): | promotion to officer candidate (Fahnenjunker)). | or at a designated infantry officer candidate training |
| NCO training (culminating in promotion to | PART TWO (up to 4 months): | school, or at a Panzer troops advanced officer |
| NCO rank). | Officer training at an appropriate officer training | candidate school. |
| All Phase I training was conducted within a | school, or at the special-to-arm infantry, Panzer | On completing Phase III of their officer training, |
| training unit of the Ersatzheer. | or artillery schools (culminating in promotion | candidates were promoted to second lieutenant |
| | to advanced officer candidate (Oberfähnriche)). | (Leutnant). |

## The Reserve Officer Standard Training Course

| Phase I | Phase II | Phase III |
|---|---|---|
| **Basic and NCO Training** | **Field Training and Officer Candidate Training** | **Advanced or Specialist Training** |
| (up to 10 months) | (up to 7 months) | (3 months) |
| PART ONE (4 months): | PART ONE (up to 3 months): | Advanced or special-to-arm training at an |
| Basic infantry training (if required). | Attachment to a field unit (culminating in promotion | appropriate officer training course, which was |
| PART TWO (6 months): | to reserve officer candidate staff sergeant | usually conducted or directed by the Wehrkreis |
| NCO training (culminating in promotion to | (Fahnenjunker-Feldwebel der Reserve)). | headquarters. |
| NCO rank). | PART TWO (up to 4 months): | On completing Phase III of their reserve officer |
| All Phase I training was conducted within a | Officer training at an appropriate officer training | training, candidates were promoted to reserve |
| training unit of the Ersatzheer, or by a designated | school, or at the special-to-arm infantry, Panzer | second lieutenant (Leutnant der Reserve). |
| infantry or artillery officer replacement unit of | or artillery schools (culminating in promotion to | |
| the Ersatzheer. | advanced reserve officer candidate (Oberfähnrich | |
| | der Reserve)). | |

for service with a normal combat unit, although their subsequent training blended military training and field experience with longer specialist courses at universities (medical officers, judge advocates), army ordnance schools (ordnance officers), army administrative academies (administrative officers) or motor maintenance technical schools (motor maintenance officers).

Once the formal periods of officer training were complete, further courses were undertaken as required at any of the army's several arm or special service schools. These included specialist training centers for the infantry, mountain infantry, reconnaissance and cavalry troops, Panzer troops, artillery, chemical warfare, engineers, signals troops, supply troops, motor maintenance technical troops and administrative officials and officers. Special courses were also conducted for senior personnel officers by the army personnel office, for battalion and company commanders (the latter often by the Feldheer within the army or army group rear area), for gas protection (chemical defense) officers (Gasabwehr-Offiziere), and for National Socialist Guidance Officers (NS-Führungsoffiziere, or "NSFO").

The NSFO courses provided intensive political training, which equipped these officers to promote Nazi ideology and conduct political indoctrination within units of the Feldheer. The NSFO became a particularly prominent and everyday fact of army life after the failed bomb attack against Hitler on 20 July 1944. As regular army officers were prohibited from direct political activity, the NSFO officers were generally recruited from reserve officers who had been Nazi party members before entering the army. Acting as the eyes and ears of the Nazi party within the army, they could report a commander who, for example, failed to obey an order to stand and fight to the last man – which would almost invariably result in that officer being relieved of his command and frequently suffering much worse disciplinary sanctions. At the same time, the NSFO was responsible for the morale and ideological indoctrination of the soldiers, combining a predominantly nationalistic or patriotic approach with additional instruction on the more political aspects of a soldier's duty wherever this was deemed necessary.

## 3. General Staff Corps

Ever since the "golden era" of Prussian and German military achievement in the mid-nineteenth century, when the army was shaped by such figures as von Roon and von Moltke, in accordance with the theories propounded by von Clausewitz, von Gneisenau and von Scharnhorst, one part of the army's officer corps had enjoyed a prestige and status that consistently exceeded all others. This was the general staff. Hitler was always suspicious of this organization and sought with varying degrees of success to constrain its power and influence once he assumed supreme command of the armed forces. However, it was only after the abortive bomb plot of 20 July 1944 (in which a number of senior

general staff officers were involved, allegedly involved or otherwise implicated) that the authority and decision-making capability of the general staff was particularly curtailed by the Nazi leadership and the SS. Even so, for most of the war the exceptionally talented and competent officers who were selected and qualified as members of the general staff corps continued to be an élite group within the wider officer corps. Access to the general staff corps was open to officers aged up to 28, typically of the rank of captain, who were recommended by their commander for general staff training. Invariably, such officers would already have been graded as exceptional based upon at least six months of front-line service and have displayed outstanding personal qualities and leadership ability, as well as possessing the necessary intellect and professional or academic qualifications to undergo general staff training. If the recommendation was accepted, it launched the successful candidate into an intensive period of training that subsequently opened the way to a "fast-tracked" career and potential employment in the highest staff and command positions of the army and the armed forces.

The formal period of general staff training lasted twelve months, during which the officer was nominally assigned to the Kriegsakademie (war school), although the first month was usually spent at the appropriate special service school to ensure that the candidate was completely up to date concerning his own arm or branch. Thereafter, the candidate completed six months of intensive centralized training at the Kriegsakademie before being attached to the general staff (Generalstab) on probation for a further five months. At the end of the year, if he had completed all the mandatory training and passed the various qualifying exercises, tests and examinations during the course and his final Generalstab attachment, the candidate was formally accepted into the general staff corps. The rigorous process of training and assessment then continued indefinitely as the officer rose through a succession of general staff appointments and service with field units. At any stage, a performance failure or serious personal indiscretion might still result in the officer's removal from the general staff corps and his return to mainstream military duties.

By 1944 the overall extent and duration of general staff training had necessarily been modified to speed up the production of much-needed and suitably trained and qualified staff officers. In early 1944 the young artillery officer Siegfried Knappe experienced these somewhat abbreviated training arrangements when he was selected for general staff training. By then he had completed almost eight years in the army (and some of his earlier service experiences are recounted later on). His experience of the general staff training process that applied during the final years of the war was fairly typical. In preparation for the formal general staff training course, he was first of all attached to the headquarters of the 71st Infantry Division in the area of Cassino in Italy, in order to gain practical experience of staff work and procedures within a major formation. Later, he also spent time with corps, army and army group headquarters. He learned the importance of knowing all of the division's key commanders and every detail of the division's plan for the battle – which at that stage of the war in Italy was the defense of part of the Gustav Line. Time was spent observing and understudying the operations officer, the intelligence officer and the quartermaster, then working directly with some of the regimental commanders, where "I observed what the different people were doing, how they received reports from the regiments, and how they put them together and sent a report to the corps [headquarters]."[3]

After three weeks with the 71st Division, Knappe was attached to the headquarters of the 14th Panzer Corps, where he noted in particular the importance of knowing the commanders and officers of his own corps and of the neighboring corps personally, rather than "from only having talked to him on the phone", as well as the value of noticing "what military decorations those people wore, because that told me a great deal about their character and their general capability."[4]

The army's system of awarding a range of battle insignia worn on the field uniform which directly reflected the wearer's actual combat experience was a useful practical arrangement, as well as a proven aid to individual and unit morale and *esprit de corps*. Later on, Knappe was attached to the army group headquarters and the theater headquarters of Generalfeldmarschall Kesselring, located to the north of Rome, where he was wounded by an Allied air attack and hospitalized in Florence. In late June he was evacuated to a hospital in Leipzig, and from there he eventually returned to duty and began the second part of his general staff preparatory training in late July 1944, attending a series of short updating courses at the Panzer, communications and engineering schools and other specialist establishments over a two-month period. (As an artillery officer, Knappe was not required to attend training at the artillery school.) With all of these preparatory activities and courses complete, Knappe was finally ready to begin the formal period of general staff training.

Knappe attended general staff training at the General Staff College, Hirschberg (in the Sudeten mountains of Silesia, the college having earlier been removed from Berlin), through the second half of 1944 and during January 1945, by which stage the Russians had already reached the Vistula and were preparing their final offensive into Germany itself. Although general staff training usually occupied up to a total of two years in peacetime, by 1944 it had been condensed into less than twelve months, with up to four months training with active units, two months at the specialized arms schools, and four months at the General Staff College. Reflecting the deteriorating strategic situation and the exigencies of the time, Knappe noted that "our only social activity was a once-a-month event during which the whole [General Staff College course] would have an evening in the ballroom, consisting of a cocktail hour and dinner." Married officers could be accompanied by their families, with two-room accommodation provided to each family and a kitchen shared between four

families, although all usually ate in the Officers' Club in any case. At Hirschberg, "We learned to lead a division in different kinds of combat situations: attacking, retreating, conducting a rearguard action, attacking across a river, attacking in mountainous terrain, establishing a bridgehead, attacking a bridgehead, and so forth. All these different situations were played out with maps or in a sand box [sand table], with tests in between. The purpose was to make us capable of assisting a general in leading a division. We learned how to write orders, how to plan an attack, how to figure out the length of a column on a road, how long it would take the column to cross a bridge, how to group troops, how to arrange for reserves, how to defend against a massive attack by an enemy, how to conduct a massive attack against a defense line, how to position infantry, how to position artillery, where to put the engineers if there is a river in the attack line and when to move them forward. We also learned intelligence and counter-intelligence work: how to find out what kind of units were opposite us and what to do with that information – how to handle all these details for the general commanding the division. In war games, we would be given the situation we were in and what was happening. Then all of a sudden something unexpected would happen, which we would learn about in a report, a radio message, or a phone call. Then we would have to react to the new situation. In [routine day-to-day] training, we

From December 1941 Hitler became closely involved in the direction and conduct of military operations. Here the Führer discusses the operational situation with Generaloberst Ferdinand Schörner and a number of senior Luftwaffe officers in 1944. Schörner headed the army's NSFO organization as well as successfully fulfilling a number of important command appointments. He retained Hitler's trust throughout the war.

Three junior non-commissioned officers are pictured in 1943 or 1944, while engaged in a training exercise using map and compass. Their uniforms and steel helmets are of the modified types produced for the Wehrmacht from 1943. All three soldiers are infantrymen and the red loops of cloth on their shoulder straps indicate the battalion to which they belong within their regiment.

would get the information and have to work out the solution overnight or over the weekend."[5]

But by late January 1945 the strategic situation had deteriorated significantly: the Russians were less than 100 kilometers away from Hirschfeld. So the training course was terminated in order for the students to be assigned immediately to general staff appointments with the front-line units.

## 4. Non-Commissioned Officers

Considerable emphasis was placed upon selecting and training the army's NCOs. The high command recognized, quite correctly, that the morale, discipline and day-to-day efficiency of the army relied

in large part upon the quality, personal application and professional competence of these men, while the NCO corps was also an important source of potential officers. The army's NCOs (Unteroffiziere) comprised two groups, each determined by rank. The more senior ranks were termed Unteroffiziere mit Portepee, while the junior ranks were Unteroffiziere ohne Portepee. The "Portepee" was a decorative and identifying cord and tassel attached to the wearer's sidearm (such as a dagger or bayonet) worn with parade or walking-out uniform; "mit" meant "with" and "ohne" meant "without". Thus only the more senior category of Unteroffiziere bore this uniform embellishment. The color and design of the Portepee indicated not only the rank of the wearer but also his precise position within the unit or organization to which he belonged. NCOs were regular career soldiers, or else they

**The Regular NCO Standard Training Course**

| Timeframe | Basic Training | Advanced Training | Supplementary Training |
|---|---|---|---|
| Until February 1944 | 4 months basic training at NCO school. | 6 months special-to-arm training at NCO school as a section (squad) commander. | |
| From February 1944 | 4 months basic training with a training unit of the appropriate arm. | 5 months special-to-arm training as a section (squad) commander at NCO school; or 3 months for some specialist branches. | 1 to 3 months with appropriate training units as necessary, to make a total 6 months of advanced and supplementary training. |

were conscripts promoted to NCO rank and termed reserve NCOs (Unteroffiziere der Reserve).* The usual engagement for a regular NCO was twelve years, although a four-and-a-half-year engagement was also available. NCOs who were also officer applicants were required to engage for an indefinite period of service. NCO promotion was based upon merit, time served and (in most cases) the existence of an appropriate vacancy in the unit's authorized organization. In broad terms, an NCO could usually be considered for promotion to the next higher rank after four months served in a combat unit, providing that he had served a total of one year in his current rank in a combat unit, or two years in a non-combat field unit.

Applications by potential regular NCOs could be made at age sixteen-and-a-half, with successful applicants entering the army at age seventeen. Alternatively, a conscript who was already serving could apply to engage for a twelve-year engagement (if not over age 38 at the end of his service) or a four-and-a-half-year engagement (for those aged up to 28) after one year's conscripted service. Subsequently, after a total of two years of military service, their enlistment was confirmed and they could be appointed as NCO applicants (Unteroffizier-Bewerber) by their unit commander, provided that they met the required leadership, instructional and disciplinary criteria. Thereafter the applicants

attended training courses at an army NCO school (Heeres-Unteroffizier-Schulen), or at a special service technical school (Waffen-Schulen), which taught subjects such as signals communications, chemical warfare or military engineering. In late 1944 there were some 22 NCO schools for the infantry, one for mountain infantry, two for the artillery, one for the signals troops, two for the engineers, and seven for Panzer troops (the latter variously specializing in tank, armored or motorized infantry, reconnaissance or anti-tank skills).

At the end of his regular NCO training the newly-qualified soldier was promoted Gefreiter (lance corporal, or private first class) and was assigned to a field unit to begin his NCO service. In addition to the arrangements for mainstream NCO applicants, special engagement and training arrangements also existed for certain technicians and specialists, including medical personnel, musicians and farriers or blacksmiths. Other non-technical NCO specialists who underwent separate or additional training included intelligence and linguist personnel, clerks, supply specialists and weapons stores account holders, and NCOs responsible for fire-fighting, gas protection (chemical defense) and catering matters. The qualifying training for what were essentially practical duties often took place within units and through actual experience of carrying out these tasks, rather than at army schools.

As well as the regular NCOs, numbers of conscripts were identified by their commanders as potential NCOs and were content to accept the rank and responsibility but did not wish to enlist formally for the twelve- or four-and-a-half-year period. These men were designated as reserve NCO applicants (Reserve-Unteroffizier-Bewerber). They usually received their qualifying training in Germany, on courses conducted under the auspices of

Although often attributed to the late summer of 1941, this well-known photograph from *Signal* magazine was probably taken during the summer of 1943. The Unteroffizier (senior non-commissioned officer) at the front is noteworthy for his Knight's Cross, Iron Cross First Class and Infantry Assault Badge. He carries issue-pattern binoculars and has an army four-color (blue, red, green and white light options) flashlight attached to his tunic button. His leather pistol holster probably contains a Walther P38. The soldiers' brown canvas or oilskin pouches contain counter-chemical (gas) attack Gasplane protective capes. The soldier on the left is an Obergefreiter (corporal). He and one other soldier are apparently wearing the Model 1943 (M43) uniform, while the Unteroffizier and other soldier wear the better-quality Model 1936 (M36) uniform (identifiable by the dark blue-green collar).

**Left:** A recruiting poster promoting a career as an army non-commissioned officer.

*The full range of German army NCO ranks is shown in Appendix 4, together with their British and US Army equivalents.

Whatever the arm or branch of the army, the training (Ausbildung) was varied, conducted robustly and always physically demanding. The pictures show (top to bottom and left to right): physical fitness training; improvised obstacle crossing; hand-grenade throwing; a first riding lesson; basic gun drills; and training with inflatable craft.

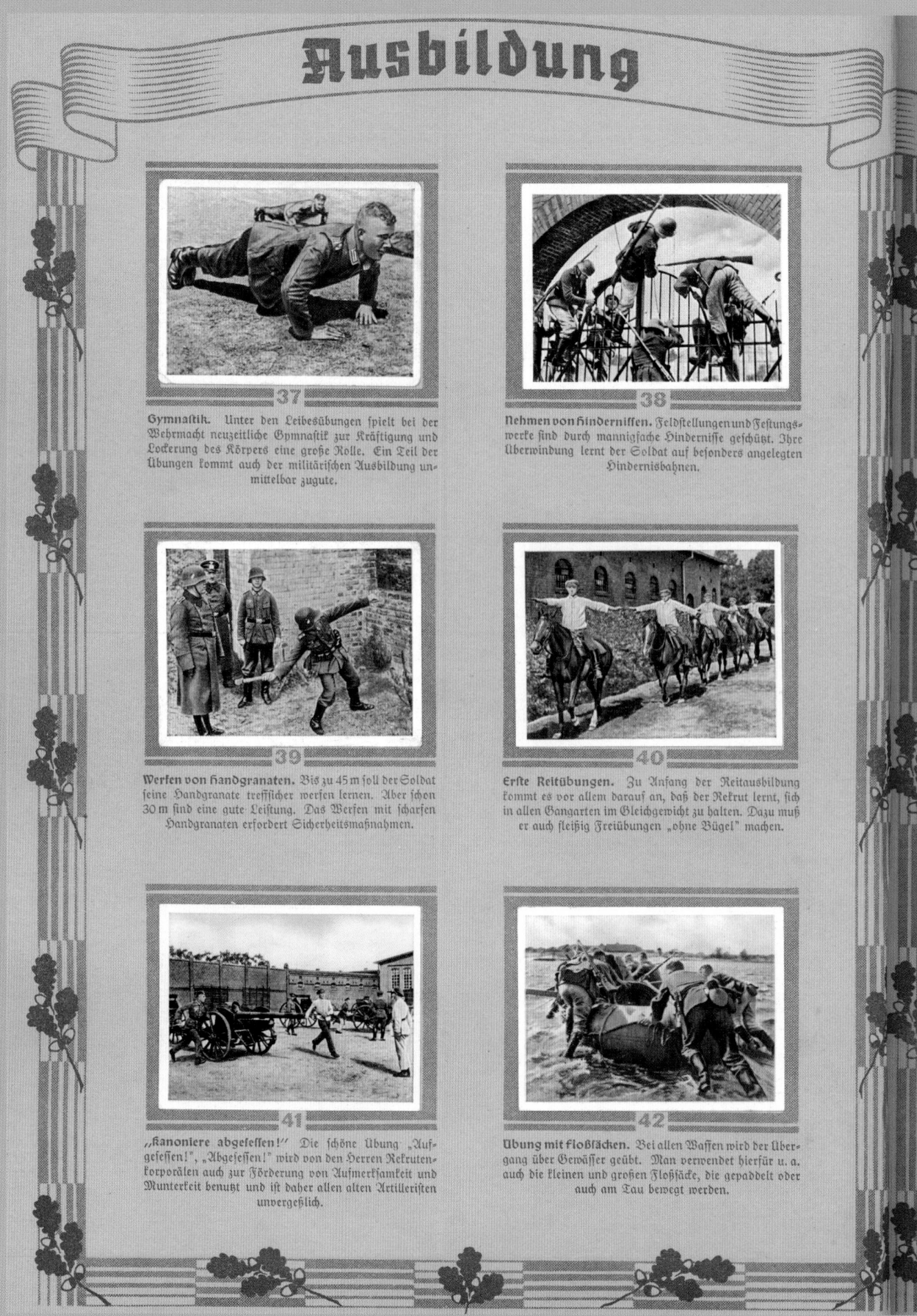

# Ausbildung

**Gymnaſtik.** Unter den Leibesübungen ſpielt bei der Wehrmacht neuzeitliche Gymnaſtik zur Kräftigung und Lockerung des Körpers eine große Rolle. Ein Teil der Übungen kommt auch der militäriſchen Ausbildung unmittelbar zugute.

**Nehmen von Hinderniſſen.** Feldſtellungen und Feſtungswerke ſind durch mannigfache Hinderniſſe geſchützt. Ihre Überwindung lernt der Soldat auf beſonders angelegten Hindernisbahnen.

**Werfen von Handgranaten.** Bis zu 45 m ſoll der Soldat ſeine Handgranate treffſicher werfen lernen. Aber ſchon 30 m ſind eine gute Leiſtung. Das Werfen mit ſcharfen Handgranaten erfordert Sicherheitsmaßnahmen.

**Erſte Reitübungen.** Zu Anfang der Reitausbildung kommt es vor allem darauf an, daß der Rekrut lernt, ſich in allen Gangarten im Gleichgewicht zu halten. Dazu muß er auch fleißig Freiübungen „ohne Bügel" machen.

**„Kanoniere abgeſeſſen!"** Die ſchöne Übung „Aufgeſeſſen!", „Abgeſeſſen!" wird von den Herren Rekrutenkorporälen auch zur Förderung von Aufmerkſamkeit und Munterkeit benutzt und iſt daher allen alten Artilleriſten unvergeßlich.

**Übung mit floßſäcken.** Bei allen Waffen wird der Übergang über Gewäſſer geübt. Man verwendet hierfür u. a. auch die kleinen und großen Floßſäcke, die gepaddelt oder auch am Tau bewegt werden.

a Wehrkreis. Although small numbers of non-infantry candidates were also trained, these courses were overwhelmingly infantry orientated and were usually run by units of about regimental size based at various permanent training areas. Reserve NCO training was not exclusively the preserve of the Wehrkreise, as the army's mainstream NCO schools also became involved in aspects of this training from time to time. Finally, due to the unavoidable exigencies of wartime service and the ever-present problems of manning the front-line combat units, long-term enlistees on active service with the Feldheer were also able to complete a much-abbreviated period of NCO training at a divisional battle training school or at a field NCO school (Feld-Unteroffizier-Schule) without having to return to Germany for formal training with the Ersatzheer. For the infantry, artillery and Panzer arms, this training sometimes lasted as little as two-and-a-half months, being conducted in the various German-occupied territories by field NCO schools organized very much as regiments of those arms. However, in response to the deteriorating strategic situation these schools were eventually forced to re-locate back to Germany.

## 5. Soldiers

Ordinary soldiers (Mannschaften) were graded into three groups, promotion to a higher grade being based upon time served and professional ability. A soldier could usually be considered for promotion after four months in a combat unit, with a qualifying service requirement in his current grade that ranged from six months to five years in combat units, one to five years in other field units, and from two to six years in all other units. However, there were various exceptions to these "time in current rank" parameters, in order that soldiers and junior NCOs who had temporarily but successfully filled appointments as section (squad) and platoon commanders in combat units for at least four months

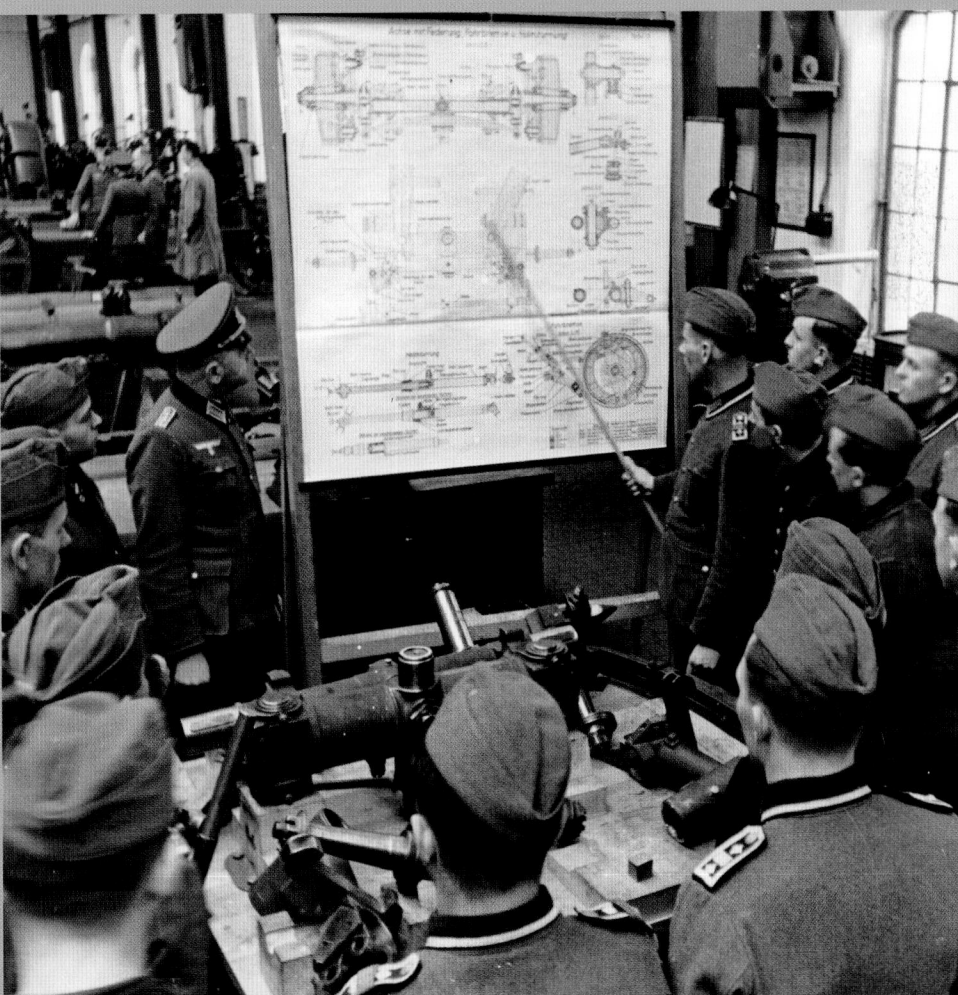

**Top:** The Wehrmacht's technical school provided specialist training for personnel serving with motor transport, engineer and similar arms and branches of the army.

**Above:** The technical training of army officers and non-commissioned officers routinely included visits to industrial plants. This group of artillery troops is learning at first-hand about the weapons they use in their units at one of the factories that produces those guns.

**Left:** As in so many armies, "spud-bashing" was an unavoidable feature of day-to-day life for the German soldier. Potato peeling by these young soldiers in February 1941 is being closely supervised by one of the unit's chefs and a non-commissioned officer.

From 1940, female auxiliaries were increasingly employed in the army's communications units and in clerical and similar supporting roles, working mainly (but not exclusively) at the higher level HQs.

could be promoted to the appropriate rank forthwith, and irrespective of other service considerations. Immediate promotions could always be made in the field (including posthumously) in recognition of an individual's distinguished conduct or achievements in battle. This flexibility rewarded leadership within the Feldheer and encouraged soldiers to take on responsibilities beyond those normally required by their rank.

# 6. Female Auxiliaries and Nurses

In National Socialist ideology, the role of German women was always considered to be of lesser importance than that of men, apart from their patriotic duty to bear and rear the future leaders of the National Socialist state. This perception and policy was

stressed, developed and confirmed from an early age in various all-female youth organizations. The Bund Deutscher Mädel (League of German Girls) was the female branch of the Hitler Jugend and catered for girls in separate groups aged from ten to fourteen and from fifteen to twenty-one. At seventeen, a girl could join the Glaube und Schönheit (faith and beauty) organization, which specifically trained them in domestic science and home-making in preparation for marriage. Subsequently, young women could join the Nazi party women's organization (the NS-Frauenschaft) at age twenty-one. Despite the Nazi view of the role and responsibilities of German women, and the ready availability of the disciplined but generally non-military training provided in the Bund Deutscher Mädel (which contrasted with the paramilitary environment experienced by the boys in the Hitler Jugend), all parts of the armed forces employed uniformed female auxiliaries from 1940, the numbers necessarily increasing as the war progressed, replacing ever more men being called to combat duties.

The first unit of female military auxiliaries was formed to support the army's communications organization, being established on 1 October 1940 by order Heeresmiteillungsblatt 40, Nr. 1085. This unit was the forerunner of a number of other female military and paramilitary auxiliary branches and organizations. In due course, compulsory military service for all females between the ages of eighteen and 40 was introduced in December 1942, with the female auxiliaries of all three branches of the Wehrmacht finally being merged into a single organization of Wehrmacht-helferinnen ("armed forces female auxiliaries") on 29 November 1944. This progressive abandonment of the traditional role of the German woman was inevitable and reflected the increasingly unsustainable numbers of male combat casualties incurred by the Wehrmacht from late 1942.

Within the army, from 1940 the female volunteers of the Nachrichtenhelferinnen des Heeres (literally, "female signals communications support assistance to the army") were mainly employed in the higher-level military headquarters. Many served in OKW and OKH, although numbers also worked in other major headquarters at lower levels of command that were regularly exposed to direct Allied air and long-range artillery attacks, as well as to partisan action on the Eastern Front. At these headquarters, female auxiliaries were organized into Nachrichtenhelferinnen-abteilungen and trained to operate wireless equipment, telegraph systems, telephone switchboards and carry out various other messaging and signals communications tasks. Others (Stabs-helferinnen) also carried out a wide range of clerical and administrative duties in support of the military staff. Nicknamed the "grey mice", they wore a grey uniform jacket and skirt, a white blouse, black shoes and grey or black gloves, and were issued with a regulation black leather handbag fitted with a shoulder strap. Strict rules limited or prohibited the use of make-up and the wearing of jewellery, while the wearing of civilian clothes off-duty was forbidden for those female auxiliaries serving with units based in the occupied territories. Grey overalls were provided for Nachrichtenhelferinnen personnel working mainly indoors in offices. A "blitz" (lightning flash) cloth arm emblem or a black-and-silver enamelled brooch identified these auxiliaries as communications personnel. These women received free rations, accommodation and uniforms. Although subject to military discipline, they were not officially considered to be military personnel, and their pay rates were those of civil servants rather than soldiers. Furthermore, their senior leader (Führerinnen) grades did not correspond to, or enjoy the status of, those of military officers. In due course, as the pool of men for military service became ever smaller, female auxiliaries in Germany also manned anti-aircraft guns (Flakwaffenhelferinnen), operated barrage balloons, and trained to serve as motor and aircraft mechanics.

Somewhat less controversially (in terms of the National Socialist female ideal), Deutsches Rotes Kreuz (German Red Cross, or "DRK") nurses served widely within the military medical services. They worked in the military hospitals in Germany and in hospitals and field hospitals in every operational theater throughout the war, during which time some were killed and others wounded, while a number of DRK nurses were decorated for their bravery under fire. The conditions in which these nurses worked is illustrated by the experience of Agnes Mertes, a DRK nurse in the military hospital at Gerolstein in the Rhineland in late December 1944, where she and the other medical staff were caring not only for German soldiers but also for numbers of wounded American prisoners-of-war. On Christmas Eve a particularly heavy Allied air raid struck the hospital, and Frau Mertes, a senior and very experienced nurse, was ordered to transfer all the patients from the part-demolished hospital to an emergency medical center established at the "Zur Linde" inn in Gerolstein, using some motor ambulances. She recalled: "The road between the two places was under heavy bombardment from Allied aircraft and when the [air raid] alarm was given we had to stop, unload the wounded and hide them (and us) in the roadside ditches. One day while unloading the stretchers at our emergency hospital, a bomb exploded near the inn 'Zur Linde'. A wall caved in and fell upon the wounded soldiers and nursing staff. I was working nearby and was slightly wounded, but after a short treatment I was able to carry on with my duty."[6]

DRK nursing sister (DRK-Schwester) Elfriede Wnuk was one of a small number of DRK personnel awarded the Iron Cross for gallantry. She received the award in September 1942 for her bravery and the example she set by continuing to tend the patients in her care while under direct attack on the Eastern Front. During her service she was also wounded on several occasions and held the Verwundetenabzeichen in silver. In similar circumstances, DRK nursing sisters Greta Fock and Ilse Schulz received the Iron Cross in April 1943 for the courage they had displayed while serving with field hospitals in North Africa. In the case of Greta Fock, she had refused to go to the shelter despite the hospital at which she was

On 22 September 1941, soldiers wounded during the army's early campaigns bid farewell to some of the DRK nurses who cared for them during their time in hospital. Most of these men would then proceed on convalescent leave to complete their recovery before rejoining their units.

> **"** *Ich Schwöre bei Gott diesen heilegen Eid, dass ich dem Führer des Deutschen Reiches und Volkes ADOLF HITLER, dem Obersten Befehlshaber der Wehrmacht, unbedingten Gehorsam leisten und als tapferer Soldat bereit sein will, jederzeit für diesen Eid mein Leben einzusetzen.* **"**
> — The Soldier's Oath, 2 August 1934

The Soldier's Oath introduced in 1934 set an inviolable standard and requirement of absolute loyalty, honor and obedience to Adolf Hitler for every member of the Wehrmacht, whatever his rank or unit.

nursing being under heavy fire, remaining at her post in order to assist a surgeon to complete a critical operation already in progress when the attack started. Some 22 DRK nurses, nursing sisters and female doctors were awarded the Iron Cross Second Class between 1942 and 1945, while DRK-Schwester Else Grossman was one of only two women awarded the Iron Cross First Class, receiving that award in January 1945.

## 7. Military Administrative Officials

A further group of "army" personnel existed, whose members were often mistaken for officers, but who were in fact neither officers nor military personnel (although some of them were accorded military status from 1944). These were the large numbers of civilian administrative specialists (Wehrmachtbeamte) employed by the armed forces. The Wehrmachtbeamten possessed existing professional qualifications or other relevant experience and carried out a whole range of civil service and "officer type" duties that were both uniformed and wholly within the army organization but which were not officially categorized as "military". Many Wehrmacht-beamten were former pre-war NCOs who had opted for civil service employment after completing their twelve-year Reichswehr engagements. In 1944 the status of certain categories of Wehr-

machtbeamte was amended, when they became military officers in the Truppensonderdienst (special troop service). Examples of those affected included judge advocates (Richter) ranked from captain to lieutenant general, higher (Intendanten) and lower (Zahlmeister) grades of administrative officers, ranked from second lieutenant to lieutenant general, and certain technical services officials (mainly dealing with motor maintenance). Several supplementary categories of administrative official were also created to take account of other Wehrmachtbeamten employed by the armed forces both in Germany and in the occupied territories but who did not fit directly into any of the main groups.

## 8. Conscription

On 16 March 1935, Hitler announced the introduction of conscription throughout Germany. The opening text of the Military Service Law dated 21 May 1935 established the legal conditions for this: "Military service is honorary service to the German people. Every German is liable to military service. In time of war, in addition to liability to military service, every German man and every German woman is liable to service to the Fatherland."[7]

Every German man was now liable to military service from the age of eighteen until the 31 March following their 45th birthday; in East Prussia the end of the military service liability extended until the 31 March following a man's 55th birthday. These were the pre-war conscription liabilities, but by 1944 the German government had used the additional powers available to it in wartime to widen these age parameters to extend from seventeen to 61.

In addition to those who were immediately eligible for active service, there were several categories of men who for a variety of reasons (primarily age, physical fitness and medical condition) were deferred or placed into Reserve, Ersatzreserve, Landwehr or Landsturm groups, all of which involved a reduced liability, or from which they could be called into the mainstream recruit training system at a later date. Prior to the war, any application for deferment was decided individually on its merits, with updated applications subsequently required. Such cases were rigorously tested and limited by quotas, although a well-made case could succeed – for example, one that was strongly supported by an employer on behalf of an employee in an essential war industry, or possibly one where an individual's military service would result in extreme family hardship. However, from 1942 the numbers of all types of deferment reduced significantly. The only automatic exemptions from conscription in peacetime were for men deemed to be entirely unfit medically for military service, and Roman Catholic priests (including those already training to become priests). Certain categories of men were automatically excluded from the selection process at the outset, and these reflected National Socialist dogma and policies. Among those excluded by

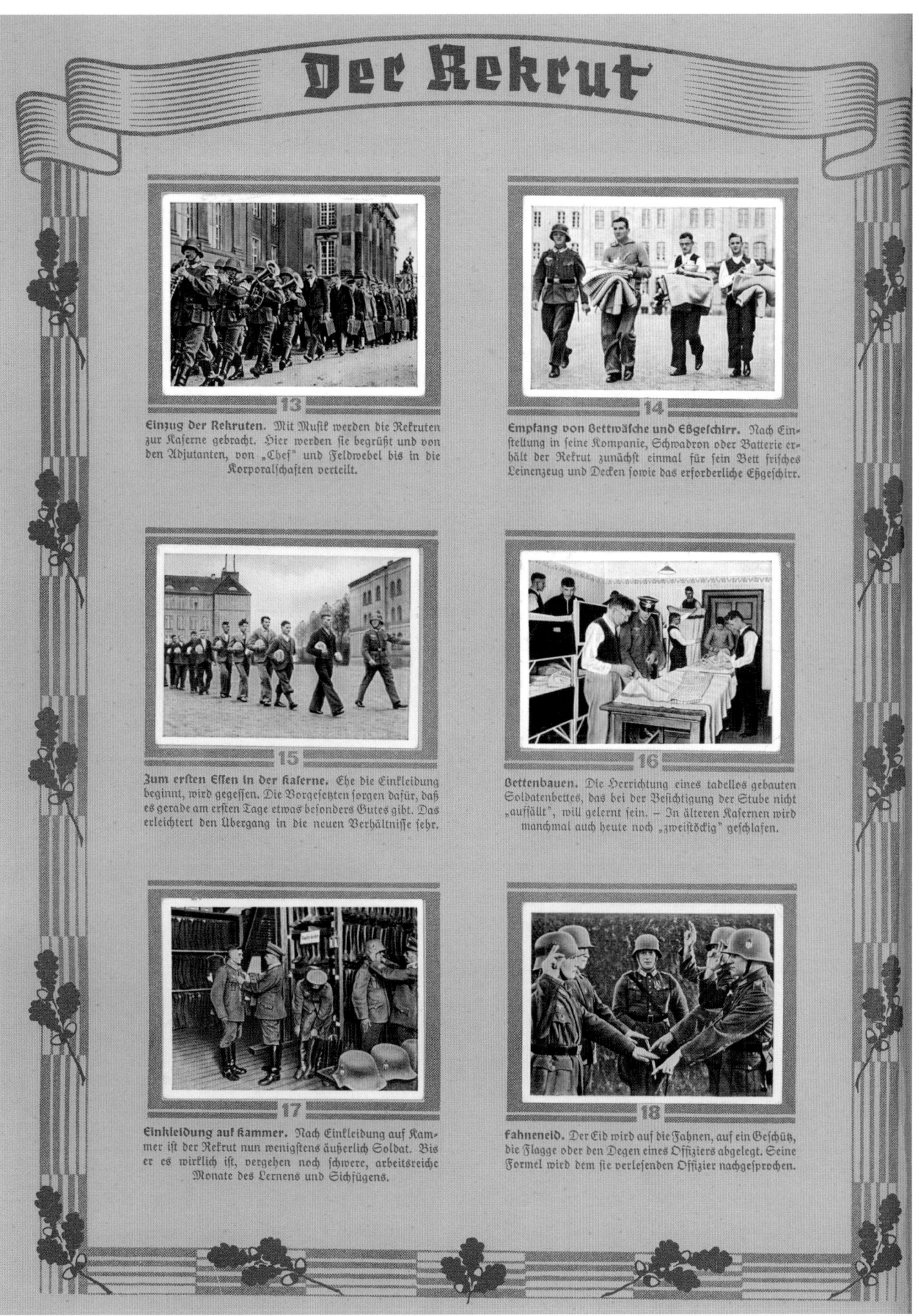

## Der Rekrut

**13** Einzug der Rekruten. Mit Musik werden die Rekruten zur Kaserne gebracht. Hier werden sie begrüßt und von den Adjutanten, von „Chef" und Feldwebel bis in die Korporalschaften verteilt.

**14** Empfang von Bettwäsche und Eßgeschirr. Nach Einstellung in seine Kompanie, Schwadron oder Batterie erhält der Rekrut zunächst einmal für sein Bett frisches Leinenzeug und Decken sowie das erforderliche Eßgeschirr.

**15** Zum ersten Essen in der Kaserne. Ehe die Einkleidung beginnt, wird gegessen. Die Vorgesetzten sorgen dafür, daß es gerade am ersten Tage etwas besonders Gutes gibt. Das erleichtert den Übergang in die neuen Verhältnisse sehr.

**16** Bettenbauen. Die Herrichtung eines tadellos gebauten Soldatenbettes, das bei der Besichtigung der Stube nicht „auffällt", will gelernt sein. – In älteren Kasernen wird manchmal auch heute noch „zweistöckig" geschlafen.

**17** Einkleidung auf Kammer. Nach Einkleidung auf Kammer ist der Rekrut nun wenigstens äußerlich Soldat. Bis er es wirklich ist, vergehen noch schwere, arbeitsreiche Monate des Lernens und Sichfügens.

**18** Fahneneid. Der Eid wird auf die Fahnen, auf ein Geschütz, die Flagge oder den Degen eines Offiziers abgelegt. Seine Formel wird dem sie verlesenden Offizier nachgesprochen.

From his first contact with the army – usually following a military band from the railway station to the training unit barracks – to his formal induction, the recruit (Der Rekrut) had quickly to adapt to a whole new way of life. The pictures show (top to bottom and left to right): the arrival of the recruits; issue of bedding, mess kit, etc.; en route to their first army meal; learning how to make their beds army-style; uniform issue; and the initial induction oath-taking before the flag.

law were Jews (and later gypsies), convicts under sentence, various categories of lesser criminal, "political undesirables" (in other words, opponents of the Nazis) undergoing "corrective training" (usually in a concentration camp such as Dachau), non-German citizens (a stipulation that eventually became ever more flexible as the war drew on), those whose civil rights had been withdrawn, and any former military personnel who had been judged unfit to bear arms by a court-martial that had convicted him of a serious criminal offense.

For the vast majority of German male citizens however, conscription was unavoidable and drew the conscript into a series of well-tried and standardized actions and events:

- Registration (based upon eligibility through age) in response to notices issued by the district civil police authorities. Local police forces routinely held details of all residents within their area of jurisdiction and were legally required to do so.
- An initial medical examination that (by the standards that were applied from December 1943) resulted in being classified fit for active service, or for reduced forms of active service, or only for the labor service, or as temporarily or permanently unfit.
- A second medical examination and drafting that confirmed or modified the assessment made by the first medical exam-

ination and then directed either a duty assignment or a deferment pending call-up.
- Call-up was triggered by a letter (Gestellungsbefehl) that ordered the individual to report to his assigned unit (in peacetime) or Ersatzheer replacement unit (in wartime). The necessary travel documents and (if required) rail ticket were included.
- When he arrived at his first unit, the conscript underwent a further medical examination. His ability and any previous experience were then fully assessed by the unit staff in order to determine his initial employment within the unit. Last of all, the soldier's oath was administered to him, at which point he became an active member of the German army; a much more formal re-affirmation or oath-taking ceremony usually took place after the first few weeks of basic training, by which stage the recruit had received sufficient drill practice to be able to play his part in this highly symbolic ceremonial parade. From 2 August 1934 the terms of this oath also bound him specifically and irrevocably to Adolf Hitler, his Führer and his supreme commander.

Those who volunteered for military service before being called up as conscripts followed a similar induction process but were usually entitled to choose the arm or branch of the army in which they served. However, for these men the age parameters were slightly different from those for conscripts. Prior to the war a volunteer could join at age seventeen; this was later reduced to sixteen-and-a-half, and then to sixteen in 1944. An Allied intelligence assessment in March 1945 noted that, "Volunteers to the ranks [of the Wehrmacht] have been numerous during the war, though much less so than in 1914–1918" … "In the past two years [i.e., in 1943 and 1944] a large proportion of the youngest age class has been induced by various kinds of pressure to volunteer, largely for the Waffen-SS."[8]

## 9. Training for War

Military training during the years before the war was in many ways a continuation of the proven training system that had served the old imperial German army and the Reichswehr well for more than :half a century. However, this training was now conducted with modern weapons and new tactical thinking and doctrine, and against a background of social change and the accelerating pace of the army's expansion. Most training took place in the training units of the Ersatzheer, with some also conducted in the Ersatzheer's replacement units. Special courses were conducted at various general training units for specialists, potential officers and potential NCOs. Special-service schools (Waffenschulen) (special-to-arm schools) also trained personnel of that arm and instructors, provided demonstration troops, assisted weapon and equipment development programs and provided specialist instruction to other arms as required. Overall responsibility for the majority of training rested upon the chief of training in the Ersatzheer, while implementation and administration of the in-Germany training was generally carried out by the Wehrkreis headquarters. Irrespective of whether the trainees were officers, NCOs or soldiers, they all entered a training system that had been assiduously developed since the 1920s and was firmly founded upon what was known as the Führung, or leadership, principle. This encouraged the soldier to think and be prepared to lead at least two levels above the rank and appointment he actually occupied, which in turn led to the army that went to war in 1939 often being termed the "Führerheer" – an indication not of the presence or influence upon it of Adolf Hitler, but of a core concept of military leadership that enabled the army to keep fighting effectively right through to 1945.

The largest training commitment was undoubtedly the transformation of newly-conscripted recruits into trained soldiers for the Feldheer and the re-training of convalescent soldiers before returning them to active duty with the Feldheer. Prior to and during the early years of the war, the training of ordinary soldiers was based upon a sixteen-week cycle of basic infantry training (Grundausbildung) divided into three succeeding parts: individual training, section (or squad) training and platoon training. Each stage took the recruit a step further in understanding and working in the larger unit. At the end of the third part the recruit could work as a trained rifleman within an infantry platoon, competent in the use of all the weapons available at that level – the rifle and bayonet, machine guns, sub-machine gun, pistol, hand grenades, light mortars, and various means of destroying tanks. He would also have acquired various fieldcraft, individual gas protection and message carrying skills.

The organization of a training unit usually mirrored the type of field unit for which it was producing manpower. The responsibility for organizing and conducting the training rested primarily upon the training company commander in an infantry training unit, with the battalion commander supervising the company-level training activities and adjudging the final standard achieved at the end of the basic training period. This allowed a certain amount of individuality on the part of these instructors, although the army's overall training priorities were (in order) combat training, weapon firing, theoretical (classroom) training, drill and sports. Although the parade march (the "goose step") was still seen on some ceremonial occasions once the war was under way, its use was increasingly viewed as irrelevant for most troops, other than those specifically required to fulfil high-profile guard or ceremonial duties in places such as Berlin. Indeed, a US military intelligence report in March 1945 noted: "The drill for the modern German soldier is far from what is generally believed [by many Allied personnel]; drilling of the famous goose-step (sic) is not permitted, and 'present arms' is not taught."[9]

In due course, certainly by late 1944, the time allocated for basic training was reduced from the pre-war sixteen weeks to as little as eight weeks for most training units. After successfully completing his basic training, the soldier moved on to advanced training (Erweiterungsausbildung), which usually continued until he was transferred to a field unit. Typically, this advanced training period involved the infantry soldier in company-level maneuvers, while those in the artillery and some other arms often progressed to battalion-level training. Clearly, the duration and level of instruction of the advanced training depended very much upon the needs of the particular arm involved. The separate experiences of several soldiers who served between 1936 and 1943 illustrates the changing nature of this training, first in peacetime, then during the early war years and finally in 1943, soon after the disastrous defeat of the German 6th Army at Stalingrad.

Werner Wagenknecht was called up in 1936, the year following the introduction of conscription. Just before his 22nd birthday he received the call-up order that required him to report to the 12th Infantry Regiment at the Prince Louis Ferdinand barracks in Halberstadt. There he was medically examined, issued with a canvas fatigue uniform and ordered to send his civilian clothes home. The basic training that followed was hard: "The first few weeks concentrated on getting us fit. One of the exercises was 'pull-ups' to a very high horizontal bar. While I was hanging there like a sack of potatoes, the sergeant would prick me on the bottom with his sword, as I tried desperately to get my chin up over the bar! … Then we trained with rifles – old World War I models and we had to wear old World War I [M1915 pattern] steel helmets too, but later we got a new Karabiner (7.92mm 98k) and new [1935 pattern] helmets which were much lighter and easier to deal with. The machine gun (08/15) was also from World War I and was water-cooled; the pistol was very heavy, again from World War I … Marching, shooting, cleaning, washing our clothes outside in stone troughs with cold water – it was all very hard training for me."[10]

Route marches often began at or before dawn and were conducted in full marching order. Sometimes they culminated at a lake or pool, where the fully-equipped recruits were required to jump in and swim ashore –any non-swimmers being pulled out by the watching corporals. Although the lowest of the army's six core training priorities, sport was also used extensively to harden and train the recruits. Some time later Wagenknecht was quite badly injured while playing a form of rugby known as Kampfball ("battle ball"), while on another occasion he was apparently knocked out during the first and last occasion on which he entered a boxing ring. Ceremonial parades also featured prominently in the 12th Infantry Regiment's program at Halberstadt, and much attention was paid to the soldiers' turnout and to practicing the parade march or "goose step" still required to be performed on such occasions during the pre-war years. The following year, during the summer of 1937, the unit travelled to the Lüneberger Heide in northern Germany to carry out more advanced and large-scale

Christmas (Weihnachten) and New Year's Eve were traditionally special times in the army, with home leave being granted to the troops whenever this was practicable. Here a group of Gebirgsjäger (mountain troops) pack their rucksacks before setting off to spend Christmas with their families in the Salzburg area.

training and maneuvers. Wagenknecht and his comrades-in-arms were transported to Celle by rail and then marched north to the barracks adjacent to the training ground at Hohne, about 25 kilometers away. He remembered: "We began training daily at 4 a.m. in full marching order, with steel helmets, water bottles filled with chlorinated water. We had to march through woods sprayed with tear-gas to test our gasmasks."[11]

At the end of four weeks' training the regiment returned to Halberstadt, but this time they marched all the way by road, completing a succession of night marches to cover a distance of just over 160 kilometers. Each night the march broke at midnight for coffee mixed with rum before continuing, while each day at sunrise a halt was called, when there was an opportunity to rest while the medical staff also inspected and treated blistered feet. When the regiment at last marched into Halberstadt, the soldiers found that a grandstand had been erected in the marketplace, before which they were required to carry out a formal parade before an assembly of generals and other prominent citizens. Many of the traditions, drill and discipline of the old imperial army were still very evident in the army of 1937, and this was particularly so in the infantry, which had long been – and continued to be – the premier branch of the German army.

Whatever the arm of service in which a soldier was subsequently destined to serve, he was first trained as an infantryman. So it had been for Siegfried Knappe, a well-educated young man from Leipzig whose father had been a naval gunnery officer during World War I. Having completed the usual six months of RAD training, he had volunteered for the artillery, expecting to be working with the new self-propelled or motorized artillery that was being increasingly showcased by the army and the National Socialist government. However, on his arrival at the artillery barracks at Jena in October 1936, it transpired that Knappe's regiment was one of very many horse-drawn artillery units upon which the army still relied, and which at that stage far exceeded the number of motorized artillery units. There, "we were issued two sets of uniforms – one for drill and stable work and another for everything else. We were also issued riding boots and riding breeches with leather seats, since we were in the horse-drawn artillery. We were especially proud when we were issued steel helmets and cartridge pouches. That made us feel more like *real* soldiers. They tried to give us the right sizes, but sometimes they could not fit us and we had to take what they had and exchange it later." Despite his previous RAD service and a reasonable expectation that he would in due course be selected for officer training due to his education and background, Knappe and his comrades then began the infantry basic training common to all arms of the army. They received only six weeks of this training, while infantry specialists completed as much as twelve months; Knappe acknowledged that "it was important, however, because the part of the artillery that accompanied the forward observation officer, called the battery troop, was always up front with the infantry." In any case, additional infantry training would later

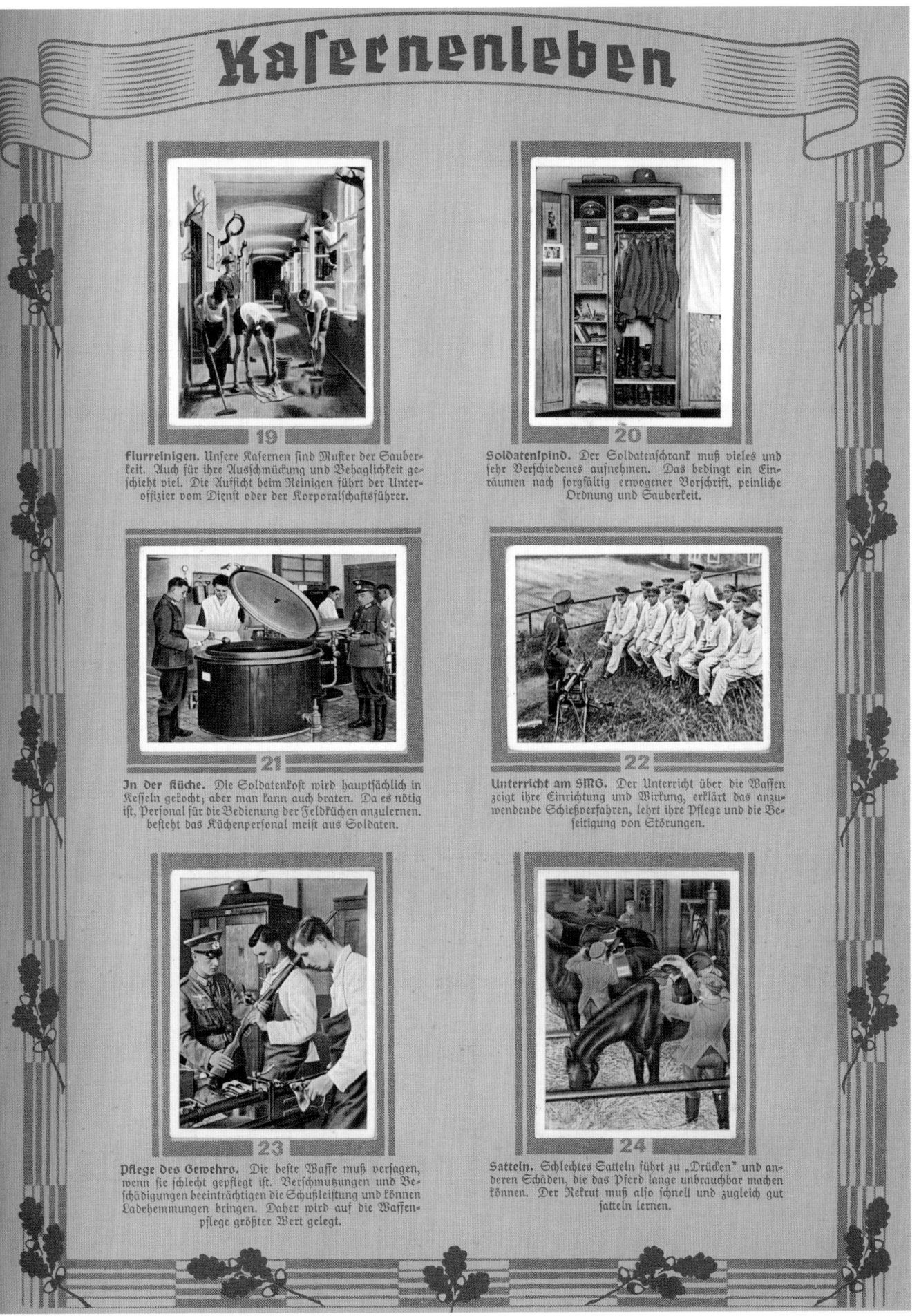

# Kasernenleben

**19 flurreinigen.** Unsere Kasernen sind Muster der Sauberkeit. Auch für ihre Ausschmückung und Behaglichkeit geschieht viel. Die Aufsicht beim Reinigen führt der Unteroffizier vom Dienst oder der Korporalschaftsführer.

**20 Soldatenspind.** Der Soldatenschrank muß vieles und sehr Verschiedenes aufnehmen. Das bedingt ein Einräumen nach sorgfältig erwogener Vorschrift, peinliche Ordnung und Sauberkeit.

**21 In der küche.** Die Soldatenkost wird hauptsächlich in Kesseln gekocht; aber man kann auch braten. Da es nötig ist, Personal für die Bedienung der Feldküchen anzulernen, besteht das Küchenpersonal meist aus Soldaten.

**22 Unterricht am SMG.** Der Unterricht über die Waffen zeigt ihre Einrichtung und Wirkung, erklärt das anzuwendende Schießverfahren, lehrt ihre Pflege und die Beseitigung von Störungen.

**23 Pflege des Gewehrs.** Die beste Waffe muß versagen, wenn sie schlecht gepflegt ist. Verschmutzungen und Beschädigungen beeinträchtigen die Schußleistung und können Ladehemmungen bringen. Daher wird auf die Waffenpflege größter Wert gelegt.

**24 Satteln.** Schlechtes Satteln führt zu „Drücken" und anderen Schäden, die das Pferd lange unbrauchbar machen können. Der Rekrut muß also schnell und zugleich gut satteln lernen.

Life in barracks (Kasernenleben) in peacetime followed a predictable and well-ordered routine of administrative duties, training, weapon and equipment mantenance and team building. The pictures show (top to bottom and left to right): barrack-room cleaning duties; the soldier's locker; the barracks kitchen; instruction on the MG 08 heavy machine gun; weapon cleaning; and the stables (of a mounted or artillery unit).

continue in parallel with artillery training. Knappe recalled: "During this infantry-training period, we would get up at five o'clock, perform stable duty, have breakfast, fall out, and begin a very full day that ended only when we fell into bed, exhausted, at ten o'clock. The training was interesting, well planned and well organized." The program included "handling our rifles, shooting them on the firing range, moving on the ground under fire, and digging in. Of course, that was in addition to marching, drilling and learning to parade. We kept [the pace] while marching by singing. We also had training with hand grenades and machine guns." Each day followed a regular pattern: "Lunch was our main meal of the day. The food was good, and it was well prepared. After lunch we would get fifteen minutes or so of rest, then we would typically change uniforms (the clothing was [precisely] prescribed for different activities) and get a lecture on espionage or German national history." Guard duty for two-hour periods in the stables was also part of the curriculum, as was physical training, including gymnastic exercises and handball.[12]

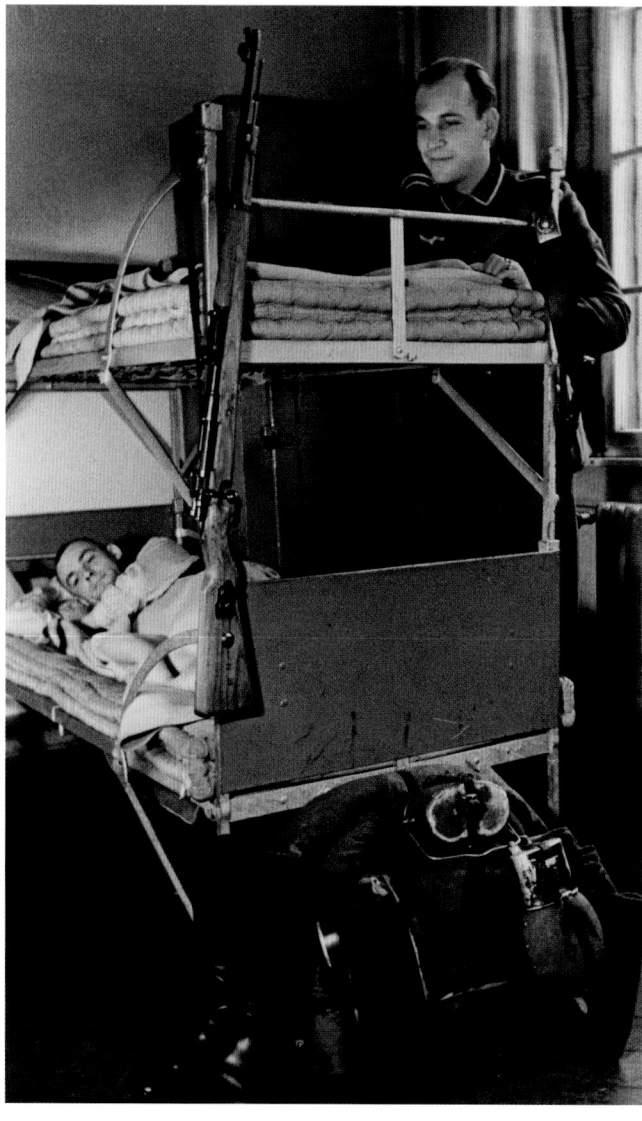

Home sweet home! A double-tiered bunk in typical barracks accommodation pictured shortly before or early in the war. Note the rifle, boots, pack and equipment laid out immediately to hand.

With his mandatory period of infantry training completed at the beginning of December 1936, Knappe began three months of basic artillery training. As his artillery regiment was horse-drawn, training in handling the guns proceeded in parallel with training in the care and handling of the horses upon which the unit depended. Knappe recalled: "We were divided into two groups: those who would handle the horses (usually those [recruits] from the farms and those [recruits] who would handle the guns (usually those from the city), although each group had to be familiar with the other's duties … Basically, the horse handlers were learning equine care and how to bridle and harness horses. Those of us who were gunners practiced going through the motions of firing: taking the gun off the ammunition cart [limber], placing the gun in the proper position, loading it with a dummy shell and bags of sawdust for powder, aiming it at a fixed point, making corrections, and firing on command. We went through these exercises every day in the training area, just going through the motions without live ammunition. The horse handlers (fahrer) and gunners (kanonier) exercised constantly but separately."[13]

After a couple of weeks training separately, the training of both groups converged, and thereafter they always trained together, with all four complete gun crews coming together to train as a battery once a week as well. Deployment on roads and cross-country, and maneuvering the guns into position – often by manhandling them – and camouflaging them, were all practiced exhaustively, as was the system of passing target information between the battery troop deployed forward with the infantry and the gun line. This was achieved using both radios and telephones, without which the guns could not carry out their task of supporting the forward units.

One of the many thousands of soldiers conscripted into the army after the outbreak of war was former mechanic Rolf Werner Völker, who was born in 1920 and came from Frankenthal, Pfalz. He was called up on 5 October 1940 and joined the 104th Infantry Rifle Regiment (which subsequently became a Panzergrenadier regiment in 1941) at the Ernst Ludwig Kaserne in Darmstadt, where he was assigned to the 4th (Machine Gun) Company. "In Darmstadt the camp was full," he recalled. "We were sixteen to a room, plus an old soldier who was in charge. We slept in double-tier bunk beds with straw mattresses. Every morning when we got up we had to shake our mattresses and make up our beds – the sheets and blankets had to be really neat and tidy with no creases. If they weren't good enough to satisfy our room 'oldster', then he pulled them on to the floor and we had to make them up again and again just to give us plenty of practice! …We couldn't grumble about the food when compared with the war rations of the civilian population. We also had china dishes, plates, cups and saucers to use in our mess hall, although we had to bring our own eating utensils. There were the usual shenanigans – you had to show that your hands and fingernails were clean before you got anything to eat! The cold food ration was delivered once a day for the morning and evening meal. It was delivered by a rations NCO direct from the kitchen to the rooms and every man had a special place in his

locker to keep his ration. Also coffee (a mixture of malt and chicory) and tea (stinging nettles and herbs). One of us fetched this from the kitchen in an aluminium can. It is said that they put something in the tea to stop the recruits from getting too sexy – the lads called it Henkolin."[14]

Völker recalled various aspects of his basic training, and his account of that period and of the growing pace of military life reflects the immediacy of the rapidly expanding war in 1940 and 1941: "There was a shortage of the new, shorter rifle (Karabiner 98K), so we had to do our drill and basic work with the old Gewehr 98 lang … I had a bit of good luck, they gave me a precision rifle made in 1913 with a walnut butt [stock], and I was such a good shot with it that I won lots of time off. We also learned how to handle stick grenades. We had to bind five or six together to use against tanks by placing them under the tracks. We did the same to destroy barbed-wire fences. They were very strict about the wearing of gasmasks and they made certain that ours worked properly with some sort of irritating gas. We also had to learn fieldcraft and tactics, for example how to advance and withdraw, how to win a few meters of territory, how to lie down and get up again, even how to take an enemy position with fixed bayonets." During one exercise, Völker and his companions had to wade through a manure heap; when he returned to camp, "I went under the shower in my steel helmet and full uniform. There was so much dirt that you couldn't even see my ammunition pouches! After our dinner break we went back on to the parade ground for drill, still

in our soaking wet clothes." The formal oath-taking ceremony took place after three weeks of basic training, and thereafter Völker and the others were instructed in subjects such as communications, judging distance, and using pistols, mortars and machine guns. They also conducted maneuvers at night and completed forced marches, on which they regularly carried heavy support weapons in addition to their individual weapons and equipment. "On Sunday afternoons," he recalled, "we were allowed to go out, but as we were very short of money all we could ever afford to buy was a cup of coffee."[15]

In the sixth week of training the recruits were issued with new uniforms, shoes, jackboots, and 98K rifles. At that stage the soldiers were confined to the camp and instructed to send their civilian clothes to their homes. The pace of life increased again, with field training that included living in the field in shelters made up of the individual tent sections (Zeltbahn) carried by each man. There were also changing parades, during which the troops were ordered to change into different orders of dress and equipment at five-minute intervals, which taught them instant obedience to orders and total familiarity with their individual equipment. Finally, Völker's recollection of the moment a couple of months later (in early 1941), when he and his comrades finally left the barracks at Darmstadt to join their Feldheer unit at Landau in the Pfalz, encapsulates both the pride and the pathos of the occasion. It also epitomizes the attitude of so many young soldiers to the conflict in which they were by then directly involved and which

Training usually blended theoretical explanations with practical exercises – as for these Panzer unit recruits receiving a briefing on tank tactics during a field training camp conducted near Berlin shortly after their conscription in 1935.

many of them viewed rather more as an adventure than as a war: "Then, with the band leading, we marched to the railway station. With our young, high spirits we could not understand why the people standing at the side of the road watching us march by, had tears in their eyes. But they were right of course, because only half of us would come back. We passed the [train] journey through Hessen and over the Rhine to Landau singing and telling stories – were we not the men who would rescue the Fatherland?"[16]

Once they arrived at their new unit in the Feldheer as trained but now it all had more sense of purpose. "All our instructors had seen active service and they now had the job of teaching us new recruits (Grünschnäbeln) – [for] we were going to fight the Englander!"[17]

Heinrich Stockoff also entered the army at about the same time as Völker. Stockoff was born in 1921, and came from Gesmold, a small village near Melle, to the northwest of Bielefeld and west of Osnabrück. After his Reichsarbeitsdienst (RAD) service he joined Infanterie-Ersatz-Bataillon Nr. 37 and was assigned to the first platoon of the 1st Company. Among his memories of those days he recalled: "I certainly liked the army better than the RAD. When we did well in our training our platoon sergeant, Unteroffizier Willi Kraft, allowed us to have free time – for example we went on a trip into Osnabrück city. On the first Sunday there was a church service and Feldwebel Stahlberg took all the [Roman] Catholics to church. The others, who said they didn't believe in God, were

taken to the kitchen. They had to peel potatoes. The next Sunday all the soldiers said they believed in God!"

Erwin Grubba was born in Marienberg, East Prussia, in 1925 and was conscripted a couple of years after Wagenknecht, Völker and Stockoff. He was called up in spring 1943 and reported to Spandau Kaserne, Berlin, in September, after a period of time with the RAD. Grubba's initial training was not a particularly happy experience, and it made a lasting impression upon him: "Spandau barracks [was] the Grenadier depot and that was where the real hell began – a couple of weeks or so of very tough training. A lot of bullying, which took the form of fatigues, packs on your backs, rifles extended at arms length for ages – it seemed like hours – with your arms breaking … crawling on your belly, running at the double everywhere, even with food on your plate. There wasn't much food anyway. You spilt half of it. And you were always being bullied and chivvied in that way … I remember one [NCO] who came into the barrack room at night when we had just swept it. He opened the little iron stove, took the ash pan out and scattered the ashes all over the floor. Then he shouted: 'This place looks like a pigsty – clean it up!' So we had to get out of bed and do it."[18]

Certainly the military training regime became harsher as the war drew on, and this was vividly described by Guy Sajer in his 1967 book *Le Soldat Oublié* (*The Forgotten Soldier*), which documented in considerable detail his experiences and service as a German soldier on the Eastern Front and in Germany from 1942 to 1945. Guy Sajer was an enlistee from Alsace-Lorraine who was half-German and half-French. He completed his basic training during the summer of 1942, and in spring 1943 transferred into the élite "Großdeutschland" Division. Although by definition already a trained soldier, this transfer brought him to his new division's battle training camp in Russia in July 1943. "Camp F" was sited in the division's rear area some twenty miles from Romny and about 160 kilometers to the west of Belgorod. Despite the fact that he already had some combat experience, the three weeks of re-training Sajer experienced before joining the "Großdeutschland" Division in the field exemplifies some of the realities of training for war in a wartime army. In many ways this follow-on training was a repetition of basic training, but in Russia in 1943 it was conducted with a new urgency by officers and NCOs who were all combat-experienced.

Days that began at sunrise, lengthy and exhausting sessions of physical training, seemingly unending forced marches in full battle order, live-firing exercises and exercises while actually under fire, little food and time to eat it, and the constant risk of injury all characterized this period. These activities were also being conducted in the blazing heat of the Russian summer. During the three weeks of Sajer's course, four men died in training accidents, twenty were injured to various extents, and two were nearly drowned. The training was organized in 36-hour periods of constant and intense activity, broken only by three 30-minute breaks for food. After the 36 hours there were eight hours' rest, but various alerts frequently interrupted these respites. One exercise

When soldiers rotated out of the front line to in-theater rest and recuperation centers, a shower with real soap was the first priority, closely followed by a proper meal and a long sleep! While there, their uniforms were thoroughly de-loused, cleaned and then issued back to them; although in many cases uniforms worn in combat were beyond reuse, when new or reconditioned uniforms would be issued.

involved an advance of almost one kilometer, crawling all the way, while the course officer, Hauptmann Fink, took up a position on a hillock designated as the "enemy position" and fired his pistol at any soldier who showed himself while moving to that objective. On another occasion one training section acted as the "enemy", firing just above Sajer's section as it moved through the cover provided by a swamp, raising themselves more than chin-deep from the water only at their peril. Agility exercises and various forms of confidence training also took their toll, including the requirement to negotiate a succession of old underground gas pipes, angled in places, where anyone who suffered from claustrophobia was forced to face his fears in the darkness. One anti-tank exercise involved the section digging a trench 150 meters long, half a meter wide, and almost one meter deep. Ordered to lie in the ditch, the soldiers then experienced four or five Pz.Kpfw.III tanks driving straight over them, the narrowly-dug earthworks protecting them and demonstrating the efficacy of a well-dug trench. In other anti-tank training, Sajer and his comrades learned how to use the Panzerfaust or magnetic mine to destroy a tank. In the latter case, the exercise called for the soldier to wait hidden in a foxhole until an approaching tank was no more than five meters away, then to leap out on to the vehicle, place the mine at the junction of turret and hull and leap off to the right side before the mine exploded.

The fears of failure, of dropping out through sheer exhaustion or of disobeying an order were ever present, any of which would inevitably result in disciplinary action. For serious cases of indiscipline Camp F had a punishment hut, the Hundehütte (literally "dog kennel"), into which soldiers were placed, manacled, and forced to remain seated on a wooden box during the eight-hour rest period between the main 36-hour training periods (from which they were still not exempted). Soup was brought to the Hundehütte in an eight-man tureen, from which the unfortunate and still-manacled soldiers under punishment had to lap their nourishment. Successive punishment periods spent confined in the Hundehütte could induce a coma in an already exhausted soldier and might ultimately prove fatal. Sajer related one story that circulated at the camp concerning a soldier called Knutke, who had apparently suffered six periods of this field punishment but still refused to obey the orders to train with his section. Finally, with Knutke already comatose, the unfortunate soldier was simply taken out and shot. With the disaster at Stalingrad having taken place just six months earlier and with the tide on the Eastern Front beginning to turn, the robust and often brutal nature of Sajer's three weeks at Camp F was specifically designed to ready these soldiers for the sort of fighting they were shortly to experience. This training regime was based upon the army's experience of four years of non-stop war, but especially of the bitter and unrelenting conflict on the Eastern Front. In simple terms, the old military adage "train hard, fight easy" was most apposite for the German army in 1943.

At the end of the training period at the battle camp these new members of the "Großdeutschland" Division re-dedicated them-selves to Germany and Adolf Hitler at a suitably formal oath-taking ceremony conducted in front of all the officers and instructors, and, before leaving Camp F to join the division, the trained soldiers were given two days of complete rest. Meanwhile, immediately after the re-affirmation parade for Sajer and his comrades, "[Hauptmann] Fink produced a glass of excellent wine for each of us, and lifted his own glass with ours, to a chorus of 'Sieg Heils.' Then he walked through our ranks, shaking each of us by the hand, thanking us, and declaring himself equally pleased with us and with himself. He said that he felt well satisfied that he was sending a good group of soldiers to the division … It seems scarcely credible that [despite the daily torments, trials and tribulations to which he had subjected us] by the time we left we all nourished a certain admiration for the Herr Hauptmann. Everyone, in fact, dreamed of someday becoming an officer of the same stripe."[19]

Sajer's comments were not particularly surprising, and in professional armies throughout the world it has ever been thus. The effectiveness of the training carried out to prepare the German soldier for war was indicated succinctly by Professor Sir Michael Howard, a distinguished historian and World War II combat veteran, in an article written in 1978 highlighting the differences between the Anglo-US and German troops: "Until a very late stage of the war the commanders of British and American ground forces knew all too well that, in a confrontation with German troops on anything approaching equal terms, their own men were likely to be soundly defeated. They were better than we were: that cannot be stressed too often. Every allied (*sic*) soldier involved in fighting the Germans knew that this was so."[20]

# 10. Rest and Recuperation in Peace and War

Although the army was frequently engaged in prolonged periods of intense fighting, there were many times when reductions of operational tempo provided an opportunity for individuals or complete units to be withdrawn to rest areas, where the troops could recuperate before returning to combat. This morale-building activity was essential to the general efficiency and combat effectiveness of the army, and complemented the equally important system of home leave for individuals in Germany that continued throughout the war. In peacetime, well-regulated and subsidized soldiers' clubs (Soldatenheim) provided short-term accommodation, a canteen, a bar and restaurant facilities, with regular programs of entertainment that ranged from film shows, professional entertainers and formal social events to in-house amateur revues and private parties. Clearly a place for the soldier to relax away from the barracks when off-duty, these clubs also enjoyed a discreet degree of military supervision that could forestall the troops coming into conflict with the civilian population or police as a consequence of misbehaving in other bars and clubs. As well as being associated primarily with the local garrison, the Soldatenheim was also used by non-garrison soldiers on leave in the local area and while in transit between assignments. When much of the army moved beyond Germany after 1938, similar facilities were established in many of the towns and cities of the newly occupied territories.

Once the army was at war there was a requirement to provide suitable rest and recreation facilities in-theater for the many thousands of troops who could not proceed on leave but who nevertheless needed a break from the front line. Each army established one or more rest and recuperation camps within its rear area. These camps were often quite extensive and routinely provided the soldiers with basic home comforts such as proper beds, tables and chairs, as well as access to a field post office, a military field library (Feldbücherei) and a canteen where they could purchase beer, cigarettes and everyday necessaries. The mobile Feldbücherei offered a range of novels and non-fiction books as well as newspapers and journals, while the army also provided a range of paperback books called Tornisterhefte, specifically designed to be carried in the soldier's pack (the Tornister). Medical personnel were available in the rest camp to treat minor ailments – such as skin inflammations, blisters and stomach disorders – that might not have justified attention while in

the front line, while also taking the opportunity to identify and deal with any more serious medical conditions that might previously have been overlooked or ignored. Meanwhile, an extensive program of recreational sport, leisure, film shows and other activities was usually available. Those staging these activities included groups of professional male and female entertainers of the Wehrmachtbühne (the organization that provided entertainment for the troops), who toured these rest camps to give performances to the troops. These Wehrmachtbühne shows included concerts and musicals, comedy and dance, as well as serious dramatic performances, all staged by a host of talented musicians, artistes and actors. However, on arriving at a rest camp directly from the front line, there were more immediate priorities for the soldiers. They entered a very necessary standard process that began with de-lousing and the removal of their uniforms for washing and sterilizing. The uniform might be re-issued, but it was often replaced in its entirety. De-lousing was followed by a hot shower – the soap provided often being the first that the soldier might have seen for many weeks, certainly on the Eastern Front – and then by a hot meal made wholly or in the main from fresh rations. This induction was followed by an initial medical assessment if required, and then by the opportunity to enjoy an uninterrupted sleep. After a further hot meal, the soldier's time at the camp was more or less his own to use as he wished. Nevertheless, during his time at the camp he might be required to attend one or more of the routine political or ideological briefings or presentations given by a NSFO (NS-Führungsoffizier) visiting from a division or higher headquarters. The written word was also an important part of the propaganda and motivating campaign conducted within the armed forces throughout the Nazi era, and as a matter of policy the high command ensured that quantities of suitably optimistic and inspiring official publications, pamphlets and news sheets were readily available at the army's rear area rest camps.

## 11. Duty and Discipline, Crime and Punishment

The ideological backdrop to the development of Hitler's army being National Socialism and the principles that flowed from it, the disciplinary code by which its officers and soldier were bound reflected an unprecedented degree of politicization, together with many of the moral and ideological concepts and norms propounded by the Nazis. Many Germans might not have realized the consequences at the time, but their enthusiastic acceptance of Hitler and Nazism resulted in the army having a disciplinary system that could remain robust but generally benign only as long as it enjoyed success on the battlefield – once it experienced its first significant defeats on the Eastern Front, notably that at Stalingrad in early 1943, military discipline became inextricably interwoven with fear, extremes of Nazi ideology, severe retribution

The camp cinema – such as this one pictured in 1935 – provided entertainment and a welcome opportunity to relax after a hard day's training, or period of front-line service.

Home leave was a vital factor affecting morale. By and large the army managed to maintain an effective leave system throughout the war – certainly until late-1944. Soldiers on leave from the front were often fêted in their home town or village, as with these two members of Panzergrenadier-division "Feldherrn-halle", veterans of the Eastern Front, pictured while on leave in Bavaria during May 1944.

and brutality against the civilian populations of occupied territories.

Prior to Operation *Barbarossa*, army discipline was firm, often physically robust, but generally fair, much as it had been in the German army for almost two centuries. Similarly, the army's conduct, including its treatment of civilians and enemy prisoners, was generally correct, although even as early as 1939 various instances of indiscipline were noted within the victorious forces in occupied Poland. There, one of the several divisions engaged, the 12th Infantry Division, reported seventeen courts-martial in September, 32 in October, and 63 in November, with a monthly average of 50 in December and in January 1940.

Some instances of the ill-treatment of prisoners-of-war occurred during the campaign against France and the Low Countries in 1940, including several cases of the summary execution of French prisoners by army units. On 7 June, a number of soldiers of the 53ème Régiment d'Infanterie Coloniale were shot, probably by troops of the 5th Panzer Division, following their

surrender after a spirited defense in the area of Airaines, near Le Quesnoy. Similar acts had also been perpetrated by soldiers of Rommel's 7th Panzer Division on 5 June against the defenders of Le Quesnoy. Rommel noted in his own account of the action that "any enemy troops were either wiped out or forced to withdraw"; at the same time he also provided the disparaging (but possibly somewhat contradictory in light of his first note) observation that "many of the prisoners taken were hopelessly drunk."[21]

Significantly perhaps, most of the French colonial soldiers involved in these particular engagements and their unfortunate aftermath were black. Soon afterwards, on 17 June, the 1st Panzer Division summarily executed seven surrendered soldiers of the 61ème Régiment Régional at Sainte-Suzanne, near Montbéliard, while on 19 June ten members of the 55ème Bataillon de Mitrailleurs were shot by the 6th Panzer Division troops at Dounoux, north of Epinal. Also in the Epinal area, soldiers of the 198th Infantry Division were responsible for shooting many members of the 146ème Régiment d'Infanterie de Forteresse at

Domptail on 20 June as soon as they surrendered. In some cases the army sought to justify or legitimize such summary executions by alleging that the French troops had used illegal ammunition (such as "dum-dum" bullets).[22]

However, the frustration of the German commanders and troops at having their advance delayed, together with the often significant casualties they had sustained at the hands of black African and North African soldiers deemed by the Nazis to be racially inferior were undoubtedly factors that provoked extreme reactions and excesses on the part of some German officers and soldiers during the campaign of 1940. Certainly, as the war progressed, such actions by army personnel were neither widespread nor comparable with the growing litany of atrocities carried out against civilians and prisoners-of-war by the SS. But the army could not escape its share of the blame for various contraventions of the Geneva Conventions on the battlefield, or which resulted from its involvement in some of the wider reprisals and punitive actions later taken against civilians and irregular forces behind the lines and in the German-occupied territories.

The army was operating alongside SS and SD units whose military agenda was wholeheartedly approved by the Nazi government and was driven by an ideology and policies that openly encouraged them to eliminate Jews and other racial and ethnically "undesirable" groups and to have no regard for the civilian population. It followed that much of the army was fully aware of what was going on from the very outset of the Polish campaign, and on 25 October 1939 Generalfeldmarschall von Brauchitsch issued a directive that specifically forbade "all criticism of the measures of the state leadership" (referring to the actions of the SS in the occupied territories) and called for "strict silence" and the "avoidance of all gossip and the spreading of rumours" concerning those matters.[23]

Almost from the start of the war, the army (but the general staff and the officer corps in particular) was presented with two options. By objecting to the excesses perpetrated by the Nazis it could follow its moral conscience and the norms of a civilized society, together with the best traditions of the former imperial German army. However, to do so would have directly contravened the oath of obedience to the Führer. Alternatively, the army could simply remain silent, passively condoning all that was being done in Germany's name. It chose the latter option, and thereafter the army as a whole became guilty by association and its acquiescence in the many war crimes committed between 1939 and 1945. This was despite the fact that many units which served only with the Afrikakorps, or managed to avoid extended service on the Eastern Front, were not directly involved in such crimes. The soldier's oath was looked upon as sacrosanct, and the power it imposed upon the German officer and soldier was absolute. At the same time it provided an all-too-convenient rationale for carrying out the unthinkable, for legitimizing the unconscionable and for justifying actions that were blatantly inhuman or illegal. During the war crimes trials at Nürnberg and elsewhere from 1945, the defendants regularly advanced the argument that a soldier was bound by his oath, and therefore obliged to obey the orders of his superior officer (who was ultimately Hitler himself) no matter what. The Allied war crimes tribunals routinely rejected this defense.

A well-documented "legalization of illegality" that exemplified the influence of National Socialist ideology upon the long-accepted rules of war was the Kommissarerlaß (commissar decree) issued by Hitler in March 1941. This pronouncement, made prior to the invasion of the Soviet Union, illustrated in a single directive the far-reaching significance of the soldier's oath and its potential implications for the army – it legitimized the summary execution of a whole category of Red Army soldiers wherever they were encountered and thus exposed the true nature of the sort of warfare that the Führer demanded of the Wehrmacht in Russia. The decree stated: "The war against Russia cannot be fought in knightly fashion. The struggle is one of ideologies and racial differences and will have to be waged with unprecedented, unmerciful, and unrelenting hardness. All officers will have to get rid of any old-fashioned ideas they may have. I realize that the necessity for conducting such warfare is beyond the comprehension of you generals, but I must insist that my orders be followed without complaint. The commissars hold views directly opposite to those of National Socialism. Hence these commissars must be eliminated. Any German soldier who breaks international law will be pardoned. Russia did not take part in the Hague Convention and, therefore, has no rights under it."[24]

This pronouncement and similar policy statements were reinforced by several propaganda publications issued in 1941 aimed primarily at the ordinary soldier in Russia. One such was *Mitteilungen für die Truppe* ("Information for the Troops"), an extract from which included the text: "Anyone who has ever looked at the face of a red commissar knows what the Bolsheviks are like ...We would be insulting the animals if we were to describe these men, who are mostly Jewish, as beasts. They are the embodiment of a satanic and insane hatred for the whole of noble humanity. The shape of these commissars reveals to us the rebellion of the Untermenschen against noble blood."[25]

Such inflammatory publications were widely circulated, their official status affording them an unjustified but undeniable authority and credibility.

Given such starkly expressed, politicized and clear direction, and the acquiescence of the high command, it was hardly surprising that *Barbarossa* became such a remorselessly brutal campaign and that the measures needed to maintain the discipline of the troops on the Eastern Front became increasingly severe and brutal. Perhaps the most telling indication of the increasing harshness of the military discipline in Hitler's army was provided by its comparison with that of the Kaiser's army during World War I. Between 1914 and 1918 the imperial German army executed 48 soldiers. However, between 1939 and 1945 the Germans executed somewhere between 13,000 and 15,000 men, including those executed summarily by officers and NCOs without formal

trial and by "flying courts-martial". In total, these executions roughly amounted to the equivalent of killing an entire infantry division.

The huge numbers of executions in Hitler's army were, however, less indicative of widespread crime than of the politicization of the military justice system, which resulted in offenses such as desertion and self-harming (to avoid military service) being categorized as treason and subversion, both of which offenses automatically attracted the death penalty. Withdrawal without orders, deserting one's post, sleeping while on sentry duty, cowardice, lateness for a duty, surrendering to the enemy, smoking during a partisan attack – these were but a few of the offenses for which soldiers were executed or received long prison sentences on the Eastern Front. Averaged out from September 1939 to April 1945, no fewer than 100 soldiers found guilty of subversion and 100 found guilty of desertion were executed each month of the war. During the final years of the war the Feldjägerkorps was created, whose units (Feldjägerkommando) were manned by army officers, NCOs and soldiers with considerable combat experience. The task of the Feldjägerkorps was primarily disciplinary and more specifically focused than that of the army Feldgendarmerie: its mandate included the apprehension of looters and deserters and pressing rear-area troops into combat units in times of operational crisis. However, the Feldjägerkorps was also authorized to conduct "flying courts-martial" and to dispense summary justice to offenders found guilty by that process.

In December 1939 there were 12,853 courts-martial, while in October 1944 there were 44,995; many of those found guilty of offenses but not sentenced to death were consigned to prisons and hard labor. Between August 1939 and mid-1944, some 23,124 soldiers received long prison sentences, 84,346 went to prison for more than one year, and 320,042 received less than one year in prison. Thousands of soldiers convicted of a whole range of lesser or essentially military offenses were dispatched to penal battalions where they could redeem themselves by their performance in combat – these units were regarded as expendable, and so a posting to one of them was virtually the same as a death sentence. In an effort to increase the wider disciplinary impact of an execution and link it to the old military concept of honor, at least sixteen men executed for desertion or self-inflicted wounds by the 12th Infantry Division between June 1941 and June 1943 were posthumously deprived of their civil rights as German citizens, which meant that their families could not claim their pensions. Similarly, during the later war years deserters were buried far from any military cemetery and without any military honors or recognition other than a sign showing their name, date of birth and date of death. The fear of reprisals against an offender's family was considerable; it prompted one deserter who managed to reach the Russian lines safely to shoot en route three German sentries who had seen him go, in order to prevent them reporting his defection.[26]

Summary justice without recourse to trial was officially authorized in February 1943 in an effort to stem desertions,

Military bands played an important part in boosting morale, entertaining the troops and the civilian population, as well as providing the martial music for most formal parades and military events. The army band shown here is performing in the Olympic Stadium in Berlin on 21 July 1940, during the interval of the final of that year's German football championship.

Whatever his arm or branch of the army, basic rifle and foot drill were core elements of every recruit's basic training. Here, a squad of young fortress engineer troops is on parade.

withdrawals and retreats by individuals or groups. Hitler directed: "every commanding officer and NCO, or in extraordinary situations every courageous man, will enforce the execution of orders, if necessary by the force of arms, and will immediately open fire in case of insubordination. This is not only his right but also his duty." Similarly, during that summer the commander of the 18th Panzer Division "expect[ed] officers to make ruthless use of all means at their disposal against men who bring about occurrences of panic and who leave their comrades in the lurch and, if necessary, not to refrain from using their weapons." In one case where seven soldiers attempted to desert, four were shot by officers before they reached the Russian positions, while another instance involved five soldiers being executed out of hand while attempting to desert. Even the army's élite formations were not exempt from desertions, and during the last six months of 1942 the "Großdeutschland" Division sentenced seven men to death and charged a further eleven with desertion, all of whom were probably executed. Significantly perhaps, all these examples related to the Eastern Front, where soldiers were well aware both of the appalling nature of the Soviet Union's prison camps, and that the Red Army soldiers routinely shot many of the German soldiers they captured; but they were still prepared to risk all this in order to escape from what they believed was an intolerably oppressive and fearful existence in their German army units as the campaign in Soviet Russia entered its second year.[27]

It is notable that few of the disciplinary issues afflicting the army in Russia affected its troops in the West or in North Africa. By and large, the ideological impact of National Socialism and consequently the "crusading" nature of the army's war against the Soviet Union made that particular campaign immeasurably more bitter, brutal and politically charged than that in the west. Whereas offenses by military personnel against the civilian population in Poland and Russia, as well as in the Balkans – including murder, rape, looting and torture – went largely unpunished, offenses judged potentially prejudicial to military effectiveness in combat were treated with the utmost severity. Conversely, in the western theater of operations, soldiers who committed murder, rape, ill-treatment, robbery or any other criminal acts against the civilian population – other than as official acts of reprisal – were punished appropriately. In that theater of operations their actions were seen to bring the army into disrepute, and even to precipitate further acts of indiscipline if not dealt with rigorously. Nevertheless, the sheer scale of the conflict on the Eastern Front meant that, once started, it soon became the principal campaign fought by Hitler's army during the war and, as such, it was largely this campaign that provided the touchstone by which history has judged the army's effectiveness in combat, together with its conduct and discipline.

A major consequence of National Socialism and Hitler's invasion of the Soviet Union was to legalize both explicitly and by default the army's subsequent actions against the civilian populations in the territories it occupied. When the tide of war turned against Germany, such officially approved behavior by

German troops undoubtedly influenced the Soviet Union's own conduct of the war and was used to justify the often extreme actions of its own forces. During the Red Army's final campaign into Germany in 1945 excesses were carried out against the German civilian population that were blatantly punitive and the fulfilment of an unconstrained desire for revenge. For many Germans this behavior also confirmed all too vividly that Hitler's 1941 warnings of the growing communist threat and an impending Asiatic onslaught that sought to annihilate the German people and their culture had been all too accurate. Indeed, the mass rapes carried out in Germany by the Red Army in 1945 were to all intents and purposes officially condoned by the Soviet high command and were systematically conducted on a scale virtually unrivalled in the history of warfare. But for the German officers and soldiers of Hitler's army, the great tragedy of Operation *Barbarossa* and all that followed was that it dishonored its officers and soldiers through their misplaced obligation to remain true to their soldier's oath no matter what, and to obey the orders and directives of a Führer whose political ambitions and National Socialist ideology bore little resemblance to the principles, martial traditions and concept of honor that had previously stood the Prussian and German army in such good stead.

# 12. Honor, Loyalty and Conscience

Rolf Werner Völker had been called up for military service with the 104th Infantry Rifle Regiment on 5 October 1940, and he remembered with considerable pride the day in late October on which he became fully a member of the German army and the regiment, when he and those who had joined with him took the soldier's oath on a parade before the assembled battalion (1,000 strong) at the regiment's barracks in Darmstadt. "After three weeks drill and 'spit and polish' without a break, confined to barracks," he recalled, "we were all waiting for the day when we would be sworn in. On the appointed day, the battalion was on the parade ground in a hollow square formation, with the band at the top. Four recruits brought the regimental flag on parade, with their 'oath finger' on the flag. Then we all took the oath: 'I swear by Almighty God …' We were all very excited and moved. We all felt that it was a good thing that we were doing and that we were sure that we would never break our oath."[28]

The significance of the soldier's oath, whether administered to a general or to a new recruit, was very great indeed, and the solemn ceremony during which it was taken was in many respects quasi-religious, as well as recalling many aspects of oath-taking ceremonies conducted in the Kaiser's army. "Meine Ehre heißt Treue" ("My Honor is Loyalty") was the motto of the Waffen-SS, and such sentiments also reflected the army's attitude to the obligation of absolute loyalty and obedience contained in the oath, by which the soldier would "swear by God this sacred oath that I

shall render unconditional obedience to Adolf Hitler, the Führer of the German Reich and its people, supreme commander of the armed forces, and that I shall at all times be prepared, as a brave soldier, to give my life for this oath." Because it was bound inextricably to much older perceptions of military culture and honor, this oath presented an insurmountable obstacle (although perhaps for some it was a more convenient obstacle) to many members of the armed forces who might otherwise have taken action against Hitler once they finally identified the disastrous path along which he was leading Germany. But as Hitler had astutely bundled together his position as head of state and supreme commander with his personal embodiment of Germany and its people, he circumvented any opposition by most officers – such action would not merely strike against an individual but against the state itself. This would be nothing short of treason, which was clearly dishonorable and therefore unthinkable for a German officer. Nevertheless, a number of army officers and others eventually dared to think the unthinkable, as the situation on the Eastern Front deteriorated, the Afrikakorps was defeated in North Africa, and the United States entered the war against Germany, making a second front in the west inevitable. In July 1944, these men finally acted in contravention of their oath and contrary to all that the traditional military code of honor, loyalty and obedience required of them. What later became known as the "July Plot" was a defining moment of the war, but nowhere was its subsequent impact greater than upon the army, the general staff and the OKH.

Although two earlier attempts on Hitler's life (both of which had failed either due to bad luck or to ineptitude) had been carried out by army officers in 1943, by far the most significant and ill-fated attack was that carried out on 20 July 1944, when Oberstleutnant Claus Schenk, Graf (or "Count") von Stauffenberg, secreted a powerful time-bomb in his briefcase and brought it to a conference at the Führer's headquarters, the Wolfsschanze (or "Wolf's Lair"), at Rastenburg, East Prussia. This plot involved many senior Wehrmacht officers, diplomats and former political leaders, who planned not only Hitler's death but also to remove the Nazi government and negotiate a separate armistice with the Allies. The bomb duly exploded with devastating effect, killing some and wounding many. However, another officer attending the conference had by chance moved the briefcase further under the conference table shortly after von Stauffenberg left the meeting to "make a telephone call". As a result, the heavy table shielded Hitler from serious injury, and although shocked he was able to walk from the devastated conference room more or less unaided. Hitler's rage was terrible, as was the retribution subsequently inflicted by the Gestapo upon the conspirators, their associates, their families, and many others. The failure of the 20 July plot was a catastrophe for the German resistance movement and for many other minor opposition groups within Germany, irrespective of whether or not they had known about, or had been actively involved with, the assassination attempt. Many of these men were senior officers, including several commanders who had already distinguished themselves fighting for the Third Reich, although they also included lieutenants as well as generals and field marshals. The purge of army officers in the aftermath of the July Plot was particularly far-reaching. Predictably, Heinrich Himmler headed the subsequent investigation, and the Gestapo and the SS carried out this task ruthlessly and with considerable enthusiasm. About 200 alleged conspirators were arrested, tried and executed. Others (including von Stauffenberg) were summarily shot within hours of the event and so were spared the horrors and humiliations of the show trials, torture and barbaric forms of execution suffered by the majority of those subsequently arrested by the Gestapo. Several conspirators chose to commit suicide. Even General-feldmarschall Rommel, who had criticized Hitler but had actually opposed the assassination attempt, was ordered by the Führer to commit suicide, this being the price of safeguarding his family by avoiding the ignominy of a public show trial and inevitable execution. Quite apart from the many executed or imprisoned for their involvement or alleged involvement, the bombing also provided the Nazi leadership with an excuse to dismiss some other senior military personnel. One such was General Kurt Zeitzler, who was replaced as chief of the general staff by Guderian on 22 July. Guderian immediately denounced the conspirators for having preferred to take the road of disgrace rather than "the road of duty and honor."[29]

The embodiment of Hitler as the very essence of the German nation and of the Fatherland itself by the words of the soldier's oath, introduced for all military personnel in August 1934, was also of particular significance in light of the July Plot. If von Stauffenberg had succeeded in killing Hitler, it might have been argued that many of those officers and soldiers who were already uneasy about the direction in which Hitler was taking Germany, but who nevertheless felt bound absolutely by their oath to the Führer, could have felt themselves released from this very specific and personalized oath by Hitler's death. Certainly any obligation to follow Nazi policies thereafter would have been tenuous, so that more expansive forms of patriotism and duty to the Fatherland could quite quickly have supplanted the residual authority of the remaining Nazi leadership. It was also true from the moment of its inception that the very specific wording and personalization of the oath meant that nothing less than the death of Hitler could realistically have enabled the aims and aspirations of the anti-Nazi German opposition groups within the Wehrmacht, despite the intolerable crisis of conscience, duty and honor that this produced for very many right-thinking army officers.

In July 1944, Siegfried Knappe was attending pre-general-staff training at the Panzer training school at Bergen-Hohne, north of Celle, when the assassination attempt was carried out. Knappe was very aware of the mood of the time and the shock waves that reverberated through the army in general and among the general staff officers in particular. "The next several days were total chaos throughout Germany. Nobody knew what would happen next or who would be arrested next. The government and the army were both in a constant state of uproar; there were endless rumours, whispered names, and some announcements on the radio. It was at least a week before the situation showed any signs of abating … Immediately, everybody in the general staff was under suspicion. The Nazi party leaders were particularly vocal and vicious in accusing general staff officers … We thought that at best the General Staff College would be abandoned, we would all be reassigned to the front, and there would be no more general staff. Many of our instructors at the General Staff College were concerned for their lives, because they knew some of the convicted general staff officers. It was a very critical time for general staff officers, especially those who had been in general staff work for some time. An officer could be arrested [simply] because a friend or relative had been arrested … even some junior officers were arrested because they had been on an implicated general's staff for some time and had become confidants of the general … Everybody knew someone who had been arrested. And with the Nazis' system of holding a man's family responsible if he did something wrong, even families were arrested and sent to concentration camps."[30]

The 20 July bombing was a defining moment in Hitler's relationship with the army. Although he had already neutralized the OKH, the July plot served to destroy any residual trust in the army and its officer corps that he might still have entertained. Himmler's widespread purge of the officer corps in the aftermath of the July plot literally tore the heart out of the army and removed many men who might well have contributed positively to the German recovery in the post-war years. At the same time, the assassination attempt enabled the SS greatly to extend its power throughout Germany, including over the Volkssturm and the Ersatzheer, when Hitler appointed Himmler as its new commander on 21 July. The increased influence of the SS was exemplified by an edict issued on 23 July, when the Wehrmacht was ordered to abandon its traditional forms of saluting – henceforth all personnel were required to use only the Nazi salute. In fact, Hitler's reaction and the punishments meted out in the immediate aftermath of the plot were by no means entirely contrary to the mood of public opinion at the time. Very many officers and soldiers, together with much of the German civilian population, condemned the conspirators as traitors to the Fatherland, who had betrayed the officer corps, and these people expressed their genuine shock and shame that Germans could have carried out such an attack against the nation's leadership. Such had been the impact of National Socialism and its propaganda during the previous decade, reinforced by its perversion of the army's traditional concepts of duty, honor and loyalty and the pervasive effects of the soldier's oath. However, notwithstanding the turmoil that followed the failed assassination attempt, its direct effects upon the operational effectiveness and fighting spirit of the army proved to be hardly discernible in practice, and the determination and vigor with which Operation

*Wacht am Rhein* was prosecuted in the Ardennes just five months later illustrates this.

Irrespective of any assessment of its more immediate effects, the July plot and its aftermath still provided the most striking evidence of the dichotomies of loyalty and honor, conscience and moral judgment, duty and patriotism within the army by 1944, while at the same time demonstrating the inner strength and professionalism of an army that continued to operate effectively despite the ensuing disruption within its leadership and while assailed on all sides by its enemies on the battlefield. For better or worse, this ability to fight on in the face of such adversity was testament to martial qualities that undoubtedly existed well before the decade during which Hitler's army existed – a decade that was in many respects a bizarre historical aberration when set against the wider history of Prussian and German militarism during the preceding three hundred years. When the commander of the 53rd Army Corps, General Graf von Rothkirch, was captured by units of the US 3rd Army late in the campaign in northwest Europe, he was asked why the Wehrmacht still continued to fight against all the odds, with defeat inevitable. The German officer's reply was predictable and would no doubt have been proferred by virtually every army officer: "We are under the orders of the High Command, and must carry on as soldiers in spite of personal beliefs and opinions."[31]

His words explain in large part, not only the timeless determination and motivation of the German fighting man, but also the distaste and condemnation with which the officers who had conspired to kill Hitler on 20 July 1944 were viewed by many members of the officer corps, even though a considerable number of those same officers had by then also lost faith in the Führer as the nation's war leader and supreme commander – their traditional perceptions of honor, loyalty and duty all too easily sublimating any such reservations.

Claus Schenk, Graf von Stauffenberg (1907–1944)

Shortly after the abortive 20 July 1944 bomb plot, Hitler and Mussolini view the devastated conference room at the Führer's "Wolf's Lair" HQ at Rastenburg, East Prussia.

An extract from a 1936 publication showing a selection of the flags, badges and uniforms in use by the army at that time.

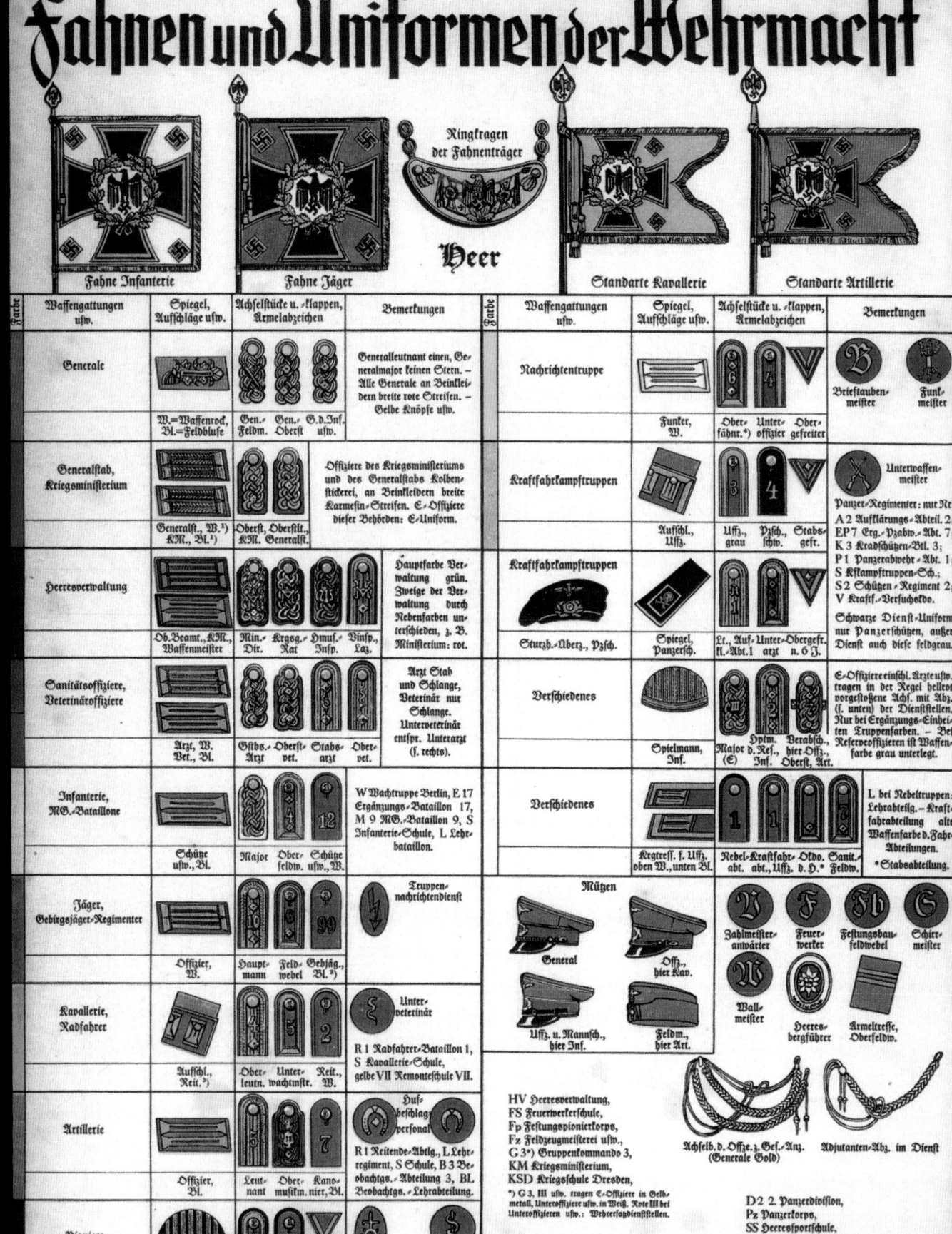

# PART VI
# Dressed to Kill: Uniforms and Equipment

The subject of German army uniforms worn during the 1933–45 period is vast and in many ways reflects the wider military heritage and traditions of that nation and its armed forces. Indeed, very many specialized and highly detailed references already deal in considerable detail with every aspect of the uniform and equipment of the German fighting man during the Nazi era. Although a traditional dress uniform (Gesellschaft-anzug), two versions of the walking-out uniform (Ausgehanzug and Meldeanzug), the parade uniform (Paradeanzug), and the service dress uniform (Dienstanzug) when not worn as a field uniform existed and were worn when appropriate, the following paragraphs deal mainly with the army's field service uniforms and personal equipment, being intended primarily to provide the reader with a clear overall picture of the appearance of the men of Hitler's army once they went to war.

## 1. Service and Field Service Uniforms

In 1939, most of the soldiers wore a field-grey (Feldgrau) service uniform jacket and trousers, with appropriate rank insignia and colored distinctions indicating the wearer's arm or branch of the army. These arm-of-service color distinctions were called "Waffenfarbe." Prior to 1935 the service uniform was all-wool, and during that year a wool-rayon mix was introduced, the percentage of rayon in the material later rising from five percent, to 25 percent, and eventually to 65 percent. The wool quality was also reduced as the war progressed, and by 1943 about 90 percent of the woollen cloth material was produced from poor-quality wool waste. Officers' uniforms were usually purchased rather than issued, and the material and tailoring were therefore generally of superior quality. Officers (together with cavalrymen and some senior NCOs) usually wore riding breeches and boots rather than the trousers worn with jackboots or ankle boots and anklets by the ordinary soldiers.

Formidable numbers of badges, awards, cuff titles, gorgets, rank insignia and so on were introduced from 1935 and throughout the war for wear on the service uniform, but only three distinguishing items were to be found on virtually every service uniform. The first of these was the national emblem (Hochheitzeichen), the eagle and swastika, worn on the right breast just above the pocket. Next, almost all officers and soldiers wore a "double-bar" pattern collar insignia of braid or lace (Doppellitze or Litzen) woven in silver wire, aluminium thread or grey cotton. This was set upon a patch (Kragenpatten) of

**Left:** As an austerity measure, a modified field service uniform was introduced in 1943, together with the ubiquitous Einheitsfeldmütze (field cap). The M 43 uniform shown is that of an Unteroffizier (here an Oberfeldwebel) of a pioneer unit. Note the poorer quality of the material, the lack of "boxed" pockets, and the mass-produced cloth collar lace and breast eagle, as well as the Iron Cross First Class and the silver-level wound badge.

**Right:** Another M 43 uniform, this time that of an infantryman of the Panzergrenadier-division "Gross-deutschland". The low-quality machined embroidery of the collar lace and chest eagle is very clear. However, the division cuff-title is still being worn.

material in the appropriate Waffenfarbe color, with the center of each bar sometimes highlighted in the same color. The only major exceptions to this were the Panzer personnel, who wore a deaths-head collar insignia, and the general officers, who wore a bright red collar patch with a stylized gold-wire oak-leaf insignia. The jacket shoulder straps were piped or had an underlay in the same Waffenfarbe color.*

As the war continued, shortages of material and the need to cut costs affected the uniform design more and more. Originally, the ordinary soldier's single-breasted jacket had four box-pleated patch pockets; plain patch pockets were introduced in 1943. At that stage the dark blue-green material from which the jacket collar and shoulder straps were made was also abandoned, with plain field-grey material used thereafter. The design of the field uniform trousers was also changed so that they had a fitted belt instead of being supported by braces. This very practical change was prompted by operational experience, which had demonstrated the need to be able to remove the trousers in the field without also having to remove the jacket and basic fighting equipment such as gas-mask container, belt and ammunition pouches. A year later, the Model 1944 field blouse was introduced, being very much an austerity measure and of poor quality, also lacking style when compared with its predecessors. It

\* Further details of the Waffenfarbe system and examples of some of the principal color distinctions are in Appendix 3.

closely resembled the British army's battledress blouse, being styled with a waistband instead of a jacket skirt and therefore losing the lower patch pockets of the earlier jacket types. The national insignia and collar patches were also manufactured in an austerity version using dull grey thread. Various styles and colors of shirt were issued in woollen, cotton and cotton drill materials during the war. A fairly impractical white collarless shirt was used pre-war and until late 1939 by all troops except armored crewmen (who were issued with grey shirts). After the Polish campaign the white shirt was superseded by field-grey and mouse-grey collar-attached shirts, and a tan cotton-drill variant was also produced later for use in North Africa.

It had originally been intended that all armored vehicle crewmen should wear a specially designed black uniform, comprising a short double-breasted jacket and black trousers. This black uniform was generally retained by tank crewmen throughout the war, while the crews of tank destroyers and assault guns were subsequently issued with uniforms of a similar design in grey, and a reed-green denim uniform was also widely used by tank crewmen. In North Africa, a lightweight cotton field service uniform was provided to the soldiers of the Afrikakorps and other Wehrmacht personnel.

Various camouflage-pattern uniform items were also issued to many army personnel, including reversible over-jackets, camouflaged on one side and white (for winter warfare) on the other. The principal camouflage patterns adopted by the army were usually described as "green splinter pattern" and "tan water pattern", while "mouse grey" and white materials were also used. Despite the increasing use of such uniforms as the war progressed, their use by the army was relatively limited compared with their proliferation within the Waffen-SS, where extensive ranges of over-jackets, overalls, helmet covers and other clothing items were produced in at least six different seasonally-based camouflage color schemes (plus white).

The army lost its original airborne battalion when the Fallschirm-Infanterie-Bataillon was absorbed into the Luftwaffe's airborne forces on 1 January 1939, but for completeness, and because virtually all of the Luftwaffe Fallschirmjäger were eventually used as élite ground forces under OKH operational command, it should also be mentioned that the Wehrmacht's paratroopers were issued with a purpose-designed jump smock variously manufactured in blue-grey, olive-green, tan or (from spring 1940) army-pattern camouflage materials.

In addition to all these variations and modifications of the basic service or field uniform there was also a whole range of special-to-purpose uniforms and protective clothing items. These included items designed specifically for mountain troops, a denim material fatigue uniform, sports clothing, winter clothing, motorcyclists' waterproofs, wind-proofs, anoraks, overalls, parade uniforms for certain élite or guard units, several styles of greatcoat (always a part of the German soldier's uniform), leather coats, fur-lined coats and so on.

but they were lighter and incorporated various production improvements. Until 1940 a black-white-red tricolor shield appeared on the right side, with a Wehrmacht eagle and swastika insignia on the left side. The shield was discontinued from 1940, followed later by the Wehrmacht insignia, and by 1943 these helmet badges were rarely seen. Helmets were painted field-grey in manufacture, had two small ventilation holes, and were fitted with an adjustable padded leather liner and black leather chinstrap. Various camouflage schemes were routinely applied to the helmets once issued, including white-washing them for winter warfare and painting the helmet with matt sand-colored paint for service in North Africa, where a coating of loose sand was often applied over the paint before it dried. Among the very many official and improvised aids to concealment regularly adopted were mud, paint, camouflage-pattern cloth covers, netting, wire mesh, canvas or leather straps, and circular bands cut from tire inner-tube rubber, by which means foliage could be secured to the helmet.

A special steel helmet was also produced for the (Luftwaffe) parachute troops. This compact and practical helmet had a distinctive shape, with a rim that was only slightly flared in order to reduce the risk of neck injury on landing and to minimize the possibility of the helmet snagging on the parachute rigging lines or harness. The helmet's anti-shock lining was of padded rubber, and a special chin harness was provided for use when parachuting, as well as a replacement chinstrap for normal field use.

## 2. Steel Helmets

The steel helmet (Stahlhelm), with its distinctive "coalscuttle" shape, was undoubtedly the single item of uniform most readily identified with the German soldier. While the old Model 1916 pattern continued in use by some home and civil defense organizations and Volkssturm units until 1945, it was successively superseded throughout the Feldheer by the Model 1935 and Model 1943. Both these helmets were essentially the same shape,

## 3. Other Headdress

Many types of headdress were worn. First, there was the field service cap (Feldmütze), manufactured in field-grey material in Model 1938 and Model 1942 versions. The Feldmütze had no peak and could be folded flat, while its sides could also be pulled down to protect the wearer's face and ears in bad weather. The Model 1938 displayed the national emblem, the national cockade (Reichskokarde) and an inverted "V-shaped" piping in Waffen-

The Model 1935 steel helmet (Stahlhelm). Use of the helmet decals had been generally discontinued by 1943.

**Above:** A group of soldiers in North Africa, showing the variety of headdress in use by the Deutsches Afrikakorps (DAK) during its campaign 1941–3.

**Above right:** The black uniform introduced for Panzer crewmen in 1935, which included the distinctive Schutzmütze beret with its well-padded rubber lining.

**Center right:** The officer's uniform cap, the Schirmmütze. Note the silver cap cords worn by officers below general officer rank.

**Bottom right:** The field cap worn by the ordinary soldier, the 1938-pattern Feldmütze. Note the yellow inverted chevron of Waffenfarbe, which was replaced by a two-button fastening on the Model 1942 Feldmütze.

farbe. The 1942 version omitted the inverted "V-shaped" piping and substituted in its place two small grey metal buttons that could be used to secure the unfolded cap sides under the chin. In several respects the Feldmütze closely resembled the sort of British army field service cap (or "side" or "forage" cap) used by that army since the late nineteenth century, while the closest US equivalent was the military "overseas cap." The officer's field service cap was either the pre-1942 version, which was a peaked cap manufactured without any shaping stiffening or, from 1 April 1942, a better-quality version of the soldier's Model 1938 Feldmütze. Apart from the quality of manufacture, the types of national insignia and other embellishments applied to these caps identified the wearer as an officer. Both types of the Offizier-feldmütze continued in use right through to 1945.

From 11 June 1943 a new field cap (the Einheitsfeldmütze) came into service. This was a very practical and popular soft-manufacture cap, with fold-down sides that could be buttoned under the chin and a prominent semi-stiff cloth-covered peak. It was loosely based on the pattern of field cap used by the Afrikakorps and was produced in a variety of colors, most commonly field-grey. Apart from the steel helmet, the Einheitsfeldmütze was probably the most widely used item of German military headdress. As with the Offizierfeldmütze, the officer's version of the Einheitsfeldmütze displayed additional piping and insignia of a better quality than that of the ordinary soldier's issue cap. The various field service caps were clearly the most practical forms of headdress for operational use, but a uniform cap (Schirmmütze) also existed, and this was worn by all ranks with service dress uniform, for parades, and when walking out off-duty. This was a well-made, traditionally-styled and suitably smart peaked cap. Its basic design was the same for all ranks and included a field-grey top, a dark blue-green cap band, and a shiny black peak. Apart from the overall quality of manufacture, a whole range of differing qualities and styles of national insignia, piping, cap cords (or chinstrap), buttons, and

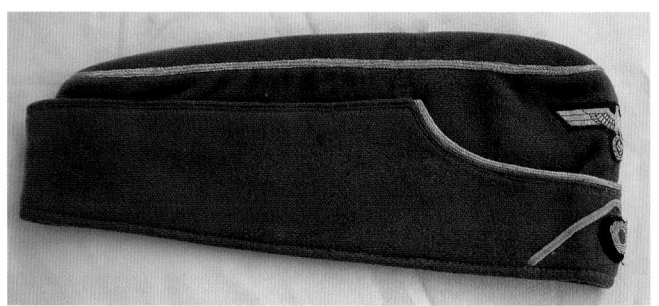

Waffenfarbe identified the wearer as a general, an officer, an NCO or an ordinary soldier, as well as indicating the branch and arm of service or unit for personnel other than generals. The Schirmmütze was also worn by officers and some senior NCOs in the field, but very often with the stiffening spring used to shape the crown removed in order to soften it and enable the wearer to customize its appearance.

Other soft head-dress included the Gebirgsjäger cap (the Bergmütze), which was similar to the Einheitsfeldmütze but also bore an Edelweiß badge on the left side. There was also the distinctive padded black beret used by the tank crewmen (the Schutzmütze) until 1940, when these berets were superseded by a black version of the Model 1938 Feldmütze. Various fur caps (Pelz Mützen), hoods, toques and other fur-trimmed items were eventually issued from 1942 for use during the Russian winter. Finally, tropical sun helmets were issued to the Afrikakorps from 1941, but these were soon discarded in favor of more practical headdress both for work and for combat.

## 4. Boots and Shoes

Foremost amongst the several types of footwear issued to the army was the familiar black leather jackboot, or marching boot (Marschstiefel). These boots were steel-tipped and well-studded. Other boots and shoes included leather riding boots (Reitstiefel), mountain-climbing boots (Bergschuhe) for the Gebirgsjäger, sports or running shoes (Laufschuhe), lace-up leather service shoes and ankle boots (Schnürschuhe), as well as leather sandals and canvas-and-leather lace-up tropical service boots (Leinen und leder Tropenschnürschuhe) for use primarily in North Africa. The experience gained during the first Russian winter eventually prompted the issue of felt over-boots, felt and leather boots, and other special-purpose footwear. An extensive range of gaiters, canvas spats or leggings, anklets, waterproof leggings and puttees was intended to supplement all but the jackboot and the riding boot, the issue of these additional protective items being dependent upon the operational theater and the role of the wearer. Special rubber-soled lace-up boots for the Luftwaffe's parachute troops were also produced, and these were widely worn by these soldiers while employed as ordinary infantrymen.

## 5. Individual Personal Equipment

The soldier's basic equipment consisted of an arrangement of straps, pouches and containers that carried all he needed to fight and survive on the battlefield – ammunition, food, water, shelter and protection against a chemical gas attack. In addition to this basic equipment, a cowhide or canvas pack Model 39 (the Tornister) was provided to carry less vital items, while a green canvas rucksack was also issued as an alternative to the Model 39

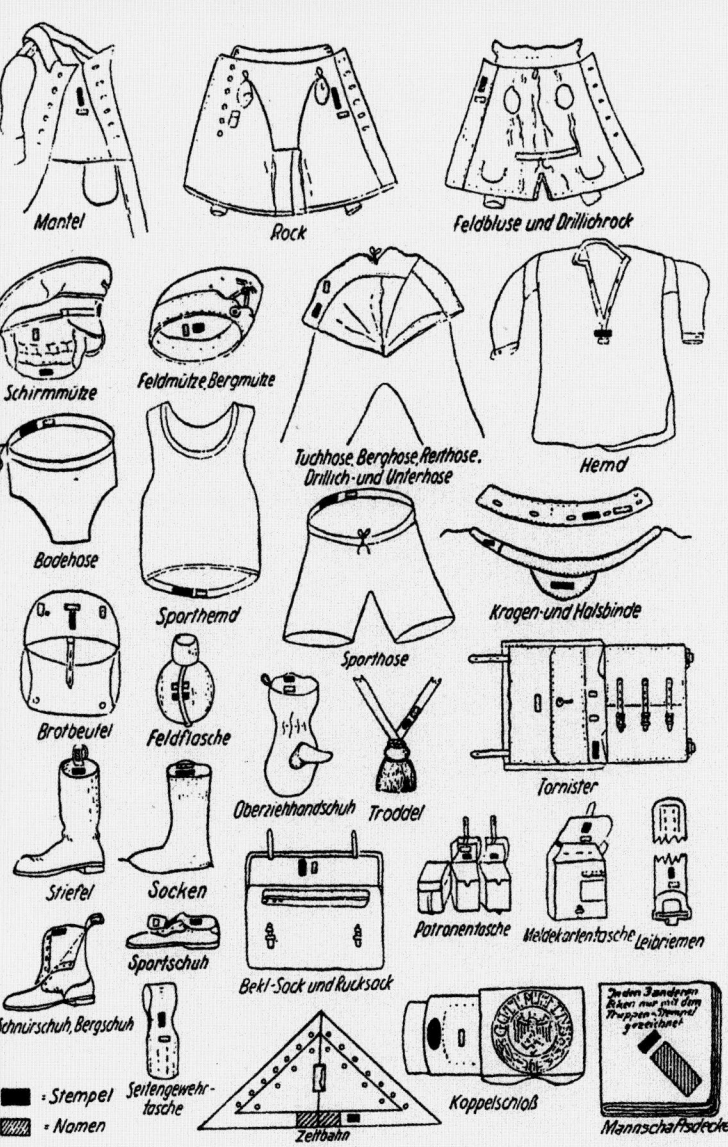

Two Unteroffiziere seen with German film director Hans Albers at the première of his film *Die Abenteur des Baron von Münchhausen*. Note the infantry assault badge and wound badges, as well as the marksmanship lanyards worn by both men. The M 36 pattern uniforms and enlisted men's belt buckles are also shown to advantage.

haversack contained a day's rations, eating utensils, washing kit, and the Feldmütze or Einheitsfeldmütze when not worn. The Brotbeutel was usually attached to the belt by web or leather straps, although a detachable shoulder strap was also provided for it. Two D-rings were fitted to the Brotbeutel, and the water bottle was attached to the right-hand ring. The army water bottle (Feldflasche) held a little over a liter and was manufactured either of aluminium or enamelled steel, those produced for the European operational theater being covered with grey, green or brown felt. In 1941 some water bottles covered with dark-brown plastic-impregnated wood were also issued. A cup (Trinkbecher) was fitted to the top of the water bottle, made of black-painted aluminium, but later of field-grey painted steel, while a small black plastic cup version also existed. The cup was secured to the water bottle by a leather or web strap, and a separate shoulder strap was also provided for the combined cup and water bottle.

The gas mask in its ribbed metal carrying canister (Gasmaske und Tragbüchse) was usually slung on a strap over the right shoulder to rest on the left hip. An additional short strap clipped this grey-green painted canister on to the main belt. These canisters were routinely painted tan for use in North Africa. Dispatch riders and drivers of horse-drawn and motor vehicles sometimes wore the canister slung across the chest for comfort and ease of access. On 11 December 1942 the OKH directed that the anti-gas cape (Gasplane) pouch should also be carried attached to the gas-mask canister strap. The types of gas mask in most common use were the GM 30 and GM 38. Both had two eye-pieces and filter canisters that attached directly to the mask, creating a "snout" appearance. These masks provided good protection against most of the war gases of the time and some other chemically generated gases. A filter canister to protect specifically against carbon monoxide gas was also available. There were special optical masks, a cavalry variant, combat engineer masks, a mask for patients with head wounds, three gas-mask variants for horses, and one for dogs.

An entrenching tool (Kleiner Spaten), a short-handled, flat-bladed shovel, was suspended from the belt on the left hip by the two straps of a black leather or olive-colored canvas carrier. Two more straps on the carrier enabled the bayonet and scabbard to be secured to the entrenching tool, so that the two items did not bump against each other. In due course a folding entrenching tool was produced, and this was used extensively by the Afrikakorps from 1942. When not attached to the Kleiner Spaten the bayonet and scabbard were suspended from the belt on the left hip in a black leather or olive webbing frog.

In order to offset the weight taken on the belt and to provide additional carrying capacity, a set of adjustable black leather "Y" straps were provided as braces (Koppeltraggestell). These straps attached to the center of the belt at the back, behind the ammunition pouches. Two D-rings set on the shoulders enabled the rucksack or the Model 39 pack to be clipped directly on to them. The mess kit (Kochgeschirr) and Zeltbahn (a rolled-up

pack or in addition to it. The basic equipment was supplemented by other items to match the specific function, specialization or rank of the soldier. The troops in North Africa were provided with canvas webbing belts, straps and other items in place of many of the leather equipment components used elsewhere.

The foundation item of the soldier's basic equipment was a black leather belt, fitted with a grey-green painted steel or alloy buckle plate. This plate bore the words "Gott mit uns" (literally, "God [is] with us") embossed on it and set above an embossed Wehrmacht eagle badge that was itself set within a wreath of oak leaves. Next, viewed from the front, two sets of three ammunition pouches (Patronentaschen) were fitted on the left and right sides of the belt adjacent to the buckle plate. These pouches were of leather, usually dyed black, and each pouch held two five-round clips of rifle ammunition. Non-infantry troops were sometimes issued a single set of the three pouches. Soldiers armed with the MP 38 or MP 40 submachine gun were usually issued two sets of the three-compartment ammunition pouches for these weapons, each compartment holding one magazine of 32 rounds. These MP 38 and MP 40 pouches were produced both in leather and in olive-green canvas versions, the latter often fitted with leather straps.

Food and water were usually carried attached to the belt on the right hip. An olive-colored canvas bread bag (Brotbeutel) or small

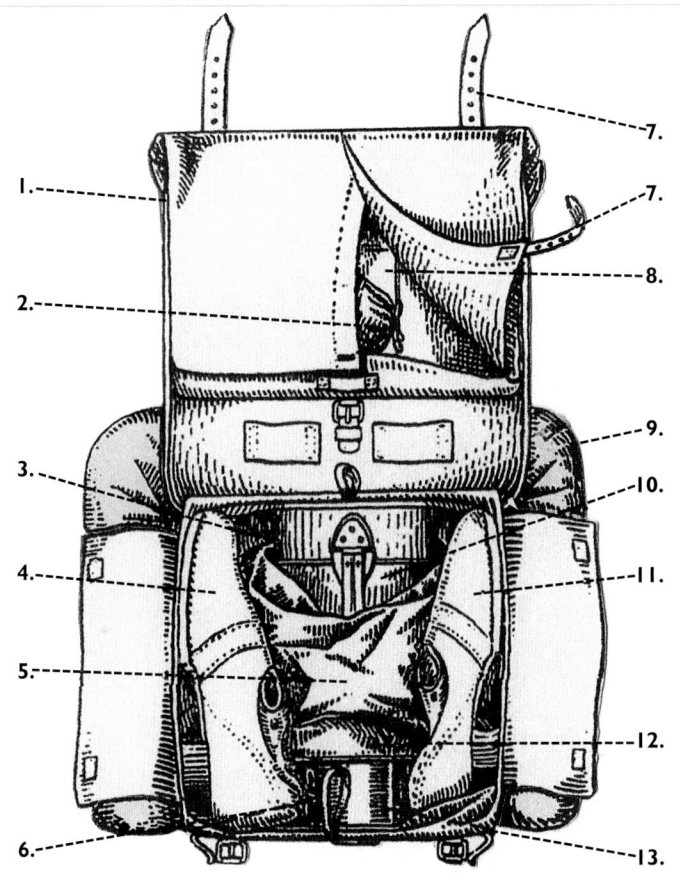

1. Cowhide flap (fur on other side) with pockets inside for small items.
2. Washing items, tent poles and pegs. (Wasch~ und Rüh~zeug)
**3.** Socks (Strümpfe)
**4.** Shoe (right) (r. Schuh)
**5.** Cover for messing and cooking kit (Kochgeschirrhülle)
**6.** Tent rope (Zeltleine)
**7.** Leather straps and reinforcing patches
**8.** Underwear, small towel (Leibwäsche, handtuch)
**9.** Rolled greatcoat (mantelrolle) or blanket
**10.** Metal messing and cooking kit (Kochgeschirr)
**11.** Shoe (left) (lk. Schuh)
**12.** Weapon cleaning kit (Gewehr~reinigungsgerät)
**13.** Canned meat ration (Fleischkonserve)

options for these various load-carrying straps and harnesses provided considerable flexibility and practicality, which in turn meant that from 1939 to 1945, many different equipment configurations were adopted.

The mess kit was manufactured of aluminium (later enamelled steel) and consisted of a deep pot with a lid or cover that could be used as a frying pan or a plate. The two parts were secured together by a black leather or olive-colored web strap and were attached either to the Sturmgepäck harness or to the left-hand D-ring on the Brotbeutel (next to the water bottle), behind the right hip. Alternatively, it could be fastened directly on to the belt on the left hip. The soldier's metal knife, fork and spoon was usually a stainless steel set that clipped together, and at least one version included a can opener and an opener for crown-type bottle caps. Another more lightweight type incorporated a riveted swivelling spoon and fork combination made of aluminium. Individual fuel-tablet stoves (Esbitkocher) made of zinc-coated steel were routinely issued, the fuel tablets being produced in four blocks each of five tablets and carried wrapped in paper inside the folded stove. These stoves were lightweight and proved to be most efficient cookers. (Virtually identical hexamine-fuelled stoves are still in use by some armies more than six decades after the end of the war.)

The Zeltbahn, as mentioned above, was a triangular shelter quarter that served either as part of a four-man tent or as a weatherproof poncho. The material was made of tightly-woven

**Far left:** The Tornister was the standard army rucksack and was designed to contain all of the essential clothing, equipment and personal effects required by the soldier on campaign.

**Left:** These three Gebirgsjäger (mountain infantry) soldiers have just arrived at a small alpine town in the Salzburg area at the start of their Christmas leave. Their Tornisters are fully packed, complete with blanket rolls, and they also have additional kit with them in canvas knapsacks, but no personal weapons; all of which might indicate that they have just completed a training course and are due posting to a new unit straight after their leave. Note the Gebirgsjäger metal Edelweiß badge on the side of the cap of the right-hand soldier, also the special climbing boots and short puttees issued to these mountain troops.

shelter tent quarter) could be attached to the rear of the "Y" straps. A triangular harness was also provided, which enabled the mess kit and the shelter tent quarter to be carried rolled together with a small canvas bag and attached below the mess tins. The canvas bag could hold one day's iron ration (tinned meat and biscuit), the rifle cleaning kit and a section of tent rope. This equipment arrangement was termed the Sturmgepäck (assault pack). In the infantry, use of the "Y" straps and Sturmgepäck was seen more in dismounted infantry units and some truck-mounted motorized infantry units, as the Panzergrenadiers usually relied upon the belt alone to support all that they required, leaving their other equipment in their armored vehicles. The combinations and

The Zeltbahn – a multi-purpose weatherproof cape and shelter half or tent – could be used in several ways. It could be configured as a poncho cape for troops operating on foot, as well as for horse riders and bicycle riders. It could also be set up as a shelter or one-man tent, or combined with others to provide a basic shelter tent for two or more soldiers. Additionally, the Zeltbahn could be packed with light foliage or other suitable material and secured with cord to form an emergency buoyancy aid for crossing a water obstacle, or for carrying an individual's weapons and equipment across a water obstacle.

water-resistant cotton drill, colored in the army "splinter-pattern" camouflage (light on one side and dark on the other). Limited numbers of tan-color Zeltbahn were also produced for the Afrikakorps.

The canvas rucksack (if issued) was provided to carry additional clothing, "make and mend" materials, miscellaneous personal items and suchlike. Meanwhile, the fur-covered cowhide Model 39 Tornister pack and a later canvas version of the Model 39 pack were part of the soldier's standard field marching order and therefore contained specific items that were usually packed in accordance with a laid-down plan. For an infantryman the Tornister typically contained underwear, a towel, mess kit, a pair of service shoes or ankle boots, rifle-cleaning kit, tinned-meat ration, a length of tent rope, socks, washing kit, tent-pole sections and tent pegs, while either a blanket or the soldier's greatcoat could be rolled about the top and sides of the pack. Where the Sturmgepäck harness was used, the requisite items were removed from the pack and attached to that harness instead, with the Tornister being left behind on transport or centralized elsewhere to be reclaimed later.

## 6. Special Equipment

Items issued or carried by individual officers and soldiers routinely included goggles to protect against dust, sand and sun, canvas hand-grenade bags (Handgranaten sack), canvas or cotton ammunition bandoliers, and leather map or dispatch cases (Meldekartentasche). These distinctive map cases were used primarily by dispatch riders and by commanders at company, platoon and section level. They had a number of internal compartments and external pockets to accommodate maps, documents, notebooks, map-reading instruments, map-measures, rulers, pens and pencils. Although they were widely available early in the war, the issue of these map cases was restricted from 1943 in order to conserve leather. Officers and NCOs in tactical command appointments usually carried a sighting compass (Marschkompaß), which enabled bearings to be taken and transferred between the ground and a map, and it also allowed troops to follow a bearing by day or night. The compass scale was graduated in 6,400 mils (rather than the 360-degree graduation still used in some other armies of the time, including the British army and the US Army) and had luminous highlighting to facilitate its use at night. A very practical military flashlight was widely issued. With a rectangular metal body and a single forward-facing lens and reflector dish, it had a switch enabling the light shown to be changed from white to red, green or blue as desired. A short leather strap with a button hole was fitted to the rear of the flashlight, which could thus be attached to any suitable coat pocket, leaving the hands free and with the light shining forward.

Every item of clothing and personal equipment issued to the soldier had to be clearly marked with his name and a stamped number or other identifying mark. Specific regulations laid down the precise place and manner in which every such item was to be marked.

## 7. Personal Documents

Three personal or individual documents were retained, carried or worn by the soldier at different stages of his service, depending upon his military status at any given time. These were the Wehrpaß, the Soldbuch, and the Erkennungsmarke. At the time of his first medical and physical examination, a service record book (Wehrpaß) was created and issued to every man on his acceptance for military service. This was a passport-sized booklet in which was recorded the man's pre-military service in the national labor service (Reichsarbeitsdienst, the RAD), his liability for military service, any military activities carried out and his official military status. While not engaged in active service the Wehrpaß was retained by the individual soldier, but once he reported for active duty it was handed into the unit for retention by his company headquarters. At that stage he was issued with a

The Wehrpaß was issued to every soldier accepted for military service but not on active duty.

The Soldbuch recorded all details of a soldier's active duty service and once on such service it was carried by him at all times, also serving as his official means of identification.

paybook (Soldbuch) in lieu, which he then retained both as an official means of identification and as a comprehensive record of his active duty service until released from that service or medically discharged. The Soldbuch contained the soldier's name, rank, service number, photograph and signature. It also recorded details of the units in which he served, the clothing and equipment issued to him, inoculations, medical treatment and hospitalizations, promotions, pay grades and rates, incidental payments made to him by other units while (for example) on detached service, leave taken, awards and decorations received, and any other pertinent personal or military information. The soldier was required to carry the Soldbuch with him at all times. In addition to the military service number issued to him at the time the Wehrpaß was created, the Soldbuch also detailed the inscription and number shown on the soldier's identity disc.

The identity disc (Erkennungsmarke) was made in two parts, with a horizontal dividing perforated "break-line" across the center. The lower half was punched with a single hole and the upper half with two holes, through which the neck cord passed. Identical information was shown on each half. The text shown on the Erkennungsmarke varied, but as a minimum it normally included the soldier's personal number, his blood group and unit designation; it might also show his pay-book number and the roll number of the relevant Ersatzheer replacement unit. Although the disc bore the designation of his original unit, any replacement disc would bear the designation of the issuing unit at that time. The soldier was required to wear the identity disc at all times when on active service. If he was killed, the disc was broken in two, the lower half being returned to the military administrative authorities in Germany while the other half (attached to the neck cord) was buried with the soldier's body. Subsequently, his Wehrpaß would be given to the next-of-kin, while his Soldbuch and all of his other military records were filed at his unit's home station (Wehrersatzdienststelle). Eventually, a report on his death and burial, together with the lower part of the Erkennungsmarke and a description of the location of the grave, were to be sent to the Wehrmacht information office for war casualties and prisoners-of-war.

# 8. Insignia, Decorations and Awards

Apart from the Waffenfarbe system of identifying an individual's branch or arm of service, the many items of insignia worn by the German army officer or soldier also included national emblems, unit identifiers, badges of rank, awards for merit, and badges for professional skills and specializations. There were also various battle insignia and campaign shields, cuff titles, decorations and medals, and special items of insignia, such as the gorgets (Ringkragen) issued to Feldgendarmerie, Feldjägerkorps and other duty personnel. In addition to the several standard items of insignia that appeared on virtually every uniform, the

proliferation of other Wehrmacht insignia produced between 1933 and 1945 reflected the long-standing German tradition of recognizing individual military achievement or campaign service by uniform distinctions. It also matched the burgeoning use of such martial symbols by the Nazi paramilitary and party organizations ever since the early days of the National Socialist party. Indeed, Hitler – himself a former soldier and holder of the Iron Cross 1st Class – knew very well the positive impact that such visible indicators of unit identity and individual merit or heroism invariably had upon military morale. Although the issue or award of individual insignia items was extensive, the criteria governing these awards were formally laid down and strictly applied. Consequently, they had enormous resonance and value in the German army and engendered huge pride in those who

The Erkennungsmarke identity disc was an important means of identifying and recording casualties. Although most commonly produced in zinc, aluminium or gunmetal, some were also manufactured from other metals and materials. As indicated in the pictures, the quality and layout of the manufacture and stamping varied considerably.

The spread-eagle national emblem (Hoheitzeichen) appeared on virtually every army uniform jacket and cap; as did the Reichskokarde headdress insignia – both with and without surrounding oak leaves. Both badges appeared in a variety of qualities and types, and embroidered or solid metal, depending upon the rank of the wearer, the time of issue, and (in the case of the Hoheitzeichen) whether it was for use on the cap or on the jacket.

Gebirgsjäger

Bergführer

Jäger

Ski-Jäger

Feldgendarmerie (officers)

Feldgendarmerie (other ranks)

received them, while at the same time spurring others to emulate their achievements.

### The National Emblem and Cockade

The two items worn by all troops were the national emblem and the cockade. The national emblem (Hoheitszeichen) consisted of the German eagle with outstretched wings clutching a wreath, within which was a swastika (Hakenkreuz). This badge appeared on the right breast of most army jackets, while a smaller version was worn on all army cloth headdress. The cockade (Reichskokarde) worn on all army caps was in the form of a roundel, which showed the national colors of Germany – black, white (or silver) and red at the center. It was surrounded by a wreath of oak leaves on the uniform cap, the Panzer troops' black beret, and the pre-1942 version of the officer's field service cap; on all other headdress the cockade appeared without the surrounding oak leaves. A slightly modified version of the Hoheitszeichen worn on the upper left arm instead of on the right breast indicated that the wearer was a member of the Waffen-SS or SS, rather of an army or other Wehrmacht unit, as did the deaths-head (Totenkopf) worn by SS personnel below the Hoheitszeichen on cloth headdress in place of the Reichskokarde.

### Badges of Rank

Badges of rank were worn on the left upper arm for ranks from private soldier (Schutze) to corporal (Obergefreiter) and on shoulder straps from junior sergeant (Unteroffizier) through to colonel (Oberst). General officer rank was indicated on the shoulder straps and the collar. In addition to these conventional badges of rank, a range of cotton-patch rank insignia for use primarily on camouflage uniforms was introduced on 22 August 1942, this insignia also being worn on some fatigue uniforms and specialist clothing. These black-green-yellow patches were available for ranks from Unteroffizier to Generalfeldmarschall and were worn on the left upper arm.*

### Trade, Specialist and Proficiency Badges

Specialist personnel below the rank of Lieutenant who had achieved the required level of proficiency in their trade or specialization wore an arm badge to indicate this. With only a couple of exceptions, these were worn on the lower left or right arm, and most were manufactured with a yellow symbol worked on to a dark blue-green, field-grey or tan backing disc or oval. Other colors were also used for the piping or symbol featured on the badge; for example, the appropriate Waffenfarbe color of the employing unit or formation was used for the "lightning flash" symbol shown on the "blitz" badge worn by its attached signals personnel.** A further category of badge indicated a soldier's particular proficiency, skill or type of unit. These included the

\* The army's badges of rank are illustrated in Appendix 4.
\*\* The principal trade and specialist badges are illustrated in Appendix 6.

Two examples of the Reichskokarde cap insignia.

The Sniper Badge (Scharfschützenabzeichen) was awarded in three classes: left to right, First Class for 60 kills (edged with gold cord), Second Class for 40 kills (edged with silver cord); and Third Class (for 20 kills).

Tank destruction badge (Panzervernichtungsabzeichen) in silver.

Left to right:

Tank battle badge (Panzerkampf-abzeichen)

Infantry assault badge (Infanterie-Sturmabzeichen)

General assault badge (Allgemeines Sturmabzeichen)

Army anti-aircraft battle badge (Heeres-Flakkampfabzeichen.

Edelweiß arm badge of the Gebirgsjäger, the oak-leaves arm badge of Jäger troops, the skis-and-oak-leaves arm badge of the Ski-Jäger, the military police (Feldgendarmerie) eagle-swastika-and-oak-leaves arm badge, and the enamelled metal Edelweiß badge awarded to qualified mountain guides (Bergführer).

### Battle Insignia

While medals were awarded for particular acts of heroism or service in combat conditions, there was also a range of badges awarded automatically to soldiers who had achieved certain laid-down levels of competence in specific aspects of combat. While not by definition medals or decorations, these badges or battle insignia were none the less highly prized by their recipients, as they provided tangible evidence of an individual's courage and success in action against the enemy, while also being less susceptible to the vagaries and politicization of the centralized system governing the awarding of conventional medals and decorations. One such battle insignia was the badge awarded to snipers, which was awarded in three classes: the 3rd for twenty kills, the 2nd (silver edged) for 40 kills, and the 1st (gold edged) for 60 kills. The basic badge (Scharfschützenabzeichen) was instituted on 20 August 1944 and featured a black eagle's head above green oak leaves, being worn on the lower right arm. A number of these badges were certainly awarded, but few if any Scharfschützenabzeichen were actually worn – and never in the combat zone in any case – as its discovery if captured would almost invariably have resulted in the wearer suffering extreme mistreatment and summary execution.

There was also a badge for the single-handed destruction of a tank (Sonderabzeichen für das niederkämpfen von Panzerkampfwagen durch Einzelkämpfer, also known as the "Panzervernichtungsabzeichen"). This was instituted on 9 March 1942 (but backdated to 22 June 1941 to include the early part of *Barbarossa*). The badge was worn on the upper right arm and consisted of a strip of silver or gold cloth on which was mounted a bronze metal tank symbol. Each silver award represented one enemy tank destroyed single-handed, while the gold award

indicated five tanks destroyed. The two grades of this badge could be combined as necessary to indicate higher numbers of tanks destroyed.

A similar concept applied to the badge awarded for downing low-flying aircraft (Tieffliegervernichtungsabzeichen). This badge was instituted late in the war on 12 January 1945 and so might not have actually been awarded before its end. Again, the silver award was for each aircraft shot down using small-arms fire, with gold awards for five aircraft shot down. The badge was to be worn on the upper right arm and consisted of a small black (gold for the gold award) aircraft symbol set on a strip of silver or gold cloth.

Other battle badges were instituted at various stages of the war, all being manufactured in metal and worn on the left breast. They included the infantry assault badge (Infanterie-Sturmabzeichen, 20 December 1939), the general assault badge (Allgemeines Sturmabzeichen, 1 June 1940), the tank battle badge (Panzer-kampfabzeichen, 20 December 1939), the army anti-aircraft battle badge (Heeres-Flakkampfabzeichen, 18 July 1941) and the anti-partisan battle badge (Bandenkampfabzeichen, 30 January 1944). A close-combat clasp (Nahkampfspange, 25 November 1942) was also available and was worn on the upper right breast.*

Another badge related directly to combat service was the wound badge (Verwundetenabzeichen) instituted on 1 September 1939 and awarded in black, silver or gold to reflect the number or the severity of the wounds sustained. A special "one off" wound badge was also produced and awarded to those injured in the abortive bomb attack against Hitler on 20 July 1944.

### Campaign Shields and Cuff Titles

A number of die-struck metal campaign shields were awarded for the appropriate length of service in a given campaign or between specified dates. Additional qualifying criteria applied to some shields. They were worn on the upper left arm and included

---

* The qualifying standards for the various grades of these battle insignia badges are shown in Appendix 6, together with illustrations of the insignia.

Left to right: Cholm campaign shield; Kuban campaign shield; and silver- and gold-level Wound badges (Verwundeten-abzeichen).

Left to right: campaign shields for Demjansk; Narvik; the Crimea (Krim); and an Anti-partisan battle badge (Bandenkampf-abzeichen).

AFRIKA (North Africa) cuff title.

KRETA (Crete) cuff title.

Close combat clasp (Nahkampfspange).

awards recognizing service in the Kuban bridgehead campaign (fought from 1 February 1943), the Demjansk Pocket campaign (8 February to 21 April 1942), the Cholm Pocket campaign (21 January to 5 May 1942), the Crimean peninsula campaign (21 September 1941 to 4 July 1942), and the Narvik campaign (9 April to 9 June 1940).

Some additional official and unofficial campaign shields were also designed, with a number produced as proofs and a few subsequently being manufactured and issued. Among these were shields to recognize combat in the Balkans during 1944 and 1945, at the defense of Dunkirk (1944–5), in Lapland during 1945, in Warsaw (1 August to 2 October 1944) and during the defense of Lorient (1944–5).

Embroidered cloth cuff titles in various colors and versions were also awarded to indicate campaign service. These were worn on the lower left arm and included cuff titles for "AFRIKA", "KRETA" (the airborne invasion and battle for Crete in 1941), "KURLAND"(the defense of Courland in 1945) and "METZ 1944" (for the defense of Metz from 27 July to 25 September 1944). These campaign cuff titles were awards in their own right, and so were not the same as the many types of unit cuff titles issued to (for example) members of the Afrikakorps, those serving in the "Großdeutschland" regiment and division,

During the war, numbers of Iron Crosses awarded during World War I were still to be seen worn by senior officers and older army veterans.

The Knight's Cross of the Iron Cross was worn as a neck decoration, and was a higher level of award than the Iron Cross First Class of World War II.

Feldpost personnel, troops serving in the propaganda companies, staff members of the Führer's headquarters and so on.

**Medals and Decorations**
Many army officers and soldiers had received decorations and awards for service during World War I, and these were worn by many senior officers, reserve officers and long-serving soldiers during the 1933–45 period. During World War II the principal medals and decorations instituted and awarded to army personnel were the Iron Cross 1939 in 2nd and 1st Class, 1939 bars to the 1914 Iron Cross 1st or 2nd Class, the War Service Cross in First and Second Class, and the Knight's Cross of the Iron Cross, which was awarded in five grades or levels. The Knight's Cross was worn as a neck decoration suspended from its black, white and red ribbon, with different clasps indicating the level of the award. The Iron Cross 1st Class was worn on the left breast without a ribbon, while the ribbon of the Iron Cross 2nd Class was usually worn in the button hole but without the actual medal. The German Cross was worn on the right side of the service uniform jacket and was awarded in gold or silver for bravery in action and distinguished leadership.

**Below:** Colonel Villamo of the Finnish army presents medals to German troops fighting on the northern front, 13 July 1942. Finland became an ally of Germany in anticipation of the German attack on Russia in June 1941.

A contemporary chart showing the decorations available to the army at that time and the correct placement of various insignia and awards on the service dress uniform (US Official, 1945).

The above figures illustrate the manner of wearing some of the more common German decorations and awards. The officer at left wears two tank destruction badges; the one at right has Crimea shield on arm, assault and wound badges on breast, 1939 bar to 1914 Iron Cross in buttonhole and the Knight's Cross on ribbon at neck.

Knight's Cross of the Iron Cross.
With gold oak leaves, swords and diamonds.

Knight's Cross of the Iron Cross.
With oak leaves, swords and diamonds.

Knight's Cross of the Iron Cross.
With oak leaves and swords.

Knight's Cross of the Iron Cross.
With oak leaves.

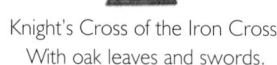

Knight's Cross of the Iron Cross.

The German Cross.
Gold or silver.

Iron Cross 1st Class.
Worn without ribbon.

Iron Cross 2nd Class.
Usually ribbon only worn.

1939 Bar to 1914 Iron Cross.
Worn in buttonhole.

War Service Cross with Swords.
Silver or bronze.

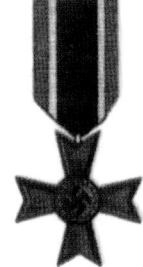

War Service Cross without Swords.
Silver or bronze.

Honor Roll Clasp.
Worn in buttonhole.

1. Iron Cross, 1914
2. Iron Cross, 1939
3. War Service Cross
4. War Service Medal

5. Eastern Winter Campaign, 1941–42
6. War Cross of Honor (Front Line Fighter)
7. Party Service Badge (24 Years)
8. Party Service Badge (15 Years)

9. Party Service Badge (10 Years)
10. German Social Service
11. Medal for Length of Military Service
12. Entry into Austria

13. Entry into Sudenland
14. Westwall Service, 1939–40
15. Memel Ribbon
16. Olympic Games Medal

17. German Mother's Cross
18. Fireman's Ribbon
19. Baltic Cross (1919–20 Freikorps Service)
20. A.R.P. Medal

21. Prussian War Effort Cross
22. Prussian Life-Saving Medal
23. Silesian Eagle (1919–20 Fighting vs Poland)
24. Baden Military Service Cross

25. Bavarian Military Service Cross
26. King Ludwig Cross
27. Prince Regent Luitpold Medal
28. Bavarian Military Service Badge

29. Bavarian Medal of Valor
30. Wurttemberg Military Service Cross
31. Austrian Medal of Valour
32. Karl Troop Cross

33. Austrian War Service Medal
34. Tirol Service Medal
35. Hamburg Hansa War Cross
36. Bremen Hansa War Cross

37. Lubeck Hansa War Cross
38. Bulgarian Medal of Valor
39. Bulgarian War Service Medal
40. Hungarian War Service (Horthy)

41. Croatian Medal of Valor
42. Slovakian Medal of Valor
43. Africa Ribbon
44. Italian Medal of Valor

45. Italian Service Medal
46. Finnish Service Medal
47. Finnish Liberation Cross I Class
48. Finnish Liberation Cross II Class

49. Finnish Liberation Cross III Class
50. Spanish Military Medal of Valor
51. Spanish Red Military Service Cross
52. Spanish White Military Service Cross

53. Spanish Campaign Medal
54. Spanish Wound Medal
55. Spanish Survivors Ribbon
56. Spanish Communist Ribbon

57. Rumanian Medal of Valor and Loyalty
58. Rumanian Faithful Service Cross (Peace)
59. Rumanian Medal of Valor
60. Rumanian Order of the Crown (Post 1932)

61. Rumanian Order of the Crown (Pre-1932)
62. Rumanian Faithful Service Cross (War)
63. Rumanian Medical Service Cross
64. Rumanian Faithful Service Medal (War)
65. Rumanian Anti-Communist Service

66. Cross of Queen Marie of Rumania
67. Rumanian Fliers' Medal of Valor
68. Rumanian Fliers' Order of Valor
69. Star of Rumania

70. Bronze Cross of Valor and Service*
71. Silver Cross of Valor and Service*
72. Gold Cross of Valor and Service*
*For Eastern Volunteers

A representative selection of medal ribbons for those medals awarded by Germany and its Axis allies for valour and service 1939-45. German military personnel awarded these medals were authorized to wear the appropriate ribbon above the left breast pocket of the service uniform (US Official, 1945).

# PART VII
# Combat Arms

## 1. The Division

Germany's ground war was waged on a vast scale, spanning virtually all of Europe while also spilling into North Africa. Although many smaller army units attracted fame or notoriety during the war and often performed deeds out of all proportion to their actual size, the army's basic tactical unit or formation for all operational planning was the division, and during the Blitzkrieg campaigns in the west in 1940 no fewer than 141 German

A comprehensive range of flags and pennants was available to designate army levels of command, headquarters and specific units and those shown are but a few examples. A combination of shape, design, annotated numbers and letters, and colors enabled the speedy identification of any unit or formation displaying one of these tactical flags. Where used on vehicles, these flags were usually painted on to a metal base, or directly on to the body or mudguard (fender) of an armored vehicle.

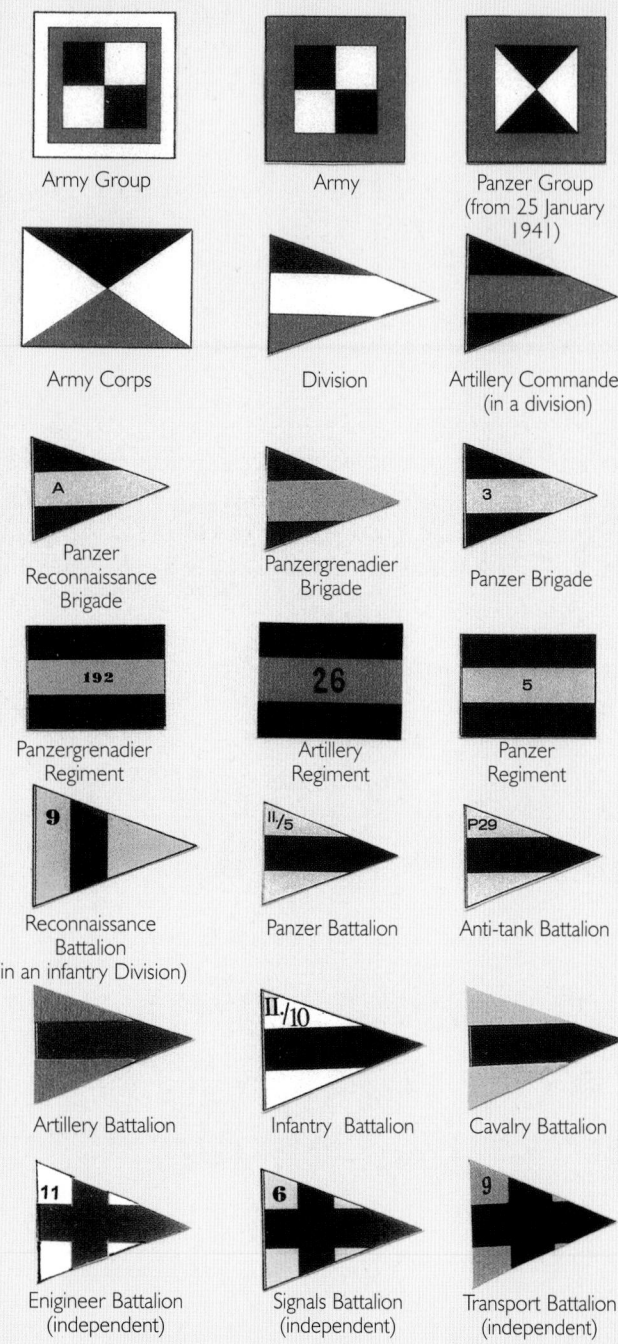

Army Group

Army

Panzer Group (from 25 January 1941)

Army Corps

Division

Artillery Commander (in a division)

Panzer Reconnaissance Brigade

Panzergrenadier Brigade

Panzer Brigade

Panzergrenadier Regiment

Artillery Regiment

Panzer Regiment

Reconnaissance Battalion (in an infantry Division)

Panzer Battalion

Anti-tank Battalion

Artillery Battalion

Infantry Battalion

Cavalry Battalion

Enigineer Battalion (independent)

Signals Battalion (independent)

Transport Battalion (independent)

divisions were engaged. These all-arms groupings of infantry, armor, artillery and service support units were self-contained, had direct control over all of the capabilities needed to carry out most offensive or defensive operations, and were sufficiently flexible to change their structure by taking under command additional combat units as necessary. Although divisions were based broadly upon a standard organizational and doctrinal framework for command and control and logistic support, most differed one from another to varying extents. This was particularly true of the type and number of combat units subordinated to them and the types of equipment operated by these units. While most army divisions fell generally into the category of infantry, infantry (motorized), Panzergrenadier, Panzer or Volksgrenadier, there were also mountain infantry (Gebirgsjäger), light (Jäger), and airborne or parachute infantry (Fallschirmjäger) divisions (although the Fallschirmjäger were actually Luftwaffe rather than army troops).

In addition to these better-known types of division, some other special-to-role divisions also existed at various stages of the war. Twenty-two Luftwaffe field divisions (Luftwaffenfelddivisionen) were formed in late 1942, primarily from Luftwaffe ground-based personnel and anti-aircraft gunners considered to be less-needed in their original role by that stage of the war. Several of these divisions, each of which was initially about 10,000 men strong, suffered heavily on the Eastern Front, and in 1943 they were fully absorbed into the army. Subsequently they were either disbanded or reorganized as standard "Type 1944" infantry divisions. Assault divisions (Sturmdivisionen) were reduced-strength infantry divisions but with enhanced firepower. Reserve divisions (Reservedivisionen) were nominally "infantry", but in practice usually consisted of a reserve-based unit and staff organization charged with managing the drafting of personnel for various active army units, although for part of the war a number of these divisions also fulfilled a conventional combat role. At the outbreak of the war a cavalry division existed to administer the army's cavalry units, but only one cavalry brigade in East Prussia maintained an operational cavalry capability above unit level. Although the army's artillery was generally organized on a regimental rather than a divisional basis, the 18th Artillery Division was formed on the Eastern Front in October 1943. The success of this division led to the creation of the 310th, 311th and 312th Artillery Divisions on the Eastern Front, while a 309th Artillery Division was also formed and served in northwest Europe.

A number of other specialist army organizations were also categorized as "divisions". Air-defense divisions (Flakdivisionen) provided ground-based air-defense and were usually manned by Luftwaffe personnel. Line-of-communication security divisions (Sicherungsdivisionen) were largely manned by older and less well-armed troops and had the task of securing the rear areas on the Eastern Front, but they were also occasionally required to engage in full-scale combat. Field training divisions (Feldausbildungsdivisionen) controlled numbers of field training regiments and supervised their training activities in the rear areas of the Eastern Front. Meanwhile, replacement division staff and special administrative division staff oversaw the induction of manpower replacements within Germany and the activities of certain Germany-based homeland and fortress (Festung) defense units (Landesschützen). Lastly, coastal defense and frontier guard (Grenzwacht) divisions dealt with the defense and security of the German littoral and borders. Such divisions were generally not organized on standard lines but according the the specific needs of their roles.

By 1945 the total number of army divisions had increased almost three-fold. However, these increases had often been achieved at the expense of the strength of the divisions themselves – certainly, the physical existence of a divisional headquarters in 1945 did not necessarily mean that it controlled manpower or combat power equivalent to that of the divisions which went to war in 1939.

**Army Divisions in 1939 and 1945**

| Division | | |
|---|---|---|
| Infantry | 86 | 176 |
| Motorized (later Panzergrenadier) | 4 | 13 |
| Jäger (or light infantry) | 2 | 11 |
| Mountain (Gebirgsdivision) | 3 | 10 |
| Airlanding | 1 | 1 |
| Volksgrenadier | 0 | 50 |
| Panzer | 6 | 31 |
| Light Armored (later Panzer) | 4 | 0 |
| Cavalry (one brigade existed in 1939) | 0 | 2 |
| Coastal Defense | 0 | 4 |
| Security | 0 | 6 |
| Total | 106 | 304 |

In addition to the army divisions, the OKH could also call upon the Luftwaffe's parachute or airborne divisions (Fallschirm-divisionen), subject to the approval of the Luftwaffe high command, and after 1941 these divisions served primarily as infantry. Only one Fallschirmdivision existed in 1939, and the number had increased to ten by 1945, with an eleventh division planned but never formed. In the meantime, subject to the agreement of the principal SS operational office (SS-Führungs-hauptamt) or the field headquarters (Feldkommandostelle RF-SS) of Reichsführer-SS Heinrich Himmler, the OKH was also able to take under command and direct the operations of up to 41 divisions of the Waffen-SS. These divisions were "army" divisions in all but name, ethos and their usual command subordination. The organization of Waffen-SS divisions more or less mirrored that of the equivalent army division (although the Waffen-SS often received better and more modern equipment), and Waffen-SS divisions regularly served alongside those of the army, often

attracting particular admiration and respect for their tenacity, motivation and fighting prowess, as well as considerable notoriety and controversy for the atrocities carried out by some Waffen-SS units. However, while Waffen-SS units sometimes had a significant operational impact upon various campaigns and battles, the Waffen-SS was a military-political tool of the Nazi state rather than a fourth arm of the Wehrmacht.*

## 2. Infantry

Most of the army's manpower was in the infantry arm, and, although a number of military thinkers already appreciated that the only way for the army to conduct a war of maneuver would

A poster promoting the traditional and superior status of the Infantry as the 'Queen of the (Fighting) Arms' within the army

KÖNIGIN ALLER WAFFEN

* The story of the Waffen-SS falls generally outside this study of the German army. Nevertheless, in order to place this important non-army military organization in context, a brief account of the Waffen-SS is included in Appendix 1, including a list of the divisions it formed.

through its development of the new Panzer arm, the infantry was still widely regarded as being the army's "Königin aller Waffen" (literally "Queen of the combat arms") and its principal war-winning force. In the German army the infantry had long held pride of place in the order of battle and, notwithstanding the new-found capabilities of the Panzer units, it was still "the infantry, supported by the other arms of the service, [which] decides the outcome of the battle by seizing and holding the enemy's positions. Its fighting ability enables it to close with the enemy and destroy him."[1]

In 1939 and during the early war years the typical infantry division consisted of three infantry regiments (each commanded by a colonel (Oberst)), together with integral engineer and artillery support. In 1938[2] the organization of an infantry regiment (with about 95 officers and 2,989 soldiers) included:

- Three battalions (each usually commanded by a major), each of three infantry companies (with integral light and heavy machine guns and light mortars), with the necessary battalion headquarters staff and communications specialists. In 1939 an infantry battalion typically numbered about 25 officers and 813 soldiers, with up to four officers and 183 soldiers in each infantry company.

- Each battalion also had a support or heavy weapons company. These included four (but sometimes six) heavy machine guns mounted on horse-drawn carriages, which could be used either in the ground role or for air defense. These support companies were also equipped with six 81mm and four 120mm mortars. Up to five officers and 183 soldiers were found in the infantry

battalion's heavy weapons or machine gun company in 1939.

- Each regiment also had a howitzer or infantry gun company of six horse-drawn light (75mm) and two heavy (150mm) howitzers, an anti-tank company with three or four platoons, each of these platoons manning three 37mm anti-tank guns (usually mounted on motorized tractors), a signals platoon, a bicycle platoon, a field engineer platoon and a logistic support detachment grouped within the regiment's headquarters company.

- A troop of cavalry was also assigned to each regiment to provide it with a mounted reconnaissance capability.

This was the basic organization on which the immediate pre-war infantry regiment was based. It was modified extensively as the war continued, especially in terms of the quantities and types of weapons and vehicles allocated to it, to reflect the changing operational situations and the introduction of new weapons and equipment.

### The Infantry Division

Traditionally and doctrinally all arms still existed to support the infantry, just as they had in Germany's nineteenth-century and early twentieth-century conflicts. However, the presence of all arms in the army's divisions meant that, while the design for battle usually centered upon the infantry, operations were conducted as a closely coordinated team, with all the separate but interdependent divisional elements fighting together to achieve the division's mission. Non-armored infantry divisions fielded up to 17,734 men at the beginning of the war, and this figure had dropped to about

The organization of an infantry division in 1940. Note that the actual organization often varied between divisions that were theoretically of the same type, especially during the later stages of the war, and that the manpower totals shown were frequently not achieved.

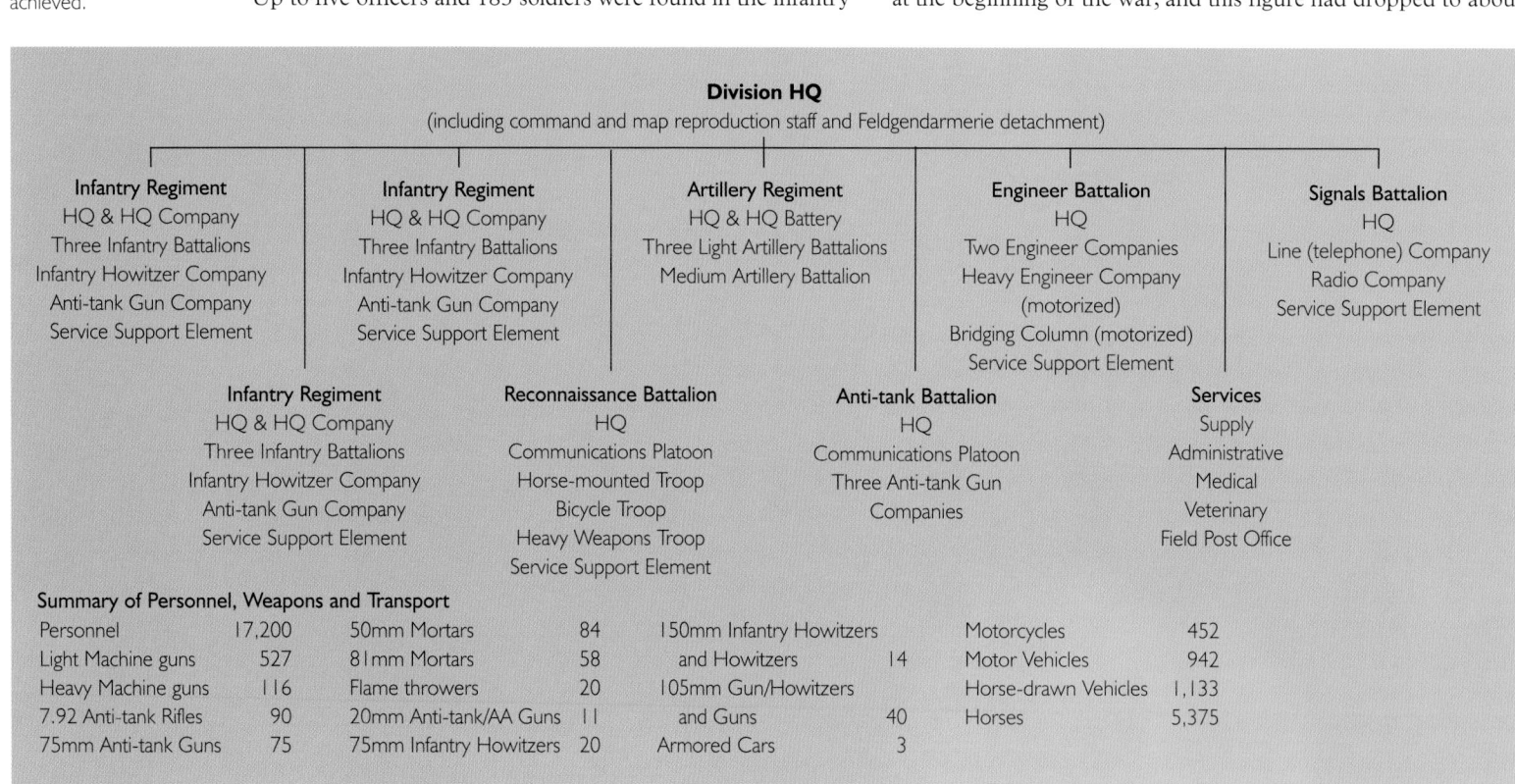

**Division HQ**
(including command and map reproduction staff and Feldgendarmerie detachment)

| **Infantry Regiment** | **Infantry Regiment** | **Artillery Regiment** | **Engineer Battalion** | **Signals Battalion** |
|---|---|---|---|---|
| HQ & HQ Company | HQ & HQ Company | HQ & HQ Battery | HQ | HQ |
| Three Infantry Battalions | Three Infantry Battalions | Three Light Artillery Battalions | Two Engineer Companies | Line (telephone) Company |
| Infantry Howitzer Company | Infantry Howitzer Company | Medium Artillery Battalion | Heavy Engineer Company | Radio Company |
| Anti-tank Gun Company | Anti-tank Gun Company | | (motorized) | Service Support Element |
| Service Support Element | Service Support Element | | Bridging Column (motorized) | |
| | | | Service Support Element | |

| **Infantry Regiment** | **Reconnaissance Battalion** | **Anti-tank Battalion** | **Services** |
|---|---|---|---|
| HQ & HQ Company | HQ | HQ | Supply |
| Three Infantry Battalions | Communications Platoon | Communications Platoon | Administrative |
| Infantry Howitzer Company | Horse-mounted Troop | Three Anti-tank Gun | Medical |
| Anti-tank Gun Company | Bicycle Troop | Companies | Veterinary |
| Service Support Element | Heavy Weapons Troop | | Field Post Office |
| | Service Support Element | | |

**Summary of Personnel, Weapons and Transport**

| Personnel | 17,200 | 50mm Mortars | 84 | 150mm Infantry Howitzers | | Motorcycles | 452 |
|---|---|---|---|---|---|---|---|
| Light Machine guns | 527 | 81mm Mortars | 58 | and Howitzers | 14 | Motor Vehicles | 942 |
| Heavy Machine guns | 116 | Flame throwers | 20 | 105mm Gun/Howitzers | | Horse-drawn Vehicles | 1,133 |
| 7.92 Anti-tank Rifles | 90 | 20mm Anti-tank/AA Guns | 11 | and Guns | 40 | Horses | 5,375 |
| 75mm Anti-tank Guns | 75 | 75mm Infantry Howitzers | 20 | Armored Cars | 3 | | |

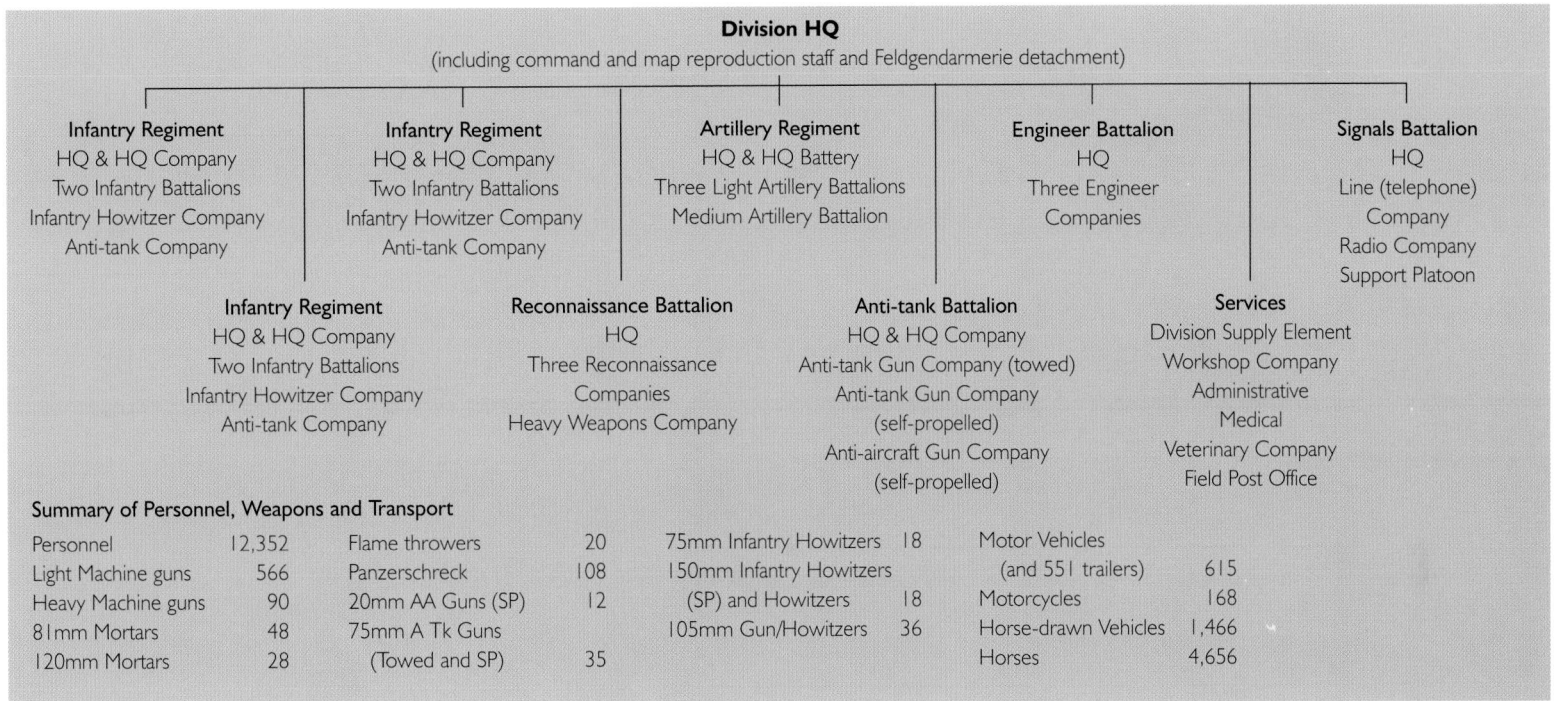

**Division HQ**
(including command and map reproduction staff and Feldgendarmerie detachment)

| Infantry Regiment | Infantry Regiment | Artillery Regiment | Engineer Battalion | Signals Battalion |
|---|---|---|---|---|
| HQ & HQ Company | HQ & HQ Company | HQ & HQ Battery | HQ | HQ |
| Two Infantry Battalions | Two Infantry Battalions | Three Light Artillery Battalions | Three Engineer | Line (telephone) |
| Infantry Howitzer Company | Infantry Howitzer Company | Medium Artillery Battalion | Companies | Company |
| Anti-tank Company | Anti-tank Company | | | Radio Company |
| | | | | Support Platoon |

| Infantry Regiment | Reconnaissance Battalion | Anti-tank Battalion | Services |
|---|---|---|---|
| HQ & HQ Company | HQ | HQ & HQ Company | Division Supply Element |
| Two Infantry Battalions | Three Reconnaissance | Anti-tank Gun Company (towed) | Workshop Company |
| Infantry Howitzer Company | Companies | Anti-tank Gun Company | Administrative |
| Anti-tank Company | Heavy Weapons Company | (self-propelled) | Medical |
| | | Anti-aircraft Gun Company | Veterinary Company |
| | | (self-propelled) | Field Post Office |

**Summary of Personnel, Weapons and Transport**

| | | | | | | | |
|---|---|---|---|---|---|---|---|
| Personnel | 12,352 | Flame throwers | 20 | 75mm Infantry Howitzers | 18 | Motor Vehicles | |
| Light Machine guns | 566 | Panzerschreck | 108 | 150mm Infantry Howitzers | | (and 551 trailers) | 615 |
| Heavy Machine guns | 90 | 20mm AA Guns (SP) | 12 | (SP) and Howitzers | 18 | Motorcycles | 168 |
| 81mm Mortars | 48 | 75mm A Tk Guns | | 105mm Gun/Howitzers | 36 | Horse-drawn Vehicles | 1,466 |
| 120mm Mortars | 28 | (Towed and SP) | 35 | | | Horses | 4,656 |

12,500 by late-1943 with the creation of the "Type 1944" infantry division. A number of two-regiment (instead of the usual three-regiment) infantry divisions of some 10,000 men were also created from mid-1941. The main parts of an infantry division were the headquarters, up to three infantry regiments, an artillery regiment, and the signals, reconnaissance, anti-tank and engineer battalions, together with the division's service support. Although there were both horse-drawn and some motorized transport in the infantry division, for most planning purposes its mobility and manoeuvrability were predicated upon the marching soldier. No tanks, self-propelled artillery or assault guns were included in the organization of the standard infantry division.

The relative lack of mobility in an infantry division is illustrated by the observations of an artillery officer whose regiment was supporting such a division during the advance into Russia in the summer of 1941: "The infantry had to move on foot, but [the artillerymen] rode either on horseback or on the equipment being pulled by our horses. Occasionally, when there was resistance up ahead, [headquarters, 9th Army] would send trucks back to rush the infantry forward more quickly. A supply column followed us to provide ammunition, hay and oats for the horses, food for the people, and fuel for the motorized equipment. If we outran our supply column, we had to live off the land, but most of the time our supply column kept up."[3]

The essential and quite extensive use of horses for motive power within these non-motorized infantry divisions was significant. Despite the progressive mechanization of the army and the pressing need to develop a sizeable armored capability – all of which was supported enthusiastically by Hitler – this critical dependence upon horses for all sorts of transport needs persisted

in most operational theaters throughout the war. Had Hitler chosen to carry out his strategic plans only after the modernization and mechanization of the army was complete, its ability to wage and to sustain the sort of protracted war that developed after the initial Blitzkrieg successes of 1939 and 1940 would have been substantially improved. More than 700 infantry divisions were created during the war, but this figure is not particularly illuminating, as the total number and identity of the army divisions that actually existed from month to month varied considerably, especially after the tide began to turn on the Eastern Front from 1942. New divisions were built from the remnants of those shattered in action while not necessarily adopting the same divisional number. Brand-new divisions were formed and others were re-roled or re-named, some adopting the titles of divisions so badly mauled in earlier battles that they had been entirely removed from the order of battle. Others were amalgamated or fragmented and their units re-assigned to satisfy the ever-changing operational needs. The only meaningful figures for a comparison of relative strengths were those for the numbers of infantry divisions actually allocated for a specific campaign or operation, with the actual strengths of the divisions engaged then also being taken into consideration.

The policy by which numbers and other designations were allocated to infantry divisions was quite complex, and there were inevitably a number of exceptions and variations within the system. In summary, the line infantry's divisions were numbered from 1 to 36, 44 to 46, 50 to 100, and 200 to 300, some divisions bearing a name rather than a number. Not all numbers were allocated or used. The division numbers 501 to 600 were kept available for new divisions formed later during the war, and some

The organization of an infantry division in 1944. Note the significant reduction in overall manpower compared with an infantry division at the start of the war.

Whatever the type of infantry division, its reputation and operational success ultimately depended upon the training, discipline, marksmanship and performance of the individual riflemen who manned its units.

of these were eventually allocated to the Volksgrenadier divisions created from 1944. The last infantry division numbers to be allocated were 702 to 704 and 707 to 719, and an exception to the overall numbering system was the 999th Penal Division. The system was further complicated by the separate numbering of the

Jäger divisions and by the later transfer to the armored forces of the motorized infantry divisions, which were then re-designated as Panzergrenadier divisions and re-numbered.

### The Infantry (Motorized) Division

Infantry (motorized) divisions of up to about 14,000 men were organized much as the ordinary infantry divisions, but usually with two infantry regiments rather than three, and with the addition of a self-propelled assault gun battalion (or sometimes a tank battalion) and an air defense battalion. Horses and bicycles were generally replaced by light vehicles and motorcycles, while the infantry regiments were transported in trucks or (infrequently) in armored half-tracks, as were the other elements of the division. The type and scale of motorization varied widely between these divisions, and in many cases horses were still found in regular use by them. Nevertheless, in principle the infantry (motorized) division was fully mobile without resorting to movement on foot and provided a pragmatic compromise between the basic infantry division and the armored infantry (Panzergrenadier) division.

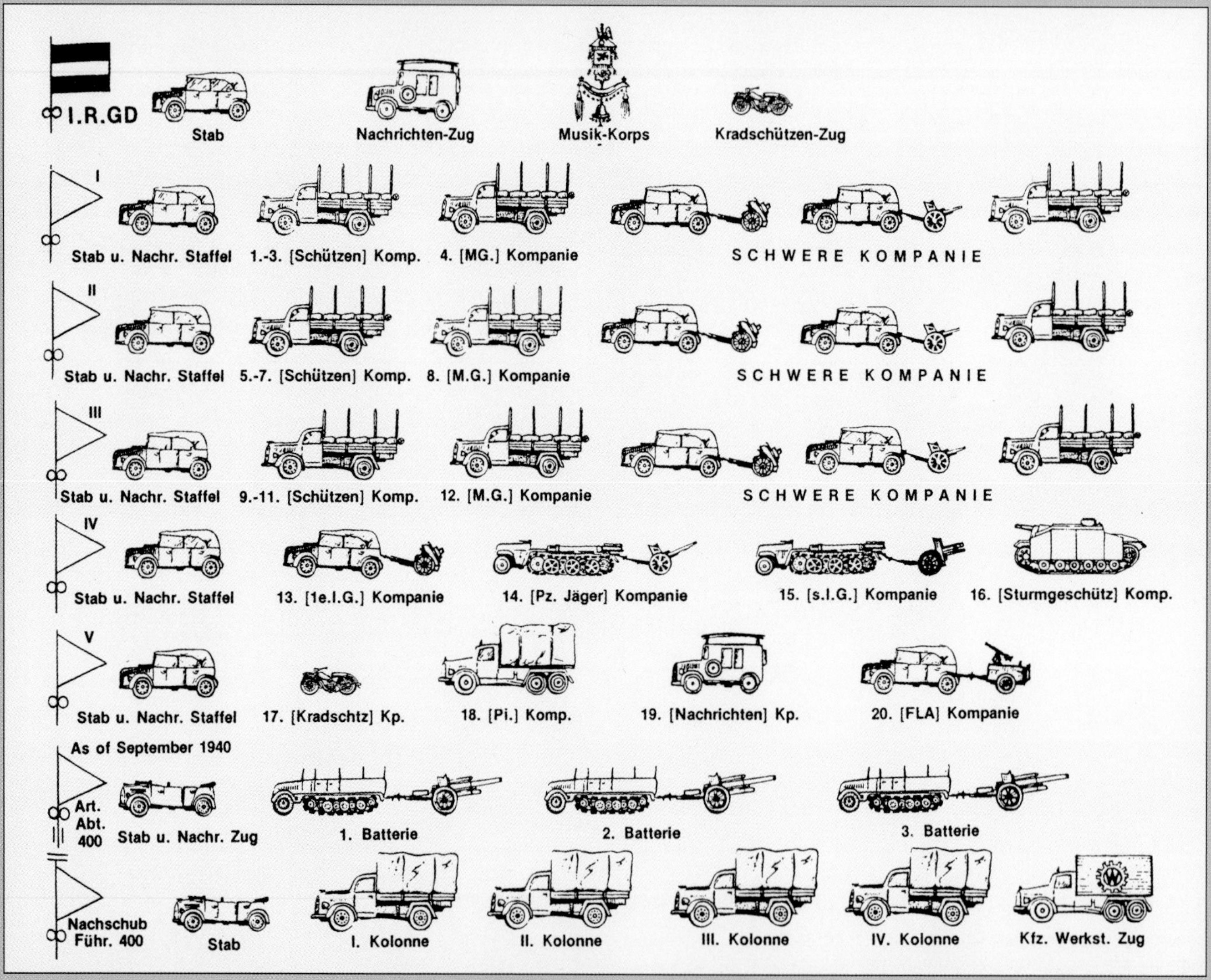

Diagram of the organization of motorized infantry regiment "Großdeutschland", December 1940, from an original German publication. Note the wide variety of vehicle types and equipment.

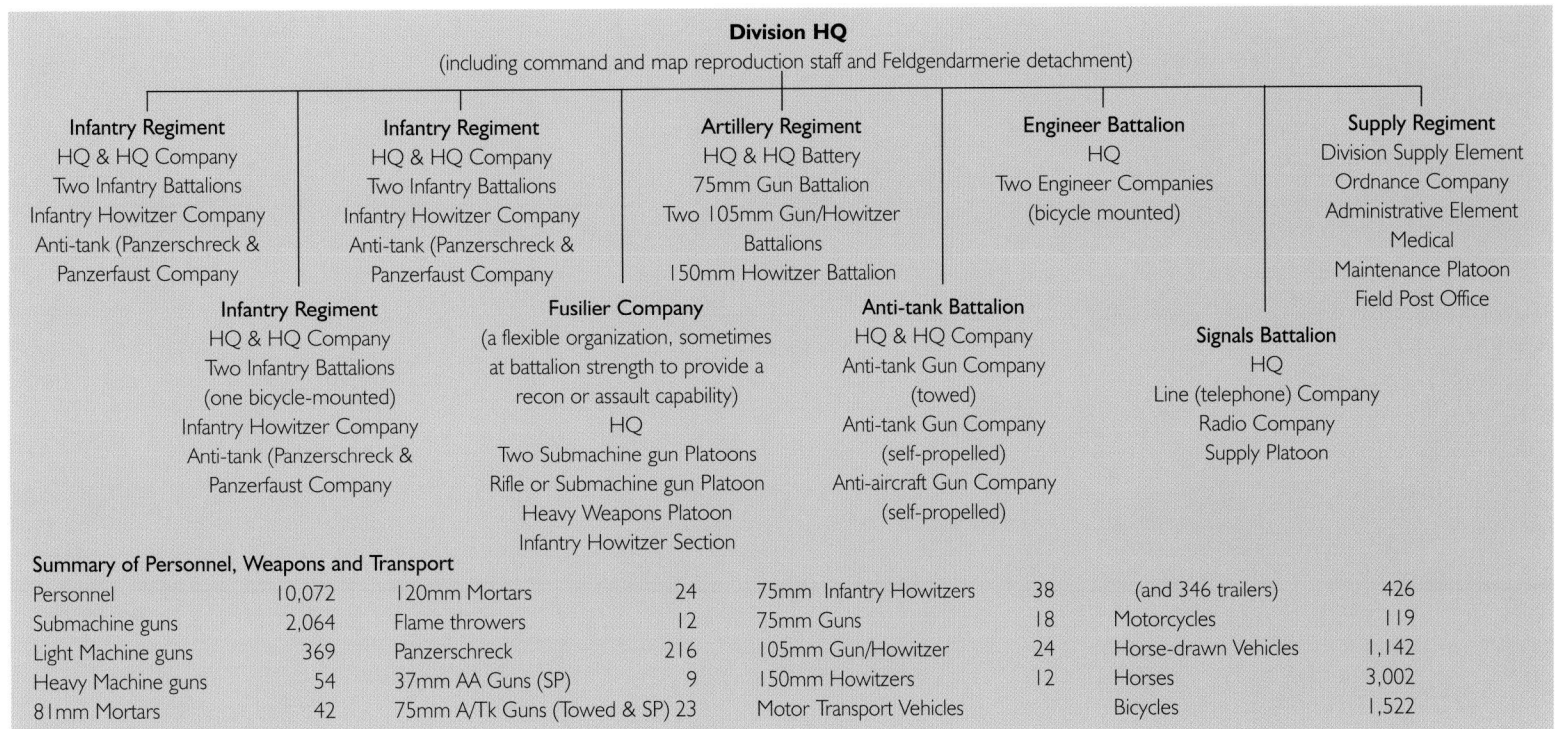

**Division HQ**
(including command and map reproduction staff and Feldgendarmerie detachment)

| Infantry Regiment | Infantry Regiment | Artillery Regiment | Engineer Battalion | Supply Regiment |
|---|---|---|---|---|
| HQ & HQ Company | HQ & HQ Company | HQ & HQ Battery | HQ | Division Supply Element |
| Two Infantry Battalions | Two Infantry Battalions | 75mm Gun Battalion | Two Engineer Companies | Ordnance Company |
| Infantry Howitzer Company | Infantry Howitzer Company | Two 105mm Gun/Howitzer | (bicycle mounted) | Administrative Element |
| Anti-tank (Panzerschreck & | Anti-tank (Panzerschreck & | Battalions | | Medical |
| Panzerfaust Company | Panzerfaust Company | 150mm Howitzer Battalion | | Maintenance Platoon |
| | | | | Field Post Office |

| Infantry Regiment | Fusilier Company | Anti-tank Battalion | |
|---|---|---|---|
| HQ & HQ Company | (a flexible organization, sometimes | HQ & HQ Company | **Signals Battalion** |
| Two Infantry Battalions | at battalion strength to provide a | Anti-tank Gun Company | HQ |
| (one bicycle-mounted) | recon or assault capability) | (towed) | Line (telephone) Company |
| Infantry Howitzer Company | HQ | Anti-tank Gun Company | Radio Company |
| Anti-tank (Panzerschreck & | Two Submachine gun Platoons | (self-propelled) | Supply Platoon |
| Panzerfaust Company | Rifle or Submachine gun Platoon | Anti-aircraft Gun Company | |
| | Heavy Weapons Platoon | (self-propelled) | |
| | Infantry Howitzer Section | | |

**Summary of Personnel, Weapons and Transport**

| | | | | | | | |
|---|---|---|---|---|---|---|---|
| Personnel | 10,072 | 120mm Mortars | 24 | 75mm Infantry Howitzers | 38 | (and 346 trailers) | 426 |
| Submachine guns | 2,064 | Flame throwers | 12 | 75mm Guns | 18 | Motorcycles | 119 |
| Light Machine guns | 369 | Panzerschreck | 216 | 105mm Gun/Howitzer | 24 | Horse-drawn Vehicles | 1,142 |
| Heavy Machine guns | 54 | 37mm AA Guns (SP) | 9 | 150mm Howitzers | 12 | Horses | 3,002 |
| 81mm Mortars | 42 | 75mm A/Tk Guns (Towed & SP) | 23 | Motor Transport Vehicles | | Bicycles | 1,522 |

When the war began in 1939, only the 2nd, 13th, 20th and 29th Infantry Divisions were categorized as "motorized", and they were subsequently re-designated as Panzergrenadier divisions or restructured as Panzer divisions. On 5 July 1942, any remaining motorized infantry divisions were redesignated as Panzergrenadier divisions, and this process was repeated over time for other divisions, with numbers of truck-mounted motorized divisions subsequently being converted into Panzergrenadier divisions, their soldiers partly or entirely mounted in armored vehicles.

**The Volksgrenadier Division**

Volksgrenadier (or "people's infantry") divisions originated in late 1944 when Heinrich Himmler was appointed commander of the Ersatzheer following the 20 July bomb plot. The target strength of these divisions mirrored that of the infantry division of the time and was 12,700 men, but in practice the Volksgrenadier divisions rarely achieved strengths that much exceeded 10,000 men. "Volksgrenadier" was presented as an honor title – while in fact, its use and the creation of the Volksgrenadier divisions actually reflected the increased pressure upon army manpower by that stage of the war. The lower level of manpower in these new divisions was achieved by reducing and streamlining the number of separate units within them, which in turn called for less command, control and support personnel. For example, all of the division's service support units were combined into a single divisional supply regiment. Such manpower reductions were offset to some extent by an increase in the division's allocation of automatic weapons (such as submachine guns) and man-portable anti-tank weapons (such as the Panzerfaust and Panzerschreck).

Due to the circumstances of their inception, the organization of Volksgrenadier divisions varied considerably when they were introduced in late 1944. Their planned organization was generally based upon that of the three-regiment infantry division, one of which regiments was bicycle-mounted. The division also benefited

from the addition of a "fusilier" company or battalion, in which were concentrated the division's infantry heavy weapons and its ground reconnaissance capability. However, the division's lack of mobility was all too evident from the fact that up to 3,002 horses were established to provide the primary motive power for a fully established Volksgrenadier division.

Volksgrenadier divisions, despite being used in the vanguard of operations such as *Wacht am Rhein* in December 1944, were often not as capable as infantry or Panzergrenadier divisions. Volksgrenadier divisions were frequently built upon a core of veterans – often the surviving troops of another combat-shattered division – but the size and quality of the pool from which its new recruits were drawn had much diminished by late 1944, as had the time available to train these men for battle.

**The Gebirgsdivision**

Nine army mountain divisions, each of some 13,000 Gebirgsjäger (literally, "mountain riflemen"), were formed between 1938 and the end of the war, and a further five such divisions were formed

**Above:** The organization of a Volksgrenadier (or "People's Grenadier") division in 1944. The overall manpower was significantly less than that of a regular infantry division at the start of the war, although the division's enhanced short-range anti-tank firepower and increased complement of automatic weapons were intended to offset this.

**Left:** Within the infantry division's regiments, weapons such as the 75mm Infantry Light Gun provided a readily available and potent source of firepower.

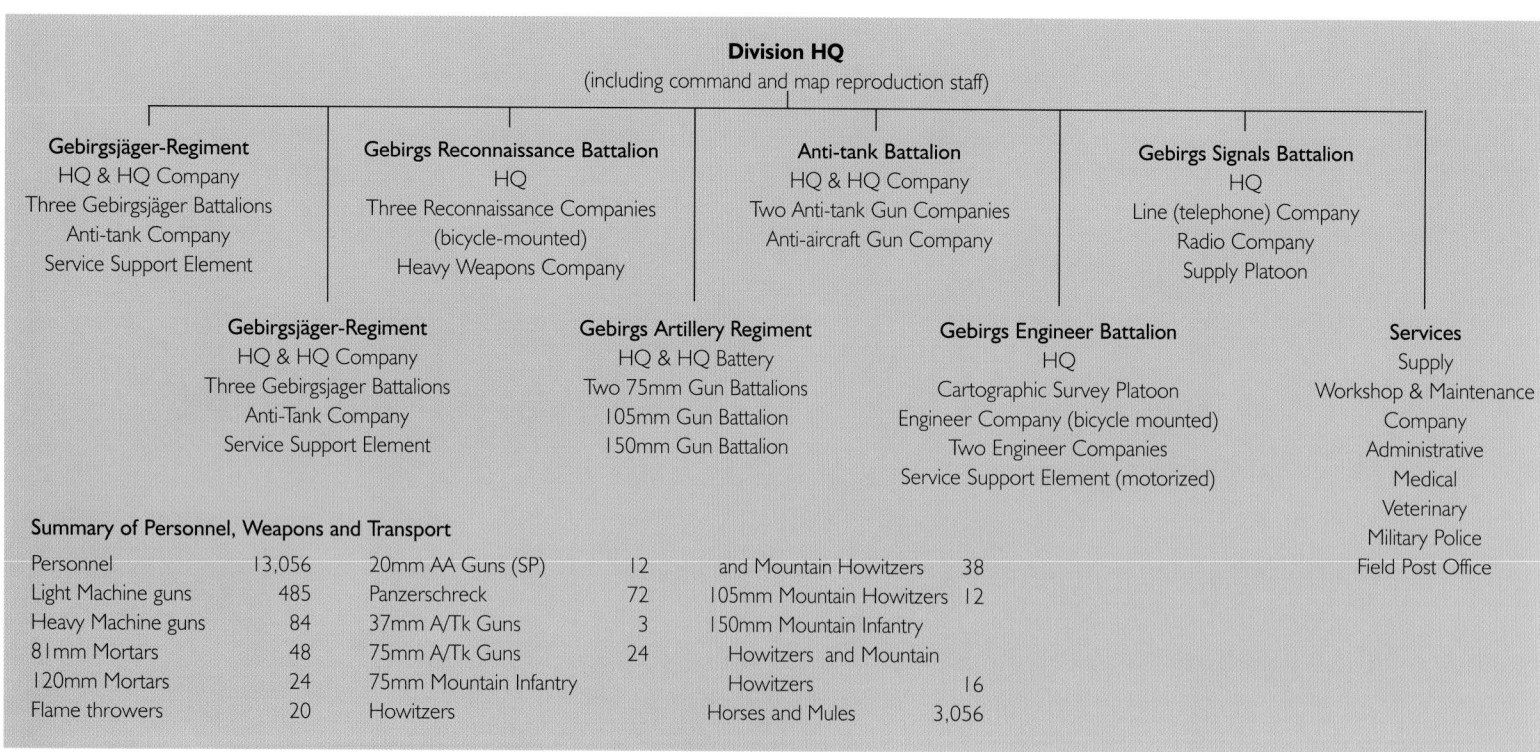

**Division HQ**
(including command and map reproduction staff)

| Gebirgsjäger-Regiment | Gebirgs Reconnaissance Battalion | Anti-tank Battalion | Gebirgs Signals Battalion |
|---|---|---|---|
| HQ & HQ Company | HQ | HQ & HQ Company | HQ |
| Three Gebirgsjäger Battalions | Three Reconnaissance Companies | Two Anti-tank Gun Companies | Line (telephone) Company |
| Anti-tank Company | (bicycle-mounted) | Anti-aircraft Gun Company | Radio Company |
| Service Support Element | Heavy Weapons Company | | Supply Platoon |

| Gebirgsjäger-Regiment | Gebirgs Artillery Regiment | Gebirgs Engineer Battalion | Services |
|---|---|---|---|
| HQ & HQ Company | HQ & HQ Battery | HQ | Supply |
| Three Gebirgsjager Battalions | Two 75mm Gun Battalions | Cartographic Survey Platoon | Workshop & Maintenance |
| Anti-Tank Company | 105mm Gun Battalion | Engineer Company (bicycle mounted) | Company |
| Service Support Element | 150mm Gun Battalion | Two Engineer Companies | Administrative |
| | | Service Support Element (motorized) | Medical |
| | | | Veterinary |
| | | | Military Police |
| | | | Field Post Office |

**Summary of Personnel, Weapons and Transport**

| | | | | | |
|---|---|---|---|---|---|
| Personnel | 13,056 | 20mm AA Guns (SP) | 12 | and Mountain Howitzers | 38 |
| Light Machine guns | 485 | Panzerschreck | 72 | 105mm Mountain Howitzers | 12 |
| Heavy Machine guns | 84 | 37mm A/Tk Guns | 3 | 150mm Mountain Infantry | |
| 81mm Mortars | 48 | 75mm A/Tk Guns | 24 | Howitzers and Mountain | |
| 120mm Mortars | 24 | 75mm Mountain Infantry | | Howitzers | 16 |
| Flame throwers | 20 | Howitzers | | Horses and Mules | 3,056 |

The organization of a Gebirgsdivision in 1944. These divisions were not equipped to conduct highly mobile or mechanized operations, and the significant numbers of horses and mules upon which they relied is noteworthy.
**Right:** The Gebirgsdivisionen (mountain divisions) were well-prepared for infantry operations in rugged and mountainous terrain, including counter-partisan operations and warfare in winter conditions. Here Gebirgsjäger troops practice ambush and raiding operations high in the mountains.

by the Waffen-SS. The army Gebirgsdivision consisted of the divisional headquarters, reconnaissance, anti-tank, engineer and signals battalions, two regiments of infantry, an artillery regiment and divisional service support units, all of which were trained and equipped for operations in mountain areas. For its mobility, a full strength division depended on its establishment of between 3,056 and 5,000 pack-mules and horses.

### The Jägerdivision

A Jäger (or "light infantry") division had a planned strength of up to 13,000, its organization being very similar to that of the Gebirgsdivision. However, it had additional motor transport in lieu of the latter's specialist mountaineering equipment and some of its pack animals. Between 1941 and the end of the war, ten Jägerdivisionen were formed either as new divisions or by re-designating and restructuring existing army divisions. These divisions were well suited for operations in close country, in urban areas and against irregular forces. They were employed mainly in the Balkans, in Greece, Poland and on the Eastern Front.

### The Fallschirmdivision

The Fallschirmdivision ("airborne" or "parachute division") or Fallschirmjäger ("parachute infantry") division had a planned strength of more than 16,000 and included both glider-borne infantry and paratroopers. Of the ten divisions raised (an eleventh was being formed when the war ended) few achieved manning levels that even approached this figure. Although designated as "paratroopers" relatively few Fallschirmjäger were in fact parachute-trained or qualified, and this number decreased further

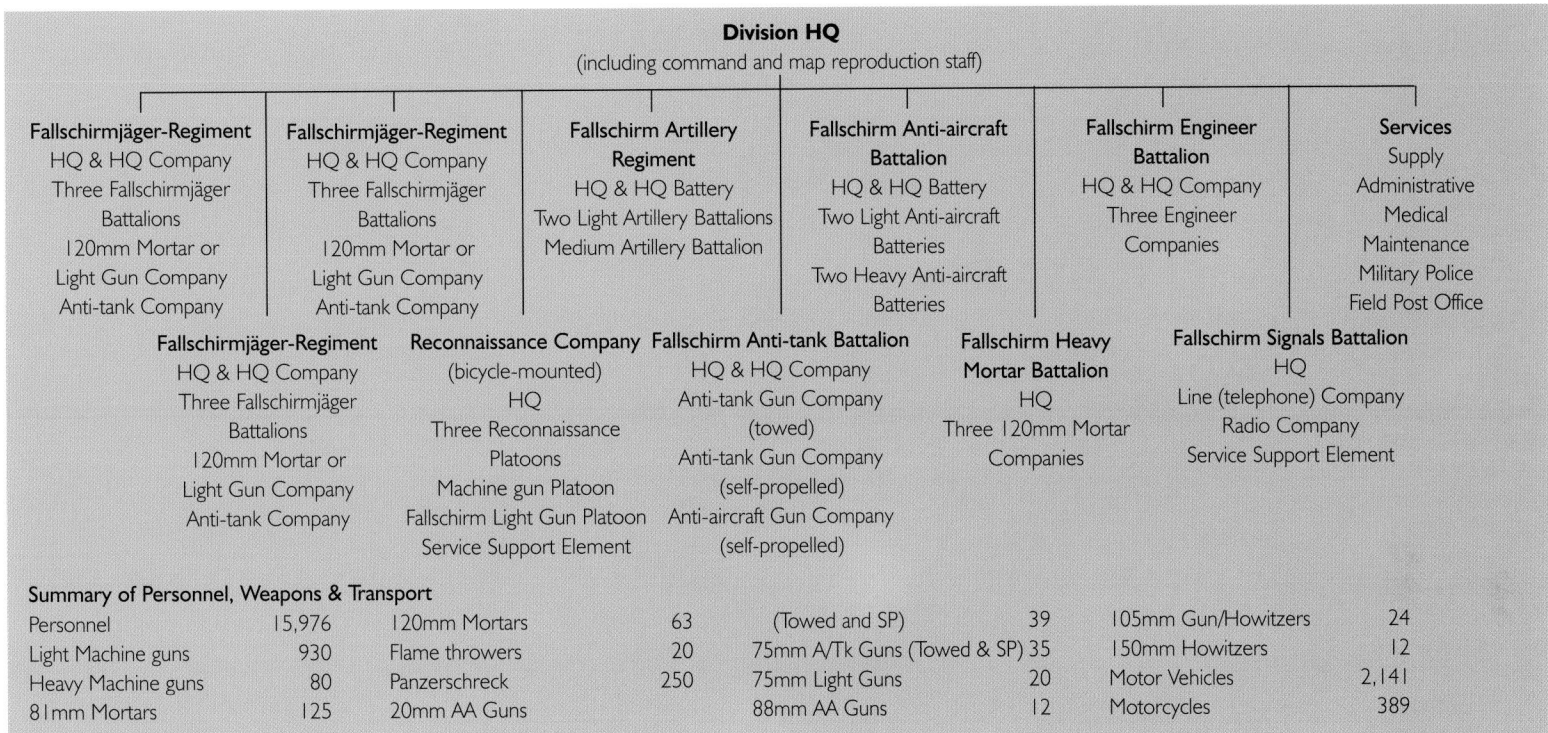

**Division HQ**
(including command and map reproduction staff)

| Fallschirmjäger-Regiment | Fallschirmjäger-Regiment | Fallschirm Artillery Regiment | Fallschirm Anti-aircraft Battalion | Fallschirm Engineer Battalion | Services |
|---|---|---|---|---|---|
| HQ & HQ Company | HQ & HQ Company | HQ & HQ Battery | HQ & HQ Battery | HQ & HQ Company | Supply |
| Three Fallschirmjäger Battalions | Three Fallschirmjäger Battalions | Two Light Artillery Battalions | Two Light Anti-aircraft Batteries | Three Engineer Companies | Administrative |
| 120mm Mortar or Light Gun Company | 120mm Mortar or Light Gun Company | Medium Artillery Battalion | Two Heavy Anti-aircraft Batteries | | Medical |
| Anti-tank Company | Anti-tank Company | | | | Maintenance |
| | | | | | Military Police |
| | | | | | Field Post Office |

| Fallschirmjäger-Regiment | Reconnaissance Company (bicycle-mounted) | Fallschirm Anti-tank Battalion | Fallschirm Heavy Mortar Battalion | Fallschirm Signals Battalion |
|---|---|---|---|---|
| HQ & HQ Company | HQ | HQ & HQ Company | HQ | HQ |
| Three Fallschirmjäger Battalions | Three Reconnaissance Platoons | Anti-tank Gun Company (towed) | Three 120mm Mortar Companies | Line (telephone) Company |
| 120mm Mortar or Light Gun Company | Machine gun Platoon | Anti-tank Gun Company (self-propelled) | | Radio Company |
| Anti-tank Company | Fallschirm Light Gun Platoon | Anti-aircraft Gun Company (self-propelled) | | Service Support Element |
| | Service Support Element | | | |

**Summary of Personnel, Weapons & Transport**

| | | | | | | | |
|---|---|---|---|---|---|---|---|
| Personnel | 15,976 | 120mm Mortars | 63 | (Towed and SP) | 39 | 105mm Gun/Howitzers | 24 |
| Light Machine guns | 930 | Flame throwers | 20 | 75mm A/Tk Guns (Towed & SP) | 35 | 150mm Howitzers | 12 |
| Heavy Machine guns | 80 | Panzerschreck | 250 | 75mm Light Guns | 20 | Motor Vehicles | 2,141 |
| 81mm Mortars | 125 | 20mm AA Guns | | 88mm AA Guns | 12 | Motorcycles | 389 |

as the war progressed – particularly after the successful but costly invasion of Crete in 1941, following which Hitler and the OKW decided not to mount any more major airborne operations. Nevertheless, these Luftwaffe-owned divisions (although they were in practice commanded and controlled by the OKH on operations) distinguished themselves in action, being engaged primarily in the Western, North African and Italian theaters. They generally served as regular infantry but quickly gained a reputation as élite troops, while earning the respect of Allied troops as formidable and professional opponents. The airborne division had a headquarters, three regiments, a reconnaissance company, an artillery regiment, a 120mm mortar battalion, an anti-tank battalion, an engineer battalion, plus divisional service support units. Although all of these divisional units were organized and equipped to be transported by air, the intention for them to be fully deliverable into battle by parachute or glider was neither pursued nor achievable after 1941.

# 3. Armored Forces

The story of the "armored mobile" or "Panzertruppe" forces – which included the tank (Panzer) regiments and the armored infantry (Panzergrenadier) regiments – cannot be separated from the story of the development of the Blitzkrieg concept that these forces supported. Doctrinally, the Panzers were regarded as a "weapon of operational opportunism", and as such they were used to achieve a breakthrough, to exploit success, to provide a highly mobile and powerful reserve force, and to paralyse the enemy by

advancing rapidly through his forward defenses to wreak havoc in his rear areas; all of which had been tasks carried out by the cavalry in former times. However, traditional pre-war perceptions and prejudices were not easily dispelled, and despite their clear potential the Panzers were not widely viewed as being the decisive weapon that would bring about the enemy's final defeat; rather, they were seen as a complementary weapon that would enable the other arms – primarily the infantry – to bring about that defeat. Such attitudes changed substantially once the efficacy of the Blitzkrieg had been demonstrated in 1940, although by then it was too late to generate new Panzer forces on the scale required either to avert or to conduct successfully the war of attrition precipitated by Operation *Barbarossa*.

Foremost among those officers championing the potential of the Panzer arm prior to the war were Heinz Wilhelm Guderian

The organization of a Fallschirmdivision in 1944. These formations remained under Luftwaffe administrative control throughout the war. However, after the successful but costly assault against Crete in 1941 these troops (Fallschirmjäger) were mainly used as high-grade infantry, generally serving under the operational command of various army headquarters.

**Left:** The Mercedes-Benz heavy armored car was used extensively in the 1930s. This Sd.Kfz. 232 variant is fitted with an overhead antenna for use as a command vehicle or for signals communications.

The Panzerdivisionen (armored divisions) provided the army's main ground offensive capability throughout the war. The numerical strength of the standard Panzer-division was reduced after 1940, but they continued to receive new and ever more powerful tanks until 1945, including the formidable Pz.Kpfw.V Panther and Pz.Kpfw.VI Tiger models. Below: the organization of a Panzerdivision in 1944.

and Otto Lutz. As a junior staff officer, Guderian was involved with the early development of the Panzer arm from the former transport battalions, together with the experiments and training conducted at Kazan in Russia from 1925. He had also studied the doctrine developed by other armies for the use of armor, and in the 1930s, while working directly for General der Panzertruppen Otto Lutz, Guderian was able to propose many of the tactical concepts and ideas which Lutz subsequently translated into workable organizations and doctrine. The sort of operations later spearheaded by the German Panzertruppe were characterized by a journalist in 1939 after the Polish campaign, when he encapsulated the rapid maneuver, all-arms cooperation, concentration of overwhelming firepower, abandonment of flank security for speed, envelopment and final annihilation of the enemy forces with the single word "Blitzkrieg", or "lightning war". In its updated form, this innovative concept epitomized the sort of war of maneuver that had eluded the imperial German army on the Western Front after 1914. It also followed the principles of Auftragstaktik that had been at the very core of German military

thinking during the final decades of the imperial army. There was initially a considerable amount of scepticism (often stemming from subjective prejudice, outdated traditionalism and inter-arm and inter-service rivalry) about the validity of the Blitzkrieg concept, but this criticism largely dissipated after the success of the campaigns of 1939 and 1940. In any case, the prospect of the army avoiding a re-run of the stagnation and attrition of 1915–18 provided a powerful argument in favor of the Panzer arm and its new form of warfare, while Hitler also supported the concept enthusiastically and so ensured its wider approval and continued funding. The Führer judged correctly that the Panzertruppe would be an absolutely essential part of the army, vital for achieving his strategic goals within his self-imposed political timeframe. The Panzers also conveyed a powerful image of modern military might, innovation and offensive spirit that sat very well with the images of Germany that the Nazis were promoting through their propaganda both domestically and internationally. Inevitably, therefore, the Panzer forces became part of the army's order of battle, although this they did on a fairly small scale as a proportion of the overall

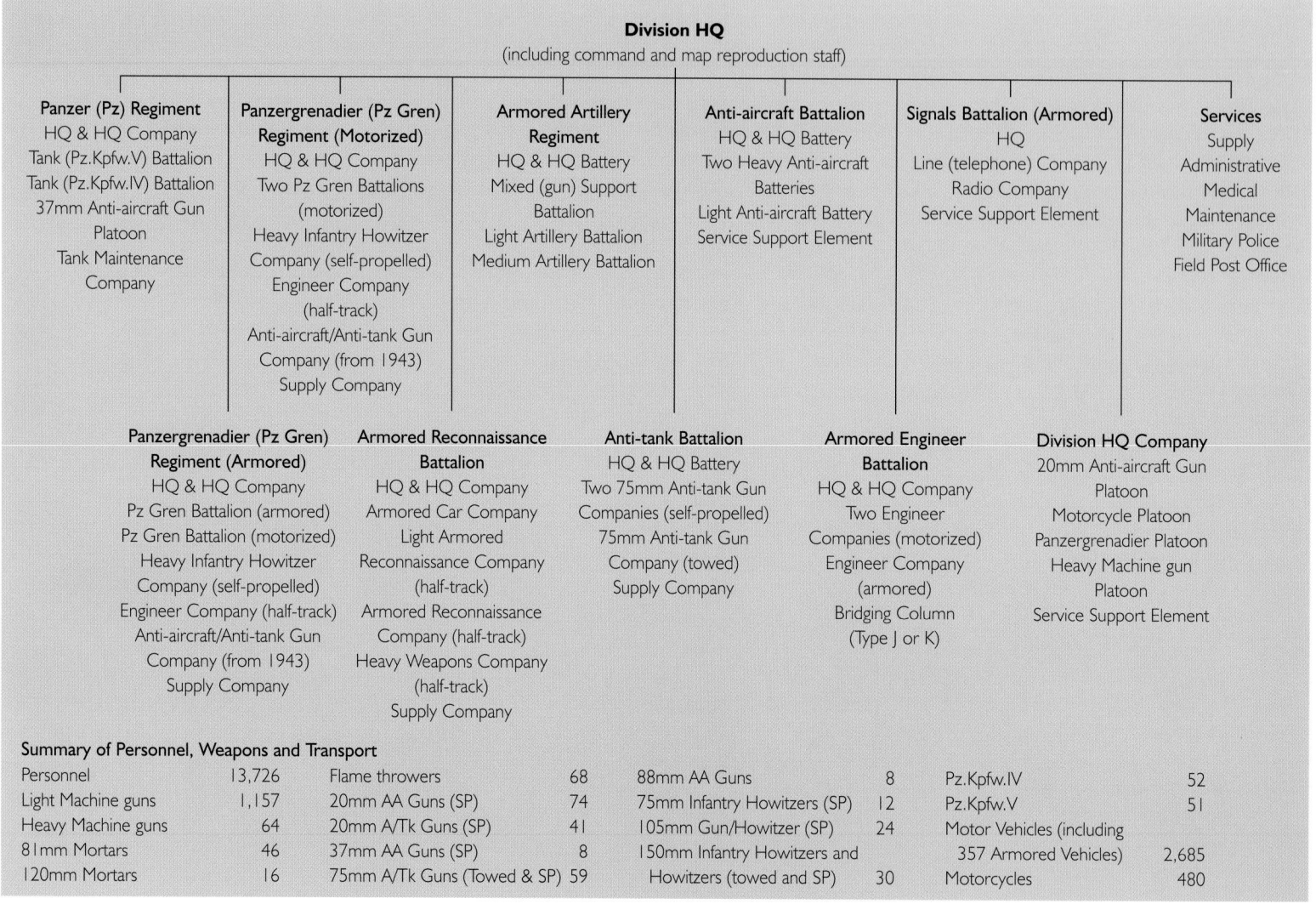

**Division HQ**
(including command and map reproduction staff)

| **Panzer (Pz) Regiment** | **Panzergrenadier (Pz Gren) Regiment (Motorized)** | **Armored Artillery Regiment** | **Anti-aircraft Battalion** | **Signals Battalion (Armored)** | **Services** |
|---|---|---|---|---|---|
| HQ & HQ Company | HQ & HQ Company | HQ & HQ Battery | HQ & HQ Battery | HQ | Supply |
| Tank (Pz.Kpfw.V) Battalion | Two Pz Gren Battalions | Mixed (gun) Support | Two Heavy Anti-aircraft | Line (telephone) Company | Administrative |
| Tank (Pz.Kpfw.IV) Battalion | (motorized) | Battalion | Batteries | Radio Company | Medical |
| 37mm Anti-aircraft Gun | Heavy Infantry Howitzer | Light Artillery Battalion | Light Anti-aircraft Battery | Service Support Element | Maintenance |
| Platoon | Company (self-propelled) | Medium Artillery Battalion | Service Support Element | | Military Police |
| Tank Maintenance | Engineer Company | | | | Field Post Office |
| Company | (half-track) | | | | |
| | Anti-aircraft/Anti-tank Gun | | | | |
| | Company (from 1943) | | | | |
| | Supply Company | | | | |

| **Panzergrenadier (Pz Gren) Regiment (Armored)** | **Armored Reconnaissance Battalion** | **Anti-tank Battalion** | **Armored Engineer Battalion** | **Division HQ Company** |
|---|---|---|---|---|
| HQ & HQ Company | HQ & HQ Company | HQ & HQ Battery | HQ & HQ Company | 20mm Anti-aircraft Gun |
| Pz Gren Battalion (armored) | Armored Car Company | Two 75mm Anti-tank Gun | Two Engineer | Platoon |
| Pz Gren Battalion (motorized) | Light Armored | Companies (self-propelled) | Companies (motorized) | Motorcycle Platoon |
| Heavy Infantry Howitzer | Reconnaissance Company | 75mm Anti-tank Gun | Engineer Company | Panzergrenadier Platoon |
| Company (self-propelled) | (half-track) | Company (towed) | (armored) | Heavy Machine gun |
| Engineer Company (half-track) | Armored Reconnaissance | Supply Company | Bridging Column | Platoon |
| Anti-aircraft/Anti-tank Gun | Company (half-track) | | (Type J or K) | Service Support Element |
| Company (from 1943) | Heavy Weapons Company | | | |
| Supply Company | (half-track) | | | |
| | Supply Company | | | |

**Summary of Personnel, Weapons and Transport**

| | | | | | | | |
|---|---|---|---|---|---|---|---|
| Personnel | 13,726 | Flame throwers | 68 | 88mm AA Guns | 8 | Pz.Kpfw.IV | 52 |
| Light Machine guns | 1,157 | 20mm AA Guns (SP) | 74 | 75mm Infantry Howitzers (SP) | 12 | Pz.Kpfw.V | 51 |
| Heavy Machine guns | 64 | 20mm A/Tk Guns (SP) | 41 | 105mm Gun/Howitzer (SP) | 24 | Motor Vehicles (including | |
| 81mm Mortars | 46 | 37mm AA Guns (SP) | 8 | 150mm Infantry Howitzers and | | 357 Armored Vehicles) | 2,685 |
| 120mm Mortars | 16 | 75mm A/Tk Guns (Towed & SP) | 59 | Howitzers (towed and SP) | 30 | Motorcycles | 480 |

army, particularly in comparison with arms such as the infantry.

Hitler's early personal interest and faith in the armored Panzertruppe persisted throughout the war. This was clearly shown in the directive he issued to Guderian on 28 February 1943 when the general was appointed inspector-general of armored troops. The document, signed personally by Hitler, stated: "The Inspector-General of Armored Troops is responsible to me for the future development of armored troops along lines that will make that arm of Service into a decisive weapon for winning the war. The Inspector-General of Armored Troops is directly subordinate to myself. He has the command powers of an army commander and is the senior officer of armored troops."[4] This gave Guderian very wide-ranging powers, as the armored troops covered by this document included the Panzertruppe (tank) troops, the Panzergrenadiere, motorized infantry, armored reconnaissance, anti-tank units, and heavy assault-gun units. Inevitably, Hitler's conferral of such extensive responsibilities and authority upon Guderian attracted various amounts of resentment from elsewhere within the high command.

**The Panzers**

The army's armored (Panzer, or tank-heavy) divisions originally had two tank regiments, but this was reduced to one by early 1941 in order nearly to double the total number of Panzer divisions prior to Operation *Barbarossa*. Wide variations in equipment availability meant that the organization of the Panzer regiment in 1938–9 was by no means standardized. The typical regiment of the time usually comprised two or three battalions, each battalion then having two or three companies, each with a headquarters and three (but occasionally four) platoons, with up to five tanks per platoon. More tanks were also available within each regimental, battalion and company headquarters, being manned by the personnel of those headquarters. There were up to eight tanks within the regimental headquarters and its headquarters company, eight tanks in the battalion headquarters and its defense platoon, and two tanks in a company headquarters. In addition to the regimental headquarters staff, each Panzer regiment was supported by various combat engineer, signals and logistic support units. The war establishment organization of the first Panzer divisions was determined and promulgated officially as at 15 October 1935. In the case of the 1st Panzer Division it consisted of:

- 1st Panzer Brigade (two Panzer regiments, each with two tank battalions of four light tank companies).
- 1st Motorized Rifle Brigade (one rifle regiment of two battalions, each of which had a motorcycle company, two motorized rifle companies, one heavy machine gun company, and one composite company with engineer, anti-tank and infantry gun platoons).
- 37th Anti-tank Battalion (three anti-tank companies).
- 4th Armored Reconnaissance Battalion (two armored car companies, one motorcycle company and one composite company).

- 73rd Artillery Regiment (two battalions, each with three batteries of light field howitzers).
- 37th Signals Battalion (two companies, one radio and the other line or telephone, with a platoon detached to the HQ of the 1st Panzer Brigade and HQ 1st Motorized Brigade).
- Light Engineer Company.

This organization was the framework upon which the Panzer divisions that went to war in 1939 and 1940 were based and developed. Apart from improvements to the type and quantity of weapons and equipment, the most obvious enhancements by 1940 were the addition of an anti-aircraft battalion, the upgrading of the engineers to battalion strength, and significant enhancements of the division's armored reconnaissance capability, together with the divisional administrative support and supply arrangements.

The quality of the tanks fielded by the Panzer regiments at the start of the war was very different from that of those in service at its end. In 1936 there were some 3,000 of the Panzerkampfwagen model 1 (Pz.Kpfw.I) in service. These two-man light tanks were armed with two machine guns and had been used to good effect during the Spanish Civil War. However, by 1935 it was already clear that they were much less capable than their Soviet and French equivalents, and production ceased in March that year, although the Pz.Kpfw.I chassis continued in use as a command vehicle, weapons carrier and ambulance. The Pz.Kpfw.II, III and IV followed in 1935 and 1936, with a 20mm gun replacing the machine guns as the main armament in the Pz.Kpfw.II. After the German occupation of Czechoslovakia in early 1939, 469 Czech T-38 light tanks were seized, as well as almost 200 of the older T-35s, and taken into use in the Panzer units, while the Czech tank production lines were also taken over and utilized by the Germans. The Czech T-38 light tanks (designated Pz.Kpfw.38(t)) had a four-man crew and mounted a 37mm gun and a machine gun. They gave valuable service to the Panzer divisions during the first part of the war, as well as making good much of the shortfall in German tank numbers at that time.

At the outbreak of the war, the Pz.Kpfw.II was the most numerous type of German tank in service. The Pz.Kpfw.III introduced from 1936 was an improvement over the Pz.Kpfw.II, although the early models still had inadequate firepower and protection. However, the

**Left:** The commander of a group of Pz.Kpfw.I Ausf. A tanks using flag signals to control the movement of his command during pre-war maneuvers. From the mid-1930s and during the early campaigns of the war, the Panzer units relied upon tanks such as the Pz.Kpfw.I, but such lightly armed and thinly armored vehicles were soon superseded by more capable fighting vehicles in light of the battlefield experience gained in Poland and France.

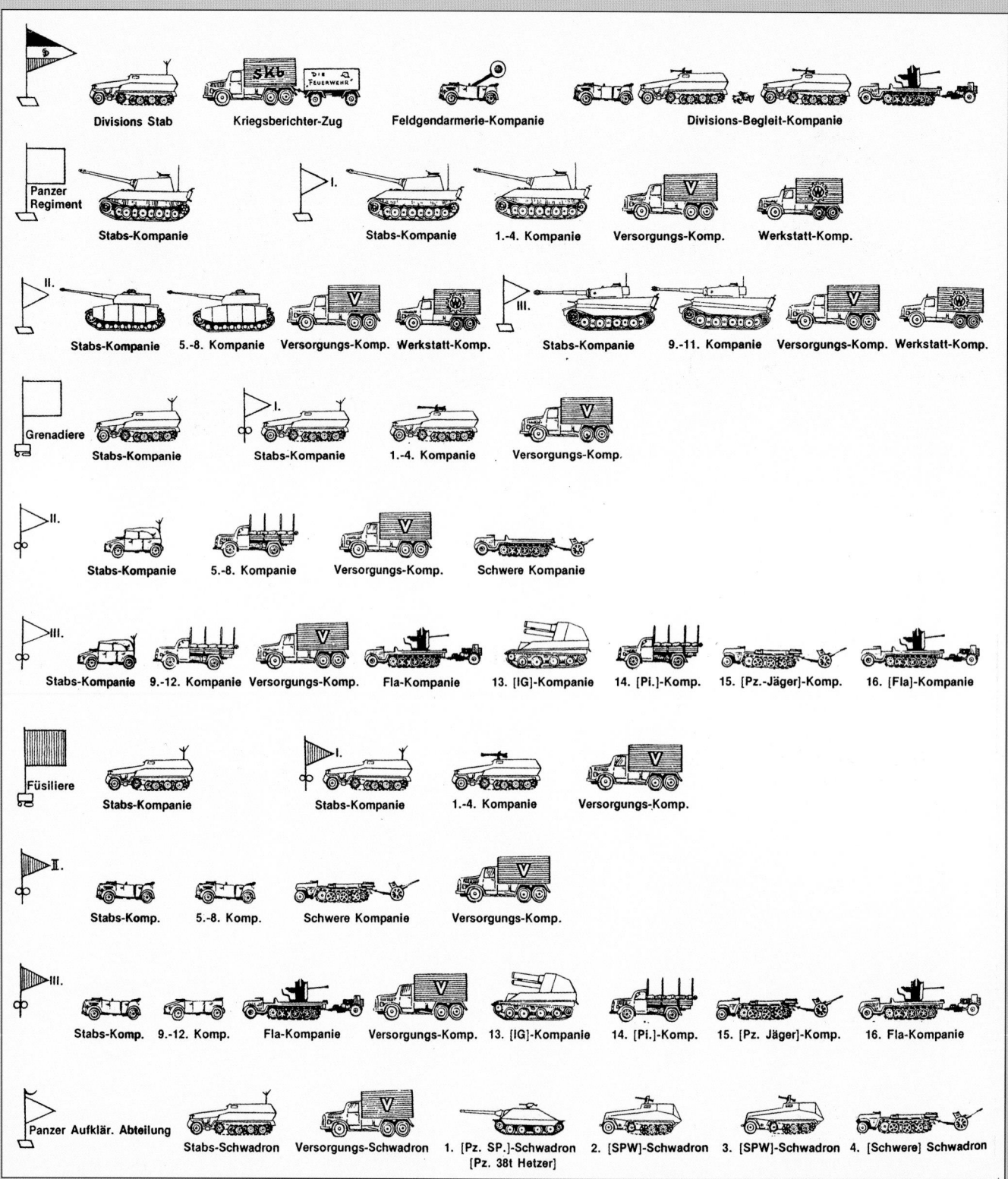

Divisions Stab · Kriegsberichter-Zug · Feldgendarmerie-Kompanie · Divisions-Begleit-Kompanie

Panzer Regiment · Stabs-Kompanie · Stabs-Kompanie · 1.-4. Kompanie · Versorgungs-Komp. · Werkstatt-Komp.

Stabs-Kompanie · 5.-8. Kompanie · Versorgungs-Komp. · Werkstatt-Komp. · Stabs-Kompanie · 9.-11. Kompanie · Versorgungs-Komp. · Werkstatt-Komp.

Grenadiere · Stabs-Kompanie · Stabs-Kompanie · 1.-4. Kompanie · Versorgungs-Komp.

Stabs-Kompanie · 5.-8. Kompanie · Versorgungs-Komp. · Schwere Kompanie

Stabs-Kompanie · 9.-12. Kompanie · Versorgungs-Komp. · Fla-Kompanie · 13. [IG]-Kompanie · 14. [Pi.]-Komp. · 15. [Pz.-Jäger]-Komp. · 16. [Fla]-Kompanie

Füsiliere · Stabs-Kompanie · Stabs-Kompanie · 1.-4. Kompanie · Versorgungs-Komp.

Stabs-Komp. · 5.-8. Komp. · Schwere Kompanie · Versorgungs-Komp.

Stabs-Komp. · 9.-12. Komp. · Fla-Kompanie · Versorgungs-Komp. · 13. [IG]-Kompanie · 14. [Pi.]-Komp. · 15. [Pz. Jäger]-Komp. · 16. Fla-Kompanie

Panzer Aufklär. Abteilung · Stabs-Schwadron · Versorgungs-Schwadron · 1. [Pz. SP.]-Schwadron [Pz. 38t Hetzer] · 2. [SPW]-Schwadron · 3. [SPW]-Schwadron · 4. [Schwere] Schwadron

newer but less numerous Pz.Kpfw.IV by then rolling off the production lines was a more capable and better-armed vehicle. The five-man crewed Pz.Kpfw.IV came fully into service in late 1939 (with just over 200 then available in Panzer units), mounting a 75mm cannon and two machine guns, with much better mobility and armor protection than that of its predecessors. However, the Panzers were still under-gunned and under-armored compared with their likely opposition, although their relatively light weight (about twenty tons, depending on the model) meant they were fast and manoeuvrable. It was not until 1942 that events on the Eastern Front resulted in the

production of the Pz.Kpfw.V "Panther", which was one of the best tanks deployed by any nation during the war.[5]

### The Panzergrenadiers

While the tanks of the Panzer regiments spearheaded the attack, the business of securing the victory fell to the Panzergrenadier troops who moved with or just behind the tanks in their armored troop carriers, usually the Hanomag Sd.Kfz.251 series of armored half-track vehicles. These units were created to solve the problems encountered in 1939 and 1940, when tank units frequently found

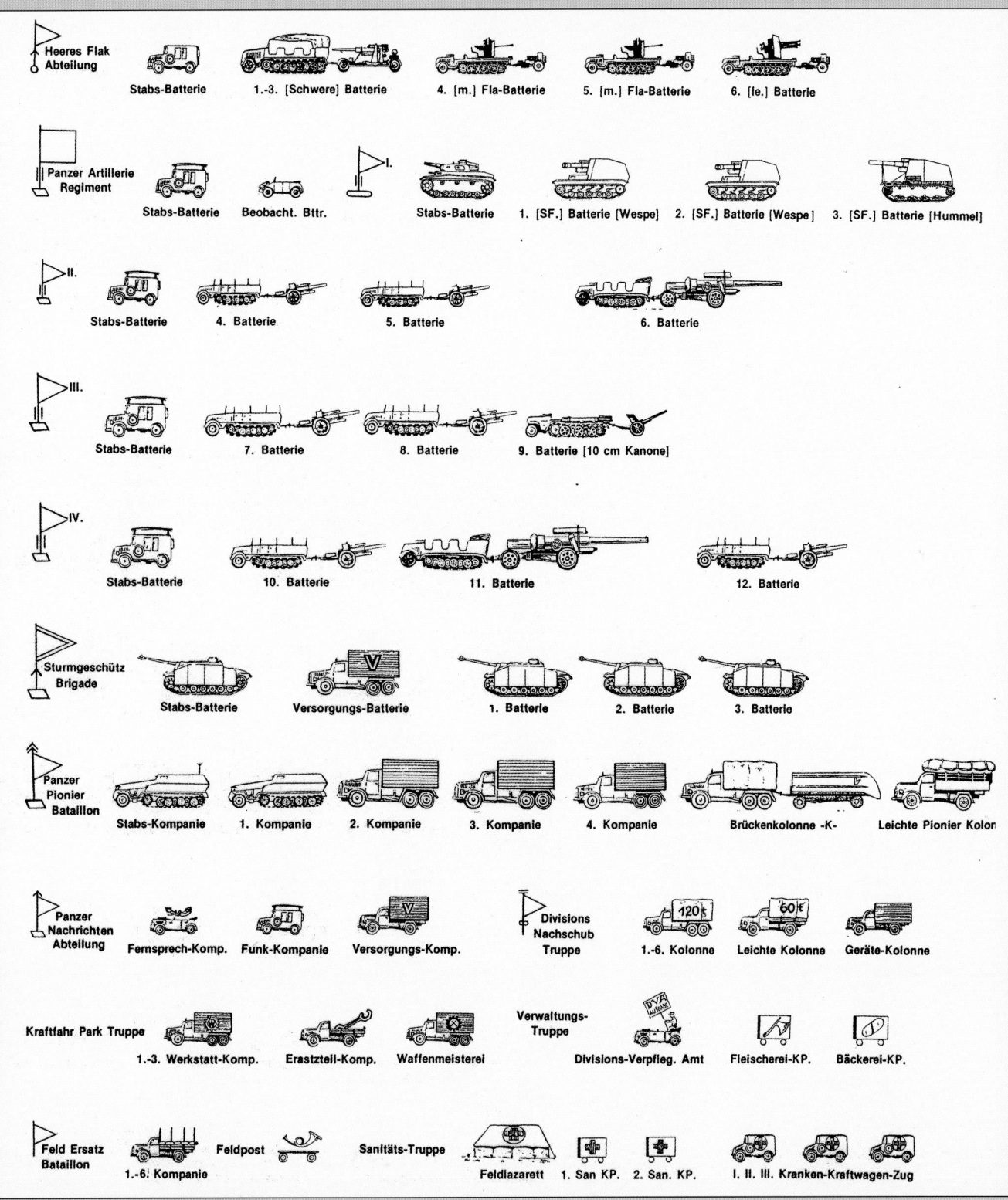

Diagram of the actual organization, vehicles and principal weapons of the élite Panzergrenadierdivision "Großdeutschland", July 1944, showing the vehicles and weapons fielded by the division.

themselves moving far ahead of the infantry and other supporting arms and became vulnerable to infantry-manned anti-tank weapons. Despite their categorization as part of the Panzer forces, the high command's aspiration to equip them with armored vehicles always exceeded Germany's industrial capacity, and it was not unusual for a Panzergrenadier regiment to be partly or wholly equipped with trucks rather than armored infantry carriers. Indeed, a similar shortfall in tank production meant that assault guns and earlier types of tanks had to provide the armored fire support for Panzergrenadier formations instead of this being

provided by the latest tanks. None the less, where they were available, the protection and vehicle-mounted weapons of the armored troop carriers allowed the Panzergrenadiers to remain mounted until the last possible moment, fighting from their vehicles if necessary, thus ensuring that the time between the initial tank attack and the infantry assault was minimal, maximizing the shock effect of the joint tank and infantry onslaught. If the infantry was the premier arm of the German army, the army's Panzergrenadiers were undoubtedly the élite infantry warriors of modern mobile warfare.

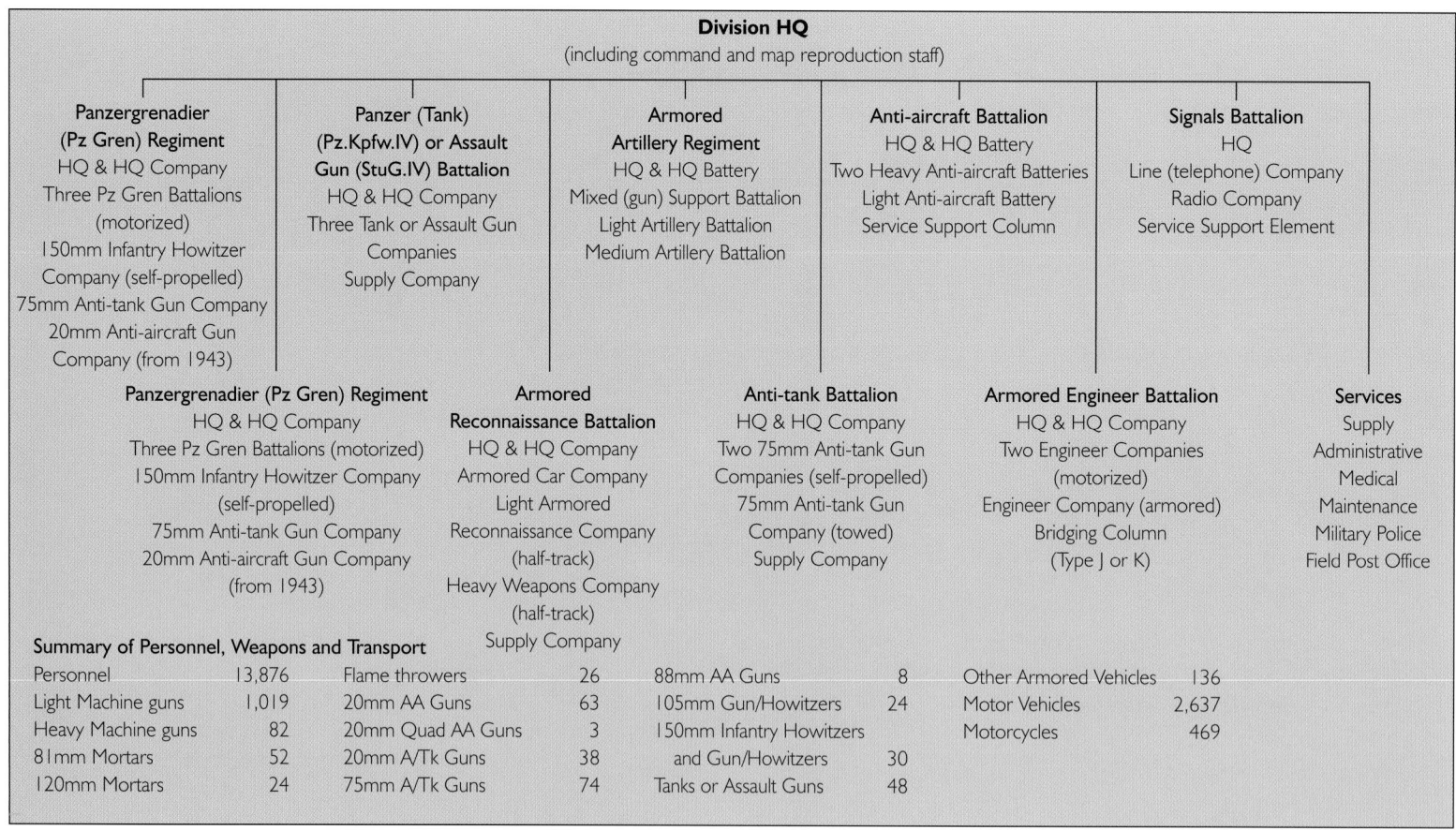

| Division HQ (including command and map reproduction staff) | | | | |
|---|---|---|---|---|
| **Panzergrenadier (Pz Gren) Regiment** HQ & HQ Company Three Pz Gren Battalions (motorized) 150mm Infantry Howitzer Company (self-propelled) 75mm Anti-tank Gun Company 20mm Anti-aircraft Gun Company (from 1943) | **Panzer (Tank) (Pz.Kpfw.IV) or Assault Gun (StuG.IV) Battalion** HQ & HQ Company Three Tank or Assault Gun Companies Supply Company | **Armored Artillery Regiment** HQ & HQ Battery Mixed (gun) Support Battalion Light Artillery Battalion Medium Artillery Battalion | **Anti-aircraft Battalion** HQ & HQ Battery Two Heavy Anti-aircraft Batteries Light Anti-aircraft Battery Service Support Column | **Signals Battalion** HQ Line (telephone) Company Radio Company Service Support Element |

| **Panzergrenadier (Pz Gren) Regiment** HQ & HQ Company Three Pz Gren Battalions (motorized) 150mm Infantry Howitzer Company (self-propelled) 75mm Anti-tank Gun Company 20mm Anti-aircraft Gun Company (from 1943) | **Armored Reconnaissance Battalion** HQ & HQ Company Armored Car Company Light Armored Reconnaissance Company (half-track) Heavy Weapons Company (half-track) Supply Company | **Anti-tank Battalion** HQ & HQ Company Two 75mm Anti-tank Gun Companies (self-propelled) 75mm Anti-tank Gun Company (towed) Supply Company | **Armored Engineer Battalion** HQ & HQ Company Two Engineer Companies (motorized) Engineer Company (armored) Bridging Column (Type J or K) | **Services** Supply Administrative Medical Maintenance Military Police Field Post Office |

**Summary of Personnel, Weapons and Transport**

| | | | | | |
|---|---|---|---|---|---|
| Personnel | 13,876 | Flame throwers | 26 | 88mm AA Guns | 8 |
| Light Machine guns | 1,019 | 20mm AA Guns | 63 | 105mm Gun/Howitzers | 24 |
| Heavy Machine guns | 82 | 20mm Quad AA Guns | 3 | 150mm Infantry Howitzers | |
| 81mm Mortars | 52 | 20mm A/Tk Guns | 38 | and Gun/Howitzers | 30 |
| 120mm Mortars | 24 | 75mm A/Tk Guns | 74 | Tanks or Assault Guns | 48 |

| | |
|---|---|
| Other Armored Vehicles | 136 |
| Motor Vehicles | 2,637 |
| Motorcycles | 469 |

The Panzergrenadier-divisionen (armored or motorized infantry divisions) had significant combat power. However, a lack of armored personnel carriers and the frequent allocation of assault guns rather than tanks to these divisions sometimes meant that they lacked the mobility and firepower to achieve their full potential.

### The Panzer and Panzergrenadier Divisions

Panzer divisions of up to about 14,000 men provided the strike force that spearheaded the Blitzkriegs in 1939 against Poland, in 1940 against France and the Low Countries, and in 1941 against the Soviet Union. In 1939 a Panzer division comprised two tank regiments and two Panzergrenadier regiments, together with the usual supporting arms and services. This meant that the Panzer divisions each controlled as many as 400 light and medium tanks at the beginning of the war. At best, only two of the division's four Panzergrenadier battalions were transported in armored half-tracks, while the remaining two or three battalions were usually transported in trucks.

During the winter of 1940, Hitler ordered that the total number of Panzer divisions should be increased from ten to 21. However, this was to be achieved not by the production of more tanks but by halving the tank strength of the existing divisions, which meant that the number of tank regiments in each division reduced from two to one, while the division's tank strength dropped to between 150 and 200. Notwithstanding any possible arguments about achieving an enhanced operational flexibility by the creation of these additional maneuver units, this would soon prove to have been an ill-judged decision. Monthly tank production between January and June 1941 averaged only 212 vehicles, so that by the start of Operation *Barbarossa* no more than 5,262 tanks were available, with only about 4,198 fully ready to conduct intensive offensive operations, of which only 1,404 were the better-armed Pz.Kpfw.III and Pz.Kpfw.IV medium tanks.[6] Amid the euphoria that resulted from the Blitzkrieg victories of 1940, and in his desire to generate sufficient numbers of Panzer divisions for *Barbarossa*, Hitler had fatally weakened the actual combat strength of those

armored divisions that were launched into Russia in June 1941. As the war continued, this meant that these divisions always lacked the overwhelming combat power necessary to realize their true potential. It also underlined the strategic consequences of the failure of the leadership of the Third Reich to place German industry and the whole nation on to a total war footing in the late 1930s – a failure motivated both by internal political considerations and by over-optimism about the duration and outcome of the war.

The types and quantities of tanks and other weapons used within the various Panzer units varied enormously. During the first two or three years of the war the typical all-arms Panzer division had anywhere between 150 and 200 tanks and self-propelled assault guns at its disposal, although sometimes as many as 300 or even 350 might be fielded for a specific operation, or by any of the several élite Panzer or Panzergrenadier divisions such as the Panzergrenadier Division "Großdeutschland" or the 21st Panzer Division. Although the numbers of other weapons in the divisions also varied widely, they usually had available more than 500 machine guns, almost 100 anti-tank guns, about 50 howitzers and some 150 mortars.

The army's Panzergrenadier divisions, each with up to 14,000 men at full strength, were officially part of the army's Panzertruppe, and as such they were administered by the Inspectorate of Mobile Forces rather than by the Inspectorate of Infantry. The Panzergrenadier division had two regiments, and its overall organization was virtually the same as that of the infantry (motorized) division. Indeed, in many cases these divisions were upgraded motorized infantry divisions, although most importantly they also had an Abteilung (a battalion-sized unit) of tanks or self-propelled assault guns. The use of armored personnel carriers (typically the half-track Hanomag Sd.Kfz.251, where available) meant that their means and speed of entering combat and their initial impact were all different from that of non-armored infantry, but once dismounted from their armored half-tracks Panzergrenadiers operated much as other infantry soldiers.

# 4. Cavalry

Although the Reichswehr had nominally fielded three cavalry divisions, by 1938 the only operationally independent cavalry formation still in existence was a single brigade based in East Prussia. During the first eighteen months of fighting from September 1939, cavalry troops were allocated to infantry divisions for reconnaissance duties, while others were deployed piecemeal to operate with the light armor of the light divisions and on various reconnaissance missions in support of the army corps and other divisions where required. But by November 1941 the cavalry had been largely supplanted by the Panzer forces, and on 3 November the army in effect lost the cavalry arm when its sole remaining cavalry division became the 24th Panzer Division. In light of the experience gained on the Eastern Front, however, the 1st Cossack Cavalry Division was formed in August 1943. This was subsequently joined by two more, and all three divisions eventually formed an army corps. In late 1944, the three divisions were re-designated as the 14th SS Corps and transferred into the Waffen-SS, which (unlike the army) had not dispensed with its cavalry arm in 1941 and retained three cavalry divisions throughout the war.

# 5. Artillery

The artillery had proved a war-winner in Germany's nineteenth-century wars and a battle winner in World War I, and in 1939 its principal mission was still to support the infantry in all phases of war, using indirect fire to engage any sort of target as required. Somewhat surprisingly, although senior artillery officers served at army group and army headquarters, it was not until quite late in World War II that artillery staff officers were assigned to the headquarters of each army corps. Meanwhile a well-justified aspiration by OKW to establish a suitably senior artillery commander at the headquarters of every infantry division to provide the division with effective fire support, by overseeing all aspects of the artillery fire planning, munitions planning, fire coordination and artillery staff work, was never realized. The commander of the divisional artillery regiment usually fulfilled these functions in addition to his more immediate command responsibilities, advising the division commander and being responsible for planning and executing the artillery fire plan to match the division commander's battle plan. In addition to a full range of field, medium, heavy and super-heavy artillery and howitzers, the artillery also fielded anti-aircraft and smoke-producing units, as well as survey, meteorological

and mapping specialists. The 75mm and 150mm infantry guns overlapped the calibers of various field artillery weapons, and anti-tank guns were originally classed as infantry weapons rather than artillery. The later use of 88mm anti-aircraft guns as anti-tank artillery blurred this distinction, the situation further confused by the fact that at the outset of the war most of these guns were manned mainly by Luftwaffe flak units.

In 1939 the standard artillery regiment in an infantry division consisted of the headquarters elements and three battalions, each of three four-gun batteries of 75mm guns. A heavy battalion of three four-gun batteries equipped with 150mm howitzers completed the 48 gun regiment. All these guns were horse-drawn. From 1943, however, evolving operational needs and a shortage of German-produced guns forced several pragmatic changes. These resulted in artillery regiments that consisted of a headquarters, a headquarters battery (incorporating communications, cartography and meteorological specialists), three battalions with two four-gun 105mm batteries and one 75mm battery, and a heavy howitzer battalion with two three-gun 150mm batteries.

In addition to the artillery regiments that supported the various divisions, a number of special-to-purpose and independent artillery regiments, battalions and other units manned the army's

Cavalry troops on pre-war maneuvers taking time to feed their mounts in the field and to inspect their hooves, dealing with any injuries or re-shoeing required. The widespread use of horses by the cavalry pre-war and by all arms (except the Panzer forces) both prior to and throughout the war depended upon the army's extensive and well-organized system to feed and care for these animals. This included a sizable veterinary organization.

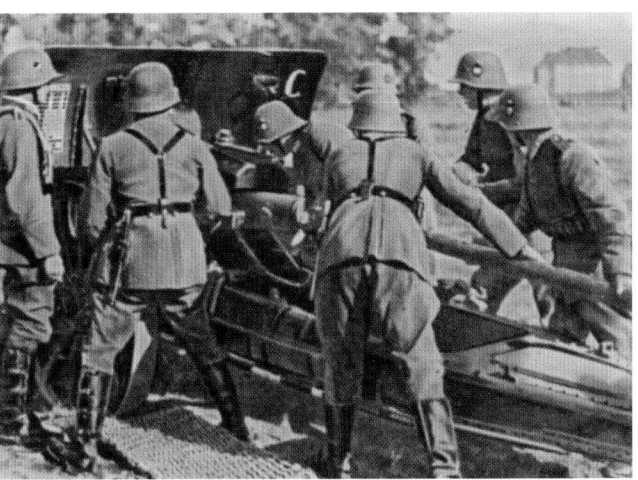

A fully manned artillery gun crew practicing their loading drills in the pre-war years.

various heavy, super-heavy and special artillery weapons. Among these weapons were assault guns, coastal and fortress artillery, and railway artillery guns (Eisenbahnlafette) – including 280mm guns, and the two massive 800mm guns "Gustav" and "Dora". Unsurprisingly, the number of army heavy artillery battalions increased rapidly once the war commenced, so that the 35 battalions that had existed in September 1939 numbered no fewer than 117 by May 1940.[7]

# 6. Engineers

The tasks carried out by the army's engineers were diverse: the engineer arm included combat or assault engineers, construction engineers and fortress engineers; there were also railway engineer units, although they constituted a separate specialized arm. Within the division, engineer platoons belonged to the arm of the unit that they served and were therefore not "engineer troops" by definition, although these personnel were trained to carry out a wide range of engineer tasks. Only the divisional engineer battalion (Pionier-bataillon) was truly an engineer unit. The engineers were organized

in regiments for administrative and command and control purposes, and were subsequently assigned to support particular operations, units and formations as necessary. The assault engineers were in many respects combat infantrymen and were regularly the first into action, operating assault boats, blowing paths through wire obstacles, clearing minefields, destroying bunkers and operating flame throwers and remotely controlled demolition-charge carriers. Engineers also surveyed, laid, marked and cleared minefields, as well as constructing forward airfields and decoy installations, while major camouflage tasks – often carried out as part of the operational deception plan – were also the responsibility of the engineers.

An engineer battalion usually comprised a battalion headquarters and three engineer companies (two in a Volksgrenadier division), while an armored engineer battalion had an additional headquarters company and a bridge construction column. Indeed, bridging was a routine engineer task, and bridge construction columns were originally found in all engineer battalions until 1943 when they were withdrawn from all but the Panzer formations and centralized under army-level control. The bridging battalions thus formed were about 900-men strong, fielding four bridging companies and a supporting

engineer park company ("park" refers here and elsewhere to a semi-static unit, usually holding quantities of equipment, vehicles or other resources). Construction engineers were formerly a separate arm dealing with such matters as road construction, obstacle building and removal, route clearances, major bridge repair work and tunnelling, but in 1943 they also came under centralized control.

The railway engineer troops (Eisenbahntruppen) were also held under central control and assigned as necessary. These regiments consisted of two battalions, each of four companies, and carried out tasks that included the maintenance and repair of railways and railway bridges. They often deployed specialist railway construction companies (Eisenbahnpionierkompanien) to create new railway systems and sometimes utilized prisoner-of-war labor for this work.

Whatever the means of transport being employed, the army's mobility was only as effective as its ability to avoid or overcome the

The army's engineer units were skilled in crossing water obstacles by a variety of means.

## Army Engineer Boats

| Type of Boat | Basic Characteristics | Remarks |
| --- | --- | --- |
| Small inflatable assault boat | Length 3 meters, weight 53 kilos, capacity three men with assault weapons and equipment or 300 kilos. | Several together could also be used to support an infantry assault bridge. |
| Medium inflatable boat | Length 5.48 meters, weight 150 kilos, capacity seven men with assault weapons and equipment or 1.35 tons. | Various numbers used together could also support rafts carrying loads of about 2.25, 4.5, or 9 tons. |
| Large inflatable boat | Length 7.93 meters, weight 290 kilos, load-carrying capacity up to 13.5 tons. | |
| Motorized assault boat (wood) | Length 6.09 meters, weight 216 kilos, capacity nine men with assault weapons and equipment. | Two crewmen are included in the nine-man capacity. |
| Motorized utility boat (steel) | Length 7.01 meters, weight 2 tons, capacity six men with assault weapons and equipment or about 1,700 kilos. | Although suitable for assault and reconnaissance tasks, this boat was used mainly for constructing bridges and towing or maneuvering rafts and bridge sections. |
| Amphibious Tractor (Sachsenberg Land-Wasser-Schlepper) | A fully tracked amphibious vehicle weighing 16 tons, equipped with twin propellers and rudders, and powered by a Maybach HL 120 engine (300 horsepower). | Able to carry up to sixteen personnel, and generally used as a tractor on land and as a tug in sheltered waters or during the construction of pontoon bridges. |

**Army Engineer Bridging Equipment**

| Type of Bridge | Basic Characteristics | Remarks |
|---|---|---|
| Infantry assault bridge | Lightweight bridge constructed to any required length across rivers with currents flowing at up to 2.24 knots, supported by inflatable assault boats. | Able to carry infantry moving across the bridge in single file. |
| Light pontoon and trestle bridge (Brückengerät C) | Timber or aluminium pontoons with decking. | Constructed either as a basic single-file footway for personnel, or with sufficient pontoons to enable a 4.5 or 5.9 tons load-bearing capacity. |
| Medium pontoon and trestle bridge (Brückengerät T) | Timber pontoons with timber roadway on timber bearers. | Constructed with sufficient pontoons to enable a 4.5 or 11 tons load-bearing capacity, or as a raft capable of carrying 10 tons. |
| Heavy pontoon and trestle bridge (Brückengerät B) | Steel or alloy pontoons with steel superstructure and timber roadway on steel bearers. | Constructed with sufficient pontoons to enable a 4.5 or 10 tons load-bearing capacity, or as a raft using half-pontoons and capable of carrying 10 tons, or using whole pontoons and capable of carrying 20 tons. |
| Assault bridge (Brückengerät K) | Lightweight metal bridge of box girder construction, capable of carrying weights up to 27 tons and bearing vehicles including light tanks. | Dependent upon the requirement and construction used, spans could be approximately 10, 14 or 19 meters. |
| Light sectional bridge (Leichte Z Brücke) | Despite its designation of "light" the bridge was constructed of steel panels, with a 3.63 meter-wide timber roadway capable of bearing tanks weighing up to 33 tons. | The span could be built up to 45 meters in length and in addition to supporting sustained movement by heavy vehicles there were also instances of the use of the Leichte Z Brücke to support railway tracks. |
| Heavy bridge (Brückengerät J 42 and J 43) | Substantial steel bridges constructed to carry sustained movement of heavy vehicles on either a single or double (two-way) trackway. | The maximum span was about 20 meters. Trestles or pontoons could support the structure if required and the J 43 bridge was primarily a reinforced version of the J 42. |

many obstacles – natural and man-made – that lay in its path. Of these, the most frequently encountered natural obstacle was usually water, while the man-made obstacles generally involved minefields. Given the time to do so, and with any nearby enemy troops effectively neutralized, minefields could usually be breached by probing or by using mine detectors to detect the metal mine casings, the mines either being lifted or marked to enable the safe passage of troops or vehicles. Crossing water obstacles invariably involved a more complex operation, with the employment of more specialized troops and equipment. Where the army's movement was obstructed by a major river obstacle, the commander first had to place troops on the opposite bank to secure the site, so that a suitable bridge could be constructed to allow the passage of men and vehicles. By and large,

both tasks usually fell to the army's assault engineers and engineer bridging units, and these troops had a number of specialized boats and bridging equipment with which to carry them out.

# 7. Close Air Support

Although the air force, the Luftwaffe, was a separate part of the Wehrmacht, the close air support it provided to the army was an essential element of the Blitzkrieg concept. Its Messerschmitt, Heinkel, Focke-Wulf and Junkers aircraft – especially the Junkers Ju 87 "Stuka" dive-bombers – were literally the army's "flying artillery", whose operational activities from 1939 presaged the sort of air and ground forces cooperation subsequently developed by the armed forces of many other nations. As such, the Luftwaffe's close air support for the army deserves mention in any study of the German army during World War II.

While the potential benefits of strategic bombing had been thoroughly considered by the Luftwaffe during the 1930s, support for the army had become its principal task by 1939, and this was reflected in the design and development of most of the Luftwaffe combat aircraft deployed during the war. Potentially, almost every type of Luftwaffe combat aircraft could be used to support the army's operations. However, the Junkers Ju 87 tactical dive-bomber, the multi-role Junkers Ju 88 fighter-bomber, and the Focke-Wulf Fw 190 and Messerschmitt Bf 109 fighters were the mainstays of the Luftwaffe's close support operations. In all, about 1,500 combat aircraft supported the invasion of Poland in 1939,

Pontoon bridges provided yet another means of crossing major river obstacles.

while some 3,500 provided close- and medium-range support for the attack against France in 1940, with 2,800 (60 percent of the Luftwaffe's total strength) being deployed for the initial air strikes against the Soviet Union in June 1941.

During the attacks on Poland, Denmark, Norway, the Low Countries and France in 1939 and 1940 the Luftwaffe's air onslaughts were frequently categorized as "terror attacks" by those nations that suffered them. In reality these attacks simply represented the true nature of modern all-arms warfare, being broadly designed to facilitate a speedy victory by the ground forces rather than to create terror for its own sake. Only the 1940 Blitz (which was in any case a strategic air campaign, not close air support) was truly designed to terrify the civilian population of Great Britain into submission and force the London government to seek an armistice. But the Blitz was a signal failure and demonstrated that conventional air power alone could not by itself subdue a nation – whereas coordinated and simultaneous action in the air and on the ground had already proved a winning combination.

Many operations during the Blitzkrieg campaigns of 1939 to 1941 showed the effectiveness of close ground-air cooperation. Conversely, as the Luftwaffe's power and its numbers of combat aircraft waned during the later years of the war, so the army's ability to mount large-scale mobile offensive operations became ever more constrained. As early as 1940 the Luftwaffe's failure to win the Battle of Britain, and thus guarantee German air superiority over the English Channel, had effectively ended the army's hopes of mounting Operation *Seelöwe* in the aftermath of the defeat of France. Much later, the vulnerability of the army's Panzer units to air attack was highlighted time and again during the counter-invasion operations mounted in the days and weeks after D-Day in the summer of 1944. The ultimate failure of the *Wacht am Rhein* offensive in the Ardennes that winter re-emphasized this and demonstrated the critical nature and interdependence of ground and air forces during mobile operations, while showing all too clearly the often parlous state of Luftwaffe close air support by that stage of the war. Indeed, from as early as 1941, the Luftwaffe could only support ground offensives by generating local air superiority on a temporary basis to support a specific operation, such as the invasion of Crete in May 1941, or by achieving complete surprise, as was the case during the opening phase of Operation *Barbarossa* in June 1941. In the face of overwhelming Allied air power, from late 1944 the Luftwaffe and army together had also to capitalize wherever possible on adverse weather conditions that effectively prevented any flying by either side, while still allowing ground movement, as they did during the early days of the December 1944 Ardennes offensive.

By definition, close air support was that which was provided within the main battle area and immediately to the rear of the enemy's front line and usually involved the direct support of troops on the ground. This meant that the targets to be attacked changed constantly, reflecting the ebb and flow of battle. In offensive

operations it was brought to bear on the flanks of attacking divisions as well as immediately ahead of advancing troops. It also involved the "counter-air" suppression of any enemy aircraft that attempted to attack the ground forces. Close air support missions usually involved bombing and strafing static and mobile ground forces, artillery positions, headquarters, bunkers and other weapon emplacements, concentrations of tanks, self-propelled guns and troop carriers, supply, fuel and ammunition dumps and logistic supply columns. Most of the French army's artillery was still largely horse-drawn in 1940, and as such it was particularly vulnerable to air attack, with much of the French 9th Army's artillery in the Sedan area immobilized as a result of pin-point bombing by the Luftwaffe's Stuka dive-bombers during the fighting that May. Other air support missions struck targets deep within enemy territory, such as railheads, communications centers, major depots, airfields and industrial sites.

Despite its clear importance, direct radio communication between Luftwaffe aircraft and ground troops was generally extremely limited below army group or army headquarters level, although where they were available Luftwaffe liaison officers (Fliegerverbindungsoffiziere, or "Flivos") were assigned to army corps and occasionally to divisional headquarters. Their task was to plan and facilitate air support for the ground forces, including the coordination of air reconnaissance, while other specially trained Luftwaffe officers (Fliegerleitoffiziere) could also be deployed with the ground forces, using ground-to-air radios to direct air strikes from forward observation positions. But these forward air observers were frequently unavailable or were not necessarily in the right place to deal with an immediate crisis. Consequently, the ground forces made much use of visual (primarily smoke and light) pre-planned and emergency signals, together with various improvised vehicle recognition devices, which included the extensive use of German flags secured flat across the rear decking of attacking armored vehicles. To avoid "friendly fire" incidents, a high standard of training in the recognition of vehicles used both by the Wehrmacht and by the Allies was a vital attribute for all Luftwaffe pilots, but particularly those who flew the fighters and fighter-bombers that provided the close air support for the army.

The Junkers Ju 87 Stuka dive-bomber provided vital close air support for the army's operations, especially during the Blitzkrieg years of 1939-1941, and commanders came to regard it as a form of "airborne artillery".

# PART VIII
# Weapons of War

The development and production of the weapons with which Hitler's army fought the Second World War was carried out during two quite different but overlapping periods. The first of these was the pre-war rearmament of Germany from 1933 to 1939, parts of this process having been already in train even before Hitler achieved power in 1933. The second period was the program of modification, further development and production of brand-new weapons as a result of the experience gained on the battlefield from 1939 to 1945. Undoubtedly the greatest influence upon the second period was the knowledge acquired on the Eastern Front from late 1941.*

## 1. Stocking the Armory, 1933–1939

A major part of the rearmament process was the development and production of the weapons with which the army would fight its future war. Although this was already well under way before Hitler achieved power, it accelerated significantly from the mid-1930s. The weapons that flowed from factories such as Mauser, Gustloff, Krupp, Grossfuss, Busch, Rheinmetall, Walther and many others were superbly engineered, innovative and accurate. Eventually weapons such as the MG 42 machine gun, the 88mm dual-role anti-tank and anti-aircraft gun and the PAK 40mm anti-tank gun were generally regarded as being the best weapons in their class fielded either by the Allies or the Axis during the war. However, their sheer quality and close engineering tolerances made some of the weapons susceptible to the extreme climatic conditions in which they would eventually be used, particularly in Russia, but also amid the dust and sand of North Africa.

Germany would ultimately find that its home-based armaments industry could not produce weapons in the huge quantities necessary to sustain a war of attrition, but the disarmament (in all but name) of the nation and its army after 1918 did mean that

The MG 34, here mounted on its tripod for use in the medium or sustained fire role, was one of the best known machine guns of World War II. The less complex and further improved MG 42 was developed from it.

Germany's armed forces were not hamstrung by a residue of thousands of obsolete weapons left over from the 1914–18 war. It could thus take a wholly fresh and innovative approach to developing new weapons for a future conflict instead of being forced to perpetuate the technology (and therefore many of the tactics) of the previous one. Necessarily, innovation went hand-in-hand with subterfuge, and in the autumn of 1934 the Heereswaffenamt (Army Ordnance Office) provided every arms manufacturing facility in Germany with a code number and letter to be stamped on to weapons in place of the traditional name and address of the manufacturer routinely applied by German arms producers in former times. This action acknowledged that a weapon with the manufacturer's address shown on it, if captured by the enemy, could provide intelligence leading to the manufacturing plant being subjected to air attack; at the same time it contributed positively to the wider policy of obfuscating international awareness of German rearmament, with the list of manufacturing code numbers being closely protected by a "Geheim" ("Secret") security caveat. During the late 1930s, large quantities of foreign weapons from Austria and Czechoslovakia were also taken into the army's inventory, subject to their acceptance by the Ordnance Office, when they were usually stamped with the office's "WaA" ("Waffenamt") and a German eagle with an approval number. Many of these foreign weapons continued in production and German use throughout the war but were given German names and numerical designations indicating their actual country of origin. With the Berlin government ever conscious of the constraints imposed by Versailles, some of the new weapons (notably artillery) produced in Germany during the 1930s were deliberately allocated the manufacturing model number "18" to imply that these were not new types but rather were weapons already in service at the end of the war in 1918. Despite the pace of German rearmament during the 1930s, weapons supply rarely met demand, and so the army was constrained to continue to use a wide range of foreign weapons throughout the war. This in turn produced significant logistics (particularly ammunition supply), maintenance and training problems.

Once Hitler came to power, German weapons development was increasingly directed toward supporting what later became the Blitzkrieg form of warfare, with much development focused upon maximizing firepower, mobility and the need to defeat the threat posed by armored or tank units. One such weapon that emerged from the rearmament activities of the 1930s was the Maschinengewehr 34 (MG 34) machine gun. This recognized the effectiveness of the medium machine guns that had caused so many casualties during the 1914–18 war, and at the same time it was acknowledged that the infantry now needed a readily portable light machine gun to support it in a fast-moving war of maneuver.

* The principal weapons with which Hitler's army fought the Second World War are shown in Appendix 7, together with their main characteristics.

In order to circumvent Versailles, the experimental work to produce a suitable weapon was carried out at the Rheinmetall plant at Solothurn in Switzerland. The result was the 7.92 mm MG 34, introduced into service from 1936 as the standard machine gun (Einheitsmaschinengewehr) of the German ground forces. This excellent, but technologically complex, weapon was air-cooled, lightweight, and had a rate of fire of 800 to 900 rounds per minute, with ammunition fed either from a 50-round box magazine, or by belts of 50 or 250 rounds. A particular feature was the ability to change the MG 34 barrel quickly and easily, thereby largely avoiding stoppages and malfunctions due to overheating. Whether used with or without its optical sight (the MG-Zieleinrichtung), the MG 34 was a very accurate weapon, which could be used as a light machine gun, a medium machine gun mounted on a tripod, an anti-aircraft machine gun using a special tripod mount, or fitted as a vehicle-mounted machine gun.

A submachine gun (machine pistol or machine carbine), the 9mm Maschinenpistole 18/I (MP 18/I), had been developed in 1918 primarily for use by assault detachments in the trenches, and from this weapon the MP 28, MP 34 and other similar weapons were subsequently developed, being based to varying extents upon designs produced by Hugo Schmeisser of the Bergmann engineering company. Then in 1938 Heinrich Vollmer and the Erma-Werke armaments manufacturer produced a much-improved Maschinenpistole (MP), the MP 38, using steel stampings and plastics. The MP 38 had a 32-round box magazine and a rate of fire of 500 rounds per minute. It combined cheapness of manufacture with firepower and robustness while also using the same ammunition as the army's standard Walther and Luger (or Parabellum) service pistols. It was suitable for use by ground

The 37mm PAK 35/36 anti-tank gun was widely used throughout the war, although more powerful anti-tank weapons were introduced by 1943. A Pz.Kpfw.IV tank is behind the PAK 35/36.

**Right:** The 7.92mm PzB 38 anti-tank rifle proved of limited effectiveness, other than against lightly armored vehicles.

**Below:** Despite their fairly limited range, flame-throwers were often used to devastating effect. Here a Flammenwerfer 35 operator is dealing with an emplacement or bunker.

troops, paratroopers, Panzer and vehicle-borne troops alike, due to its size, weight and folding metal stock. In due course the MP 38 (and its successor the MP 40 even more so) proved to be one of the most effective and best-known submachine guns of World War II (being frequently but quite incorrectly called the "Schmeisser").

The impact of the tank upon the campaign on the Western Front in 1917 and 1918 had been well noted by the army high command, but the Versailles treaty did not permit Germany to possess either tanks or anti-tank weapons. However, a later relaxation of these constraints eventually allowed the development of the 37mm Panzerabwehrkanone (anti-tank gun, or PAK) L/45, which came into service in 1928. This gun was drawn by horses, but it could also be manhandled over short distances. From 1934 the 37mm Panzerabwehrkanone 35/36 was produced for the army, being a lighter and improved version of the PAK L/45 and which could also be towed by motor vehicles. These guns provided the foundation upon which the highly successful 75mm PAK 40 was later based. These weapons provided the infantry with an adequate counter to many types of armored threat, but all efforts to produce a hand-held anti-tank weapon were generally unsuccessful until the appearance of anti-tank rocket launchers much later during the war. Two anti-tank rifles – the 7.92mm Panzerbüchse (PzB) 38 and the PzB 39, both of which fired a tungsten carbide armor-piercing projectile – were taken into service before the war and subsequently proved to be ineffective against all but lightly-armored vehicles such as armored cars.

A much more successful weapon was the Flammenwerfer (flame thrower) 35 which entered service from 1935. The flame thrower was originally a German invention, and both the Flammenwerfer 35 and later types of this weapon built upon the considerable experience of their use during World War I. Having noted the usefulness of the light (or "trench") mortars used by the British army during that conflict, the German army also developed a medium mortar (the 81mm Granatwerfer 34), which entered service in 1934. This was followed by a light mortar (the 50mm leichter Granatwerfer 36) in 1936. These weapons had maximum ranges of 2,400 meters and 520 meters respectively and could provide immediate fire support for infantry units.

For its longer range fire support the army looked to the artillery, just as it had for the previous hundred years. German artillery had acquired a formidable reputation during the wars of the nineteenth century, especially the Austro-Prussian War of 1866 and the Franco-Prussian War of 1870–1. During World War I the guns that supported the Kaiser's army further enhanced that reputation, when the quality of weapons made by Krupp, the principal manufacturer of artillery both for the national army and for export, was already legendary. In response to the deluge of new government orders for artillery placed from 1933, Krupp, Rheinmetall and many other manufacturers rose to the challenge with alacrity. The vital need for mobility greatly influenced the design of the new guns, and existing pieces were modified where necessary to facilitate being towed by vehicles or drawn by horses,

**Far left:** The 50mm light mortar Type 36 provided rapid and effective short-range HE fire support to troops in close contact with the enemy.

**Left:** The 81mm medium mortar is shown here with some of the ammunition types and other equipment used to operate it, including a 70cm range-finder.

while suitable prime-movers and other vehicles were also specifically developed to tow artillery guns on the battlefield and cross-country. By the 1930s much of the work to circumvent the limitations imposed upon the Reichswehr by Versailles was in any case already well in hand both within Germany and by armaments contractors and manufacturers in Switzerland, Sweden and the Netherlands. There, much of the heavy artillery specifically

prohibited by the Versailles treaty was developed, tested and produced in secret, with the use of the number "18" type designator applied extensively to further disguise the existence and actual modernity of these guns by implying that they had already been in service in 1918.

The army's artillery requirements fell into four broad categories: light artillery was needed to support infantry and mountain

The 75mm leIG 18 infantry light gun in the foreground was not classed as an artillery weapon, being specifically designed to provide close supporting fire to the infantry divisions within which it was found. The gun in the background is a 105mm leFH 18 field artillery howitzer.

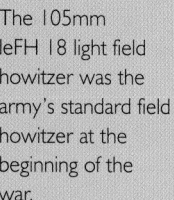

The 105mm leFH 18 light field howitzer was the army's standard field howitzer at the beginning of the war.

infantry units directly; field artillery supported the army's divisions; medium artillery provided longer-range supporting fire; and heavy artillery carried out long-range bombardment and special fire missions. A fifth category was anti-aircraft artillery, these guns generally being manned by Luftwaffe personnel. Arguably, a further category existed – the self-propelled artillery, such as assault guns (Sturmgeschütz) – but these guns, mounted on tank chassis, were really a part of the Panzer forces rather than the artillery arm, and in any case did not appear until after the war had started.

To satisfy the needs of the army's infantry divisions, two types of light (or "infantry") gun were produced in quantity during the 1930s, both of which continued in use and production throughout the war. These were the 75mm leichtes Infanteriegeschütze 18 (the infantry light gun type 18) and the 150mm schweres Infanterie-geschütze 33 (the infantry heavy gun type 33). The 75mm gun was originally designed to be drawn by horses, but a modified gun carriage enabling it to be towed by vehicles was soon developed and produced after 1933. This gun could be manhandled into position by its six-man crew with relative ease. For the mountain infantry troops, two equivalent but specialized types of gun were produced, both of which could be dismantled and carried on pack animals or manhandled. These mountain guns were the 75mm leichtes Gebirgsinfanteriegeschütz 18 (the mountain infantry light gun type 18) and the 75mm Gebirgsgeschütz 36 (the mountain gun type 36). The Type 36 was intended to replace the earlier model, but both guns remained in service during the war.

During the 1930s the army's field artillery units relied mainly upon two guns, the 75mm Feldkanone 16 (the field gun type 16) and Rheinmetall's 105mm leichte Feldhaubitze 18 (the light field howitzer type 18). In accordance with the policy set for the post-1933 artillery modernization program, the 105mm leichte Feldhaubitze 18 entered service as the army's standard field howitzer in 1935, while the 75mm Feldkanone 16 was replaced with an improved gun produced by Rheinmetall-Krupp, the 75mm leichte Feldkanone 18, which entered service in 1938. In the meantime, the development and production of a whole range of brand-new medium and heavy artillery proceeded apace, so that by 1939 most of the old 1914–18 gun types had either been replaced or extensively modernized, although some heavy artillery dating back to the pre-1914 era was retained for special bombardment tasks. Generally, the medium artillery guns were of

105mm to 155mm caliber, while the heavy artillery included guns larger than 155mm – some of which were railway guns and self-propelled howitzers with calibers as great as 280mm, 420mm, 600mm and even 800 mm.

Although motorized trucks and tractors were used to tow some of the guns, and a number were self-propelled, the vast majority of the artillery's field guns in all but the armored divisions were still drawn by horses, each gun typically served by nine soldiers: a gun commander (an Unteroffizier or Unterwachtmeister), five gunners and three horse handlers. The principal gunner was responsible for the gun-sight and for aiming the piece as ordered, while the other four men prepared the ammunition and managed its supply, loaded the gun, and manhandled and camouflaged it as necessary. The process of coming into action during an advance followed a well-rehearsed sequence. Once the battery commander and forward observation officer had reviewed the situation with the infantry unit the guns were supporting, the battery commander returned to the battery gun line and briefed the battery officer on the mission, at the same time indicating where he wished the individual gun positions to be. The guns were unhitched and manhandled into position while the ammunition was unloaded from the limbers and piled adjacent to the guns. The horse handlers then took the horses and limbers back into cover well clear of the gun line. Reference points were selected, and the forward observation officer passed back to the battery officer all the target details and information about his own position. One gun then fired on the target, its fall of shot being adjusted by the forward observation officer. Once that gun was firing right on target, the other three guns would set their own sights accordingly, and the whole battery could proceed to engage the enemy. At the end of the action the horse handlers brought the limbers forward, the deployment process was reversed, and the battery could be quickly on the move again, all ready to respond to the next call for fire support.

Two prerequisites for successful mobile offensive operations were air superiority and a comprehensive and guaranteed anti-aircraft defense, and to ensure the latter the high command knew that large numbers of Flugabwehrkanone (literally, "air defense guns") would be needed. Versailles had prohibited Germany from producing or acquiring these weapons, so even before 1933 the Reichswehr had taken action to remedy this deficiency. The development of these weapons was carried out secretly in Switzerland, Sweden and the Netherlands during the 1920s, so that by the time Hitler ordered full-scale rearmament a formidable range of Flugabwehrkanone (or "Flak") guns had already been designed and tested and were ready to go into production. These included the 37mm Flak 18, the 20mm Flak 30, and later the 20mm Flak 38, and the four-barrelled Flugabwehrkanonevierling, while larger-caliber anti-aircraft guns were also produced, such as the 105mm Flak 38. The most versatile and potent anti-aircraft weapon to have emerged by 1939 was the 88mm Flak 18, later followed by the similarly impressive 88mm Flak 36 and Flak 37 – the true potential of these weapons as dual-role anti-aircraft and anti-tank guns was only fully realized once they were used in action. The 88mm Flugabwehrkanone 18 was originally developed by Krupp personnel working secretly in Sweden during 1931, and production of the gun began in Germany from 1933, with full testing carried out in Spain, including during the civil war from 1936. Most of these anti-aircraft guns played a key part in many of the army's operations, but they were in almost every case manned by Luftwaffe gunners despite being routinely deployed under the operational control of army units and formations.

The weapons of war that best exemplified the renewed energy and changing operational focus of the army in the 1930s were undoubtedly those of the emerging mobile or Panzer arm, foremost among which was the tank, already widely recognized as being an essential element of any offensive operation. Versailles had forbidden the possession or production of tanks by Germany, but even before the advent of Hitler's National Socialist government the high command of the Reichswehr had put in train the programs to develop a range of armored vehicles. The existence of these embryo tanks was disguised by describing and documenting them officially as "farm vehicles" – the so-called "Leichter Traktor" and "Großtraktor" ("light" and "heavy" tractors). These lightly armored "tractors" were produced during the late 1920s and provided the army with a suitable, if somewhat rudimentary and artificial, means of conducting trials of its concepts and tactics for armored warfare, and for determining its future requirements for armored vehicles. By 1933 the high command had identified the need for a mix of types of tank (Panzerkampfwagen or Pz.Kpfw.) for the army's new Panzer divisions, and in December 1935 the high command formally stated its requirements for a light tank armed either only with machine guns or with machine guns and a 75mm cannon, for a medium tank with a 75mm or 105mm cannon, and for a heavy

The 88mm anti-aircraft gun, sited here in an emplacement on the Channel coast and manned by a Luftwaffe gun crew, proved to be one of the most versatile artillery guns of the war – being used successfully both against ground and air targets.

tank armed with a 105mm cannon. From this was born the tank development program that had already produced the Pz.Kpfw.I in 1934 in time for its experimental employment during the Spanish Civil War in 1936. By this time no fewer than 3,000 Pz.Kpfw.I tanks had been manufactured. The Pz.Kpfw.II followed in 1935, and the Pz.Kpfw.III and Pz.Kpfw.IV from 1936, with successive adaptations, marks and types (Ausführung or Ausf.) of each tank following on from the first production models.

The civil war in Spain provided the army with a valuable opportunity to carry out trials of some of these new vehicles on the battlefield. Although very effective against infantry and non-armored vehicles, the Pz.Kpfw.I, armed only with two machine guns, proved to be under-gunned for the sorts of tasks by then being envisaged for the Panzer forces. These tasks would involve fighting other tanks as well as breaking through infantry defense lines, in addition to operating independently in order to maintain the momentum of an attack, and pursuing and destroying a withdrawing enemy. The Panzers were not required to engage in major tank battles in Spain, but it became clear that the armor of the Pz.Kpfw.I provided inadequate protection against anything other than small-arms fire and light-artillery shell fragments. As a result, production of the Pz.Kpfw.I ceased in March 1935, although the vehicle was subsequently adapted for use as a command vehicle, and some other specialized variants were also developed. The Pz.Kpfw.II, which mounted a 20mm cannon, first appeared in 1935 and also saw limited employment in Spain, where its success against what were recognized to be generally inferior forces nevertheless suggested that it might be used effectively against other tanks. After 1940, however, its armament and armor protection both proved inadequate for this task. The first version of the Pz.Kpfw.III was produced in 1936 with a 37mm gun, and entered service in September 1939, subsequently being improved by a series of modifications and upgrades as the war progressed. The ubiquitous Pz.Kpfw.IV also first appeared in

1936 and was taken into service in September 1939. Mounting a 75mm gun, this tank too was extensively modified and improved in response to the later experience gained in combat, and more than 8,650 Pz.Kpfw.IV tanks were produced between November 1938 and February 1945.

In addition to the various Pz.Kpfw. tanks produced within Germany, a considerable boost had been given to Hitler's rearmament program, and to the effectiveness of the Panzer forces especially, shortly before the war when the German occupation of Czechoslovakia in early 1939 enabled the army to seize almost 700 Czech T-35 and T-38 light tanks, together with that country's tank production lines, which offset significantly the serious shortfall in tanks that still existed within the Panzer arm at that stage. The acquisition and exploitation of what were subsequently re-designated by the Germans as the "Pz.Kpfw.35(t)" and "Pz.Kpfw.38(t)" tanks also accorded with the high command's deliberate policy of using captured foreign weapons and equipment wherever possible, notwithstanding the considerable maintenance and logistic problems invited by this policy.

Those, then, were some of the most important weapons developed and produced to enable the achievement of Hitler's military aspirations, being in accordance with the national program of rearmament from 1933 to 1939, as well as with the initiatives taken by the Reichswehr during the preceding decade. From 1939 began a further period of weapons development, during which the army's weapons of war were conceived, modified and produced in direct response to the lessons learned on the battlefield and to the ever-changing operational and strategic situation over the following six years.

## 2. Exploiting the Armory, 1939–1945

In addition to the extensive range of modern weaponry available to the army in 1939, other weapons of all sorts were already under development, and no time was lost learning the lessons of combat to improve, reject or replace any in-service items that failed to live up to expectations or to meet the challenges of the battlefield. Indeed, while innovation and experimentation fuelled a constant process of modernization and improvement, the plethora and diversity of new weapons and equipment developed, produced and taken into service after 1939 eventually diluted the resources available for the overall armaments procurement program once the tide of war turned against Germany.

### Small-arms: Rifles, Machine guns, Pistols and Submachine Guns

When the army went to war in September 1939 the vast majority of its soldiers were armed with the well-proven Mauser 7.92mm Karabiner 98 (Kar 98) rifle, of which the Kar 98K was the version most widely in service. This bolt-action weapon had a five-round

On the morning of 10 May 1940 German forces invaded the Netherlands, Belgium and Luxembourg. These Pz.Kpfw.II tanks of the 2nd Panzer Division are pictured shortly after crossing the Belgian frontier.

The 7.92mm KAR 98K was the army's standard rifle during the pre-war years and during the first two years of the war.

The 7.92mm Gewehr 41 was issued widely in late 1942, being the forerunner of a series of self-loading rifles.

box magazine and an effective range of about 600 meters (although it was sighted to 2,000 meters), and a ten-inch bladed bayonet could be fitted to the rifle. Although based upon a design that dated back to 1898, the Kar 98K was a reliable, robust and accurate weapon, remaining in service throughout the war. The final version of this rifle was the Mauser Gewehr 98/40, which entered service in October 1941 and continued in use and production throughout the rest of the war. Add-ons for the Kar 98K and other rifles included telescopic sights (although only commercial versions were available until well into 1940), grenade dischargers, which entered service from about mid-1941, and a silencer (Schalldämpfer) introduced in 1944, which was used primarily by snipers firing special low-velocity ammunition (Gewehrnahpatrone) whenever the silencer was fitted. In anticipation that the Kar 98 rifle would continue as the army's principal small-arm, weapons manufacturers such as Mauser, Haenel, Walther and Genschow had, ever since 1919, produced air rifles and .22 caliber rifles that in all other respects mirrored the size, weight and main operating characteristics of the Mauser Kar 98. This had enabled the widespread availability of "service rifles" for training purposes while not breaching the constraints on the holdings of rifles of the military (7.92mm) caliber imposed by Versailles.

Development of a 7.92mm self-loading rifle began early in the war, and this resulted in the production of separate designs by Walther and Mauser respectively. Following troop trials in 1941, Walther's weapon, the Gewehr 41(W), was accepted for general service and was issued widely from December 1942 as the Gewehr 41. This weapon was subsequently modified and made lighter, when it became the Gewehr 43, which went into production in early 1943, and the following year it was re-designated as the Karabiner 43 (Kar 43). This self-loading weapon had a ten-round box magazine and an effective range of about 600 meters, although sighted to 1,200 meters. A special automatic rifle developed for parachute troops entered service in 1942, with an improved

version following in 1943. Paratroopers were, of course, Luftwaffe rather than army personnel, so this weapon, the 7.92mm Fallschirmjägergewehr 42 (FG 42), was officially a Luftwaffe weapon. It featured a twenty-round box magazine (fitted on the left side), automatic or single-shot fire, a bipod and a spike bayonet, which meant that the FG 42 was really a cross between a rifle or assault rifle, a light machine gun and a submachine gun. It was effective to about 600 meters, with sight settings to 1,200 meters.

In September 1939 the army's principal machine gun was the 7.92mm MG 34, with an effective range of 2,000 meters in the light role and up to 5,000 meters mounted on its tripod in the medium role. However, insufficient numbers of MG 34s were available to equip the whole army, so various other types and Czech machine guns made up the deficit until March 1941, by which time the MG 34 was on general issue throughout the army. Development of a cheaper and less complex successor to the MG 34 was already under way when the war started, but it was not until early 1941 that the MG 39/41 was submitted for troop trials. Following its acceptance, production of the re-named "MG 42" commenced in 1942, quantities of the new machine gun being issued to units by the end of the year. With a high rate of fire (up to 1,200 rounds per minute), robustness, reliability and a maximum effective range of almost 6,000 meters, the MG 42 was in all respects an outstanding weapon – probably the best multi-role machine gun produced by any side during the war. By November 1943 sufficient numbers of this gun had been produced to supplant the MG 34, although very many MG 34s continued in use until the end of the war. Some minor modifications of the MG 42 were made in 1943 and 1944, when it was re-designated the "MG 43". Perhaps the best testament to the effectiveness of the MG 42 was the fact that when the post-war West German armed forces (the Bundeswehr) were created in 1955, the army's standard general-purpose machine gun was based directly upon the MG 42 design and hardly differed from it in appearance.

The 7.92mm KAR 43 was developed from the Gewehr 41, and went into production in 1943.

The 7.92mm Fallschirmjäger-gewehr 42 (FG 42) was a unique weapon, being specifically designed for Germany's paratroopers.

Among the other small-arms with which the army went to war was the 9mm self-loading Luger pistol. Originally manufactured by Borchardt-Luger in smaller calibers in order to satisfy the rules set by Versailles, these pistols were specifically manufactured in such a way that they could readily be upgraded to accept 9mm Parabellum military ammunition. The Luger 08 pistol had a magazine holding eight rounds and was accurate up to about 100 meters, but as a close-quarters weapon it was rarely employed at such ranges. While less famous than the Luger 08, the 9mm Walther P38 pistol displayed the same general characteristics and in addition operated on the "double action" principle. The P38 began to replace the Luger 08 from May 1940, although both weapons continued in service throughout the war alongside a

whole range of privately purchased pistols, foremost amongst which were those made by Mauser, Walther and Sauer. Several types of signal pistol (Leuchtpistole) were also available in 1939, with other models and upgrades introduced as the war progressed; in addition to signal flares, some of these weapons (such as the Kampfpistole, issued from early 1943) were also able to fire special bulleted cartridges and grenades.

The MP 38 was officially the army's standard submachine gun when the war began, but too few had been produced by September 1939, so various other weapons manufactured by Bergmann, Schmeisser, Erma and Steyr-Solothurn were also taken into service as a temporary measure. These stop-gap weapons were eventually replaced when the output of MP 38s caught up with the army's

The 7.92mm MG 42 was probably the best multi-role machine gun produced by any nation during World War II.

requirement for them, but by then a new version of the MP 38, the MP 40, had already appeared late in 1940. By 1942 the MP 40 and MP 38 had been produced in sufficient numbers to enable them to replace all the other types of submachine gun then in use. Although these weapons were widely used by all sorts of troops, the so-called 'Schmeisser' Maschinenpistole symbolized the offensive spirit of the German assault trooper throughout the war.

While the MP 38 and MP 40 achieved their place in history, it was actually a weapon developed late in the war as their intended successor that provided a model upon which several post-war automatic weapons were based (notably the Soviet Union's Kalashnikov AK-47 assault rifle, which attracted both fame and notoriety during the Cold War era). Work to develop a new Maschinenpistole had begun in 1941 and was carried out by the designers at Walther and Haenel, and in 1943 numbers of the first version of the new German weapon, the 7.92mm Maschinen-pistole 43 (MP 43), entered service. Although categorized as a Maschinenpistole, however, it bore little resemblance to the MP 38 and MP 40, for the MP 43 was really an automatic carbine or

**Above:** Although the Luger 08 (left-hand picture) was better-known, the Walther P38 pistol on the right was widely issued from 1940, and was generally considered to be the better weapon.

**Left:** The versatile Kampfpistole entered service in 1943. It fired signal flares and other special cartridges, as well as projecting grenades.

**Below left:** Two of the best-known weapons of World War II were the MP 38 and MP 40 "Schmeisser" machine-pistols. The 9mm MP 40 is shown here.

The 7.92mm StuG 44 assault rifle was an excellent weapon but entered service too late to fulfil its potential.

(in modern military parlance) an assault rifle. This fact was properly recognized when the much-improved and modified second production model, the MP 44, was renamed the Sturm-gewehr 44 (literally, assault rifle 44, or StuG 44), although it was also known as the "Karabiner 44" (Kar 44 or K44). It was cheap and simple to produce, its parts largely being pressed rather than machined. It had a rate of fire of 800 rounds per minute, and the curved box magazine held 30 of the shortened (Kurz) rounds, which had been specially developed for the MP 43 and MP 44. Both these weapons had an effective range of 300 meters. Had the StuG 44 arrived on the scene much earlier and in greater numbers it would almost certainly have entirely supplanted the "Schmeisser" weapons, while further modifications and improvements might also have allowed it to replace many of the standard service rifles. It was only in service during the final two years of the war; enhancements in 1943 and 1944 included a telescopic sight attachment and a rifle grenade discharger (the special explosive and armor-piercing grenades for which were never produced). Another unique and highly innovative StuG 44 refinement was a 30-degree curved barrel and linked periscope attachment (the "Krummer Lauf"), which enabled the firer to engage targets without exposing himself to do so (literally making it possible to shoot round corners and through the firing ports or hatches of armored vehicles). Ten thousand of these special curved barrel attachments were ordered in August 1944, quantities of which finally reached the army early in 1945.

The last full-scale production runs of most of the main types of German small-arms ended in late 1944 as ever-increasing numbers of armaments factories were destroyed by Allied bombing or faced the threat of being overrun by ground forces. With a continuing need to replace the army's weapons and to arm the new Volksgrenadier and Volkssturm units, the OKH necessarily placed much reliance upon various cheap, basic and easily manufactured (but consequently often inferior) substitute weapons. Among the most numerous of these was a mass-produced submachine gun whose design was based closely upon that of the British Sten submachine gun of the period.

### Grenades

In addition to small-arms, various types of hand grenades featured prominently in the inventory of those units likely to engage in close-quarters combat. "Offensive" hand-grenades relied primarily upon their blast effect and could be thrown safely during an advance, while "defensive" hand grenades fragmented to cause direct casualties, and so required the thrower to be protected from the explosion. Ignition was either by a friction igniter and time fuse, or by a percussion fuse that exploded the grenade on impact. The best-known type of German hand-grenade was the stick-handled Stielhandgranate 24. It was ignited by first removing a cap on the end of the handle to expose a porcelain ball and cord; once the ball was pulled, the grenade would detonate four to five seconds later. The basic Stielhandgranate 24 relied upon blast rather than fragmentation, and so a serrated steel sleeve was provided, which could be clipped over the grenade's explosive head to produce a much more lethal effect if required. The head of this grenade, containing almost a quarter kilogram of explosive, could be detached from the handle and combined with a number of others to form an improvised demolition charge. Similarly, by connecting several grenade heads in series, all of them being detonated simultaneously, a "Bangalore torpedo" type of demolition charge could be created and used to breach wire obstacles. A properly manufactured Bangalore torpedo charge (Gestreckte Ladung) also existed, being made up with the requisite number of sections of steel pipe packed with high-explosive all connected together and then ignited at one end with a cap igniter set or using a striker match and safety fuse. Although similar in appearance to the Stielhandgranate 24, the Stielhandgranate 43 (introduced in 1943) had a solid wooden handle and incorporated a friction primer and detonator fitted to the head of the grenade. The thrower simply unscrewed the blue metal cap on top of the head, pulled it and threw the grenade, which exploded after four-and-a-half seconds. Another type of hand grenade in general use was the egg-shaped Eierhandgranate 39, which was made of thin sheet metal and produced multiple shards of metal when it exploded. To ignite the Eierhandgranate 39

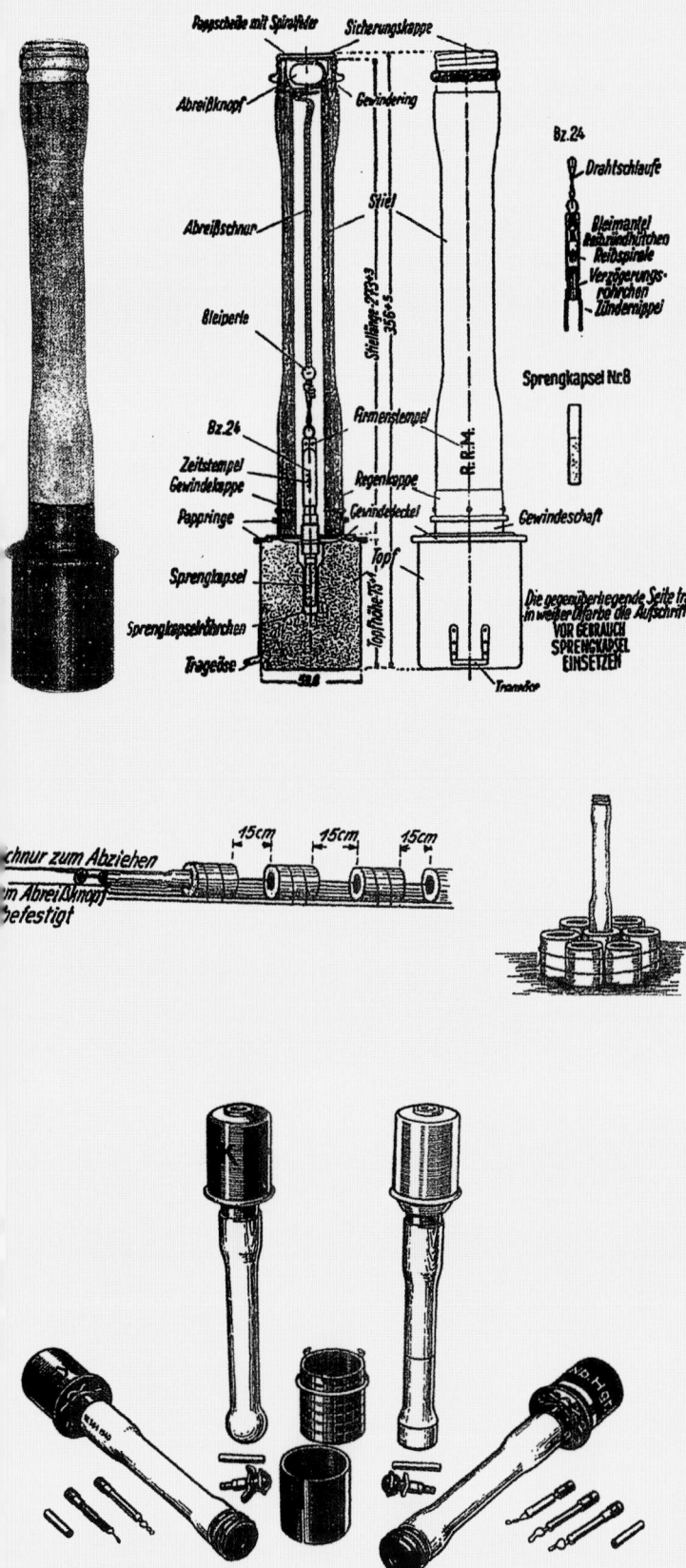

the thrower unscrewed a blue metal cap on top of the grenade and pulled the igniter, the grenade exploding after four to five seconds. As well as high-explosive hand grenades, smoke grenades were also available in both the stick-type and egg-shaped configurations, while other sorts of hand grenade included a hollow-charge anti-tank hand grenade (Panzerwurfmine) and special glass smoke grenades (Blendkörper) for use against the occupants of pill-boxes, bunkers and trenches. Various rifle grenades were also used during the war, including high-explosive, hollow-charge and anti-armor types, all of which could be fired from a cup attachment (Schießbecher) fitted to the Kar 98K rifle.

## Flame throwers

Another weapon used against bunkers and pill-boxes with considerable success was the flame thrower, which was usually operated by assault engineers. The Flammenwerfer 35 system already in service continued to perform well, although the particular nature of this sort of weapon always incurred various hazards, not least of which was the way in which the distinctive shape of the fuel pack (either cylinders or a "lifebuoy" shape) and projector attracted enemy fire, while there was also a significant problem of concealment when the weapon was fired. Several improved versions – including the man-portable Flammenwerfer types 40, 41, and 42 – were taken into service during the war,

**Above and top left:**
Stick hand grenade type 24 (Stielhand-granate 24). The cutaway shows the firing mechanism type 24 and detonator type 8.

**Below left:**
Stielhandgranate 24 multiple heads assembled as improvised explosive charges (top), with other stick hand grenades and component options (bottom)

Granatwerfer 34 fired a two-and-a-quarter kilogram bomb to 1,200 meters.

## Anti-armor Weapons

Post-1939, it was in the area of hand-held anti-tank weapons that some of the greatest changes and weapon advances occurred. Although the Panzerbüchse 38 and 39 anti-tank rifles continued in service during the early part of the war (the Panzerbüchse 39 being later modified to become the 7.9mm Granatbüchse 39 to enable it to fire anti-tank grenades), their failings prompted the urgent development of an alternative means by which the individual soldier could defeat an enemy tank. Research began in 1941, and in 1942 a weapon (the Püppchen, or Raketenwerfer 43) was produced that fired an 88mm rocket-propelled projectile. However, it was not man-portable, and, although its rocket technology had shown the way forward, it was not until 1943 that a series of lightweight and easily manufactured anti-tank rocket launchers began to enter service. Foremost among these were the Raketenpanzerbüchse 54 (or Panzerschreck – the "tank terror") and several varieties of the one-shot, disposable Faustpatrone (usually known as the "Panzerfaust"). With the introduction of these weapons, the individual soldier at last had in his hands the means to stop or even destroy an enemy tank single-handed.

The Raketenpanzerbüchse 54 resembled a stove-pipe (and it was often referred to as such, the Ofenrohr) from which an 88mm hollow-charge rocket could be fired to a distance of about 120 meters, penetrating up to 100mm of armor. A small shield was fitted to later models of the weapon to protect the firer from the rocket's back-blast. The principal drawback of the Panzerschreck was the rearwards flame and blast produced when it was fired, which disclosed the firer's position. Two men usually operated the

**Top:** An MG 42 machine-gunner in Normandy, summer 1944. He is wearing the army green splinter-pattern camouflage clothing and helmet cover.

**Above:** Flame throwers mounted on half-tracks enabled these weapons to accompany and support armored units effectively.

**Right:** An 81mm medium mortar in action on the Eastern Front.

differing in size, fuel capacity, weight and the ignition system used. All these portable flame throwers projected jets of flame at temperatures of 700–800 degrees centigrade for bursts of between one and three seconds duration, each burst being projected some 30 to 40 meters. Much larger vehicle-mounted flame throwers also existed and had much greater fuel capacity, but were still unable to project their flames much beyond 60 meters.

## Mortars

The infantry battalion's 81mm Granatwerfer 34 medium mortar remained in service throughout the war, but the company-level 50mm leichter Granatwerfer 36 proved over-complicated and expensive to produce, so a new 81mm Granatwerfer Kurz 48 (the "short mortar type 48") was produced in 1942 to serve as the standard mortar for the infantry company. It was later termed the "Stummelwerfer". Its general ussue was forestalled by the introduction of a new 120mm Granatwerfer 42 into infantry units that same year and the Stummelwerfer was subsequently abandoned in favor of the 120mm weapon. The Granatwerfer 42 could fire a sixteen kilogram bomb up to 6,600 meters, while the

The Panzerschreck anti-tank rocket launcher provided the infantry with a simple and effective means of defeating tanks at close quarters.

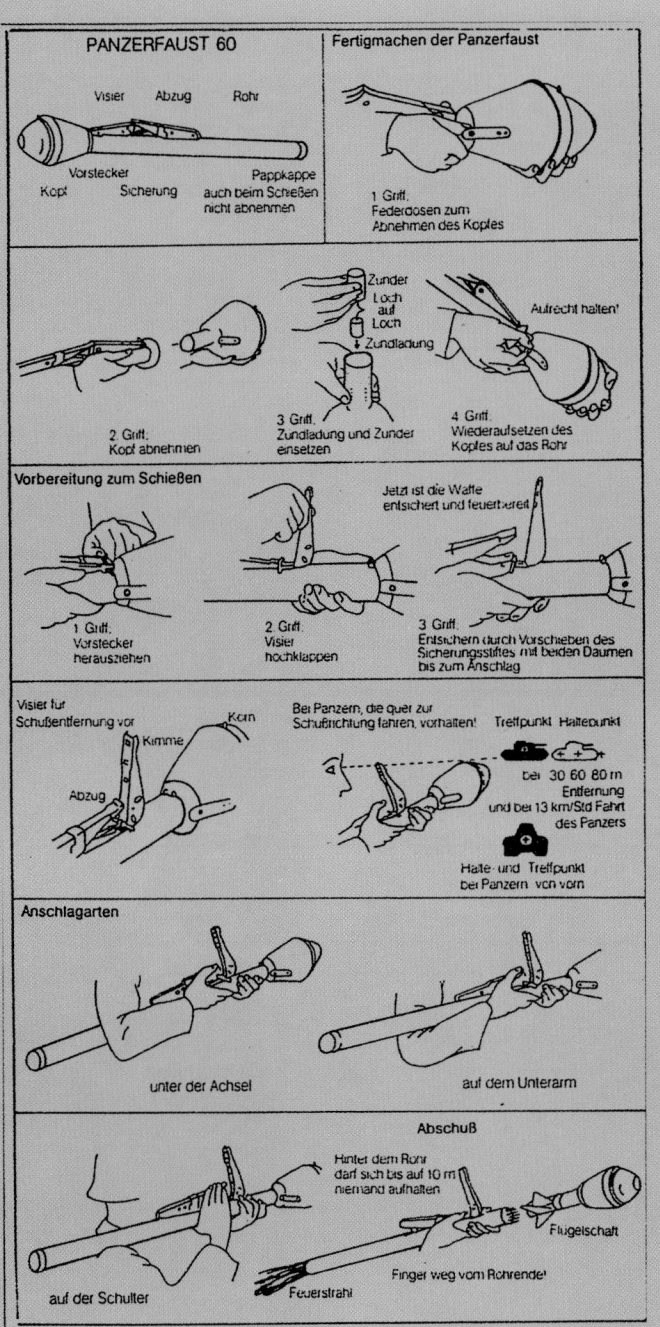

Panzerschreck, working as loader and firer; once the weapon was loaded, an individual could fire it unaided. Even more basic, however, was the disposable Panzerfaust, which was developed and produced with model numbers 30, 40, 60 and 100. All featured a simple launching tube on to which a large, hollow-charge, rocket-propelled anti-tank grenade was fitted. The weapon's sighting system was rudimentary and simply required the firer to align a folding sight on the tube with the top of the projectile itself. Once the rocket projectile had been fired, the firing tube could be thrown away. Some early models of the Panzerfaust (notably the Panzerfaust 30) proved positively dangerous to the firer, but such deficiencies were speedily rectified, and the weapon quickly gained widespread popularity throughout the Wehrmacht when even the redoubtable Soviet T-34 tank proved vulnerable to it. Certainly the Panzerfaust's rocket projectile could penetrate 200mm of armor at ranges up to 100 meters, although accurate engagements at 30–50 meters were usually more realistic – provided the firer could keep his nerve and his aim steady with an enemy tank so close.

Left and below: The Panzerfaust 60 was cheap to produce and straightforward to use. Preparation, aiming and firing of the weapon are shown, together with the internal construction of the weapon's shaped-charge warhead.

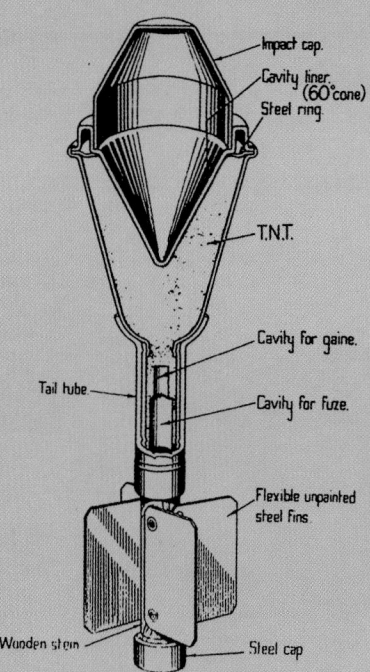

The development of hollow-charge warheads and anti-tank rocket technology signified a real breakthrough in the matter of anti-tank defense, but until 1943 the principal means of destroying tanks remained the anti-tank gun and the landmine. Based on the experience gained with the 37mm Panzerabwehrkanone 35/36 (PAK 35/36), a new 50mm PAK 38 was designed and entered service early in 1940, while its successor, the 75mm PAK 40, used extensively from 1941, proved to be the best of the army's conventional towed anti-tank guns. The PAK 40 could engage targets with various types of ammunition out to 1,800 meters, and its armor-piercing round could penetrate 100mm of armor. Other Panzerabwehrkanone were produced, but the PAK 40 was the most ubiquitous and best-known purpose-designed anti-tank gun.

Once hostilities began, it was not only the traditional Panzer-abwehkanone that were used to defeat tanks, for as early as 1940 it was discovered that the Luftwaffe's 88mm Flak 36 anti-aircraft gun was also most effective against armored vehicles. The engagement between units of Rommel's 7th Panzer Division and the Matilda tanks of the British Expeditionary Force (BEF) at Wailly on 21 May 1940 is widely quoted as the moment at which the wider potential of the 88mm gun was fully appreciated. In fact, the broad concept of using anti-aircraft guns in the anti-armor role and against other ground targets had already been proved by the Germans during the Spanish Civil War, so a number of Flak guns were routinely deployed as multi-role weapons throughout the war. In North Africa, Rommel made particularly good use of the

Until the introduction of various hand-held anti-tank weapons from 1943, the army relied upon anti-tank guns and mines to attack armored vehicles. The 50mm PAK 38 (top) and 75mm PAK 40 (center) towed anti-tank guns entered service in 1940 and 1941 respectively, remaining in use throughout the war. Bottom: Although usually manned by Luftwaffe personnel, the 88mm anti-aircraft gun was used extensively against ground targets, and was a particularly effective long-range anti-tank gun.

experience he had gained during the 1940 Blitzkrieg, and from 1941 to 1942 the 88mm Flak 18 guns of the Deutsches Afrikakorps exacted a very heavy toll upon the British armor, these weapons at first being assessed by the British intelligence staff as some sort of new secret weapon.

The series of 88mm Flak guns used and produced both before and during the war – the Flak 18, 36, 37 and 41 – were the most powerful and effective long-range anti-tank guns used by either side. These guns were usually manned by a crew of seven (almost invariably Luftwaffe gunners) and were able to fire about fifteen rounds per minute with considerable accuracy and devastating effect against targets up to 2,000 meters away, although about 1,500 meters was generally the optimum range. The principal drawback of these particular guns was their size and high silhouette, which meant that they were difficult to conceal in the forward combat areas and attracted enemy fire. A shield was added to later variants to provide a measure of protection for the gun crew, while from 1943 a version of the Flak 41 designed primarily for anti-tank use entered service. Designated the PAK 43, this gun exposed a much lower silhouette by being ground-mounted on to a cruciform base once it had been placed in its firing position.

The command and control of 88mm Flak guns used as anti-tank guns did give rise to difficulties from time to time, as the Luftwaffe high command retained overall control of these weapons and was often reluctant to authorize their use by the army in the anti-tank role. One such occasion occurred in the aftermath of the Allied invasion of Normandy in 1944 – the threat posed by Allied armor was very evident, but the Luftwaffe high command nevertheless denied the local army commander the use of these guns in the anti-tank role.

## Landmines

Guns and rocket-propelled munitions were not the only means of attacking enemy armored vehicles, and the army's engineers had a comprehensive range of anti-tank mines available for this purpose. No fewer than forty different types were used during the war, of which the circular Tellermine (literally, "plate mine") was probably the type most widely deployed. These dinner-plate-size high-explosive mines were usually detonated by the pressure of a vehicle passing over them. With up to five-and-a-half kilograms of explosive, varying pressures required to detonate them, and a range of casings and ignition systems, the Tellermine types 29, 35, 42, 43 together provided a sure way to stop any tank, and in many cases also causing crew casualties and severely disabling or even destroying the tank, while many less robust vehicles would simply be blown apart. In addition to the Tellermine, a bar-shaped Riegelmine 84 (bar-mine type 84) provided a means of increasing the area across which the mine's detonation might be initiated, as well as increasing the blast effect under the vehicle instead of only upon the wheel or track. Anti-handling devices, performance and ignition modifications and enhancements, wood- or aluminium-cased mines and various

foreign mines all appeared in the German army's anti-tank minefields at various times during the war.

Anti-personnel mines were also available, and these were sown either together with anti-tank mines or separately. The most widely used anti-personnel mines were the S-Mine types 35 and 44, the Schützenmine (Schü-Mine) 42 and various wood-cased and cardboard-cased mines, some of which could be exploded either by pressure or by a trip wire, and could be set to detonate in various ways. The best-known anti-personnel mines were probably the S-Mine 35 and 44, which featured a "bounding" or jumping effect. With these mines, the main explosive charge would be projected one to two meters into the air within three to four seconds of the mine being triggered, exploding half a second later to blow its 360 steel ball-bearings, scrap steel or steel rod filling in all directions, killing or severely wounding unprotected personnel up to twenty meters away and injuring others up to 100 meters distant. Ever since they were invented, the function of the anti-

Left: The explosive charge within the Tellermine being laid by this Obergefreiter on 27 January 1941 was powerful enough to stop any tank.

Below: A selection of mines in common use. Left to right: S-Mine type 35 (interior), S-Mine type 35 (exterior), Schü-Mine type 42. In the foreground is an improvised mine or booby trap, fitted with a pull-switch (Zugzünder) igniter.

**Above:** The well-proven 105mm leFH 18 field gun in action.

**Right:** The 150mm sFH 18 was the division's standard medium artillery howitzer.

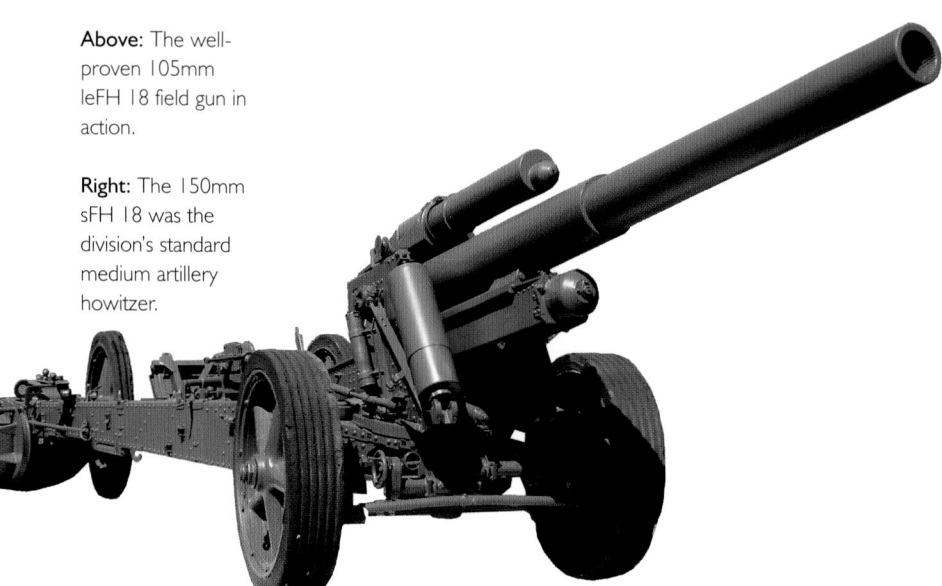

during its campaigns, or subsequently manufactured by armaments factories in the occupied territories. Consequently, the inventory of artillery that supported Hitler's army between 1939 and 1945 was very extensive and contained a considerable variety of weapon types and calibers.

In the infantry division, the well-tried 75mm leichtes Infanteriegeschütz 18 and the 150mm schweres Infanteriegeschütz 33 continued in service throughout the war, providing very effective direct fire support to the front-line troops (although the size and weight of the 150mm gun sometimes meant that it could not be deployed as far forward as the 75mm gun). The field artillery's 105mm leichte Feldhaubitze 18 was modified in 1940 so that it could fire a more powerful shell, and subsequently this proven field gun received additional modifications in light of the experience of its use in combat. Another useful field gun which pre-dated the war, the 100mm Kanone 18, was modified and re-issued as the 100mm Kanone 42 from 1942, while the 75mm leichte Feldkanone 18 also provided valuable service as a field gun throughout the war. These were the principal German field guns, but there were other types as well, and alongside all of these weapons were deployed the many foreign-made field guns, more captured and foreign field guns being used by the army than any other category of artillery.

Prominent among the army's medium and heavy artillery were the 150mm schwere Feldhaubitze 18, with a range of 13,300 meters, a gun that was further improved and modified in 1942; the 150mm Kanone 18, with a maximum range of 24,500 meters; and the 170mm "Kanone 18 in Mörserlafette" (literally, "mounted on a mortar (howitzer) gun carriage"). This last was an impressive gun that could engage targets 29,600 meters away. The 210mm Mörser 18 could fire a 113 kilogram shell – almost double the weight of the 150mm gun shells – some 16,700 meters; it was largely superseded by the 170mm Kanone 18 in Mörserlafette from 1942. Other guns and howitzers with calibers of 210mm, 240mm, 280mm, 380mm, 406mm, 420mm, 600mm and 800mm, together with a miscellany of predominantly foreign large-caliber guns acquired during the conflict, were also used, many of these heavy guns eventually being permanently sited in emplacements on the Western Front in anticipation of the Allied invasion of northern France.

personnel mine has been as much to cause serious injury as to kill the enemy, thereby creating casualties who immediately became a burden upon the logistics and medical system and required able-bodied troops to evacuate them – and the German S-Mine achieved this pragmatic aim all too efficiently.

### Field, Medium and Heavy Artillery

When the army invaded Poland in September 1939 it was already well provided with diverse types of artillery developed, modified or introduced into service since 1933, together with some guns that well-preceded the Hitler era. However, the army's virtually insatiable need for ever more firepower, and therefore for ever more artillery, meant that the Heereswaffenamt had to approve and accept into service very many of the foreign guns captured

### Super-heavy Artillery and Railway Guns

The super-heavy artillery included some guns that were truly spectacular, such as the two massive 800mm railway guns "Dora" and "Gustav", which had been designed and built by Krupp from 1937. Although such huge guns were potentially vulnerable to air attack, Europe's extensive railroad system and the ability of the railway artillery troops to move their guns on what were often poor-quality or rapidly repaired railway tracks (together with the prodigious efforts of the army's railway engineer units) generally validated the continued use of railway guns. The first gun, "Dora", was test-fired in 1942, being manned by 1,420 men commanded by a major general, and it was subsequently employed to good effect during the campaign in the Crimea in mid-1942, firing more than 50 seven-ton shells almost 50 kilometers into Sevastopol in mid-1942; later it fired some 30 rounds into Warsaw during the 1944 uprising. "Gustav" was never used in action.

The procedure for preparing, loading and firing "Dora" involved several separate operations. First, the huge shell was brought forward from the ammunition car on a special ammunition transporter, which was then placed on to the electrical lift and raised to the platform at breech level. Once at that level, the shell was transferred on to the loading table and pushed into the breech chamber by a hydraulic rammer. Next, the bagged charges of propellant were raised to the platform on a second lift and placed into the chamber. Finally, the breech was closed and the loading table moved away from it. The barrel could then be elevated to its firing position using electric power, while the position of the whole gun could also be laterally adjusted as necessary by moving it along its twin railway tracks. Movement on these tracks was powered by two diesel-electric railway engines. With all target engagement computations complete – including consideration of the air temperature, weather conditions, wind direction and the actual temperature of the charges – and any final checks and adjustments carried out, the gun was ready to be fired. Its very first use in combat was at 0535 on 5 June 1942, during the siege of Sevastopol: "The bright flash and thunderous roar was unlike any gunshot the observers could remember. Everyone in the area had been warned to plug their ears at the time of firing. The recoil of the gun made even its massive carriage tremble, but all components functioned properly."[1] The target, a barracks and a series of fortified artillery batteries, had been selected by the commanders of the 11th Army and 54th Army Corps in consultation, and the first round scored a direct hit, "shaking the very earth and causing a pillar of smoke to climb high into the sky."[2] With the firing of a round complete, the barrel had then to be lowered to the horizontal position so that the empty brass-plated steel shell case could be removed and the chamber cleared and cleaned, ready for the next shell to be loaded for firing. In the days that followed, more than 50 high-explosive and concrete-penetrating shells were fired against Sevastopol's fortifications, mostly with a considerable degree of success.

Self-propelled "Karl" super howitzers ("Karl" was but the first of a number of these huge 600mm howitzers) were also used at Sevastopol and elsewhere with truly devastating results. Meanwhile, other railway guns were also used to bombard the French Maginot Line forts during the Blitzkrieg offensive of 1940, to shell southern England after the Dunkirk evacuation, during the siege of Leningrad, and in Italy during 1944, where the 280mm railway gun "Leopold" regularly bombarded the Allied beachhead at Anzio. Wherever these large shells landed on target they caused considerable destruction. Despite their slow rate of fire sometimes reducing the more immediate operational impact of these massive guns, the morale-sapping effect of being regularly shelled with

**Below left:**
Although the "Karl" series of 540mm and 600mm heavy mortars had limited mobility their firepower was devastating – as was shown during the army's bombardment of Sevastopol in 1942.

**Below right:**
The 210mm Mrs 18 gun was the army's standard heavy artillery howitzer and the only gun of that caliber that could be vehicle-drawn and transported without disassembly.

The 210mm K12 (E) railway gun was manufactured by Krupp during the late 1930s and entered service in 1940. Note the relatively simple box girder construction of the gun carriage and the two rail trucks; also the extensive barrel-bracing, designed to avoid the 31.5 meters-long barrel whipping and drooping during firing. This was the forerunner of the 280mm K5 (E), eventually the army's standard super-heavy railway gun.

propulsion, rather than being propelled solely by the explosion of a single charge, although there was still a significant back-blast when the Nebelwerfer was fired). Therefore, the Nebelwerfer could be towed, maneuvered and man-handled much more easily than a field gun while also being suitable for mounting on a vehicle chassis. More than twelve Nebelwerfer variants were taken into use during the war, four types featuring particularly prominently from 1942 until 1945. These were the six-barrel 150mm Nebelwerfer 41, the five-barrel 210mm Nebelwerfer 42 (which could also fire 150mm rockets), the 280mm/320mm Nebelwerfer 41 (which fired 280 mm high-explosive rounds and 320mm incendiary projectiles), and the ten-barrel 150mm Panzerwerfer 42, which was mounted on an armored vehicle. All but the last type were mounted on two-wheeled trailers similar to gun carriages. Nebelwerfers were fired electrically, the operator being sited in cover some fifteen to twenty meters away in order to stay clear of the blast. Although the rockets were usually launched in salvoes, each barrel of a multi-barrel Nebelwerfer discharged its projectiles in sequence over about ten seconds, this staggered firing being necessary to prevent the weapon being overturned by the combined blast of a simultaneous firing of all its barrels. Indeed, the combination of back-blast, smoke and the smoke trail of each rocket in flight meant that these weapons almost inevitably revealed their position as soon as they opened fire. The maximum range of the Nebelwerfer 41 was 7,500 meters; that of the Nebelwerfer 42 was 8,500 meters; while the ten-barrel Panzerwerfer 42 could engage targets out to 7,300 meters from the half-track armored vehicle (typically the Büssing-NAG schwerer Wehrmachtsschlepper) on which it was mounted. Other multi-barrel Nebelwerfer systems, both mobile and static, also existed, and these were able to fire a variety of smoke, chemical, and high-explosive rockets. All these projectiles produced a loud screaming or roaring noise in flight, which added a useful psychological effect to their more conventional destructive power, and the Allied troops nicknamed the Nebelwerfer the "Screaming Meemie".

The Propagandawerfer was a special short-range projector for a 73mm rocket that could be filled with up to 227 grams of propaganda leaflets or other paper products.

apparent impunity by such formidable weapons from up to 80 kilometers away certainly had an adverse effect upon the activities of those Allied troops selected as their targets.

### Rocket Launchers – the Nebelwerfer

Before the war, Germany was already experimenting with various forms of rocket projectors, and in 1941 the first of these appeared on the battlefield. The widespread use and effectiveness of the Red Army's rocket launchers also influenced the speed with which these weapons were developed and brought into service by Germany. The original role of the Nebelwerfer (smoke projector) had been to lay down blanket barrages of smoke or chemical munitions covering an area target rather than pin-point targets. The troops manning these projectors were called Nebeltruppen (literally "smoke troops", where "smoke" encompassed any sort of chemically generated gas or smoke), whose usual employment of these weapons reflected the inherent inaccuracy of rocket launchers compared with conventional artillery. However, these low-velocity weapons were generally lighter than an artillery piece and had minimal recoil (as the projectile carried its own means of

### The Panzers

Nowhere did the experience of war produce greater changes to the army's weapons inventory than in the Panzer arm – the upgrading and modification of its tanks, the development of new tanks and the introduction of self-propelled artillery or assault guns based upon the chassis of tanks already in service. There were also highly mobile wheeled armored cars, used extensively for reconnaissance and command purposes, among which were the leichter Panzerspähwagen (light reconnaissance armored car) Sd.Kfz.221, 222 and 223, with armament options that included a 20mm gun and MG 34 machine gun. From 1944 the impressive eight-wheeled schwerer Panzerspähwagen (heavy reconnaissance

The Pz.Kpfw.I Ausf. A (Sd.Kfz.101). Note the white "Balkenkreuz", used during the Polish campaign, which was replaced by the more familiar black and white cross soon thereafter.

Nebelwerfer rocket projectors were originally designed to deliver chemical munitions. However, weapons such as the 150mm Nebel-werfer 41, shown here firing HE projectiles, were widely used against suitable area targets throughout the war.

armored car) Sd.Kfz.234/1 also came into service. This technologically very advanced vehicle had an operating range of 600 kilometers, a top speed of 82 kilometers per hour and mounted a 20mm, 50mm or 75mm gun. A number of armored and semi-armored half-track vehicles were also introduced, mounting a wide variety of machine guns and other light guns. However, it was always the tank that occupied pride of place,

always a key element of the operational and tactical doctrine of the Panzer forces, as well as being central to Hitler's own ideas of war-fighting and the Blitzkrieg concept.

Non-German-manufactured and captured armor continued in use by the army throughout the war, and as late as the spring of 1941, Czech armor still accounted for no less than 25 percent of the total German tank fleet. When Operation *Barbarossa* began,

**Above:** During the Blitzkrieg in 1940, the Panzer forces made extensive use of the Czech Pz.Kpfw.35(t) and 38(t) tanks seized by Germany in 1938 and 1939. The command parentage of the tank shown here is somewhat uncertain, since the "ghost" symbol was that of the 11th Panzerdivision and was used between 1940 and 1945, while the "Y" symbol indicated the 7th Panzerdivision, 1941–5.

**Right:** This Pz.Kpfw.II Ausf. F-J (Sd.Kfz.121) is shown with the older type Ausf. C turret fitted. The Ausf. F-J turrets had a storage "bustle" at their rear.

the 6th Panzer Division was still using some 103 of the Pz.Kpfw.35(t) vehicles, while the 7th, 8th, 12th, 19th, 20th and 22nd Panzer Divisions also entered Russia with significant numbers of Pz.Kpfw.38(t) tanks in their armored units. Meanwhile, the Czech tank factory at Milowitz near Prague was employed to convert a number of the submersible Tauchpanzer III tanks originally readied in 1940 for Operation *Seelöwe* for a new role in assault river crossings, and a number of Tauchpanzer III and IV tanks were so employed by the 18th Panzer Division for its crossing of the River Bug at Patulin on 22 June 1941.[3]

### Pz.Kpfw.I and II and the Czech Tanks

The army entered the war with its Pz.Kpfw.I, II, III and IV tanks, together with the Pz.Kpfw.35(t) and 38(t) light tanks seized during

the occupation of Czechoslovakia, but the hard lessons it learnt in Poland in 1939, in France in 1940 and – most significantly – on the Eastern Front from late 1941 soon prompted the development of new types of armored fighting vehicles for the ongoing conflict. The Pz.Kpfw.I continued in use as an armored command vehicle, the kleiner (small) Panzer-Befehlswagen, with a lengthened chassis, a more powerful engine, an additional generator to support the enhanced radio installation, a single MG 34 and a raised and enlarged body to accommodate a small map table and increase in crew numbers from two to three. This vehicle was intended to provide Panzer commanders with a means of observing and controlling the mobile battle while moving well forward in the battle zone. The pre-war types of Pz.Kpfw.II finally dropped out of service during 1941 when a lack of spares made them increasingly difficult to maintain. However, even though the Pz.Kpfw.II had originally been intended only to provide an interim capability while the heavier Pz.Kpfw.III and IV tanks were developed, the Pz.Kpfw.II development program continued apace, and types (Ausführung or Ausf.) A to L appeared in quick succession between 1941 and 1943, although in many cases the type differences involved modifications rather than significant upgrades. Some of the more major changes to the Pz.Kpfw.II turned this tank from an under-gunned and inadequately protected vehicle in 1939 into an effective light tank by the end of 1942. These modifications included a complete re-working of its suspension, so that the Ausführung D, E and finally L, the Sd.Kfz.123 or Luchs ("Lynx"), versions lost the return rollers retained on the other types and adopted a Christie-type suspension. The 20mm cannon and a 7.92mm MG 34 were

retained, but its engine horsepower was increased from 140 to 180, its speed from 40 kilometers per hour to 60, and its range of action from 160 to 250 kilometers, while the overall weight of the vehicle was gradually increased from about nine tons to almost twelve. The final Ausführung L version was crewed by four rather than the three men carried by its predecessors. Some Ausführung D and E vehicles were also used as flame thrower tanks, though most of these two variants were withdrawn from service in March 1940.

As a light tank used for tasks such as reconnaissance, escort duties, exploiting a breakthrough, or against infantry and partisans, or similar lightly armored or soft-skinned vehicles, the Pz.Kpfw.II served the army well, and the Ausführung L (with its Christie-type suspension mirroring that of the Soviet T-34) proved to be a particularly useful general-purpose fighting vehicle. However, with its basic armor protection never more than 10–30mm thick (bolt-

on sections of armor plate were also added by user units in the combat zone) and its main armament still only a 20mm cannon, the Pz.Kpfw.II was never able to take on other tanks as the high command had originally intended.

### Pz.Kpfw.III

The Pz.Kpfw.III first appeared in 1936 and was intended to be the army's standard light tank, also being able to destroy other tanks. The Ausführung E version was finally adopted in September 1939, when quantity production commenced. The Pz.Kpfw.III had a crew of five, armor protection 10–30mm thick, a weight of almost twenty tons, an engine output of 300 horsepower, a range of operation that extended to 175 kilometers and a top speed of 40 kilometers per hour. It was armed with a 37mm cannon and three MG 34 machine guns but by mid-1941 most had been up-gunned

The first version of the Pz.Kpfw.III, the Ausf. A shown here, appeared in 1936. However, after extensive trials the five-bogie wheel chassis was not adopted.

Many versions of the Pz.Kpfw.III were manufactured. This is the Pz.Kpfw.III Ausf. M (Sd.Kfz.141/1).

by the introduction of a 50mm cannon and an improved tank machine gun. Later models featured various improvements to the suspension, turret, ventilation, access hatches and vision ports, and the thickness of armor protection, as well as the addition of smoke dischargers and further improved versions of the 50mm cannon. One version, the Ausführung N, produced from February 1943, mounted a 75mm gun and had armor 10–57mm thick, together with the added protection afforded by large side skirts (Schürzen) of 5mm armor plate specifically designed to defeat anti-tank rifle fire and hollow-charge warheads. Most variants of the Pz.Kpfw.III at various stages of modification (including both those with the 50mm gun and those with the 75mm gun) continued to operate side-by-side throughout the war. Between December 1938 and August 1944 at least 5,445 Pz.Kpfw.III tanks were produced, of which some 150 were the Pz.Kpfw.III Ausf. N. The Pz.Kpfw.III proved to be a better tank than the II, but it still lacked the

capability and armor protection to take on the main Soviet tanks successfully (especially the T-34 and the KV-1 heavy tank). Indeed, the potential vulnerability of the Pz.Kpfw.III had been recognized in an army order dated 21 October 1939 directing that neither the Pz.Kpfw.III nor the IV were to deploy more than 100 meters ahead of the infantry.

### Pz.Kpfw.IV

Although it was by no means the final solution to the armor imbalance on the Eastern Front (which would emerge only with the arrival of the Pz.Kpfw.V Panther and Pz.Kpfw.VI Tiger tanks from 1943 and 1942 respectively) the Pz.Kpfw.IV, accepted into service in late 1939, was used to good effect in every theater of operations. Work on this tank had begun as early as 1934, with various prototypes produced during 1934 and 1935, and while its overall appearance was quite similar to the Pz.Kpfw.III, the IV was a much more capable tank. It eventually became the core of the army's Panzer units throughout the war, with more than 8,651 of the Pz.Kpfw.IV Ausführung A to J produced and taken into service between November 1938 and February 1945. The first version of this tank was operated by five crewmen and weighed just over eighteen tons, having a 250-horsepower engine, an operating range of 150 kilometers, a speed of 30 kilometers per hour, and armor 10–30mm thick. It was armed with a 75mm cannon and two 7.92mm MG 34 machine guns. Numerous modifications ensued, with the Ausführung F appearing in 1941 and the Ausführung F2 in 1942, the latter mounting a new high-velocity 75mm gun capable of penetrating up to 89mm of armor. Further mod-

Eventually outmatched by some Allied tanks, the Pz.Kpfw.IV (Sd.Kfz.161) medium tank was a mainstay of the Panzer forces throughout the war. The Pz.Kpfw.IV Ausf. D pictured belongs to the 15th Panzerdivision of the DAK – indicated by the triangular device on its front and sides.

Regular maintenance periods and the ready availability of spare parts were vital to the success of the Panzer forces. Here a Pz.Kpfw.IV has its power pack removed for repair or replacement at an armored unit's maintenance area on the Eastern Front.

The Pz.Kpfw.IV chassis was also used for a number of other armored vehicles, including the 88mm Nashorn ("Rhinoceros") (originally titled the Hornisse or "Hornet") self-propelled assault gun shown here.

The Pz.Kpfw.V Panther (Sd.Kfz.171) was one of the best tanks used by any army in World War II. However, this well armored tank with its 75mm gun and good mobility arrived on the battlefield too late in the war to realize its true potential. **Top:** A Pz.Kpfw.V Panther Ausf. A is pictured in Italy on 24 July 1944, and below it a Panther in France during the summer of 1944. Note the infantrymen being carried on the rear deck of the tank – a common practice when out of contact with the enemy. **Bottom:** Several other armored vehicles were based upon the Pz.Kpfw.V chassis, one such being the Jagdpanther self-propelled assault gun (Sd.Kfz.173), mounting a powerful 88mm PAK 43/3 or 43/4 gun.

ifications were made, with Ausführung H and J being the final production versions. The type of Schürzen side screens that had been applied to the Pz.Kpfw.III were also fitted to these models from March 1943 once they arrived with Panzer units, which added a further 5mm of armor protection to the suspension and hull area and 8mm to the turret. In these final two versions, the vehicle's weight increased to 25 tons, the engine output to 300 horsepower (delivering a top speed of 42 kilometers per hour), the operating range to 200 kilometers, and the maximum armor thickness to 80mm. The Ausführung H and J were armed with an improved 75mm cannon and two 7.92mm machine guns. By default, the Pz.Kpfw.IV became the army's standard tank during the war: although outmatched by the T-34, it nevertheless fulfilled that function with a considerable degree of success until the arrival of numbers of Tiger and Panther tanks in 1942 and 1943 swung the qualitative balance in Germany's favor.

The Pz.Kpfw.IV chassis was also used for various other specialist vehicles, including the munitions carriers for the artillery's super-heavy 600mm "Karl" Mörser (Gerät 040), the "Nashorn" ("Rhinoceros") or "Hornisse" ("Hornet") 88mm-gun tank destroyer (which was based on a hybrid Pz.Kpfw.III and IV chassis), and the Sturmpanzer "Brummbär" ("Grizzly Bear"), which mounted a powerful 150mm close-support howitzer on a Pz.Kfpw.IV chassis.

**Pz.Kpfw.V Panther**

Despite the proliferation of Pz.Kpfw.IV tanks, probably the best-known German tanks of the war were the two new vehicles produced somewhat belatedly to counter the T-34 tanks encountered on the battlefield shortly after the start of Operation *Barbarossa*. Until mid-1941, the OKH had been confident that the Pz.Kpfw.III and Pz.Kpfw.IV tanks were a match for any tank that might be fielded by the Red Army. However, within a few weeks of the invasion of Russia the high command had been thoroughly disabused of this belief, and just six months later, following an intensive investigation of the design of captured T-34s, two prototypes of a completely new type of German tank were produced. One was an almost exact copy of the T-34, while the second had similarly sloped armor, but otherwise featured a number of significant differences. Production models of the latter type were subsequently ordered for testing in November 1942, but production difficulties prevented these, the first Pz.Kpfw.V Panther tanks, appearing before February 1943.

The Panther was undoubtedly the most successful of the several tanks produced by Germany prior to and during the war, and had it already been widely available in June 1941 the Russian T-34s would almost certainly not have enjoyed the battlefield success and the legendary reputation that they did. The Panther was much larger than its predecessors – the early model Ausführung D weighed 43 tons, had a 650-horsepower engine, 15–80mm of armor, a speed of 46 kilometers per hour, and an operating range of 168 kilometers, while its five-man crew manned a 75mm cannon and one machine gun. The Ausführung A production model that appeared in late 1943 saw the engine power increased to 700 horsepower, the operating range increased to 177 kilometers, and two additional machine guns fitted. Finally, the Ausführung G model entered service in 1944, by which time the usual upgrades had been introduced, the most apparent of which was the use of sloped rather than vertical side plates on the hull. With its well-sloped armor, powerful motive power, well-proven high-velocity 75mm gun and robust suspension system, the Panther was both formidable and (for its size and weight) agile, being more than capable of taking on any Allied tank with relative impunity. Unfortunately for the army's Panzer troops, it simply arrived on the scene too late.

In addition to the basic tank, a tank-destroyer version without a turret but mounting an 88mm gun was produced from December 1943, with 382 of this Jagdpanther (literally, "hunting Panther") variant completed during the war. Other Panther variants included a command tank (Befehlspanzer), artillery observation post tank (Beobachtungspanzer) and a special recovery vehicle (Bergepanzer), this last type being required due to the significant weight of the Panther. In total, more than 5,738 Panther tanks were produced between February 1943 and February 1945, plus 58 Bergepanzer recovery vehicles.

## Pz.Kpfw. VI Tiger I

Although the Panther was certainly the best tank fielded by the army during the war, the tank most feared by Allied troops was probably the Pz.Kpfw. VI Tiger (which actually entered service in June 1942, despite its type number being later than that of the Panther introduced in 1943). The Tiger, produced both in Tiger I and Tiger II versions, captured the imagination of friend and foe alike, and this was especially so on the Western Front, where its armor and armament outclassed that of most Anglo-US tanks.

Following the usual exhaustive tests, mass production of the Tiger began at the Henschel tank factory in August 1942, the first Tigers being committed to the fighting at Leningrad just a month later. The Pz.Kpfw. VI Tiger I Ausführung E was a heavyweight at 57 tons, but its 650-horsepower engine (later upgraded to 700 horsepower) still provided a top speed of 38 kilometers per hour, although with an operating range of only 100 kilometers. Its increased weight enabled the Tiger to mount an 88mm cannon (derived from the 88mm Flak 18), with armor protection of 25–100mm. A five-man crew operated the tank, its cannon, and two machine guns. Between June 1942 and February 1945 more than 1,534 Tiger I tanks were produced. Tank destroyers based upon the Tiger I chassis were also produced, including the Panzerjager Tiger (P) Elefant or Ferdinand, which mounted a fixed 88mm gun with full elevation but limited traverse.

### The Pz.Kpfw. VI Tiger I in action, Eastern Front, winter 1943

The men of the Panzertruppe who fought in the army's Tigers and its earlier tanks always considered themselves to be an élite band of armored warriors, and it was undeniable that these were the men who had in large part delivered Germany's Blitzkrieg victories. The demanding nature of tank warfare called for a challenging mix of technological skills and knowledge, personal daring and initiative, physical resilience and raw courage.

The air heavy with the smell of fuel, cordite, engine oil, exhaust fumes and sweat, the inside of the Tiger I was an armor-plated and claustrophobic world within which its black-uniformed crewmen could all too easily become detached from the world outside. These men knew that constant vigilance was their best defense (however effective their tank's armor protection), as well as the only way in which they could acquire and engage enemy tanks at the optimum

Although relatively late on the scene, the Pz.Kfw. VI Tiger I (Sd.Kfz.181) and Tiger II (Sd.Kfz.182) were two of the best-known tanks of the war. Here a Tiger I of the 1st SS-Panzerdivision "Leibstandarte SS Adolf Hitler" moves into action in France during the summer of 1944.

**Above:** The Tiger I on the right is being passed by what appears to be a heavily camouflaged Sd.Kfz.166 "Brummbär" 150mm self-propelled gun on a road close to the Anzio–Nettuno front in Italy on 14 March 1944.

**Above right:** As soon as they arrived from Germany, armored vehicles had to be painted to camouflage them appropriately for the operational theater. Here a newly arrived Tiger I is being spray-painted by a Panzer crewman on 11 July 1943.

range, using the Tiger's powerful 88mm gun to deadly effect. In action, the commander was responsible for identifying targets and directing the engagement from his position in the turret cupola: "Enemy tank, at right side of ruined barn, right one o'clock – load AP (armor piercing) 40!" The commander has decided to move the Tiger forward to engage the T-34 at much less than 1,000 meters, when the high density core of the APCR (armor piercing composite rigid) PzGr 40 ammunition, with its muzzle velocity of 3,000 feet per second, could be used to best effect. The gun loader takes a black-nosed APCR round from its rack in the ammunition bin (other types of round available included black-and-white PzGr 39 APCBC [armor piercing capped ballistic cap], grey HEAT [high explosive anti-tank] and yellow HE ammunition) and places it into the gun's breech trough, ramming it fully into the open breech chamber with his fist, pushing against the brass base-plate. The breech closes with no more than the slightest of clicks as he reports: "All safe – Loaded!"

This target acquisition and preparation of the gun for firing routinely had to be carried out while the tank sped across the battlefield, rocking and lurching, the crewmen bracing themselves against the turret, the hull and their seats as they were thrown about inside. Only the driver and commander had any real warning of the next ditch, shell-hole, or other obstacle that could cause even a tank as heavy as the Tiger to buck out of control for a few seconds while the driver fought to set it back on course, during which the crewmen endured the same sort of risks of cuts, bruises and broken bones as that of a sailor below decks in a small boat on a stormy sea. The tank reaches a suitable firing position to engage the Russian tank by the barn. "Driver, halt!" the commander orders, and the weight of the tank is thrown forward on its tracks and suspension as its rear deck bucks upwards and its nose and 88mm gun dip down. The hull stabilizes immediately, and the position of the enemy tank relative to the Tiger has hardly changed: "Traverse right – three o'clock!" At this stage the gunner

pulls in the high-speed power traverse, using the take-off from the main drive shaft to turn the turret at best speed, while controlling this movement with his right foot-pedal or rocker plate. As soon as the tank stopped, the driver would automatically have increased the engine revolutions to about 2,000 in anticipation of this call on its power, although the gunner would routinely shout "Rev up!" as he prepared to traverse the turret and lay the gun on to the target. As the 88mm swings round 90 degrees to the three o'clock position, the commander finally confirms the type of target and the range to it: "T-34 tank, beside ruined barn, 400 meters!" Having moved the gun on to the approximate position of the enemy tank, the gunner releases the power traverse and uses his hand elevation and traverse wheels to fine-tune his aim. He now has a clear view of the Russian tank through the gunner's binocular sight. A side or rear shot was always preferable, as a tank's frontal armor was invariably the thickest. The gunner takes a point just below the junction of the hull and the turret – the turret ring – as his point of aim.

"Fire!" is ordered, as everyone braces for the concussion, "Firing now!" shouts the gunner as he pushes the firing button. There is a roar as the gun fires and the tank shudders briefly, the 88mm gun recoils, the breech opens and the empty brass shell case is ejected and drops into a canvas tray, which is positioned to collect "empties" so that they do not accumulate on the floor of the hull and obstruct the crew or the tank's equipment. Some smoke escapes into the tank, while outside smoke and hot air from the gun muzzle temporarily impair the gunner's view. Wet snow and a spray of mud are also thrown up briefly by the shock wave generated by the shell as it exits the gun muzzle, at the muzzle brake. However, sitting slightly above and to the rear of the gunner in the commander's turret cupola the commander has a clear view of the shot, and he watches the shell's green tracer marker as it flies toward the T-34. A split-second later there is a flash of orange and red as the AP shell hits the tank and punches straight through its armor, to fly about inside the tank at great speed, killing the Russian crewmen, igniting the fuel and ammunition, and enabling the Tiger's commander to claim yet another enemy tank "killed". Meanwhile, the radio operator and loader man the hull and turret MG 34 machine guns, ready to engage any Russian crewmen who might try to escape the inferno. However, the destruction is complete. Disregarding the shattered, smoking ruin of the T-34, the Tiger's commander is already seeking his next target and preparing to move to a new firing position before an enemy tank or anti-tank gun can acquire and engage the Tiger: "Driver, advance ... Anti-tank gun and infantry emplacement, left ten o'clock, 600 meters – load HE, machine-gunners, stand by ..."[4]

### Pz.Kpfw.VI Tiger II

If the Tiger I was an awe-inspiring fighting vehicle, the Tiger II was even more so. By the time the Tiger II first appeared in early 1944, its designers had already taken full account of the design success of the Panthers, and of that tank's sloped armor in particular, so the Tiger II had well-sloped armor on both hull and turret. Depending upon which turret type was fitted (either a Henschel or a Porsche) it weighed in at more than 68 tons or almost 70 tons. Its armor was between 26 and 150mm thick, it carried three machine guns and mounted the most advanced version of the renowned 88mm cannon, able to penetrate 182mm of armor. (The same gun was mounted on the Jagdpanther, but in the Tiger II it was fitted into a fully rotating turret.) The Tiger II was designated the Königstiger ("King Tiger", also known as "Royal Tiger" by the Allied troops), and, although it was less agile than many Allied tanks, its armament and armor protection were in all other respects more than a match for any of them. A total of 198 Tiger II "Königstiger" tanks were manufactured from January to August 1944, plus a Panzerbefehlswagen (command vehicle) variant, only a few of which entered service.

The only armored fighting vehicle that carried an even more powerful gun than that of the Tiger II and the Jagdpanther was the Jagdtiger (literally, "hunting Tiger"), a tank destroyer derived from the Tiger II, mounting a 128mm anti-tank gun and protected by armor 250mm thick. Only about 70 of the 150 Jagdtigers ordered late in 1943 or early in 1944 were actually delivered before the war ended. Similarly, only about ten of the Sturmtiger self-propelled assault guns based on a Tiger chassis, which entered service in 1944 and mounted a 380mm mortar or short-barrelled howitzer, were actually used in action.

The most powerful tank of the war was the Pz.Kpfw.VI Tiger II (Sd.Kfz.182), also known as the Königstiger (King Tiger). It was produced with two types of turret, the model shown here being fitted with the Porsche turret. Both types mounted an 88mm gun.

**Right:** This Königstiger is fitted with the Henschel turret. It is pictured in Budapest during the summer of 1944. The crewman is apparently adjusting the 88mm gun's muzzle cover.

**Below:** The Tiger II chassis was adapted to produce other armored vehicle variants. These included the heavily armored Jagdtiger self-propelled assault gun (Sd.Kfz.186), which mounted a formidable 128mm PAK 44 gun.

Clearly, the Panther and the Tiger were both tanks that the army had really needed at the beginning of the war but, by the time that the requirement had been identified and full-scale production was finally approved, Germany's tank production plants were already suffering severe constraints and an ever-diminishing supply of essential raw materials due to Allied bombing. Consequently, these vehicles simply could not be manufactured in the numbers that the army by then so urgently needed. This situation similarly applied to many other providers of the army's weapons of war as the tide turned on the Eastern Front and in North Africa, and when second and third fronts were eventually opened up by the Allies in Italy and France. The quantity – if not necessarily the overall quality – of many of the weapons of war that Hitler's army needed to continue its operations declined steadily during the last three years of the conflict relative to the ever-increasing quantities of weaponry fielded by the Allied armies.

While by no means a unique example, the story of German tank production from 1940 to 1944 provides evidence of the problem

faced by the Wehrmacht, and later by Albert Speer personally, in trying to sustain what were predominantly German national forces engaged in an expanding global conflict conducted on multiple fronts against a formidable alliance of nations that included at least two major military-industrial powers. In 1940, tank production within Germany was a little over 1,500. By 1944 Speer had been instrumental in increasing this to almost 8,000, and during the war about 25,000 tanks and 12,000 assault and self-propelled artillery guns of various types were produced. However, by 1944 Germany's tank production had neither kept pace with demand nor could it compete with the rates of production achieved by the Allies – especially that of the Americans and the Russians. From 1943, the Allies' strategic bombing campaign further depleted the number of tanks produced (a typical example was the single USAAF raid on Henschel's factory at Cassel in 1944 that destroyed no fewer than 200 brand-new Tiger tanks) or frustrated the delivery of those vehicles that were completed by destroying them in transit. The German-controlled Czech armaments factories were generally beyond the reach of air strikes, and so the production of assault guns and tank destroyers by these factories actually increased in late 1944, with 766 vehicles produced in August and 1,199 in November. But these particular vehicles were primarily defensive in nature and so could not substitute for the tanks that were so desperately needed by the Panzer forces at that stage of the war. Also, despite a deteriorating strategic situation, political imperatives and perceptions once again frustrated military pragmatism in mid-1944 when Hitler directed that the bulk of these new armored vehicles should go to the newly-created Volksgrenadier divisions rather than to the embattled front-line units that by then urgently needed them to counter the Allied armor and forestall its advances from both east and west.

# PART IX
# Supporting Arms and Services

## 1. Logistics and Supply

The full industrial capacity of the Third Reich was not mobilized until the war was well under way, when it at last became clear that the speedy total victory Hitler had expected to win by the end of 1941 was no longer possible. Nevertheless, Germany was in many respects already a nation in arms by 1939, as Hitler well understood that having a strong, modern war machine at his disposal was critical to achieving his political objectives. This meant that the acquisition of raw materials, the means of industrial production and the provision of resources had to be coordinated and controlled at the highest level, together with the high command's estimates of need and statements of requirement for everything that the Wehrmacht and the Waffen-SS needed to prosecute the war. In terms of sheer scale and diversity, the army was the largest consumer of day-to-day resources, and the logistic needs of the OKH were met by a two-tier system of procurement and supply, the first of which was centered upon Germany itself, while the second tier provided the means of logistic support and supply to the army in the field.

While the weapons of war taken into service between 1933 and 1945 were the essential tools with which the army fought its battles, campaigns could not be won by weapons alone – the army's divisions also needed the means to move wherever the OKH required and the mobility to deploy or redeploy once arrived there. At the same time, the huge quantities of supplies necessary to sustain these forces in combat also had to be moved. In addition, the army needed reliable means of command and control by which messages and orders could be passed and reports submitted

immediately, irrespective of whether the senders and recipients were static or on the move. As well as the transport, technology and other resources developed to meet these needs, many other mechanical and electronic machines, devices and equipment were produced to satisfy a myriad of requirements and maximize the army's combat effectiveness.*

### Logistic Support within Germany

Within Germany a complex system of procurement and supply dealt with all sorts of military equipment and *matériel* and managed its passage from the factory and other sources to the depots at which items were held ready for dispatch to the Feldheer. The supply, storage and repair of weapons, ammunition and most of the army's equipment was controlled by the ordnance branch, headed by the chief army ordnance officer (Feldzeugmeister), while the process of research, design, development and acceptance was conducted by the army ordnance office (Heereswaffenamt) in cooperation with the weapons and manufacture group (Amtsgruppe für Industrielle Rüstung). Once manufactured, equipment was moved to army equipment depots (Heereszeugämter) and branch equipment depots (Heeresnebenzeugämter), where it was stockpiled. Many of these permanent depots in Germany covered sizeable areas and were often constructed entirely or partially underground, frequently having substantial manufacturing facilities as well as an extensive storage capacity. Although the army was responsible for supplying some major

* Details of the principal weapons, vehicles and other equipment operated both by the combat arms and by the supporting arms and services are shown in Appendix 7.

Germany's autobahns provided an indispensable network of through routes, along which troops and the means to sustain them could be moved speedily as required. Autobahn construction was an important feature of Hitler's strategic planning, as well as one of several measures used by the Nazis to eliminate domestic unemployment. Here, the Führer is seen at the formal opening of the Leipzig autobahn in 1937, which marked the completion of more than 1,600 kilometers of autobahn construction.

equipment items (such as tanks) to the Waffen-SS, the SS maintained a separate supply system within Germany to provide both the Waffen-SS and the Allgemeine SS with most of their equipment needs – an arrangement that resulted in much logistics duplication and inter-service rivalry, with the politically-favoured Waffen-SS frequently enjoying priority over the army when competing for scarce equipment. Each depot was subdivided into a storage depot (Lager) and a workshop (Werkstatt), with other subdivisions and specializations as necessary to fulfil the depot's particular function. They were manned primarily by ordnance branch personnel, but many civilians, non-specialist soldiers, foreign labourers and sometimes prisoners-of-war also worked in these storage centers, with the latter personnel used as a pool of unskilled labour. Army equipment depots dealt with an almost infinite variety of items, including weapons, armored and motor vehicles and spare parts, assault boats, radios and ancillaries, chemical warfare protective equipment, bridging equipment, engineer plant and machinery, special clothing, reference documents and training manuals. However, fuel, rations, general purpose clothing, and individual, medical and veterinary equipment were generally processed by specialist depots, while specialist corps area equipment parks also complemented these depots and the army equipment depots with supply facilities geared to specific areas and units of the field army, as well as having certain repair and maintenance responsibilities.

The Berlin-based medical park (Hauptsanitätspark) and corps medical parks (Wehrkreissanitätsparke) were the principal providers of all medical supplies and equipment, as well as processing and re-

issuing captured medical supplies, while the Hauptsanitätspark in Berlin was also responsible for testing and evaluating medicines and equipment and for developing medical usage policies and directives. For the veterinary services, a main veterinary park (Heereshaupt-veterinärpark), home veterinary parks (Heimatveterinärpark), remount depots (Heeresmonteämter) and subsidiary horse parks (Heimatpferdepark) were responsible for acquiring, processing and supplying the Feldheer's horses as required, as well as dealing with the full range of veterinary stores and equipment. Ammunition depots (Heeresmunitionsanstalten) and branch depots (Heeres-munitionsnebenanstalten) – very many of which were sited underground – not only stored and issued ammunition but also assembled and filled shells as well as making fuzes and other items. The supply of all non-specialist clothing and individual equipment for the Wehrmacht was controlled by the Berlin-based armed forces clothing and procurement office (Wehrmachtbeschaffungsamt Bekleidung und Ausrüstung), while army clothing policy and provision were dealt with by the general army office (Allgemeines Heeresamt) through a chain of clothing depots (Heeres-bekleidungsämter). In addition to storing, supplying and repairing clothing, individual equipment and other items to the field army, these depots also received the raw materials from which they manufactured clothing, insignia, blankets, tents, water-bottles, messing items, leather straps and belts, shoes and other textile-based equipment.

In recognition both of its critical importance and later of Germany's gradually diminishing access to oil stocks and other raw materials during the later years of the war, the provision of

This picture taken during army maneuvers in Hessen in the mid-1930s illustrates the diversity of the army's vehicle types. This further increased as the war progressed, imposing a significant logistic burden upon the Wehrmacht.

fuel and lubricants was controlled at the highest level. This was the responsibility of the ministry of economic affairs and the central petroleum office, which together ascertained and authorized the quantity of fuel allocated to the Wehrmacht and that made available to civilian users. Once fuel had been allocated to the army it was stored and distributed by OKH-controlled depots (OKH Nachshubtanklager) and army fuel supply depots (Heeres-nachshubtanklager), from which it was provided to the Feldheer.

The procurement and policy for the supply of food and animal (primarily horse) forage were controlled by the OKH administration office (OKH Heeresverwaltungsamt), and managed by the rations and procurement group through higher rations stores (Ersatzverpflegungsmagazine). These stores held sufficient rations for about 300,000 men for one month (about 10,000 tons of food), with the main rations depots (Heeresverpflegungs-hauptämter) each holding some 3,000 tons of rations, while the garrison and army rations depots (Heeresverpflegungsämter) each held several hundred tons of rations. For planning purposes, the higher ration stores were required to ensure that the army had sufficient rations available at all times to meet its requirements for about ten days, the required amounts being based upon projected figures provided 28 days in advance. These higher-level ration depots usually had integral bakeries and access to good rail links, and the size and capability of a depot usually reflected the size and nature of the garrisons and Feldheer formations it supported. Forage and rations were processed in parallel, depots often holding several thousand tons of oats alongside tons of rations, while depots sited in rural areas often had special responsibilities for collecting and storing fodder.

### Logistics Support for the Field Army (Feldheer)

Once the Feldheer was actively engaged in operations, the fundamental principle governing its re-supply and logistics support was that all the resources expended by it daily in combat should be replaced by the start of the following day. Underlying

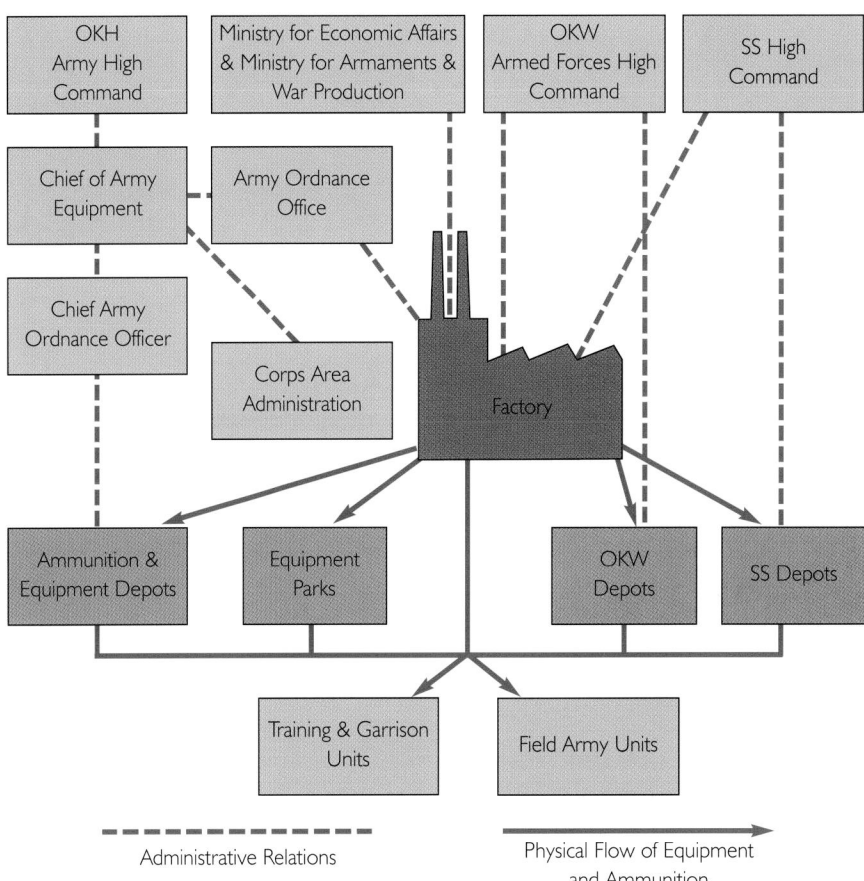

The control and supply of weapons, ammunition and equipment, showing the inter-relationship between industrial production and the army; together with the discrete chain of command used by the SS for its equipment and ammunition needs (US Official, 1945).

this principle and offsetting these daily replenishment requirements were close control of expenditure at all levels, the recovery and repair of equipment wherever possible, the salvaging and use of enemy equipment, and the forward positioning of stocks to ensure their ready availability. Considerable flexibility of action was accorded to the logistics staff officers responsible for all this. The headquarters staff branch that dealt with logistics at Feldheer headquarters and at army group, army, corps and divisional level

### Responsibilities of Logistics Staff Officers

| Level of Command or Headquarters | Principal Responsibilities |
|---|---|
| Field Army (Feldheer) | The 1b staff provided statements of requirement for the subordinate armies, which were then submitted to the OKH for action. They also oversaw and coordinated army supply systems, controlled major logistics stocks, logistic transport and repair facilities, and regulated the evacuation of wounded personnel and prisoners-of-war. Feldheer headquarters usually dealt directly with the subordinate army headquarters on logistic supply matters. |
| Army Group | Security of logistic stocks and depots in the rear area (within the Feldheer, army group headquarters were not usually involved directly in the supply chain). |
| Army | The 1b staff collated, developed, validated and passed to the Feldheer headquarters the requisitions and statements of requirement. They also directed and controlled the distribution of supplies to the divisions and units under their command while also being responsible for the supply dumps, collecting points, depots and repair facilities under its command or in its operational area. |
| Army Corps | Although involved in the supply of matériel to any integral corps troops, army corps headquarters were not directly involved in the supply chain other than receiving and endorsing supply requests received from the divisions. |
| Division | The 1b staff controlled the distribution of all supplies to the division's units, while also ensuring that sufficient reserve stocks were generated to facilitate anticipated needs and future operations. These 1b staff officers processed the unit requisition requests and thus initiated the flow of statements of need that eventually comprised the consolidated supply request submitted by the Feldheer for action by the supply depots within Germany. |

Much of the vast quantity of Allied equipment abandoned at Dunkirk in June 1940 was subsequently salvaged and taken into use by the Germans.

army on mainland Europe came as far forward as practicable by rail, these having been loaded at home depots and eventually arriving at army railheads, ideally without any cross-loading during the journey from Germany. The railway system within Germany was a key part of the military logistic support system, and had been carefully designed to fulfil that role, with other European rail networks also being incorporated into the army's rail movement plan as the war and extent of German-occupied territory expanded. For the supply of military vehicles, there were field army equipment parks (Heereskraftfahrpark), which dealt with the repair of vehicles as well as with their storage, supply and the provision of spare parts. These equipment parks might hold reserves of as many as 200 new vehicles. Once arrived in the army's operational area, supplies were distributed to divisions, corps troops and units through a series of dumps, distribution points and collection points. Each of these usually dealt with a specific type of commodity – rations, ammunition, fuel, clothing, vehicles and so on – although ration dumps often also processed individual equipment, clothing and office equipment and consumables. An army ration dump (Armeepflegungslager) typically stocked up to 100 tons of rations, while an army ammunition dump (Armeemunitionslager) usually stocked between 3,000 and 6,000 tons of ammunition, with infantry and artillery ammunition usually being separated before being issued from division ammunition distribution points (Divisionsausgabestellen) and moved onwards to division ammunition dumps (Divisionsmunitionslager) established in the divisional areas. Thereafter, ammunition was received by units via regimental, battalion and company supply points. As far as practicable, empty shell cases and ammunition packaging, together with any unused or defective ammunition, had to be returned to Germany through the supply chain, with the reclamation and recycling of these items accorded the same priority as the forward movement of new ammunition. Meanwhile, fuel and lubricants were passed forward to divisional and unit fuel points from army railheads via a similar supply chain, with fuel packed in twenty-liter and 200-liter metal containers.

was designated "1b". These staff officers were responsible to their respective commanders and chiefs of staff for all matters pertaining to supply; the primary responsibilities of the principal 1b staff officer at each level of command varied according to the level of headquarters in which he served.

An early opportunity for the logistics staff officers and their commanders to exploit the spoils of war and offset some of the army's quantitative deficiencies occurred in mid-1940, following the evacuation of the BEF and other Allied troops from Dunkirk. There the Germans were left with a massive haul of abandoned weapons and equipment that included some 600 tanks of various types, no fewer than 75,000 motor vehicles, 1,200 field guns and heavy artillery guns, 1,350 anti-aircraft and anti-tank guns, 6,400 anti-tank rifles, 11,000 machine guns and many tens of thousands of rifles, together with 7,000 tons of ammunition.[1] Although various attempts had been made by the Allies to disable or destroy this *matériel* before it was abandoned, the sheer scale and nature of the evacuation meant that great quantities remained entirely serviceable, were readily restorable or were suitable for cannibalizing. Consequently, much of this *matériel* (and that later produced by factories in occupied territories) subsequently supplemented the army's vehicles and equipment in North Africa, Europe and on the Eastern Front, with captured French armored vehicles, tracked carriers and other motor vehicles being particularly in evidence, as were the Czech 35(t) and 38(t) tanks seized in 1939, and the further 6,500 armored fighting vehicles subsequently produced for the army by Czech factories between 1939 and 1945.

In most cases, armies in the field received combat supplies, vehicles and equipment directly from the Germany-based depots and equipment parks. Although variations to the standard supply chain were necessary to accommodate forces overseas – such as the Deutsches Afrikakorps – most of the supplies provided to the

All other equipment was dealt with by army parks (Armee Park), which issued items directly to the divisions and received defective or damaged equipment from them for repair or backloading for cannibalizing, more extensive repair or disposal. Army parks were required to hold a reserve of between five and ten percent of the arms and equipment of the army they supported, and to that end the army established a number of specific-to-purpose equipment parks. These included an infantry park (infantry weapons and vehicles), an artillery park (artillery weapons and vehicles), a signals park (radio, line and other communications items), a motor transport park (vehicles and spare parts), and an engineer park (engineer stores and materials). Further more specialized equipment support was provided by a chemical protection (or "anti-gas") park (protective clothing, gas masks, decontamination clothing, and smoke (Nebel) equipment), a medical park, a veterinary park, and a horse park (for draught and riding horses). Finally, an army equipment park dealt with a multiplicity of general items, including cooking equipment, horse carts, horse harness and suchlike.

Although the troops manning these and any other service support and supply units and depots were primarily logistics specialists, they would all have completed a period of infantry basic training shortly after their conscription. This was both prudent and essential, as there were countless occasions – especially on the Eastern Front – when supply troops (no matter how far to the rear) necessarily found themselves fighting as infantrymen. One example of the vulnerability of the army's supply lines in Russia was revealed in an account provided by Gunter Toepke, quartermaster of the 6th Army at Stalingrad, which came about while he was en route to Chir from Karpovskaya to supervise the loading of some horses. His journey coincided with the start of the Russians' Operation *Uranus*, designed to close off Stalingrad, when, "on the way through Kalach I heard all sorts of rumours from the supply troops stationed there … It was said that the Russians had already broken deep into our lines … Suddenly it dawned on me … it looked like the Russians were attempting a large-scale pincer movement to box the 6th Army into Stalingrad. Kalach was the meeting point … The divisions inside Stalingrad had no idea of what was going on, of what was being played out deep in their rear. Around that time I put my supply units on alert: bakers, butchers, mechanics, horse grooms and drivers were formed up into battle units and made to man a line around our headquarters."[2]

*Ammunition* The ammunition of a unit or formation was expressed and calculated in standard "units of issue" (Munitions-ausstattung) for every weapon held by that unit or formation. For a Volksgrenadier division in early 1945, examples of the single Munitionsausstattung included:

| Weapon | Number of rounds |
| --- | --- |
| 9mm pistol | 17 |
| 9mm submachine gun | 601 |
| 7.92mm rifle (infantrymen) | 87 |
| 7.92mm rifle (non-infantry) | 22 |
| 7.92mm light machine gun | 2,977 |
| 7.92mm light machine gun (artillery and anti-tank troops) | 1,185 |
| 81mm mortar | 138 |
| 120mm mortar | 120 |
| 75mm infantry howitzer | 171 |
| 75mm anti-tank gun | 125 |
| 105mm gun | 175 |
| 150mm howitzer | 105 |

*For the same type of division's artillery units the following Munitionsausstattung applied:*

| | |
| --- | --- |
| 37mm anti-aircraft gun | 1,500 |
| 75mm anti-aircraft gun | 300 |
| 88mm anti-aircraft gun | 300 |
| 105mm gun | 125 |
| 150mm howitzer | 125 |
| 150mm gun | 75 |
| 210mm howitzer | 50 |

Two Munitionsausstattung were carried within the division at all times for every weapon on its establishment, being both distributed among the forward units and held within the divisional reserve, with one further Munitionsausstattung held in the army reserve. As and when ammunition stocks were expended, they were replenished as quickly as possible to restore the division's holdings to the mandated Munitionsausstattung levels.

*Fuel and Lubricants* Fuel distribution was calculated in terms of "consumption units" (Verbrauchsatz), each of which was the amount of fuel necessary to move a given type of vehicle a distance of 100 kilometers. As with ammunition, fuel holdings were replaced as soon as practicable, with army formations usually carrying up to five Verbrauchsatz (reconnaissance units carried six-and-a-half). Meanwhile, divisions maintained a reserve stock of three further Verbrauchsatz at army fuel dumps. Despite the excessive and misplaced reliance of Hitler and the OKW on Germany seizing and holding the Caucasus oilfields, the provision of fuel to the army generally worked efficiently into 1944. However, Allied air bombardment and the loss of the oilfields in

Fuel was the lifeblood of a modern army, without which the Panzer divisions could not function.

the Soviet Union during the final two or three years of the war meant that much of the civilian population of Germany had to rely increasingly upon cars, buses and trucks modified to run on charcoal or other solid-fuel-powered engines and on horse-drawn wagons from 1943; while the Wehrmacht generally managed to supply fuel to its combat units, albeit often at much-reduced levels. But by early 1945 even the Wehrmacht began to run out of fuel, this being exemplified by incidents such as the Panzer Lehr armored division being rendered immobile at Mönchengladbach, and the 12th SS Panzerdivision "Hitler Jugend" having to destroy a consignment of brand-new tanks at Memmingen in southern Germany when it was discovered that there was no fuel available to drive them into action from the delivery point. Late in the war, a substitute fuel was produced for the Wehrmacht, using a

combination of gasoline and alcohol, but this mixture damaged engine carburettors and filters as well as requiring tank exhaust manifolds to be pre-heated with blow-torches.[3] The fuel crisis deepened, and by early spring of 1945 many army combat units were forced to emulate the civilian population by using horse-drawn carts and solid-fuelled transport vehicles, or else by simply abandoning the use of all motor vehicles for non-combat transport purposes.

***Rations*** The daily ration for each serviceman was set by OKW, with full account taken of the man's employment and theater of operations. As a matter of policy, the army planned to live off the land in the territory it occupied, and it therefore confiscated or purchased food for men and animals wherever possible, using

**Below:** Field bakeries provided fresh bread wherever practicable. Here a catering officer and a unit administrative officer check the quality of the product.

**Below right:** The field kitchen – the "Gulaschkanone" – was an efficient means of providing large quantities of nourishing hot meals with the minimum of resources. Meal menus regularly included potato soup, pea and ham soup, and all sorts of stews. Generally, such meals were accompanied by a bread or biscuit ration.

| Ration Type | Application and Description |
| --- | --- |
| Type I (Verpflegungssatz I) | Normal rations for troops engaged in combat, recovering from combat, or serving in extreme cold climates. 1.698 kilograms, plus seven cigarettes. |
| Type II (Verpflegungssatz II) | Normal rations for occupation forces and service or line of communication troops. 1.654 kilograms, plus six cigarettes. |
| Type III (Verpflegungssatz III) | Normal rations for garrison troops serving within Germany. 1.622 kilograms, plus three cigarettes. |
| Type IV (Verpflegungssatz IV) | Normal rations for office-based personnel and all nurses serving within Germany. 1.483 kilograms, plus two cigarettes. |
| Iron rations (Eiserne Ration) | Iron rations consisted of biscuits (250 grams), preserved cold meat (200 grams), preserved vegetables (150 grams), coffee (25 grams) and salt (25 grams), a total weight of 650 grams, or 825 grams including packing. Half iron rations were also issued and comprised biscuits (250 grams) and preserved cold meat (200 grams), weighing a total of 450 grams, or 535 grams inclusive of packaging. These were categorized as emergency rations and were usually held in reserve, being used only when ordered and when full rations were unobtainable. |
| Combat and close-combat ration packs (Großkampf-päckchen) and (Nahkampf-päckchen) | High-energy and easily carried emergency rations issued to troops actively engaged in combat, usually made up of biscuits, chocolate bars, sweets and fruit bars, and cigarettes. |
| March ration (Marschverpflegung) | Issued to troops in transit (on foot, by rail or vehicle-borne). A cold ration of bread (700 grams), cold meat or cheese (200 grams), spreads (60 grams), coffee (9 grams) or tea (4 grams), sugar (10 grams) and cigarettes (6), with a total weight of 980 grams. |
| Animal rations | The daily ration allowance (Rationssatz) for animals depended upon the type of animal (i.e., horse – with four sub-types, mule, ox, dog, carrier pigeon), the operational theater and the ration composition, which frequently included locally-procured items such as corn, barley or oats. |

these foodstuffs to supplement or replace military rations. An army usually maintained a ten-day ration reserve for every soldier on its established strength. The daily ration (Portionsatz) included three meals, to include (expressed proportionally in relation to the total daily amount) breakfast (one-sixth), lunch (one half), and evening meal (one-third). The various categories of Portionsatz (to each of which was added a small issue of wine during the summer months) included the items shown in the table opposite.

Where fresh meat was provided for butchery and inclusion in the various types of full rations (Verpflegungssatz I–IV), divisional butchery platoons could process 40 beef cattle (40,000 meat rations), 80 pigs (24,000 meat rations) or 240 sheep (19,000 meat rations) per day. Meanwhile field bakery companies could produce between 15,000 and 19,200 bread rations per day. Wherever practicable, meals were cooked centrally by horse-drawn wood-burning field kitchens (so-called Gulaschkanone) in non-mechanized units and by equivalent field cooking ranges mounted on trucks for Panzer and Panzergrenadier units. Field kitchens were categorized either as large (catering for 125–225 men) or small (catering for 50–125 men), with other types of field cooking equipment issued to units of less than 60 men.

*Expenditure Rates* Actual expenditure rates clearly depended upon the operational situation, the type of unit and the nature of the fighting, and the average daily expenditure rates of all commodities (consolidated and expressed in tons). For an infantry division on the Eastern Front during the period between June and December 1941 these were 80 tons while the division was not in action and 1,100 tons during any 24-hour period of continuous combat. For a Panzer or Panzergrenadier division these figures were 30 tons and 700 tons respectively. The planned daily total supply requirements for all commodities (but primarily combat supplies) for an individual soldier on the Eastern Front in late 1941 were:

| | |
|---|---|
| Troops not engaged in combat | 2.5–5 kilos |
| Troops engaged in low-intensity operations | 7.5–10 kilos |
| Troops engaged in defensive combat (normal rate) | 10–12.5 kilos |
| Troops engaged in defensive combat (intensive rate) | 12.5–25 kilos |
| Troops engaged in offensive combat | 12.5–25 kilos |

**Far left:** Field cooking in the desert presented a whole range of special problems, foremost of which were the availability and use of water and the storage of fresh rations.

**Near left, top to bottom:** This sequence of pictures illustrates rations being carried forward to front-line positions from the main field kitchen; their further distribution at a company or platoon headquarters; and finally the rations being eaten by troops in the forward trenches. The first and last pictures were taken of the same unit on 5 December 1941, while the Gebirgsjäger photograph (middle) dates from 22 October 1943.

So it was that the OKW, OKH and the army logistics and supply organization sought to provide an uninterrupted and appropriate flow of everything that the army needed to maintain its operational effectiveness. However, the efficient and timely movement of such vast quantities of supplies and huge numbers of men also depended upon having an effective transport system, and especially upon access to railways.

## 2. Movement and Transportation

The army's extensive transport and movement organization was responsible for coordinating and carrying out the movement of troops, equipment and supplies by road, rail and inland waterways. At the highest level, the OKW chief of transportation directed and controlled a network of regional transportation headquarters (Transport-Kommandanturen) located throughout Germany and the occupied territories. These headquarters were generally under army control but acted in support of the wider Wehrmacht, interfacing with the state railways (Deutsche Reichsbahn) and inland waterways authorities. Any rail or water movement of personnel, vehicles or equipment by the army had to be authorized and coordinated by the appropriate Transport-Kommandanturen and was carried out by movement detachments assigned to major railway stations and inland harbours. Rail transport was used extensively, with military trains enjoying priority on any railway lines also used by civilian trains.

### Rail Movement

The German railway system was so well developed and with so many lines and routes in place that it continued to operate effectively until the final few months of the war. This reflected the assiduous development of the national railway system by the general staff ever since the mid-nineteenth century, when rail movement became a core element of Germany's mobilization plans and its support for military operations. Accordingly, the importance of the railways to the war effort cannot be overstated, while they also facilitated routine movement by rail virtually everywhere within Germany right through the war – albeit with ever-increasing delays and diversions caused by the Allied air campaign, especially from 1944. Despite such interruptions and inconveniences, ammunition, rations, fuel, equipment, replacement vehicles, horses and mail consigned by rail all moved more or less as planned during most of the war, as did the many thousands of personnel proceeding on duty, leave, convalescence and so on. Wherever possible, standard trains – made up of predetermined numbers and types of wagon – were used for troop movement, so that a complete unit such as a company or battalion could be moved by a single train, complete with all its weapons, essential equipment and provisions for the journey. Typically, these trains were made up of between 30 and 60 wagons, flat-beds and box-cars, the precise mix depending upon the type of unit to be transported. The operational situation and ease of access to the train wagons in the loading area directly affected loading times; loading a troop train might take anything between two and twelve

The army relied upon rail movement throughout the war. Here, a trainload of Pz.Kpfw.V Panther tanks is en route to the front in Normandy during the summer of 1944.

hours, with unloading usually taking about half the loading time. Infantry regularly detrained as close to the combat area as possible and then moved forward on foot, while the mobility of armored units and the particular need to conceal their arrival in an operational area meant that they usually detrained well to the rear. An infantry division required between 35 and 40 standard trains to move it, while a Panzer or Panzergrenadier division might require as many as 80 such trains to transport all of its men, vehicles (including tanks and self-propelled artillery) and equipment. Some examples of special-to-purpose military trains included:

- Special trains (Sonderzüge), for the movement of heavy tanks and self-propelled artillery. These trains of 30 to 35 wagons carried about 125 personnel with (for example) four to six Pz.Kpfw.VI Tiger tanks or six to eight Pz.Kpfw.V Panthers, plus other equipment.
- Motor-vehicle-carrying trains, with about 51 wagons, carrying 250 personnel, twenty heavy vehicles and twenty light vehicles, plus equipment.
- Special tank trains (Sonderpanzerzüge), of about 33 wagons, carrying about twenty medium tanks (such as the Pz.Kpfw.II or IV), their crews and other equipment.
- Infantry trains (Infanteriezüge), with about 55 wagons, typically carrying some 350 personnel, ten heavy vehicles, ten light vehicles and 70 horses, and other equipment; up to 800 troops could be carried in lieu of some of the vehicles, horses or equipment.
- Replacement troop trains, with between 50 and 60 wagons, moving as many as 2,000 soldiers carrying only their personal equipment and basic rations for the rail journey.
- Engineer construction trains, each of about 40 wagons (including 39 open or flat-bed wagons) transporting 820 tons of engineer stores plus a small escort or handling detachment.
- Armored trains (Eisenbahnpanzerzüge), whose primary function was in fact that of a combat unit protecting the rail lines of communication on the Eastern Front and supporting counter-partisan operations. These trains typically comprised

six heavily armored wagons manned by about 113 personnel to serve the multiplicity of weapons carried on board the armored wagons. Two wagons carried infantry equipped with two medium mortars, one heavy machine gun, and as many as 22 light machine guns, while two more each carried a 105mm howitzer. Lastly, two wagons provided air defense, mounting a multi-barrelled 20mm anti-aircraft gun on each, sometimes with an additional anti-tank or artillery gun. Further wagons could each carry a light tank, such as the Czech-manufactured 38(t), or two light armored cars to provide the train with additional protection and also to enable reconnaissance tasks to be carried out some distance from the train itself.
- Horse supply trains (Pferdeersatzzüge) of 55 wagons, each wagon containing eight horses, or up to six heavy draught horses, with a total of between 330 and 440 horses transported per train.
- Combat supplies trains, carrying rations, ammunition or fuel, might transport loads made up as shown in the table below.

Another train carrying Pz.Kpfw.V Panther tanks and their crews. This one is also in France during the summer of 1944 – the potential vulnerability of such rail movement once the Allies achieved air superiority is all too clear.

| Category of Train | Average number of Wagons | Details of Load (and Total Weight) |
|---|---|---|
| Rations (Verpflegungszüge) | 40 | 300,000 combat ration packs and 300,000 combat half-ration packs (442 tons). |
| Rations | 40 | 180,000 full rations (including bread) and 40,000 animal rations (454 tons). |
| Rations | 40 | 300,000 full rations, less bread but including baking materials (450 tons). |
| Rations | 40 | Flour sufficient for 833,000 rations (450 tons). |
| Rations | 40 | Oats sufficient for 90,000 animal rations (450 tons). |
| Rations | 40 | Animals for butchery: 360 cattle or 1,200 pigs or 1,800 sheep (72–180 tons). |
| Ammunition (Munitionszüge) | 30 | Unit-loaded trains, containing a mix of ammunition types to cater for all of the receiving unit's weapons. |
| Ammunition | 30 | Trains carrying a mix of ammunition of specific calibers, with each wagon containing about fifteen tons of ammunition of a given caliber. |
| Ammunition | 30 | Single-caliber ammunition trains, all wagons loaded with ammunition of the same type and caliber. |
| Fuel (Betriebsstoffzüge) | 20 | Tanker wagons, together containing up to 529,000 liters of fuel. |
| Fuel | 30 | Twenty-five wagons carrying fuel in 200-liter and 20-liter containers (about 480,500 liters), plus five wagons carrying lubricants, paraffin and anti-freeze solution in various oil drums and containers. |

### Water-borne Movement

Sea moves by the army were relatively few, but those that were carried out included movement to and from North Africa, the invasion of Norway and subsequently the invasion of Crete, operations in the Black Sea and the Crimea, and routine moves to and from the occupied Channel Islands, as well as the extensive preparations and training for the cancelled Operation *Seelöwe*. Inland, canals and major rivers were used whenever appropriate, with barges and any available cargo or passenger vessels routinely requisitioned as necessary. Whether by sea or on inland waterways, the planning for these moves was based upon the "gross registered ton", although volume rather than weight was critical to determine the size and type of vessel required, and for staff planning purposes each gross registered ton equated to a volume of 2.83 cubic meters. Under this system a man equated to two gross registered tons, a horse to eight, a light vehicle to ten, a truck or field gun to twenty and a medium tank to 25. This in turn indicated embarkation planning times of eight minutes for 100 men, one hour for 100 horses led on board, and six hours for 100 horses or 100 light vehicles embarked by crane, while a vessel of 2,000 tons capacity would take sixteen hours to load with freight. From these figures, it was assessed that an infantry division would require between 50,000 and 70,000 tons (or the equivalent cargo volume) to conduct a sea move.

Merchant vessels were usually employed to carry out major moves of troops or equipment by sea. Here Pz.Kpfw.III tanks for the DAK are off-loaded at a North African port. Meanwhile, in September 1942, the Gebirgsjäger unit pictured at a European or Baltic port will embark once its vehicles, heavy weapons and equipment have been loaded.

### Road Movement

Although much road movement was unavoidably still carried out on foot, the army also had a large road transport organization. This included at least 50 transport regiments as well as many independent transport battalions and companies, the latter often having specialized vehicle maintenance, recovery and repair responsibilities. However, a continuing lack of wheeled vehicles for troop movement and cargo-carrying meant that the army had to confiscate or requisition large numbers of vehicles in order to meet its needs, while many of the so-called military trucks in army service were actually civilian vehicles adapted for military use, which often lacked the durability or motive power for the tasks demanded of them. By and large, only the army's élite units and formations were properly equipped with military-grade transport vehicles and one estimate indicated that for every purpose-built military transport vehicle used by the Wehrmacht during the war, there were a further 100 civilian types in service. Since large numbers of captured military vehicles (especially from Czechoslovakia and France) were also taken into use, and did offset the wheeled-vehicle deficit to some extent, the overall mix of military, civilian and foreign vehicles created significant repair and maintenance difficulties throughout the Wehrmacht. The disparity between foot and vehicle movement in an army that had actively placed mobility at the center of its operational doctrine was

illustrated by the general staff planning figures. These indicated that an infantry division without troop transports could march between fifteen and 30 kilometers per day, while a motorized division with wheeled or possibly some half-track transport could cover between 150 and 250 kilometers per day; a Panzer or Panzergrenadier division could drive between 100 and 150 kilometers per day.

So, apart from its armored combat vehicles and horse-drawn wagons, the army used a wide array of motorized transport vehicles. These included motorcycles and motorcycle combinations, the unique semi-tracked Kettenkraftrad, light vehicles such as the ubiquitous Volkswagen Kübelwagen and its amphibious variant the Schwimmwagen, numerous light, medium and heavy automobiles, trucks, and ambulances, and a whole range of light, medium and heavy half-track and fully-tracked vehicles. Road movement was also conducted using horses or mules, and even oxen, with a horse-drawn transport column covering between twenty and 30 kilometers per day, resting on alternate days. Pack

**Above:** Whether for reconnaissance, liaison, traffic control or a multiplicity of other tasks, motorcycles were used extensively by the army throughout the war.

**Top right:** The Volkswagen Kübelwagen light utility vehicle was employed in every operational theater.

**Right, center and bottom:** The light amphibious car Kfz.1/20 Schwimmwagen (VW designation Kdf.166) was used extensively by Panzer and Panzergrenadier units for reconnaissance, liaison and command and control.

**Right:** These heavy motorcycle combinations pictured on the Eastern Front almost certainly belong to a reconnaissance unit. The motorcycles are the BMW R75 or Zündapp KS750.

**Center right and below:** Bicycles provided the army with an important, low-maintenance and flexible means of transport for thousands of soldiers both prior to and during the war. The bicycle troops shown here are operating in the Balkans, 4 October 1943. The robust and versatile German military bicycle (Truppen-fahrrad) was manufactured in several versions, including a folding bicycle (Klappfahrrad) for parachute troops. It could be configured to carry a range of weapons, ammunition and equipment in addition to the rider, and to tow a light trailer.

trains (Tragtierkolonnen) of some 40 mules or horses could transport up to five tons of weapons and equipment across mountainous terrain and other ground impassable to vehicles.

The army also made extensive use of bicycle-mounted troops (Radfahrtruppen) for straightforward movement, reconnaissance and message carrying. Although German army bicycle units pre-dated World War I, they still proved their worth in the West during 1940 and on the Eastern Front from 1941, providing a low-maintenance movement capability for lightly-equipped troops when the threat of direct enemy air or ground action was not high. The machines used by the army's bicycle squadrons (Radfahr-schwadronen) were specially constructed to carry the soldier's personal equipment and weapons – including grenades, ammunition, or parts of a machine gun – as well as special attachments that enabled a number of cyclists to be towed on roads by a motor vehicle. Other modifications allowed special equipment such as food containers or signals equipment to be carried, and there was even a light trailer that could be attached to the bicycle and towed. Folding bicycles that could be dropped by parachute were also developed, as were tandems and other unofficial modifications of the basic military bicycle.

Very many different types of transport vehicles were employed by the army to carry out a virtually infinite range of tasks. Among the many German manufacturers of the army's buses and ambulances, and light, medium and heavy cars, tractors and trucks were such well-known names as BMW, Mercedes-Benz and Daimler-Benz, Opel, Büssing-NAG, Hanomag, MAN, Porsche, Audi, Maybach, and Volkswagen. Even the Ford Motor Company indirectly found itself providing vehicles for the Wehrmacht in the pre-war period, when Ford's factory near Köln (Cologne) was taken over by the German authorities, who then paid the US company for its use. Civilian vehicles were often taken straight into military use with little or no modification other than a new paint scheme. Once gasoline and diesel fuel started to become scarce, numbers of the Wehrmacht's wheeled utility vehicles were converted to run on compressed gas, usually being fitted with gas producers manufactured by Imbert. A less technical modification that appeared late in the war was prompted by Allied air supremacy: a metal seat fitted on the front right wing of many trucks. This seat was occupied by an air observer, who could warn of an impending air attack and also direct the truck driver into one of the many shelter bays that had been constructed beside German roads by that stage of the war. A further standard modification was a system of blackout and convoy lights and driving aids, including an ingenious display system of rear convoy lights that enabled a driver to assess whether or not he was the correct distance behind the vehicle in front. While the overall effectiveness of much of the army's general-purpose wheeled vehicle fleet lacked the robustness of vehicles specifically designed for military use, the half-track vehicles used widely throughout the war as personnel carriers and prime-movers provided outstanding mobility on roads and across country.

Many trucks were modified to accommodate an air observer seated on the right-side wing. His task was to give warning of air attack. The photograph shows Feldgendarm-erie troops of a Fallschirmjäger unit in Normandy, summer 1944.

One of the best known light utility cars used by the army was the soft-top Volkswagen (KdF) Kraftfahrzeug (motor vehicle) leichter Personenkraftwagen (light personnel carrier) K1 Type 82, usually known as the "Kübelwagen". About 52,000 of this four-wheel, two-wheel-drive (4×2) vehicle were produced by the end of the war, its several variants including vehicles for desert use. Between 1942 and 1944 Volkswagen also manufactured 14,265 amphibious 4×4 versions fitted with a hinged three-bladed propeller at the rear, and these vehicles were generally known as the "Schwimmwagen". Both vehicles seated up to five personnel, the space available dependent upon what radios or other equipment was fitted, and their air-cooled engines developed twenty-five horsepower providing a top speed of about eighty kilometers per hour. Porsche also produced a Schwimm-wagen, and several vehicles similar to the Kübelwagen were produced by Tatra, Opel, Mercedes-Benz, Stöwer, Hanomag, BMW and others. The Kübelwagen was used in every theater of operations, while the Schwimmwagen's superior mobility meant that it was regularly employed well forward within Panzer and Panzergrenadier units, as well as being used as a reconnaissance vehicle.

The army's medium and heavy classes of automobile were much more robust and often carried as many as eight to ten personnel. They included 4×2, 4×4 and 6×4 vehicles and most of the heavier types could also tow a trailer or light artillery gun if required. Many of the heavy automobiles (including 6×4 types) served as staff cars and as radio vehicles for command and control tasks. The several types of wheeled ambulance were based mainly upon the chassis of various heavy automobiles or light trucks and typically accommodated eight seated casualties or four stretcher cases. Among these ambulances was a 6×4 version produced for the army by Steyr in Austria until 1941.

The Krupp-manufactured 6×4 Kfz.70 (Krupp designation L2H143) was typical of the light cargo, troop-carrying and general-purpose trucks employed by the army throughout the war.

Below: Another example of the variety of transport used. A Horch medium car negotiates a congested roadway, together with motorcycle troops, other wheeled vehicles and an Sd.Kfz.223 light armored car during the invasion of Poland.

Below right: An AU/Horch 4×4 Kfz.15 medium car pictured in service with a medical unit of the DAK in Tobruk main square shortly after the capture of the town in 1942.

At least eighteen types of light truck were in service during the war, including 4×2, 4×4, 6×4, and 6×6 variants. Foremost among the many roles of these trucks were personnel and cargo transport, prime-mover, reconnaissance, light anti-aircraft gun platform, artillery observation and sound ranging, command and control, communications and casualty evacuation. Next came the medium trucks, those with a load-carrying capability of about three tons, and once again extensive use was made of commercially available types, including some pre-war American trucks made by Ford, Oldsmobile and Chevrolet which served alongside trucks produced by most of the major German vehicle manufacturers. During the early stages of the war some commercial trucks had the metal cab replaced with a soft-top canvas version, which was in turn replaced with a standardized substitute or Ersatz cab known as the Einheitsfahrerhaus from 1944, being a cheaply-constructed cab made of wood and pressed cardboard. As well as carrying cargo and personnel, medium trucks were frequently configured as radio vehicles, fuel tankers, and headquarters staff support vehicles. Although 4×2 versions predominated in this class of truck before the war, operational experience soon prompted the development of 4×4 vehicles, and several types of former 4×2 trucks were converted to 4×4. Probably the best known medium truck was the Opel Blitz, which existed as the 3.6-36S (commercial), the 3.6-36S

(military), both of which were 4×2 with rear-wheel drive, and the 3.6-6700A (the 4×4 version). There was also a heavy version of the 3.6-47 Blitz that featured a lengthened chassis intended for use on coaches (which could also be converted into ambulances or command vehicles). All of these Opel trucks had gasoline engines developing about 68 horsepower. Other medium trucks widely used by the army included commercial Ford G 917 T and G 997 T vehicles modified to meet military needs, the robust diesel-powered Mercedes-Benz LCF 3000 and the powerful 6×4 Büssing-NAG III GL6. The chassis of the army's versatile range of 6×4 medium trucks often provided the vehicle platform for fuel tankers, searchlights, fire-fighting appliances, mobile telephone exchanges and similar specialist functions.

The last type of all-wheeled trucks were those categorized as "heavy," which featured substantial load-carrying and towing capabilities. These included 4×2, 4×4, 6×4 and 6×6 load-carriers and prime-movers ranging from about six tons to eleven tons, as well as vehicles designed to carry mobile operating theaters, and for use as heavy fuel tankers, recovery vehicles, winch vehicles, buses and tank transporters (such as the Faun L900D567); there were even versions (such as the 4×2 Henschel 6J2) fitted with special wheels and modified to run on railway lines. Mercedes-Benz, Büssing-NAG, Henschel, Opel, MAN, and later Skoda and Tatra all featured prominently among the manufacturers of these heavy trucks.

The very nature of the procurement and development of the Wehrmacht's wheeled vehicles resulted in fleet management difficulties, and an Allied assessment made in 1945 stated: "In general, German automotive equipment consists of adaptations of civilian types, and these in most cases do not reach the high standard of American or British vehicles either in reliability or performance." However, this was not the case in respect of the army's half-track vehicles, and the same Allied report went on to state: "With half-tracked prime-movers and personnel-carriers, however, the Germans have excelled; in this class they have

produced vehicles which have given excellent service and which are unrivalled for cross-country performance."[4] Although half-track or semi-track vehicles were also used by the Allies, especially by the US forces later in the war, these remarkable and distinctive vehicles were particularly associated with the Wehrmacht, for which considerably more than 25,000 were eventually produced. Half-track vehicles had been under development since the 1920s, and most of the production models that emerged from about 1936 continued more or less unaltered until the end of the conflict apart from upgrading modifications. They ranged in size from the small NSU Kettenkraftrad motorcycle tractor to heavy prime-movers such as the eighteen-ton Famo Zugkraftwagen, with the various classes of half-track chassis used both for soft-skin and armored vehicles – the latter including the troop carriers adopted by the Panzergrenadiers, but never in the numbers the army required. Half-tracks also provided the automotive platforms on which a diverse range of weaponry and special equipment was mounted.

With the exception of the particular suspension arrangements used on the range of so-called "Maultier" ("Mule") semi-track cargo variants, which were half-tracks that had been converted

from conventional wheeled drive systems, all the army's half-tracks (including those used by Luftwaffe anti-aircraft gun crews as prime-movers for their 88mm Flak 18 guns) featured a torsion-bar suspension system with rubber-padded drive sprockets and between five and eight overlapping rubber-tired metal "bogie" wheels, which also supported the top run of the track. The metal track had detachable rubber pads, with vehicle steering carried out both via the tracks themselves and by using the conventional front-wheel steering system. The motive power for most half-tracks was provided by a Maybach six-cylinder or V-12 engine developing between 90 and 230 horsepower. The half-tracks most widely used by the army included the remarkable motorcycle-based Kleines Kettenkraftrad made by NSU, which was used for various tasks including that of light tractor, for laying telephone line and as a light transport vehicle. There were also several light (one-ton) variants such as the Demag D11-3 and D7 series, which included the Sd.Kfz.10/4 mounting a 20mm anti-aircraft gun, the Sd.Kfz.10 Panzergrenadier vehicle, and the Sd.Kfz.250/1 armored personnel carrier, which carried a crew of six and mounted two machine guns. Adler also produced various models, some carrying up to eight personnel. Among the best-known light half-track vehicles were those manufactured by Hanomag, including the Sd.Kfz.251/16, which mounted no fewer than three flame throwers and a machine gun. Almost 15,000 Hanomag armored personnel carriers and variants were produced during the war. Medium and heavy half-tracks – both soft-skinned and armored – provided the mobile platforms for 20mm and 37mm anti-aircraft guns, Panzerwerfer 42 multi-barrel rocket launcher systems and other types of artillery guns. They also served as snow ploughs, gas (chemical warfare) detection and decontamination vehicles, vehicle recovery tractors and mobile cranes, as well as meeting the army's more straightforward prime-mover and load-carrying needs. These vehicles ranged from five to eighteen tons, with Krauss-Maffei, Mercedes-Benz, Hanomag, Büssing-NAG, Daimler-Benz, Famo, Vomag and Tatra the principal manu-

**Left, top:** The army's Opel Blitz medium cargo truck had a 3-ton capacity and typified this class of transport vehicle.

**Below left:** AU/Horch medium vehicles were much used as staff cars. Here Generalfeldmarschall Rommel is seated in the rear of his AU/Horch, having just arrived at a farmhouse in northern France for a meeting with some of his senior commanders, summer 1944.

**Below:** The army made great use of half-tracked vehicles throughout the war. Among its many roles, the ubiquitous Hanomag Sd.Kfz.251 served as a weapons platform – including as a flame-thrower vehicle, designated Sd.Kfz.251/16.

**Right and far right:**
The Hanomag Sd.Kfz.251 also served as a troop carrier for Panzer-grenadiers (right), as a command vehicle, for reconnaissance tasks, and as a cargo or ammunition carrier. The symbol on the left front of the vehicle on the opposite page is that of the 21st Panzer-division.

**Below:** These Krauss-Maffei medium half-tracks (Sd.Kfz.7) are towing 105mm sK 18 medium artillery guns, with all members of each gun's crew travelling in the vehicle towing it. The half-track was also used to tow the 88mm anti-aircraft gun.

facturers. Probably the most widely used half-tracks in this class were the five-ton Krauss-Maffei BN 9 Sd.Kfz.6 and the eight-ton Krauss-Maffei KM 11, the twelve-ton Mercedes-Benz DB 9 Sd. Kfz.8, and the eighteen-ton Famo F3 Sd. Kfz.9/1 (which carried a six-ton crane).

**Air Movement**

Although the vast majority of routine army movement was conducted by rail, road vehicle or foot, aircraft were sometimes used to move troops to or from an operational theater and to evacuate casualties (such administrative movement being separate from the movement of airborne forces such as the Luftwaffe's Fallschirmjäger units). One theater of operations that relied heavily upon the air link was North Africa, where the Royal Navy and the British presence in Gibraltar and Malta constantly threatened the sea lines of communication in the Mediterranean to Rommel's Afrikakorps. Later, the air bridge to the beleaguered 6th Army at Stalingrad from late 1942 exemplifies a situation in which the army was entirely dependent upon this form of air support – and

graphically illustrates the consequences of the Luftwaffe's inability to meet this operational remit. The best-known of the Luftwaffe's transport aircraft was the three-engined Junkers Ju 52, with a crew of three or four, a speed of 265 kilometers per hour and a range of 335 kilometers. The Ju 52 could transport 22 men with their personal equipment or up to 2,272 kilograms of cargo; although it was essentially a transport aircraft, it was armed with up to five machine guns for self-defense. The Ju 52 continued as the mainstay of the air transport fleet throughout the war, although other Junkers and Messerschmitt transports, together with some converted bombers, were also developed and used in this role. When the Blitzkrieg was launched against France and the Low

The Junkers Ju 52 was the Luftwaffe's principal troop transport aircraft, as well as being used by the Fallschirm-jäger for airborne assault operations. The troops shown above are boarding a Ju 52 in southern Russia in 1944. Note the self-defense machine gun position on the aircraft roof.

A Messerschmitt Bf 323 pictured at Tunis, North Africa, in 1942. This aircraft could transport up to 100 personnel.

Countries in May 1940, the Luftwaffe had no less than 475 transport aircraft available; however, as the war expanded and the Wehrmacht's requirement for air transport steadily increased, the Luftwaffe was eventually unable to provide the required levels of this support.

Meanwhile, the Fiesler Fi 156 "Storch" and Henschel HS 126 light aircraft were the two principal liaison and air reconnaissance aircraft that supported the army, carrying out a multiplicity of tasks and providing sterling service throughout the war.

## 3. Intelligence

The army's attitude to intelligence during much of the war often belied its traditional diligence and attention to this subject in earlier times, while also underlining the pervasive influence of Hitler himself and of wider institutional and political attitudes and agendas within the Third Reich. This was especially so at the higher levels of command, where – in order to maintain his control of them – Hitler deliberately allowed the intelligence agencies of the Wehrmacht, the state and the SS to operate competitively and in relative isolation, without any sort of high-level centralized controlling authority. In January 1940, Hitler ordered that nobody was to receive intelligence or information additional to that which he required in order to carry out his duties. This "need to know" principle was sound when applied sensibly, but its literal interpretation by far too many personnel at all levels of command undoubtedly stifled the cross-fertilization of intelligence and information. Consequently, while the collection and analysis of intelligence was theoretically accorded a high priority, the disparate nature of the Third Reich's intelligence organization and the diversity of intelligence units, often constrained by their discrete lines of command and channels of information, meant that in many cases the Wehrmacht's intelligence capabilities were not enhanced significantly or properly coordinated until the final few years of the war, by which time Germany had lost the strategic initiative and was fighting a primarily defensive war.

Misplaced attitudes toward the business of intelligence within the army were also shaped by more traditional influences. The military intelligence staff branch (department 1c) was always subordinate to the operations staff branch (1a) in any headquarters, while the traditional concept of the primacy of the offensive had long implied that it was leadership, firepower, valorous men and sheer determination that won battles, rather than intelligence. The operational impact of such views was not immediately evident during the victorious Blitzkrieg years, but from 1942 only a steadily improving intelligence capability could compensate for the gradually diminishing strength of the Wehrmacht as it was forced to adopt a defensive posture in the East, and then in the West from 1944. Some overestimates of German military prowess and underestimates of the enemy – both of which gained a false measure of validity with the Blitzkrieg

The Henschel Hs 126 was a two-seat reconnaissance and observation aircraft, well thought of for its good short takeoff and flying characteristics at low speeds.

The Fiesler Fi 156 "Storch" provided the reconnaissance "eyes" of the army at longer ranges, as well as fulfilling a host of other liaison and other observation missions.

victories of 1939 and 1940 – also contributed to the downplaying of the importance of operational and tactical intelligence prior to and during the early years of the war.

At the strategic and operational levels, intelligence for the ground forces was provided to the OKW by the Abwehr, which had agencies in occupied and neutral countries as well as in areas where army operations were in progress. In addition, its signals intelligence (or "SIGINT") organization intercepted, decoded, interpreted and assessed Allied radio transmissions. Throughout the war, SIGINT was the single most important intelligence source for the OKW and OKH, providing details of enemy orders of battle, situation and intentions. Other important sources included ground and air reconnaissance and the human information and intelligence (HUMINT) gained from prisoners-of-war. At the OKH, operational intelligence was evaluated by two branches of the general staff. These were the Third, which covered foreign armies in the West (Fremde Heere West, or FHW) and the Twelfth, covering the East (Fremde Heere Ost, or FHO). The FHW's area of responsibility included the western hemisphere and initially focused on the forces of Great Britain, other western European states and the upper Balkans, while the FHO covered Scandinavia, Poland, Africa, the lower Balkans, the Far East, the USSR and the USA. However, FHO responsibility for the USA passed to the FHW in December 1941, and in 1942 the new head of the FHO, Colonel Reinhard Gehlen, reorganized the branch and upgraded its capabilities in response to the rapidly growing top-priority need to gather intelligence on Soviet forces. At the same time, the Abwehr's Warsaw station, which had previously conducted all spying and counter-intelligence operations against the Soviet Union, came under FHO control.

From 1944 the SS, specifically the Reichssicherheitshauptamt (RSHA), took control of the Abwehr and all higher-level intelligence operations, which adversely affected the work of many non-SS intelligence officers because the SS routinely adjusted potentially unpalatable assessments of Allied capabilities and strengths to provide more acceptable assessments to Hitler. As a result, the OKW-endorsed assessments passed to the OKH from early 1944 were frequently neither impartial nor accurate. One example of the consequences of the RSHA's control of intelligence matters involved the crucially important assessments of the Allied order of battle for D-Day, provided initially by the FHW. Although the head of the FHW, Colonel Baron von Roenne, was a professional military intelligence staff officer trusted by Hitler, the Sicherheitsdienst (SD) none the less denied him direct access to the Führer. Accordingly, in the certain knowledge that the SD staff routinely halved his estimates of Anglo-US strengths before presenting them to Hitler, he simply doubled all of the order of battle figures provided for these enemy forces. However, in May 1944 the SD officer who had automatically halved the FHW assessments in earlier months was re-assigned, and his successor accepted in good faith von Roenne's deliberately inflated pre-invasion "FHW Assessment of the Enemy Order of Battle" in its entirety, endorsing it and passing it on to Hitler unamended. Consequently, for some time after the Allied landings in Normandy, Hitler and the OKW persisted in the belief that the remaining unaccounted for or uncommitted part of the main invasion force was still based in the Dover area, preparing to carry out the main landing at Calais. So it was that the domination and politicization of the intelligence organization by the RSHA from 1944, together with the long-standing rivalries between the principal agencies, all contributed to the disastrous intelligence failures of May to July 1944, which in turn contributed significantly to the success of the Anglo-US invasion on 6 June.[5]

Such fundamental flaws in the system at the OKW and OKH inevitably had various impacts lower down the army's chain of command, as the medium and longer-term plans of most units relied to varying degrees upon the intelligence assessments they received from above. Only at the tactical level were such assessments based largely upon the real-time intelligence and information provided by the reconnaissance and surveillance forces and capabilities directly controlled by the army and division headquarters 1c staffs. At major headquarters down to army level, general staff officers with experience of intelligence duties filled the 1c branch positions, while at the lower levels of command non-specialist (but suitably trained) officers usually fulfilled this function. The work of all these officers was usually sound, resulting in accurate and timely operational and tactical intelligence, the provision of appropriate advice to commanders and the effective tasking of the ground reconnaissance units under their control. However, at divisional and regimental level these same officers often had responsibility for matters such as propaganda, censorship and troop welfare as well, and this tended to perpetuate some of the army's long-standing perceptions about the relative importance of intelligence.

## 4. Communications

Effective operational command and control always depended upon the timely, reliable, secure and efficient passage of information and orders. The responsibility for this fell to the signal troops (Nachrichtentruppen), which included both specialist signallers and non-specialist signals troops trained to support the communications needs of their own parent unit. The Wehrmacht's communications included conventional radio, telephone, telegraphy, teleprinting, communications security, coding and decoding messages, intercept and various related functions. Until early 1943 the army's propaganda troops (Propagandatruppen) were also part of the signals arm, using communication skills and information as a complementary weapon of war. At the highest level, a signals regiment (Nachrichtenregiment) supported the OKW and provided communications between Hitler's head-quarters (the Führerhauptquartier) and the headquarters of the army groups and armies. At lower levels of command, signals

The signals (Nach-richtendienst) units provided the army's communications in a wide variety of ways. These included the use of message dogs, flags (semaphore), carrier pigeons, telephone lines and radios. Signals training routinely involved operating while wearing gas masks. The pictures show (top to bottom and left to right): a message-carrying dog; using flag signals in the mountains; a carrier pigeon transport truck (carrying 50-60 birds); departure time for a carrier pigeon at the front; testing telephone communications; and a radio station at the front line.

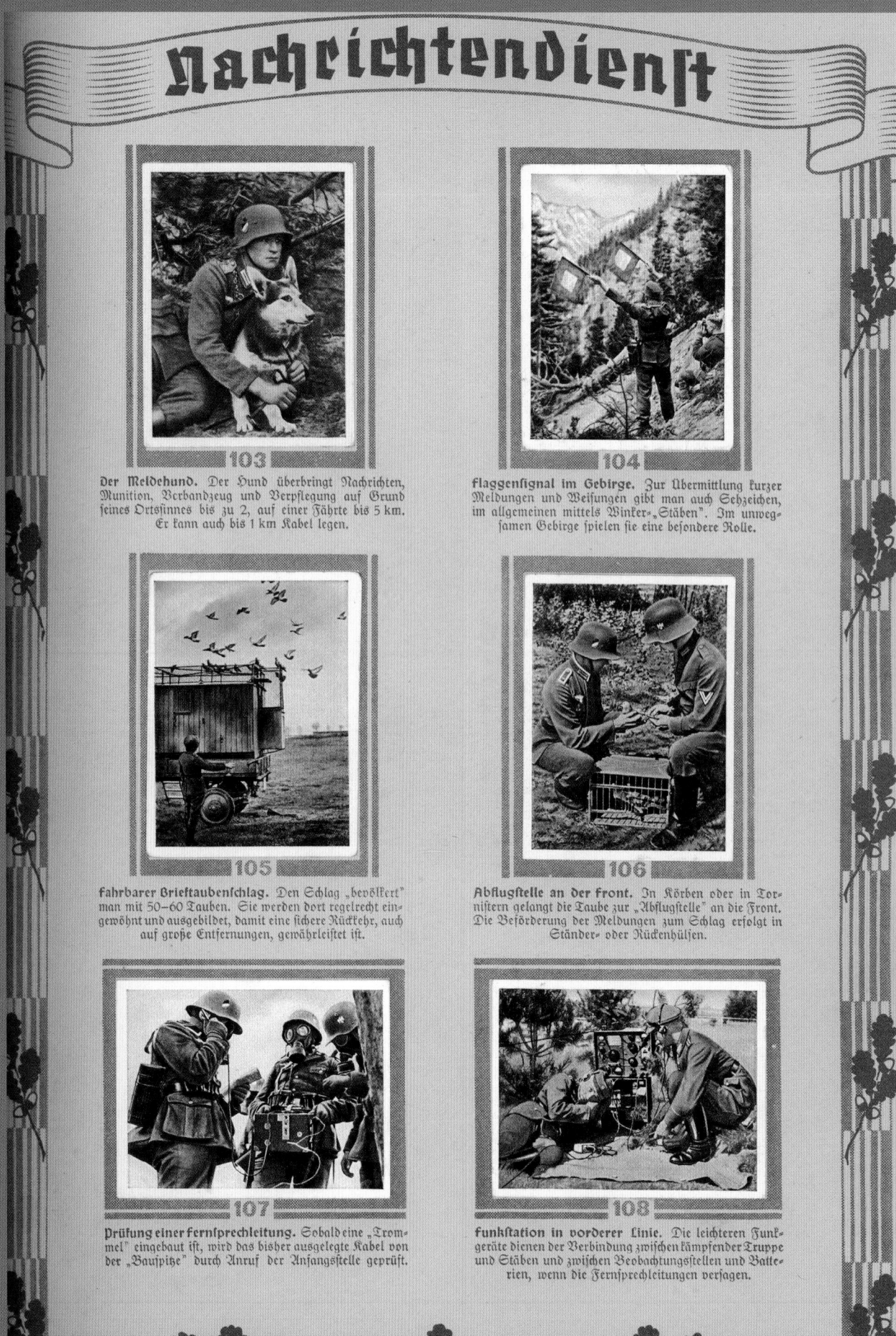

# Nachrichtendienst

**103**

**der Meldehund.** Der Hund überbringt Nachrichten, Munition, Verbandzeug und Verpflegung auf Grund seines Ortsfinnes bis zu 2, auf einer Fährte bis 5 km. Er kann auch bis 1 km Kabel legen.

**104**

**flaggensignal im Gebirge.** Zur Übermittlung kurzer Meldungen und Weisungen gibt man auch Sehzeichen, im allgemeinen mittels Winker-„Stäben". Im unweg-samen Gebirge spielen sie eine besondere Rolle.

**105**

**fahrbarer Brieftaubenschlag.** Den Schlag „bevölkert" man mit 50–60 Tauben. Sie werden dort regelrecht ein-gewöhnt und ausgebildet, damit eine sichere Rückkehr, auch auf große Entfernungen, gewährleistet ift.

**106**

**Abflugstelle an der front.** In Körben oder in Tor-niftern gelangt die Taube zur „Abflugstelle" an die front. Die Beförderung der Meldungen zum Schlag erfolgt in Ständer- oder Rückenhülsen.

**107**

**Prüfung einer fernsprechleitung.** Sobald eine „Trom-mel" eingebaut ift, wird das bisher ausgelegte Kabel von der „Baufpitze" durch Anruf der Anfangsstelle geprüft.

**108**

**funkstation in vorderer Linie.** Die leichteren funk-geräte dienen der Verbindung zwischen kämpfender Truppe und Stäben und zwischen Beobachtungsstellen und Batte-rien, wenn die fernsprechleitungen versagen.

regiments provided mobile communications, while a separate field signals command (Feldnachrichtenkommandantur) was responsible for any static signals installations within an army's operational area. At divisional level, an integral signals battalion (Nachrichten-bataillon) provided the communications support and adopted an appropriate identifying prefix in its own unit title, using "Motorisiert" where their parent formation was a Panzer or Panzergrenadier division or "Gebirgs" where it was a mountain division's signals battalion. The particular importance of rail movement to the Wehrmacht was illustrated by the existence of a specialist railway signals regiment (Eisenbahnnachrichtenregiment), which had a number of railway signals battalions under its command, while other specialist signals units and independent companies also existed to support specific operational needs, their function usually being indicated in the unit title. In addition to the army's male signals personnel, many volunteer female auxiliary signallers (Nachrichthelferinnen des Heeres) were employed on army communications duties. These mainly consisted of operating telephone switchboards, and other wireless and telegraphy equipment, in the army's higher-level headquarters and static installations. The army's signals equipment included a full range of vehicle-mounted radios, man-pack radios, field and other telephones, telephone exchanges and switchboards, radio and line intercept equipment, teleprinters, speech scramblers, telegraphy and line-laying equipment, together with electricity generating, testing, repair and maintenance equipment.

Signals troops were organized into units that ranged in size from regiment to company, the divisional signals battalion being the most widely deployed signals unit, comprising a radio company, a telephone company and a resources or support platoon. Typically, an infantry division's signals battalion numbered 379 men (sixteen officers and 363 NCOs and other ranks), while that of a Panzer or Panzergrenadier division numbered 515 (sixteen officers and 499 NCOs and other ranks), reflecting the more complex communications needs and mobility of the last two types of division. The scale of transport allocated to a signals battalion was based primarily on the amount required to carry the unit's communications equipment, and although an infantry division's signals battalion had about 76 motor vehicles and thirteen motorcycles, the only troop-carrying vehicles were its fourteen horse-drawn wagons. Even then, the signallers would ride only if these wagons were not required to carry signals equipment, and during non-tactical movement an infantry division's signallers were routinely expected to march alongside the infantrymen they supported. However, signals battalions in Panzer or Panzer-grenadier divisions had no fewer than 114 motor vehicles, of which twenty were armored, with no official allocation of horse-drawn vehicles.

The army's radios were robust and generally reliable, as well as relatively straightforward to operate. Unitary or modular construction enabled the speedy replacement of an electrical function complete, rather than time being wasted tracing the

specific part that had failed. The majority of radio casings were manufactured of precise metal castings in alloys made predominantly of magnesium and aluminium, and most radios featured user-friendly controls, displays and dials, and internal electrical connectors that were each specifically numbered to aid servicing, construction and the correct connectivity. Electrical power for vehicle radios (including those in armored vehicles) was generally provided by electrical converters working from the twelve-volt vehicle batteries, while ground stations used storage batteries, dry cells, gasoline generators, or pedal-operated generators. Man-pack radios were powered by storage batteries or dry cells. About twenty different types of radio equipment were fitted to the army's armored vehicles, with typical transmission distances for the standard tank radio (the ten-watt Fu.5 radio) ranging from 4 to 6 kilometers for carrier wave (CW) Morse transmissions and 2 to 4 kilometers for voice transmissions, depending on whether or not the tank was stationary. The twenty-

This Kettenkraftrad (SD.Kfz.2) is being used to lay signal cable on 6 March 1944. The "WL" registration plate indicates that it is a Luftwaffe vehicle, and might therefore belong to an 88mm anti-aircraft unit.

The Feldfern-sprecher 33 field telephone was the army's principal means of line communication at tactical level.

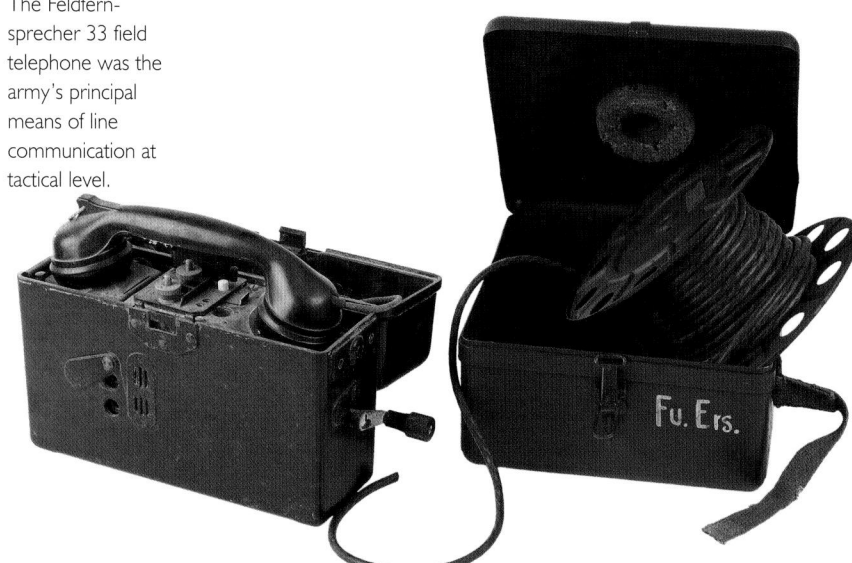

watt Fu.6 radio fitted in some command tanks could achieve ranges of 8 to 10 kilometers for CW and 6 to 8 kilometers for voice, while some other types of vehicle-borne radio could transmit and receive successfully over distances of up to about 80 kilometers when stationary and using an elevated antenna.

The infantry and other non-vehicle-borne troops also used at least twenty different types of radio, with a wide span of outputs and frequency bands providing mainly short- and medium-range communications for a multiplicity of tasks. These included artillery observation and fire control, observation-post and small-unit communications in the forward areas, patrol communications, liaison between dismounted infantry and the armored vehicles supporting them, internal communications within a defensive position, and chain of command communications between an infantry regimental or brigade headquarters, its battalions and their companies. These radios supported voice transmissions over distances up to between 30 and 50 kilometers, although the smallest sets had ranges as short as 3.2 and 4.8 kilometers. However, those radio sets that had a CW capability could transmit and receive such messages up to almost 100 kilometers in some cases, while a number of larger and significantly more powerful (up to 1,000 and 1,500 watts) ground station radios were also used, some of which could transmit and receive voice and CW over distances up to several hundred kilometers. These powerful sets met the command and control needs of higher-level headquarters, such as those at division and corps, and supported communications between corps and army headquarters.

While radio communications were essential to support the army's fast-flowing mobile operations, there was still a huge reliance upon telephone – or line – communications. While a radio message could be intercepted, line messages were generally secure,

Right: Some armored vehicles had comprehensive signals equipment, enabling effective radio communic-ations and command and control on the move. An Sd.Kfz.260/261 Kleiner Panzer-Funkwagen (light armored radio car) is on the left, with an Sd.Kfz.250 half-track radio vehicle. Both vehicles are serving with Heeresgruppe Kleist in Russia during August/September 1943.

# Nachrichtendienst

**109**

**Bau einer Fernsprechleitung.** Fernsprechleitungen werden vom Kraftwagen, vom Pferde aus oder zu Fuß gebaut. Man legt sie zum eigenen Schutz und zur Vermeidung von Verkehrsunfällen baldmöglichst hoch.

**110**

**Fernsprechvermittlung.** Die Sprechleitungen laufen in Vermittlungen zusammen, die mittels Klappenschränken die gewünschten Verbindungen herstellen. Ihr Ausfall kann ernste Folgen haben.

**111**

**Funkstelle.** Das stärkere Ft.-Gerät unserer Nachrichtentruppen dient Zwecken der höheren Führung, z. B. der Verbindung zwischen Heeresteilen und der Verständigung mit weit voraus befindlichen Aufklärungskräften.

**112**

**Doppelleitungsbau auf Stangen.** Bei guten Doppelleitungen kann der Feind nicht „mithören". Ihr Bau auf Stangen erhöht die Betriebssicherheit. Die Leute auf dem Bilde ziehen das ausgelegte Kabel an, während andere gleichzeitig die Stangen aufrichten.

**113**

**Blinktrupp.** Die Blinkstellen dienen zur Verbindung im vorderen Kampfbereich. Ihre Leistung ist abhängig von Lampenstärke, Hintergrund, Beleuchtung und Wetter.

**114**

**Befehlsstelle im Walde.** Die Nachrichtenverbindungen der Division laufen im Gefechtsstand des Divisionsstabes zusammen. Dieser muß Sicht und Feuer möglichst entzogen sein. So legt man ihn auch gern in Waldungen.

Inevitably, most signals troops were trained to operate an extensive range of technical communications equipment. These troops carried out tasks such as laying telephone cables above or at ground-level, using light signalling equipment and operating radios, telephones and telephone exchanges. They were vital to the effective command and control of operations, establishing, manning and maintaining the army's communications links at and between all levels of headquarters. The pictures show (top to bottom and left to right): laying a telephone line; a telephone exchange in the field; a vehicle-mounted radio station; constructing a double communications line carried on poles; a signalling light in position; and a command post sited in woodland.

**Right:** The T.FuG.k radio shown here had effective ranges of 11 kilometers (voice) and 24 kilometers using CW (Morse). It was used primarily by the artillery to communicate between the gun line and the battery command post but was also used by all other arms except the infantry.

**Far right:** "Enigma" encoding machines were used for the army's strategic radio communications. An "Enigma" machine could also be mounted in an armored vehicle, as seen here (in the foreground) during June 1940 inside one of General Heinz Guderian's HQ 19th Armee-korps command vehicles. Guderian is standing behind the radio operators.

provided that the line itself was suitably protected against eavesdropping or line tapping and (where necessary) a scrambler device was used. Various telephones and types of cable were used by the army, although permanent in-place telephone systems were utilized wherever they were available. The general purpose field telephone (Feldfernsprecher) was the battery-powered type 33, which weighed less than six kilograms and was the standard telephone used (for example) to interconnect infantry platoons with their company headquarters in a defensive position, and that company headquarters with its battalion headquarters. A mains (AC) or battery-powered amplifier unit was also available to improve the performance of the type 33 Feldfernsprecher telephone. A comprehensive range of switchboards and telephone exchanges was also available, catering for two to ten lines with the basic Vermittlungskätchen exchange, and from ten to 300 lines with other switchboard units and combinations of these. The army's inventory of line equipment also included several types of teleprinter and telewriter, these being used mainly in the rear areas.

As well as transmitting and receiving messages, the army's signallers also had several pieces of equipment that were designed to jam radio transmissions, while other equipment was provided to intercept radio and line transmissions and thus provide the operations staff with valuable intelligence about enemy operations.

Ever aware of their own capabilities in this area, the Germans developed a range of encoding and scrambling equipment, with signals troops operating the army's "Enigma" coding machines, an electro-mechanical encryption machine used by the Wehrmacht for its strategic radio communications, which was sufficiently robust for it to be mounted in vehicles and used in armored command vehicles as well as in static headquarters. It employed a battery-powered keyboard, and when the operator typed a letter it struck wheels or rotors (three originally; a more secure four-rotor version was introduced for the U-boats in 1942) which then randomly registered substitute letters for transmission, the substitution process being controlled by using a secure key setting applied earlier. Throughout the war the Germans had great confidence in "Enigma" and assumed that this encoding system was entirely secure. This was a serious miscalculation. The British already possessed a Polish-designed decoding machine constructed from information provided by a young Pole who had previously worked in the German factory producing the "Enigma" machines, and in due course the British secret intelligence service also managed to acquire an "Enigma" machine for detailed analysis. Without the relevant key, breaking the coded intercepts depended upon thousands of hours of message analysis and mathematical calculations carried out manually by cryptanalysts,

and it was only the successful development of electro-mechanical and electronic computers by the Allies that eventually speeded up this process significantly. The high-value intelligence material derived from "Enigma" that was intercepted and successfully decoded at Bletchley Park in England was known to the Allies as "Ultra" and played a very significant part in the eventual defeat of the Third Reich.

# 5. Propaganda Troops

Although propaganda troops were officially removed from the army signals organization in early 1943 to become a separate arm, they fulfilled an important role conducting "information warfare" operations throughout the war, first as signals troops and later as specialist propaganda troops. A propaganda company usually consisted of a headquarters, three war reporter platoons, a propaganda platoon and a support detachment, with about 48 officers or officer-status officials and 262 NCOs and other ranks; the company was provided with 56 motor vehicles and 26 motorcycles. Most of the officers and soldiers functioned as news reporters, photographers, radio commentators and film

**Left and below left:** Message-carrying pigeons and dogs were widely used by the army signals troops during the war.

**Below right:** *Signal* magazine fulfilled propaganda and information functions, as did the less well-known *Die Wehrmacht* magazine, with *Signal* setting virtually unprecedented high standards for color photography and war reportage.

cameramen, many bringing existing civilian media skills to their military service, having been selected and assigned accordingly. Although the company's primary function was war reporting, it was also required to direct propaganda against the enemy, as well as political and morale-building propaganda toward German troops. An important example of this last function was the production of *Signal*, the Wehrmacht's own in-house magazine, which utilized much of the front-line color photography produced by the propaganda companies. *Signal* magazine was originally devised and then developed by Doctor Paul Leverkühn, who served as a military intelligence officer in World War I. The first issue of *Signal* appeared in April 1940. Representing the government's official view of the war through high-quality color photographs and a superlative standard of journalistic writing, *Signal* enjoyed virtually unlimited resources and financial support, and at the height of its success the print run for each edition was almost two and a half million copies, being published in twenty languages and distributed not only within the Wehrmacht but also throughout every German-occupied country of Europe. Although indisputably a propaganda tool, throughout its relatively short life *Signal* nevertheless set technical standards for publishing that were unprecedented in the 1940s, especially in the area of color photography and printing. Other more specifically directed propaganda publications issued at various stages of the war

included *Wofür Kämpfen Wir* ("For Which We Fight"), an illustrated 144-page pamphlet issued by the Heerespersonalamt, and a booklet titled *Frankreich – der ewige Reichsfeind* ("France – the Eternal Enemy of the Reich") issued by the OKW in 1940–1, together with an equivalent OKW publication dealing with and justifying Germany's attack on the Soviet Union. The management and dissemination of such propaganda material within the army also involved the NSFO officers based at division and higher headquarters.

# 6. Field Security and Military Police

The military police operated throughout the rear areas and in the occupied territories but were also employed close to the front line when their duties required this. The military police services were grouped within two main organizations, with the principal group – the military policing arm (Feldgendarmerie) – further subdivided into security and discipline and traffic-control branches. The military police traffic regulators (Verkehrsregelung-polizei) were directly responsible for traffic control, which was a key task as the timely movement of tracked and wheeled vehicles, men, horses and all sorts of towed equipment and loads on the correct routes was always critical to the success of the army's operations in every theater. Military police independent guard battalions (Wachtruppen) were assigned to army groups and armies as necessary, with responsibility for guarding key installations as well as for processing and escorting prisoners-of-war from the battle area and the divisional prisoner-of-war collecting point (Divisionsgefangenensammelstelle) to the army-level collecting point (Armeegefangenensammelstelle) in the rear area. Feldgendarmerie soldiers were readily identified by a special police arm badge, a "Feldgendarmerie" cuff title, and a metal gorget worn at the neck when on duty. This gorget featured an eagle and swastika symbol, and the word "Feldgendarmerie" on a scroll, with all of these details and the two studs or bosses securing the neck chain highlighted with luminous paint to facilitate their ready identification at night and while engaged on traffic duties.

A Feldgendarmerie battalion of three (sometimes four) companies, each of three platoons, was usually assigned to each army-level organization, with sub-units distributed throughout the army as required, but with Feldgendarmerie units invariably found at divisional-level and higher. Typically, a Feldgendarmerie company comprised four officers, 90 NCOs, and 22 other ranks.[6] These men were all trained as infantrymen in addition to undergoing special police training and were responsible for a wide range of routine security, disciplinary, investigative and movement control duties, including the control of ports and airfields. The company had 22 cargo trucks, seven smaller vehicles and 28 motorcycles. During offensive operations the Feldgendarmerie would follow behind the leading units, dealing with stragglers and

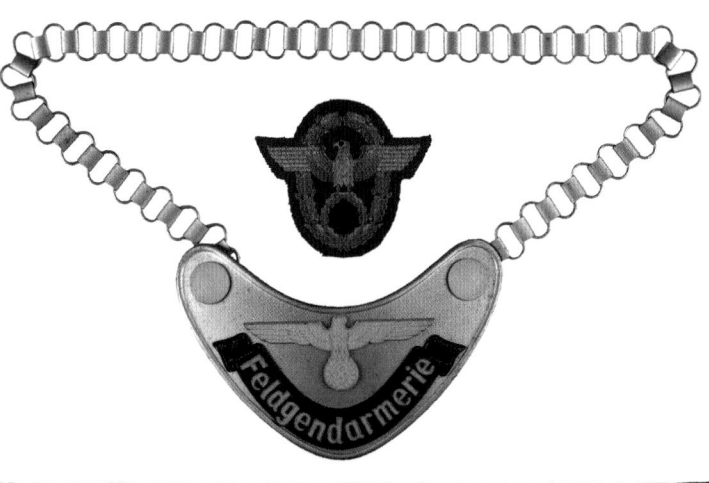

refugees, gathering up prisoners-of-war prior to their evacuation rearwards, accounting for the weapons discarded by both sides, guarding property, preventing looting and establishing immediate military control over occupied towns and villages. Their administrative and law-enforcing duties in occupied territories also involved the control and regulation of civil matters as diverse as hunting, fishing, cattle disease, business administration, forestry and agriculture, Feldgendarmerie personnel working closely with operational and district commanders, and with army officers appointed as local "town majors."[7] Within Germany itself – including the area of the "Greater Reich" from 1938 – the Feldgendarmerie (often in close cooperation with the secret field police, the Geheime Feldpolizei) was responsible for detaining deserters and for matters affecting troop discipline, as well as dealing with its usual tasks of military traffic control and the marshalling and evacuation of prisoners-of-war and refugees.

The men of the Geheime Feldpolizei (or GFP) were usually assigned to work closely with the intelligence staff – their mission was to prevent sabotage and espionage as well as investigate corruption or the undermining of morale within the army unit or formation to which they were assigned. When in uniform, members of the GFP were readily identifiable by the letters "GFP" in gold or silver on their shoulder straps. Sometimes operating in civilian clothes, they were usually assigned as groups organized for specific tasks, a company-strength GFP group supporting an army or army group, while a GFP battalion might support an army of occupation. In addition to its primary tasks, the GFP also gathered the evidence for courts-martial and assisted troops engaged in hunting down deserters. Its members worked closely with the Feldgendarmerie to implement measures ordered by the formation or army headquarters to restore, maintain or instil military discipline. When operating in civilian clothes, GFP personnel carried a special light-green photo identity card and military badge with which they would identify themselves when required, although in this case the investigative powers and authority of the GFP personnel were more limited than when they were in uniform.

## 7. Chemical Warfare Troops

Together with the jackboot and the distinctive "coalscuttle" helmet, the cylindrical metal gas-mask canister carried by all ranks was immediately identifiable with the German soldier of World War II, while the protective gas sheets (Gasplane) attached to these canisters were also much in evidence during the campaigns of 1939 and 1940. Certainly the army fully expected that chemical agents – primarily poison gases – would be used both against it and by it, based upon its experience during World War I. Many military illustrations and photographs during the pre-war years show German soldiers wearing gas masks while carrying out their normal duties in the field. To that end, the army had developed

**Left:** A special arm badge and cuff title identified military police personnel, while a metal gorget was also worn by these troops when engaged on policing duties.

**Below left:** A Feldgendarmerie traffic control point somewhere on the Eastern Front. Note the duty gorget worn by the right-hand soldier; also the lollipop-style disk (red center, white outer) used to direct the traffic. The motorcycle appears to be a NSU 251 OSL and the padlocked panniers might indicate a dispatch rider or courier, while the tactical sign on the left-hand pannier is that of an infantry unit.

**Above and below:** The GM 38 gas mask (left) had a synthetic rubber face-piece and entered service in 1938. It replaced the GM 30 (right), with its four-layer grey fabric face-piece. Chemical warfare defense featured prominently in the army's training both before and during much of the war, and the photograph below is dated 2 January 1941.

comprehensive offensive and defensive chemical warfare capabilities, although use of the former was banned by Hitler personally and it was not employed during the war. Nevertheless, numerous guns, mortars, howitzers and multi-barrel rocket launchers were capable of delivering chemical munitions, and a number of medium, heavy and mountain rocket-launcher battalions had been specifically earmarked as chemical warfare units. Hitler's policy banning such operations (although a form of toxic smoke was used during the siege of Sevastopol in 1942) meant that in practice they were only used as conventional rocket-launcher units. In 1939 the Germans possessed some 2,900 tons of chemical warfare gas agents, and German scientists had also developed the nerve gas Tabun to production stage in 1942, followed by Sarin soon afterwards. As late as March 1945, US

Army intelligence assessments continued to state: "Offensively or defensively the German Army is in a position to wage chemical warfare at any time."[8] This threat did not materialize, but the army was undoubtedly well prepared to defend against it and, if so ordered, to initiate chemical strikes or to respond in kind to such strikes carried out by the Allies.

The possible need for chemical (or "gas") defense was taken very seriously throughout the army, with a comprehensive organization of gas detection and decontamination units and trained personnel at all levels of command. Every headquarters down to battalion level had a suitably trained gas officer, with a gas NCO in each company, and these men were responsible for conducting gas training and for inspecting the unit's chemical defense protective equipment. In every unit there were also non-specialist teams trained to carry out gas defense duties as detection (Gasspürtrupps) and decontamination (Entgiftungstrupps) teams. A detection team consisted of one NCO and three men, while a decontamination team comprised an NCO and six men, these teams being equipped with protective clothing, detectors, warning devices and decontamination equipment. Various types of gas mask and protective sheets and clothing were issued to all personnel (including gas masks designed for troops with special tasks and for those who had sustained head wounds), as well as for horses and dogs. The belief that a chemical warfare threat existed was also illustrated by the general issue of a whistling cartridge (Pfeifpatrone) for use with the army's standard signal pistol, this cartridge being specifically intended to warn of a gas attack.

Apart from the suitably trained non-specialist personnel within the army's units and formations, various medical and veterinary units were specifically organized and trained to carry out large-scale, chemical decontamination of men and equipment. These units included motorized decontamination companies able to decontaminate and re-clothe 150 men per hour, and decontamination platoons that were also able to treat gas casualties. Horse decontamination units drawn from within the main divisional veterinary organization were capable of decontaminating up to twenty horses per hour. The special chemical detection and mass-decontamination equipment used by these units and personnel was carried on various light trucks, as well as by half-track vehicles such as the Sd.Kfz.10 and Sd.Kfz.11 series prime-movers.

## 8. Medical Services

The operational benefits of having soldiers returned to active duty as soon as possible, and who were physically fit and medically, dentally and optically healthy in the first place, were obvious. However, fitness was also very much in tune with the Aryan image of the German fighting man so actively promoted by the Nazis prior to and during the early war years, which was intended to motivate both the nation and its armed forces to achieve and maintain high standards in the areas of health, hygiene and

physical resilience. Once in the army, the soldier's physical health was managed and maintained by the medical services, which were responsible for preventive and remedial measures and health promotion, as well as for the treatment and evacuation of casualties. Chemical contamination and infestations of personnel, equipment or buildings were also dealt with by the medical services.

In all, some 1,782,798 members of the German ground forces died between September 1939 and 31 January 1945 (including 160,237 through non-combat causes, but excluding a further 1,646,316 missing, presumed dead). Many of these fatal casualties received immediate emergency medical aid on the battlefield, albeit unsuccessfully. However, no fewer than 4,145,863 ground forces personnel were wounded and survived, virtually all of whom would have been assessed, processed and treated by the military medical services.[9] Undoubtedly the highest casualties were those sustained on the Eastern Front, whether from enemy action or from the conditions in which the war in the Soviet Union was conducted – during the first six months of *Barbarossa* the army suffered almost 750,000 casualties, which increased to more than a million (including more than 250,000 killed or missing) by the end of March 1942.[10] This amounted to no less than a third of the entire army in the east. Such huge losses imposed a severe and continuing strain upon the army medical services at all levels throughout the war from mid-1941 onwards. Nevertheless, their sound organization and an efficient system of medical evacuation from the front line, all the way back to hospitals in Germany if necessary, generally provided a high level of care and treatment.

The framework of the medical services organization was based

upon army medical battalions (Armeesanitätsabteilungen), each army being assigned one battalion responsible for controlling up to four field hospitals. Depending upon the tactical situation, the battalion's subordinate companies were usually allocated to the army's divisions, with each medical company able to control one field hospital (Feldlazarett) as well as forming several platoon-strength casualty clearing stations and a motorized ambulance unit. Within an infantry division, the medical staff typically numbered about 21 officers and up to 448 NCOs and soldiers. Until 1943 every division was automatically allocated a field hospital, but from that year field hospitals were retained under army-level control and were allocated to divisions according to operational needs.

The casualty evacuation system was flexible, seeking to treat and return soldiers to their units as quickly as possible. This meant that the formal evacuation system was routinely circumvented when appropriate, and at all levels of command medical officers would decide whether to return a soldier to action or to order his evacuation for additional treatment or convalescence. A soldier wounded in combat went first to his battalion's aid post, where emergency first aid was provided, unit stretcher bearers carrying him there if necessary. Next, he walked or was transported to the regimental aid post (Truppenverbandplatz), which was usually sited about 500 meters behind the front line, and further treatment was available here. The regimental medical officer also divided stretcher cases from walking wounded before evacuating the serious cases by ambulance to the regiment's main dressing station (Hauptverbandplatz). There, straightforward surgery (including amputations), injections, transfusions, splinting and halting major

**Above left:** Medical staff deal with casualties after a road convoy is hit by an Allied air attack near Arnhem, Netherlands, September 1944.

**Above:** A medical unit on the move in Russia. The original German caption indicates that the leading vehicle is a mobile operating theater.

bleeding were carried out. In the meantime, the less serious cases and walking wounded were processed at a separate medical facility (often co-located with the main dressing station) for the "slightly wounded" – the Leichtverwundetensammelplatz – from which numbers of soldiers would return to combat within a few days unless their condition deteriorated and further evacuation was ordered. Thereafter, casualties moved via a chain of casualty collecting points (Krankensammelstellen) and casualty clearing stations to various hospitals in the rear area or in Germany. These might be a 200-bed divisional or army field hospital, a 500-bed general base hospital (Kriegslazarette), a base hospital for minor cases (Leichtkrankenkriegslazarette), which could accommodate up to 1,000 in-patient casualties for up to four weeks, or a general hospital with the full range of treatment facilities for long-term patient care. Although necessarily mobile and able to set up and function virtually anywhere, field and base hospitals were established in buildings whenever possible in order to access existing water, electric power and sewerage facilities, while existing civilian hospital facilities were usually appropriated if available. In addition to the military medical personnel, male and female members of the German Red Cross (Deutsches Rotes Kreuz, or DRK) also worked in these various field, base and general hospitals, experiencing the day-to-day bombardments, ground fire and the privations of war alongside the soldiers they cared for while inevitably sustaining casualties themselves.

The range of transport used by the army for casualty evacuation was extensive and often diverse. In addition to motorized ambulances (which could accommodate either four stretcher cases, or two stretcher and four seated cases or eight seated cases) evacuation was also carried out by horse-drawn wagons, sledges (on the Eastern Front) and any available military or civilian vehicles, while casualties were also occasionally evacuated by air, as they were from Stalingrad during the winter of 1942/3, when the 6th Army's main field hospital was based at Pitomnik airfield. Wherever it was practicable to do so, casualty evacuation to a general hospital in Germany was usually by hospital train (Lazarettzüge), each of which typically transported up to 386 stretcher cases or 920 seated casualties. The facilities categorized as "general hospitals" in Germany included a number of permanent military and civilian medical centers and major civilian hospitals.

Oberleutnant Siegfried Knappe was wounded on the Eastern Front in December 1941, and his experience of medical evacuation and the treatment system was not untypical. On 5 December 1941 the division that his artillery regiment supported was at Peredelkino, just outside Moscow and no more than twenty kilometers from the Kremlin, where it was barely managing to operate effectively because of the bitter cold. Suddenly a Russian tank attack burst upon the troops in their forward positions, during which an exploding shell killed and wounded several officers inside a peasant hut, where they had been seeking a short respite from the severe cold. (Although the Germans did not know it at the time,

this attack marked the beginning of the Russian counter-offensive designed to save Moscow and force a German withdrawal.) Knappe, a battery commander, was one of those wounded in the head and arm. After the medical orderlies had applied first aid dressings to his wounds, he entered the medical evacuation system. With others, he was taken back to the battery command post by hand-hauled sleds, where despite his wounds he was able to hand over command of the battery before embarking on a 120-kilometer truck journey to the field hospital at Vyazma. There were nine wounded lying on the floor in the in the back of the truck, and travelling over the frozen ground they endured an unavoidably "cold, jolting, painful ride."[11] Three or four hours later the group arrived at the field hospital, where their wounds were checked and dressed again. By the time he was put aboard an ambulance train bound for Warsaw the next day, Knappe already had lice under his bandages – but could not deal with them without disrupting the dressings! The rail journey took two days, during which the wounded men were at last warm again and relatively well fed. During the rail journey they were segregated into different coaches depending upon whether they were able to sit up or were bed-ridden. A high standard of medical care was provided by the on-board medical staff, and the absolute reliance of the army upon the railway was reinforced yet again. In Warsaw, the army had taken over a civilian hospital, and there Knappe's wounds were again dressed, cleaned – with the eviction of the lice at last – and there was an opportunity to bathe and wash properly, with plenty of hot water and real soap available. Doctors reassessed the wounds at that stage to determine whether further evacuation and more specialized treatment were necessary, and within a few days Knappe was evacuated to hospitals first at Olmütz and then Brno (Brünn) in Czechoslovakia, before reporting as "walking wounded" (but, having sustained a head wound, to be kept under observation) to the main military hospital in Leipzig. There Knappe was treated as an out-patient and convalesced before eventually returning to duty with his artillery battery in the spring of 1942.

# 9. Veterinary Services

Despite the emphasis upon Blitzkrieg warfare and the ascendancy of the Panzer arm, the army still employed thousands of horses and mules, as individual mounts, to draw artillery and supply wagons, and as pack animals. Mules were used extensively and to particularly good effect during the fighting in Italy, and were the principal means of transportation in the army's Gebirgsjäger units. The cavalry arm had been reduced to brigade strength prior to 1939, but throughout the war about 80 percent of the army's motive power was still provided by horses, mainly to pull the artillery guns and supply wagons. These animals were used in every theater in which the army fought. Huge numbers died in the intense cold of the winters on the Eastern Front from 1941, some of those that succumbed to the ravages of the Russian winter subsequently supplementing the rations of the troops that they had previously served as working animals. Indeed, of 625,000 horses (some estimates suggest a grand total of 750,000 horses and mules) that accompanied the army into the Soviet Union on 22 June 1941, at least 180,000 died during the first Russian winter, and by the beginning of summer 1942 only about half of the horses that had set out on Operation *Barbarossa* still lived. In all, more than two and a half million horses and mules were used on the Eastern Front during the war, and possibly as many as 1,000 died each day due to sickness, the harsh climate, enemy action or the strain of pulling carts and artillery through the mud and snow – seventeen percent of all horse fatalities probably resulting from heart failure.[12] At the same time, as the campaign in the east developed, the army's pre-war reduction of the cavalry was shown to have been premature, with various army mounted units now being created as a matter of urgency – first on a local or *ad hoc* basis and then formally from 1943 – to carry out long-range

patrolling and reconnaissance duties in the many areas in which the terrain or bad weather prevented vehicle movement.

In order to maintain the health of these many thousands of animals, to treat those that were wounded or injured, and to oversee and advise on their acquisition, selection for military service, care, and subsequent employment, the army maintained a comprehensive veterinary (Veterinär) service. The Veterinär officers of 1933–45 built upon the considerable experience gained by the imperial German army during the second half of the nineteenth century and during World War I, and so provided a high standard of practical veterinary expertise at all levels of command. Veterinär officers (identifiable by the snake insignia on their shoulder straps) of various ranks – including colonel (Oberstveterinär), lieutenant colonel (Oberfeldveterinär), major (Oberstabs-veterinär), captain (Stabsveterinär), lieutenant (Oberveterinär), and second lieutenant (Veterinär) – were found at all major headquarters, as well as in all formations and units with horses on their establishment. This was essential, as by 1939 an infantry

Horse-drawn artillery units parade in Paris in 1940 following the defeat of France.

The army depended upon large numbers of horses and mules to maintain its mobility throughout the war. Consequently, the veterinary services were always much in demand. Horses were employed in very many ways: to draw artillery guns and limbers, cargo wagons and field kitchens, as well as being used for reconnaissance patrols. Meanwhile, mules were the primary means of transport in the mountain divisions.

division needed between 4,077 and 6,033 horses in order to move its support weapons, ammunition and other combat supplies and equipment. Even as late as the beginning of 1945, the establishment tables for various types of infantry division showed that 4,662 horses were still authorized for a Type 1944 division, 3,002 horses for a Volksgrenadier division, 2,734 for the newly created two-regiment division and between 3,056 and 5,000 horses and mules for a mountain division – although these authorized complements of horses and mules were rarely achieved in practice. Each non-armored infantry division usually included a veterinary company (Veterinärkompanie) of four officers and up to 152 NCOs and soldiers, with the company organized into a horse collecting platoon, a horse hospital (Pferde-Lazarett) and a fodder platoon. (Meanwhile, although not formally established for veterinary support, some motorized infantry and Panzer divisions also used horses when the situation required.) The sheer scale of equine support and the army's absolute reliance upon these animals right through the war were indeed significant.

When a horse fell sick, was injured or wounded, it was first moved to a Veterinär dressing station (Pferdeverbandplatz) for emergency treatment, then to the divisional treatment station if necessary, where up to 150 horses could be treated simultaneously. Movement by road between these veterinary facilities was usually in groups of about 40 animals, each group constituting a horse transport road column. Thereafter, horses were moved back either via collecting points established at each level of command or directly

to an army horse hospital (Armeepferdelazarett), or to the field army horse hospital (Heerespferdelazarett) where more extensive treatment could be carried out, with up to 500 animals able to be dealt with at the same time. Even better-equipped horse hospitals (Heimatpferdelazarette) and other veterinary facilities existed within Germany itself, and animals requiring more extensive treatment were usually moved there by special trains (Pferdetransportzüge) carrying six horses per rail wagon, with up to about 350 horses on each 55 wagon train. Similar levels of skilled veterinary care were also provided in those occupied territories where the terrain or operational situation necessitated the widespread use of horses and pack animals – as was the case in the hills and mountains of Italy.

## 10. Postal Services

Each division had a field post office (Feldpost), staffed by eighteen personnel, whose army uniforms bore a "Feldpost" cuff title, and the letters "FP" on their shoulder straps. Feldpost specialist officers – such as the Feldoberpostdirektor, Feldpostinspektor and Feldpostsecretär – were actually civilian specialists operating in support of the army, and although they had officer status and were uniformed and armed as soldiers, they were usually shown as "armed forces administrative officials" (Wehrmachtbeamte) on military organization tables. Feldpost sorting offices, mail collection points and post offices were established throughout the military

This army supply column of horse-drawn vehicles is en route to surrender to US forces near Orléans, 19 September 1944. Note the field kitchen behind the first wagon, continuing to cook or heat food while on the move.

The arrival of the mail was one of the most important boosts to morale in any unit!

chain of command to provide a comprehensive postal service. The Feldpost was responsible for the collection, carriage and delivery of the army's personal and official mail (including that of Germany's Axis allies where applicable) to and from every military unit and Germany, and within every occupied area and region in which German military forces were based or operating. The Feldpost was usually accorded priority for road movement, its duty vehicles readily identifiable by the "FP" prefix on the registration plates. The Feldpost enjoyed an enviable reputation throughout the war for ensuring that mail reached the troops, and the impact of its work upon morale was well appreciated by senior commanders and ordinary soldiers alike. As late as 22 December 1942, a full delivery of Christmas post was delivered to the beleaguered 6th Army in Stalingrad, with further intermittent deliveries until a final delivery was made on 18 January 1943 – just two weeks before the surrounded army surrendered. Apart from the unavoidable, but usually temporary, delays occasioned by operational activities, the only protracted break in Feldpost deliveries was that which affected the garrison of the occupied Channel Islands during the winter of 1944/5, by which time France had been liberated and the troops on Jersey and Guernsey were already isolated from the remaining German forces in the west.

Behind the front line the essential paperwork continued apace – even within units actively committed in the field. Efficient battalion- and company-level administrative offices ensured that postings, mail, leave travel, promotions, ration indents, personnel replacements and an almost infinite range of other administrative actions were completed in a timely way. These were important, not only for the welfare and management of the soldiers and their morale, but also directly affected the unit's wider operational performance.

# PART X
# Tactics and Special Operations

## 1. General Principles and Doctrine

The army's organization, weapons and equipment favored the offensive over the defensive. Its tactical doctrine, historically and during 1939–45, recognized that military success could only be achieved through conducting such operations, an essential element of which was usually surprise. This belief underlined the development and application of the Blitzkrieg concept of war-fighting and was entirely in accordance with the principle of Auftragstaktik. This mission-orientated system of ordering and conducting operations originated in the nineteenth century, during the days of the great military reformers Gneisenau, Scharnhorst and Clausewitz, and its subsequent refinement conferred an enviable operational flexibility upon the German army. Auftragstaktik emphasized the mission's required end result, its wider operational context and the higher commander's intentions, rather than specifying in detail the means by which the mission was to be achieved. Allied to this, all of the army's commanders were trained to operate at least one level – but usually two – above their own level of command, unlike many of their Anglo-US opponents, whose national doctrine for command and control usually afforded junior commanders little room for flexibility or initiative concerning the way in which they were to carry out their missions. Nevertheless, Auftragstaktik in no way negated the absolute requirement for commanders to be fully conversant with the army's laid-down way of conducting every military activity and operation of war, since this guaranteed that routine inter-unit operations and cooperation required few if any additional orders – and this in turn enabled the concept of Auftragstaktik to work.

However, while the equipment and actions of the army's Panzer units reflected the intentions of this operational doctrine and the concept of Auftragstaktik, the preponderance of non-armored and non-motorized units, and horse-drawn artillery and supply units, meant that this doctrine could only be achieved for limited periods and where the necessary quantity and type of units could be concentrated. In the meantime, the belated total mobilization of German industry to support the war effort meant that the vast quantities of munitions, fuel and other war *matériel* necessary to sustain large-scale offensive operations could only be provided and maintained for limited periods, particularly during the final two years of the war. Even so, the army displayed a remarkable ability to take offensive action in support of its defensive and withdrawal operations as the war drew on, particularly once the fortunes of war began to turn against it from late 1942, and there were countless examples of resolutely held and masterfully sited defensive positions established primarily as a means of forcing the Allies into a situation that could be exploited by a successful counter-stroke. Similarly, if a German position was overrun, it was well understood that an *ad hoc*

reserve should be assembled as quickly as possible and an immediate counterattack mounted to regain the position. In order to apply this doctrine effectively, commanders at all levels would always be sited well forward to observe and influence the developing situation directly – a sound but costly principle that inevitably resulted in a significant number of German senior officers being killed in action.

## 2. The Blitzkrieg Concept

Blitzkrieg was simply a logical extension of the principle of the primacy of the offensive. Even before it was accorded the "Blitzkrieg" name, the concept underwrote much of the Wehrmacht's wider strategic, operational and tactical thinking immediately prior to the war, being further developed and refined once hostilities had commenced. In Blitzkrieg operations the tanks, supported by motorized or armored infantry, self-propelled or mobile artillery, combat engineers and close air support, cut through the enemy defenses. They ignored, bypassed or avoided any areas where resistance was strong, moving on to attack headquarters, communications sites, depots and other vital command and support functions in depth, thereby rendering the enemy's front-line units ineffective. At the heart of this concept was the Panzer or tank division.

Concerning the campaigns against Poland and France in 1939 and 1940, Generaloberst Heinz Guderian, one of the foremost exponents of armored warfare, observed: "The tank crews did not fight alone. From the inception of the new [Panzer] weapon, its creators' thinking about modern tank warfare led to the close involvement of support units that were fully motorized and to some extent armored. The German Army created tank divisions that formed large self-contained units which included all arms of the service. After reconnaissance, in combat the tanks and the supporting riflemen and motorcycle troops, artillery, engineers and signal corps, could exploit their joint successes instantly, thanks to the mechanization common to all these arms. Further backing was given to the tank divisions by motorized infantry. The tank divisions became the natural partners of the air force, with whom they soon formed the closest bonds of comradeship. The enforced [strategic] delay imposed upon the forces by the winter conditions of 1939–40 was utilized to build up the tank formations. In May 1940, they advanced with renewed vigor in the west. Their achievements exceeded all expectations."[1]

At the strategic and operational levels, this form of offensive action comprised seven distinct but complementary and inter-dependent phases, with the liberal use of air power in close support of the ground operations an essential prerequisite for all but the first phase of the Blitzkrieg:

- The preparatory disruption of the enemy's rear areas and command, control and fixed communication facilities by fifth columnists, saboteurs and small groups of infiltrated special

Right: "The attack," a poster highlighting the infantry's decisive role at the point of main effort of every offensive operation.

DER ANGRIFF
Im Schwerpunkt der Schlacht stürmt
unwiderstehlich die Infanterie

The armored assault by Panzer units and their supporting arms, to achieve deep penetrations, seize key objectives, and to shock, overrun and destroy enemy forces, but bypassing major urban areas and well-defended strongpoints. These operations continued and reinforced the envelopment of the enemy forces, thus enabling their subsequent annihilation by Panzer units and follow-on ground forces.

The follow-up assault by non-motorized infantry divisions and their supporting arms, to destroy the enemy in detail, establish secure rear areas including the suppression of any irregular resistance forces, impose military administration upon occupied areas, and deal in detail with any locations bypassed earlier by the mobile forces. Finally, these less mobile forces linked up with the Panzer formations to complete the operation or campaign.

The seven phases of the Blitzkrieg concept provided the Wehrmacht with a broad operational framework for strategic planning, and into which most military operations and activities could be fitted.

## 3. Offensive Operations

The aim of offensive action was to encircle and destroy the enemy, using sufficient firepower, numbers and surprise. In order to achieve this, the point of main effort (Schwerpunkt) was first identified, at which the attacking troops, support weapons and reserves would be concentrated to produce a local superiority while other forces conducted diversionary and holding operations elsewhere. Factors affecting selection of the Schwerpunkt included the enemy's deployment and perceived weaknesses, terrain, the need to maximize the weight of artillery fire and the extent of combined-arms involvement. The Schwerpunkt might well need to be changed as the battle developed, and alternative plans were made in anticipation of this. The types of attack included flank (Flankenangriff), envelopment (Umfassungsangriff), encirclement (Einkreisung), wing (Flügelangriff) and frontal (Frontalangriff); the follow-up to a successful attack included penetration (Einbruch) and breakthrough (Durchbruch), which in turn enabled further flanking attacks while reserve and armored forces exploited the initial penetration. The frontages allocated to dismounted infantry for their attack sectors depended upon various factors, including the terrain and presence of any obstacles, but these were typically up to 150 meters for a platoon, 350 meters for a company, 700 meters for a battalion and 3,500 meters for a division.

Many accounts of the German army's campaigns in 1939, 1940 and 1941 focus upon the operations conducted by the armored forces. However, while the rapid and wide-ranging advances by the Panzers understandably caught the imagination of military observers and of the civilian population at the time,

troops. This neutralized his overall military capability and prejudiced his mobilization plans, as well as creating fear and uncertainty and lowering his morale. Such operations were regarded as long-term, being conducted over as much as ten to twelve months prior to overt offensive action where practicable.

The destruction of the enemy's air power on the ground by a surprise bombing attack in overwhelming strength. The enemy air force always posed the single greatest threat to the ground forces of an attacker moving in the open.

The interdiction of enemy troop movement and command facilities by bombers and ground attack aircraft. This prevented the movement of reserves and logistic re-supply to counter the attack and sustain the defense.

The neutralization (by preventing their redeployment or movement out of protected cover) or destruction of enemy units and formations by air attack, usually by dive-bombers such as the Ju 87 Stuka.

Infiltration and exploitation of gaps in the defense lines by light armored and motorized all-arms forces to carry out reconnaissance in depth, identify undefended routes and exploit opportunities as they presented themselves. These operations signalled the start of the envelopment of the enemy forces.

numerous hard-fought battles were also conducted by the non-motorized infantry divisions advancing behind the armored forces, or who were required to deal with enemy defensive positions judged too strong for the Panzers to overcome and which had therefore been by-passed by these armored forces. Such separations between the armored and non-motorized forces frequently occurred during the early stages of the advance into Russia in 1941, when non-armored infantry divisions routinely carried out lengthy advances on foot and then became involved in what were predominantly infantry battles once they made contact with the enemy. Typical of such an advance was that conducted in late July 1941 by the 87th Infantry Division, 9th Army, in Army Group Center, the ultimate objective of which was at that stage the capture of Moscow. Oberleutnant Siegfried Knappe's artillery regiment was in support of the division and although some of the artillery was motorized, the vast majority was horse-drawn. Consequently, where little or no resistance was offered, the army group's tanks and motorized infantry moved far ahead of the non-motorized units and formations – which therefore regularly had to conduct dismounted infantry attacks. Knappe describes how on one such occasion contact was made when "our forward scouts – usually motorcycle troops, although we had some cavalry – went ahead of us, reconnoitring. When they drew fire, the point battalion would immediately spread out. The troops behind the point battalion would also spread out from the road on which we were marching. Once we knew how strong the resistance was, we would prepare an attack."[2] The initial assessment of enemy strength took account of the type and weight of incoming fire: rifle and machine gun fire were to be expected; where it was supplemented by mortar, artillery or (especially) tank fire, this provided an indication of the nature and level of command of the opposing force. Apparently, "the forward scouts were rarely killed, and far more often than not they were not even hit. The Russian soldiers firing at them were usually not there to fight, but only to stop us momentarily and then very quickly get back to report to their superiors what they had seen."[3]

Having encountered a well-established line of defense, the infantry division initiated a set series of well-tried actions and procedures. First, the troops would prepare their own hastily-dug defensive positions, and from these conduct further reconnaissance to identify, assess and confirm the extent and type of enemy force. Once this had been done, with similar intelligence from flanking divisions and corps factored into the assessment, a set-piece or deliberate attack would be prepared, which would usually be launched at dawn the day after the first contact. During the night the point or assaulting battalion would be reinforced and replenished as necessary and move into its assault positions. The Russian defensive positions usually consisted of successive lines of trenches. As the attacking infantry overran each line, the defenders therein usually surrendered quite promptly, being rounded up by the follow-up troops and sent to

the rear. Meanwhile the assault troops would move on to overcome the other lines of trenches as speedily as possible, so that the momentum and shock effect of the attack were maintained.

On one occasion during such an infantry attack at Orsha, between Minsk and Smolensk, Knappe relates how the first line of trenches had been overcome and the assault moved on, when, "we were suddenly aware that we were taking rifle fire from behind as well as from in front of us. The Russian soldiers in the first line of trenches, who should have surrendered, had turned and were shooting us in the back, and some of our people were killed and wounded by this fire."[4] The German soldiers regarded this as a breach of an unwritten code of combat, and as a result, "Our soldiers went berserk, and from that point on during the attack they took no prisoners and left no one alive in a trench or foxhole."[5] Arguably, had the Russians been disarmed immediately, they could not have resumed shooting. In any event the incident unsettled Knappe, who admitted in a private conversation with his superior officer that, while he "did not like" the retribution meted out by the assault troops, he had

A Panzer division in full flood – tanks of Generalmajor Erwin Rommel's 7th Panzer Division advance into France in 1940.

A battle-winning team – infantrymen with a Pz.Kpfw.IV tank move through woodland.

An Unteroffizier of the Panzertruppe – the men whose tanks spearheaded the Blitzkriegs of 1939, 1940 and 1941. This particular soldier, pictured in October 1942, had considerable combat experience, as he wears the Spanish campaign medal and Cross of Military Merit as well as the German Iron Cross First Class, the tank assault badge and the wound badge in silver.

"understood" what he had witnessed and why it had occurred. As the campaign on the Eastern Front ground on, many of the niceties, assumptions and codes of conduct of the army of 1939–41 would be ignored and become increasingly irrelevant.

Good light was generally considered essential for an attacking force, and if night fell before the attack was completed the assaulting troops would usually dig in or occupy the trenches already captured and then send out patrols to find weaknesses in the enemy line and gain intelligence before resuming the attack the next day. However, where the night was well illuminated by moonlight, or if the soldiers were already very familiar with the ground, they might continue attacking through the night, while in these circumstances as an alternative the whole attack might be launched during the night instead of at dawn.

The leading tank regiment in an attack with motorized or armored infantry in support might attack on a frontage of 700–1,000 meters, with a depth extending some 2,000 meters. If assault guns were also used to protect the flanks of an armored attack, possibly with anti-tank guns also advancing in bounds on the flanks, this might increase the overall frontage of a regimental attack to about 2,000 meters. Although always a viable tactical option, pre-planned non-armored infantry attacks – including such attacks supported only by assault guns and indirect artillery fire – became less frequent after 1941 (other than where the enemy might be defending an urban or wooded area, or other difficult terrain in which armor could not operate).

Combined-arms attacks were therefore the norm. The army's tactical doctrine called for these to be launched in three waves, tanks spearheading the assault unless the objective had well-prepared anti-tank obstacles and anti-tank guns deployed forward – in which case an infantry assault had first of all to overcome these anti-tank defenses in detail and open the way for the Panzer force. Where such defenses did not exist, however, the first wave of attacking tanks would overrun the forward positions, destroying or neutralizing any easily identifiable positions with their guns, machine guns and tank tracks. The tanks then drove on to penetrate as far as the anti-tank positions sited in depth and the artillery gun lines, bypassing any strongly held defensive positions where necessary. At that stage the first wave would adopt suitable positions from which to provide covering fire to support the next wave's advance and attack. The leading elements of the second wave of a regimental attack usually moved about 100 meters behind the rear elements of the first one, in order to maintain the attack's momentum and exploit its success as quickly as possible. This wave, including the Panzergrenadiers in their half-track armored carriers, closed up to the first wave, dismounting as close as possible to the anti-tank positions, machine gun posts, infantry trenches and bunkers in order to to deal with them. Finally, the third wave consisting of the remaining Panzergrenadiers moved up to complete the destruction of the enemy. In the meantime, the first and second waves might well have resumed the advance and attack. The commander of the tank

unit was usually in overall command of the attack as his unit possessed greater combat power and radio communications than the infantry, while he was also best able to assess the developing situation, normally being well forward in the first wave. However, his attack plan would also take full account of the capabilities of the Panzergrenadiers, artillery, anti-tank, assault gun and engineer units within his command, and the advice of their respective commanders. The artillery commander usually moved with the attacking force commander, the artillery observers moving with the first wave either in their own armored vehicles or (if necessary) as passengers in assaulting tanks. In addition to these pre-planned attacks, the army's tactical doctrine also dealt with variations such as the meeting engagement (Begegnungsgefecht), the counterattack and other unanticipated or responsive offensive actions. In all such offensive operations, individual initiative by all ranks, a sound training standard to obviate the need for detailed orders, speed and aggression were identified as critical factors.

The infantry were to the fore in virtually every attack and were usually responsible for securing the victory while cooperating with the other combat arms, which inevitably meant that they routinely bore the brunt of the close-quarter fighting. One such typical attack was carried out at Ishun in the Crimea on 26 October 1941: "At 0800 the massed guns of the artillery opened fire. As the hail of shells struck the Soviet positions it obliterated some of the enemy observation posts. Patches of dried-out steppe grass burned freely and reddish clouds of dust and smoke enveloped the area, depriving the Russians of visibility in some places. Meanwhile, the first German assault wave moved forward. When NCOs with 27mm flare pistols fired a signal flare to indicate they were entering the Russian defensive positions, the artillery fire was shifted. The assault detachments opened gaps in the center and the difficult task of ferreting out the enemy force dug-in began. The assault forces fanned out from the initial points of penetration and moved forward firing well-aimed bullets at anything that moved. Whenever Russians from a nearby foxhole or bunker returned the fire, they were silenced by a well-placed hand grenade. The main fortified positions were neutralized by teams carrying portable flame-throwers. Whenever a particularly fanatic[al] Russian force could not be flushed out by the assault troops, they fired a signal flare to pinpoint the target for the German artillery pieces and mortars. Dive-bombers, flying in waves, made low-level attacks against tanks, dug-in tanks, and anti-tank guns, while the infantry continued to storm Russian machine gun nests and strongpoints. This bloody fighting continued for days."[6]

In close country – wooded and urban areas – and where obstacles obstructed the advance, infantry units would carry the attack forward.

# 4. Defensive Operations

Despite the deeply-enshrined primacy of the offense over the defense, from 1942 the army was increasingly obliged to conduct defensive operations. Although this was in many cases merely the precursor to an offensive operation, the switch from offense to defense was often ordered as a matter of military necessity to allow reinforcement, refurbishment, replenishment and planning to be completed. Nevertheless, the gradual slowing of the campaign on the Eastern Front from December 1941, the success of the Allied counter-offensive in North Africa from late 1942, and the build-up of US forces in England from 1942 all prompted the army to develop, adapt and apply its defensive doctrine and tactics ever more frequently; apart from the short-lived *Wacht am Rhein* Ardennes offensive in December 1944, the heady Blitzkrieg days of 1939, 1940 and mid-1941 had all but ended by the end of 1941. Meanwhile, in the west the development of the Atlantic Wall and Siegfried Line defenses demonstrated the German skill and ingenuity in the development and construction of major fortifications and obstacles, although here also deficiencies and weak points emerged as the Third Reich's manpower, industrial resources, and raw materials became evermore scarce or inaccessible due to Allied action. At the same time, the army's armored mobility and ability to generate reserves also diminished, with operations such as *Zitadelle* at Kursk in July 1943 and in the Ardennes in 1944 only made possible by concentrating the required quantities of tanks, troops and troop carriers and other resources at the expense of other theaters and operational areas. Although the strategic balance had swung toward the defense (Verteidigung), the army applied itself to these operations just as energetically as it had to the offense, while always emphasizing that defense was merely a temporary situation, being designed to defeat an attack and enable a counterattack, or to gain time and shape the battlefield for future offensive action. Probably the army's most successful defensive campaign of the war was that conducted in Italy from late 1943, where the rugged terrain particularly favored the defense.

Defensive positions usually consisted of an advanced position (Vorgeschobene Stellung), outpost positions (Gefechtsvorposten) and a main line of resistance (Hauptkampflinie). Reconnaissance forces were mainly deployed within and just forward of the advanced position, and a reserve or secondary position might also be developed and occupied by a mobile reserve or used as a rallying point from which a counterattack could be launched. Frontages depended upon many factors, including the terrain and the perceived enemy threat, but in principle a unit's frontage

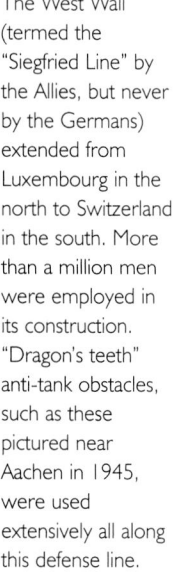

The West Wall (termed the "Siegfried Line" by the Allies, but never by the Germans) extended from Luxembourg in the north to Switzerland in the south. More than a million men were employed in its construction. "Dragon's teeth" anti-tank obstacles, such as these pictured near Aachen in 1945, were used extensively all along this defense line.

in defense was usually about twice that when attacking – a platoon might occupy a frontage of 350 meters, a company 700 meters, a battalion 1,500 meters, a regiment 2,000 meters, and a division might be responsible for a frontage of between 4,000 and 7,000 meters.

The advanced position was designed to provide information on the enemy, inflict casualties, and deceive the enemy into deploying early and in the wrong direction. It was sited up to 4,500 meters forward of the main position and so could be supported by the medium artillery. The predominantly armored-car, reconnaissance, artillery observation, machine gun, and anti-tank units in the advanced position were not required to hold ground and would withdraw before a determined enemy attack was launched against them.

Outpost positions were sited about 1,200 to 3,200 meters forward of the main line of resistance and were usually manned by infantry in up to company-strength, supported by light guns, mortars, machine guns and anti-tank guns, also being sited with interlocking fields of fire and integrated with natural and man-made obstacles. Their task was to provide information, to deny the enemy information by destroying his reconnaissance forces, and to disrupt the build-up for an attack. The outpost plan included alternate and dummy positions, which would be variously occupied, vacated and re-occupied by the defenders by day and night and as the tactical situation changed. Withdrawal of the outposts would be ordered with an enemy attack judged to be imminent, when these troops retired into the main defensive position along carefully pre-planned routes, often via the flanks in order not to baulk fire from the main position. However, some outposts might remain in place to observe and harass the attackers in depth. All the outposts would be pre-registered by the artillery in anticipation of the enemy occupying them.

The main line of resistance was the point at which the defenders planned to break the enemy attack or to force its deflection or abandonment. The commander's assessment of the threat again applied the Schwerpunkt principle, in that his concentration of defensive force would be deployed at the point at which it was believed the enemy's main effort would be directed. Defensive positions were sited on reverse slopes as a matter of policy, in order to avoid them coming under the observed long-range fire that forward-slope positions invariably attracted once they had been unmasked or were otherwise identified by reconnaissance beforehand. Wooded areas were usually avoided unless plenty of time was available to develop them into defended areas, in which case woods often proved to be at least as effective as reverse slope positions, as well as becoming significant obstacles in their own right – such as that created in the Hürtgenwald forest near Aachen, where the army inflicted 24,000 battle casualties upon the advancing US 1st Army between October and early December 1944. The main line of resistance confronted an attacker with a complex blend of infantry positions, machine gun emplacements, support and anti-

tank weapons, bunkers, minefields, barbed wire and natural obstacles such as rivers, swampland and ravines. These positions and obstacles were supported by a comprehensive artillery and mortar-fire plan able to engage all parts of the defended area as well as the ground well to its front, including any gaps or dead ground between the fixed positions. Alternative positions would also be constructed, so that key weapons could be redeployed during the battle if necessary, as the tactical situation changed.

The priorities for construction were usually the combat trenches and emplacements, counter-infantry obstacles (such as wire and mines), machine gun and anti-tank gun positions, and clearing fields of fire. Wherever possible, positions were dug along the line of hedgerows, field edges, tree lines, rivers, or by buildings, in order to aid their concealment. Trench systems were zig-zagged and continuous, often running for between 200 and 400 meters, depending upon the terrain. Individual machine gun trenches were about two meters in length. To aid concealment and protection, the earth spoil was distributed as a gradually rising slope to the front of the trench, with a greater amount piled behind to reduce silhouetting and to trap, and so neutralize, any fire that might otherwise have continued onwards to strike other positions farther to the rear. Natural foliage was retained wherever possible, with overhead protection (when available) formed from three layers of logs and packed earth, or the equivalent of this using whatever materials might be to hand.

Other construction tasks, in priority order (although many would be carried out concurrently) were artillery observation posts, infantry heavy-weapons positions, command posts, artillery gun positions and finally anti-tank ditches, dummy positions and alternative positions. The latter would be constructed far enough to the rear to ensure that they could not be engaged by enemy artillery supporting the main attack unless it redeployed forward to do so – thereby remaining protected from indirect fire, or forcing the enemy to disrupt or suspend his

Huge quantities of mines and barbed wire, always covered by fire, were used in the construction of the Atlantic Wall in 1943.

artillery support for the main attack. Based on experience, anti-tank ditches and obstacles were usually dug and constructed within the main position rather than forward of it, as it was found that they might otherwise provide cover for attacking infantry, whereas placing them just forward of the artillery gun positions protected the gun lines and could halt the attack under the concentrated fire of the dug-in defenders, thereby creating an opportunity for a counterattack. All obstacles were covered by fire, and any safe lanes through them would be capable of being blocked or destroyed at short notice if necessary, by blowing pre-placed demolition charges.

The anti-tank defense plan was accorded a high priority, with these guns usually dug into positions from which they could produce enfilade (flanking) fire at ranges up to 1,000 meters. Single guns would aim to take out command vehicles and other key targets at that range, while the massed anti-tank guns would probably hold their fire until the enemy armor was less than 200 meters away. The anti-tank defense plan would also include pre-positioned and roving tank-hunting teams armed with mines, grenades, flame throwers and light anti-armor weapons such as

the Panzerfaust and Panzerschreck, coordinated with the anti-tank guns. Where available, the Luftwaffe's 88mm anti-aircraft guns could also be used in the anti-tank role, firing at ranges out to 2,000 meters, although their size and high profile meant they were often less easily dug in and concealed. Once a tank attack developed, smoke shells were fired into the area between the first and second assaulting echelons to prevent them supporting each other during the assault, as well as silhouetting the first line of tanks against the smoke so that the anti-tank gunners could engage them. Once an attack had been repulsed, the anti-tank guns and other weapons might redeploy to alternative positions if it was thought that their original positions had been compromised during the first attack. Once the enemy attack had begun, the pattern of the developing defensive battle could not be pre-determined, although in principle the artillery would seek to break the attack before it breached the main defensive line, and artillery observers were positioned to direct fire from first contact until the point at which a successful enemy penetration might be approaching the gun lines. In any event, locally constituted reserves were identified and maintained at all levels of command,

Well-protected and well-sited artillery positions were emplaced throughout the Atlantic Wall. This battery of 150mm guns was at Longues-sur-Mer, in Normandy.

ready to carry out immediate counterattacks, while at a higher level the principal commander would hold a suitably strong combined-arms reserve force under a single commander, in readiness to launch a pre-planned counterattack if required.

Although many defensive operations took place in the open countryside and semi-rural areas, with a consequent need to construct the positions in their entirety, wherever built-up areas were available they were frequently utilized. Whether single houses, farm complexes, hamlets, villages, towns or cities, most urban areas offered protection and concealment, with the cellars found beneath many European buildings much used for command posts, aid posts and suchlike. Urban areas also usually denied an attacker full use of his tanks and other vehicles. In urban areas the main line of resistance was sited within a town rather than at its edge, in order to conceal it and to draw the attackers into the streets, although anti-tank guns and artillery observers might also engage approaching vehicles from the edge before withdrawing to alternative positions. However, an infantry attack usually posed the greatest threat and the whole urban area was developed as an integrated network of strongpoints,

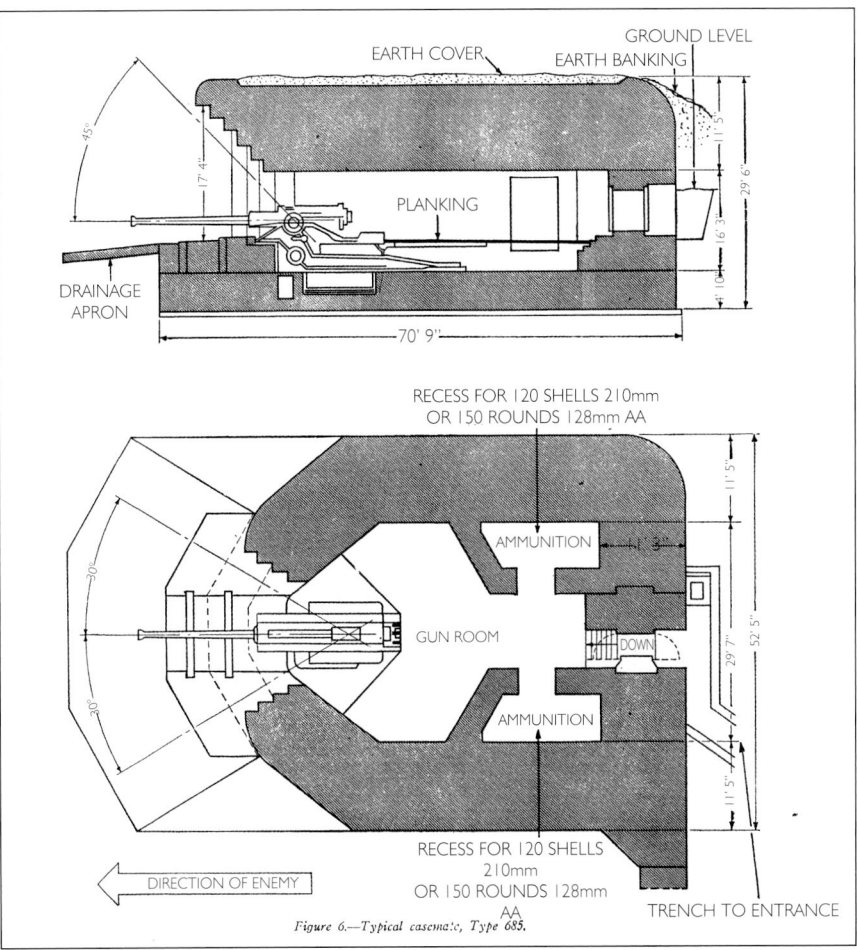

Figure 6.—Typical casemate, Type 685.

outposts, road blocks and tank traps, with all of the buildings either occupied and fortified or booby-trapped and left unoccupied. Communication routes were opened between all defended buildings through the cellars and attics and over the roofs; rooms were darkened and windows left open, with fire positions constructed well within them; machine guns were usually sited to fire from basement windows and ground-level ventilation shafts; individual bricks and roof tiles were removed to provide loopholes; anti-tank and anti-personnel mines were laid; and some armored vehicles, such as assault guns, were often concealed within buildings. Reserve forces were held both within and outside the urban area, the former ready to launch immediate counterattacks and the latter with the task of preventing the urban positions being outflanked. Where a village or similar area was developed into a self-contained strongpoint, the commander of the main unit defending the location was often designated as a battle commandant (Kampfkommandanten), with authority over all military units and civilian organizations and personnel within that immediate area.

The close-combat nature of fighting in a built-up area is illustrated by one soldier's account of the action in Stalingrad in late 1942 – "the front is a corridor between burned-out rooms. It is the thin ceiling between two floors. Help comes from nearby buildings via fire escapes and chimneys. There is ceaseless struggle from morning until night. From floor to floor, we bombard each other with grenades amid explosions, clouds of dust and smoke, heaps of mortar, floods of blood, fragments of furniture and fragments of human beings."[7] Whether attacking or

**Above:** Diagram of a typical German casemate or gun position, published by the US Department of Defense in March 1945.

**Left:** German doctrine emphasized that defense was merely the prelude to resuming the offensive. As soon as practicable, the soldiers would emerge from their bunkers and trenches to carry the fight to the attacker.

defending, fighting in towns and cities almost invariably consumed more men, ammunition and other material than any other sort of combat, and imposed significantly higher levels of stress and exhaustion upon the troops committed to such operations.

At the highest levels of command, the OKW and OKH carried the doctrine for defensive operations into their plans for the defense of the Atlantic Wall along the north coast of France and the Low Countries, together with those for the construction of the West Wall or Siegfried Line on Germany's Western Front. In the army, the construction and maintenance of the necessary defenses was managed and overseen by specially qualified fortress engineers. This defensive strategy led to the development of a whole range of gun batteries, emplacements, bunkers, storage sites, command posts, headquarters and suchlike, all on a massive scale and using vast quantities of reinforced concrete, iron and steel. But the Maginot Line thinking that had so debilitated the French army's defensive planning between the two world wars was not allowed to develop in the German army. In the Wehrmacht, the troops manning these great defensive works were trained to use them as a means of disrupting or destroying an enemy attack, subsequently using them as a secure base from which to launch a counterattack. The West Wall in particular was actively portrayed as a protected area from behind which offensive operations could be launched (as was the case with *Wacht am Rhein* in December 1944) rather than just as a line of defense. Even if a bunker or other fixed position was entirely cut off, its continued resistance could aid others and support a counterattack – everyone understood that, while fortifications could delay and degrade the enemy attacking force by fire, the

Rommel advocated defeating the Allied invasion of northern France on the beaches. To that end, thousands of obstacles – such as these in Normandy in 1944 – were emplaced on the beaches to frustrate a landing at high tide and to baulk vehicle movement on the beaches.

battle would ultimately be decided by the counter-offensive action conducted outside and among these massive emplacements. Arguably, it was the failure of Hitler and the OKW to authorize the early release of the reserve Panzer forces to counter the Allied landings in Normandy on 6 June 1944 that denied the German defenders of the Atlantic Wall the opportunity to apply this concept against the Anglo-US forces lying under their guns on the beaches by destroying them with a decisive armored counter-stroke. Had full operational command of this potent armored reserve force been delegated to Generalfeldmarschall Rommel well before the Allied landings took place, the outcome of the battle for the Normandy beachheads might well have been somewhat different. Indeed, the experience gained by the Germans when countering the Allied invasions of Sicily and Italy should have been applied in Normandy. During these invasions, armored counterattacks had come close to dislodging the US landing at Gela in Sicily, and to overwhelming the Allied beachhead at Salerno in Italy, and the later landing carried out at Anzio.

# 5. Withdrawal and Delaying Operations

Just as events from 1942 increasingly forced the army on to the defensive in several theaters, so it also needed to become ever more adept at conducting planned withdrawals (Abbrechen des Gefechts) and enforced retreats (Rückzug). Withdrawals were usually carried out to extract forces where an impending defeat

was assessed inevitable, where no further advantage could be gained by continuing a battle, or where the engaged troops were required elsewhere – possibly to reinforce another theater or area, or to form a reserve prior to offensive action. Such withdrawals were carried out by night wherever possible (especially where the Allies had air superiority), contact being broken simultaneously across the whole front. This would be followed by rearward moves on multiple routes via a series of defensible positions (for use if required) and finally either to a prepared new defensive position or into a secure area in the rear pending other operations. During the withdrawal, reconnaissance units or other mobile forces might provide a covering force to deceive the enemy and prevent any disruption of the withdrawing forces while they were leaving the defensive positions, at which stage they were at their most vulnerable.

As the situation deteriorated both on the Eastern Front and later in the west, the army was obliged to carry out an increasing number of enforced retreats. In these circumstances the overriding aim was always to maximize the distance between the retreating forces and the enemy as quickly as possible, this subsequently enabling the retreat to be transformed into an orderly withdrawal, and eventually into a newly-constituted defense well to the rear of the original defensive line. Those troops already in contact with the attacking enemy were usually required to form a covering force in order to maintain for as long as possible the illusion that the positions were still fully occupied, while the normal levels of artillery fire were also maintained to reinforce this deception. In order to provide time and security to the retreating units, it was accepted that some or all of this covering force, including some anti-tank and artillery guns, might have to be sacrificed. While the covering force continued to engage the enemy and win time, the retreating force would have used their own short respite out of contact with the enemy to form a rearguard (Nachhut) and a main body.

A division retreating on two routes would usually employ an infantry battalion group on each route, the three companies of each battalion alternating as they moved rearwards in bounds. The group normally comprised the infantry battalion, some mobile reconnaissance units for flank protection, light guns and possibly self-propelled guns or howitzers for fire support (with half of these guns deployed with the rearmost company), combat engineers to carry out demolitions and possibly assault guns or tanks if available. The divisional artillery usually remained with the main body in order to re-establish itself at the new position as speedily as possible, ready to come into action if the pursuing enemy followed the retreating troops too closely. However, the success of the retreat depended upon the rearguard conducting a series of delaying actions, by which the enemy could be increasingly distanced from the retreating main body. To that end, the rearmost company commander decided when it was necessary to move his company back to the main part of the rearguard, while the main body commander decided when the whole rearguard was to move back to its next delaying position. Where available, armored reconnaissance units would be used to support or provide the rearguard, as their firepower enabled them to engage pursuing enemy armor at long or short range, and their mobility allowed them to mount ambushes and local counterattacks against the pursuers.

In order to maximize the delay imposed on the enemy during a retreat or a withdrawal, lines of resistance (Widerstandslinien) for rearguards, special battlegroups or other forces were set far enough apart so that not more than one line could be engaged by the enemy artillery simultaneously. At the same time, the aim was to deny the main enemy force the opportunity to close up to a distance that was less than that to the next line of resistance, in order to give the retiring troops sufficient time to reach the next line safely. As a result, the intervening area between the two lines (the Zwischenfeld) sometimes had to be contested by a counter-attack or rearward fire and maneuver if more time was required to prepare the next line. These lines of resistance were not sited in depth and were often complemented and supported by specially constituted mobile "strongpoint" detachments sited on forward slopes, using pre-planned and concealed, but unprepared, positions in order to minimize the chance of their identification from the air. These detachments might include a couple of self-propelled guns or assault guns, or a few tanks, supported by two heavy mortars and up to six machine gun teams. During any retreat or withdrawal, extensive use was also made of engineers to carry out demolitions, to construct obstacles, and to lay mines and booby traps, while at the same time assisting the rearwards movement of men and vehicles as necessary.

## 6. Mines and Minefields

Extensive use was made of mines (Minen) to protect defensive positions, to cover withdrawals and retreats, and to protect the flanks during offensive operations, with at least eight types of anti-personnel mine and nineteen types of anti-tank mine used by the army during the war. German minefield doctrine initially called for dense protective minefields to be laid in front of the line of main resistance; later this policy changed, these dense minefields now being sited within the main battle position together with numbers of well-dispersed mines laid irregularly in the area forward of this. While the broad siting policy might have changed, it was still axiomatic that minefields should be covered by fire – whether direct fire such as that from machine guns or light guns, or indirect artillery or mortar fire initiated by artillery observers, or possibly by listening posts or standing patrols sited to the rear of the minefield. The engineers were responsible for laying, marking and recording minefields, while other troops might also be co-opted to assist or to carry out this task when necessary. Combat units occupying or moving into a defended

Right: Many thousands of mines were laid by the DAK in North Africa, complemented by wire obstacles, booby traps and anti-tank ditches.

Below right: Teller mines, seen here carried by an Obergefrieter on the Eastern Front, were the type of anti-tank mine most widely used by the army.

Below: Minefield marker signs were used to indicate the position, type and extent of the German-laid minefields to their troops. These markers included purpose-made signs and improvised forms of marker.

area would expect to receive written instructions, sketches and maps from the local engineer commander detailing the location and extent of any minefields in that area, all of which were carefully surveyed, with existing natural or man-made reference points noted and used in laying out the minefield and producing minefield maps. These reference points also had wider applications, being related to any other significant features of the defensive position such as strongpoints, bunkers, and obstacles, which ensured that the minefield was integrated into the overall defense plan. Although the locations of all mines that were laid were required to be recorded, only those minefields that were within the operational area – where offensive and defensive actions were anticipated – were laid strictly in accordance with the standard density, pattern, composition and marking. In areas where no future movement of troops or vehicles was anticipated, mines were laid irregularly and only as densely as the quantity and types of mines available permitted.

Anti-tank minefields were laid with anti-personnel mines at the forward edge to hamper any attempts by enemy infantry or combat engineers to lift them, while booby traps, anti-handling devices and tripwires were also set among the mines. Similarly, anti-personnel minefields were laid with anti-tank mines at the forward edge, to discourage armored vehicles driving through to clear a lane for the infantry. Wood-cased demolition charges fitted with pressure fuses were also positioned at the forward edges of all minefields, serving both as anti-vehicle and anti-personnel mines that could not be detected electronically. The random laying of a number of both types of mine was also carried out in the area forward of the main minefield to deceive the enemy as to its limits and true configuration or orientation, as well as to protect cleared lanes through the minefield.

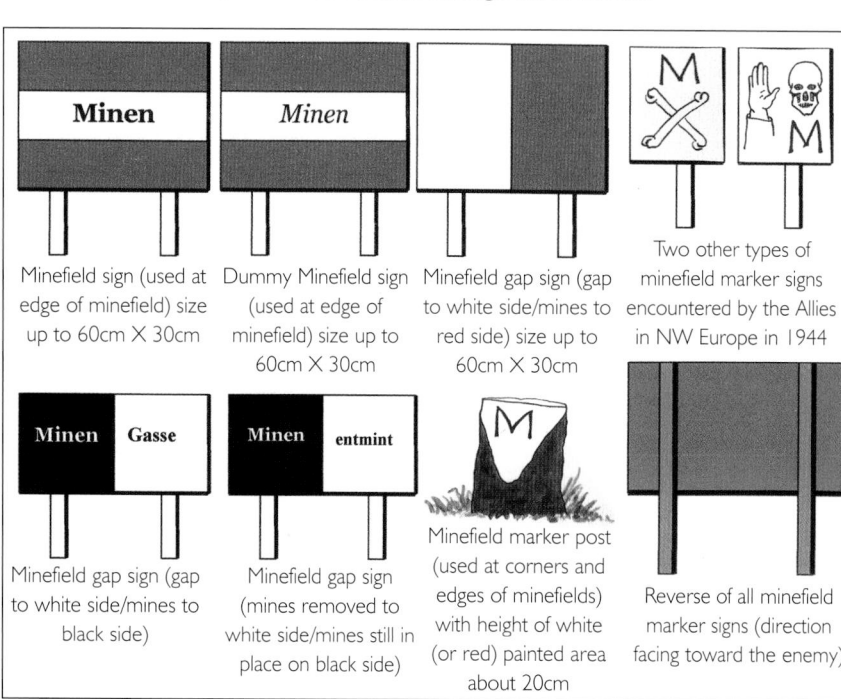

Minefield sign (used at edge of minefield) size up to 60cm X 30cm

Dummy Minefield sign (used at edge of minefield) size up to 60cm X 30cm

Minefield gap sign (gap to white side/mines to red side) size up to 60cm X 30cm

Two other types of minefield marker signs encountered by the Allies in NW Europe in 1944

Minefield gap sign (gap to white side/mines to black side)

Minefield gap sign (mines removed to white side/mines still in place on black side)

Minefield marker post (used at corners and edges of minefields) with height of white (or red) painted area about 20cm

Reverse of all minefield marker signs (direction facing toward the enemy)

The pressure-initiated mines in the main minefield were laid out in lines, their precise spacing determined by the use of a measuring wire (Minenmeßdraht) 24 meters long, with various markers along its length indicating the correct spacing, and four rings at one end enabling the correct off-setting or staggering of successive rows, which together ensured that all lines of approach were covered. The density of the minefield (that is, the distance between individual mines and the number of rows of mines laid) was determined by the type of mine used, whether it was surface-laid or buried, and the tactical situation, while the patterns used for minefield sections included echeloned lines, arrowheads and inverted arrowheads, with a series of minefield sections forming the main minefield.

In addition to standard minefields, the army also used hastily-laid unmarked nuisance minefields (typically, as part of a delaying operation or withdrawal) and properly marked dummy minefields to delay and deceive the enemy. Several other mine-laying ruses were also employed, such as burying anti-tank mines about fifteen centimeters deep in soft soil so that the mine would detonate only after several vehicles had already passed over it – each vehicle would successively compress the earth above the mine's detonating mechanism and eventually the direct pressure exerted by a subsequent vehicle would explode it. Wood-cased mines were used to defeat electronic mine detection, and tire marks could be impressed on to the ground through a minefield by hand, creating the impression that vehicles had already passed through safely. Anticipation of the enemy's likely actions was also important, with anti-tank mines surface-laid on verges adjacent to road obstacles and just beyond the brow of a hill on a road or track, while anti-personnel mines were laid around demolition sites, in roadside ditches where troops might take cover, and by road signs and kilometer markers where drivers and vehicle commanders might dismount to check their route. Mines might

be linked together and initiated by tripwire rather than direct pressure, while they could be similarly connected to form an improvised demolition charge. Metal battlefield debris and dummy mines were sometimes buried and used to frustrate and confuse electronic mine detection, although such ploys frequently involved the use of booby traps as well.

# 7. Reconnaissance Operations

Prior to offensive action, a reconnaissance of the area and the objective would be carried out as extensively as time and resources permitted, the ground reconnaissance being complemented or preceded by aerial reconnaissance wherever this was available. Reconnaissance and surveillance tasks would continue during periods of time spent in defense, and in anticipation of resuming offensive operations. Reconnaissance operations were carried out at all levels of military activity, including operational (Operative Aufklärung), tactical (Taktische Aufklärung) and battlefield (Gefechtsaufklärung). As well as gaining information by observation, the army's reconnaissance doctrine encouraged the use of initiative and aggressive action wherever appropriate, including the use of speculative fire (both direct and indirect) and deploying armored car and motorcycle patrols to draw fire, thereby encouraging the enemy to unmask his positions prematurely. During offensive operations the reconnaissance forces would dominate the area and maintain contact with the enemy with a view to preparing and shaping the battlefield for the attack force, but without becoming involved in the main battle at the expense of the reconnaissance mission. At battlefield level the various types of reconnaissance units, patrols and associated tasks included armored car patrols (usually of three vehicles such as the Panzerspähwagen Sd.Kfz.234/1 or 234/2, which was also known as the

The open nature of the North African terrain allowed Rommel's DAK to use reconnaissance aircraft such as the Fiesler Fi 156 to particularly good effect.

Right: In all theaters of operations, armored reconnaissance cars – such as this highly manoeuvrable 8 X 8 Sd.Kfz.234/3, with a 4-man crew and mounting a 75mm gun and a machine gun – ranged ahead and on the flanks of German units and formations to gain tactical intelligence information for their commanders.

Far right and below right: Luftwaffe Fallschirmjäger paratroopers prepare for an operational or training drop. Note the protective padding, the special jump boots, and the badge of rank on the arm of the parachute smock.

Puma), composite armored car and motorcycle patrols, sound-ranging and flash-spotting units and foot patrols. The missions set for foot patrols might include gaining tactical or terrain information, manning an observation post, capturing a prisoner for interrogation, or carrying out specific minefield, demolition, engineer, route-proving or other specialist tasks.

# 8. Airborne Operations

The airborne infantry (Fallschirmjäger) forces, which included parachute troops and glider-borne troops, were nominally Luftwaffe units, not part of the army. However, while retaining their Luftwaffe uniform distinctions and heritage, these well-trained and highly motivated forces were increasingly used as non-specialist infantrymen, serving alongside army units and under army operational command. They were also trained by army personnel and were largely equipped (apart from some special-to-role weapons and equipment) and supported by the army prior to and during operations. A Fallschirmjäger division usually consisted of three Fallschirmjäger regiments, each regiment having three battalions, with each regiment supported by a heavy (120mm) mortar or light (75mm) gun company and an anti-tank company. A total of eleven Fallschirmjäger divisions were created between 1943 and 1945.

The Fallschirmjäger were employed "in-role" on small-scale, *coup de main* and commando-style operations. Among these were the glider-borne assault against fortress Eben-Emael in May 1940, the rescue of Mussolini by a glider-borne assault in September 1943, an unsuccessful combined parachute and glider assault designed to kill or capture Tito in Bosnia in May 1944, and parachute drops in support of the Ardennes offensive in December 1944. Fallschirmjäger were also dropped immediately prior to the major ground offensives against Denmark and

Norway in April 1940. Groups of Fallschirmjäger were also used in up to battalion strength in Russia and the Balkans as well as in the Ardennes, being delivered by parachute and by glider to carry out sabotage missions, to seize key points and communications sites, to divert or draw away enemy reserves, and to hold tactically important ground ahead of the advancing or maneuvering ground units.

Had Operation *Seelöwe* (the intended invasion of England in 1940) taken place as planned, the 7th Fallschirmjäger Division would have landed in the Hythe–Lympne–Lyminge area to seize key points and secure the coastal area ahead of the seaborne invasion. The greatest German parachute assault of the war was that launched against the island of Crete in May 1941, where the large number of casualties sustained by the paratroopers resulted in a decision by Hitler and the OKW not to authorize any more large-scale airborne operations. Thereafter, the Fallschirmjäger divisions were routinely deployed as élite infantry units in most theaters (particularly distinguishing themselves during the Italian campaign), with ever-diminishing numbers of their men being parachute-trained.

The Fallschirmjäger remained under the organizational command and control of the Luftwaffe throughout the war and should not be confused with the Luftwaffe field divisions (Lw.-Felddivisionen) formed from Luftwaffe personnel in 1942 to offset the army's growing losses on the Eastern Front. By 31 October 1943, these non-airborne Lw.-Felddivisionen were reorganized and fully incorporated into the army as Type 1944 infantry divisions, in accordance with an order from the Führer's headquarters dated 20 September that year.

# 9. Mountain Warfare

The army deployed ten mountain infantry divisions (Gebirgsjäger divisions) during the war, all trained to deal with the extreme weather conditions, limited routes, difficult communications, and rugged terrain encountered in the mountain regions. The possibility of these troops becoming isolated due to the terrain or enemy action determined many of the special skills of the Gebirgsjäger, which included the ability to conduct small-unit actions by (for example) reinforced company-strength groups supported by an engineer platoon and a mountain artillery battery, the use of short-range, high-trajectory mortars and howitzers, and radio rather than line communications. The Gebirgsjäger used a two-echelon supply system, one echelon based in a valley and a forward echelon on a mountain; they were often entirely dependent upon men and mules to transport their weapons and supplies, and the Gebirgsjäger division had an established strength of about 13,056 officers and soldiers and some 3,065 pack animals to achieve this. The sort of mountain operations conducted by the Gebirgsjäger might include securing the flanks of conventional formations

Gebirgsjäger troops were thoroughly trained to conduct operations in mountainous terrain and in harsh winter conditions. Their specialist skills included rock climbing, skiing, and cold-weather and high-altitude movement and survival. Unlike the army's other units, these troops were proficient in using mules rather than vehicles to transport their heavy weapons and supplies, with their heavy machine guns and light mountain howitzers specifically designed to be dismantled and transported by the unit's mule trains.

operating on the adjacent plains, manning observation posts and seizing mountain passes. When attacking, the Gebirgsjäger usually infiltrated to an assembly area as close as possible to the objective, in order to minimize the assault time and distance. In defense, they usually manned a number of well-concealed and protected forward-slope positions, with their support weapons (mortars and artillery) positioned on the reverse slope, together with a strong reserve ready to mount a counterattack. Although they were used successfully in the mountains of Norway, the Balkans, Crete and Europe's Alpine regions, Gebirgsjäger divisions lacked the combat power and mobility that the normal infantry and Panzer divisions could bring to the conventional battlefield.

# 10. Winter Warfare

As a direct consequence of the invasion of the Soviet Union in June 1941, much of the army became involved in winter warfare during the late-autumn of that year, when it was forced to continue the campaign during the Wehrmacht's first Russian winter spent in the field. From the end of October 1941 to early April 1942, the troops on the Eastern Front learned by bitter experience many of the skills necessary to fight, to operate equipment and to survive in extreme conditions of cold, snow and ice. Although the harshest conditions were encountered on the Eastern Front, the army also used winter warfare techniques and specialized equipment during its operations in Norway and other mountainous regions during the winter periods. Meanwhile, at the tactical level, the Gebirgsjäger (who were specifically trained to operate in severe winter conditions) and units of ski troops performed valuable service patrolling, securing flanks and moving cross-country through deep snow and ice where roads were impassable. The ability to ski was a skill that many German soldiers living in rural areas would already have acquired prior to their military service, so the use of ski troops was not limited to specially trained winter warfare units. Special reconnaissance tasks for ski troops included assessing snow depth, avalanche threats and the load-bearing strength of ice, as well as marking viable trails and snow-covered roads with poles, stakes or other markers. Ski troops were also used for raids, small-scale assaults and harassing the enemy's flanks, while in defense ski troops were often held in reserve for use as a rapidly deployable counterattack force. While white camouflage clothing was eventually issued widely, during the winter of 1941/2 demand far exceeded supply, with many soldiers on the Eastern Front forced to adopt camouflage over-suits improvised from white sheets and suchlike.

With the end of the Blitzkrieg-style advances in the summer of 1941, the troops soon began to experience the hard realities of

fighting on the Eastern Front, where winter warfare all too quickly became an unavoidable way of life for up to five months of each year they were in Russia. By early December the daytime temperature in Russia was routinely 40 degrees Fahrenheit below zero. The army's morale generally held up remarkably well during the winter of 1941/2, but it was evident that the OKW and OKH had been woefully unprepared in June 1941 for a campaign that continued into the Russian winter. No general issue of winter clothing had been authorized, so as the temperature plummeted the soldiers were still wearing summer combat uniforms. Lubricants froze, so vehicles and weapons refused to work. Vehicles that had sunk into mud one day were inextricably frozen into it by the next morning, and explosives sometimes had to be used to break up the ground and free them. To touch any sort of bare metal without gloves was to risk the flesh instantly freezing on to it. Periods of sentry duty in the open were reduced from the usual one or two hours to no more than 30 minutes, but sometimes even less.

Large numbers of the horses upon which the army depended – especially the artillery and supply units – simply collapsed and died during the bitterly cold nights. At Stalingrad, as well as elsewhere on the Eastern Front, horsemeat was an unavoidable part of the soldiers' diet during the winter of 1942/3. Sergeant Helmut Werner of the 16th Panzer Division recollected that, "meat was being cut from horses lying in the street … to begin with no one wanted to eat horsemeat, but hunger is really painful, and so everyone devoured it. We looked like skeletons or walking corpses, some of us on a ration of just a handful of oats and a little water." Another soldier writing home on New Year's Eve, recorded that, "This evening we cooked up some horse again. You will have

**Below:** The Russian winter frequently posed almost insurmountable problems for the army. While these horse-drawn sledges are clearly appropriate for the task, the soldiers' uniforms are woefully inadequate to combat the ravages of winter.

**Opposite page:** The miseries and morale-sapping effect of winter warfare endured without the appropriate clothing and equipment is very evident from the faces of the soldiers in this 27 April 1944 photograph.

Suitable camouflage clothing for winter warfare was widely improvised from white sheets where necessary, although proper winter clothing was provided in due course, together with skis and other special equipment. However, this was rarely in sufficient quantities to meet the army's needs.

*Nächste Annahmestelle*
von Schaf-, Ziegen-, Wild-, Hasen- und Kaninchenfellen:

The parlous situation of the troops during the Russian winters was emphasized by this poster seeking public donations of all sorts of furs and fleece-lined clothing for delivery to the front-line soldiers on the Eastern Front.

7.62mm PPSh-41 generally meant that the soldier using it had to rely upon the continued availability of captured Russian ammunition, since the MP 40 used 9mm ammunition.

Self-help measures taken to combat the cold included packing newspaper into boots and simply wearing as many layers of clothing as possible, but this slowed movement and reduced agility. Commanders soon learnt the dampening effects of snow on the explosive power and lethality of artillery shells, and its effect on armored movement – any unpacked snow deeper than twenty centimeters severely inhibited the tactical movement of tanks and tracked assault guns. The troops soon developed the means of excavating (often with explosives) shelters and bunkers in hard-frozen terrain, subsequently using snow and ice with any locally-found materials, usually no more than logs, to construct and camouflage them. Wherever any sort of man-made building or shelter existed, it was usually utilized – even if that meant casting the civilian occupants out into the snow. In many cases such shelter was no more than a peasant hut or livestock shed and the troops gradually learned and adopted some of the survival skills of the Russian civilians who had endured their country's harsh winter climate for generations, often emulating their primarily vegetable-based subsistence diet on occasions when the military supply system broke down.

From December 1941, successive Russian winters transformed the army on the Eastern Front from the fast-moving technologically advanced force of the Blitzkrieg years and Operation *Barbarossa* into one that slowly became "de-modernized", less mobile and more defense-orientated, although the army's growing reliance upon defensive operations was in any case virtually inevitable in light of the burgeoning strength of the Red Army from late 1942. However, the experience of combat during the Russian winter immeasurably hardened many of the soldiers and units who fought on the Eastern Front, significantly enhancing their effectiveness when they were later engaged elsewhere – including against the Anglo-US forces in the West after June 1944.

to imagine how it tastes, without salt or any other seasoning, and when the animal gave up the ghost a month ago and has been lying under the snow ever since."[8]

At the same time, many infantry companies were reduced to platoon strength as frostbite and cold injuries and illnesses escalated, and all the while the winter clothing that could have prevented some of this failed to materialize. The army's supply lines extended over many hundreds of miles of barren winter landscape, which regularly frustrated early attempts to remedy the high command's original omission, and so wherever the opportunity presented itself, the soldiers would take the felt over-boots and white camouflage clothing from the corpses of the better-clothed Red Army troops. They would also take and use the Russian PPSh-41 submachine guns, which were prized for their simplicity and reliability in cold weather compared with the German MP 40 weapon – although the MP 40 was technologically more sophisticated and accurate, it was less reliable in extreme winter conditions. Clearly, his adoption of the

# 11. Desert Warfare

The desert campaign from February 1941 to May 1943 was unlike any other conducted by the army. Not only was it prosecuted in a manner widely recognized as being positively civilized in comparison with much of the war in Europe and on the Eastern Front, but the uncluttered and largely uninhabited desert wastes also allowed the German commander, General Erwin Rommel, to apply the principles of Auftragstaktik in their purest form and to especially good effect. The army's tactics in Libya, Cyrenaica and Tunisia by and large accorded with its existing doctrine and battlefield experience in Poland, Western Europe and the Balkans, but were modified as necessary to take specific account of the harsh desert environment. One factor that

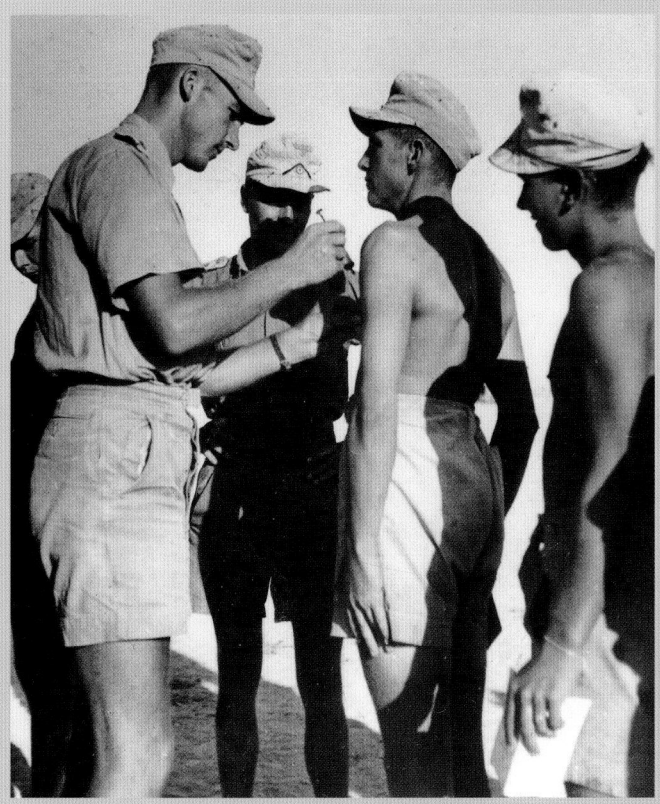

always determines tactics is the ground, and it was the nature of the North African desert terrain and climate – sand, mountains, lack of water, intense heat – that made the Deutsches Afrikakorps (DAK) two-year campaign so different. The OKH and the army were well-prepared for the operations against France and the Low Countries in 1940, but the sudden need for the army to conduct operations in the North African desert from early 1941 was largely unanticipated and precipitated by the succession of reverses suffered by Italy during 1940. Taken more or less by surprise, the OKH preparations for this campaign were somewhat limited, the short-notice deployment meaning that the troops involved had time to concentrate upon little more than the essentials.

Among the preparations that could be implemented were ensuring that the troops earmarked for North Africa were medically fit for tropical service (particularly rigorous standards were applied) and training them on those aspects of health and hygiene that were peculiar to desert regions. The normal training program was also adapted where practicable to reflect the anticipated nature of desert warfare, especially the command and control of armor and mobile operations in the open desert. To that end, all personnel were briefed extensively on the various types of desert terrain and their advantages and limitations, as well as about the Italian allies alongside whom they would fight and the British and Commonwealth forces that would oppose them. Meanwhile, the potentially arduous and unhealthy nature of desert service was recognized by the payment of an extra daily allowance of two Reichsmarks for enlisted ranks and three Reichsmarks for officers, warrant officers and NCOs. There was no time for the first troops who deployed to North Africa in February 1941 to receive any practical training for desert warfare. (Reinforcing units later benefited from the experiences of those who had gone before, Grafenwöhr in northern Bavaria in due course being designated the army's "hot weather training area" during the summer months.)

Training was largely limited to attending a series of lectures about tropical medicine and by officers who had by chance travelled in various desert regions before the war, this information being supplemented by individual research carried out in military libraries. Even General Rommel had no time to prepare – he was briefed by Generalfeldmarschall von Brauchitsch on 6 February, arrived in Rome on 11 February and flew to Tripoli on 12 February – while the principal headquarters staff for this generally unexpected mission had only formed up in late 1940, mainly on a contingency basis, and moved to North Africa on 24 February 1941. This situation was hardly ideal, but the inherent skills, flexibility and professionalism of the German army in early 1941 meant that the arrangements made by the OKH for the upcoming campaign would generally prove adequate in the circumstances.

From the outset the OKH had, correctly, identified the provision of water as a particularly high priority. Special

Health, hygiene and prophylactic vaccinations were especially important for the soldiers of the DAK operating in the dust, dirt, heat and flies of the North African desert.

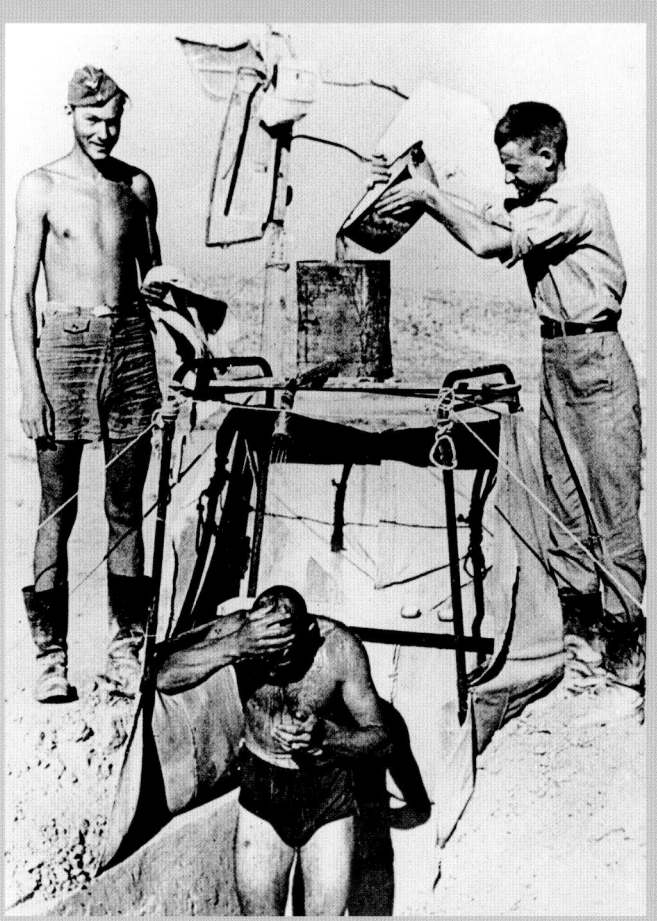

Necessity once again proves to be the mother of invention – here Luftwaffe personnel enjoy an improvised shower in the North African desert.

Water was as important as fuel in the desert. At this water replenishment point, pictured on 9 May 1941, the water cans are clearly distinguishable from fuel containers of the same pattern by the painted white crosses.

men working in a tropical climate, and the lack of fresh food resulted in various diet-related illnesses, especially during the first four months of the campaign. The bread problem was alleviated from March, when Bakery Company No. 531 began operations, but its dependence (and that of the army's field kitchens) upon wood for fuel continued to hamper the whole business of baking and cooking in the arid and sandy desert wastelands, since most of the German field cooking equipment was the same as that used in Europe, where wood was plentiful. Eventually, both fuel oil and logs for the army's bakeries and field kitchens in North Africa were imported from Italy.

A comprehensive range of lightweight cotton tropical uniforms was provided from the outset of the campaign, and in due course other special uniforms and personal equipment were developed specifically for desert use. The leather belt and other leather items of the soldier's load-bearing equipment were replaced with similar items made of olive-green web material, and the familiar leather jackboot was supplanted by knee- and ankle-length canvas desert boots, with canvas ankle gaiters also issued. A tropical sun (or "pith") helmet was initially provided to all troops, but the ubiquitous peaked field cap was universally preferred by the combat troops, who had in any case to wear steel helmets (usually painted sand color) while in the front line. Purpose-made improvements to the vehicles destined for desert service were less easily accomplished, and, apart from being camouflaged with sand-colored paint, many of the vehicles sent to North Africa during early to mid-1941 proved ill-prepared for desert warfare. The tanks had no enhanced cooling systems and were not fitted with the special air and oil filters essential to overcome the desert dust and sand. Various technical modifications did eventually appear, but overheating engines and other breakdowns constantly constrained the DAK's tactical options. Many tank engines lasted little more than 1,400 kilometers (half that of the British tanks), and the wheeled vehicles regularly broke down, while the need to avoid vehicle movement in the heat of the day meant that most armored movement had to be conducted by night, over relatively short distances, and with frequent halts.

An entry in the war diary of the 1st Panzergrenadier Regiment during the advance in March 1941 noted, "with vehicles designed for European road and terrain conditions, with maps that proved to be unusable … The farther we travel away from the coast into the limitless desert the higher soar the daytime temperatures which, despite the time of the year, approach 50 degrees centigrade." Then, while moving during the dark of the desert night with the vehicles following an officer walking ahead with a prismatic compass, "all the rest of us follow in his tracks. However, it is soon impossible to make progress in the deep, soft sand, so we have to rest and wait for the morning. At daybreak we set off again, after pulling and pushing those vehicles that had got stuck during the night. Now at last we can recognize the soft sand and bypass it."[9] In conditions like these, the vehicle maintenance and recovery

companies were created specifically to source, purify and transport drinking water, and these companies arrived in North Africa with the first combat formation, the 5th Light Division (5. leichte Division), on 14 February. The army's water-supply transport columns operated as a part of the normal supply system but had no role other than the transportation of water, which was carried in twenty-liter metal cans (dubbed "Jerricans" by the Allies). These containers were exactly the same type as those used for fuel, apart from being painted black with a white cross to identify them as "water only". Water-supply companies were manned by engineer troops, who had the capability to drill for, pump, purify and distil water, and the DAK and its successors rarely ran short of water, which remained a critical logistic factor for all the forces fighting in the desert.

Rations were more of a problem however: the army's usual European-theater staples of bread and potatoes, together with everyday items such as butter, eggs, bacon, ham, and fresh fruit and vegetables, could not easily be provided or stored in the desert. As a result, black bread, tinned sardines and olive oil were substituted, to which the Italians added an individual issue of coffee beans, cooking oil (170 grams), marmalade and grated cheese (85 grams), while Italian canned meat was also used extensively by the German troops. Although this diet provided an adequate amount of nutrition and protein, it was not ideal for

DAK units on the move in the North African desert – tanks, half-tracks, motorcycles and trucks all faced differing movement and maintenance challenges, as well as the ever-present vulnerability of ground forces to air attack.

units were absolutely critical to the success of the highly mobile operations conducted by Rommel's DAK. Consequently, the strategic outcome of the desert campaign and the defeat of the DAK were to be determined in large part by the superiority of the British logistic capability, when that of the Germans was becoming ever more stretched, as much-needed resources were either withheld or diverted to the Eastern Front.

Tactically, the German army benefited enormously from its professionalism, its doctrine of Auftragstaktik, and from the experience that many of its commanders had already gained in the art of maneuver warfare in Poland in 1939 and in France and the Low Countries in 1940. Rommel well understood the need for the integration and close cooperation of armor, infantry and artillery, and close air support (although the Luftwaffe was much less in evidence supporting the DAK in the desert than had been the case in Europe). In France, when dealing with an unexpected threat posed by an attacking British tank unit, Rommel had noted the effectiveness of the 88mm Flak anti-aircraft gun used as an anti-tank gun, and the DAK used these guns (which had been provided with armor-piercing shells by 1941) to exploit the desert's unrestricted fields of fire to devastating effect. Rommel also understood that capturing and holding ground was largely irrelevant in the desert, so the DAK moved fast and moved often, its commander's objective always being to fix and destroy the

British forces on ground of his choosing. He compensated for the DAK's lack of numbers by concentrating his combat power and committing the maximum force to offensive operations, entirely unbalancing the less imaginative and often inflexible British forces with a succession of German victories from February to June 1941. Indeed, the perpetual lack of German manpower meant that guarding prisoners-of-war was a recurring problem, and on one occasion during April 1941 the 1st Panzergrenadier Regiment was constrained to release several hundred British prisoners – sending them off unarmed and on foot toward the Allied lines – in order that the Germans would have sufficient fighting soldiers left to continue their own mission.

Hitler and the OKW were unprepared for the early success of Rommel's offensive and urged caution, at the same time directing the DAK to adopt a primarily defensive posture, since the Wehrmacht's strategic priorities were by then the campaign in Greece and the impending invasion of the Soviet Union. Nevertheless, what had by then become Panzergruppe Afrika was reinforced by the 15th Panzer Division before it was struck by the British 8th Army (already much stronger in armor and air support) counter-offensive (Operation *Crusader*) at Sidi Rezegh in November 1941. There, serious losses and the DAK's over-extended supply lines forced its temporary withdrawal, despite the Germans having inflicted proportionally greater losses upon could also actually conceal movement. During the final stage of the advance to an attack at Acroma on Trigh Capuzzo on 1 June 1941, "an immense wall of dust loomed up in front of us, blocking Tommy's vision. We were able to get within 600 meters of the strongpoint before the defensive fire began."[10] But dust clouds and sandstorms also resulted in "friendly fire" incidents: there were several reported instances of the Luftwaffe bombing DAK units, while individual and columns of vehicles of both sides often drove into the midst of the other's positions or convoys by mistake.

Intelligence was just as critical to both sides in the desert as elsewhere, and at the operational and tactical levels, the army's reconnaissance units (including the élite Brandenburger "special forces" commando units, Sonderverband 288 and later Brandenburger "Abteilung von Koenen", which were specially created for sabotage and reconnaissance work behind the Allied lines in North Africa) provided a steady flow of information and intelligence to Rommel and his commanders. During its advances, the DAK's reconnaissance units used armored vehicles and motorcycles (usually motorcycle combinations armed with a machine gun) ranging far ahead and on the flanks of the main force, gathering intelligence that could offset the inferiority of German numbers and resources.

However, at the strategic level – without the knowledge of either Rommel or the German high command – a great deal was already known in London and Washington about the German plans and intentions through the successful Allied intercepts of "Enigma" coded messages. Eventually, this significant intelligence advantage combined with the steadily increasing amounts of Allied combat power on the ground to halt the German advance in North Africa and seal the fate of Rommel's remarkable campaign. With its manpower and resources already strained to the limit, Panzerarmee Afrika at last suffered a decisive defeat at El Alamein during a two-week battle of attrition that began on 23 October 1942.

Rommel was forced to withdraw through Libya and into Tunisia, but throughout this withdrawal and the subsequent fighting in Tunisia the army employed many of the maneuver skills and tactics that had been honed during its successful advances in 1941 and 1942, while also benefiting from the reducing length of its supply lines as it moved westwards. In February 1943 it even managed to inflict a potentially devastating blow against the recently arrived US forces at the Kasserine Pass. There, 6,500 US soldiers were killed, wounded or captured, along with the loss by the Allies of almost 400 armored vehicles, 200 guns and 500 other vehicles to the Germans. However, the Allied naval blockade in the Mediterranean continued to deny Panzerarmee Afrika the reinforcements and *matériel* it needed to sustain its operations, while simultaneously enabling a largely unrestricted flow of men and resources to the Allies. The result was inevitable, and on 13 May 1943 the last German and Italian forces in North Africa finally surrendered.

A typical DAK soldier wearing tropical uniform and equipment, although the tropical helmet was largely abandoned in favor of the cap or steel helmet quite early during Rommel's North Africa campaign.

the British attackers. In January 1942, Rommel resumed the sort of operations that characterized both his own concept of mobile warfare and the army's desert campaign. With a series of rapid advances and outflanking moves, the Germans first of all seized Benghazi, outmaneuvering the British and Free French at Bir Hakeim, before defeating the British at Gazala and finally capturing Tobruk on 21 June. However, the farther the newly-designated Panzerarmee Afrika moved east toward its strategic objective, Cairo, the more extended its lines of communication became, and with so few routes across the desert suitable for high volumes of vehicle movement these supply lines became increasingly vulnerable to the growing threat posed by Allied air attack. Any vehicle movement was instantly betrayed by clouds of dust, while the availability of natural cover to mask observation of static vehicles from the air was also virtually non-existent. At the same time, however, the dust produced by artillery fire or bombing frequently blinded the observers of both sides and so

# 12. Amphibious Operations

Most of the army's war was land-based, and there were few large-scale amphibious operations. One such was the invasion of Norway in April 1941, for which a special staff was formed to command the joint land-air-sea operation. The initial seaborne invasion was carried out by troops transported on various warships, subsequent waves of reinforcements and supplies coming in on merchant ships. Later, small-scale amphibious operations were carried out in the Baltic Sea in June 1941 and in the Black Sea area (including the Kerch strait) from late 1941 to mid-1944. In the Baltic this activity centered mainly on the capture and recapture of various islands, while the Black Sea amphibious operations included troop evacuations as well as attacks. Numerous river-crossing and water-transiting operations were also carried out, usually using requisitioned civilian craft, small inflatable assault boats or larger motorized rigid assault boats, these craft being operated by the engineer or pioneer units. An example of one such operation was on the Meuse in May

1940, where assault engineers spearheaded the crossing, first manning and operating the inflatable assault craft, and then engaging in direct combat once across the river rather than acting merely as ferrymen.

The army was also involved in the preparation for the planned invasion of England (Operation *Seelöwe*) in 1940. Had it taken place, this would have been one of the largest and most complex amphibious operations in modern military history, with two armies (9th and 16th) of Army Group A embarking at French ports from Dunkirk to Étaples, and Le Havre, as well as at Rotterdam, Ostend and Antwerp in the Netherlands, before crossing the Channel and landing from Brighton in the west to Hythe in the east. The 7th Fallschirmjäger Division would have supported the seaborne invasion with an advance airborne assault on to the Lyminge, Lympne and Hythe area. The army group objective was to seize a line running northeast from north of Brighton to Ashford and Faversham, while the follow-on forces were to advance to a line from Portsmouth to Guildford and across to Gravesend – thus directly threatening London. But for any such amphibious operation local air superiority and maritime security were prerequisites, and the Royal Navy and RAF (during the Battle of Britain in 1940) ensured that these were not achieved. This strategic failure, primarily by the Luftwaffe, and the higher-priority need to prepare for the invasion of the Soviet Union led Hitler to postpone the planned invasion of England in October 1940, which in practice amounted to its cancellation. However, *Seelöwe* had an indirect resonance almost four years later: the extensive planning carried out by the OKW and OKH for this operation undoubtedly colored Hitler's belief, and that of the OKW, that the Allied main invasion in mid-1944 would be at the Pas de Calais. It mirrored the crossing that the German high command had studied exhaustively, assessed as being feasible and believed most likely to succeed in 1940.

The army's engineers had a very comprehensive range of rafts, ferries, inflatable craft and bridging equipment to carry out water-crossing operations.

# 13. Counter-Partisan Operations

An inevitable consequence of Hitler's conquests was the emergence of partisan groups, such as the *Maquis* in France, the resistance groups in Scandinavia and the Low Countries, and the guerrillas or partisans in Yugoslavia, Russia and elsewhere. Although the principal focus for counter-partisan operations was always the SS and the paramilitary police units, the sheer scale of the problem meant that virtually all parts of the Wehrmacht became involved with it. In the rear areas of every theater of operations, the army lines of communication and supply provided prime targets for sabotage and low-level offensive action by these groups. As a result, the army was actively involved in counter-partisan operations, which included large-scale search-and-destroy operations as well as a whole range of security and guarding duties, policing, and occasionally carrying out reprisal and punitive actions. The omnipresent nature of the partisan threat meant that every soldier was potentially a counter-partisan fighter. As a matter of policy, special training of counter-partisan troops was introduced, which also involved the close coordination of the Wehrmacht, SS, police and local civil authorities in the occupied areas, with territorial and pre-existing administrative boundaries being disregarded. The units employed against partisans included entire divisions as well as special task forces consisting of motorized infantry, cavalry, service units, locally recruited forces, and even (on the Eastern Front) armored trains. While the full range of weaponry was used by these units, the need for mobility favored lighter weapons capable of producing maximum firepower and shock effect – machine guns, flame throwers, sniper rifles, and light anti-armor and anti-aircraft guns. Appropriate clothing and equipment and supply arrangements were also developed to allow counter-partisan operations to carry on unconstrained by weather conditions or reliance upon the standard military supply system.

The need for intelligence was quickly appreciated, and the summary execution of captured partisans was discouraged in light of the information they might reveal during subsequent interrogation. On the Eastern Front, however, the conventional understanding of "partisan" was reinterpreted and expanded in September 1941 to include regular units of the Red Army that had been overrun by Axis forces but which subsequently reformed behind the forward combat zone – which meant that all such "irregular combatants" could be shot out of hand. Intelligence was acquired through collaborators, captured documents, radio and telephone intercepts, routine patrolling, and aerial reconnaissance, while long-term monitoring by army patrols of areas from which the partisans drew their support and supplies often led to the identification of partisan bases or to successful ambush operations mounted by special counter-partisan units. Understandably, the capture or elimination of partisan leaders was a prime objective, with rewards regularly offered or coercion used to achieve this. Direct assaults were launched against partisan groups and individuals whenever they were identified, while on the Eastern Front large-scale encirclement operations were mounted to destroy partisan groups in their bases. This was usually achieved either by overwhelming firepower, by progressively compressing the perimeter on all sides or from one side, by attacking into the encircled area directly or by launching containment attacks into the area to subdivide it and then destroy the smaller pockets separately.

SS units routinely carried out reprisals and punitive operations, such as the summary execution of partisans and sometimes of entire communities, the taking and execution of hostages, and the destruction of whole villages. It is undeniable that some army units also employed such extreme measures while attempting to achieve security and impose what they considered to be the rule of law within the occupied territories.

Such action was routinely justified as being necessary to discourage or punish local civilian support for the partisans, or as the unavoidable response to a particularly brutal action carried out by partisans. Predictably, these counter-partisan campaigns often produced extreme violence, with atrocities carried out by both sides. This was especially evident on the Eastern Front, where the German perception that the Russian partisans were not only irregular fighters (and therefore "illegal" combatants) but also "Untermenschen" further dehumanized and brutalized the troops ordered to carry out these counter-partisan operations.[11]

On 30 January 1944, Reichsführer-SS Heinrich Himmler instituted a special anti-partisan battle badge (Bandenkampf-abzeichen) to reward and distinguish members of the SS, the police and the Wehrmacht who had been actively engaged in counter-partisan operations. The badge was awarded in gold, silver and bronze respectively for 100, 50 or twenty days in action against partisans and was worn on the left breast pocket of the jacket. The main elements of the Bandenkampfabzeichen included a sword, a swastika "sun wheel" and a death's head, its most prominent feature being a writhing multi-headed serpent (impaled by the sword), which represented the partisans, while also symbolizing the German soldier's traditional loathing of these and all other irregular fighters and what were (from a German perspective) "illegal" combatants.

# 14. Forces of Occupation

To protect against attacks by partisans or similar armed resistance groups or Allied commandos within the occupied territories, large numbers of troops had to be permanently dispersed throughout the German-held areas. In recognition of the nature of the threat posed to them, these local security units, often based in isolated outposts, were usually deployed in no less than company strength, their outposts and bases organized for all-round defense, with a designated guardroom as the base strongpoint and rallying-point in the event of attack. The overall responsibility for the security of all the troops within a given area usually rested with the senior military commander of that area. Potentially vulnerable strategic facilities and key points such as railways, roads and inland waterways were often protected by lines of blockhouses established at intervals all along their length, while industrial facilities, communications centers and similar sites all had various levels of permanent protection. Inevitably, the large number of troops required to man these static strongpoints was a significant drain on the Wehrmacht's combat strength.

The army's attitude to the civilian population in the occupied territories differed markedly between that in the East and the often relatively benign regime imposed in the West (provided of course that the civilian population remained broadly passive or acquiescent to the requirements set by the military command or collaborative civilian government). On the Eastern Front the brutality and hostility exhibited by many troops toward the Russian civilian population stemmed in large part from the unremitting flow of Nazi propaganda that depicted Soviet Russia as the epitome of evil, as the instigator of a so-called Bolshevist-Jewish conspiracy designed to destroy Germany, and as the home and last refuge of the "Untermenschen" whose aim was the annihilation of the German nation and its culture. Such extreme generalizations might appear bizarre today, but by 1941 many young soldiers had been comprehensively indoctrinated with these ideas in school and then in the Hitler Jugend, while numerous Germans of the older generations had succumbed both to the Nazi propaganda and to the old "stab in the back" concept of 1918 – the latter often reinforcing the former through Hitler's manipulation of the historical legacy of World War I. Meanwhile, in some occupied areas on the Eastern Front, commanders actively encouraged fear and distrust of the civilian population, in order both to discourage fraternization and to enable them to impose an increasingly harsh disciplinary regime in some units; this was especially so from 1943, once the army began to suffer significant reverses on the battlefield. Indeed, quite apart from the official reinterpretation of "combatants" applied to counter-partisan campaigns, the semi-automatic categorization of any civilian suspect as a "spy" or "agent" indicated a presumption of guilt. This routinely resulted in violent interrogation, culminating in summary execution. As early as July 1941, troops of the 12th Infantry Division were ordered to shoot all refugees trying to cross the German lines westwards, on the grounds that any refugee incursions into German-occupied territory were indicative of espionage activities. In an address to an officers' conference in 1941, the commander of that division ordered that, "prisoners [taken] behind the front-line ... shoot as a general principle. Every soldier shoots (sic) any Russian found behind the front-line who has not been taken prisoner in battle."[12]

The 18th Panzer Division followed a similar policy with regard to its treatment of refugees during its first year in Russia until it finally acknowledged in June 1942 that its treatment of "suspects" and "agents" had possibly been excessively harsh – thereafter any such "suspects" arrested by the division were handed over to the GFP (where they almost certainly suffered the same fate).[13] While the SS and SD were the principal perpetrators of such actions, the OKH and a number of senior Feldheer commanders actively supported and promoted such policies, and it would therefore be disingenuous to suggest that the army's involvement in such excesses, punitive operations and summary executions was merely incidental, or that the progressive dehumanizing of the army on the Eastern Front was simply an inevitable consequence of the often horrific nature of the fighting that took place in Russia.

Reflecting Nazi dogma, relations between German forces of occupation and the civilian population were generally much better on the western front, as pictured here in France during June 1940, than in Poland, Czecho-slovakia, the Balkans or on the Eastern Front. Nevertheless, resistance movements emerged in all of the occupied territories.

The only part of the British Isles to be occupied by the Germans was the Channel Islands, where the island authorities were constrained to conduct a pragmatic if uneasy collaboration with the occupying forces. This police sergeant is pictured at one of the German administrative headquarters on the islands on 8 September 1940.

*Die Letzte Handgranate*, a painting by Elke Eber, 1937. Although painted some two years before the outbreak of the war, the drama and pathos captured by Eber's picture – "The Last Grenade" – proved prophetic and, apart from its completion date, it might well depict an incident during the army's final battle for Berlin in 1945 or a unit's last stand on the Eastern Front in 1944 or 1945.

# PART XI
# The End of Hitler's Army

During less than six years of war the armed forces of the Third Reich had been devastated, the Wehrmacht as a whole losing almost four-and-a-half-million killed and missing, plus a further four-and-a-half-million wounded. Of these casualties, the majority were soldiers, with almost two million killed, more than one-and-a-half-million missing and well over four million wounded. As a result, by May 1945 the once powerful and highly-respected army that had conquered much of Europe so speedily and efficiently in 1939 and 1940, and the western Soviet Union during mid to late 1941, had literally ceased to exist. The totality of its demise was in some ways reminiscent of the ancient tales and legends on which German culture was founded, the same tales that the Nazis had used to misrepresent aspects of the military heritage of the army and the Third Reich. Ultimately one such legend had particular resonance – a large part of the German army had finally been consumed by a modern Götterdämmerung amid the flames and rubble of the Third Reich's capital during the wholesale devastation and slaughter of the Russian assault on Berlin.[1] And by then many thousands of its soldiers were already incarcerated in the huge prisoner-of-war camps that had been established by the Allies within Germany as the war drew to a close.

The privations suffered by many of those held by the Russians were already well-known, but during the final months of the war the sheer numbers of prisoners taken imposed an almost unmanageable situation upon the Western Allies as well. The British generally coped with the prisoner-of-war crisis effectively, often by pragmatically allowing the disarmed German units they captured to continue to administer themselves as formed units, albeit under close British military control. However, the Americans usually broke up the units they captured, segregated the ranks, and destroyed any existing chains of command as a matter of policy, so that any residual sense of discipline or unit cohesion was entirely destroyed. In many instances the principle of "survival of the fittest" prevailed. As a result, even more than the horrendous litany of Wehrmacht casualty figures, the often appalling conditions in these hastily built camps – frequently no more than barbed-wire enclosures without accommodation, latrines or any shelter from wind, rain and sun – truly demonstrated the full extent of Germany's defeat and the depths into which its army had finally sunk. In the camp administered by the US Army at Rheinbach, for example, starving German prisoners ate the fields of clover and grass bare, and then the foliage on the hedges; while at Bad Kreuznach 560,000 prisoners were held in a US Army camp designed for no more than 45,000.

Often these unfortunate men were guarded by young and inexperienced US Army replacements who had recently arrived

German prisoners-of-war are escorted through a devastated village in the Roer river area by soldiers of the 9th US Army in February 1945. They are only a handful of the hundreds of thousands of prisoners taken by the Allies during the final months of the war.

in Europe and were frustrated at having just missed the closing campaign of the war while at the same time being all too well aware of the horrors that their comrades and their allies had discovered at Dachau, Belsen, Buchenwald and other concentration and death camps during the spring of 1945 – all of which had already been widely reported by numerous newspapers, photo journals and radio broadcasts, as well as being shown on cinema newsreels. Even more immediately, attitudes to the Germans within the US military forces in Europe had been considerably inflamed and hardened by official reports of the so-called "Malmédy Massacre" of US prisoners-of-war that had been carried out by Waffen-SS troops on 17 December 1944 during the Ardennes offensive.[2] At about the same time or soon thereafter the flow of stories of the severe hardships endured by many Allied prisoners in German camps increased dramatically, as a succession of prisoner-of-war camps were liberated or simply abandoned by their guards. Many of those released had been prisoners for several years, but their circumstances during the final six months of the conflict had worsened significantly as a direct consequence of the accelerating collapse of the Third Reich's administrative infrastructure and supply arrangements.

The experiences of many of the young, combat-untested, American soldiers captured in the Ardennes during the early days of Operation *Wacht am Rhein* in December 1944, so soon after their arrival at the front line in Europe, were particularly harrowing. The sheer scale of the numbers of US soldiers captured during the offensive virtually overwhelmed the Wehrmacht's ability to deal with them, and the majority of these prisoners – many of them wounded or in various states of shock or combat fatigue – had been transported on lengthy rail journeys or on foot from Stalag to Stalag in midwinter, with minimal supplies of food, water or medical attention. By then Germany and its own armed forces

Following the German capitulation in Denmark, troops surrender their weapons at an Allied control point on the German-Danish frontier, spring 1945, before moving on into Germany.

were suffering extreme austerity measures and struggling to manage their own survival – Allied prisoners-of-war were a low priority. Frequently the men captured that December and January were moved in railway box-cars by trains subsequently subjected to sustained attacks by USAAF and RAF aircraft within Germany, the Allied aircrew unaware of the human cargo these trains carried. Meanwhile, the German authorities sought continually to move these prisoners ever farther away from the rapidly advancing Allies; which meant that in some cases Allied tactical successes actually compounded the hardships of Allied prisoners-of-war. Once they had arrived at a prisoner-of-war camp, the prisoners often fared little better. Among the network of Stalags and Oflags set up in Germany, Stalag XIB at Fallingbostel, Stalag XIIIC at Hammelburg and Stalag VIIA at Moosberg attained particular notoriety within the US forces in Europe once the experiences of their American former inmates became known, these tales circulating just as the particularly harsh European winter of 1944/5 at last began to give way to spring. Cumulatively, these events and news stories – the concentration camps, the Malmédy Massacre and the experiences of Allied prisoners-of-war – and the widespread publicity accorded them by the Allied high command and the Anglo-US news media early in 1945, undoubtedly had a significant and generally adverse effect upon the way in which large numbers of German prisoners-of-war were subsequently processed and confined by their Allied captors.

As a result, by the closing months of the war, often little sympathy or compassion was shown for the exhausted, starving and frequently sick or wounded Wehrmacht prisoners by the GIs tasked to guard and administer them. Instances of the deliberate ill-treatment or disregard of prisoners in the several vast and hastily established camps were commonplace. Huge numbers of these captured German soldiers therefore had to survive in the open, without any protection from the torrential downpours of April or the beating sun of May, sometimes standing propped against each other with as many as 3,000 to a hectare. Numbers of them sought to gain a small degree of protection from the elements by digging out "survival holes" in ground that was often contaminated by the lack of latrines, using cutlery, empty tins, sticks or their bare hands. Despite the US Army's abundance of supplies for its own troops, the system simply could not cope with such vast numbers of captives. At Bad Kreuznach, for example, food was in such short supply that for a considerable time only four tarpaulin bundles of biscuits were provided for 1,000 prisoners per day, and for many weeks the official ration for each prisoner at Bad Kreuznach was just "three spoonfuls of vegetables, a spoonful of fish, two prunes, one spoonful of jam and four biscuits." Dysentery and death, despair and disorder dominated life within the Rhineland prisoner-of-war camps during the spring and early summer of 1945, as thousand upon thousand of soldiers of Hitler's army who had managed to survive the war now experienced the full consequences of Germany's defeat, its unconditional surrender and the disintegration of its armed forces.[3] However, the seeds of the German army's own destruction had been sown long before, by its political passivity and detachment, and by its often self-interested willingness to accept and obey without question the extreme and expansionist internal and external policies and actions of a perverse but charismatic Führer who lacked the ability to be both head of state and commander-in-chief. (Indeed, Hitler's historic decision to invade the Soviet Union in 1941 without first ensuring that Britain could never provide a secure base from which to mount an invasion of continental Europe was probably his greatest strategic error of judgment, one that ultimately determined the outcome of the war.) The extreme nature of Hitler's National Socialist ideology, his sidelining and neutralization of the old general staff system and his deliberately divisive management of the command and control of the Wehrmacht *vis-à-vis* the SS, all gradually but comprehensively undermined the Wehrmacht and the army in particular. The extent of this was such that not even the army's long-standing qualities of professional competence, technological innovation and operational flexibility – together with its historical touchstones of loyalty, honor and duty – could withstand the National Socialist propaganda onslaught. Not least amongst the promises made by Adolf Hitler in the sometimes tumultuous, frequently exciting and militarily intoxicating years following his coming to power in 1933, had been the prospect of new military glory for Germany and the overturning of the humiliations imposed by the Allies at Versailles in 1919. Irrespective of their political views, for most professional army officers these aspirations were particularly enticing and compelling in the political and economic chaos of Germany in the 1930s. Indeed, it would be both naïve and arrogant for non-Germans to suggest that in analogous circumstances of national humiliation, strategic insecurity and political and financial turmoil, their own nation could never have been lured by a vision and promises similar to those presented to the German populace by Adolf Hitler from the late 1920s. Ultimately, however, the desire of countless Germans to achieve the National Socialist vision of a Germanic utopia and international military dominance that had been portrayed so convincingly by Hitler proved illusory.

Hitler's army was finally defeated when Nazi Germany at last stood alone in Europe, fighting a war of attrition on two major fronts, while opposed by the combined and overwhelming military and industrial might of the Soviet Union, the United States and Great Britain, and their various United Nations and British Commonwealth allies. For just over a decade the path of National Socialism and that of the German army had run closely in parallel, frequently converging and overlapping, and sometimes virtually impossible to distinguish as being separate paths. Despite increasing opposition to Hitler within parts of the army from 1943 – exemplified by the failed attempt to kill him in July 1944 – the fortunes and fate of Germany and the army were inextricably bound together. The euphoria following the campaigns of 1939 and 1940, the cumulative effect of years of Nazi propaganda and the traditional German attitudes to honor, duty and the Fatherland

meant that once the armed forces had acknowledged Hitler's status as Führer and supreme commander, coupled with the obligations that this imposed upon every soldier through his oath of loyalty, this outcome was inevitable. However, while the coincidence of the German military renaissance in the 1920s and 1930s with the rise of National Socialism was particularly unfortunate for the wider world and an absolute catastrophe for Germany, it is none the less undeniable that the army created to carry through Hitler's foreign policies was a truly remarkable fighting force. This was perhaps all the more so because, against all the odds, it had risen from the ashes of defeat, disorder and despair in 1918, and the national humiliation inflicted upon it by the Versailles treaty in 1919, to become by 1939 the most powerful and forward-thinking military force in Europe.

This young soldier's face epitomizes the sheer scale and impact of the German defeat in 1945.

# Conclusion

As well as being one of the most formidable fighting forces in the history of modern warfare, the development of Hitler's army also exhibited many contrasts, extremes and ambiguities, and as such it has understandably inspired more analysis and writing since 1945 than most other armies, especially as it existed for such a short period of time – a total of just over ten years. This has resulted occasionally in a degree of stereotyping and misperception about its actual nature and capabilities.

By 1939, the army was one of the most modern in Europe, with a whole range of new or proven weapons and equipment in service or under development. The new tanks, half-tracks, guns, small-arms and close-support aircraft exemplified and visibly demonstrated this modernity, but the true strength of the German army lay in its officers and soldiers, its general staff system, its training and support arrangements, its command and control arrangements and battle procedures – all of which aspects have been described in some detail in the various parts of this work. Similarly, rather than its equipment, much of which was actually of a comparable or lesser quality and quantity than that fielded by France and Great Britain in 1939, it was the innovative nature and all-arms cohesion of the army's strategic and operational concepts and planning that placed it in a class of its own. Certainly the army that went to war in 1939 was better-prepared than any that opposed it; but, contrary to the oft-stated myth of the Panzer forces' overwhelming technological advantage, it was the way in which the army organized and used its armored and other forces to confound the Allies in 1939 and 1940 that carried the day so convincingly, not merely the physical existence of mobile or armored forces and weapons that were in reality not unique to the German army. Indeed, the army's early successes stemmed from the way in which it used the vehicles and equipment that it had, some of which were undoubtedly less than ideal for the purpose, and from the speed with which it learned from, and remedied, deficiencies identified in combat.

Several factors conspired to influence the subsequent development and fortunes of the army as the war progressed. Therein were to be found many of the contrasts, extremes and ambiguities that made a German victory virtually impossible after 1941 and eventually resulted in the defeat of the Wehrmacht and the downfall of the nation. Strategic issues, such as Germany's lack of any militarily effective Axis allies in Europe,[1] the failure to defeat or effectively neutralize Great Britain in 1940, and the creation of a war on two fronts following Hitler's invasion of Russia in 1941 were pivotal. However, the failure of German industry to move on to a total war footing until 1942 also meant that neither Hitler's strategic war aims nor the generally sound plans and operational concepts of the army high command could be realized. Much of this operational planning was predicated upon an ever-increasing availability of armoured vehicles and the resources to sustain them, the army's Panzer forces being at the very core of its doctrine of offensive action. However, although much new equipment (especially tanks and artillery) was of excellent quality,

it could not be produced in sufficient numbers to meet the army's operational needs. The German campaign on the Eastern Front is often portrayed as being dominated by armored mobile warfare – but in reality, apart from major but brief encounters such as that at Kursk in 1943, much of the army was primarily engaged in defensive and often quite limited armored and mobile operations from 1942. Indeed, the state of the army on the Eastern Front might reasonably be described as one of gradual de-modernization from 1942, as the numbers of its machines and resources essential for mechanized warfare gradually diminished, being stretched ever more thinly as the war continued.

Similarly, one of the great ambiguities of Hitler's army was the extent to which its artillery and service support units had to rely upon horses for motive power right through the war. At the same time, the majority of the army's infantry units still marched to battle rather than riding in motor vehicles. The army's extensive use of bicycles throughout the war was practical and pragmatic, but it was nevertheless a somewhat slow and anachronistic means of transport for a modern fighting force and hardly fitted the image of armored warfare inspired by the Blitzkrieg concept. Frequent time and space disconnects between the movement of the Panzer divisions and those of the follow-on non-motorized infantry divisions in 1939, 1940 and 1941 were therefore inevitable and served to highlight the urgent need for more Panzer and other motorized units to be created. However, yet again there was an unbridgeable gulf between such aspirations and what could be achieved with the industrial and manpower resources available.

Of course, the army made much use of railways and did so to good effect wherever these existed or could be built. Germany's excellent internal railway system was a key contributor to the success of mobilization in 1939, and of the Wehrmacht's early campaigns thereafter. The army's railway units and railway engineers were undoubtedly the best of any European army, and they needed to be, for its absolute dependence upon rail transport, not only for mobilization but then also to support the field army once deployed, meant that these specialist troops had to be totally proficient. However, placed in its historical context, this particular form of military transport had been innovative when the Prussian army and its South German allies had used it during the Franco-Prussian War of 1870–1; but from 1939, once the initial mobilization and deployment had been successfully completed, railways would always lack the operational flexibility necessary to satisfy the needs of forces engaged in mobile armored warfare.

Nowhere was the increasingly dated nature of the army's means of mobility and the inadequacy of its industrial capacity more evident than in Northwest Europe following the Allied invasion of Normandy in 1944, where the overall modernity and quantities of vehicles and equipment fielded by the Allies were in particularly stark contrast to those of the defending German troops. Even though some weapon systems, such as the Pz.Kpfw.V Panther and Pz.Kpfw.VI Tiger I and II tanks, were superior to any of the Western Allied tanks that opposed them, the army never received sufficient quantities of these potentially battle-winning weapons. Similarly, if every German infantry division had been a motorized or Panzergrenadier division in 1939, fully equipped with armored personnel carriers, a supporting tank regiment, and the considerable amounts of ammunition, fuel and other resources to sustain them, the Blitzkrieg successes of 1939 and 1940 would probably have been accomplished even more speedily and with significantly greater military and political impact. The invasion of Russia in 1941 might also have taken a very different course, with Moscow probably being captured before the onset of winter, Stalin's communist government destroyed, and the industrial, oil and other natural resources of the Soviet Union brought firmly under German control by the end of that year.

But perhaps the final irony for Hitler's army was more indirect, being the legacy of its defeat in 1945 and which emerged during the re-militarization of what then became West Germany (the BRD) and East Germany (the DDR) in the Cold War years that followed.[2] In West Germany, a rigorously de-Nazified Bundeswehr was created in 1955, serving within NATO as a vital counter to the growing Soviet and Warsaw Pact threat. By the early 1970s this new German army was equipped with high-quality weapons and vehicles on a scale that the former OKH of the Third Reich had always needed but never achieved, while the design of this equipment took full account of the bitter lessons learned by Hitler's army on the Eastern Front, as the Bundeswehr anticipated that the principal focus of the next war would also be on what had become NATO's eastern flank. Had the Cold War become a "hot war" in Europe, the Bundeswehr's new Leopard tanks, Marder infantry fighting vehicles, Gepard mobile anti-aircraft systems, Luchs reconnaissance armoured cars, and M2 amphibious bridge-ferry systems would certainly have been key contributors to a NATO victory in Europe. Such equipment, together with a whole range of rugged, high-wheelbase trucks and other fighting vehicles, modern self-propelled artillery and all sorts of other weapons would undoubtedly have proved more than adequate first to counter a Warsaw Pact attack, and then – alongside those of West Germany's new-found Western allies – to spearhead any new campaign on NATO's eastern flank in Europe. However, while the Bundeswehr at last had the necessary weapons and equipment, during its early years the active policy of de-Nazification and the wave of anti-militarism actively promoted throughout West Germany meant that many members (especially officers) of the former wartime army were automatically denied the opportunity to participate in and contribute positively to the development of West Germany's new defence force. By debarring these former members of Hitler's army from joining the Bundeswehr much useful military experience and expertise was lost.

Meanwhile, and in stark contrast to the story of the Bundeswehr, just across the Inner German Border to the east, the Russians created the National People's Army (NVA) in the German Democratic Republic, ostensibly as a counter to West Germany's incorporation into NATO. Despite the so recent and bitterly-contested ideological and armed struggle between Nazism and communism, the Russians and the East German communist regime actually employed many of the presentational, practical and management characteristics of the former Third Reich in its creation of the NVA, communist ideology conspicuously replacing that of the Nazis. Many aspects of the NVA resembled the army of the Nazi era – uniform, the use of grand military parades (including the revival of the old pre-war parade march or "goose step"), public displays of massed military hardware and the liberal use of martial-style flags, banners and insignia, together with incessant propaganda that included many blatant misrepresent-ations of German cultural and military history. Even the use by East Germany's new army of suitably trained political officers and informers would have resonated with former members of Hitler's army who had experienced the day-to-day activities of the Nazi NSFO political officers; while the new communist state's security organization, the MfS, bore many of the hallmarks of the former SD and SS security organizations. And, unlike the West Germans, the East German regime often adopted a less-principled and more pragmatic approach to its employment of those who had served in the armed forces and other organizations of the Third Reich.

The very last word on Hitler's army should perhaps broaden the matter and return to the wider subject of German militarism and the underlying but intangible qualities of military profes-sionalism, patriotism, honor, discipline and commitment that have characterized the German army and the nation that it serves ever since the emergence of Prussia in 1648, and arguably since even earlier times. Despite the awesome scale of the Wehrmacht's defeat in 1945, it was noteworthy that by the 1970s Soviet military intelligence assessments routinely rated the combat effectiveness of the West German army above that of any other NATO nation's ground force deployed in Central Europe, while at the same time NATO intelligence assessments throughout the Cold War consistently rated the East German NVA as the best of the non-Soviet Warsaw Pact armies. So it was that even an apocalyptic defeat on the scale of that suffered in 1945 could neither extinguish the legend nor prevent the resurrection of German military prowess. Meanwhile, set against the three and a half centuries of German history that have passed since the end of the Thirty Years War in 1648, Hitler's army was in many ways an historical aberration. Certainly Hitler was the architect of the war machine that he created, but in the end he was also the principal instrument of its destruction, as his flawed military judgment and ideologically driven obsessions continued unchecked, eventually consigning to oblivion both the Third Reich and the fighting force upon which Germany had depended so absolutely.

# APPENDIX I
# The Waffen-SS

The Waffen-SS was not a part of the army, nor indeed was it even a fourth branch of the Wehrmacht, but the eventual impact of Waffen-SS units and divisions upon the course of many land battles and campaigns was often significant and frequently controversial. Therefore, because of its necessarily close operational and command relationships with the army throughout the war and because of the extent to which the Waffen-SS regularly had to compete with the army for finite quantities of modern equipment and other resources (usually successfully, which frequently led to friction between the Waffen-SS and the OKH), a brief account of the development, scale and nature of this formidable fighting force is included as an appendix to the main work. This account also places in context the principles upon which the Waffen-SS was founded, which in turn shaped the way in which its troops conducted themselves in combat.

Prior to and during the early war years, membership of the Waffen-SS was voluntary and highly selective.

WAFFEN-SS

EINTRITT NACH VOLLENDETEM 17. LEBENSJAHR

Historically, the concept of the Waffen-SS (literally, the "armed SS") had its origins in the post-1918 Freikorps, and it was eventually born out of the political turmoil and street violence of 1920s and 1930s Germany. It was spawned specifically by the paramilitary organization that supported and physically protected the Nazi party during much of that turbulent period – the Schutz-Staffel (or SS). Hitler distrusted many members of the high command of the existing armed forces (that of the army especially so); the SS, and later the Waffen-SS, emerged in response to his desire for the Nazi party to have at its immediate disposal a totally reliable armed military or paramilitary force that was not part of the national armed forces and owed its allegiance only to him, personally, its political and ideological *raison d'être* being the fulfilment of the Nazi aims and objectives. In the course of developing his ideas on the desired nature of the SS, Hitler appropriated elements of the theories and writings of the nineteenth-century German philosopher Friedrich Nietzsche concerning the creation of a race of Ubermenschen (or supermen). In defining the qualities required of the Waffen-SS soldier, Hitler stated: "The SS man's basic attitude must be that of a fighter for fighting's sake; he must be unquestionably obedient and become emotionally hard; he must have contempt for all 'racial inferiors' and for those who do not belong to the order [of the SS]; he must feel the strongest bonds of comradeship with those who do belong, particularly his fellow soldiers, and he must think nothing impossible."[1] Over time, in parallel with the rapidly increasing size of the army, the SS grew significantly from the relatively small beginnings of its original formation in 1923 as the SS-Stabswache in Berlin (which became the Leibstandarte SS "Adolf Hitler" in March 1933) and (in 1925) as the SS-Verfügungstruppe (SS-VT) and the SS-Totenkopfverbände (SS-TV).

Originally, the SS-VT was little more than a militarized security force for the Nazi party, recruited exclusively from party members "with Aryan blood", and as such it was by no means as well trained or capable as a regular army unit. Most of its troopers certainly displayed few of the characteristics set out by Hitler for membership of this highly politicized private guard force. Meanwhile, the SS-TV was originally formed as a source of guards for the Nazi concentration camps and to provide a politically reliable internal security force for Germany in time of war. However, at the end of June 1934 the SS finally achieved primacy over its SA rivals during the so-called "blood purge" – the "Night of the Long Knives" of 30 June – and thereafter its power and influence increased rapidly, while the subsequent rise of its commander, Heinrich Himmler – already one of the most powerful men in Germany – was positively meteoric.

Certainly the events of 30 June 1934 and the few days that followed proved particularly significant for Germany and the army alike, for as well as consolidating Hitler's power and establishing the Nazis' political course for the next decade, the "blood purge" also eliminated the SA and replaced it with the much more effective and ideologically focused SS. This later enabled the creation of the Waffen-SS, after which it developed separately from the Allgemeine SS (or "general SS") while still remaining a part of the wider SS organization. By 1936 an SS-VT Inspectorate had been established to oversee the administration and development of what had become, by late 1939, the "armed" or Waffen-SS headed by Reichsführer-SS (RF-SS) Heinrich Himmler.

The military role of the Waffen-SS and its independence from the Wehrmacht were formally confirmed by Hitler on 17 August 1938. Initially, in order to achieve the organization's rapid expansion from 1939, many Waffen-SS junior officers were necessarily found from among the army's NCO corps, while many of the organization's more senior officers were transferred directly to the Waffen-SS from the Wehrmacht and the police forces. Waffen-SS officer training was conducted at officer cadet schools

Serried ranks of Waffen-SS troopers on parade during a Nazi party rally at Nürnberg in the mid-1930s.

at Braunschweig and Bad Tölz, and although it was patently not part of the German army, the military story of the Waffen-SS increasingly overlapped that of the army from 1939, with Waffen-SS units regularly fighting alongside or under the command of army formations. Similarly, at various stages of the war army formations were also commanded by Waffen-SS headquarters.

With the establishment of the SS-VT Inspectorate in 1936, the terms of service for the Waffen-SS were formalized, requiring its officers to serve for 25 years, its NCOs (sergeants and above) for twelve years, and ordinary SS men for four years. Prior to the formal establishment of the Waffen-SS in 1940, units of the SS-VT's first three numbered motorized infantry regiments (the 1st "Deutschland", 2nd "Germania", and 3rd "Der Führer") and the Leibstandarte SS "Adolf Hitler" (the LAH) participated in the German occupation of the Sudetenland and Austria and the campaign in Czechoslovakia. Each regiment consisted of three battalions, each of four companies, with three platoons of four sections. The regiments had their own artillery, engineer, reconnaissance, air defense and communications support. In general, the performance of these units during the early campaigns up to and including that in Poland fell well short of that of the army. After the Polish campaign the Waffen-SS underwent extensive reorganization and re-training, and thereafter it increasingly came to be regarded – albeit somewhat grudgingly by many within the army who resented its existence and its competing calls upon Germany's always scarce military resources – as an élite military force. In June 1941 four Waffen-SS divisions took part in Operation *Barbarossa*, and in Russia and the Balkans these and other Waffen-SS divisions

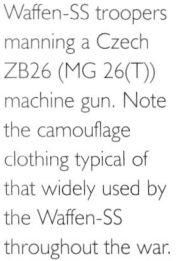

Waffen-SS troopers manning a Czech ZB26 (MG 26(T)) machine gun. Note the camouflage clothing typical of that widely used by the Waffen-SS throughout the war.

subsequently performed well. Later, Waffen-SS divisions were also employed in the Western theater and generally acquitted themselves well in combat. From September 1939 to May 1945 20–25 percent of Waffen-SS troops were killed in action, and more than 400 Waffen-SS officers were awarded the Knight's Cross (Ritterkreuz). Over the course of the war no fewer than 38 Waffen-SS divisions were formed, and almost a million men of some fifteen nationalities served in these divisions, the only operational theater in which Waffen-SS troops were not used being North Africa.

Despite the legendary fighting reputation gained by the Waffen-SS on the battlefield, its successes were frequently marred by the atrocities perpetrated by certain of its units. On the Eastern Front this was probably inevitable, given the nature of Himmler's statement at the outset of *Barbarossa* that, "This is an ideological battle and a struggle of races. National Socialism is based on the value of our Germanic, Nordic blood – a beautiful, decent, socially equal society. On the other side stands a population of 180 millions, a mixture of races, whose very names are unpronounceable, and whose physique is such that one can shoot them down without pity or compassion. These animals have been welded by the Jews into one religion, one ideology that is called bolshevism."[2] With such invective firmly implanted in their minds, the Waffen-SS set about the destruction of the Soviet Union and its people with an ideological fervour that assumed much of the significance of a crusade. Consequently, although other parts of the German armed forces were by no means blameless in this particular matter, at the end of the war in 1945 the SS as a whole became "the alibi of the German nation", with responsibility for virtually all of the war

# APPENDIX 2
# The Oberkommando des Heeres: Staff Branches and Other Elements

The following information amplifies the outline organizational details shown in the diagram of the OKH in Section 3 of Part IV. Other than where indicated otherwise, it represents the OKH organization as at late 1944 and early 1945, as documented by the Allied intelligence staff in TME-E 30-451 dated 15 March 1945, from which this information has been extracted and reproduced in simplified summary form. Some minor errors of terminology found in the original document have also been corrected.

### Army General Staff (Generalstab des Heeres) and the Central Branch of the General Staff

Located at the OKH forward field headquarters during war, with only a small rear element remaining in Berlin, the Army General Staff personnel were the main advisers to the commander-in-chief on all matters concerning operations, intelligence, supply, organization and policy. The OKH Army General Staff was originally intended to consist of twelve branches (Abteilungen) grouped under five senior general staff officers (Oberquartiermeister). However, the operations function was progressively subsumed into the operations staff of the OKW, while the extent and significance of several other OKH General Staff branch functions also reduced or were transferred to the OKW from early 1942. As the war progressed, some functions were also delegated to other specialist branches within the OKH, while others devolved on to the Germany-based Ersatzheer soon after hostilities commenced.

The breadth of the responsibilities of the Generalstab des Heeres that the OKH had originally intended is evident from a listing of the principal functions of the twelve original Abteilungen of the Generalstab des Heeres in the pre-war period (the number of the responsible Abteilung is shown in brackets):

- Operations, tactical and warfare policy (1).
- Organization and authorized scales of men and equipment (2).
- Intelligence on eastern foreign armies (Soviet Union, lower Balkans, Scandinavia, Africa, Far East; this Abteilung also originally covered the Western Hemisphere until Pearl Harbor and the US entry into the war in December 1941) (3).
- Training within the operational theater (4).
- Transport (5).
- Rear echelon administration (6).
- Military history (7).
- Technical services (8).
- Topography (9).
- Large-scale maneuvers and operational planning (10).
- Military schools and officer training (11).
- Intelligence on western foreign armies (Great Britain, upper Balkans, and (from January 1942) the Western Hemisphere) (12).

Finally, the Central Branch of the General Staff was responsible for the selection, training, posting and promotion of all General Staff Corps officers until March 1943, when this task passed to Branch P3 of the main Army Personnel Office.

### Supply and Administration Groups (Quartiermeister-Gruppen)

A powerful and wide-ranging OKH staff branch headed by the chief of supply and administration (Generalquartiermeister), this organization consisted of a number of supply sections or groups (Gruppen) that dealt with the following functions (the number of the responsible Gruppe is shown in brackets):

- Overall planning and organization of supply to and within the field army, lines of communication and supply, control of service troops not allocated to specific army groups or armies (1).
- Civil affairs policy in the rear areas, including exploitation of resources, evacuation measures, prisoners-of-war, and the collection, control and exploitation of plundered military and non-military matériel (2).
- Coordination and processing of army group and army requisitions for combat supplies and engineer equipment (3).
- Personnel and security matters (IIa).
- Legal administration, jurisprudence and military law in the field (III).
- General administrative matters, including personal equipment, billeting, rations, pay and other financial matters, and the control of administrative personnel throughout the Feldheer (IVa).
- Control of all medical matters and personnel throughout the Feldheer (IVb).
- Control of all veterinary matters and personnel throughout the Feldheer (IVc).
- Control of all mechanical transport maintenance troops throughout the Feldheer and in Germany, as well as for general matters of mechanical transport availability and utilization (V).
- Non-military matters affecting civil administration of occupied areas within theaters of operations ("Section Z", with Gruppe 2 and Gruppe III).
- Control of all general headquarters supply troops (in collaboration with Gruppe 3).
- All matters relating to army postal services in the Feldheer (FP).
- Organization and employment of technical troops in the Feldheer (no Gruppe number was allocated).
- All matters pertaining to the organization and employment of military police in the Feldheer (no Gruppe number was allocated).

### Branch Chiefs attached to the General Staff

The following specialist senior officers were attached to the OKH Army General Staff, representing the combat arms and providing advice to the commander-in-chief on the organization, training,

crimes committed during the Third Reich period devolving directly upon that organization. Indeed, the SS organization taken as a whole – including both the Waffen-SS and the Allgemeine SS – evolved rapidly after 1934 into a dangerous and insidious form of self-contained and militarized internal Nazi state at the very heart of the Greater German Third Reich.

The Waffen-SS was by no means an exclusively German fighting force, for Himmler had always hoped and intended that it would become a racially pure Germanic or Nordic organization, and as such it was often presented on recruiting posters and in literature as a European army to fight the evil of communism. But, as the war drew on, and the numbers of Waffen-SS casualties rose, the organization was forced to admit increasing numbers of non-Germanic, "non-Aryan" personnel – Yugoslavs, Latvians, Estonians, Slovenes, Ukrainians, Romanians, Hungarians, Belorussians, Albanians and Croatians – the last two manning what were predominantly Muslim formations! The designation of Waffen-SS divisions indicated their racial composition, with the "SS-Division" containing only German volunteers, the "SS-Freiwilligendivision" containing ethnic German or Germanic volunteers such as Norwegians, Danes, Netherlanders and Belgians (Walloons), and the "Division der Waffen-SS" containing eastern Europeans. The Waffen-SS divisions[3] that existed during the period 1939–45 included:

These soldiers of the 12th SS-Panzerdivision "Hitler Jugend" pictured on the western front in June 1944 were formidable and highly motivated fighters.

1st SS-Panzerdivision "Leibstandarte SS Adolf Hitler" (LSSAH)
2nd SS-Panzerdivision "Das Reich"
3rd SS-Panzerdivision "Totenkopf"
4th SS-Polizei-Panzergrenadierdivision
5th SS-Panzerdivision "Wiking"
6th SS-Gebirgsdivision "Nord"
7th SS-Freiwilligen-Gebirgsdivision "Prinz Eugen"
8th SS-Kavalleriedivision "Florian Geyer"
9th SS-Panzerdivision "Hohenstaufen"
10th SS-Panzerdivision "Frundsberg"
11th SS-Freiwilligen-Panzergrenadierdivision "Nordland"
12th SS-Panzerdivision "Hitler Jugend"
13th Waffen-Gebirgsdivision der SS "Handschar"
14th Waffen-Grenadierdivision der SS
15th Waffen-Grenadierdivision der SS
16th SS-Panzergrenadierdivision "Reichsführer-SS"
17th SS-Panzergrenadierdivision "Götz von Berlichingen"
18th SS-Freiwilligen-Panzergrenadierdivision "Horst Wessel"
19th Waffen-Grenadierdivision der SS
20th Waffen-Grenadierdivision der SS
21st Waffen-Gebirgsdivision der SS "Skanderbeg"
22nd SS-Freiwilligen-Kavalleriedivision "Maria Theresa"
23rd Waffen-Gebirgsdivision der SS "Kama" (existed in 1944 only)
23rd SS-Freiwilligen-Panzergrenadierdivision "Nederland" (existed in 1945 only)
24th Waffen-Gebirgskarstjägerdivision der SS

25th Waffen-Grenadierdivision der SS "Hunyadi"
26th Waffen-Grenadierdivision der SS
27th SS-Freiwilligen-Grenadierdivision "Langemarck"
28th SS-Freiwilligen-Grenadierdivision "Wallonie"
29th Waffen-Grenadierdivision der SS (existed in 1944 only)
29th Waffen-Grenadierdivision der SS (existed in 1945 only)
30th Waffen-Grenadierdivision der SS
31st SS-Freiwilligen-Panzergrenadierdivision "Böhmen-Mähren"
32nd SS-Panzergrenadierdivision "30. Januar"
33rd Waffen-Kavalleriedivision der SS (existed until early 1945)
33rd Waffen-Grenadierdivision der SS "Charlemagne" (formed early 1945)
34th SS-Freiwilligen-Grenadierdivision "Landstorm Nederland"
35th SS-Polizei-Grenadierdivision
36th Waffen-Grenadierdivision "Dirlewanger"
37th SS-Freiwilligen-Kavalleriedivision "Lützow"
38th SS-Panzergrenadierdivision "Nibelungen"

However, with the exception of the 22nd SS-Freiwilligen-Kavalleriedivision, the divisions numbered from 21st to 38th did not exceed regimental or (in a few cases) brigade strength in practice. Of the remainder, probably no more than ten divisions, including the "Liebstandarte SS Adolf Hitler", "Das Reich", "Totenkopf", "Wiking", "Hohenstaufen", "Frundsberg" and "Prinz Eugen", achieved the status of truly élite fighting formations, being at least as effective as the equivalent first-rate army divisions.

equipment and tactical employment of these arms in the field (amplifying detail is only provided where appropriate):

- Chief Infantry Officer (General der Infanterie).
- Chief of Armored Trains (Kommandeur der Eisenbahn-Panzerzüge).
- Chief Artillery Officer (General der Artillerie).
- Chief of Mapping and Survey (Chef des Kriegskarten und Vermessungswesens).
- Chief Signals Officer (Chef des Heeresnachrichtenwesens).
- Chief Engineer and Fortifications Officer (General der Pionere und Festungen).
- Chief Officer of Smoke/Fog Forces (General der Nebel-truppen).
- Chief of Volunteer Units (General der Freiwilligenverbände). This section or branch was formed in January 1944, from when this officer and his staff dealt with the organization, equipment, training and employment of units formed from Soviet prisoner-of-war volunteers. In 1942 this branch was called General der Osttruppen (Chief of Eastern Forces) with an inspector of the "turkvölkischen Verbände." In 1944, a branch merger created the General der Freiwilligenverbände.
- Chief Army Transportation Officer (Chef des Transportwesens).
- General for Special Employment (Discipline) (General zur besonderen Verwendung). This section or branch was responsible for counter-espionage, discipline, penal matters and legal matters throughout the Feldheer in the field. As such, it overlapped and supplanted aspects of the responsibilities of Supply and Administration Gruppe III.

### Chief Medical Inspector (Heeres-Sanitätsinspekteur)

Directed and advised medical and surgical matters as appropriate within the Feldheer, and controlled medical matters in the Ersatzheer.

### Chief Veterinary Inspector (Veterinärinspekteur)

Directed and advised veterinary matters as appropriate within the Feldheer, and controlled veterinary matters in the Ersatzheer.

### Army Personnel Office (Heerespersonalamt)

Consisted of seven main groups (Amtsgruppen) and branches (Abteilungen) and two special sections, most of which were based with the OKH rear headquarters element in wartime, with a representative presence at the field headquarters to facilitate speedy decision-making on important personnel issues. The Heerespersonalamt dealt only with military personnel and with certain non-military officials who were none the less categorized as military officers. In summary, the Heerespersonalamt dealt with the following matters:

- Amtsgruppe P1 was responsible for all officer records, appointments, postings, promotions and personnel policy. Its seven Abteilungen (numbers shown in brackets) dealt with: policy and inter-service transfers (1); infantry and cavalry officers (2); panzer and supply troops officers (3); artillery and chemical warfare officers (4); engineer and signals officers (5); reserve officers and officers recalled to active duty (6); specialist (e.g., veterinary, medical, ordnance, mechanical maintenance) officers (7), until the responsibility for this particular category of officers passed to Amtsgruppe P6 in early 1944.
- Amtsgruppe P2 was responsible for officer education and welfare, including (from August 1942) the ideological – or political – training of officers. Its three Abteilungen (numbers shown in brackets) dealt with: policy, education, officer corps honor issues, political matters, and any non-specific issues affecting senior officers (1); final decisions on individual officers concerning behavior, courts-martial and breaches of the code of honor (2); officer representations and complaints, Aryan ancestry issues, marriage, welfare and related matters concerning officers and their families (3).
- Heeres-Personalabteilung P3 was responsible for the selection, training, posting and promotion of all General Staff Corps officers (in place of the Army General Staff Central Branch from March 1943).
- Heeres-Personalabteilung P4 was responsible for officer replacements and related policy directives.
- Heeres-Personalabteilung P5 was responsible for decorations and awards.
- Amtsgruppe P6 was formed in May 1944, taking on the responsibility for the specialist officers formerly administered by Amtsgruppe P1. It now also dealt with administrative officers (Intendanten) and judge advocates (Wehrmachtsrichter). Its four Abteilungen (numbers shown in brackets) dealt with: specialist officers (7); general policy and directives concerning those officers administered by the Amtsgruppe (8); other specialist categories of officer and (from May 1944) those former armed forces officials (Wehrmachtbeamten) who had been accorded military officer status (Truppensonderdienst) (9 and 10).
- Heeres-Personalabteilung P7 was formed in October 1944 and was responsible for all army officers employed within Feldheer units under the control of Reichsführer-SS Heinrich Himmler. This principally concerned the Volksgrenadier formations created late in the war.
- Gruppe zbV was a special purpose section responsible for managing the physical distribution of decorations and awards, and for other ceremonial functions.
- The Lehrgänge für höhere Adjutanten administered the Army Personnel Office's in-house six-to-eight-week specialist courses on personnel policy, management and organization provided to senior personnel officers.

### Chief of Army Equipment and Commander of the Replacement Army (Chef der Heeresrüstung und Befehlshaber des Ersatzheeres)

A powerful and wide-ranging organization that dealt within Germany – the "zone of the interior" – with personnel conscription, replacement and training; procurement, storage and provision of equipment; and the military administration of the territory, including control of the OKH rear headquarters elements (apart from the Army Personnel Office). Originally intended to be the deputy to the army commander-in-chief in wartime, the post of Chef der Heeresrüstung und Befehlshaber des Ersatzheeres became even more significant when Hitler dismissed Generalfeldmarschall von Brauchitsch in December 1941 and assumed direct command of the armed forces. However, the Ersatzheer came increasingly under SS control after Himmler was appointed its commander by Hitler, following the failed July 1944 assassination attempt against the Führer; in the wake of which its former army commander, General Fromm, was executed in March 1945.

### General Army Office (Allgemeines Heeresamt)

In practice the secretariat and coordinating organization for the OKH, miscellaneous branches and inspectorates, and various agencies in the Feldheer and within Germany including direct support for the commander of the Ersatzheer.

### Staff (Stab)

Approved and issued publications such as manuals, equipment and organization tables, army regulations, clothing and uniform directives, and technical publications.

### Inspectorates (Inspektionen) of Arms and Service Branches (Waffenabteilungen)

The separate OKH inspectorates included those for the infantry, horse riding and driving, artillery, anti-aircraft artillery, engineers, fortifications engineers, panzer troops (transferred to a separate newly-created panzer troops inspectorate after 1943), signals (with three sub-branches), supply, chemical warfare and air raid protection, railway engineers, technical troops, motor transport (with two sub-branches), medical (with three sub-branches), veterinary and ordnance. Arms inspectors in the OKH were usually accorded the title "General der …"

### General Troop Matters (Amtsgruppe Ersatzwesen und Allgemeine Truppenangelegenheiten)

Had a similar role to that of the Army Personnel Office, but dealt with enlisted personnel issues, policies and directives as opposed to those for officers. Its work was conducted on a general basis, rather than dealing with individuals. It had three sub-branches. The first dealt with all aspects of the regulations for troop postings, promotions, welfare, personal issues, non-commissioned officer matters, penal affairs and German prisoners-of-war held by the Allies. The second was responsible for army chaplains. The third dealt with requisitioning accommodation and training areas for military use.

### Army Judge Advocate General's Group (Amtsgruppe Heeresrechtswesen)

The Judge Advocate's branch and a supporting legal staff section.

### Unit Deactivation Staff (Abwicklungsstab)

A special-purpose staff element created in 1943 to resolve the affairs (including any residual financial matters) of the units destroyed with the German 6th Army at Stalingrad at the beginning of that year. It also dealt similarly with the units of Heeresgruppe Afrika and the Afrikakorps after their surrender to the Allies in May 1943. From mid-1944 this staff element assumed responsibility for deactivating army units destroyed in any theater of operations.

### Demobilization Branch (Abteilung Demobilisierung)

Dealt with policies and directives concerning projected demobilization issues and associated arrangements.

### Chief of Army Museums (Chef der Heeresmuseen)

Responsible for policy and providing direction affecting army museums.

### Chief of Training in the Replacement Army (Chef des Ausbildungswesens im Ersatzheer)

This important post was created in October 1942, with the incumbent immediately subordinate to the commander of the Ersatzheer. Through and assisted by the inspectors of arms and services, the Chef des Ausbildungswesens im Ersatzheer was responsible for controlling all training conducted within the Ersatzheer apart from that of the specialist medical, veterinary, ordnance and motor maintenance troops. The principal subordinate arm and service inspectors were those for the infantry, horse riding and driving troops, artillery troops, anti-aircraft troops, engineers and railway engineers, construction troops, signals troops, supply troops and chemical troops.

### Training Film Branch (Abteilung Lehrfilm)

Controlled the production, distribution and archiving of army training films and the training of film projectionists and production staff.

### Army Ordnance Office (Heereswaffenamt)

This sizeable office comprised eight major groups, most of which controlled numerous sub-sections and branches, and it had overall responsibility for the design, testing, development, proving and acceptance of all ordnance equipment. Its staff cooperated closely with the ministry of armament and war production (Reichsministerium für Bewaffnung und Kriegsproduktion), which also maintained representatives at the Heereswaffenamt.

The sub-sections and branches of the Central Group (Zentral-Amtsgruppe des Heereswaffenamts) dealt with organizations, administration, plant efficiency, regulations, ordnance premises and their security.

The many separate branches of the Development and Testing Group (Amtsgruppe für Entwicklung und Prüfung) dealt with all types of ballistic ammunition, infantry weapons and equipment, artillery weapons and equipment, engineer and railway engineer equipment, fortress engineer equipment, panzer and motorized equipment, signals equipment, optical survey, meteorological, artillery fire control, and cartographic printing equipment, gas (chemical warfare) protection research and equipment, special equipment (such as some of the V-weapons developed late in the war), and the control of the various proving grounds on areas under military control (such as military training and maneuver areas).

The Group for Weapons and Equipment Manufacture (Amtsgruppe für Industrielle Rüstung – Waffen und Gerät) dealt with all ordnance material except ammunition, including placing orders with industry. Its seven separate branches comprised those that dealt with general equipment (including medical and veterinary), weapons, engineer, railway engineer and fortress engineer equipment, tanks and tractors, signals equipment, optical and precision instruments, and motor vehicle equipment.

The Group for Ammunition Manufacture (Amtsgruppe für Industrielle Rüstung (Munition)) comprised five branches, each dealing with separate aspects or natures of ammunition manufacture and procurement.

The Acceptance Group (Amtsgruppe für Abnahme) had three sub-branches responsible for ensuring that all ordnance material met the required specifications and subsequently for accepting it into army service.

The Chief Ordnance Engineer Group (Amtsgruppe Chefingenieur) controlled six branches, each of which dealt with the technical design, development and manufacture of various types of ordnance equipment.

The Group for Anti-aircraft Artillery Development (Amtsgruppe für Flakentwicklung) controlled five branches, each of which dealt with a separate aspect of anti-aircraft artillery defense.

The Ordnance Research Branch (Forschungsabteilung) carried out or directed additional research tasks as and when required.

### Army Administration Office (Heeresverwaltungsamt)

The Heeresverwaltungsamt bore overall responsibility for the procurement of pay, rations, accommodation and clothing for the army. Until May 1944 much of this work was carried out by uniformed armed forces officials (Wehrmachtbeamten), but from that date these (together with the army judge advocates) were re-categorized as special duty troops (Truppensonderdienst) and accorded military officer status – being administered thereafter by the army Personnel Office, although their duties with the Heeresverwaltungsamt continued as before. This office comprised five main groups, each with various sub-sections, branches and departments:

- The Group for Officials and Civilian Workers (Amtsgruppe Allgemeine Heeresbeamten-, Angestellen-, Arbeiter- und Kassenangelegenheiten) had seven branches and dealt with salaries, terms of employment, financial accounting and administration of these personnel.
- The Group for Real Estate, Agriculture and Forests (Amtsgruppe Liegenschaften, Land- und Forstwirtschaft) had three branches, which dealt with the procurement of garrison real estate and quartering, the administration of maneuver areas, and army forestry matters.
- The Rations and Procurement Group (Amtsgruppe Heeresverpflegungs- und Beschaffungswesen) had three branches, each dealing with various aspects of ration procurement, inspection and supply.
- The Construction Group (Amtsgruppe Bau) had two branches and these together dealt with matters affecting all army construction activities.
- The Budget Group (Amtsgruppe Haushalts- und Besoldungswesen) was created within the Heeresverwaltungsamt in February 1944, when the overall responsibility for army pay, general finance and budgetary matters was removed from the commander of the Ersatzheer. The group included four sub-branches.

### Inspector General for Potential Officers and Non-commissioned Officers (Generalinspekteur für den Führernachwuchs des Heeres)

Originally, this organization and appointment was that of the Inspector of Army Training and Education, before its remit was broadened and its name was changed in March 1944. This important, politically sensitive and influential appointment was subordinate to the commander of the Ersatzheer, and the incumbent was responsible for the recruitment, training, and National Socialist ideological instruction of all potential officers and non-commissioned officers. He also bore responsibility for all officer candidate (i.e., officer cadet) and non-commissioned officer schools, including course content, methods of instruction used and the political training included. To achieve this he controlled four branches:

- The Branch for the Procurement of Leaders (Abteilung Heeresnachwuchs) was placed under the control of this office early in 1944 and represented the army in all matters affecting the procurement of potential leaders.
- The Cadet School Branch (Abteilung Kriegsschulen) administered all the army officer candidate schools.
- The Non-commissioned Officer School Branch (Abteilung Unteroffiziervorschulen u. -schulen) administered all of the army non-commissioned officer schools.
- The appointment of Inspector of Officer Procurement (Inspekteur der Annahmestellen für Offizierbewerber des Heeres) was originally established in 1943 within the Army Personnel Office, and was subsequently transferred to the

Generalinspekteur für den Führernachwuchs des Heeres in 1944. It controlled the officer candidate selection and acceptance centers in each German Wehrkreis.

### Signals Communications Branch (Nachrichten-Betriebsabteilung des Ch H Rüst u. BdE)

Subordinate to the commander of the Ersatzheer, this independent organization comprised a telegraph company, a signals communications exploitation company, a radio transmission center and a telephone operating company.

### Army Raw Materials Branch (Heeres-Rohstoffabteilung)

Subordinate to the commander of the Ersatzheer, this independent agency procured raw materials for the OKH.

### Army Cartographic Service (Heeresplankammer)

Subordinate to the commander of the Ersatzheer, this independent agency held stocks of foreign-area maps and produced all sorts of mapping for OKH as required.

### Army Technical Bureau (Heerestechnisches Büro)

Subordinate to the commander of the Ersatzheer, this independent organization provided specialist engineer expertise to the OKH.

### Women's Auxiliary Corps (Nachrichtenhelferinnen-Einsatzabteilung)

The female members of this corps were organized into battalions (Einsatzabteilung) and deployed to provide communications, administrative and clerical support within the OKH and the higher-level headquarters of the Feldheer and the Ersatzheer.

### National Socialist Guidance Staff of the Army (Nationalsozialistischer Führungsstab des Heeres)

Established in March 1944, the members of this staff organization were attached to the army high command but were directly subordinate to Hitler. Their task was to oversee and control the overall program of National Socialist ideological indoctrination within the army and to develop and issue appropriate directives to National Socialist Guidance Officers (NSFO) assigned to units in the field.

### Führer's Official Military Historian (Der Beauftragte des Führers für die militärische Geschichtsschreibung)

Established in 1942 to record the military history of the war, this appointment was attached to the OKH but remained directly subordinate to Hitler. It controlled five sub-branches, which included the Army Historical Branch (Kriegsgeschichtliche Abteilung des Heeres), Military History Research Institute (Kriegswissenschaftliches Institut), Chief of Army Archives (Chef der Heeresarchive), Chief of Army Libraries (Chef der Heeresbüchereien), and the Captured Documents Exploitation Center (Wehrmacht-Sichtungsstelle).

### Inspector General of Panzer Troops (Generalinspekteur der Panzertruppen)

This most important post and supporting staff organization was established in 1943 when the OKH responsibility for panzer troops was separated from that originally borne by the Chief of Mobile Troops (General der Schnellen Truppen) within the Army General Staff organization. The Generalinspekteur der Panzertruppen was directly subordinate to Hitler but remained attached to the OKH, with responsibility for the organization, training and replacement of all panzer troops – including those of the Waffen-SS and Luftwaffe panzer units. To fulfil this extensive remit there were four branches:

- Chief Anti-tank Officer for All Arms (General der Panzerabwehr aller Truppen), who was appointed in November 1944 with responsibility for anti-tank tactics throughout the Wehrmacht and liaison on panzer matters with the Army General Staff.
- Inspector of Panzer Troops (Inspekteur der Panzertruppen), who (unlike the other OKH arms inspectors) carried out this function independently of the chief of training of the Ersatzheer.
- The Field Army Branch (Abteilung Feldheer) was responsible for liaison between the Generalinspekteur der Panzertruppen and the Feldheer, and for the evaluation and development of the panzer arm's organization, training and tactics in the light of combat experience.
- The Training Branch (Ausbildungs-Abteilung) was created early in 1944, when it assumed responsibility for administering the training of all panzer troops, a function previously carried out by the panzer branch of the General Army Office's Inspectorates of Arms and Services. The Ausbildungs-Abteilung also produced as a training publication a monthly account of the combat experiences of the panzer troops.

# APPENDIX 3
# Waffenfarben
# (Arm or Branch of Service Colors)

| Arm or Branch of Service | Waffenfarbe | Arm or Branch of Service | Waffenfarbe |
|---|---|---|---|
| Infantry | | Smoke (Nebelwerfer) troops<br>Military justice staff | |
| Artillery<br>General Officers<br>Ordnance | | Medical troops<br>Supply officers | |
| Cavalry | | Engineers<br>Pioneers | |
| Panzer (armored) troops<br>Anti-tank units | | Wehrmachtbeamten<br>(Administrative officials) | |
| General Staff officers<br>(OKW and OKH)<br>Veterinary personnel | | Transport and mechanized supply<br>troops | |
| Signals | | Feldgendarmerie<br>(military police)<br>Recruiting personnel | |
| Military clergymen | | Motorized reconnaissance troops | |
| Jäger (rifles, light infantry)<br>Gebirgsjäger (mountain infantry) | | Propaganda troops | |
| Panzergrenadier<br>(armored infantry) | | Specialist officers | |

Only the Waffenfarben of some of the principal arms, branches, organizations and functions are shown. Waffenfarbe appeared on the shoulder straps of the service jacket throughout the war. It was also used as piping on head-dress and as part of the jacket collar insignia, although these particular applications often lapsed during the final years of the conflict. Numerous anomalies and extensions of this complex identification system existed, and it was compounded by the same Waffenfarbe being shared by some units or organizations with unrelated functions. The Waffenfarbe identification system was refined by the use of identifying metal insignia (symbols, numbers or letters) on the service jacket shoulder strap to indicate a particular unit, function or individual specialization.

# APPENDIX 4
# Military Ranks and their US and British Equivalents

| German Army Rank | British Army Equivalent | US Army Equivalent | Waffen-SS Equivalent |
|---|---|---|---|
| **GENERALE (GENERALS)** | | | |
| Generalfeldmarschall | Field Marshal | General of the Army | SS-Oberstgruppenführer |
| Generaloberst | | General | SS-Obergruppenführer |
| General (der Infanterie, Artillerie, Pionere, Panzertruppe, etc.) | General (of the arm or branch indicated) | Lieutenant General | SS-Obergruppenführer |
| Generaloberstabs -arzt, -veterinär | General (head of medical or veterinary branch or service) | | |
| Generalstabs -arzt, -veterinär | General (deputy head of medical or veterinary branch or service) | | |
| Generalstabsintendant | Administrative or commissariat (supply services) senior commander | | |
| Oberreichskriegsanwalt | Judge Advocate General | | |
| Generalleutnant | Lieutenant General | Major General | SS-Gruppenführer |
| Generalmajor | Major General | Brigadier General | SS-Brigadeführer |
| | Brigadier | | SS-Oberführer |
| **STABSOFFIZIERE (FIELD OFFICERS)** | | | |
| Oberst | Colonel | Colonel | SS-Standartenführer |
| Oberstarzt | Colonel (medical) | | |
| Oberstveterinär | Colonel (veterinary) | | |
| Oberstleutnant | Lieutenant Colonel | Lieutenant Colonel | SS-Oberststurmbannführer |
| Oberfeldarzt | Lieutenant Colonel (medical) | | |
| Oberfeldveterinär | Lieutenant Colonel (veterinary) | | |
| Major | Major | Major | SS-Sturmbannführer |
| Oberstabsarzt | Major (medical) | | |
| Oberstabsveterinär | Major (veterinary) | | |
| **HAUPTLEUTE (CAPTAINS)** | | | |
| Hauptmann | Captain | Captain | SS-Hauptsturmführer |
| Rittmeister (in cavalry and horse-drawn supply units) | Captain | | |
| Stabsarzt | Captain (medical) | | |
| Stabsveterinär | Captain (veterinary) | | |
| **LEUTNANTE (LIEUTENANTS)** | | | |
| Oberleutnant | Lieutenant | First Lieutenant | SS-Obersturmführer |
| Oberarzt | Lieutenant (medical) | | |
| Oberveterinär | Lieutenant (veterinary) | | |
| Leutnant | Second Lieutenant | Second Lieutenant | SS-Untersturmführer |
| Assistenzenarzt | Second Lieutenant (medical) | | |
| Veterinär | Second Lieutenant (veterinary) | | |
| **UNTEROFFIZIERE MIT PORTEPEE (SENIOR NCOS)** | | | |
| Hauptfeldwebel | Warrant Officer Class 1 (Regimental Sergeant Major) | | |
| Stabsfeldwebel | Warrant Officer Class 1 (Staff Sergeant Major) | Master Sergeant | |
| Oberfeldwebel | Warrant Officer Class 1 | Technical Sergeant | SS-Oberscharführer |
| Feldwebel | Warrant Officer Class 2 | | |
| Staff Sergeant | SS-Oberscharführer | | |
| **UNTEROFFIZIERE OHNE PORTEPEE (JUNIOR NCOS)** | | | |
| Fähnrich | Ensign (but, in practice, equivalent to an officer candidate or cadet) | | |

Continued on page 252

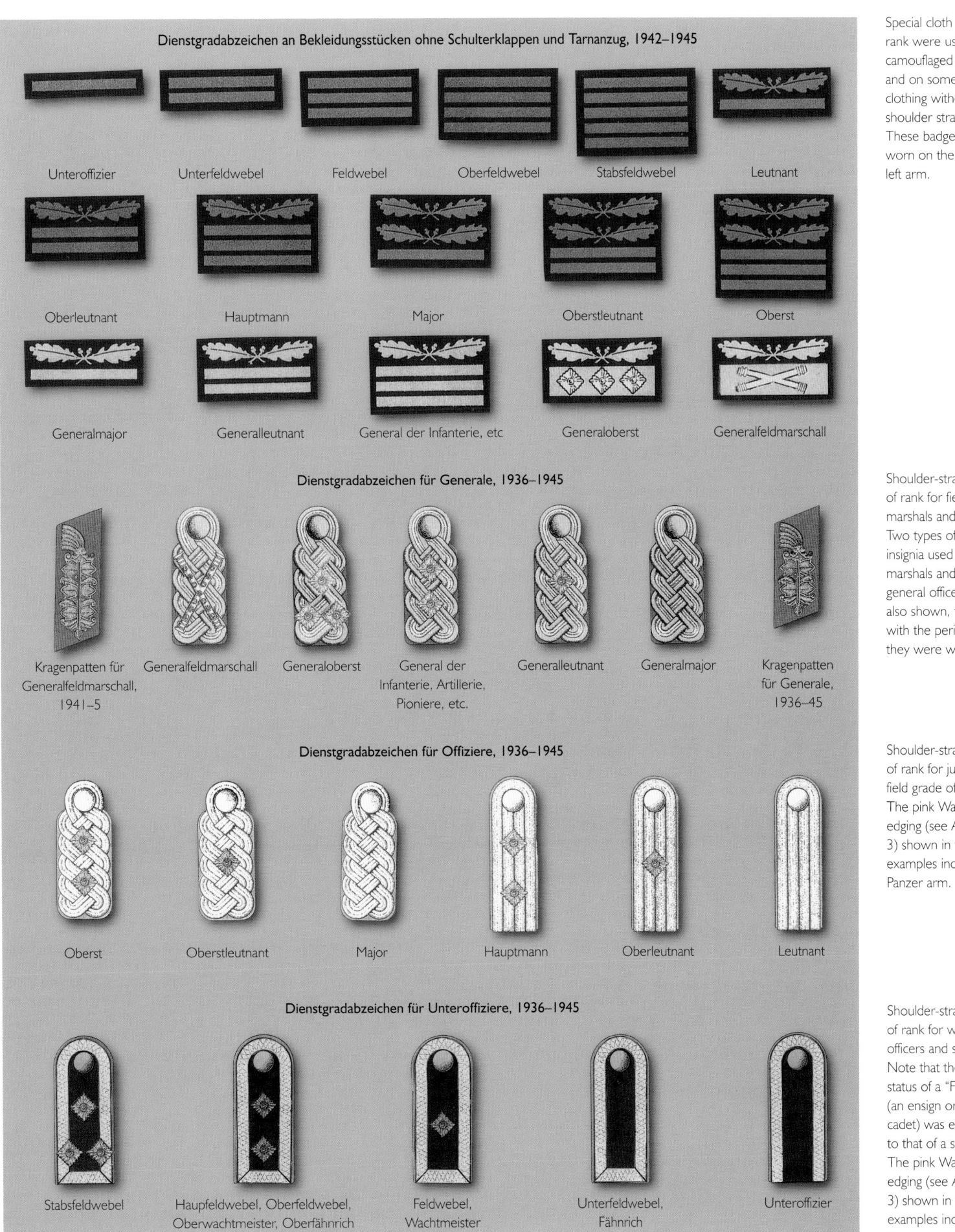

Dienstgradabzeichen an Bekleidungsstücken ohne Schulterklappen und Tarnanzug, 1942–1945

Unteroffizier | Unterfeldwebel | Feldwebel | Oberfeldwebel | Stabsfeldwebel | Leutnant

Oberleutnant | Hauptmann | Major | Oberstleutnant | Oberst

Generalmajor | Generalleutnant | General der Infanterie, etc | Generaloberst | Generalfeldmarschall

Special cloth badges of rank were used on camouflaged clothing and on some other clothing without shoulder straps. These badges were worn on the upper left arm.

Dienstgradabzeichen für Generale, 1936–1945

Kragenpatten für Generalfeldmarschall, 1941–5 | Generalfeldmarschall | Generaloberst | General der Infanterie, Artillerie, Pioniere, etc. | Generalleutnant | Generalmajor | Kragenpatten für Generale, 1936–45

Shoulder-strap badges of rank for field-marshals and generals. Two types of collar insignia used by field-marshals and by general officers are also shown, together with the period that they were worn.

Dienstgradabzeichen für Offiziere, 1936–1945

Oberst | Oberstleutnant | Major | Hauptmann | Oberleutnant | Leutnant

Shoulder-strap badges of rank for junior and field grade officers. The pink Waffenfarbe edging (see Appendix 3) shown in these examples indicates the Panzer arm.

Dienstgradabzeichen für Unteroffiziere, 1936–1945

Stabsfeldwebel | Haupfeldwebel, Oberfeldwebel, Oberwachtmeister, Oberfähnrich | Feldwebel, Wachtmeister | Unterfeldwebel, Fähnrich | Unteroffizier

Shoulder-strap badges of rank for warrant officers and sergeants. Note that the wider status of a "Fähnrich" (an ensign or officer cadet) was equivalent to that of a sergeant. The pink Waffenfarbe edging (see Appendix 3) shown in these examples indicated the Panzer arm.

| German Army Rank | British Army Equivalent | US Army Equivalent | Waffen-SS Equivalent |
|---|---|---|---|
| **Unteroffiziere ohne Portepee (Junior NCOs)** *continued* | | | |
| Unterfeldwebel (in infantry, engineer, motorized supply, panzer and smoke (chemical warfare) units) | Sergeant | Sergeant | |
| Unteroffizier | Sergeant (junior or Lance Sergeant) | Corporal | SS-Unterscharführer |
| **Mannschaften (Soldiers)** | | | |
| Stabsgefreiter | Corporal (senior) | Private First Class | |
| Obergefreiter | Corporal | Private First Class | SS-Rottenführer |
| Gefreiter | Lance Corporal | Private First Class | SS-Sturmann |
| Oberschütze | Private (senior) | Senior Private | |
| Schütze, Grenadier, Fusilier, Musketier, Jäger, Reiter, Kanonier, Panzerschütze, Panzergrenadier, Pionier, Funker, Fahrer, Kraftfahrer, Musikerschütze, Sanitätssoldat, Trompeterreiter, Beschlagschmied-schütze, Beschlagschmiedreiter, Soldat, etc. | Private (of various infantry types, light infantry (or rifle),cavalry, artillery, tank crew, armored infantry, engineers, signals, driver (horse-drawn), driver (motorized), musician, medical, cavalry trumpeter, farrier, cavalry farrier) | Private | SS-Grenadier, etc. |

**Notes:**

1. Ranks listed are not exhaustive, especially in respect of the non-commissioned ranks and a number of specialized and special-to-arm functions and appointments.
2. In some cases, no corresponding British army rank existed, so literal translations are also used to describe or clarify some German army ranks.
3. Ranks for army administrative officials (Wehrmachtbeamten) are not shown, apart from the Generalstabsintendant and Oberreichskriegsanwalt. In practice, there were numerous Wehrmachtbeamte ranks or appointments, which were grouped within four classes that broadly approximated to and bracketed the six separate classes of army officer and non-commissioned officer ranks.

4. From time to time between 1935 and 1945, minor changes in army ranks and terminology were made. These were often carried out for presentational or morale reasons and mainly affected the lower ranks. One such example was Hitler's order in November 1942 that all infantrymen apart from Gebirgsjäger and Jäger were henceforth to be termed "Grenadier" instead of "Schütze" in recognition of their contribution to the war. Similarly, armored infantrymen had already been accorded the title "Panzergrenadier" instead of "Panzerschütze". Another example: certain infantrymen of Panzer Corps "Großdeutschland" were designated "Musketier" from November 1944. "Fusilier" was a similar honor title that was conferred upon certain infantry units, and was consequently adopted by their infantrymen.

Badges of rank worn on the upper left arm by senior private soldiers and corporals.

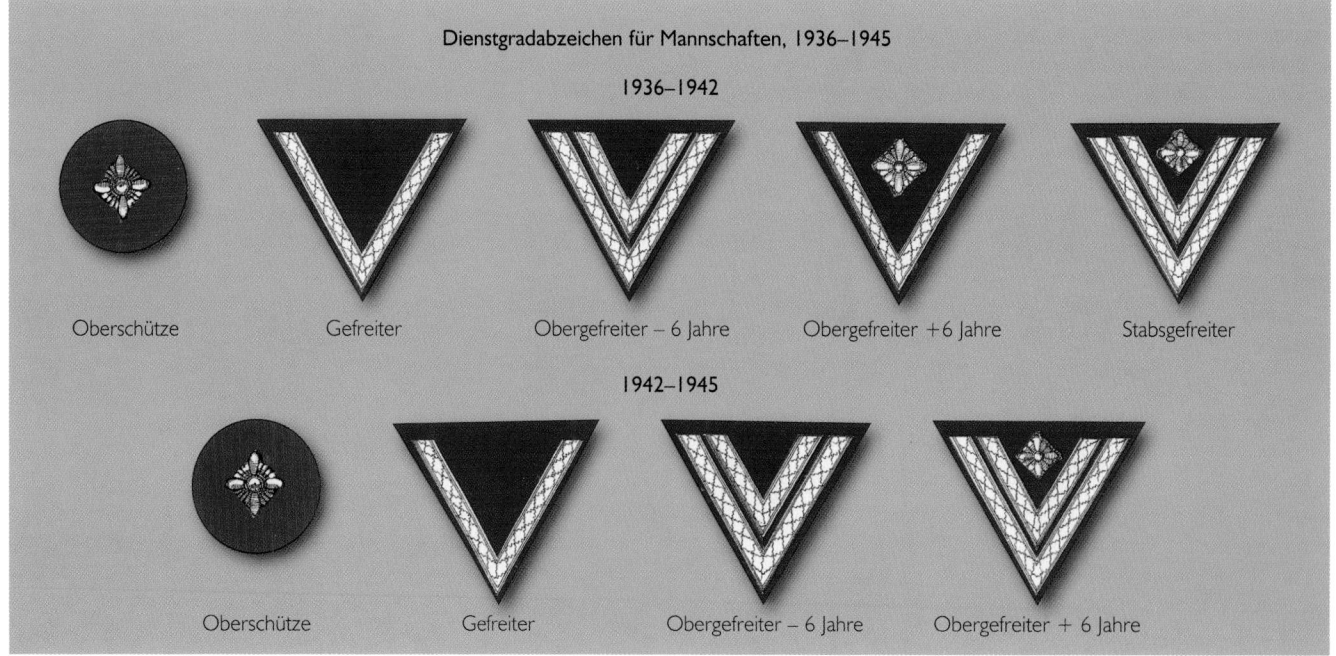

Dienstgradabzeichen für Mannschaften, 1936–1945

1936–1942

Oberschütze    Gefreiter    Obergefreiter – 6 Jahre    Obergefreiter +6 Jahre    Stabsgefreiter

1942–1945

Oberschütze    Gefreiter    Obergefreiter – 6 Jahre    Obergefreiter + 6 Jahre

# APPENDIX 5
# Army Pay and Allowances

**Armed Forces Regular Pay (Wehrmachtbesondung)**
The professional or regular soldier continued to receive his normal or peacetime rate of pay throughout his war service (including any period during which he was a prisoner-of-war). This peacetime rate of pay (Friedenbesoldung) was made up of his basic pay (Grundgehalt) (from which income tax was deducted), an allowance for accommodation (Wohnungszuschlag) and for any dependent children (Kinderzuschlag). In wartime a special deduction (Ausgleichsbetrag) was made from the taxable Friedenbesoldung, and for all ranks above that of Hauptmann this was more or less equivalent to the non-taxable special payment of war service pay (Wehrsold) that was made to all ranks in time of war.

The total adjusted rate of the regular soldier's pay in wartime was termed Wehrmachtbesoldung, which was administered by a

Always a high point of the month, the soldiers' pay was usually issued on a formal pay parade – such as this one in a unit serving in the western theater of operations on 29 November 1939.

suitable garrison pay office and paid directly into the soldier's bank account one month in advance (from January 1945, Wehrmachtbesoldung was paid two months in advance). No additional financial support was provided to the soldier's dependants as part of the Wehrmachtbesoldung, although once he was in receipt of war service pay (in other words, in time of war) this family welfare safeguard applied to him and his family as well.

On discharge, various benefits were paid to all regular officers and soldiers, and these depended primarily upon length of service. In addition to a cash payment, a pension was also admissible in some cases. Additional assistance was provided with job-seeking, entry to civil service employment and land-purchase for agricultural use.

## War Service Pay (Wehrsold)

This was paid tax-free in advance, monthly or at intervals of not less than ten days, to all officers and soldiers by the unit pay staff. An additional allowance was paid direct to the soldier's dependants by the civil authorities, and this continued if the soldier became a prisoner-of-war, although in those circumstances the soldier became non-effective and so payment of the Wehrsold (but not of

| Rank | Regular Pay (Wehrmacht-besoldung) (RM) | Tax Deducted from Regular Pay (RM) | War Service Pay (Wehrsold) (RM) |
|---|---|---|---|
| Generalfeldmarschall | 2,250–2,800 | 985–1,095 | 300 |
| Generaloberst | (not shown) | (not shown) | (not shown) |
| General (der Infanterie, Artillerie, Pionere, Gebirgstruppen, Panzertruppen, etc.) | 1,928 | 738 | 270 |
| Generalleutnant | 1,763 | 660 | 240 |
| Generalmajor | 1,400 | 508 | 210 |
| Oberst | 930 | 313 | 150 |
| Oberstleutnant | 710 | 218 | 120 |
| Major | 593 | 170 | 108 |
| Hauptmann | 428 | 98 | 95 |
| Oberleutnant | 273 | 40 | 80 |
| Leutnant | 200 | 18 | 70 |
| Hauptfeldwebel, Stabsfeldwebel, Oberfeldwebel | 155–175 | 10–15 | 60 |
| Feldwebel | 150–160 | 10 | 53 |
| Unterfeldwebel | 138–158 | 8–10 | 45 |
| Unteroffizier | 114–140 | 1–5 | 40–45 |
| Stabsgefreiter | 78–90 | 0–1 | 35 |
| Obergefreiter, Gefreiter | 78–90 | 0–1 | 35 |
| Oberschütze | 78 | 0 | 35 |
| Schütze, Grenadier, Fusilier, Musketier, Jäger, Reiter, Kanonier, Panzerschütze, Panzergrenadier, Pionier, Funker, Fahrer, Kraftfahrer, Soldat, etc. | 78 | 0 | 30–35 |

the Wehrmachtbesoldung, which included the various specific allowances if applicable) to him ceased. A mechanism also existed for non-regular soldiers to apply for wartime regular rates of pay (Kriegsbesoldung); however, this could result in the loss of any support provided by the civil authorities for his dependants, and so only men with no dependants or who calculated that the Kriegsbesoldung was worth more than this family support would usually apply for this pay rate. Meanwhile, non-regular soldiers who later contracted for regular service were entitled to a one-off bonus payment (Kapitulantenhandgeld) of RM 300.00 for signing on to a twelve-year contract or RM 100.00 for the four-and-a-half-year contract; although by November 1944 such conversions to regular service were already becoming somewhat academic in light of the wider strategic situation.

## Monthly Rates of Pay

The examples of monthly rates of army pay for selected ranks shown in the table are based upon information extracted from a US war department briefing document published in 1945 (TM-E 30-451, dated 15 March 1945), which reflected the situation as at 9 November 1944. The rates are expressed in Reichsmarks (RM) rounded up to the nearest RM 1.00 and are approximate, having been calculated and converted from a November 1944 exchange rate of approximately 1 RM = US $ 0.40. The precise pay rate for an individual officer or soldier depended upon a number of factors; for some grades this included length of service, and so the rate or ranges of rates shown in the table are necessarily indicative rather than definitive.

## Miscellaneous Allowances

For duty journeys all ranks received a quartering allowance plus an incidental expenditure allowance of RM 6.00. As accommodation was provided to regular soldiers free of charge, together with free leave travel, rations and (apart from officers) free clothing, no separate allowance for quarters was admissible. However, non-regular soldiers who were in receipt only of the Wehrsold were also entitled to financial support for their family (who, it was assumed, were still living in their peacetime non-military accommodation).

While soldiers received free clothing, officers were expected to purchase their own uniforms, for which they received a single payment of about RM 450.00 followed by a monthly uniform upkeep allowance of RM 30.00. Meanwhile, the hardships (but not the danger) of front-line service were recognized by a daily payment (Frontzulage) of RM 1.00 to all ranks serving in a combat area.

Although leave travel remained free, and leave was granted quite readily during the early war years, by 1944 the deteriorating operational situation meant that applications for leave generally needed to be extremely well justified – for example, convalescence following wounding or a period of hospitalization.

# Insignia

## TRADE, SPECIALIST AND PROFICIENCY BADGES 1935–1945

 Brieftaubenmeister (pigeon-post master)

 Sanitätsunterpersonel (medical personnel)

 Schirrmeister (motor transport NCO)

 Steuermann (qualified engineer assault boat helmsman)

 Feuerwerker (NCO artificer or ordnance technician)

 Waffenfeldwebel (ordnance warrant officer)

 Truppensattlermeister (troop saddler NCO)

 Festungsbaufeldwebel (fortress construction warrant officer)

 Nachrichtenpersonal (signals communications operators)

 Zahlmeisteranwärter (trainee paymaster)

 Gebirgsjäger (mountain infantry)

 Festungspionierfeldwebel (fortress engineer warrant officer)

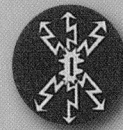 Funkmeister (radio operator)

 Wallfeldwebel (fortifications warrant officer)

 Jäger (light infantry)

 Gerätverwaltungsunteroffizier (supply NCO)

 Kraftzeug, Panzer Warte I, or Kraftzeug, Panzer Warte II (motor or armored vehicle mechanic 1st and 2nd Class), Handwerker (technical artisan), or Vorhandwerker (master technical artisan) – dependent upon the color of the badge edging (the cogwheel (Zahnrad) device being colored pink in every case)

 Zeugmeister (clothing stores NCO)

 Ski-jäger (infantry units qualified and in-role as ski troops)

 Gasschutzunteroffizier (gas or chemical defense NCO)

 Hufbeschlagmeister, Geprüfte Anwärter (candidate farrier)

 Feldgendarmerie (military police)

 Nachrichtenmechaniker (signals communications technician)

 Geprüftes-Hufbeschlagpersonal (qualified farrier)

 Bergführer (mountain guide)

 Hafbeschlag Lehrmeister (farrier instructor)

 Richtabzeichen für Artillerie (Richtkanonier) (artillery gun layer)

 Veterinärpersonal (veterinary personnel)

 Regimentsuntersattlermeister (regimental saddler NCO)

 Richtabzeichen für Nebeltruppen (smoke or multi-barrelled rocket projector [Nebelwerfer] operator)

The prowess and courage of an individual in battle and various forms of specialist combat was recognized by the award of a range of "battle insignia" badges that in many respects equated to and had the status of gallantry medals. These badges were usually of metal and worn on the lower left breast pocket. However, the much-prized "Nahkampfspange" was worn above the pocket on the left breast; the "Panzer-vernichtungsabze-ichen" on the upper right arm; and the "Scharfschützen-abzeichen" on the lower right arm.

## BATTLE INSIGNIA 1939–1945

Scharfschützenabzeichen (sniper badge) – in three classes, for 20, 40, (silver) and 60 (gold) kills

Allgemeines Sturmabzeichen (general assault badge) – for non-infantry and non-Panzer troops engaged in at least three entirely seperate assaults, with further grades of the badge recognizing engagement in 25, 50, 75 and 100 separate assaults

Infanterie-Sturmabzeichen (infantry asssault badges) – for infantrymen engaged in at least three entirely separate assaults

Panzerkampfabzeichen (tank battle badge) – for Panzer crewmen engaged in at least three entirely separate assaults – a silver badge for tank crewmen and a bronze badge for non-tank crew-men and with further grades of the badge recognizing engagement in 25, 50, 75 and 100 separate assaults

Heeres-Flakkampfabzeichen (army anti-aircraft battle badge) – for anti-aircraft, sound detector and searchlight crews based upon vari-ous criteria and involvement in numbers of anti-aircraft engagements

Bandenkampfabzeichen (anti-partisan battle badge) – in three classes for 20 (bronze), 50 (silver) and 100 (gold) days' action against partisans

Verwundetenabzeichen (wound badge) – in three classes for first wounding (black), for three wounds or a serious or partially disabling wound (silver) and for five wounds or a severely disabling wound (gold)

Verwundetenabzeichen 20 Juli 1944 (wound badge for personnel wounded in the explosion at Hitler's headquarters, 20 July 1944) – in three classes, black, silver, and gold and silver

Panzervernichtungsabzeichen (tank destruction badge) – in two classes, for single tanks destroyed (silver) and for five tanks destroyed (gold)

Tieffliegerverichtungsabzeichen (aircraft destruction badge) – in two classes, for single aircraft destroyed (silver) and for five aircraft destroyed (gold)

Nahkampfspange (close combat clasp) – in three classes for 15 (bronze), 30 (silver) and 50 (gold) days engaged in close combat fighting

# APPENDIX 7
# Weapons and Equipment

| Pistols | | | | |
|---|---|---|---|---|
| Weapon | Caliber | Maximum Effective Range | Ammunition | Remarks |
| Self-loading Pistol 08 (Luger) | 9mm | 100 meters | 9mm Parabellum in 8-round magazine | First manufactured under the name "Borchardt-Lüger". A butt (shoulder stock) was also available and could be fitted for longer-range fire up to about 200 meters. |
| Self-loading Pistol P38 (Walther) | 9mm | 100 meters | 9mm in 8-round magazine | Double-action weapon. |
| Self-loading Pistol PPK S.L. (Walther) | 7.65mm | 100 meters | 7.65mm in 7-round magazine | In service use 1939–45, but often purchased privately. |
| Self-loading Pistol 3A (Walther) | 7.65mm | 100 meters | 7.65mm in 7-round magazine | In service use 1939–45, but often purchased privately. |
| Self-loading Pistol (Sauer) | 7.65mm | 100 meters | 7.65mm in 8-round magazine | In service use 1939–45, but often purchased privately. |
| Self-loading Pistol (Mauser) | 7.63mm | 100 meters | 7.63mm in 10- or 20-round magazine | A World War I weapon issued with a wooden holster that could be fitted as a butt (stock) for longer-range fire up to about 200–300 meters. Capable of single-shot and automatic fire. |
| Grenade Pistol (Kampfpistole) (Walther) | 27mm | 100 meters | HE and smoke grenades, and signal cartridges | A modified version of this weapon (Sturmpistole) also allowed it to fire a small-caliber anti-armor grenade. |
| Signal Pistol (Leuchtpistole) (Walther) | 26.7mm | 75–100 meters | Colored light and illuminating cartridges, and a whistling gas- warning cartridge (Pfeifpatrone) | A modified version of this weapon (Sturmpistole) also allowed it to fire a small-caliber anti-armor grenade. |
| Double-barrel Signal Pistol (Walther) | 26.7mm | 75–100 meters | Colored light and illuminating cartridges, and a whistling gas- warning cartridge (Pfeifpatrone) | Either one or both barrels could be fired simultaneously. |

| Rifles | | | | |
|---|---|---|---|---|
| Weapon | Caliber | Maximum Effective Range | Ammunition | Remarks |
| Rifle Type Kar 98K (Mauser) | 7.92mm | 600 meters | 7.92mm ball or armor-piercing in 5-round box magazine | Bolt-operated. Sighted to 2,000 meters, with maximum range 3,000 meters. Also used as a sniper rifle. Bayonet fitted as required. |
| Rifle Type G98/40 (Mauser) | 7.92mm | 600 meters | 7.92mm ball or armor-piercing in 5-round box magazine | Bolt-operated. Sighted to 2,000 meters, with maximum range 3,000 meters. Also used as a sniper rifle. Bayonet fitted as required. Introduced October 1941. |
| Self-loading Rifle Type G41M (Mauser) | 7.92mm | 600 meters | 7.92mm ball or armor-piercing in 10-round magazine containing two 5-round clips | Self-loading, gas-operated. Sighted to 1,200 meters. Also used as a sniper rifle. Bayonet fitted as required. |
| Self-loading Rifle Type G41W (Walther) | 7.92mm | 600 meters | 7.92mm ball or armor-piercing in 10-round magazine containing two 5-round clips | Self-loading, gas-operated. Sighted to 1,200 meters. Also used as a sniper rifle. Bayonet fitted as required. |
| Self-loading Rifle Type Kar 43K (also known as the G43) | 7.92mm | 600 meters | 7.92mm ball or armor-piercing in 10-round magazine containing two 5-round clips | Self-loading, gas-operated. Sighted to 1,200 meters. Also used as a sniper rifle. Bayonet fitted as required. Developed from G41W. |

*Continued*

| Rifles (continued) | | | | |
|---|---|---|---|---|
| Weapon | Caliber | Maximum Effective Range | Ammunition | Remarks |
| Assault Rifle Fallschirmjägergewehr FG 42 | 7.92mm | 600 meters | 7.92mm in a 20-round box magazine mounted horizontally on the left side of the weapon | Automatic and single shot. Sighted to 1,200 meters. Spike bayonet and folding bipod fitted for use when required. Also used as a sniper rifle. Designed originally for use by Luftwaffe airborne (parachute) infantry forces. |
| Assault Rifle MP 43 | 7.92mm | 300 meters | 7.92mm in a 30-round curved magazine | Single shot and automatic. Sighted to 800 meters. The MP 44 was the production model of the MP 43, a superior type of assault rifle (Sturmgewehr) rather than a submachine gun, despite the "MP" designation. Could be fitted with a grenade launcher when required. A curved barrel attachment also allowed the MP 44 to fire around corners or from within "closed-down" tanks. Ammunition for both rifles was the 7.92mm short (Kurz) or "intermediate" round, developed specifically for this weapon. |
| Assault Rifle MP 44 (also known as the Kar K44) | 7.92mm | 300 meters | 7.92mm in a 30-round curved  magazine | |

| Submachine guns | | | | |
|---|---|---|---|---|
| Weapon | Caliber | Maximum Effective Range | Ammunition | Remarks |
| MP 18 (Bergmann) | 9mm | 200 meters | 9mm Parabellum in a 32-round magazine | Also known as the MP 18/I, first introduced in 1918. Single shot and automatic. In army use until 1943. Sighted to 1,000 meters. Originally based on designs of Hugo Schmeisser. |
| MP 28 (Schmeisser) | 9mm | 300 meters | 9mm Parabellum in a 32-round magazine | Single shot and automatic. Sighted to 1,000 meters. |
| MP 28 (Steyr-Solothurn) | 9mm | 300 meters | 9mm Parabellum in a 30-round magazine | Single shot and automatic. Sighted to 500 meters. |
| MP 34 (Bergmann) | 9mm | 200 meters | 9mm Parabellum in a 32-round magazine | Single shot and automatic. Sighted to 1,000 meters. |
| MP 34 (Erma) | 9mm | 300 meters | 9mm Parabellum in a 32-round magazine | Single shot and automatic. Sighted to 1,000 meters. Produced by Erma-Werke at Erfurt. |
| MP 38 (Beretta) | 9mm | 300 meters | 9mm Parabellum in a 10, 20 or 40-round magazine | Single shot and automatic. Sighted to 500 meters. |
| MP 38/42 (Beretta) | 9mm | 300 meters | 9mm Parabellum in a 10, 20 or 40-round magazine | Single shot and automatic. Sighted to 500 meters. |
| MP 38 | 9mm | 200 meters | 9mm Parabellum in a 32-round magazine | Automatic fire only. Fitted with a folding stock. Sighted to 200 meters. Designed by Hugo Vollmer, and commonly but incorrectly known as the 'Schmeisser'. |
| MP 40 | 9mm | 200 meters | 9mm Parabellum in a 32-round magazine | Automatic fire only. Fitted with a folding stock. Sighted to 200 meters. Developed from the MP 38 and originally intended for use by airborne troops, but soon taken into general and widespread use. Became one of the best known small-arms of the war, and also commonly but incorrectly known as the "Schmeisser". A double-magazine version was produced in 1943. |
| MP 3008 (Neumünster) | 9mm | 100–200 meters | 9mm Parabellum in a 32-round magazine | A mass-produced, low-cost copy of the British Sten gun, intended primarily for home defense units in the closing months of the war; relatively few were actually manufactured. Probably not used by the army apart from Volkssturm and possibly some Volksgrenadier troops. |
| EMP 44 | 9mm | 75–150 meters | 9mm Parabellum, with a double 32-round magazine capacity | An unsophisticated, mass-produced, low-cost weapon designed for use in close-quarter combat by troops with minimal training (such as the Volkssturm) and intended primarily for home defense units in the closing months of the war; few, if any, were manufactured. |

## Anti-tank and Grenade Rifles

| Weapon | Caliber | Maximum Effective Range | Ammunition | Remarks |
|---|---|---|---|---|
| Anti-tank rifle PzB 38 | 7.92mm | 100 meters (30mm armor); 300 meters (25mm armor) | 7.92mm armor-piercing, tracer and tear gas capsule, with each round loaded individually | |
| Anti-tank rifle PzB 39 | 7.92mm | 100 meters (30mm armor) 300 meters (25mm armor) | 7.92mm armor-piercing, tracer and tear-gas capsule round, with each composite round loaded individually | A slightly improved development of the PzB 38. |
| Grenade rifle Grb 39 | 7.92mm | Up to 250 meters | Two types of hollow-charge anti-tank grenades and an anti-personnel grenade, fired using a special "bulleted blank" 7.92mm cartridge | Converted from a pre-war type of anti-tank rifle and fitted with a standard-size rifle grenade discharger cup. |

## Hand and Rifle Grenades

| Weapon | Caliber | Maximum Effective Range | Ammunition | Remarks |
|---|---|---|---|---|
| Hand grenade (stick type) (Stielhandgranate) Types 24, 43 and variants, plus Types 39 and 39B smoke grenades and all-wood and combined wood and concrete types | — | Up to 50 meters, dependent upon the strength and skill of the grenade thrower | HE (blast or fragmentation) and smoke versions, plus a separate metal fragmentation collar that could be fitted to enhance lethality | Fuse delay options from 4 to 7 seconds dependent on type. Ignition systems varied, including pull cords and friction strikers. Multiple grenades could also be combined to construct improvised demolition charges or wire-cutting demolition charges. |
| Hand grenade (egg type) (Eierhandgranate) Types 39 (HE) and 42 (smoke) | — | Up to 25 meters, dependent upon the strength and skill of the grenade thrower | Type 39 grenade was HE in a thin sheet-metal casing; Type 42 smoke grenade was filled with smoke-producing compound; smoke emitted from three holes in the casing | Fuse delay 4 to 5 seconds. |
| Hand grenade (glass) Types 1H and 2H (smoke) | — | Up to 25 meters, dependent upon the strength and skill of the grenade thrower | Titanium chloride (Type 1H) or titanium chloride and calcium chloride (Type 2H) | For use against bunkers, cellars and vehicles. The Type 2H was specifically designed for use in low humidity, and temperatures down to minus 40 degrees centigrade. |
| Hand grenade anti-tank, hollow-charge Type 1L | — | Up to 30 meters, dependent upon the strength and skill of the grenade thrower | Shaped, HE hollow-charge | Fin-stabilized once thrown, so that the charge strikes the armored vehicle at the correct angle. Exploded on impact. |
| Rifle grenades, including anti-personnel, anti-tank, hollow-charge, parachute illuminating and propaganda (leaflet-carrying) | — | 100–250 meters for most practical purposes, dependent upon type; one HE anti-personnel type could achieve 700 meters, and the propaganda grenade 500 meters | Propelled by a 7.92mm blank or (wooden) "bulleted blank" cartridge dependent upon type, and fired from a standard rifle grenade discharger cup | Numerous types and variants, including HE anti-personnel type that could also be hand-thrown (with 4.5 second delay fuse). Anti-tank hollow-charge versions armed on launch and exploded on impact, penetrating about 30mm of armor. |

## Anti-tank Rocket Launchers

| Weapon | Caliber | Maximum Effective Range | Ammunition | Remarks |
|---|---|---|---|---|
| Panzerschreck 54 (also known as the Raketen Panzerbüchse 5) | 88mm | 100 meters | Hollow-charge HE rocket, penetrating 100 mm of armor | Copied from the US Army bazooka rocket launcher. A fitted metal shield protected the firer's face from the rocket's significant back-blast on firing. |

*Continued*

| Anti-tank Rocket Launchers (continued) | | | | |
|---|---|---|---|---|
| Weapon | Caliber | Maximum Effective Range | Ammunition | Remarks |
| Type 43 (also known as the Püppchen) | 88mm | 500 meters | Hollow-charge HE rocket, penetrating 100 mm of armor | A heavy, longer range, version of the Panzerschreck sighted to 700 meters, mounted on a basic two-wheel gun carriage fitted with a protective shield. Unlike the Panzerschreck, it employed a base cap which, rather as a shell or cartridge case, had to be cleared from the breech after firing. Entered service in late 1944, but not on the large scale originally intended. A follow-on, improved version of the Püppchen, the Panzertod ("Panzer Death"), firing a 105mm rocket, was under development in 1945 but never entered service. |
| Panzerfaust (Faustpatrone) Types 30, 40, 60 and 100 | 44mm | 100 meters; 150 meters for the Type 100 | Hollow-charge HE grenade, fin-stabilized and rocket-propelled, penetrating up to 200mm of armor | Early safety problems with the Type 30 were speedily overcome in subsequent types. A simple, cheap, disposable and very effective infantry anti-armor weapon for use at close range. |

| Flame Throwers | | | |
|---|---|---|---|
| Weapon | Maximum Effective Range | Application of Fire | Remarks |
| Type 35 | 40 meters | 10–12 second discharge (in 2–3 second bursts) | Usually operated by assault engineers, but could also be operated by non-engineer combat troops. Fuel contained in a single cylindrical back-pack. |
| Type 40 | 40 meters | 8 seconds discharge (in 2–3 second bursts) | Usually operated by assault engineers, but could also be operated by non-engineer combat troops. Fuel back-pack configured in a "lifebuoy" shape. |
| Type 41 | 40 meters | 8 seconds discharge (in 2–3 second bursts) | Usually operated by assault engineers, but could also be operated by non-engineer combat troops. Fuel back-pack consisted of two horizontal cylinders. |
| Type 42 | 40 meters | 8 seconds discharge (in 2–3 second bursts) | Usually operated by assault engineers, but could also be operated by non-engineer combat troops. A modified and improved version of the Type 41. |
| Flame thrower, medium | 40 meters | 25 seconds discharge (total) | Usually operated by assault engineers, but could also be operated by non-engineer combat troops. A larger version of the Type 35, mounted on a two-wheeled trolley. |

| machine guns | | | | |
|---|---|---|---|---|
| Weapon | Caliber | Maximum Effective Range | Ammunition | Remarks |
| Light machine gun MG 15 | 7.92mm | 600 meters | 7.92mm in a 75-round saddle-type magazine | Used as an LMG, but also fitted in some armored fighting vehicles. |
| Light machine gun (Bergmann) | 7.92mm | 600 meters | 7.92mm, magazine-fed | Used as an LMG, but also fitted in some armored fighting vehicles. |
| Light machine gun ZB 26 (Czech) | 7.92mm | 600 meters | 7.92mm in a 30-round top-mounted box magazine | Very similar to the British Bren gun. |
| Light machine gun MG 13 (Dreyse) | 7.92mm | 600 meters | 7.92mm in a 25-round magazine | A World War I-era air-cooled LMG from which the MG 34 was later developed. |
| Light machine gun (Madsen) | 8mm | 600 meters | 8mm in belts | Sighted to 1,000 meters. Single shot and automatic fire. Introduced as an emergency stop-gap measure in 1941 and generally issued only to garrison or home defense units. |
| General purpose machine gun MG 34 | 7.92mm | 2,000 meters (LMG role), 3,800 meters (MMG role), maximum 5,000 meters | 7.92mm ball, armor-piercing, semi-armor-piercing, and tracer in 50-round metal disintegrating link belts or 50-round drum box magazine | Sophisticated, finely machined, air-cooled weapon, which could not readily be mass-produced. Single shot and automatic fire. Could be used in the LMG role firing from a bipod or in the MMG/HMG role with a tripod or as single or multiple anti-aircraft guns when fitted on to the appropriate mounting. Many were also fitted as armored fighting vehicle machine guns. |

*Continued*

| machine guns (continued) | | | | |
| --- | --- | --- | --- | --- |
| Weapon | Caliber | Maximum Effective Range | Ammunition | Remarks |
| General purpose machine gun MG 42 | 7.92mm | 2,000 meters (LMG role), 3,800 meters (MMG role), maximum 5,000 meters | 7.92mm ball, armor-piercing, semi-armor-piercing, and tracer in 50-round metal disintegrating link belts | A relatively cheap and mass-produced but very effective general purpose machine gun, although wasteful of ammunition with its high rate of fire (900–1,200 rpm). Automatic fire only. Could be used in the LMG role firing from a bipod or in the MMG/HMG role with a tripod or as single or multiple anti-aircraft guns when fitted on to the appropriate mounting. One of the best known machine guns of the war. |

| Mortars | | | | |
| --- | --- | --- | --- | --- |
| Weapon | Caliber | Maximum Effective Range | Ammunition | Remarks |
| Light mortar Type 36 | 50mm | 520 meters | HE only | Rate of fire about 12 to 20 rpm. |
| Light mortar (automatic) | 50mm | 750 meters | HE only in 6-round clips | A longer version of the Type 36, with a power-operated loader. Only deployed emplaced in special concrete turrets within fixed defensive positions. |
| Medium mortar Type 34 | 81mm | 2,500 meters | HE, smoke, airburst, target indicating | Range achieved was dependent upon the charge used (main charge to 500 meters, charge 1 to 1,000 meters, charge 2 to 1,500 meters, charge 3 to 2,000 meters, charge 4 to 2,500 meters). Rate of fire about 10–12 rpm. Operated by an NCO and five men. |
| Medium mortar Type 42 | 81mm | 1,200 meters | HE, smoke, airburst, target indicating | A shortened version of the Type 34, designed for greater portability. Maximum range achieved with HE using charge 2. |
| Heavy mortar Type 42 | 120mm | 6,600 meters | HE only (four types of HE projectile) | Mounted on a two-wheeled carriage. |
| Medium (smoke) mortar 105mm Type 35 (105mm Nebelwerfer 35) | 105mm | 3,000 meters | HE, smoke and chemical munitions | A larger version of the Type 34. |
| Medium (smoke) mortar 105mm Type 40 (105mm Nebelwerfer 40) | 105mm | 6,170 meters | HE, smoke and chemical munitions | Breech-loading. Mounted on a two-wheeled carriage. |

| Infantry Close Support Guns | | | | |
| --- | --- | --- | --- | --- |
| Weapon | Caliber | Maximum Effective Range | Ammunition | Remarks |
| Infantry light gun leIG 18 | 75mm | 3,375 meters | HE and HE hollow-charge shells | Infantry close support gun mounted on a two-wheeled gun carriage with pneumatic-tire wheels or wooden-spoke wheels, a split trail, and either with or without a protective shield. Horse-drawn or vehicle-towed. |
| Infantry light gun leIG 37 | 75mm | 5,000 meters | HE and HE hollow-charge shells | Infantry close support gun mounted on a two-wheeled gun carriage with pneumatic-tire wheels, a split trail, and a protective shield. Horse-drawn or vehicle-towed. |
| Infantry light gun leIG 42 | 75mm | 5,000 meters | HE and HE hollow-charge shells | Infantry close support gun mounted on a modified Type 37 gun carriage with an angled protective shield. Horse-drawn or vehicle-towed. |
| Infantry heavy gun sIG 33 | 150mm | 4,700 meters | HE and smoke, also a HE bomb-type projectile for use against minefields and wire obstacles | High- and low-angle fire options. Horse-drawn or vehicle-towed. Mounted on a two-wheeled box trail gun carriage with protective shield. |

## Mountain Infantry Guns

| Weapon | Caliber | Maximum Effective Range | Ammunition | Remarks |
|---|---|---|---|---|
| Mountain light howitzer Geb G 36 | 75mm | 9,150 meters | HE and HE hollow-charge shells | Horse-drawn, sledged, or mule-packed (broke down into eleven parts). No shield fitted. |
| Mountain howitzer Geb H 40 | 105mm | 16,740 meters | HE, smoke, illuminating and HE hollow-charge shells | Horse-drawn, mule-packed, or packed on to a horse-drawn wagon (broke down into nine parts). No shield fitted. |

## Recoilless Guns (Airborne)

| Weapon | Caliber | Maximum Effective Range | Ammunition | Remarks |
|---|---|---|---|---|
| LG 40 | 75mm | 6,800 meters | HE, APCBC (armor-piercing capped ballistic cap), and hollow-charge shells | In service with the Luftwaffe Fallschirmdivision. Mounted on a lightweight split-trail, light metal alloy gun carriage. Could be packed into two air-droppable wicker containers. |
| LG 40 | 105mm | 7,950 meters | HE, and hollow-charge shells | In service with the Luftwaffe Fallschirmdivision. |
| LG 42 | 105mm | 7,950 meters | HE, smoke, HE incendiary and hollow-charge shells | In service with the Luftwaffe Fallschirmdivision. |

# 2. ARTILLERY GUNS

## Dual-role Anti-tank Guns

| Weapon | Caliber | Maximum Effective Range | Ammunition | Remarks |
|---|---|---|---|---|
| Flak 30 | 20mm | 4,700 meters | HE incendiary and armor-piercing (various types, including armor-piercing incendiary) | Anti-aircraft and anti-armor gun. Vehicle towed or self-propelled. 1,000 meters maximum range for effective penetration of armor. |
| Flak 38 | 20mm | 4,700 meters | HE incendiary and armor-piercing (various types, including armor-piercing incendiary) | Anti-aircraft and anti-armor gun. Vehicle towed or self-propelled. A mountain lightweight version (Geb Flak 38) also existed. 1,000 meters maximum range for effective penetration of armor. |
| Flakvierling 38 multiple gun | 20mm | 4,700 meters | HE incendiary and armor-piercing (various types, including armor-piercing incendiary) | Anti-aircraft and anti-armor multiple gun system. Four Flak 38 guns mounted together and carried on a towed trailer or half-track vehicle. Single shot or automatic fire on each gun. 1,000 meters maximum range for effective penetration of armor. |

## Anti-tank Guns

| Weapon | Caliber | Maximum Effective Range | Ammunition | Remarks |
|---|---|---|---|---|
| Pz B 41 | 28mm | 500 meters | HE and armor-piercing | Broke down into a five-man load, carried on a towed trailer, or by air. Split trail gun carriage with protective shield. A variant for use by airborne troops also existed. Caliber also described as '28/20mm' due to the tapered barrel. |
| PAK 35/36 | 37mm | 500 meters | HE and armor-piercing, including an HE hollow-charge armor-piercing stick projectile | Split trail gun carriage with protective shield. |
| PJK 41 | 42mm | 1,000 meters | HE and armor-piercing | Caliber also described as "42/28mm" due to the tapered barrel. Split-trail gun carriage fitted with a double (spaced) armor protective shield. |
| PAK 38 | 50mm | 1,000 meters | HE and armor-piercing | Split-trail gun carriage fitted with solid rubber tires and a double (spaced) armor protective shield. Usually towed by half-track vehicle. Could also be transported by air. |

*Continued*

## Anti-tank Guns (continued)

| Weapon | Caliber | Maximum Effective Range | Ammunition | Remarks |
|---|---|---|---|---|
| PAK 40 | 75mm | 1,800 meters | HE, armor-piercing (various types), HE hollow-charge and smoke | Split-trail gun carriage fitted with solid rubber tires and a double (spaced) armor protective shield. |
| PAK 41 | 75mm | 2,000 meters | HE and armor-piercing | Split-trail gun carriage fitted with a protective shield. Caliber also described as "75/55mm" due to the tapered barrel. |
| PAK 97/38 | 75mm | 1,800 meters | HE, armor-piercing and HE hollow-charge | French 75mm field gun Model 1897 converted for anti-tank use and mounted on the PAK 38 gun carriage. |
| PAK 43 | 88mm | 2,000 meters | HE and armor-piercing (various types) | Electrically fired, semi-automatic gun mounted on a cruciform base. A protective shield was fitted. |
| PAK 43/41 | 88mm | 2,000 meters | HE, armor-piercing (various types) and HE hollow-charge | Split-trail gun carriage fitted with a protective shield. |
| PAK 44 | 128mm | 3,000 meters | Armor-piercing, using tungsten-core munitions in conjunction with a muzzle velocity of more than 4,200 fps | Developed from 1942 and produced in small numbers by Rheinmetall, achieving an armor-piercing capability of 120mm armor at 1,000 meters. However, the rifled barrel life never exceeded 200 rounds and, with Germany's supplies of tungsten also reducing, further development of the gun was abandoned. |
| PAK 36(r) | 76mm | 2,000 meters | HE and armor-piercing (various types) | Russian 76.2mm field guns converted to anti-tank guns. |
| PAK 39 | 76mm | 1,800 meters | HE and armor-piercing (various types) | Russian 76.2mm field guns converted to anti-tank guns. |

## Field Artillery

| Weapon | Caliber | Maximum Effective Range | Ammunition | Remarks |
|---|---|---|---|---|
| leFK 18 | 75mm | 9,425 meters | HE, HE hollow-charge, smoke and armor-piercing | Light field gun, mounted on a split-trail gun carriage with wooden-spoke wheels. |
| leFH 18 | 105mm | 10,675 meters | HE, smoke, incendiary, illuminating, armor-piercing and propaganda (leaflet) shells | Light gun/howitzer, in service throughout the war as the standard divisional field howitzer. Subsequent modifications and improvements were the leFH 18(M) and le FH 18/40. |
| K 18 | 100mm | 19,075 meters | HE and armor-piercing | Standard medium artillery gun throughout the war. Horse- or vehicle-drawn. |
| sK 18 | 105mm | 18,980 meters | HE and armor-piercing | Standard medium artillery gun. Split-trail, two-wheel gun carriage with solid rubber tires and detachable two-wheel bogie. Usually vehicle-drawn. |
| sFH 18 | 150mm | 13,250 meters | HE, armor-piercing, anti-concrete and smoke | Standard divisional medium howitzer. Split-trail, two-wheel gun carriage with solid rubber tires and additional two-wheel detachable bogie or trailer at end of the trails when in transit. Horse- or tractor-drawn. |
| K 18 | 150mm | 24,500 meters | HE, armor-piercing and anti-concrete | Vehicle-towed medium artillery gun. Two-wheel detachable bogie or trailer was fitted at end of the trails when in transit. Vehicle-drawn. |
| K 18 | 170mm | 29,600 meters | HE and armor-piercing | Long-range, vehicle-drawn mobile gun with enhanced 360-degree traverse and speedy into/out of action capability. |
| Mrs 18 | 210mm | 16,700 meters | HE and various anti-concrete munitions | Standard heavy howitzer. Vehicle-drawn. |
| K 38 | 210mm | 32,760 meters | HE | Heavy artillery. Box trail configuration. Transported to gun position in two loads. |
| K 39 | 210mm | 29,850 meters | HE, armor-piercing, semi-armor-piercing and anti-concrete | Heavy artillery. Carriage in three parts on a four-wheeled limber. Modified versions K 39/40 and K 39/41. |
| K 3 | 240mm | 37,500 meters | HE | Heavy artillery. Transported to gun position in five loads. |

## Field Artillery

| Weapon | Caliber | Maximum Effective Range | Ammunition | Remarks |
| --- | --- | --- | --- | --- |
| Mrs Karl | 540mm | 11,830 meters | HE, armor-piercing and anti-fortification | Heavy mortar mounted on a self-propelled tracked gun carriage that could be disassembled into four loads and carried on special multi-wheeled trailers for movement into and out of an operational theater. "Karl" was the mortar type name, but each individual weapon was allocated its own name. |
| Mrs Karl | 600mm | 6,650 meters | HE, armor-piercing and anti-concrete | Heavy mortar mounted on a self-propelled tracked gun carriage that could be disassembled into four loads and carried on special multi-wheeled trailers for movement into and out of an operational theater. "Karl" was the mortar type name, but each individual weapon was allocated its own name. |

## Railway Artillery

| Weapon | Caliber | Maximum Effective Range | Ammunition | Remarks |
| --- | --- | --- | --- | --- |
| K (E) | 150mm | 22,500 meters | HE and anti-concrete | |
| K 12(E) | 210mm | 115,000 meters | HE | |
| KzBr K(E) | 240mm | 29,500 meters | HE | |
| LgBr K(E) | 280mm | 36,600 meters | HE | A longer-barrel version of the KzBr K(E). |
| K 5 (E) | 280mm | 86,500 meters | HE (rocket-assisted shell) | |
| K(E) Siegfried | 380mm | 55,700 meters | HE | |
| K(E) Gustav | 800mm | 47,000 meters | Anti-concrete | |

## Coastal Defense Artillery

| Weapon | Caliber | Maximum Effective Range | Ammunition | Remarks |
| --- | --- | --- | --- | --- |
| SK L/60 | 105mm | 17,500 meters | HE | |
| Tbts C/36 | 150mm | 19,525 meters | HE | |
| SK L/40 | 170mm | 27,200 meters | HE | Permanently emplaced in prepared gun positions within coastal defenses. Some other ammunition options available. |
| SK L/50 | 280mm | 39,100 meters | HE | |
| K Siegfried | 380mm | 55,700 meters | HE | |
| K Adolf | 406mm | 56,000 meters | HE | |

## Self-propelled Artillery

| Weapon | Caliber | Maximum Effective Range | Ammunition | Remarks |
| --- | --- | --- | --- | --- |
| leFH 18/2 Wespe | 105mm | 12,300 meters | About 30 rounds of HE, HE hollow-charge and smoke | 105mm light field howitzer FH 18/2 mounted on the Pz.Kpfw.II tank chassis (Sd.Kfz.124). Five-man crew. |
| Stu.Pz.43 Brummbär | 150mm | 4,500 meters | About 38 rounds of HE, HE hollow-charge and smoke | Short-barrel 150mm sIG 33 howitzer mounted on the Pz.Kpfw.IV tank chassis (Sd.Kfz.166). Five-man crew. Other self-propelled mounts for the 150mm sIG 33 howitzer included the Pz.Kpfw.IB, Pz.Kpfw.II and 38(t) tank chassis. |

*Continued*

## Self-propelled Artillery (continued)

| Weapon | Caliber | Maximum Effective Range | Ammunition | Remarks |
|---|---|---|---|---|
| Hummel | 150mm | 13,250 meters | About 18 rounds of HE, HE hollow-charge and smoke | 150mm field howitzer sFH 18/1 mounted on a modified Pz.Kpfw.IV tank chassis also utilizing PzKpfw.III components (Gw.III/IV Sd.Kfz.165). Six-man crew. In a similar configuration to the Brummbär, 150mm sFH 13 howitzers were also mounted on French Lorraine tank chassis. |
| StuG III K40 (SP assault gun) | 75mm | 2,000 meters | About 54 rounds of HE, armor-piercing (various types), smoke and HE hollow-charge | Close support and assault weapon. Short-barrel 75mm K40 gun mounted on the Pz.Kpfw.III tank chassis (Sd.Kfz.142/1). Four-man crew. Other self-propelled mounts for the 150mm sIG 33 howitzer included the Pz.Kpfw.IB, Pz.Kpfw.II and 38(t) tank chassis. Maximum effective range for penetration of armor 1,000 meters. |
| StuG 38(t) (SP assault gun) | 75mm | 1,800 meters | About 41 rounds of HE, armor-piercing (various types), smoke and HE hollow-charge | Close support and assault weapon. 75mm PAK 39 gun mounted on the 38(t) chassis (PzJ 38(t)). Four-man crew. Maximum effective range for penetration of armor 1,000 meters. |
| PzJ IV (SP assault gun) | 75mm | 1,800 meters | About 79 rounds of HE, armor-piercing (various types), smoke and HE hollow-charge | Close support and assault weapon. 75mm PAK 39 gun mounted on the Pz.Kpfw.IV tank chassis (PzJ IV). Four-man crew. Maximum effective range for penetration of armor 1,000 meters. |
| PzJ IV K42 (SP assault gun) | 75mm | 2,000 meters | About 55 rounds of HE, armor-piercing (various types), smoke and HE hollow-charge | Close support and assault weapon. 75mm K42 (L/70) gun mounted on the Pz. Jäger IV tank chassis (Sd.Kfz.162). Developed from the StuG K40. Five-man crew. Maximum effective range for penetration of armor 1,000 meters. |
| StuG III H42 (SP assault gun) | 105mm | 7,760 meters | About 36 rounds of HE, smoke and HE hollow-charge | Close support and longer-range assault weapon. Fired HE only. 105mm Stu H42 gun mounted on the StuG III chassis (Sd.Kfz.142/2). Four-man crew. |
| PzJ III/IV Nashorn (or Hornisse) (SP assault gun) | 88mm | 2,000 meters | About 48 rounds of HE, armor-piercing (various types), and HE hollow-charge | Anti-tank, close support and assault weapon. 88mm PAK 43/1 gun mounted on a modified Pz.Kpfw.IV chassis also utilizing PzKpfw.III components (Gw.III/IV Sd.Kfz.164). Five-man crew. |
| StuG K43 Elefant (or Ferdinand) (SP assault gun) | 88mm | 2,000 meters | About 90 rounds of HE, armor-piercing (various types), and HE hollow-charge | Anti-tank, close support and assault weapon. 88mm K43 gun mounted on a modified Pz.Kpfw.VI Tiger P tank chassis (Sd.Kfz.184). Six-man crew. |
| Jagdpanther (SP assault gun) | 88mm | 2,000 meters | About 57 rounds of HE, armor-piercing (various types), and HE hollow-charge | Anti-tank and close support weapon. 88mm PAK43/3 or 43/4 gun mounted on the Pz. Jäger V Panther tank chassis (Sd.Kfz.173). Six-man crew. |
| Jagdtiger (SP assault gun) | 128mm | 3,000 meters | About 40 rounds of HE and various armor-piercing | Anti-tank and close support weapon. 128mm PAK 44 gun mounted on the Pz. Jäger VI Tiger B tank chassis (Sd.Kfz.186). Six-man crew. |

## Mobile Anti-aircraft Artillery

| Weapon | Caliber | Maximum Effective Range | Ammunition | Remarks |
|---|---|---|---|---|
| Flak 30 | 20mm | 3,000 meters | HE incendiary, tracer and various armor-piercing | 20mm anti-aircraft gun mounted on various half-tracks, towed trailers and other vehicles. |
| Flak 38 | 20mm | 3,000 meters | HE incendiary, tracer and various armor-piercing | 20mm anti-aircraft gun mounted on a 38(t) tank chassis. |
| Flak 43 Ostwind | 37mm | 4,800 meters | HE incendiary, tracer and armor-piercing (various types, including armor-piercing incendiary) | 37mm anti-aircraft gun mounted on a Pz.Kpfw.IV tank chassis. |

*Continued*

## Mobile Anti-aircraft Artillery (continued)

| Weapon | Caliber | Maximum Effective Range | Ammunition | Remarks |
|---|---|---|---|---|
| Flak 38 Wirbelwind | 20mm | 3,000 meters | HE incendiary, tracer and armor-piercing (various types) | Four 20mm anti-aircraft guns (Flakvierling) mounted together on a Pz.Kpfw.IV tank chassis. |

## Multi-barrel Rocket Launchers

| Weapon | Caliber | Maximum Effective Range | Ammunition | Remarks |
|---|---|---|---|---|
| Nebelwerfer 41 | 150mm | 7,000 meters | HE and smoke rockets, fired from six barrels or tubes | Also capable of firing chemical munitions. Mounted on a split-trail lightweight PAK gun-carriage. Fired electrically from a remote firing position. Ninety seconds required to load and fire six rounds. A single-barrel version also existed for use by airborne troops. |
| Nebelwerfer 42 | 210mm | 7,800 meters | HE rockets, fired from five barrels or tubes | Also capable of firing chemical munitions. Mounted on a split-trail lightweight PAK gun-carriage. Fired electrically from a remote firing position. Ninety seconds required to load and fire five rounds. |
| Panzerwerfer 42 | 150mm | 6,700 meters | HE and smoke rockets, fired from ten barrels or tubes | Also capable of firing chemical munitions. Mounted on various half-track vehicles, including the Klöckner-Humboldt-Deutz armored Maultier chassis and the Büssing-NAG armored half-track. |
| Wurfgerät 40 | 280mm/320mm | 1,900 meters | 280mm HE and 320mm incendiary rockets | Rockets were fired from pre-loaded crates mounted on a wood-frame launch platform. |
| Wurfgerät 41 | 280mm/320mm | 1,900 meters | 280mm HE and 320mm incendiary rockets | Rockets were fired from pre-loaded metal containers mounted on a steel-frame launch platform. |
| Wurfrahmen 40 | 280mm/320mm | 1,900 meters | 280mm HE and 320mm incendiary rockets, fired from six tubes | Rockets were fired from six tubes mounted on a half-track armored vehicle. |
| Nebelwerfer 41 | 280mm/320mm | 1,900 meters | 280mm HE and 320mm incendiary rockets, fired from six tubes | Rockets were fired from six tubes. In transit these were mounted on a framework fitted on to a two-wheeled trailer. The trailer was removed for firing. |
| Nebelwerfer 42 | 300mm | 4,500 meters | HE rockets only, fired from six tubes | Rockets were fired from six tubes. In transit, these were mounted on a framework fitted on to a two-wheeled trailer. The trailer was removed for firing. |

## Notes

1. Anti-aircraft guns were generally manned by the Luftwaffe rather than the army, so only anti-aircraft guns that were also used as anti-tank guns or to provide close and mobile anti-aircraft protection to units of the ground forces at divisional level are shown.

2. The ranges shown for anti-tank guns are the maximum ranges at which a static target might reasonably be engaged. In order to achieve a successful engagement using armor-piercing ammunition against a moving tank, the target would often need to be engaged at much shorter ranges, while the angle of attack and whether the target was front-, rear- or side-on to the attack would also bear directly upon the success of the engagement. Generally, a planning range of 1,000 meters was the maximum distance at which armor could be penetrated by most types of anti-tank round.

3. The ranges shown for artillery guns are the maximum ranges to which they could fire effectively, usually with HE ammunition. Lesser ranges might apply for different natures of ammunition. The ranges shown for SP assault guns are indicative of the usual ranges up to which they would be expected to fire in the close support role, although they could also engage more distant targets in some cases.

4. The list of artillery guns shown is not exhaustive, and several foreign types taken into use by the army are not shown. The designations of artillery guns are those commonly used by most sources, although variations existed within the army, where designations changed at later stages of the war, and where the Allies applied their own designations for guns used by the German army. Note also the occasional use of the same number designator for different weapons, differentiation between them being indicated only by the weapon caliber.

5. Where shown in the designation of an artillery weapon, "le" indicated "light"; "s" indicated "heavy"; "K" indicated "cannon"; "H" indicated "howitzer"; "F" indicated "field"; "E" indicated "railway"; "PAK" indicated "anti-tank"; "StuG" indicated "assault (or close support) gun"; "Mrs" indicated "mortar"; and "Pz. Jäger" or "PJK" indicated a gun or self-propelled gun designed primarily (but not exclusively) as a "tank destroyer".

## 3. TANKS

| Type | Armament | Weight | Armor | Crew | Power Speed Range | Remarks |
|---|---|---|---|---|---|---|
| Pz.Kpfw.I (Sd.Kfz.101) Ausf. A | Two 7.92mm MG 13 | 5.4 tons | 6–13mm | 2 | 57 bhp 40 kph 144 km | Light tank. In service 1934. Chassis later also used for various self-propelled light guns etc. |
| Pz.Kpfw.I (Sd.Kfz.101) Ausf. B | Two 7.92mm MG 34 | 5.8 tons | 7–13mm | 2 | 100 bhp 43 kph 141 km | |
| Kl.Pz.Bef.Wg (Sd.Kfz.265) | One 7.92mm MG 34 | 5.8 tons | 23–30mm | 3 | 100 bhp 43 kph 160 km | Command vehicle variant. |
| Pz.Kpfw.II Ausf. 'c' | One 20mm KwK 30 or 38 gun One 7.92mm MG 34 | 8.8 tons | 10–30mm | 3 | 140 bhp 40 kph 160 km | Light tank. In service 1935. |
| Pz.Kpfw.II (Sd.Kfz. 121) Ausf. A, B and C | One 20mm KwK 30 or 38 gun One 7.92mm MG 34 | 9.5 tons | 10–30mm | 3 | 140 bhp 40 kph 160 km | |
| Pz.Kpfw.II (Sd.Kfz.121) Ausf. F to J | One 20mm KwK 30 or 38 gun One 7.92mm MG 34 | 9.5 tons | 20–35mm | 3 | 140 bhp 40 kph 200 km | |
| Pz.Kpfw.II (Sd.Kfz.121) Ausf. L | One 20mm KwK 38 gun One 7.92mm MG 34 | 11.8 tons | 10–30mm | 4 | 180 bhp 60 kph 250 km | Also known as Luchs. |
| Pz.Kpfw.III (Sd.Kfz.141) Ausf. E | One 37mm KwK L/45 gun Three 7.92mm MG 34 | 19.5 tons | 10–30mm | 5 | 300 bhp 40 kph 175 km | Light or medium tank. Into service 1939. Chassis also used for various other applications. |
| Pz.Kpfw.III (Sd.Kfz.141) Ausf. F | One 50mm KwK L/42 gun Two 7.92mm MG 34 | 20.5 tons | 10–30mm | 5 | 300 bhp 40 kph 175 km | |
| Pz.Kpfw.III (Sd.Kfz.141) Ausf. G | One 50mm KwK L/42 gun Two 7.92mm MG 34 | 20.3 tons | 10–30mm | 5 | 300 bhp 40 kph 175 km | |
| Pz.Kpfw.III (Sd.Kfz.141) Ausf. H | One 50mm KwK L/42 gun Two 7.92mm MG 34 | 21.6 tons | 10–30mm | 5 | 300 bhp 40 kph 175 km | |
| Pz.Kpfw.III (Sd.Kfz.141/1) Ausf. J | One 50mm KwK 39 L/60 gun Two 7.92mm MG 34 | 21.5 tons | 20–50mm | 5 | 300 bhp 40 kph 175 km | |
| Pz.Kpfw.III (Sd.Kfz.141/1) Ausf. L | One 50mm KwK 39 L/60 gun Two 7.92mm MG 34 | 22.7 tons | 10–50mm | 5 | 300 bhp 40 kph 175 km | |
| Pz.Kpfw.III (Sd.Kfz.141/1) Ausf. M | One 50mm KwK  39 L/60 gun Two 7.92mm MG 34 | 22.3 tons | 10–57mm | 5 | 300 bhp 40 kph 175 km | |
| Pz.Kpfw.III (Sd.Kfz.141/2) Ausf. N | One 75mm KwK 37 L/24 gun Two 7.92mm MG 34 | 22.3 tons | 10–57mm | 5 | 300 bhp 40 kph 175 km | In service 1942. With additional side-plate armor. Also used as an assault gun. |
| Pz.Kpfw.IV (Sd.Kfz.161) Ausf. A | One 75mm KwK 37 L/24 gun Two 7.92mm MG 34 | 18.4 tons | 10–30mm | 5 | 250 bhp 30 kph 150 km | Medium tank. In service 1939. Chassis later also used for various self-propelled guns, etc. |

*Continued*

| Tanks (continued) | | | | | | |
|---|---|---|---|---|---|---|
| Type | Armament | Weight | Armor | Crew | Power<br>Speed<br>Range | Remarks |
| Pz.Kpfw.IV (Sd.Kfz.161)<br>Ausf. B and C | One 75mm KwK 37 L/24 gun<br>Two 7.92mm MG 34 | 18.8 tons | 10–30mm | 5 | 320 bhp (B)<br>300 bhp (C)<br>40 kph<br>198 km | |
| Pz.Kpfw.IV (Sd.Kfz.161)<br>Ausf. D | One 75mm KwK 37 L/24 gun<br>Two 7.92mm MG 34 | 20 tons | 10–30mm | 5 | 300 bhp<br>40 kph<br>198 km | |
| Pz.Kpfw.IV (Sd.Kfz.161)<br>Ausf. E | One 75mm KwK 37 L/24 gun<br>Two 7.92mm MG 34 | 21 tons | 10–50mm | 5 | 300 bhp<br>42 kph<br>198 km | |
| Pz.Kpfw.IV (Sd.Kfz.161)<br>Ausf. F1 | One 75mm KwK 37 L/24 gun<br>Two 7.92mm MG 34 | 22.3 tons | 10–50/<br>80mm | 5 | 300 bhp<br>42 kph<br>198 km | |
| Pz.Kpfw.IV (Sd.Kfz.161)<br>Ausf. F2 and G | One 75mm KwK 40 L/43 gun<br>Two 7.92mm MG 34 | 21 tons | 10–50/<br>80mm | 5 | 300 bhp<br>38 kph<br>198 km | |
| Pz.Kpfw.IV (Sd.Kfz.161)<br>Ausf. H and J | One 75mm KwK 40 L/48 gun<br>Two 7.92mm MG 34 | 25 tons | 10–50/<br>80mm | 5 | 300 bhp<br>42 kph<br>198 km | |
| Pz.Kpfw.V (Sd.Kfz.171)<br>Ausf. D, Panther | One 75mm KwK 42 L/70 gun<br>One 7.92mm MG 34 | 43 tons | 15–80mm | 5 | 650 bhp<br>46 kph<br>168 km | Heavy tank. In service 1943. Chassis also used for tank destroyer Jagdpanther. |
| Pz.Kpfw.V (Sd.Kfz.171)<br>Ausf. A, Panther | One 75mm KwK 42 L/70 gun<br>Three 7.92mm MG 34 | 44.8 tons | 15–80mm | 5 | 700 bhp<br>46 kph<br>176 km | |
| Pz.Kpfw.V (Sd.Kfz.171)<br>Ausf. G, Panther | One 75mm KwK 42 L/70 gun<br>Three 7.92mm MG 34 | 45.5 tons | 15–80mm | 5 | 700 bhp<br>46 kph<br>176 km | |
| Pz.Kpfw.VI (Sd.Kfz.181)<br>Ausf. E, Tiger I | One 88mm KwK 36 L/56 gun<br>Two 7.92mm MG 34 | 57 tons | 25–100mm | 5 | 650 bhp<br>38 kph<br>100 km | Heavy tank. In service 1942. Chassis also used for Panzerjäger Tiger (P) Ferdinand. |
| Pz.Kpfw.VI (Sd.Kfz.182)<br>Ausf. B, Tiger II<br>Königstiger | One 88mm KwK 43 L/71 gun<br>Three 7.92mm MG 34 | 68.4 tons (Porsche turret)<br>69.4 tons (Henschel turret) | 25–100mm | 5 | 700 bhp<br>38 kph<br>100 km | Heavy tank. In service 1944. |

## 4. WHEELED AND HALF-TRACK VEHICLES

| Type | Manufacturer | Motive Power, etc. | Carrying Capacity, etc. | Remarks |
|---|---|---|---|---|
| Heavy Motorcycle R12 | BMW | 745cc OHV, 2-cylinder, 18 bhp, 112kph | One (occasionally plus one on the pillion) | Could be fitted with sidecar. Used for liaison, traffic control, reconnaissance etc. |
| Light Motorcycle 2510SL | NSU | 241cc OHV, 1-cylinder, 10 bhp, 96kph | One | Used for liaison, traffic control, reconnaissance etc. |
| Heavy motorcycle combination R75 | BMW | 745cc OHV, 2-cylinder, 26 bhp, 96kph | One plus one in the sidecar (occasionally plus one more on the pillion) | Used for reconnaissance and by field security units and military police. Sidecar often fitted with machine gun. |

*Continued*

| Wheeled and Half-track Vehicles (continued) | | | | |
|---|---|---|---|---|
| Type | Manufacturer | Motive Power, etc. | Carrying Capacity, etc. | Remarks |
| Semi-track Motorcycle Tractor Kettenkraftrad Sd.Kfz.2 | NSU | 1,478cc, 4-cylinder, 36 bhp, Opel engine | One plus two | Used as a light tractor, signals cable layer, light (20mm) self-propelled gun platform etc. |
| Light Car Kfz.1 (KdF 82) | Volkswagen | 985cc, 4-cylinder, 24 bhp, 4×2 | One plus three (variable, dependent upon configuration) | Basic light utility vehicle, the equivalent of the Allied forces' Jeep. Subsequently modified and also produced by numerous other manufacturers. Generally known as the Kübelwagen. Extensive range of uses. |
| Light Amphibious Car KfZ. 1/20 (KdF 166) | Volkswagen | 4-cylinder, 25 bhp, 4×4, speed 6.4 kph in water (using rear propeller) | One plus three (variable, dependent upon configuration) | Variant also produced by Porsche. Generally known as the "Schwimmwagen". Wide range of uses, but especially reconnaissance and liaison. |
| Medium Car Kfz.11 (Horch 830) | Horch | 3-liter, 8-cylinder, 4×2 | One plus three or four (variable, dependent upon configuration) | Utility vehicle for personnel and light equipment. |
| Medium Car Kfz.15 | Horch Opel | Horch V-8, 80 bhp, 4×4 Opel 6-cylinder, 68 bhp, 4×4 | One plus three or four (variable, dependent upon configuration) | Utility vehicle for personnel and light equipment. Convertible, also used as staff car |
| Heavy Car Kfz.69 | Auto-Union/Horch | V-8-108, 8-cylinder, 81 bhp, 4×4 | One plus five (variable, dependent upon configuration) | Utility vehicle for personnel and light equipment. Also as light artillery tractor, ambulance etc. |
| Heavy Car G4/W31 | Mercedes-Benz | 8-cylinder, 100 bhp, 6×4 | One plus five (variable, dependent upon configuration) | Convertible, widely used as a staff car, including by Hitler. Later models had a 5,401cc, 110 bhp engine. |
| Heavy Car 1500A/02 | Steyr (Austria) | V-8, 8-cylinder, 85 bhp, 4×4 | One plus seven | Utility vehicle for personnel. |
| Ambulance Kfz.31 (Steyr 640/643) | Steyr (Austria) | 2,260cc, 6-cylinder, 55 bhp, 6×4 | Four stretchers or eight seated, dependent upon configuration. | |
| Ambulance Kfz.31 (Phänomen Granit 1500A) | Phänomen Granit | 4-cylinder, 50 bhp, 4×4 | Four stretchers or up to eight seated, dependent upon configuration. | |
| Light Cargo Truck (Adler 60/61) | Adler | 6-cylinder, 58 bhp, 4×2 | Up to 2 tons | |
| Light Cargo Truck Kfz.76 (Büssing-NAG G31) | Büssing-NAG | 4-cylinder, 65 bhp, 6×4 | Up to 2 tons | Utility vehicle for personnel and equipment, also used as reconnaissance vehicle and light tractor. |
| Medium Cargo Truck (Borgward 3 To.GW) | Borgward | 6-cylinder, 63 bhp, 4×2 | Up to 3 tons | Utility vehicle for personnel and equipment. |
| Medium Truck Fuel Tanker (Opel Blitz 3,6-36S/MB L701) | Opel | 6-cylinder, 68 bhp, 4×2 | Up to 3 tons fuel equivalent. | Typical specialist application of standard truck chassis. |
| Medium Cargo Truck (Opel Blitz 3,6-6700A) | Opel | 3.6-liter, 6-cylinder, 73.5 bhp, 4×4 | Up to 3 tons | Utility vehicle for personnel and equipment. |
| Medium Cargo Truck (Mercedes-Benz L3000A/066) | Mercedes-Benz | 4-cylinder (diesel), 75 bhp, 4×4 | Up to 3 tons | Utility vehicle for personnel and equipment. |

*Continued*

| | | **Wheeled and Half-track Vehicles** (continued) | | |
|---|---|---|---|---|
| Type | Manufacturer | Motive Power, etc. | Carrying Capacity, etc. | Remarks |
| Medium Cargo Truck (Krupp L3H 163) | Krupp | 6-cylinder, 110 bhp, 6×4 | Up to 3 tons | Utility vehicle for personnel and equipment, also for engineer, signals and other specialist applications. |
| Heavy Cargo Truck (Mercedes-Benz L4500A) | Mercedes-Benz | 6-cylinder (diesel), 112 bhp, 4×4 | Up to 5 tons | Utility vehicle for personnel and heavy equipment. |
| Heavy Cargo Truck (Henschel 6J2) | Henschel | 6-cylinder (diesel), 125 bhp, 4×2 | Up to 6.5 tons | Utility vehicle for personnel and heavy equipment. |
| Heavy Truck Tank Transporter (Faun L900D567) | Faun | Deutz 13.5-liter F6M517, 150 bhp, 6×4 | Up to 9 tons | Typical load might be one Pz.Kpfw.II tank. |
| Heavy Cargo Truck (Mercedes-Benz LG4000) | Mercedes-Benz | 6-cylinder (diesel), 100 bhp, 6×6 | Up to 5 tons | Utility vehicle for personnel and heavy equipment. |
| Wheeled Heavy Tractor (Hanomag SS100) | Hanomag | 6-cylinder (diesel), 100 bhp, 4×2 | Various trailers, specialized towed equipment, guns, vehicle recovery and other towing tasks | Typical heavy-duty prime mover. |
| Light Half-track APC Sd.Kfz. 250/1 | Demag | 6-cylinder, 100 bhp | Six Panzergrenadier troops, two machine guns | Armored personnel carrier (APC). A non-armored variant carried 8 troops. Used extensively by the Panzer forces. |
| Half-track Armored Flame Thrower Sd.Kfz. 251/16 | Hanomag | 6-cylinder, 100 bhp | Five crewmen, three flamethrowers, one machine gun | Specialized version of standard Sd.Kfz. 251 APC chassis and body which was used for more than 20 variants. Used extensively by the Panzer forces. |
| Medium Half-track Sd.Kfz.6 | Büssing-NAG | 6-cylinder, 100 bhp | Eleven troops or up to 5 tons equivalent load dependent upon configuration | Troop transport, prime mover (especially artillery), and cargo. |
| Medium Half-track Sd.Kfz.7 | Krauss-Maffei | 6-cylinder, 140 bhp | Eleven troops or up to 8 tons equivalent load dependent upon configuration | Troop transport, prime mover (especially artillery), and cargo. |
| Heavy Half-track Sd.Kfz.9 | Famo | 12-cylinder, 230 bhp | Up to 18 tons dependent upon configuration | Troop transport, prime mover, vehicle recovery and cargo. |
| Half-track Truck Sd.Kfz. 3 Maultier (Opel Blitz 3,6-36S/SSM) | Opel | 3.6-liter, 6-cylinder, 68 bhp | Up to 2 tons | Typical example of the several Maultier vehicles produced, in which the rear wheels of a standard wheeled truck were replaced with a tracked drive. |
| Light Armored Car Sd.Kfz.223 | Auto Union/Horch | 3.5-liter, V-8-cylinder, 75 bhp, 4×4 | Three crewmen, one machine gun | Reconnaissance, command and control and signals functions. Sd.Kfz. 222 mounted a 20mm cannon and a machine gun. |
| Heavy Armored Car (Mercedes-Benz G3a/P) | Mercedes-Benz | 6-cylinder, 68 bhp, 6×4 | Three or four crewmen, turret machine gun, 20mm cannon or other armament | Primarily for reconnaissance, but variants were also produced for command and control and communications functions. 1930s forerunner of the 8*8 Puma armored cars. |
| Heavy Armored Car Sd.Kfz.231 (and later variants 232, 234, 234/1, 234/1 and 263) | Büssing-NAG | V-8-cylinder, 180 bhp, 8×8, delivering 82 kph on roads and 30 kph cross-country | Four crewmen, co-axial turret machine gun and a 20mm, 50mm or 75mm cannon | Designed as an armored combat vehicle primarily for reconnaissance tasks; variants were also produced for command and control and communications functions. Versions in use from 1944 were known as the Puma. |

**Note**

Very many types of wheeled, half-track, armored, semi-armored, fighting, cargo and special-purpose vehicles and motorcycles were used by the army. Those shown are selected examples that are typical and therefore generally representative of some of the more widely used types; however, this list is by no means exhaustive. Foreign vehicles manufactured beyond Greater Germany or subsequently seized and taken into service by the army are not shown.

## 5. ENGINEER TRACKED DEMOLITION VEHICLES

| Type | Motive Power | Control System & Range | Explosive Charge | Remarks |
|---|---|---|---|---|
| Goliath | 2-cylinder gasoline engine or twin 12-volt Bosch electric motors, both delivering a speed of 5–12 mph | Three-core 500-meter cable | About 100 kilograms of HE | Remote-controlled mini-tank for demolition and mine-clearance tasks and against bunkers, pill boxes and emplacements. Used by engineer troops. |
| B-IV | 6-cylinder gasoline engine, enabling it to be driven to its task area | Radio-controlled by the driver once dismounted | About 350 kilograms of HE mounted in a container on the sloping front plate of the vehicle body | Remote-controlled mini-tank for demolition and mine-clearance tasks and against bunkers, pill boxes and emplacements. The B-IV vehicle was not expendable and was steered remotely to its target, where the explosive pack would be dropped from the front of the vehicle, which then withdrew prior to detonation. Used by engineer troops. |
| Springer Sd.Kfz. 304 (NSU) | Opel 4-cylinder engine, delivering 36 bhp | Radio-controlled to about 500 meters, or controlled manually | About 300 kilograms of HE | Mini-tank produced in 1944 for demolition and mine-clearance tasks. Used by engineer troops. |

## 6. SELECTED MISCELLANEOUS EQUIPMENT

| Equipment | Details | Remarks |
|---|---|---|
| Mine Detector Type B "Berlin" | Back-mounted detector; registered a change of audio tone in operator's headphones when a buried metal object was swept by the search coil. | |
| Mine Detector Type 41 "Tempelhof" | Back-mounted loudspeaker; registered a change of audio tone in operator's headphones when a buried metal object was swept by the search coil. | |
| Mine Detector Type 40 "Frankfurt" | Back-mounted detector; registered a change of audio tone in operator's headphones when a buried metal object was swept by the search coil. | |
| Coincidence 70cm Range Finder Types 14 and 34 | Portable range finder. Operating range 200–7,000 meters, with a magnification of ×11. | Used by machine gun and mortar troops to determine ranges to ground targets; also used with MG 34 deployed in the anti-aircraft role. |
| Stereoscopic 1 meter Range Finder Type Em.R.1 meter and Em.R.36 1 meter. | Portable range finder. Operating range 200–7,000 meters dependent upon type, both with a magnification of ×11. | Used by anti-aircraft gunners equipped with 20mm and 37mm guns. |
| Stereoscopic 1.5 meter Range Finder Type Em.R.1.5 meter. | Tripod-mounted range finder. Operating range 400–13,600 meters, with a magnification of ×11. | Used to determine precise ranges to static ground targets. Larger, longer-range, crew-served range finders were also available for use with heavy anti-aircraft guns and coastal artillery. |
| Wire Cutters (two types in general use) | The large type was 0.7 meters long and weighed 2 kilograms, while the small type was 0.3 meters long and weighed 1 kilogram. | Both cutters pivoted on two hinge links and had insulated tubular steel handles. Used by all troops, particularly by engineers and signallers. |
| Chain Saws (two types in general use) | The light type weighed 50 kilograms; the heavy-duty type weighed almost 80 kilograms. Both had a cutting saw (chain) blade about 1 meter long. | Used primarily by engineers. |
| Haversack Water Filter | Capable of purifying between 100 and 250 liters of water per hour, but could not remove chemical agents or any attendant smell. | Issued to all units down to company level. |
| Zeltbahn Individual Shelter Tent | Manufactured of camouflage-pattern, water-repellent, closely-woven cotton duck material, the Zeltbahn served as a shelter and as a poncho. An individual Zeltbahn section was a triangle about 2 meters by 2.5 meters (two sides), with buttons and eye-holes along all three edges. | Usually four were combined to form a four-man pyramid tent. Each soldier carried two tent pegs and a section of tent pole. Eight and 16-man tents could also be constructed, the top of the latter standing about 3 meters high. |

*Continued*

| Selected Miscellaneous Equipment (continued) | | |
|---|---|---|
| Equipment | Details | Remarks |
| Entrenching Tool | A folding shovel with a 21cm pointed steel blade attached by a hinge to the 46cm wooden handle. A plastic nut was fitted at the hinge and allowed the blade to be locked for use either as a shovel or (at right-angles) as a pick, or folded back against the handle when carried on the belt. | |
| Sleds | In addition to improvised sleds, three types were provided to troops operating in winter conditions for moving equipment and supplies, as a means of moving heavy weapons, and for evacuating casualties. All three types were about 2 meters long and resembled flat-bottomed canoes. | Routinely used by mountain troops but also by others in winter conditions. Extensively used both in issued and in improvised forms by many units on the Eastern Front during the winters. |

## 7. LUFTWAFFE CLOSE AIR SUPPORT AND TRANSPORT AIRCRAFT

| Aircraft | Armament | Crew | Range (km)* | Cargo or Personnel Load |
|---|---|---|---|---|
| Focke Wulf Fw 190 Fighter/Fighter Bomber | Two machine guns Two to four 20mm cannon Two 210mm rockets | 1 | 1,536/280 | |
| Messerschmitt Bf 109 Fighter/Fighter Bomber | Two machine guns Three 20mm cannon Two 210mm rockets | 1 | 640/280 | |
| Messerschmitt Bf 110 Fighter Bomber | Six machine guns Two to four 20mm cannon | 2 | 1,472/456 | |
| Junkers Ju 87 Stuka Dive-bomber | Three machine guns Up to three 37mm cannon could be fitted externally as required Up to 1,000 kilogram bomb load | 2 | 680/448 | |
| Heinkel He 111 Bomber | One 20mm cannon Three or five machine guns Up to 1,000 kilogram bomb load | 5 to 6 | 1,344/344 | |
| Junkers Ju 52 Transport | Five machine guns | 3 to 4 | 848/336 | 22 fully-equipped troops or about 2,500 kilograms of cargo. |
| Messerschmitt Bf 323 Transport | Eighteen machine guns | 8 to 10 | 880/408 | 60 to 100 personnel (dependent upon equipment carried) or up to about 12,500 kilograms of cargo. |
| Henschel Hs 126 Reconnaissance and Liaison | Five machine guns | 2 | 705/336 | 100 kilograms. |
| Fiesler Fi 156 Storch Reconnaissance and Liaison | One machine gun | 2 or 3 | 320/152 | 100 kilograms. |

\* Normal cruising range / operating radius.

**Note**
The selected Luftwaffe aircraft shown are those that were most closely associated with the provision of close air support to the army, with transporting or supplying the ground troops, or with carrying out reconnaissance and liaison tasks in support of the army.

# German–English Glossary

The glossary includes all German words and phrases used in the main text. It does not include German words used in the appendices, all of which are explained where they are used. The German words shown are generally those that appeared in various military publications during 1939–45 and may therefore differ from their modern military or civilian usage or meaning in some cases.

| German | English Translation or Explanation |
|---|---|
| Abbrechen des Gefechts | Planned tactical withdrawal |
| Abteilung | Branch (staff), unit, detachment; also used for some battalion-sized or equivalent units |
| Abwehr | Defense (but in the military organizational context it was the name of the national counter-espionage organization) |
| Abzeichen | Insignia or badge, including some awards or decorations |
| Afrikakorps | Literally, "Africa Corps": the German ground forces in North Africa |
| Allgemeine | General (i.e., non-specialist) |
| Allgemeine Kriegsschule | General (i.e., non-specialist) military school |
| Allgemeines Heeresamt | General army office |
| Allgemeine SS | General SS (organization) |
| Allgemeines Sturmabzeichen | General Assault Badge |
| Amt | Office |
| Amtsgruppe für Industrielle Rüstung | Weapons and Manufacture Group |
| Angriffsschlacht | Offensive battle |
| Anschluß | Union (of Germany and Austria in 1938) |
| Anwärter | Aspirant, candidate |
| Anzugordnung | Routine orders or regulations for the uniform or dress of the day |
| Appell | Routine (usually daily) inspection or muster parade |
| Arbeitsanzug | Fatigue uniform or overalls |
| Armeeverpflegungslager | Army-level ration dump |
| Armeegefangenen-sammelstelle | Army-level prisoner-of-war collecting point |
| Armeemunitionslager | Army-level ammunition dump |
| Armee Park | Army-level equipment park (depot) |
| Armeepferdelazarett | Army-level horse hospital of the veterinary service |
| Armeesanitäts-abteilungen | Army-level medical battalions |
| Artillerie | Artillery |
| Aufklärung | Reconnaissance |
| Aufmarsch | Approach march immediately prior to tactical deployment |
| Auftragstaktik | Mission-led operational concept focusing upon the wider aims and objectives rather than specifying in detail the means by which they should be achieved |
| Ausführung (Ausf.) | Production mark, type or variant of vehicle or equipment (typically tanks) |
| Ausgehanzug | Walking-out uniform (one of two versions, see also "Meldeanzug") |
| Balkenkreuz | Black and white-edged square cross used extensively as identifying vehicle insignia, especially on armored vehicles |
| Bandenkampfabzeichen | Anti-partisan Battle Badge |
| *Barbarossa*, Fall | *Barbarossa*, Case (literally "Operation *Barbarossa*") |
| Bataillon | Battalion |
| Batterie | Battery (of artillery) |
| Befehlshaber | Commander |
| Befehlspanzer | Command tank |
| Befehlswagen | Command vehicle |
| Befestigung | Fortification |
| Beobachtungspanzer | Artillery observation tank |
| Berg | Mountain |
| Bergepanzer | Tank recovery vehicle (on a tank chassis) |
| Bergführer | Mountain guide |
| Bergmütze | Field service cap of mountain troops (Gebirgsjäger) |
| Bergschuhe | Mountain climbing boot |
| Blendkörper | Glass smoke hand-grenade, used to force the evacuation of (for example) a bunker or pill-box |
| Blitzkrieg | "Lightning war" |
| Böhmen und Mähren | Bohemia and Moravia, Protectorate of |
| Brotbeutel | Canvas bread bag (haversack) carried by individual soldiers as part of their personal basic field equipment |
| Brückengerät | Literally, "bridging equipment" (usually followed by the type description or letter designating the type) |
| Brummbär | "Grizzly bear", a tank destroyer based on the Pz.Kfpw.IV chassis |
| Bund Deutscher Mädel (BDM) | League of German Girls |
| Chef der Heeresleitung | Chief of the Army High Command |
| Deutsches Afrikakorps (DAK) | German Africa Corps |
| Deutsche Reichsbahn | German National Railways |
| Deutsches Rotes Kreuz (DRK) | German Red Cross organization |
| Dienst | Duty or service |
| Dienstanzug | Service dress uniform |
| Dienststelle | Place of duty |
| Dienstgradabzeichen | Rank insignia |
| Dienstgrade | Rank |
| Divisionsausgabestellen | Division ammunition distribution points |
| Divisionsgefangen-ensammelstelle | Divisional prisoner-of-war (PW) collecting point |
| Divisionsmunitionslager | Division ammunition dump |
| Doppellitze | Double bars of lace on the service uniform jacket collar |
| "Dora" | An 800mm caliber railway gun |
| Dreibein | Tripod (e.g., for the MG 34 machine gun) |
| DRK-Schwester | German Red Cross nursing sister |
| Durchbruch | Tactical or operational breakthrough |
| Edelweiß | White Alpine flower, used as the badge of mountain troops (Gebirgsjäger) |
| Ehrenwache | Guard of honor |
| Ehrenzeichen | Decoration, medal or award |
| Eierhandgranate | An egg-shaped hand grenade |
| Einbruch | Tactical or operational penetration |
| Einheit | Unit |
| Einheitsfahrerhaus | Standardized truck cab of pressed cardboard on timber frame, introduced from 1944 as an economy measure to replace metal cabs |
| Einheitsfeldmütze | Peaked field service cap introduced in 1943 |

| German | English Translation or Explanation |
|---|---|
| Einjährig-Freiwillige | One-year period of voluntary full-time military service completed in the course of obtaining a reserve officer commission |
| Einkreisung | Encircling attack |
| Einsatzgruppen | Special task groups or task forces |
| Einsatzkommandos | Special units operating as "killer groups" |
| Eisenbahn | Railway |
| Eisenbahnkanone | Railway gun (as opposed to a mortar or howitzer) |
| Eisenbahnnachrichten-regiment | Specialist railway signals communications regiment |
| Eisenbahnpanzerzüge | Armored trains (used as combat units) |
| Eisenbahnpionier-kompanien | Railway engineering construction companies |
| Eisenbahntruppen | Railway engineering troops |
| Eiserne Ration | Iron ration (a basic combat ration) |
| Eisernes Kreuz | Iron Cross (medal) |
| Entfaltung | Tactical action of moving from the line of march into an attack formation |
| Entgiftungstrupps | Gas or chemical decontamination teams |
| Entwicklung | Tactical action of moving from an attack formation into an assault formation |
| Ergänzung | Substitute or replacement (see also "Ersatz") |
| Ergänzungseinheiten | Replacement unit (see also "Ersatzeinheit") |
| Ergänzungsoffizier | Re-employed retired officer |
| Ergänzungsstelle | Recruiting office or replacement center |
| Erkennungsmarke | Identification disc |
| Ersatz | Substitute or replacement |
| Ersatzeinheit | Replacement unit (see also "Ersatzabteilung") |
| Ersatzheer | Replacement Army |
| Ersatzverpflegungs-magazine | Higher-level rations stores |
| Ersatzabteilung | Replacement unit |
| Esbitkocher | Fuel tablet (hexamine) individual cooking stove |
| Exerzierplatz | Parade ground, drill square |
| Fahnenjunker | Officer cadet on active duty, also a non-commissioned officer aspirant |
| Fall (Gelb) | Case or situation (i.e., "Plan" or "Operation") (Yellow) |
| Fallschirmjäger | Airborne (parachute) soldier |
| Fallschirmjägergewehr | Special weapon (assault rifle) developed for Luftwaffe parachute troops (specifically, the Fallschirmjägergewehr 42 or "FG 42") |
| Faustpatrone | A single-shot, disposable, rocket-propelled anti-tank grenade launcher, also known as the Panzerfaust |
| Feld | Field, also slang for "Feldwebel" |
| Feldanzug | Field uniform |
| Feldausbildungs-divisionen | Field training divisions |
| Feldausrüstung | Field equipment |
| Feldartillerie | Field artillery |
| Felddivisionen | Luftwaffe field divisions employed as ground forces |
| Feldflasche | Water bottle |
| Feldgendarmerie | Military police |
| Feldgrau | Field grey (uniform color adopted in 1914) |
| Feldhaubitze | Field howitzer |
| Feldheer | Field Army |
| Feldjägerkorps | Special army units established late in the war to apprehend deserters and exercise summary |

| German | English Translation or Explanation |
|---|---|
|  | discipline in the field, including conducting "flying courts-martial" |
| Feldkanone | Field gun |
| Feldkommando | Field command post |
| Feldkommandostelle RF-SS | Field headquarters of RF-SS Heinrich Himmler |
| Feldlazarett | Field hospital |
| Feldmütze | Field service cap worn in the field and in barracks |
| Feldnachrichten-kommandantur | Field signals communications command (static installations) |
| Feldpost | Military field post (office) |
| Feld-Unteroffizier-Schule | Field non-commissioned officer school |
| Feldwebel | sergeant major (warrant officer) |
| Feldzeug | Ordnance |
| Feldzeugmeister | Chief army ordnance officer |
| Feldfernsprecher | Field telephone |
| Fernmelde (~bataillon) | Signals or communications (battalion) |
| Festung | Fortress |
| Flakdivisionen | Anti-aircraft divisions |
| Flakwaffenhelferinnen | Female anti-aircraft gun crews |
| Flammenwerfer | Flamethrower |
| Flankenangriff | Flanking attack |
| Flasche | Bottle, flask |
| Fliegerleitoffiziere | Luftwaffe forward air controllers with army units |
| Fliegerverbindungs-offiziere ("Flivos") | Luftwaffe liaison officers allocated to army corps and (sometimes) divisional headquarters |
| Flugabwehr (~regiment) | Air defense (regiment) |
| Flugabwehrkanone ("Flak") | Anti-aircraft ("Flak") gun |
| Flügelangriff | Attack against the enemy's wing |
| Freikorps | Literally "free corps" and variously used over time to describe local militia, irregular and other armed groups and paramilitary forces, including the post-1918 right-wing paramilitary groups raised by the post-war German government of the day |
| Freie Stadt (Danzig) | Free city (of Danzig). Danzig was an independent city with special status and some sovereign rights, which also enjoyed particular political and strategic significance |
| Fremde Heere Ost (FHO) | OKH intelligence branch dealing with foreign armies in the east |
| Fremde Heere West (FHW) | OKH intelligence branch dealing with foreign armies in the west |
| Frontalangriff | Frontal attack |
| Führer | Any leader, driver etc; also applied directly to Hitler |
| Führerhauptquartier | Hitler's operational supreme headquarters |
| Führerinnen | Senior leadership grades of female auxiliaries |
| Führungshauptamt | Operational-level headquarters |
| Funken (Fu.) | Radio |
| Funker | Radio operator |
| Garde | Guard |
| Garnison | Garrison |
| Gas | Gas (chemical warfare, poison) |
| Gasabwehr-Offiziere | Gas (chemical warfare, poison gas) defense officers |
| Gasmaske | Gas mask |

| German | English Translation or Explanation |
|---|---|
| Gasplane | Anti-gas (chemical) protective cape or sheet |
| Gasschutz | Chemical warfare (poison gas) defense |
| Gasspürtrupps | Gas or chemical detection team |
| Gebirgs (~division) | Mountain (division) |
| Gebirgsgeschütz | Mountain gun |
| Gebirgsinfanterie-geschütz | Mountain infantry gun |
| Gebirgsjäger | Mountain troops |
| Gefangenschaft | Imprisonment (e.g., of prisoner-of-war) |
| Gefechtsaufklärung | Battlefield reconnaissance |
| Gefechtsvorposten | Outpost positions |
| Gefreiter | Junior corporal |
| Geheime Feldpolizei (GFP) | Secret Field Police |
| Geheime Staatspolizei | State Secret Police ("Gestapo") |
| General | General (rank) |
| General der Infanterie, Panzer, Artillerie (etc.) | General of infantry, armor, artillery (etc.) |
| Generale | General officers (as a group or category) |
| Generalfeldmarschall | Field marshal |
| Generalgouvernement | Government General (of Poland) |
| Granatwerfer, leichter Granatwerfer | Mortar, light mortar |
| Grenzwacht | Frontier guards |
| Generalleutnant | Lieutenant general |
| Generalmajor | Major general |
| Generaloberst | Colonel general |
| Generalstab, im | General staff, on the |
| Generalstabsoffiziere | General staff corps officers |
| Gerät | Equipment |
| Gericht | Justice, tribunal, court of law |
| Gesellschaftanzug | Traditional formal dress uniform |
| Gestellungsbefehl | Official "call up" to report for military duty |
| Gestreckte Ladung | "Bangalore torpedo" type of explosive charge for breaching wire obstacles |
| Gewehr | Rifle |
| Gewehrgranate | Rifle (projected) grenade |
| Gewehrnahpatrone | Low-velocity ammunition (for use with the Mauser Kar 98K rifle when fitted with a silencer) |
| Glaube und Schönheit | "Faith and Beauty" (organization) |
| "Goliath" | A tracked, remotely controlled (by wire), demolition-charge carrier |
| Gott | God |
| Götterdämmerung | "Twilight of the gods" |
| "Gott mit uns" | "God [is] with us", the motto embossed on the soldier's belt plate |
| Graben | Grave, trench, ditch |
| Granate | Shell (artillery) |
| Granatwerfer | Literally, "grenade thrower", refers to "trench" mortars, and infantry mortars |
| Grenze | Border, frontier |
| Grenzschutz | Border security, frontier control |
| Grenzwacht | Frontier guard force, border patrol |
| Grossdeutschland, Großdeutschland | Greater Germany, incorporating the Saarland, Rhineland, Austria and the Sudetenland; also the title of a specific élite army formation |
| Großdeutsches Reich | Greater German Empire (concept of an expanded Germany incorporating all German-speaking and Germanic peoples into a single political entity) |

| German | English Translation or Explanation |
|---|---|
| Großkampfpäckchen | Combat ration |
| "Großtraktor" | "Heavy (agricultural) tractor" (Reichswehr period) |
| Grundausbildung | Military basic training |
| Gruppe(n) | Group(s) |
| Gruppenkommando | (Army) group headquarters |
| "Gulaschkanone" | Literally "goulash cannon" – standard mobile field kitchen, usually horse-drawn, but sometimes vehicle-mounted |
| Hakenkreuz | Swastika or hooked cross |
| Hakenkreuzfahne | Swastika flag |
| Handgranate | Hand grenade |
| Handgranaten sack | Hand grenade carrying sack |
| Haubitze | Howitzer |
| Haupt | Head, main |
| Hauptkampflinie | Main line of defense or resistance |
| Hauptmann | Captain |
| Hauptquartier | Headquarters |
| Hauptsanitätspark | Principal medical supplies park (in Berlin) |
| Hauptverbandplatz | Regimental main medical dressing station |
| Hauptzeugamt | Central ordnance depot |
| Heer, das | Army, the |
| Heeresbekleidungsämter | Clothing depot |
| Heeres-Entlassungsstelle | Army demobilization depot |
| Heeres-Flakkampf-abzeichen | Army Anti-aircraft Battle Badge |
| Heeresgruppe | Army group (of two or more armies) |
| Heereshauptveterinär-park | Principal veterinary supplies park (depot) |
| Heeresmunitions-anstalten | Main ammunition depots |
| Heeresmunitions-nebenanstalten | Branch ammunition depots |
| Heeresnachshubtank-lager | Army fuel supply depot |
| Heeresnebenzeugämter | Army branch equipment depot |
| Heerespferdelazarett | Field army horse hospital of the veterinary service |
| Heeresremonteamt (~ämter) | Remount (horse) depots |
| Heeres-Unteroffizier-Schulen | Army non-commissioned officer schools |
| Heeresverpflegungs-ämter | Army rations depot |
| Heeresverpflegungs-hauptämter | Army main rations depot |
| Heereswaffenamt | Army Ordnance Office |
| Heereszeugämter | Army equipment depot |
| Heimat | "Homeland", in Greater Germany |
| Heimatpferdelazarette | Horse (veterinary service) hospitals based in Germany |
| Heimatpferdepark | Subsidiary horse park (depot) |
| Heimatveterinärpark | Main veterinary park (depot) in Germany |
| Hoheitsabzeichen | German national emblem (eagle and swastika) insignia |
| Hoheitszeichen | German national emblem (eagle and swastika) |
| Hornisse | "Hornet", a tank destroyer based on a hybrid Pz.Kfpw.III and IV chassis |
| Infanterie | Infantry |
| Infanteriegeschütz | Infantry gun |

| German | English Translation or Explanation |
|---|---|
| Infanteriegerät | Infantry equipment |
| Infanterie-Sturmabzeichen | Infantry Assault Badge |
| Infanteriezüge | Trains carrying infantry units with their equipment |
| Infanterist | Infantryman |
| Inspekteur | Inspector (e.g., inspector of infantry, artillery, etc.) |
| Inspektor | Inspector (see also "inspekteur") |
| Inspektion | Inspection |
| Instandsetzungs (bataillon) | Repair and maintenance (battalion) |
| Intendant(en) | Higher-grade administrative officer(s) |
| Jagdkommando | Pursuit or raiding detachment |
| Jagdpanther | Tank destroyer variant of the Panther (Panzer V) tank |
| Jagdpanzer | Tank destroyer (tracked armored vehicle) |
| Jagdtiger | Tank destroyer variant of the Tiger II (Panzer VI) tank |
| Jäger | Literally "hunter", but used to indicate light infantry, chasseur, rifleman |
| Jugend | Youth |
| Kaiser | Emperor |
| Kaiserschlacht | The "Kaiser's Battle", the final German offensive in 1918 |
| Kadett | (Officer) cadet |
| Kampf | Battle, struggle, fight |
| Kampfgruppe | Battlegroup |
| Kampfpistole | A type of signal pistol with a rifled bore that was produced for offensive use, firing bulleted cartridges and grenades |
| Kampfwagen | Tank |
| Kampfwagenkanone | Tank gun |
| Kanone | Cannon |
| Karabiner | Carbine |
| Karabiner 98K (Kar 98K) | Carbine or rifle type 98K (the standard army rifle, made by Mauser) |
| Kaserne | Barracks |
| Kavallerie | Cavalry |
| Kettenkraftrad | Part-tracked light motor or motorcycle vehicle |
| Kleiner Spaten | Entrenching tool (spade) |
| Kochgeschirr | Mess kit (metal pot with lid) |
| Kokarde | Cockade (insignia) |
| Kommando | Special task detachment |
| Kommissarerlaß | "Commissar Decree" (issued March 1941), which directed the summary execution of Red Army political commissars if captured |
| Kompanie | Company |
| Königstiger | "King Tiger", the Pz.Kpfw. VI Tiger II tank |
| Koppeltraggestell | Adjustable "Y" straps forming part of basic personal equipment |
| Kraftfahrabteilungen | Motor transport unit |
| Kraftfahrzeug | Motor vehicle |
| Kraftfahrzug (~züge) | Motorized transportation platoon(s) |
| Kraftrad | Motorcycle |
| Kragenpatten | Patch of material in Waffenfarbe color, forming part of service uniform jacket collar insignia |
| Krankenhaus | Hospital |
| Krankensammelstellen | Casualty collecting points |
| Krankenträger | Stretcher bearer |

| German | English Translation or Explanation |
|---|---|
| Krankenwagen | Ambulance |
| Krieg | War |
| Kriegsakademie | Military higher-level staff training academy or "war college" |
| Kriegsberichter | Official war correspondent |
| Kriegsflagge | National war flag |
| Kriegsgefangener | Prisoner-of-war |
| Kriegsgericht | Court-martial |
| Kriegsgliederung | Order of battle (organization) |
| Kriegsheer | Field army in wartime (see also "Feldheer") |
| Kriegskommissariat | Military service support organization |
| Kriegslazarette | General or base hospital |
| Kriegsmarine | German navy (1935–45) |
| Kriegsministerium | Ministry of War |
| Kriegsoffiziere | Wartime temporary commissioned officers or reserve officers, usually due to their special civilian qualifications or skills |
| Kriegsrecht | Martial law |
| Kriegsschule | Military training or "war" school |
| Kriegsspiel | Literally "war game", or military exercise for commanders with or without troops deployed |
| Kriegsverwaltung | Military administration within occupied territories |
| krummer Lauf | Curved barrel and periscope attachment for the Sturmgewehr 44 assault rifle |
| Kübelwagen | Light Volkswagen truck (Jeep or Land Rover equivalent) |
| Ladungsträger; schwere Ladungsträger | Remote-controlled (radio or wire) demolition-charge carrier; heavy remote-controlled demolition charge carriers |
| Lafette | Gun mounting |
| Lager | Camp, base, depot, storage depot |
| Landsmannschaften | Concept whereby the local regions of Germany were directly involved in the provision of their manpower for locally-based and regionally-linked military units |
| Landespolizeigruppe | Regional police group |
| Landesschützen | Defense units (based in Germany) |
| Landser | Descriptive term for ordinary German soldier |
| Landsknecht | Mercenary soldier (15th and 16th centuries) |
| Landsturm | Secondary reserve, home guard or local defense force (men aged over 45) |
| Land-Wasser-Schlepper | An amphibious load carrying vehicle (see also "Sachsenberg Land-Wasser-Schlepper") |
| Landwehr | Reserve or militia force (men aged 35–45) |
| Lastkraftwagen | Truck |
| Laufschuhe | Sports or running shoe |
| Lazarett | Hospital, field hospital |
| Lazarettzüge | Hospital train |
| Lehr | Instruction or training |
| Leib (~standarte "Adolf Hitler") | Literally "life" or "lifeguard", but used in the military context to indicate "bodyguard", e.g., Leibstandarte-SS "Adolf Hitler" |
| leicht, leichter | Light(weight) |
| "Leichter Traktor" | "Light (agricultural) tractor" (Reichswehr period) |
| Leichtes Gebirgs-infanteriegeschütz | Mountain infantry light gun |
| Leichtkrankenkriegs-lazarette | Base hospital dealing with minor and less serious cases |

| German | English Translation or Explanation |
|---|---|
| Leichtverwundet-ensammelplatz | Medical aid station for the lightly or non-seriously wounded |
| Leinen und leder Tropenschnürschuhe | Canvas and leather lace-up tropical boot |
| Leuchtpistole | Signal or flare (projecting) pistol |
| Leuchtspurmunition | Tracer ammunition |
| Leutnant | Lieutenant (junior or 2nd lieutenant) |
| Litzen | Lace (on the service uniform jacket collar) |
| Luchs | "Lynx", a version of the Pz.Kpfw. II light tank |
| Luftwaffe, die | German air force, the (1935–45) |
| Major | Major |
| Mannschaften | Ordinary soldiers (as a group or category) |
| Marschkompaß | Military sighting and "marching" compass (graduated in mils) |
| Marschstiefel | Black leather half-length marching boot (or "jackboot") |
| Marschverpflegung | March ration (for troops in transit) |
| Maschinengewehr | machine gun |
| Maschinenkanone | Automatic cannon |
| Maschinenpistole | Submachine gun, machine pistol, machine carbine |
| Marine (oder Kriegs-marine), die | German Navy, the (1935–45) |
| "Maultier" | "Mule", name given to class of cargo trucks converted from conventional wheeled drive to half-tracked drive |
| "Meine Ehre heißt Treue" | "My Honor is Loyalty" (the Waffen-SS motto) |
| Meisterschütze | Marksman |
| Meldeanzug | Walking-out uniform (one of two versions; see also "Ausgehanzug") |
| Meldekartentasche | Map or dispatch case (usually made of black leather) |
| Melder | Messenger, runner |
| Meldestelle | Message center |
| MG-Zieleinrichtung | machine gun optical sight (for MG 34) |
| Minen | Mines (e.g., anti-tank, anti-personnel) |
| Minenmeßdraht | Length of wire used to measure distances within minefields and between rows of mines |
| "Mit Gott für König und Vaterland" | "With God for King and Fatherland" |
| Mörser | Mortar |
| Motorisiert | Motorized, mechanized, mobile |
| Motorradfahrer | Motorcyclist |
| Munitionsausstattung | Ammunition "unit of issue" (for a given weapon) |
| Nachrichten | Signals communications |
| Nachrichtenbataillon | Signals communications battalion (usually at division-level) |
| Nachrichtendienst (ND) | Intelligence service, specifically the national secret intelligence organization, including espionage and similar activities (and which should not be confused with use of the word "Nachrichten" in connection with "signals communications") |
| Nachrichtenhelferinnen des Heeres | Army female auxiliary communications support |
| Nachrichtenhelferinnen-abteilungen | Female auxiliary communications support unit |
| Nachrichtenregiment | Signals communications regiment |

| German | English Translation or Explanation |
|---|---|
| Nachrichtentruppen | Signals communications troops (including electronic warfare, reconnaissance or information-gathering troops) |
| Nachrichtenwesen | Signals communications organization (higher HQs and levels of command) |
| Nachschub | Supply service |
| Nahkampfpäckchen | Close combat (emergency or assault) ration packs |
| Nahkampfspange | Close combat clasp (insignia) |
| Nashorn | "Rhinoceros", a tank destroyer based on a hybrid Pz.Kfpw. III and IV chassis |
| Nationalsozialistische Deutsche Arbeiterpartei (NSDAP) | National Socialist German Workers Party (Nazi party) |
| Nationalsozialistische Frauenschaft | National Socialist women's organization |
| Nebel | Fog, mist, artificial smoke |
| Nebeltruppen | Smoke (including chemical (gas) warfare) troops |
| Nebelwerfer | Smoke shell or rocket-projector or rocket-launcher |
| Oberbefehlshaber | Commander-in-Chief |
| Oberfähnrich | Advanced officer candidate |
| Oberfeldveterinär | Veterinary lieutenant colonel |
| Oberfeldwebel | Senior warrant officer |
| Obergefreiter | Corporal |
| Obergruppenführer | SS rank equivalent to army general |
| Oberkommando des Heeres (OKH) | High command (HQ) of the army |
| Oberkommando der Luftwaffe (OKL) | High command (HQ) of the air force |
| Oberkommando der Kriegsmarine (OKM) | High command (HQ) of the navy |
| Oberkommando der Wehrmacht (OKW) | High command (HQ) of the armed forces |
| Oberleutnant | Senior or 1st lieutenant |
| Oberst | Colonel |
| Oberstleutnant | Lieutenant colonel |
| Oberststabsveterinär | Veterinary major |
| Oberstveterinär | Veterinary colonel |
| Oberveterinär | Veterinary lieutenant |
| Ofenrohr | Literally, "stove-pipe", a slang name for the Raketenpanzerbüchse or Panzerschreck |
| Offizier | Officer |
| Offizieranwärter | Officer candidate |
| Offizierskaste | Officer class (as a social or hierarchical group) |
| Oflag (Offizierlager) | Prisoner-of-war camp for officers |
| OKH Nachshubtank-lager | OKH-controlled fuel supply depot |
| OKH Heeres-verwaltungsamt | OKH administration office |
| Operative Aufklärung | Operational reconnaissance |
| Ordnungspolizei | Order Police (the main civil police organization) |
| Ostfront | Eastern Front |
| Ostpreußen | East Prussia |
| Panzer | Tracked armored vehicle, usually referring to a tank or armored formation or unit |
| Panzerabwehrkanone (PAK) | Anti-tank gun |

| German | English Translation or Explanation | German | English Translation or Explanation |
|---|---|---|---|
| Panzerbüchse | Anti-tank rifle | Radfahr | Bicycle |
| Panzerdivision/~brigade | Tank or armored division/brigade | Radfahrer | Bicyclist |
| Panzerfaust | A single-shot, disposable, rocket-propelled anti-tank grenade-launcher, also known as the Faustpatrone | Radfahrschwadronen | Bicycle-mounted squadron or unit |
| | | Radfahrtruppen | Bicycle-mounted troops |
| | | Rangabzeichen | Badges of rank |
| Panzergrenadier | Armored infantry(man) | Rationssatz | Daily ration for animals |
| Panzergrenadier/ ~division/~brigade | Armored infantry division/brigade | Reich | National state, empire |
| | | Reichsarbeitsdienst (RAD) | (German) National Labor Service |
| Panzerhaubitze (PzH) | Self-propelled howitzer | | |
| Panzerjäger | Tank destroyer (tracked armored vehicle) | Reichsbahn | (German) National Railways |
| Panzerkampfabzeichen | Tank battle badge | Reichsführer-SS (RF-SS) | National leader of the SS (Heinrich Himmler) |
| Panzerkampfwagen (Pz.Kpfw. or PzKw) | Armored vehicle, usually a tank | | |
| | | Reichsführung-SS | High command of the SS and Waffen-SS |
| Panzerschreck | Literally, "tank terror", an alternative name for the Raketenpanzerbüchse | Reichsheer, das | National Army, the (1920s and 1930s) |
| | | Reichskriegsflagge | National war flag or banner of the Third Reich |
| Panzerspähwagen | Eight-wheeled reconnaissance armored car (such as the Pz.Sd.Kfz.234/1 used for reconnaissance) | Reichsmark (RM) | German national unit of currency (RM1.00 value in early 1945 was equivalent to US $0.40) |
| | | Reichspost | National Postal Service |
| Panzertruppe | Panzer or armored troops or forces | Reichswehr, die | National Armed Forces, the (1920s and to 1935) |
| Panzervernichtungs- abzeichen | Single-handed Tank Destruction Battle Badge | | |
| | | Reichskokarde | National cockade insignia (black, white, red) |
| Panzerwagen | Armored vehicle, including armored cars | Reichssicherheits- hauptamt (RSHA) | SS central (main) security office, incorporating and controlling the merged Security Service (SD), Secret State Police (Gestapo) and Criminal Police (KriPo) from September 1939 |
| Panzerwurfmine | Anti-tank hand grenade | | |
| Paradeanzug | Parade uniform | | |
| Patronentaschen | Ammunition pouches | | |
| Pelzmützen | Fur caps (issued on Eastern Front from 1942) | | |
| Personenkraftwagen | Personnel-carrying vehicle | Reservedivision | Reserve division |
| Pfeifpatrone | Whistling cartridge for signal pistols, used to warn of gas or chemical attack | Reserveoffiziere | Reserve officers |
| | | Reserve-Offizier- Anwärter | Reserve officer candidate |
| Pferd | Horse | | |
| Pferde-Lazarett | Literally, a "horse hospital" of the veterinary service | Reserve-Offizier- Bewerber | Reserve officer applicant |
| | | Reserveoffizierskorps | Reserve officers corps |
| Pferdeersatzzüge | Trains carrying replacement horses | Richter | Judge advocate |
| Pferdetransportzüge | Trains carrying horses requiring veterinary treatment | Riegelmine | Bar-shaped anti-tank mine |
| | | Ringkragen | Uniform gorget (of Feldgendarmerie for example) |
| Pferdeverbandplatz | Veterinary dressing station providing emergency treatment | | |
| | | Ritterkreuz, Ritterkreuz des Eisernen Kreuzes | Knight's Cross of the Iron Cross (a high-level medal or decoration) |
| Pickelhaube | Traditional spike- or ball-topped German military helmet (19th century to 1920s) | | |
| | | Rückzug | Enforced tactical retreat |
| Pionierbataillon | Engineer battalion | Rüstung | Armament, military equipment |
| Pioniere | Pioneer or engineer, including combat engineer | Sachsenberg Land- Wasser-Schlepper | A fully-tracked amphibious load and personnel carrier, with propeller propulsion in water |
| Polizei | Police | | |
| Portepee | Decorative side-arm tassel for bayonet, dagger etc.; also used specifically to distinguish categories of Unteroffiziere as "mit" (with) or "ohne" (without) Portepee | Sanitäts | Medical, first aid |
| | | Sanitätsmannschaften | Medical service troops or orderlies |
| | | Schalldämpfer | Silencer (for use with the Mauser 98K rifle) |
| | | Scharfschützen- abzeichen | Sniper Proficiency Battle badge |
| Portionsatz | Daily (three meals) ration | | |
| "Pour le Mérite" | Imperial Germany's highest military award "for merit" | Schießbecher | Rifle grenade projector cup (for Kar 98K rifle) |
| | | Schirmmütze | Uniform peaked cap (for parades, walking out etc.) |
| Propagandatruppen | Propaganda troops | | |
| Propagandakompanie | Propaganda company (of uniformed war correspondents) | Schlepper | Tractor, as in Wehrmachtschlepper |
| | | Schmeisser | Name commonly given to MP 38 and MP 40 submachine guns |
| Propagandawerfer | Rocket-launcher used to fire special 73mm projectiles containing propaganda leaflets | | |
| | | Schnürschuhe | Lace-up leather service shoes or ankle boots |
| Protektorat | "Protectorate" (of Bohemia and Moravia) | Schürzen | Side skirts (additional armor plates fitted to the sides of tanks to protect the suspension and hull against anti-tank rifle fire and hollow- charge warheads) |
| Quartier | Military accommodation, quarters or billets | | |
| Raketenpanzerbüchse | Anti-tank rocket-projector (similar to the US Army's "Bazooka" and the British army's 3.5- inch rocket launcher) | Schützen | Rifle troops |
| | | Schützenmine (Schü-Mine) | Anti-personnel mine |

| German | English Translation or Explanation |
|---|---|
| Schützenpanzerwagen | Armored personnel carrier |
| Schutzmütze | Padded black beret used by Panzer (tank) crewmen until 1940 |
| Schutzstaffel (SS) | Elite guard (of the NSDAP and Third Reich period) |
| Schwerpunkt | Point or focus of main operational effort |
| Schwester (DRK) | Nursing sister (of the German Red Cross) |
| Schwimmwagen | Amphibious variant of the VW Kübelwagen (light motor vehicle) |
| Seitengewehr | Bayonet |
| Selbstladegewehr | Self-loading or automatic rifle |
| Sicherheitsdienst (SD) | SS security service |
| Sicherung | Security, security forces etc. |
| Sieg | Victory |
| *Signal* | Wehrmacht-produced propaganda magazine |
| S-Mine | Anti-personnel mine (of the "bounding" or jumping type) |
| Soldbuch | Soldier's pay book and personal identification document (carried by every officer and soldier) |
| Sonder~ | Special |
| Sonderabzeichen für das niederkämpfen von Panzerkampfwagen durch Einzelkämpfer | See "Panzervernichtungsabzeichen" |
| Sonderkraftfahrzeug (SdKfz) | Special-purpose motor vehicle |
| Sonderzüge | Special trains (for moving tanks and self-propelled artillery) |
| Spaten | Spade, shovel |
| Spieß | Senior warrant officer (slang) |
| Sprengstoff | Explosive |
| SS-Führungshauptamt | Principal operational office of the SS |
| Stab | Staff |
| Stabshelferinnen | Female administrative and clerical headquarters staff |
| Stabsoffiziere | Field officers (as a group or category) |
| Stabsquartier | Headquarters |
| Stahlhelm | German steel helmet introduced in 1916; also subsequently adopted as the name of the post-1918 veterans' association |
| Stalag (Stammlager) | Prisoner-of-war (PW) camp for non-officer PWs; also used generically to describe all types of PW camps |
| Stielhandgranate | Stick-type hand-grenade |
| Stoßtruppen | Shock troops (originally in World War I) |
| Stuka (Sturzkampf-flugzeug) | Literally "dive-bomber", but usually applied to the Junkers 87 (Ju 87) |
| Stummelwerfer | Type of infantry mortar introduced into service on a very limited scale in 1942 |
| Sturm | Storm, assault |
| Sturmabteilung (SA) | Storm troops, known as the "Brownshirts" (of the NSDAP and Third Reich period) |
| Sturmdivision | Assault division |
| Sturmabzeichen | Badge (decoration) awarded for participation in assaults |
| Sturmgepäck | Triangular webbing harness to support various essential equipment items necessary for short-term assault or similar operations |
| Sturmgeschütz | Self-propelled assault gun |
| Sturmgewehr (StuG) | Assault rifle (such as the Sturmgewehr 44, or StuG 44) |
| Sturmhaubitze | Self-propelled assault howitzer |

| German | English Translation or Explanation |
|---|---|
| Sturmkompanie | Storm or assault company |
| Sturmpanzer | Assault gun (self propelled) |
| Sturmpionier | Assault engineer |
| Sturzkampfflugzeug (Stuka) | Dive-bomber (typically the Ju 87) |
| Swastika (Hakenkreuz) | Emblem or symbol adopted by the NSDAP in the 1920s, but already in use by various right-wing groups |
| Tagesbefehl | Order of the day |
| Taktische Aufklärung | Tactical reconnaissance |
| Tellermine | Dinner-plate shaped anti-tank mine |
| Tieffliegervernichtungs-abzeichen | Low-flying Aircraft Destruction Battle Badge |
| Tornister | Standard field pack made of cowhide or canvas |
| Totenkopf | Death's head |
| Traditionsträger | Literally "tradition carrier", maintaining the heritage and lineage of a former unit through the creation of a new unit |
| Tragtier | Pack animal (typically mules) |
| Tragtierkolonnen | Pack animal load-carrying trains or columns |
| Tragbüchse | Carrying container (for gas mask) |
| Traktor | Tractor (typically, agricultural) |
| Transport-Kommandanturen | Regional transportation headquarters (located throughout Germany) |
| Trinkbecher | Drinking cup (as part of water bottle set) |
| Troddel | Side-arm knot (indicating unit subordination, arm of service, etc.) |
| Truppenamt | Military office established to administer and exert command over the army (1919) |
| Truppensonderdienst | Special troop service branch (for legal and administrative officers) |
| Truppenteil | Unit |
| Truppenübungsplatz | Military training ground or maneuver area |
| Truppenverbandplatz | Regimental medical aid post |
| Übungslager | Training ground |
| Umfassungsangriff | Enveloping attack |
| Untermenschen | Subhuman (relating to race or ethnicity) |
| Unteroffizier | Non-commissioned officer (typically sergeant) |
| Urlaub | Leave, holiday |
| Vaterland | Fatherland |
| Vaterlandspartei | Right-wing "patriotic party" (1919) |
| Verbandpäckchentasche | Pre-packed field dressing |
| Verbrauchsatz | Fuel "consumption unit" (amount required to move a given vehicle 100 kilometers) |
| Verkehrsregelungpolizei | Military police traffic regulators |
| Vermittlungskätchen | A small-size, basic type of telephone exchange |
| Verpflegungssatz, Verpflegung | Ration (linked to type) |
| Verteidigung | Defense (position) |
| Verwaltung | Administration |
| Verwundetenabzeichen | Wound Badge |
| Veterinär | Veterinary, veterinary second lieutenant |
| Veterinärkompanie | Veterinary company |
| Volksgrenadierdivision | Literally "people's division" and presented as an honor title when introduced in late 1944; despite some successes, these divisions were often second-rate and poorly equipped, – especially in terms of serious major equipment and mobility deficiencies |

| German | English Translation or Explanation |
|---|---|
| Volkssturm | Home guard or "people's army" employed during the final year of World War II |
| Volkswagen | Literally "people's car", made by the Volkswagen motor manufacturing company (which also made various military wheeled vehicles) |
| Vorgeschobene Stellung | Forward or advanced defensive positions |
| Wacht | Guard |
| Wachtruppen | Military police independent guard battalions, including prisoner-of-war camp guard units |
| "Wacht am Rhein" | "Watch on the Rhine", the Ardennes offensive operation in December 1944 |
| Waffe(n) | Weapon(s), arm or branch of service |
| Waffenfarbe | System of distinctive colored shoulder and collar insignia embellishments identifying arm or branch of service |
| Waffenprüfung | Weapons proving and testing |
| Waffenprüfungsstelle | Weapons proving and testing center or site |
| Waffenschulen | Special service technical schools |
| Waffen-SS, die | Armed SS, the |
| Wehrersatzdienststelle | Home station (of a soldier or unit) in Germany |
| Wehrkreis(e) | Military district(s) (within Germany) |
| Wehrkreissanitätsparke | Corps-level medical parks (supply depots) |
| Wehrmacht, die | Armed Forces, the (1935–45) |
| Wehrmachtbeamte(n) | Civilian administrative official(s) and specialist(s) in military service but not categorized as soldiers |
| Wehrmachts- beschaffungsamt Bekleidung und Ausrüstung | Armed Forces Clothing and Procurement Office (in Berlin) |
| Wehrmacht-Heer (WH) | Armed Forces – Army; the letters "WH" appeared before the number on the vehicle registration or licence plates of all army vehicles |

| German | English Translation or Explanation |
|---|---|
| Wehrmacht-Luftwaffe (WL) | Armed Forces – Luftwaffe; the letters "WL" appeared before the number on the vehicle registration or licence plates of all air force vehicles |
| Wehrmacht-Marine (WM) | Armed Forces – Marine; the letters "WM" usually appeared before the number on the vehicle registration or licence plates of vehicles used by the navy (Kriegsmarine) |
| Wehrmachtschlepper | Literally, armed forces tractor (such as the schwerer (heavy) Wehrmachtschlepper on which the ten-barrel Panzerwerfer was mounted) |
| Wehrpaß | Service record book (for an officer or soldier) |
| Werfer | Projector (typically of rocket or shell) |
| Werkstatt | Workshop |
| Widerstandslinie | Line of resistance |
| Winkel | Non-commissioned officer's rank insignia chevron |
| Wolfsschanze | Literally "wolf's lair": the name of Hitler's headquarters in East Prussia 1941–4 |
| X-Uhr | X-hour, the equivalent of H-hour, the planned or actual start time for any military operation |
| Zahlmeister | Lower grade of administrative officer |
| Zapfenstreich | Military musical tattoo or ceremonial parade |
| Zeltbahn | Section of four-man tent; also served as a foul-weather cape or groundsheet; could also form an eight- or sixteen-man tent |
| Zug | Railway train; but also a platoon or section |
| Zugkraftwagen | Half-track heavy prime-mover tractor |
| Zweibein | Bipod (typically for small-arms such as machine guns) |
| Zwischenfeld | Area between two lines of defense or resistance (Widerstandslinie) |

# Notes

**Part I. The German Army in Peacetime, 1918–1939**

1 Subsequently the tale was produced in manuscript form, with several versions appearing in the thirteenth century and a first complete edition published in Switzerland in the mid-eighteenth century.
2 Rosinski, p. 170.
3 Rosinski, p. 177.
4 Rosinski, p. 180.
5 Rosinski, pp. 185–6.
6 Rosinski, p. 189.
7 Quoted in Kurowski, p. 485.
8 By the main Rapallo Agreement the Soviet Union waived its claim to post-war reparations, while Germany waived its claims for compensation for its territorial losses. In practice both countries had grievances with the Western Powers – the Soviet Union over their support for the White Russians, the Germans for the terms they had imposed at Versailles. As well as offering a measure of German-Soviet reconciliation Rapallo provided the Soviet leadership with an opportunity to unsettle and divide the Western Powers. It was also the first significant act of foreign policy conducted both by the Soviet Union and by Germany in the post-war period.
9 In 1925 von Hindenburg became president of Germany, and a period of relative stability ensued within Germany during the next few years. With much of his work accomplished, von Seeckt's power and influence declined in the new era of political rather than military activity. In late 1926 the minister of war, Gessler, forced his resignation after he allowed the Crown Prince of Prussia's son – a member of the politically unacceptable Hohenzollern royal family – to take part in military maneuvers as a temporary officer. General Hans von Seeckt, architect and principal creator of the Reichswehr, died in 1936, having spent much of the ten years of his retirement actively involved in politics and in writing his memoirs, as well as for a short time as a military adviser to Chiang Kai-shek.
10 In the spring of 1935, Hitler effectively terminated the Soviet-German military cooperation that had been agreed at Rapallo in 1922, and which had so benefited the Reichswehr during the following decade.
11 Uniform regulation references quoted in Davis, p. 10 and Hormann (volume II), p. 23. Simpson also states (p. 123) that, "in February 1934 … Blomberg ordered that the Nazi Party's emblem … was to be worn on the uniforms of all members of the armed forces."

**Part II. The German Army at War, 1939–1945**

1 When they signed the Tripartite Pact in 1940 and 1941, the pro-German leaders of these European nations viewed the rise of the Third Reich and the Wehrmacht's victories as the means by which they could also gain international, territorial and political advantage through their support for Hitler's policies and strategic aspirations. At the time they joined the pact, Hungary was led by the Regent Admiral Miklós Horthy, Romania by the dictator General Ion Antonescu, and Slovakia by Premier Dr. Joseph Tiso. Creation of the so-called Independent State of Croatia had been enabled by the German campaign in the Balkans in 1941, and it was headed by the right-wing radical Ante Pavelić. As the war progressed, Italian, Hungarian, Romanian and Bulgarian troops were all involved to varying extents in the Third Reich's war in Europe and the Balkans, while Italian army units and formations were also committed in North Africa. However, the Croatian military contribution was generally confined to operations within the fragmented former Yugoslavia, primarily against members of the indigenous Serb population and later the partisan groups. The motivation, training, and professionalism of these often disparate forces varied widely, as did the quality and quantity of their equipment. As such, with a few exceptions, they generally did little more than to complement the German armies alongside which they served, or to release German units for front-line deployment. Nevertheless, the increasingly serious losses sustained by the Wehrmacht from 1942 (with casualties on the Eastern Front exceeding one and a half million by spring that year) needed to be offset urgently, and so the full implications – and ultimately the often catastrophic costs – of the military obligations imposed upon the armies and civilian populations of Hitler's European allies by the pact signatories of 1940 and 1941 proved inescapable.
2 Tucker-Jones quoted in James Lucas, *Battle Group! Kampfgruppen Action of World War Two*, London, 1993, p. 19.
3 Guderian, p. 72.
4 While France had long posed the main and most immediate threat to Germany in the west, the rise and growing military strength of imperial Russia during the late nineteenth century arguably represented an even greater potential threat to Germany in the future.
5 This plan was originally developed by General Alfred von Schlieffen from 1891 during his time as chief of the general staff. It was designed to produce the speedy and comprehensive defeat of France, thus allowing the army to turn its attention to what was regarded as the potentially greater long-term strategic threat posed to Germany by Russia.
6 Statistical information drawn primarily from John Williams, *France: Summer 1940*, London, 1969, pp. 16–17. In some cases, the figures provided for the numbers of divisions finally deployed for Fall Gelb shown in some other sources such as Macksey, Pimlott and Simpson vary slightly.
7 As ever, the precise figures for the forces involved vary between sources, and those quoted in the main text reflect a reasonable consensus. Pimlott (pp. 65–7) quotes 600,000 vehicles, 3,580 tanks, 7,184 guns, 1,830 aircraft and a total of 120 divisions. Simpson suggests a total of 145 divisions 'in the east' (p. 150), albeit that a number of these were almost certainly not involved in the initial campaign. Bartov (pp. 14–15) quotes 3,600,000 troops, 3,648 tanks and 2,510 supporting aircraft. Some sources also quote an overall manpower figure of 'three million', while others quote 'four million'. Beevor, in Stalingrad, quotes 3,050,000 German troops within the total of four million. In sum, the best available information indicates that some three million German soldiers were committed on 22 June 1941, plus up to a million other Axis and complementary military, non-army and paramilitary forces.
8 Bastable pp. 17–18.
9 Beevor, *Stalingrad*, pp. 14–17. Hassell was later implicated in the unsuccessful assassination attempt against Hitler on 20 July 1944 and was hanged at Plötzensee prison, Berlin, on 8 September 1944.
10 Knappe and Brusaw, p. 201.
11 Simpson, p. 156.
12 Bastable, pp. 87–8.
13 Bastable, pp. 20–1.
14 Bastable, p. 208.
15 Bastable, p. 209.
16 Bastable, p. 207.
17 Bastable, p. 214.
18 Bastable, p. 99.
19 Yet again, the relative strengths at Kursk quoted by different sources vary. These variations are generally not great, although Pimlott does suggest that as many as 5,000 tanks may have been available to the Soviets at Kursk rather than the 3,300–3,600 quoted in most other sources; Pimlott's higher figure might possibly have included self-propelled guns and tank destroyers as well as tanks. In any event, it is noteworthy that the Russian forces committed at Kursk were (if expressed as percentages of the total strength and capability of the whole of the Red Army in mid-1943) no less than twenty percent of its men and guns, at least 33 percent of its tanks, and 25 percent of its combat aircraft.
20 The total number of tanks engaged in the core tank battle between 4th Panzer Army and 5th Guards Tank Army was probably no more than 850, with the balance of up to 1,400 or 1,500 deployed in adjacent area. Some sources imply that as many as 1,000 (Pimlott) and 1,500 (Orgill) armored vehicles were engaged in the central part of the battle.
21 Orgill, p. 121.
22 Pimlott, p. 127.
23 Orgill, pp. 121–3.
24 Whiting, *Battle of the Ruhr Pocket*, Pan/Ballantine, 1972, p. 145.
25 Public Record Office, PRO WO218/311, dated 17 January 1945 (also quoted by Hastings, p. 169).

**Part III. The Creation of Hitler's Army: Rearmament, 1933–1939**

1 Rosinski, pp. 251–2.
2 Rosinski, p. 251.
3 Guderian, p. 28.
4 Guderian, p. 30.
5 The creation of an army paratrooper or airborne capability followed the successful formation of a parachute infantry battalion from the Landespolizeigruppe (later Regiment) "General Göring" in January 1936. This battalion had been part of the Luftwaffe from 1 October 1935, and overall command of all of the German parachute forces was transferred to the Luftwaffe in January 1938, when army parachute units were also subsumed into it. The Luftwaffe had already gained control of the army's air defense artillery units in 1935. The decision to transfer these units from the army to the Luftwaffe was political rather than operational and reflected Göring's considerable influence with Hitler at that time, rather than military common sense, as both the airborne forces and the anti-aircraft artillery were logically part of the German ground forces rather than of the air force.
6 US War Department, TM-E 30-451, p. I-2.
7 TM-E 30-451, p. I-2.
8 See Bartov, pp. 12–28.

**Part IV. The Structure of Military Power**

1 Von Blomberg and Eva Gruhn left Germany and went into voluntary exile in Capri, taking no further part in German military affairs. However, his previous work in enabling Hitler's military aspirations was recalled at the end of the war, and he died in a US military prison at Nürnberg on 4 March 1946. Meanwhile, von Fritsch was publicly rehabilitated on 11 August 1938. He remained in Germany, fulfilling various duties; in August 1939 he assumed command of Artillery Regiment No. 12 in East Prussia immediately prior to the Polish campaign. On 22 September 1939, he was hit by Polish machine gun fire in open ground on the outskirts of Warsaw and was killed.
2 Simpson, p. 136.
3 Both Beck and Halder suffered the consequences of their continued resistance to Hitler. In the aftermath of the July 1944 assassination attempt against Hitler, Beck attempted unsuccessfully to commit suicide and was subsequently shot, while Halder was sent to a concentration camp but survived the war.
4 See Stone, *War Summits*, pp. 5–6.
5 Rosinski, p. 267. General Erich Ludendorff (1865–1937) was chief

of staff to von Hindenburg during World War I, and as his deputy subsequently planned and directed the German offensives of 1917 and 1918.

6  Lucas, p. 8.
7  Compiled primarily from Lucas, pp. 4–9.
8  Bartov, p. 40–3.
9  Bartov, p. 40–2.
10 Bartov, p. 41–2.

### Part V. Officers and Soldiers

1  Knappe and Brusaw, p. 117.
2  Bartov, p. 39.
3  Knappe and Brusaw, p. 245.
4  Knappe and Brusaw, p. 246.
5  Knappe and Brusaw, pp. 256–7.
6  Forty, p.75.
7  US War Department, TM-E 30-451, p. I-55.
8  TM-E 30-451, p. I-57.
9  TM-E 30-451, p. I-71.
10 Forty, p. 16.
11 Forty, p. 17.
12 Knappe and Brusaw, pp. 91, 92–3.
13 Knappe and Brusaw, p. 94.
14 Forty, p.26.
15 Forty, p. 28.
16 Forty, p. 28.
17 Forty, p. 28.
18 Forty, p. 19.
19 Sajer, pp. 197–208.
20 *Times Literary Supplement*, 21 April 1978 (also quoted by Hastings, p. 170).
21 Pallud, *Blitzkrieg in the West*, pp. 476 and 479.
22 Pallud, p. 566.
23 Bartov, p. 64.
24 Snyder, p. 199 (also quoted in other sources).
25 Bastable, p. 62.
26 The number of soldiers found guilty of various criminal capital offenses and executed by France and by Great Britain in World War II was just 40 and 100 respectively. However, these executions resulted from due judicial process dealing with what were recognized as criminal actions and so cannot be compared with the often extra-judicial and summary military executions carried out within the armed forces of the Third Reich.
27 Bartov, pp. 95–101 (includes all of the statistics for trials, executions and prison sentences).
28 Forty, p. 28.
29 Guderian subsequently served with von Rundstedt and Keitel on the three-man court of honor convened by Hitler to investigate the conduct of the army officers arrested in connection with the July plot. Those who were found guilty by this court were dismissed from the army and consigned to the so-called "People's Court" presided over by the notorious Roland Freisler for trial as civilians, which was followed in virtually every case by their execution.
30 Knappe and Brusaw, pp. 254–5.
31 Quoted in Hastings, p. 395

### Part VII. Combat Arms

1  Lucas, p. 30 (after Reibert).
2  Rosinski, p. 253
3  Knappe and Brusaw, p. 184.

4  Guderian, p. 289.
5  See also Bender and Odegard, pp. 206–78, and Davies, pp. 20–31.
6  Lucas, p. 98.
7  Lucas, p.132.

### Part VIII. Weapons of War

1  Sweeting, p. 167.
2  Sweeting, p. 167.
3  Tucker-Jones, p. 15.
4  The engagement sequence is an edited summary compiled from various accounts.

### Part IX. Supporting Arms and Services

1  Tucker-Jones, p. 29.
2  Bastable, p. 162.
3  See Hastings, p. 393.
4  US War Department, TM-E 30-451, p. VIII-1.
5  Hughes-Wilson, p. 17 and pp. 31–7.
6  The high number of NCOs in the Feldgendarmerie unit reflected the practice common in many armed forces and meant that these military policemen had sufficient rank and authority to carry out their routine duties when dealing with ordinary soldiers.
7  The term "town major" was widely used, irrespective of the actual rank of an officer appointed to this administrative task, although the appointment of an officer with the experience and seniority of a major was the norm.
8  US War Department, TM-E 30-451, p. VIII-103.
9  Bundesarchiv-Militärarchiv, RM 7/810D, OKW/WFst/Org (Vb) Nr. 743/45 v. 17 Mar 1945.
10 Bartov, p. 39.
11 Knappe and Brusaw, p. 208.
12 Lucas, p. 142.

### Part X. Tactics and Special Operations

1  Quoted in Bance, p. 8.
2  Knappe and Brusaw, p. 181.
3  Knappe and Brusaw, pp. 181–2.
4  Knappe and Brusaw, p. 193.
5  Knappe and Brusaw, p. 193.
6  US Department of the Army, Historical Study, *Small Unit Actions During the German Campaign in Russia*, Department of the Army Pamphlet No. 20-269 (Washington, D.C.: GPO, 1953), pp. 61–2 (quoted by Sweeting, pp. 38–9).
7  Bastable, p. 137.
8  Bastable, p. 215.
9  Forty, p. 45.
10 Forty, p. 48.
11 See Bartov, pp. 92–5.
12 Bartov, p. 84.
13 Bartov, p. 93.

### Part XI. The End of Hitler's Army

1  Although there is a continuing public awareness of the wartime destruction of such cities as Berlin, Dresden, Hamburg, etc., in fact no fewer than 131 major German towns and cities were effectively reduced to rubble by Allied aerial bombardment and (to varying extents) by artillery fire and ground attack. In the course of direct Allied attacks against the German homeland, at least eight million

Germans were made homeless, and more than 600,000 civilians were killed. Commenting on the sheer scale of the destruction within Germany itself, the historian Alex Kershaw observed in 2004 that, "The extent of such destruction was so vast, so utterly lacking in historical precedent, that to this day its impact has yet to be widely understood in Germany itself." (Kershaw, p. 175). During World War I, the German homeland and civilian population had been largely untouched by direct attack; by 1945 the disasters ultimately visited upon the forces of the Third Reich in World War II had been largely mirrored by their equivalent and catastrophic impact upon the German civilian population as a whole.

2  On 17 December 1944, up to 86 US prisoners-of-war were killed by Waffen-SS soldiers of Kampfgruppe Peiper (part of the 1st SS-Panzer-Division Leibstandarte "Adolf Hitler") in a field at Baugnez crossroads, just over two miles to the southeast of Malmédy. The "Malmédy Massacre" probably occurred in the immediate aftermath of a confused skirmish between retreating US troops and the advancing Germans. A situation developed in which some US soldiers had already surrendered and accepted prisoner-of-war status while at the same time others had attempted to resume or continue the fight, or simply to escape capture in the general confusion. Although the true facts of the Malmédy Massacre will probably never be known (and many of these "facts" were misrepresented during what was later shown to have been a flawed investigative process and at the subsequent war crimes trial convened by the US military authorities at Dachau after the war), there is no evidence that these killings constituted a premeditated or officially-sanctioned execution of prisoners-of-war. Nevertheless, in addition to the fact that the American personnel were clearly unarmed, the deliberate dispatch of the wounded survivors in the aftermath of the initial spontaneous period of firing unquestionably transformed the incident into a war crime. Soon after the discovery of the massacre in December 1944, the incident was widely publicized by the US Army and its propaganda impact maximized. The widespread anger it provoked was exemplified by a number of somewhat extreme retaliatory orders being promulgated by the Americans. One such order, issued on 21 December by the headquarters of the 328th Regiment of the US 26th Infantry Division, stated that, "No SS troops or paratroopers will be taken prisoner but will be shot on sight." See also Pallud, pp. 183–92.

3  A West German commission subsequently investigated the treatment of German prisoners-of-

war by the Allies and recorded its findings in *Bericht des Wissenschaftlichen Kommission der Bundesregierung z. Geschichte der deutschen Kriegsgefangen des 2ten Krieges*. See also Whiting, pp. 147–8.

### Conclusion

1  Italy could have achieved this, but Mussolini's strategic ineptitude and his army's failures in North Africa precipitated the previously unplanned need for Germany to provide military assistance, which ultimately depleted German resources much needed elsewhere.

2  The magnitude of the re-militarization task in Germany in response to the new threats posed by the Cold War was enormous, particularly in West Germany. The following policy statement agreed by the Allied powers at Potsdam in August 1945, dealing with their plans for the occupation of post-war Germany, indicated the extent of de-militarization and de-Nazification carried out from 1945: "All German land, naval and air forces, the SS, SA, SD and Gestapo with all their organizations, staffs and institutions, including the General Staff, the Officers' Corps, Reserve Corps, military schools, war veterans' organizations and all other military and quasi-military organizations, together with all clubs and associations which serve to keep alive the military tradition in Germany shall be completely and finally abolished in such manner as permanently to prevent the revival or reorganization of German militarism and Nazism."

### Appendices

1  Snyder, p. 366.
2  Snyder, p. 367.
3  The total number of divisions and their designating numbers as shown reflect Stein, Keegan, and Fosten and Marrion, these are considered authoritative, although they do vary slightly from Reitlinger's list of the Waffen-SS divisions. In any event, several of these particular formations were created at relatively short notice during the final three years of the war and often existed for only a brief period of time, with much of their war record undocumented or lost in the chaos of their defeat, surrender or annihilation during 1944 and 1945.

# Select Bibliography and Other Sources

Bance, Professor Alan (Tr.), *Blitzkrieg In Their Own Words*, Pen & Sword Military, Barnsley, 2005 (a literal translation of *Mit Den Panzern In Ost Und West*, Germany, 1942)

Bartov, Omer, *Hitler's Army*, Oxford University Press, Inc., New York, 1992

Bastable, Jonathan, *Voices from Stalingrad: Nemesis on the Volga*, David & Charles Ltd, Cincinnati, USA, 2006

Beevor, Antony, *Stalingrad*, Penguin Books, London, 1999

— *Berlin: the Downfall, 1945*, Penguin Books, London, 2003

Bender, Roger James, *The Luftwaffe*, R. James Bender Publishing, Mountain View, California, 1972

— and Taylor, Hugh Page, *Uniforms, Organization and History of the Waffen-SS*, R. James Bender Publishing, Mountain View, California, 1971

— and Law, Richard D., *Uniforms, Organization and History of the Afrikakorps*, R. James Bender Publishing, Mountain View, California, 1973

— and Odegard, Warren W., *Uniforms, Organization and History of the Panzertruppe*, R. James Bender Publishing, San Jose, California, 1980

— and Petersen, George A., *Hermann Göring: from Regiment to Fallschirmpanzerkorps*, R. James Bender Publishing, San Jose, California, 1975

Biddiscombe, Perry, *The Denazification of Germany: A History 1945–1950*, Stroud, Gloucestershire, 2007

Carr, William, *A History of Germany, 1815–1990*, Arnold (Hodder Headline Group), London, 1991

Chambers, Walker W. and Wilkie, John R., *A Short History of the German Language*, Methuen, New York, USA, 1981

Citino, Robert M., *The German Way of War: From the Thirty Years War to the Third Reich*, University Press of Kansas, Lawrence, Kansas, 2005

Craig, Gordon A., *Germany 1866–1945*, Oxford University Press, Oxford, 1981

Davies, W. J. K., *Panzer Regiments: Equipment and Organization*, Almark Publishing Co. Ltd., New Malden, Surrey, 1978

Davis, Brian L., *German Army Uniforms and Insignia 1933–1945*, Arms & Armor Press, London, 1971

Deutscher Schulverein Südmark, *Deutscher Volkskalender 1939*, Deutschen Schulverein Südmark, Graz, Österreich, 1939 (including "Die Heimat des Führers" (Linus Refer), "Der Kurier" (Karl Springenschmid), "Kunst und Character" (Dr. Wilhelm Huber) and various other articles)

Deutsches Historisches Museum, Berlin, *Pictures and Objects from German History: A Concise Guide*, Deutsches Historisches Museum, Berlin, 1995

Forty, George, *German Infantryman at War, 1939–1945*, Ian Allan Publishing Ltd., Hersham, Surrey, 2002

Fosten, D. S. V., and Marrion, R. J., *Waffen-SS: Its Uniforms, Insignia and Equipment 1938–1945*, Almark Publishing Co. Ltd., New Malden, 1972

Fowler, Will, and Rose, Mike, *Their War: German Combat Photographs from the Archives of 'Signal'*, Combined Publishing, Conshohocken, Pennsylvania, 2000

Guderian, General Heinz (Tr. Constantine Fitzgibbon), *Panzer Leader*, Futura Publications Ltd, London, 1979

Hanisch, Prof. Dr. Ernst, *Obersalzberg: The 'Eagle's Nest' and Adolf Hitler*, Berchtesgadener Landesstiftung, Bad Reichenhall, 1998

Hastings, Max, *Armageddon: The Battle for Germany 1944–45*, Pan Macmillan Ltd., London, 2004

Haus Neuerburg, *Das Reichsheer und Seine Tradition*, Haus Neuerburg, Germany, c.1936

Hinrichsen, Horst, *Radfahrschwadronen: Fahrräder in Einsatz bei der Wehrmacht 1939–1945*, Podzun-Pallas-Verlag, Wölfersheim-Berstadt/ Freiburg, 1996

Hogg, Ian V., *The Guns: 1939–45*, Macdonald & Co, (Publishers) Ltd., London, 1970

Hormann, Jörg M., *Uniforms of the Infantry, 1919 to the Present* (volume 2), Schiffer Publishing, Pennsylvania, USA, 1989

— *Uniforms of the Panzer Troops, 1917 to the Present* (volume 1), Schiffer Publishing, Pennsylvania, USA, 1989

Hughes-Wilson, Colonel John, *Military Intelligence Blunders and Cover-Ups*, Constable & Robinson Ltd., London, 1999

Hunt, Robert (Ed.), and Hartman, Tom (Ed.), *Swastika at War*, Leo Cooper Ltd., London, 1975

Keegan, John, *Waffen SS: the Asphalt Soldiers*, Macdonald & Co. (Publishers) Ltd., London, 1970

Kershaw, Alex, *The Longest Winter*, Penguin Books (imprint Michael Joseph), London, 2004

Kershaw, Ian, *The Nazi Dictatorship: Problems and Perspectives of Interpretation*, Arnold (Hodder Headline Group), London, 1993

Knappe, Siegfried, and Brusaw, Ted, *Soldat: Reflections of a German Soldier, 1936–1949*, BCA with Airlife Publishing, London, 1993

Kolb, Eberhard (Tr. P. S. Falla), *The Weimar Republic*, Routledge, London, 1995

Kurowski, Franz, *Infantry Aces: The German Combat Soldier in Combat in WW II*, Stackpole Books, Mechanicsburg, Pennsylvania, USA, 2005

Laffin, John, *Jackboot: The Story of the German Soldier*, Cassel & Company Ltd, London, 1965 (subsequently republished by Sutton Publishing Ltd., Stroud, 2003)

Le Tissier, Tony, *Berlin Then and Now*, After the Battle Publications, Plaistow Press Ltd., London, 1992

— *The Third Reich Then and Now*, After the Battle Publications, Battle of Britain International Ltd, London, 2005

Lucas, James, *German Army Handbook*, Sutton Publishing Ltd., Stroud, Gloucestershire, 1998

Macksey, Major K. J., *Panzer Division: the Mailed Fist*, Macdonald & Co., (Publishers) Ltd., London, 1968

— *Afrika Korps*, Macdonald & Co, (Publishers) Ltd., London, 1968

Montgomery of Alamein, *A History of Warfare*, Collins, London, 1968

Orgill, Douglas, *T-34: Russian Armor*, Macdonald & Co (Publishers) Ltd., London, 1970

Pallud, Jean Paul, *Battle of the Bulge Then and Now*, After the Battle Publications, Battle of Britain Prints International Ltd., London, 1984

— *Blitzkrieg in the West Then and Now*, After the Battle Publications, Battle of Britain Prints International Ltd., London, 1991

Pimlott, Dr. John, *Wehrmacht: The Illustrated History of the German Army in WW II*, Aurum Press, London, 2001

Price, Alfred, *Luftwaffe: Birth, Life and Death of an Air Force*, Pan/Ballantine, London, 1973

Reibert, Major W., and Ullmendinger, Major G., *Der Dienstunterricht im Heere: Ausgabe für den Panzerabwehrschützen*, E. S. Mittler & Sohn, Berlin, 1939

Reibert, Major W., *Der Dienstunterricht im Heere: Ausgabe für den Schützen der Schützenkompanie*, E. S. Mittler & Sohn, Berlin, 1940

Reibert, Oberstleutnant W., *Der Dienstunterricht im Heere: Ausgabe für den Schützen der Schützenkompanie*, Berlin, 1943

Reitlinger, Gerald, *The SS: Alibi of a Nation*, William Heinemann Ltd., London, 1957

Reynolds, Michael, *The Devil's Adjutant: Jochen Peiper, Panzer Leader*, Spellmount Ltd., Staplehurst, 1997

— *Sons of the Reich: II SS Panzer Corps, Normandy, Arnhem, Ardennes, Eastern Front*, Spellmount Ltd., Staplehurst, 2002

Rosinski, Herbert, *The German Army*, The Hogarth Press, London, 1939

Sajer, Guy, *The Forgotten Soldier*, Sphere Books Ltd, London, 1984

Scheibert, Horst, (Ed. Bruce Culver) *Panzergrenadier Division Grossdeutschland*, Squadron/Signal Publications, Inc., Warren (Michigan, USA), 1977

Schmidt, Heinz Werner, *With Rommel in the Desert*, Panther Books Ltd, London, 1968

Seligmann, Dr. Matthew, with Davison, Dr. John, and McDonald, John, *In the Shadow of the Swastika: Life in Germany under the Nazis, 1933–1945*, Spellmount Ltd., Staplehurst, 2003

Snyder, Professor Louis L., *Encyclopedia of the Third Reich*, Wordsworth Editions Ltd., Ware, 1998

Stein, G. H., *The Waffen SS: Hitler's Elite Guard at War, 1939–1945*, Oxford University Press, 1966

Stone, David, *War Summits: The Meetings that Shaped World War II and the Postwar World*, Potomac Books, Inc., Dulles, Virginia, 2005

— *Fighting for the Fatherland: The Story of the German Soldier from 1648 to the Present Day*, Anova Books Ltd., London, 2006

Strachan, Hew, *The First World War*, Simon & Schuster UK Ltd., London, 2003

Sweeting, C. G., *Blood and Iron: the German Conquest of Sevastopol*, Potomac Books, Inc., Dulles, Virginia, 2004

Tucker-Jones, Anthony, *Hitler's Great Panzer Heist: Germany's Foreign Armor in Action 1939–45*, Pen & Sword Books Ltd, Barnsley, 2007

US War Department, *Handbook on German Military Forces*, TM-E 30-451 (15 March 1945), US War Department, Washington, 1945

Vanderveen, Bart H., *The Observer's Fighting Vehicles Directory World War II*, Frederick Warne & Co. Ltd., London and New York, 1969

Vogelsang, Reinhard, *Im Zeichen des Hakenkreuzes: Bielefeld 1933–1945*, Stadtarchiv und Landesgeschichtliche Bibliothek, Bielefeld, 1986

Whiting, Charles, *'45: The Final Drive from the Rhine to the Baltic*, Century Publishing Co. Ltd., London, 1985

Williams, John, *France: Summer 1940*, Macdonald & Co. (Publishers) Ltd., London, 1969

Williamson, Gordon, *World War II German Battle Insignia*, Osprey Publishing Ltd., Oxford, 2002

— *World War II German Women's Auxiliary Services*, Osprey Publishing Ltd., Oxford, 2003

Woodman, Dorothy (Ed.), *Hitler Rearms: An Exposure of Germany's War Plans*, John Lane the Bodley Head Ltd., London, 1934

The author also drew variously and to varying extents upon the exhibits and archives of the following German and British military institutions and museums:

Celler Garnison-Museum e.V., Celle (Hafenstrasse 4, D-29221 Celle)

Deutsches Historisches Museum, Berlin (Unter den Linden 2, D-10117 Berlin)

Kreismuseum Wewelsburg (Burgwall 19, D-33142 Büren-Wewelsburg)

Militärhistorisches Museum der Bundeswehr (Olbrichtplatz 2, D-01099 Dresden)

Panzermuseum Munster (Hans-Krüger-Strasse 33, D-29633 Munster)

Preussen Museum Nordrhein-Westfalen, Minden (Simeonsplatz 12, D-32427 Minden)

Preussen Museum Nordrhein-Westfalen, Wesel (An der Zitadelle, D-46483 Wesel)

The Imperial War Museum, London (Lambeth Road, SE1 6HZ)

The Rifles (Berkshire and Wiltshire) Museum, Salisbury (58 The Close, Wiltshire SP1 2EX)

# Index